STUDIES IN ANCIENT ORIENTAL CIVILIZATION • No. 54

THE ORIENTAL INSTITUTE OF THE UNIVERSITY OF CHICAGO

The Mechanics of Ancient Egyptian Magical Practice

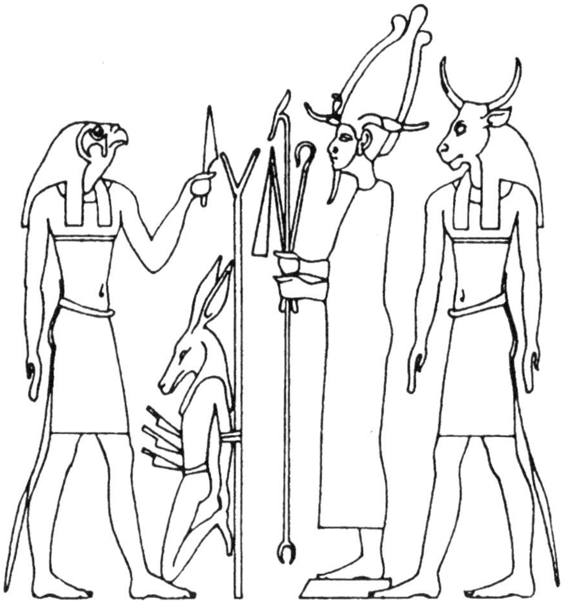

by

Robert Kriech Ritner

Is it not a silly sort of argument to reckon by the same works
that one man is a god whilst his rivals are mere "sorcerers"?

Celsus. On the True Doctrine

R. J. Hoffmann 1987, p. 66

THE ORIENTAL INSTITUTE OF THE UNIVERSITY OF CHICAGO
STUDIES IN ANCIENT ORIENTAL CIVILIZATION • No. 54
CHICAGO • ILLINOIS

Library of Congress Catalog Card Number: 92-61830
ISBN: 0-918986-75-3
ISSN: 0081-7554

The Oriental Institute, Chicago

Published 1993. Printed in Canada.

SECOND PRINTING 1995
(with minor corrections on pages 67, 69, 100, 140, 141, 152, 153, 204, 206, 231, 245, 275, 293, 303, and 320)

THIRD PRINTING 1997
(with minor corrections on pages 44, 195, 211, and 320)

FOURTH PRINTING 2008
(with minor corrections on pages 59, 114, 115, 116, 193, 194, 198, 253, 282, 303, 304, 316, 317, and 320)

Winner of the 1994 Heyman Prize for Outstanding Scholarly Publication in the Humanities, Yale University

REVIEWS

Robert Steven Bianchi. *Journal of the American Oriental Society* 114 (1994): 513–14.
Bob Brier. *KMT: A Modern Journal of Ancient Egypt* 4:4 (1993–94): 86–87.
Heinz Felber. *Enchoria* 21 (1994): 119.
Ogden Goelet. *The Egyptian Book of the Dead* (1994): 171.
Willem Hovestreydt. *Annual Egyptological Bibliography 1993* (1995): 214–16.
László Kákosy. *Journal of the American Research Center in Egypt* 31 (1994): 223–25.
Jean Vercoutter. *Revue d'Égyptologie* 46 (1995): 247–48.

COVER ILLUSTRATION AND FRONTISPIECE

Seth Bound and Stabbed before Osiris at Dendera (see fig. 14g, p. 167).

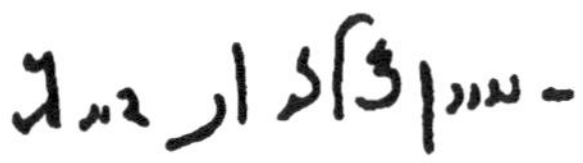

TO MY PARENTS

TABLE OF CONTENTS

FOREWORD

The present publication is a revised and expanded edition of my 1987 doctoral dissertation at The University of Chicago. *Chapter 3* is a wholly new addition, using material originally gathered for the earlier work. Other modifications in the body of the text are relatively minor; the passage of five years has entailed no changes in the original analyses or opinions but has necessitated an expansion of the footnotes to incorporate subsequent bibliography. The manuscript was closed as of May 1992, and only sources available to me by that date have been included. The reader may be struck by an apparent inconsistency in the use of hieroglyphic fonts throughout this volume. The use of "Normalschrift" fonts has been confined only to generic references to individual words and signs. In contrast, whenever a specific textual passage or edition is excerpted (whether in hieroglyphic, hieratic, or Demotic script), an attempt has been made to reproduce the original text or edition by computer scanner. It is hoped that any loss in aesthetics will be counterbalanced by an increase in accuracy.

In the preparation of this study, I have benefited from the sagacity, experience, and endurance of many, and it is a pleasure to acknowledge their contributions. The original dissertation committee comprised Drs. Klaus Baer, Robert D. Biggs, Janet H. Johnson, and Edward F. Wente, chairman and early source of inspiration. As teachers and colleagues, they have contributed to the fruition of this project in countless ways. In particular, Janet Johnson has continued to provide unflagging support, and our association on the Chicago Demotic Dictionary Project has been of primary importance for my scholastic development. Her invaluable computer skills have also enabled the use of textual scans in this volume. The untimely death of Klaus Baer has deprived Egyptology of a singularly rigorous scholar and irreplaceable teacher. His insistence on precision in methodology and detail has shaped the themes of my own work, from our first lessons in the Egyptian language. His enthusiasm for the present study remains a source of pride. Dr. George R. Hughes, who came out of retirement to guide my initial study of Demotic, has been a constant source of encouragement—especially helpful on days when the thought of researching yet another footnote was unendurable. Additional thanks are due to colleagues and students who offered support, advice, or information: William Brashear, Hans D. Betz, Susan Clark, Walter Farber, Richard Jasnow, Charles Jones, Joe Manning, John Nolan, Martha Roth, Terry Wilfong, and the late David Wilmot. Proffered suggestions and references are acknowledged individually within the relevant footnotes; responsibility for all other phraseology, opinions, and citations remains exclusively that of the author.

Family and friends have been unstinting in their support. Chief among them are my parents, Robert and Margaret Ritner, and my brother and sister-in-law, Richard and Jody Ritner, and their family. My parents, to whom this work is dedicated, have been instrumental in its completion, for without their exhortations to "finish the dissertation" I would still be inserting additional references to my discussion of *pẖr*. For enduring the brunt of my daily bouts with academia, an additional dedication is made to Dr. Neil J. Krakauer and Fínghin. Neil in particular acted as a sounding board for each thought as I conceived it, each sentence as I penned it. His relief at the completion of this task can be no less than my own.

To John Larson, Oriental Institute Archivist, I am especially indebted for the photographic material which accompanies this work. His efforts have been thorough, tireless, and far above the requirements of duty and friendship. Further thanks are owed to my dissertation editor, Joan Hives, who patiently labored with this manuscript in various incarnations through the endless petty tomfoolery of bureaucracy and computer. Her Herculean efforts have rendered the subsequent publication a simple matter.

For overcoming the ultimate technicalities of publication, I wish to thank the Oriental Institute's Publications Office directed by Tom Holland, and especially my careful editor, Richard Schoen. A final, but heartfelt gratitude, is owed to my graduate students at Yale, Jennifer Houser, Mark Stone, and Pascale Teysseire, who assisted me in the laborious but crucial task of proofreading the completed manuscript. *Dwꜣ=ỉ n=ṯn nṯr*.

LIST OF FIGURES

LIST OF TABLES

LIST OF ABBREVIATIONS

In general, abbreviations are based on W. Helck and E. Otto, eds., *Lexikon der Ägyptologie*. 7 vols. Wiesbaden: Otto Harrassowitz, 1975–89.

AcOr	*Acta Orientalia*, Leiden and Copenhagen
ADAIK	Abhandlungen des Deutschen Archäologischen Instituts Kairo, Glückstadt, Hamburg, and New York
AEB	*Annual Egyptological Bibliography*, Leiden and Warminster
ÄF	Ägyptologische Forschungen, Glückstadt, Hamburg, and New York
AfO	*Archive für Orientforschung*, Berlin and Graz
ÄgAb	Ägyptologische Abhandlungen, Wiesbaden
AH	Aegyptiaca Helvetica, Basel and Geneva
AJA	*American Journal of Archaeology*, Baltimore and Norwood
AJSL	*American Journal of Semitic Languages and Literatures*, Chicago
AnAe	Analecta Aegyptiaca, Copenhagen
AnOr	Analecta Orientalia, Rome
AOAT	Alter Orient und Altes Testament, Kevelaer and Neukirchen-Vluyn
ArOr	*Archiv Orientálni*, Prague and Paris; Stuttgart and Prague
AS	Assyriological Studies, Chicago
ASAE	*Annales du Service des Antiquitiés de l'Égypte*, Cairo
ASAW	Abhandlungen der Sächsischen Akademie der Wissenschaften zu Leipzig, Phil.-hist. Kl., Berlin
ASE	Archaeological Survey of Egypt, London
B (superscript)	Bohairic Coptic Dialect
BD	Book of the Dead (spell)
BdE	Bibliothèque d'Étude, Cairo
BdEC	Bibliothèque d'Études Coptes, Cairo
BIE	*Bulletin de l'Institut d'Égypte*, Cairo
BIFAO	*Bulletin de l'Institut Français d'Archéologie Orientale*, Cairo

BiOr	*Bibliotheca Orientalis*, Leiden
BM	The British Museum, London
BMMA	*Bulletin, Metropolitan Museum of Art*, New York
BSAC	*Bulletin de la Société d'Archéologie Copte*, Cairo
BSFE	*Bulletin de la Société Française d'Égyptologie*, Paris
CAD	*The Assyrian Dictionary of the Oriental Institute of the University of Chicago*, 16 vols. (to date). Chicago: The Oriental Institute, 1956–1989
CdE	*Chronique d'Égypte*, Brussels
CGC	Catalogue Général des Antiquités Égyptiennes du Musée du Caire, Cairo
CNI	Carsten Niebuhr Institute of Ancient Near East Studies, Copenhagen
col(s).	column(s) [citations given as follows: column no./line no(s).]
CRIPEL	*Cahier de Recherches l'Institut de Papyrologie et d'Égyptologie de Lille*, Lille
CSCO	Corpus Scriptorum Christianorum Orientalium, Louvain and Paris
CT	Coffin Texts (spell)
DAIK	Deutschen Archäologischen Instituts Kairo, Cairo
DFIFAO	Documents de Fouilles de l'Institut Français d'Archéologie Orientale du Caire, Cairo
EEF	Egypt Exploration Fund, London
EES	Egypt Exploration Society, London
EPRO	Études Préliminaires aux Religions Orientales dans l'Empire Romain, Leiden
fig(s).	figure(s)
GM	*Göttinger Miszellen*, Göttingen
GMAÄ	H. Grapow et al., eds., Grundriss der Medizin der alten Ägypter, 9 vols. Berlin: Akademie-Verlag, 1954–73
GOF	Göttinger Orientforschung, IV. Reihe: Ägypten, Wiesbaden
HO	"Hieratic Ostraca" texts as catalogued in Jaroslav Černý and Alan H. Gardiner, *Hieratic Ostraca*. Oxford: Oxford University Press, 1957
HPBM	Facsimilies of Egyptian Hieratic Papyri in the British Museum, London
IEJ	*Israel Exploration Journal*, Jerusalem
IFAO	L'Institut Français d'Archéologie Orientale du Caire, Cairo
JAOS	*Journal of the American Oriental Society*, New Haven
JARCE	*Journal of the American Research Center in Egypt*, Boston
JCS	*Journal of Cuneiform Studies*, New Haven
JdE	Journal d'Entrée (Egyptian Museum, Cairo)
JEA	*Journal of Egyptian Archaeology*, London
JEOL	*Jaarbericht van het Vooraziatisch-Egyptische Genootschap* (Gezelschap) "Ex Oriente Lux," Leiden
JNES	*Journal of Near Eastern Studies*, Chicago

KHwb	W. Westendorf, *Koptisches Handwörterbuch*. Heidelberg: Carl Winter, 1965–77
l(l).	line(s)
LÄ	W. Helck and E. Otto, eds., *Lexikon der Ägyptologie*. 7 vols. Wiesbaden: Otto Harrassowitz, 1975–89
MÄS	Münchner Ägyptologische Studien, Berlin
MDAIK	*Mitteilungen des Deutschen Archäologischen Instituts, Abteilung Kairo*, Berlin, Wiesbaden, and Mainz
MFA Bulletin	*Museum of Fine Arts Bulletin*, Boston
MIFAO	Mémoires publiés par les Membres de l'Institut Français d'Archéologie Orientale du Caire, Cairo
MIO	*Mitteilungen des Instituts für Orientforschung*, Berlin
MMA	The Metropolitan Museum of Art, Department of Egyptian Art, New York
MMAF	Mémoires publiés par les Membres de la Mission Archéologie Française au Caire, Paris
MPER	Mitteilungen aus der Papyrussammlung der Österreichischen Nationalbibliothek (Papyrus Erzherzog Rainer), Vienna
Ms.	Manuscript
n(n).	note(s)
n.d.	no date
no(s).	number(s)
n.p.	no place
N. S.	New Series
O.	Ostracon
OBO	Orbis Biblicus et Orientalis, Freiburg, Switzerland and Göttingen
OIC	Oriental Institute Communications, Chicago
OIM	The Oriental Institute Museum, Chicago
OIP	Oriental Institute Publications, Chicago
OLP	*Orientalia Lovaniensia Periodica*, Leuven
OLZ	*Orientalische Literaturzeitung*, Berlin
OMRO	*Oudheidkundige Mededeelingen uit het Rijksmuseum van Oudheden te Leiden*, Leiden
OrSu	Orientalia Suecana, Uppsala
O. S.	Old Series
p(p).	page(s)
Pap.	Papyrus
PGM	"Papyri Graecae Magicae" texts as catalogued in Karl Preisendanz, *Papyri Graecae Magicae*. 2 vols. Stuttgart: B. G. Teubner, 1973–74 (reprint of Leipzig, 1928–31; supplemental texts in H. D. Betz 1986)
pl(s).	plate(s)
PMMA	Publications of the Metropolitan Museum of Art, Egyptian Expedition, New York

PSBA	*Proceedings of the Society of Biblical Archaeology*, London
PT	Pyramid Texts (spell)
RdE	*Revue d'Égyptologie*, Cairo, Paris, and Louvain
RdT	*Recueil des Travaux relatifs à la philologie et à l'archéologie égyptiennes et assyriennes*, Paris
ro.	recto
S (superscript)	Sahidic Coptic Dialect
S.	Stela
SAK	*Studien zur Altägyptischen Kultur*, Hamburg
SAMPh	*Society for Ancient Medicine and Pharmacy Newsletter*, Madison, Wisconsin, and Philadelphia
SAOC	Studies in Ancient Oriental Civilization, Chicago
SASAE	Suppléments aux Annales du Service des Antiquités de l'Égypte, Cairo
SCO	*Studi Classici e Orientali*, Pisa
SSEA Journal	*Journal of the Society for the Study of Egyptian Antiquities*, Toronto
TT	Theban Tomb
UGAÄ	Untersuchungen zur Geschichte und Altertumskunde Ägyptens, Leipzig and Berlin (reprinted Hildesheim 1964)
Urk.	Urkunden des aegyptischen Altertums, founded by Georg Steindorff
var.	variant
vo.	verso
vol(s).	volume(s)
Wb	Adolf Erman and Hermann Grapow, eds., *Wörterbuch der ägyptischen Sprache*. 6 vols. Berlin and Leipzig, 1st ed.: 1926–31, 2nd ed.: 1957
Wb Beleg.	Adolf Erman and Hermann Grapow, eds., *Wörterbuch der ägyptischen Sprache, die Belegstellen*. 5 vols. Berlin and Leipzig, 1940–59
Webster's	*Webster's Third New International Dictionary of the English Language*. Springfield, MA: G. & C. Merriam Co., 1971
WZKM	*Wiener Zeitschrift für die Kunde des Morgenlandes*, Vienna
ZÄS	*Zeitschrift für Ägyptische Sprache und Altertumskunde*, Leipzig and Berlin
ZDMG	*Zeitschrift der Deutschen Morgenländischen Gesellschaft*, Leipzig and Wiesbaden
ZPE	*Zeitschrift für Papyrologie und Epigraphik*, Bonn

INTRODUCTION

The category of "magic" has long been a descriptive tool within the field of Egyptology, though no shared criteria have existed for defining the concept. Most often, the determination of "magic" has relied solely upon the subjective interpretation of the attitude of the ancient practitioner as surmised from the contents of recited spells. In keeping with the early anthropological theories of Frazer and Malinowski, "magic" was to be distinguished from "religion" by the former's threatening attitude and its limited, personal goals. Unfortunately, these criteria are inadequate for delineating Egyptian practice, as they frequently characterize standard cultic ("religious") texts as well. As a result, the same texts have been labeled "magical" by certain scholars though "religious" by others. A common solution has been the adoption of the noncommittal phrase "magico-religious," and certain scholars, following Claude Lévi-Strauss, have suggested that the category be abandoned altogether.

Justification for the retention of the category "magic" is suggested by the existence of native terminology (*ḥkꜣ*) which was ultimately equated with Western "magic" in the Coptic (Christian) period. However, an examination of the older Egyptian concept and its associated vocabulary, mythology, and theology reveals fundamental distinctions between the range and meaning of "magic" within the two cultures. Rather than imposing a universal definition of "magic" on both, the present thesis adopts an "emic" approach in which Egyptian and Western concepts are evaluated independently, and in their own terms. In order to obtain a "working definition" of the Western definition of "magic," a new method was selected in which *activity* serves as the diagnostic criterion. For the purposes of this study, any activity that seeks to obtain its goal outside the natural laws of cause and effect is designated as "magical" in the modern Western sense. Using such a "working definition," the identification of "magical" elements within spells, rituals, literature, and archaeological artifacts is relatively simple, and a brief selection of these are surveyed regarding both synchronic distribution and diachronic development: circumambulation, spitting, blowing, licking, swallowing, the use of images, superposition, trampling, binding, the use of red, breaking, the use of sand, burning, numerological symbolism, piercing, decapitation, reversal, burial, the use of the dead, and oracular consultations. Cross-cultural parallels are noted for contrast and comparison. The identity of the magician, his social role, and his significance in the continuity of this tradition are also examined. The "private" magician is revealed to be none other than the cultic priest, in "private practice" during interims in temple service. Thus can be explained the identity of "magical" acts in private and public ceremonies, as well as the similarity of ritual texts and "magical" spells; all were composed, compiled, and performed by the same individuals.

To date, no treatment of Egyptian magic has concentrated upon the actual practice of the magician. Both general studies and textual publications have emphasized instead the religious elements in the contents of recited spells, while the accompanying instructions with their vignettes and lists of materials, instruments, and ritual actions remained uninvestigated. This study represents the first critical examination of such "magical techniques," revealing their widespread appearance and pivotal significance for all Egyptian "religious" practices from the earliest periods through the Coptic era, influencing as well the Greco-Egyptian magical papyri. Performed by priests as the technique of religion, Egyptian "magic" cannot be opposed to religion, and the Western dichotomy of "religion vs. magic" is thus inappropriate for describing Egyptian practice. This continuum of "magical mechanics" vitiates as well the oft-repeated suggestion of religious decline and magical increase in the later periods.

Corresponding to the merger of Egyptian religion and magic as obtained from the Western definition, Egyptian concepts of magic are shown to be pivotal for indigenous religious life, underlying not merely cultic practice but all sacral speculation, forming an "imagistic theory" that bonds the tenets of religion to the techniques of religion. Only with the conversion of Egypt to Christianity is this theology abandoned, and "magic" reinterpreted in the debased meaning which it maintains in the modern West.

CHAPTER 1

TOWARD A DEFINITION OF MAGIC

Denn die Zauberei und alles was damit zusammenhängt, ist uraltes Erbgut des Ägyptertums

Wilhelm Spiegelberg 1932b, p. 101

Ten measures of magic have come into the world.
Egypt received nine of these, the rest of the world one measure.

Talmud, b. Qid. 49b

In any discussion of magical spells and techniques, one is at once confronted by the complete absence of any shared criteria for exactly what constitutes "magic." All too often, the religious and medical practices of one culture or era become "magic" when viewed from the perspective of another. Perhaps nowhere is this clearer than in the case of the developing Christian church, which was prosecuted for magical acts by pagan Rome, in turn persecuted pagans and "heretics" for the same offense when it attained power, and, finally, was again the subject of denunciations for magical practices by schismatic Protestant groups.[1] Similarly, many of the medical prescriptions of the Roman author Pliny would certainly be considered "magical" today, despite the author's denunciation of magicians and their practice.[2] This vagary inherent in the modern word "magic"—being applied by personal whim to beliefs stigmatized as evil or false—parallels the derogatory evolution of the word "myth" and, like it, seems to be a legacy of the Greco-Roman world.[3] So ingrained has this viewpoint become in Western thought that two very serious consequences have arisen for all modern Egyptological studies of the concept. First, the negative connotations of "magic"—whether as fraudulent sham or misguided "science"—have prevented truly sympathetic treatments of the phenomena in Egypt. Thus previous scholars, when constrained to discuss the topic, expressly state their distaste for the material.[4] Bounded by religion on the one hand, and on the other by medicine, magic has been considered inferior to both and has often received only perfunctory treatment in the

1. For an overview of the reciprocal accusations of magic by pagan and Christian, see Poupon 1981; Brown 1970; Barb 1963; and MacMullen 1966, pp. 95–127. Protestant accusations of magic against Catholicism are discussed in Thomas 1971, pp. 51–77 and passim.

2. Compare Pliny, *Natural History*, 30.25 for the use of a dead serpent as an amulet, 30.49 for aphrodisiacs, and note 30.30, where Pliny turns to magical remedies in the case of quartan fevers for which "ordinary medicine" was felt to be useless. These prescriptions all appear in a chapter which begins with an exposé of magic as "the most fraudulent of arts" (30.1). The question of Pliny's relationship to Roman magic is discussed in Tavenner 1916, pp. 56–59 and 74–75.

3. The pejorative use of the term "magic" to describe the beliefs and practices of one's enemies (in contrast to the term "religion" reserved for one's own beliefs and practices) is skillfully traced in Segal 1981. The complexity of this development, and the consequent confusion of categories of "religion" and "magic" within the Greco-Roman world itself, is clearly surveyed in Morton Smith 1983.

4. E.g., H. Brugsch 1891, p. 77: [Magical texts] "haben kaum einen andern wissenschaftlichen Werth als den, welchen sie den Studien der Schrift und Sprache darbieten"; Budge 1901, p. xi: "beliefs and superstitions of the most degraded character"; Erman 1907, p. 148: "it is precisely the youthful unsophisticated nations that are most readily attracted by it"; and Lexa 1925, vol. 1, p. 12: "Plus la culture nationale est basse et plus le nombre d'hommes éclairés est restreint, plus est grande l'influence de la magie." These last statements are demonstrably false. In western Europe, the social repercussions of belief in magic and witchcraft were far greater in the Renaissance than in the Middle Ages, and the beliefs were stronger among the educated than among the general population (Douglas 1970, pp. xxxi–xxxiii).

study of either.[5] Second, the very uncertainty of the exact lines of demarcation (if any exist) of the boundaries between religion, magic, and medicine has rendered the theoretical distinctions between them untenable in practice. The designation of any given text as "magical" as opposed to "religious" or "medical" is often highly problematic and subjective. The very presence of a spell within a medical context has sufficed to stigmatize that recipe as "magical" even when the accompanying format for treatment is indistinguishable from others within the same papyrus.[6] With regard to religion, emphasis has been placed upon the phraseology of the recitation and the attitude of the speaker. Seen always from a Western perspective, "religion" was to be distinguished from magic by the pious attitude of the practitioner, the humble supplication of its prayers, and the noble, all-inclusive world view of its rituals and theology. In contrast, magic demanded *hubris* and blasphemy of its devotees, its spells did not beg but threaten, and its goals were immediate, limited, and personal.[7] The limitations of this approach become readily apparent when one attempts to apply it to actual texts. Most notably, the funerary literature—Pyramid Texts, Coffin Texts, Book of the Dead, and various texts in the royal tombs of the New

5. For the supposed inferiority of magic to religion, see n. 3, above. With regard to medicine, the magisterial nine volume Grundriss der Medizin der alten Ägypter, edited by Grapow, van Deines, and Westendorf (1954–73) devotes only sixteen pages (Grapow 1955, pp. 11–26) to magic, and then only to a discussion of recited spells. Techniques of medical magic are not analyzed. Similarly, magical practitioners are dismissed as "non-medical" in Ghalioungui 1983, p. 68 and compare p. 48: "I also exclude any magicians who were not at the same time *swnw*." This reflects modern—not ancient—categorization. An early reaction against this common disinterest was voiced by W. M. Müller in his review of Erman's *Zaubersprüche für Mutter und Kind*: "So viel Interessantes bieten nun freilich nicht alle magischen Texte, aber man sieht es: es dürfte sich verlohnen, über das herrschende Vorurteil gegen Magisches etwas öfter wegzusehen" (1902, col. 349).

6. Papyrus Edwin Smith, case 9, col. 4/19–5/5, in Breasted 1930, pp. 217–24. Despite Breasted's rather harsh judgment (p. 217) of this prescription as a "grotesque product of superstition" and a "characteristic product of the recipe-hawking physician (as contrasted with the surgeon)," it is not so aberrant in its composition, which comprises an examination and treatment including a compress and bandaging. The presence of magical elements in this prescription need not reflect, as Breasted thought, an interpolation by a later scribe, but more likely results from the nature of the injury to be treated, a fractured skull incurable by contemporary medicine. Compare the reaction of Pliny to magical treatment of quartan fever in n. 2, above. The absence of additional magical elements in Pap. Edwin Smith seems equally a result of the type of injuries discussed. Most are simple fractures of obvious physical origin and correspondingly straightforward treatment. Had the text dealt with disease, recommendations for magical practice might well have been more numerous (Wilson 1952). Magical treatments are increasingly recognized as complementary, rather than opposed, to "rational" Egyptian medical practice (Walker 1990).

7. See Moret 1906; H. I. Bell 1953, p. 12; Morenz 1973, p. 98; and Barb 1963, pp. 100–01. The most complete formulation of this theory is found in Goode 1949, pp. 172–82 and 1951, pp. 50–55. These distinctions have recently been adopted for New Testament study in Aune 1980, pp. 1512–16 and were already traditional in Festugière 1932, pp. 281–328, especially p. 289.

Kingdom—have proved resistant to consensual classification. Clearly designed for a single individual (the tomb owner), these "personal" texts yet provide the greatest insights into the broader religious concerns of the country, including the relation of gods to men, the conception of the afterlife, the judgment of sins, et cetera. Moreover, there is little hesitancy on the part of the speaker of these spells to mingle praise and threats, respectful "prayer" and demands.[8] Opinions as to the nature of this literature has, accordingly, varied.[9]

These limitations become far more acute, however, when one finds that the same text may appear in both "magical" and "religious" contexts. Thus the Harris "Magical" Papyrus whose title describes it as containing spells to enchant crocodiles includes well-known hymns to the god Shu found equally in "mainstream" religious usage upon temple walls at Philae and Hibis.[10] Divorced from their context, these texts are indistinguishable. Primary dependence upon the spoken spell as the indicator of a magical text is thus clearly unreliable, and editors are often at a loss to make any formal distinction. T. G. H. James may be said to exemplify the problem, while seeking to avoid it, by styling a papyrus "magico-religious."[11] Nowhere is the subjective nature of present classification more evident than in the treatment accorded Papyrus Salt 825 (= Papyrus BM 10051). First published by Birch in 1863, the papyrus was felt to pertain to "la magie la plus absurde."[12] In preparing the second edition of 1965, Derchain was at first of the same opinion.

> ... j'ai pu difficilement me défendre d'un mouvement défavorable. Écriture facile, sans doute, mais quelle littérature![13]

During the course of his analysis, however, Derchain became aware of correspondences between the text and contemporary rituals, and radically re-evaluated the papyrus.

8. In refutation of the assumption that prayer is antithetical to magic, see the comments on the image of the god of magic (Heka) praying the universe into being in te Velde 1970, p. 183.

9. Compare Erman 1907, p. 100: "All these anxieties and all this magic scarcely appear in the Pyramid texts, with the exception of a series of spells against snakes," with Borghouts 1974, p. 7: "It is a current opinion that the whole body of Pyramid Texts and its successors ... may be called magical in its approach to the world of things unseen," following Morenz 1973, p. 99: "... mortuary texts, although they contain religious material, are not themselves religious but magical in nature and purpose," and ibid., p. 229: "To put it in a nutshell, mortuary texts are magical texts."

10. See Lange 1927, pp. 35–36 and 43–44 and Mark Smith 1977.

11. T. G. H. James 1962, p. 74. The term is almost traditional, appearing already in Erman 1893, p. 120. A similar trend in anthropology is noted in Aberle 1966; but compare the "reactionary" remarks of E. O. James 1963.

12. Birch 1863a, quote on p. 119; see also idem 1863b and 1876.

13. Derchain 1965, quote on p. ix of vol. 1.

> ... j'ai découvert tout l'intérêt de ce document qui se révélait contenir les restes d'un authentique rituel, au lieu d'être ce manuel de magie d'assez basse qualité qu'on avait vu jusqu'ici.[14]

Although the century's worth of advances in the understanding of Egyptian that are incorporated in Derchain's translation cannot be disregarded, a comparison of the two translations reveals that the essential content of the text—the properties ascribed to plants and the making of a wax figure—remains the same in 1965 as it had been in 1863.[15] The "rehabilitation" of Papyrus Salt 825 from a "poor quality magical manual" to an "authentic ritual" derives not from any improvements in the translation, but exclusively from the changed perspective of the editor. The originally perceived magical elements were still clear to Borghouts in 1972 when he felt compelled to include the papyrus in his study of magical texts, even while accepting its reclassification as "ritual."[16]

If present methods have been unsuccessful in uniformly isolating magical materials, the fault may lie not only in undue emphasis placed upon the spoken spell, but also in the operative definitions of "magic" utilized by different scholars. Such variance in the underlying definition of magic has obviously influenced the differing interpretations of Papyrus Salt 825 as mentioned above. Most often, no formal definition of magic accompanies studies of the subject as the investigator has assumed—wrongly—that his personal understanding of the term is both appropriate for an Egyptian context and implicitly shared by his colleagues.[17] To the evidence already adduced in refutation of the latter assumption of shared criteria may be added the common disagreement, encountered also in Classical and anthropological studies, whether oracles and divination are to be included among magical practices.[18] Certain scholars, most notably Budge among

14. Derchain 1965, vol. 1, p. ix. As an index of the effect of this reclassification, contrast the initial reaction of Derchain, just noted, with that of Herbin (1988, p. 95) concerning the rediscovery of the first half of Pap. Salt 825 in 1986: "Tous les éléments qu'un premier contact pouvait permettre d'apprécier, tant l'écriture, très particulière mais d'une parfaite lisibilité, que le contenu même du texte et la présence de tournures littéraires, s'accordaient pour le classer dans la catégorie des récits mythologiques."

15. For the magical properties of plants and the use of the wax figure, compare Birch 1863a, pp. 121 and 123–24 and Derchain 1965, pp. 138, 5*–6*.

16. Borghouts 1974, pp. 15–16.

17. A similar observation is made by Lexa 1925, vol. 1, p. 13. His overview of suggested definitions is found on pp. 12–15.

18. Thus Preisendanz 1931, pp. 153–54 (PGM XXVI), 155–56 (PGM XXXa–f), and 157 (PGM XXXIa–c), includes oracular responses while the re-edition of this material by Betz (1986) excludes them as non-magical. A similar lack of unanimity is found in anthropological treatments; see the comments in Evans-Pritchard 1937, p. 8. This uncertainty follows a long tradition in Western thought; compare the lack of consensus among late Roman rulers regarding the distinction between divination and magic; discussed in MacMullen 1984, pp. 96 and 162, n. 28.

Egyptologists, have tended to lump together all manner of "superstitious" activities within the realm of "magic." Thus not only oracles, but also calendars of lucky and unlucky days, dreams, horoscopes, and even animal worship have been rather incongruously associated as "magical."[19] Objections yet more serious can be raised with regard to the assumption of the applicability of modern "standardized" dictionary definitions of magic to an ancient Egyptian context. A cursory survey of entries offered by just one such source will suffice to reveal the imprecision of modern parlance for ancient practice.

> Magic may be loosely defined as an endeavour through utterance of set words, or the performance of set acts, to control or bend the powers of the world to man's will.[20]

Such a definition places undue stress upon the role of *man* in the practice of magic, for as is seen below, it is primarily the *gods* who were felt to excel in the art. Indeed, most private magical texts require the assimilation of the practitioner to a deity in order to be successful. This sanctioning of the use of magic by the gods has profound implications for attempts to distinguish magic from religion.

Magic is "the use of means (as ceremonies, charms, spells) that are believed to have supernatural power to cause a supernatural being to produce or prevent a particular result (as rain, death, healing) considered not attainable by natural means."[21]

Within this definition a clear dichotomy is postulated between the *supernatural* methods of magic and a normative *natural* system of cause and effect. For the Egyptian, however, the activity which he designated "magic" was felt to be *not* supernatural but *quintessentially a part of nature*, being coeval with the creation of the natural order and used daily by the gods to maintain—not violate—that order.[22]

> Magic is 'the art of producing unusual illusions of legerdemain.'[23]

No suggestion of trickery is ever implied in Egyptian terms for magic. Even where theatrical feats are described in literature, there is no indication that writer or audience

19. Budge 1901, pp. 206–34; so also in Wiedemann 1905, pp. 9–11.

20. *Webster's*, p. 1358.

21. Ibid., p. 1358.

22. The question of the natural status of magic is a complicated one, and is discussed below with regard to the term *ḥkꜣ*. It must be admitted, however, that this power has been described as "prenatural or supernatural" even in the study which most clearly shows its fundamental importance in the maintenance of the natural created order. See te Velde 1970, especially contrast p. 176 "prenatural" and pp. 179–80 "vital potential or creative energy" (for the creation of the cosmos, the birth of children, the preservation of the sun, etc.).

23. *Webster's*, p. 1358.

disbelieved the *possibility* of such feats.[24] In this, the Egyptian attitude is to be sharply distinguished from that of the Greco-Roman world in which the early terms for magic (γοητεία) and magician (γόης) rapidly acquired the meanings "fraud" and "huckster."[25] This highly divergent attitude between even contemporary cultures should serve as a further warning of the general inapplicability of culturally or temporally bound definitions of magic.

A similar need for greater precision in the terminology of magic has led anthropologists to repeated attempts at systematization. Social anthropology in particular has been highly influential in its formulations of magical theory, and as certain of its tenets have recently found acceptance in Egyptological literature,[26] it is of some importance to examine its conclusions within an Egyptian context. Although it is beyond the scope of the present work to trace anthropological trends in any but a most cursory manner, even this brief overview will suffice to show the original parallelisms and present divergences of the two disciplines.

Among the earliest and most persistently influential of anthropological theories of magic is that propounded by Sir James G. Frazer in his epochal *The Golden Bough*, which—despite its age—yet underlies all discussions of the subject in Egyptology. Like his Egyptological contemporaries, Frazer postulated an explicit dichotomy between religion and magic based on the pious or threatening attitude of the practitioner.[27] His more distinctive contribution, however, is his definition of magic as sympathetic in nature, being divided into two categories: *Homeopathic* and *Contagious*. The former variety makes use of the belief that "like produces like, or that an effect resembles its cause," whereas the second operates on the principle that "things which have once been in contact with each other continue to act on each other at a distance after physical contact has been severed."[28] These principles could be readily combined in practice so that, for example, the manipulation of a voodoo doll would embody *Homeopathic* magic, while the inclusion of

24. Compare the miraculous events narrated in Pap. Westcar, Setna I, and Setna II, in Lichtheim 1973, pp. 215–22 (Pap. Westcar) and 1980, pp. 125–51 (Setna I and Setna II). Further tales of magicians appear in Spiegelberg 1912 (Jug A for magician *Ḥỉ-Ḥr* and Jug B for magician *Sỉ-Wsỉr*); idem 1917b (magician *Ḥỉ-Ḥr*); idem 1932 (magician *Nꜣ-nfr-kꜣ-Skr*); and Posener 1985 (magician *Mry-Rꜥ*).

25. Liddell, Scott, and Jones 1940, p. 356a. For the evolution of these terms see Tavenner 1916, pp. 1–5; Morton Smith 1978, pp. 69–74; and idem 1983.

26. Thus Evans-Pritchard's definition of "witchcraft" is adopted in Borghouts 1980, col. 1144: "witchcraft (in the sense of evil influence by natural predisposition, without material manipulation)."

27. Frazer 1910, pp. 220ff., especially p. 225: "it [*scil.* magic] constrains or coerces instead of conciliating or propitiating them [*scil.* spirits] as religion would do."

28. Frazer 1910, pp. 52ff.

personal effects in the doll would represent *Contagious* magic. Nor were these categories limited to any particular magical act, culture, or era; all magical practice fell under one or both of these principles. So pervasive has this theory become outside of the social sciences that few authors since the publication of *The Golden Bough* have been able to resist the term "sympathetic magic."[29] Egyptology has yet to question its "Frazerian" attitude to the subject, and finds its perfect analog in the writings of B. Malinowski. Expanding upon the work of Frazer, Malinowski's *Magic, Science and Religion* upholds the religion/magic distinction, stresses the spoken spell, and insists that the primary focus of magic is man, not nature.[30] The fundamental difficulties arising from the application of these criteria to Egyptian magic are detailed above. In the social sciences, the recognition of similar deficiencies has long since led to a re-evaluation of Frazer's theory, which has ultimately been challenged as much on the question of its usefulness as on its validity. By virtue of its reductionistic nature, it is incapable of distinguishing the differences in magical practices of one culture or era from another; for both Frazer and Malinowski the activities of magicians among the tribesmen of modern Australia are to be analyzed no differently from those among the sophisticated classes of antique Rome.[31] Moreover, Frazer's theory fails to account for the remarkable persistence of the "pathetic or ludicrous" activities which he finds so devoid of truth or value.[32]

As a reaction to these deficiencies, newer theories have arisen stressing the functional role of magic, its inseparability from religion, and its value in individual societies. Chief among these theories is that of E. E. Evans-Pritchard. In attempting to avoid the indifference of general theories to cultural distinctions, Evans-Pritchard devised a new vocabulary for magical acts based exclusively upon and designed to represent a specific culture: the Zande of the Sudan.[33] Concentrating primarily upon the harmful aspects of magic, he distinguished two sub-categories: witchcraft and sorcery. The latter designates the conscious performance of illicit or immoral magic by external methods such as spells or rites, while the former refers to a "supposed psychic emanation" from an internal bodily

29. See *inter alia* Gardiner 1922, p. 265b and Wilson 1952, p. 76. The term is far from obsolete in anthropological discussions as well. Thus Tambiah (1968, p. 194) feels compelled to dispute Frazer's interpretation, and it is still used with approval in Becker 1980, p. 20.

30. Malinowski 1948, pp. 19ff. and 50–71, especially p. 54: "To the natives knowledge of magic means knowledge of spell"; 56: "It is not directed so much to nature as to man's relation to nature"; and 68: "It is always the affirmation of man's power to cause certain definite effects by a definite spell and rite."

31. Frazer 1910, p. 55 and Malinowski 1948, p. 51.

32. Frazer 1971, p. 127.

33. Evans-Pritchard 1937, pp. 8–12.

substance "which is believed to cause injury to health and property."[34] Like Frazer before him, Evans-Pritchard has spawned a school of magical theory, the "structural-functionalist" approach, which has dominated anthropological discussion since the appearance of *Witchcraft, Oracles and Magic among the Azande* in 1937.[35] Emphasizing the social processes which surround accusations of magic, he stressed the normative role of magical beliefs in sustaining the moral system and social codes of the Zande. Magic was to be viewed not as the "great delusion" of Frazer, but as an important force in sustaining a static society by providing an expedient explanation for misfortune.[36]

Despite a change in emphasis from a homeostatic to a confrontational model,[37] the analysis of Evans-Pritchard has so far replaced that of Frazer in social anthropology that collections of essays devoted to "witchcraft and sorcery" presume the knowledge of his theories and terms, and a special memorial volume was dedicated to the thirtieth anniversary of his initial study of the Azande.[38] In Egyptological literature, his terminology was introduced for the first time in 1980.[39] It is particularly ironic that the culturally-specific terms selected by Evans-Pritchard should have become standardized for general application to dissimilar cultures, since he was among the first to advance a so-called "emic" approach "whereby definitions, distinctions, and values are derived from the actors themselves rather than imposed on them by the observer."[40] The dubious wisdom of generalizing Zande concepts was clearly evident to M. Douglas in her introduction to the

34. Evans-Pritchard 1937, p. 9 (*mangu*).

35. For a discussion of the critical importance of Evans-Pritchard's study on successive theorists, see Douglas 1970, pp. xiii–xxxviii.

36. Evans-Pritchard 1937, pp. 109–17. For an appraisal, see Douglas 1970, pp. xvi–xviii.

37. In reaction to the model of witchcraft accusations as an institution for the maintenance of social harmony, recent theories have noted the increase of such accusations during periods of crisis and stressed their role as a challenge to authority when social relations are ill-defined. This interpretation has the advantage of accommodating both African and European data (Douglas 1970, pp. xviii–xxxvi).

38. Compare Marwick 1970, p. 19. For the memorial volume on the anniversary of the publication of Evans-Pritchard's study of the Azande, see Douglas 1970.

39. Borghouts 1980, col. 1144. The terminology enters Mesopotamian studies a decade earlier (Walters 1970–71).

40. Aune 1980, p. 1510, n. 4; see Evans-Pritchard 1937, pp. 4–5, especially p. 5: "I have sought to provide it [*scil.* explanation] from the statements of Azande themselves ... Explanations, therefore, will be found embodied in my descriptive account and are not set forth independently of it." The term "emic" is discussed in Harris 1968, especially p. 571: "Emic statements refer to logico-empirical systems whose phenomenal distinctions or 'things' are built up out of contrasts and discriminations significant, meaningful, real, accurate, or in some other fashion regarded as appropriate by the actors themselves."

memorial volume for Evans-Pritchard, for she expressly declines to follow her colleagues in their use of terminology.[41]

The failure of more recent scholars to adhere to this "emic" approach is all the more surprising in the case of ancient Egypt, for the superimposed term "witchcraft" that was so crucial in Zande belief is without any Egyptian referent, save only the "Evil Eye." Egyptian magic was definitely believed to reside in the body of the magician, but its use required the conscious manipulation of spell and rite.[42] Egyptian magic thus cuts across the distinction inherent in its Zande counterpart. Moreover, neither the methodology of Evans-Pritchard nor that of his successors can be perfectly consonant with that of the Egyptologist. For the anthropologist, the malevolent sorcerer or witch is a fictitious creature, and all accusations of witchcraft are presumed false.[43] The Egyptologist, on the other hand, is confronted by unmistakable archaeological and textual evidence of hostile magic, and must presume that accusations of magical practice could well be true. Although the efficacy of the practice may be subject to belief, its existence is not.

Just as a simplistic adoption of anthropological terminology provides no deeper insights into the nature of Egyptian magic, so the present vogue for sociological terminology regarding magic in the fields of comparative religion and biblical study is equally ill at home within Egyptology. Seizing upon the early theories of Emile Durkheim and Marcel Mauss which stigmatize magic as anti-social and illegal behavior, Jonathan Z. Smith has recently argued that illegality is the "one universal characteristic" of magic.[44] In response, David Aune has preferred to place magic within the framework of recent studies of social deviance, and considers magic to be "universally regarded as a form of deviant behavior," where the latter term is defined as "conduct that departs significantly from the norms set for people in their social statuses."[45] Neither of these generalizations is satisfactory, for

41. Douglas 1970, p. xxxvi, n. 1.

42. Compare CT spells 30, 33–37, and passim. For discussion, see Borghouts 1980, col. 1140.

43. See Douglas 1970, p. xxxiv: "Anthropologists have usually approached witchcraft from the point of view of the accuser, always assuming that the accusation is false. This has made it hard for us to interpret witchcraft confessions." This stance, noticeable also in the works of cultural historians, derives from a basic confusion between belief in sorcerers/witches and belief in the efficacy of sorcery/witchcraft. Admittedly, misfortunes have often been attributed to unknown and very likely fictitious witches, but this does not mean that individuals who practice witchcraft (and are therefore witches) do not exist. For a similar distinction between the witches of European folk belief and actual contemporary practitioners of sorcery, see Cohen 1970, pp. 11–12.

44. J. Z. Smith 1978, p. 192, following Brown 1970 and Morton Smith 1973, pp. 220–37. All of these theories ultimately derive from Roman law as extrapolated by Mauss 1972 and Durkheim 1965, pp. 57ff.

45. Aune 1980, p. 1515. The definition of social deviance is adopted by Aune from Merton and Nisbet 1971, p. 824.

neither is correct. However magic may be defined, in Egypt the practice was in itself quite legal. Only one trial for sorcery is preserved from ancient Egypt, involving the use of wax figures in a plot against the throne, but the trial record is careful to state that the books of magic used by the prisoners came from the king's own collection.[46] Sorcery against the king, not sorcery *per se*, was illegal. In other instances, kings, priests, and commoners used the same methods on a daily, normative, and legal basis. Thus King Amenophis II states on the Amada Stela (l. 5) that "he made execration figures of his enemies and the Nine Bows (the traditional enemies of Egypt) likewise."[47] Similar figures made by priests for foundation deposits are well known.[48] Private individuals are specifically urged to use the same methods in the so-called "Apophis Book" (Papyrus BM 10188), making figures of the enemies of Re, Pharaoh, and "all foes male and female whom your heart fears."[49] The thematically similar "Rite for Repelling the Angry One" (Papyrus Louvre E 3129) is even more precise: "If this spell is recited against any enemy of NN, evil will happen to him for 7 days."[50] In both texts the reciter is said to participate in the destruction of divine, royal, and personal enemies with no distinction as to method or legality. It should be stressed that both texts were also performed in the daily liturgies of the chief temples of Amon-Re and Osiris, and are thus an integral part of the religious norm, and by no means constitute "deviant" behavior. So inextricably mixed do magic and religion seem in these instances that any formal distinction between them might well seem artificial and improper. Indeed, E. E. Evans-Pritchard has suggested that anthropology abandon the terms "religion" and "magic," while the sociologist David Pocock, following Claude Lévi-Strauss, would dispose of the category of "magic" altogether.[51] Is there any rationale for maintaining the concept "magic" in Egyptology, and can it be distinguished from religion? The answer to the first question must be yes, and the answer to the second forms the substance of this study.

46. Papyrus Lee, col. 1/2–3: "He gave to him a book of the library(?) of Usermaatremeriamon (Ramses III), l.p.h., the great god." For the trial and term *rꜣ-ʿ-ẖt*, here provisionally translated "library," see below, pp. 195–97.

47. See Reinisch 1873, pl. 7, l. 5 and Helck 1955b, p. 1291. For discussion, see Ritner 1989a, p. 91 and below, p. 187.

48. See Vila 1973. Complete discussion, below, pp. 153–78.

49. Faulkner 1933, p. 69, col. 28/17–18 and 1937b, p. 175. See below, p. 184.

50. Schott 1929, p. 61, ll. 17–18. See pp. 189–90 and n. 884, below.

51. See Evans-Pritchard 1965, p. 111; Pocock 1972; and Lévi-Strauss 1950, pp. xviiff.

HEKA

If magic is to be retained as a category in the study of Egyptian thought, it is because the Egyptians themselves gave a name to a practice which they—not others—identified with the Western concept of magic: ϩⲓⲕ. Selected by Coptic scribes to translate the Greek μαγεία, this term appears in Acts 8:9 to describe the "magic" of Simon Magus: ⲣ̄ ϩⲓⲕ, "to do ϩⲓⲕ" = μαγεύων.[52] The clear equation of these terms is shown by the frequent parallel usage of the native ⲣⲉϥⲉⲣϩⲓⲕ, "a man who does ϩⲓⲕ, magician" with the Greek loan word ⲙⲁⲅⲟⲥ. Thus, the sorcery of Simon Magus mentioned above in Acts 8:9 (ⲣ̄ ϩⲓⲕ) is termed ⲧⲙⲛ̄ⲧⲙⲁⲅⲟⲥ, "the quality of ⲙⲁⲅⲟⲥ, magic" in Acts 8:11.[53] Similarly, in the *Oration in Praise of Saint Georgios Diospolis* by Theodotos of Ancyra, the saint, when accused of being a magician (ⲡⲁⲓ ⲙⲁⲅⲟⲥ), is berated for ⲧⲉⲕ ⲙⲉⲧⲣⲉϥⲉⲣϩⲓⲕ, "your magic practices."[54] Succinct explanation is offered in the *Martyrdom of Georgios*:

ⲡⲁⲓⲣⲱⲙⲓ ⲟⲩ ⲣⲉϥⲉⲣϩⲓⲕ ⲡⲉ ϫⲉ ⲉ̄ⲃⲟⲗϩⲓⲧⲉⲛ ⲛⲉϥⲙⲁⲅⲓⲁ̄
ⲁϥⲧⲁϩⲟ ⲛ̄ϩⲁⲛⲇⲉⲙⲱⲛ ⲉ̄ⲣⲁⲧⲟⲩ ⲙ̄ⲡⲉⲛⲙ̄ⲑⲟ ⲉ̄ⲃⲟⲗ
This man is a magician (ⲣⲉϥⲉⲣϩⲓⲕ) because by means of
his magic (ⲙⲁⲅⲓⲁ̄) he set demons before us.[55]

As an explanation of the foreign term, the words are conjoined in the Coptic Ms. 40, 50 of the Pierpont Morgan Library: ⲙⲁⲅⲟⲥ ⲛ̄ⲣⲉϥⲣ̄ϩⲓⲕ, "a magician-ⲙⲁⲅⲟⲥ."[56] In the form ⲣⲉϥⲣ̄ϩⲓⲕ, the word translates other Greek terms for "magician" as well, including φαρμακός, "sorcerer" in Deuteronomy 18:10, and ἐπαοιδός, "enchanter" in Daniel 4:4.[57]

52. For ϩⲓⲕ, see Crum 1939, p. 661a and Černý 1976, p. 276. For Acts 8:9, see Horner 1922, pp. 164–65 and H. Thompson 1932, p. 22.

53. For Acts 8:11, see Horner 1922, pp. 166–67 and H. Thompson 1932, p. 22.

54. Balestri and Hyvernat 1924, p. 228, ll. 19 (ⲡⲁⲓ ⲙⲁⲅⲟⲥ) and 21 (ⲧⲉⲕⲙⲉⲧⲣⲉϥⲉⲣϩⲓⲕ).

55. Balestri and Hyvernat 1924, p. 292, ll. 19–20 (folio 46). In a similar fashion, Father Dios is called "this magician" (ⲡⲉⲓ ⲙⲁⲅⲟⲥ) because of his successful prediction of the future (Rossi 1893, p. 88, col. a, ll. 6–7 [folio LII]). Saint Victor is denounced by his father for conjuring with the Christians: "Do you not know that I have already learned that you are among them receiving instruction to practice magic (ⲙⲁⲅⲓⲁ) in this name Jesus" (Budge 1977a, pp. 8 [text] and 260 [translation]). In contrast, Saint Anthony states that the casting out of demons by Christian practice is anti-magical, though pagan exorcisms constitute magic. See Garitte 1949, p. 84, §§78–79 (Anthony challenging pagans): "And in the place in which there is the sign of the cross, magic (ⲙⲁⲅⲓⲁ) is powerless, and sorcery (ⲙⲛⲧⲣⲉϥⲡⲁϩⲣⲉ) is without effect. Tell us, then, where now are your magical powers (ⲛⲉⲧⲛ̄ⲙⲁⲅⲓⲁ)? Where are the enchanters (ⲛ̄ⲣⲉϥⲙⲟⲩⲧⲉ) of the Egyptians? Where are the fantasies of the Egyptians by which they made magic (ⲣ̄ϩⲓⲕ)?"; and compare p. 85, §80: "Through your words which are filled with guile or by the technique which you wish or magic (ⲟⲩⲙⲛⲧⲣⲉϥⲣ̄ϩⲓⲕ), invoke your demons and cleanse them." For such accusations of magic against (and by) saints, see n. 1, above.

56. Cited in Crum 1939, p. 661a.

57. Cited in Crum 1939, p. 661a.

The lexical ancestor of the Coptic ϩⲓⲕ is the pharaonic , *ḥkꜣ(w)* and its inseparable divine "personification," 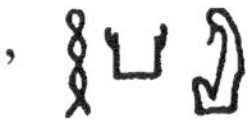, *Ḥkꜣ* (Heka).[58] The recipient of several incisive studies, the concept of *ḥkꜣ* necessarily provides the basis for any attempt to understand Egyptian magic on its own terms.[59] Both deity ("Magic/Magician") and concept ("magic") are attested from the Old Kingdom through the Roman period, with the last mentions of the god being contemporary with the Coptic formulation of ϩⲓⲕ = μαγεία.[60] The earliest mention of the god is on a wall of the funerary temple of the Fifth Dynasty king Sahure, where Heka heads a procession of nome deities bearing offerings to the king.[61] From the end of the same dynasty derive stelae of physicians who are both *swnw* ("doctors") and *ḥm-nṯr Ḥkꜣ* ("prophets of Heka").[62] References multiply in the late Fifth and early Sixth Dynasties, with the god's name compounded with that of the reigning king in the name of funerary estates: *Mr-Ḥkꜣ-ʾIssỉ-ʿnḫ* ("Heka desires that Izezi live"), *Sḥtp-Ḥkꜣ-Wnỉs* ("Heka satisfies Unis"), *Sḥtp-Ḥkꜣ-Ttỉ* ("Heka satisfies Teti"), *Ḥw.t-Mr-Ḥkꜣ-Ttỉ-ʿnḫ* ("The Mansion called Heka desires that Teti live").[63] Only two of these estates can be assigned geographic locations, but the presence of both "Heka satisfies Unis" and "Heka satisfies Teti" in the third Lower Egyptian nome may indicate a local cult of the god.[64] The first theological

58. *Wb* 3: 175–77; and see Westendorf 1965–77, p. 361 and Vycichl 1983, pp. 293–94. Vycichl's suggested link between Egyptian *ḥkꜣ* and Arabic *siḥr* is no more convincing in his 1984 article (pp. 233–37).

59. The most important studies of *ḥkꜣ* are: Gardiner 1915; Piankoff 1935–38; Bonnet 1952, pp. 301–02; te Velde 1970; and Kákosy 1977.

60. The latest mention of Heka known to me occurs in col. 6/35 of the Demotic Magical Pap. of London and Leiden, dating from the third century A.D. (Griffith and Thompson 1904, pp. 10–11 [for date] and pp. 56–57 [for Heka, written *Ḥke*]). The god's name probably appears also in phonetic spelling in the lists of magical names in cols. 7/30: *hʿke* (glossed ϒⲁⲕⲉ) and 29/10: *hʿkyꜣ* ([glossed ϒⲁⲕⲓⲉ] ibid., pp. 62–63 [col. 7/30] and 166–67 [col. 29/10]). The epithet *wr-ḥyk*, "Great of Magic" is found in col. 6/17 (pp. 52–53).

61. Borchardt 1913, p. 99 and pl. 20.

62. Known "prophets of Heka" include *ʾIpy*, *Ny-ʿnḫ-Rʿ*, and *Rʿ-ḥw=f*. For *ʾIpy*, see Mariette 1976, p. 96 (tomb B 4 at Saqqara); Ghalioungui 1983, pp. 16–17 and 48–49 (no. 4); and Gardiner 1915, pp. 261–62. For *Ny-ʿnḫ-Rʿ*, see Lepsius 1972–73, Abteilung II, pl. 91a (grave 55 at Giza); Ghalioungui 1983, pp. 19 and 48–49 (no. 26); Gardiner 1915, pp. 261–62; and for dating, Baer 1960, p. 85. For *Rʿ-ḥw=f*, see Ghalioungui 1983, pp. 21 and 48–49 (no. 38). See further, n. 116, below.

63. For the estate, *Mr-Ḥkꜣ-ʾIssỉ-ʿnḫ*, mentioned in the Giza tomb of *Sndm-ỉb* known as *Mḥỉ*, see Lepsius 1972–73, Abteilung II, pl. 74d (upper left) and Jacquet-Gordon 1962, p. 299 (no. 6). For *Sḥtp-Ḥkꜣ-Wnỉs* and *Sḥtp-Ḥkꜣ-Ttỉ*, both mentioned in the tomb of *Mḥw*, see Jacquet-Gordon 1962, p. 426 (nos. 38 and 39). For *Ḥw.t-Mr-Ḥkꜣ-Ttỉ-ʿnḫ*, mentioned in the tomb of Mereruka at Saqqara, see Duell 1938a, pl. 49, figure 11 and Jacquet-Gordon 1962, p. 413 (no. 13). An additional estate is found in the tomb of one *Mry-ʾIssỉ* with the broken name *Mr-Ḥkꜣ-[...]-ʿnḫ* (Jacquet-Gordon ibid., p. 427 [no. 4]).

64. See Jacquet-Gordon 1962, p. 99 and see also below, pp. 26–27 and n. 119.

evidence concerning *Ḥkꜣ/ḥkꜣ* is found in the Pyramid Texts. Spell 472 begins by invoking the power of magic over the cosmos:

> The sky trembles, the earth quakes before NN.
> The Magician is NN. NN possesses magic.[65]

Pyramid Texts spell 539 enlarges upon this theme and presents Heka as chastiser of the gods:

> Every god who will not build the staircase of this Mery-Re for him ... will have no offering bread, will have no sunshade ... It is not Pepi who says this against you, O gods; it is Magic who says this against you, O gods. This Mery-Re is bound for the mound containing Magic.[66]

Typical of texts which concern Heka from all periods, these spells are inconsistent regarding the inclusion of a divine determinative in the orthography of the word *Ḥkꜣ* to distinguish the god, "Magician," from the title, "magician," or the concept, "magic."[67] So enmeshed are god and concept that little distinction is made between them in Egyptian writings.[68]

65. For the text, see Sethe 1910, p. 11 (§§924a–b). Translations are found in Sethe 1935d, p. 203; Faulkner 1969, p. 160; and Gardiner 1917, p. 31. Both Faulkner and Gardiner translate "a magician" rather than "the Magician." For the ambiguity in writings of *Ḥkꜣ* as opposed to *ḥkꜣ*, see below, nn. 66 and 67.

66. For the text, see Sethe 1910, pp. 234–35 (§§1322–24) and especially p. 235 (§1324a–c) for *Ḥkꜣ/ḥkꜣ*. Translations are found in Sethe 1962a, pp. 234 and 246; Faulkner 1969, p. 208; and Gardiner 1915, p. 261. In §1324b, Sethe understands "my magic" (p. 246), while Faulkner translates "Magic," and Gardiner "Heka."

67. See Sethe 1910, p. 11 (§924b), where texts P (Pepi I) and M (Merenre) have 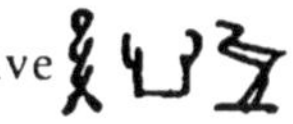, but text N (Pepi II) has 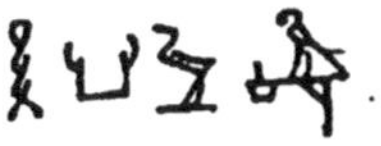. Note also the varying interpretations of the term in the translations cited in nn. 65 and 66, above. For additional discussion, see now Baines 1985, pp. 20–21.

68. In addition to these Old Kingdom writings, compare the varying orthography of the very common epithet *wr-ḥkꜣ*, "great of magic." Applied to deities, kings, staves and crowns, the usual writing of the epithet is 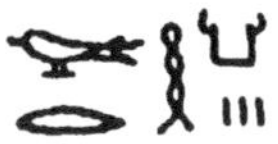; (*Wb* 1: 328/3–11). However, king Ahmose is described as *wr-ḥkꜣw pw*, "He is one great of magic," where the epithet is written . See Sethe 1927, p. 20, l. 2, versus Lacau 1909, p. 3: . See also the title of Thoth as  in Piankoff 1935–38, p. 351. The title "Great of Magic" appears rarely as *ꜥꜣ ḥkꜣ(w)*, see Schott 1929, pp. 78–79 (col. 79/21): "Horus, "; and Rochemonteix et al. 1984–87, p. 99: the king as "Horus Great-of-Magic (), who places amulets (, *sꜣ.w*) around his father."

Nonetheless, a clear picture of the god emerges from the more prolix statements of the Coffin Texts. Spell 261, a charm "To Become the God Heka," constitutes the longest theological exposition on magic, placed in the mouth of the deity himself. Within the spell, Heka addresses the gods in the presence of the creator and declares his origin and powers.

> O noble ones who are before the Lord of the universe ("the All"),[69] behold, I have come before you. Respect me in accordance with what you know. I am he whom the Unique Lord made before two things ("duality") had yet come into being in this land by his sending forth his unique eye when he was alone, by the going forth from his mouth ... when he put Hu ("Logos") upon his mouth.
>
> I am indeed the son of Him who gave birth to the universe ("the All"), who was born before his mother yet existed. I am the protection of that which the Unique Lord has ordained. I am he who caused the Ennead to live ... I have seated myself, O bulls of heaven, in this my great dignity as Lord of *kas*, heir of Re-Atum.
>
> I have come that I might take my seat and that I might receive my dignity, for to me belonged the universe before you gods had yet come into being. Descend, you who have come in the end. I am Heka.[70]

The role of Heka thus outlined presents most of the salient features of this god and the concept he embodies. First of the creations of Re-Atum, Heka appears *before* the emanation of Hu (the creative word or "Logos") from the mouth of the creator. This "authoritative utterance" he infuses with his magic vitality, thereby bringing the gods and the cosmos into existence. The intimate association of magic and word is here given ontological explanation; magic resides in the word itself.[71] Described as a son of the creator, Heka is in actuality the hypostasis of the creator's own power which begets the natural order. This primordial generative aspect of Heka is further stressed in Coffin Texts spell 648:

> His powers put fear into the gods who came into being after him, his myriad of spirits is within his mouth. It was Heka who came into being of himself, at seeing whom the gods rejoiced, and through the sweet savor of whom the gods live, who created the mountains and knit the firmament together.[72]

69. The word *tm* (de Buck 1947, pp. 382b and 384d) has been translated by scholars as either "the universe" or the god, "Atum," but even in the former case a clear pun would be intended on the name of Atum who is expressly mentioned as the father of Heka (ibid., p. 388c). For the various translations of this spell, see Gardiner 1915, p. 254; Faulkner 1973, pp. 199–200; and te Velde 1970, p. 180.

70. For the text, see de Buck 1947, pp. 382–89.

71. For the equivalence of magic and the spoken word, see *inter alia*, Pap. Ebers §356: *ḏd ḥr=k m ḥkꜣ.w*, "you say as magic," in Wreszinski 1913, p. 101; Grapow 1958, p. 87; and von Deines, Grapow, and Westendorf 1958, p. 51. See further pp. 22–24 and 35–49, and nn. 95 and 98, below.

72. See de Buck 1956, p. 270 (text) and Faulkner 1977, pp. 223–24 (translation). These clear pronouncements disprove the attempt by Borghouts 1987a, pp. 34 and 38–40, to deny creative force to Heka.

The creative act of Heka is not limited to a single event, for in Egyptian theology the creation is cyclical, being re-enacted with each sunrise.[73] In company with Hu and Sia ("Perception"), "Heka who opens his two eyes that the two lands might see" takes his place daily upon the solar bark of Re, or is seen in prayer, invoking the separation of heaven and earth.[74] In rare instances, he replaces the air god Shu and performs this separation himself.[75]

This creative benefaction of Heka by day is balanced by his role as protector of the bark by night. In the seventh hour of the book "What is in the underworld" (Amduat), Re confronts and defeats his adversary Apophis/Apep, the serpent of chaos, by virtue of the magic (*ḥkꜣ*) of Isis and the "Elder Magician" (*Ḥkꜣ smsw*).[76] The qualification of Heka as

73. "He (the sun god Re) traverses the sky without wearying until the new day comes, when the arms of his majesty (Re), as 'Great of Magic,' form again the two heavens"; Drioton 1926, p. 18. For discussions of the cyclical creation, see *inter alia* Wilson 1946, pp. 42–61; and compare Assmann 1984b for bibliography.

74. The quotation is from the "Apophis Book" ([Pap. BM 10188, col. 26/9] Faulkner 1933, p. 57 and 1937b, p. 171). For depictions of Heka in the solar boat, see te Velde 1970, pls. xxvi–xxviii; for Heka with Hu and Sia, see Piankoff and Rambova 1957, papyri 10 (*Pꜣ-tì-ꜣImn*) and 11 (*Ḫnsw-rnp*); for Heka with Maat adoring Re, see Piankoff and Rambova ibid., papyrus 16 (*Ḫnsw-ms* A) (= te Velde 1970, pl. xxxii). For representations of Heka praying, see te Velde 1970, p. 183 and pl. xxix; and Badawi 1956, p. 170 and pl. XI (unrecognized).

75. E.g. on the inner cover of the coffin of the god's father of Amon *Ns-pꜣ-wr-šfy*, Fitzwilliam E. 1. 1822 ([tenth century B.C., Thebes] Rundle Clark 1959, pl. 18, opposite p. 241 [= te Velde 1970, pl. xxixc]). See also Lanzone 1974, pl. CLVIII. The identification is based on the appearance of Heka's glyph atop the deity's head. These representations have been interpreted by Piankoff as images of Shu "en tant que dieu de la magie." Where the hieroglyph for Heka is replaced by the writing determinative , Piankoff considers Shu's act to be accomplished by written, presumably ritualistic, spells (Piankoff 1935–38, pp. 351–52). Compare also BD spell 54, §S1: "(I am) this great magical protection (*sꜣw.t*) that came into being and separated Geb from the earth," in Allen 1974, p. 53 and Naville 1886, vol. 1: pl. LXVI, l. 2. Both Heka and Shu have claim to the status of eldest son of Atum, and earlier scholars conflated the two. See Griffith and Thompson 1909, p. 61, no. 614: "Heke, a form of Shu." The corresponding—and occasionally conflicting—roles of Heka and Shu in the Coffin Texts have been carefully analyzed by te Velde 1970, pp. 182–83. A transformation of Shu into Heka is mentioned in the "table hymn" at Edfu; see below, p. 25 and n. 111.

76. See Hornung 1963, vol. 1, pp. 117–18 and 1967, pp. 14–15. See also CT Spell 1130: "Hu together with Heka defeat the 'One of evil character' (*Ḏw-qd* = Apophis) for me," in de Buck 1961, p. 466b. The interpretation of *Ḥkꜣ smsw* is questioned by Baines 1985, pp. 20–21, who proposes "elder (*wr*) magic." The reading of the phrase as the god's name is, however, certain; see n. 77, following.

"elder" should be seen as a reference to his primordial status as first-born son of Re-Atum.[77] Moreover, it serves to distinguish him from younger magician deities—here Isis—whose power (*ḥkꜣ*) is ultimately derived from his own (*Ḥkꜣ*).[78] As Heka protects the passage of the sun through the netherworld he defends the very existence of the created order itself, serving as "the protection of what the Unique Lord ordained" (Coffin Texts

77. Although Hornung would identify the "Elder Magician" as an epithet of Seth, te Velde has shown that the god Heka is preferable. Compare Hornung 1963, vol. 2, pp. 131ff. and te Velde 1970, pp. 177–78. Hornung's interpretation is based on a passage in the Sphinx Stela of Tuthmosis IV, which follows a mention of Seth by one of *Ḥkꜣ smsw*. The text in Helck 1955b, p. 1542, l. 3, reads as follows:  (original direction reversed), and 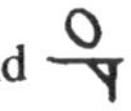 was understood by Hornung as an error for . However, the sign following the Seth animal has been re-edited by Zivie to read *Dwꜣw* ( ; see Zivie 1976, pp. 128 and 140, n. cc). There is thus no interrelationship between Seth and *Ḥkꜣ-smsw*, but rather a list of independent gods, as recognized already by Kees (1930). Most recently, Hornung's interpretation has been restated in Cannuyer 1985, pp. 83–84, who recopies the critical sign as an unambiguous writing of *Ḥkꜣ*: . Because of the general disagreement on the form of this hieroglyph, I personally inspected the Sphinx Stela on June 24, 1986 in the company of Dr. Ann Roth with the assistance of Dr. Ahmed Moussa of the Egyptian Antiquities Organization. The sign (in line 7) is undamaged, unaltered, and absolutely clear: . Cannuyer's reading is thus completely excluded, and although the sign does not show the "kidney-bean" shape often attested for *Dwꜣw*, the form is well within the range of "ovals" used to write the god's name at Giza. Only the raised and slanted positioning of the "oval" above its standard on the Sphinx Stela distinguishes the writings. Compare S. Hassan 1941, pl. 37 (= p. 117): . The Sphinx Stela may thus provide further evidence for the existence of a local cult of *Dwꜣw* in the vicinity (Kees 1980, p. 109 [near Heliopolis?]; denied by Helck 1954, p. 37).

78. This transfer of power from single deity to general divine property finds its inverse development in the evolution of *wr(.t)-ḥkꜣ.w* ("Great of Magic") from a common divine epithet to a specific divine personification as a protective cobra goddess. Thus, on a "magical wand" from the New Kingdom in the collection of University College London, the relation between Hu ("Logos") and Heka is transformed: "Hu, son of the *ka*s of She-who-is-Great-of-Magic" (Petrie 1974, p. 58 [§112, no. 318] and pl. 51). For the epithet and goddess, see Nebe 1986; Simpson 1972b, pp. 70–73; Bosse-Griffiths 1973; idem 1976; and Hari 1976. See also nn. 60, 68, and 73, above, and n. 298, below. Confusion with this cobra deity may account for the depiction of Heka as female in a traditional barque scene on a late coffin in Maspero, Gauthier, and Bayoumi 1939, p. 140 (n. 3) and pl. XLIII (top). Though Nebe (1986, col. 1223, n. 32) denies the independent existence of this goddess in the Late Period, see Norman de Garis Davies 1953, p. 4 and pl. 4 (Sanctuary, third register, right end): *Wr.t-Ḥkꜣ.t n ꜣbt(w)*, "She who is 'Great-of-Magic' of Abydos"; and Naville 1892, p. 19 and pl. 7 (right of §18): [*Wr.t*]-*Ḥkꜣ.t*. In these scenes, the implied association with Isis represents the common fate of all independent goddesses in the Late Period.

spell 261) through his destructive powers which "put fear into the gods" (Coffin Texts spell 648). This defensive aspect of magic may thus be used imitatively—and legitimately—by other deities (such as Isis) and even mankind to preserve existence and destroy enemies. The Tenth Dynasty "Instructions for King Merikare" are explicit in their allotment to mankind of the defensive powers of magic. A list of the benefactions of God for mankind concludes the mention of the creation of heaven, earth, air, food, and government by stating:

ir.n⸗f n⸗sn ḥkꜣw r ꜥḥꜣ.w r ḫsf ꜥ n ḫpry.t
It was in order to be weapons to ward off the blow of events
that he made magic (*ḥkꜣw*) for them (*scil.* "men").[79]

There can thus be no question of the legitimacy of magic in pharaonic Egypt. This is not to say that all magical practice was uncritically applauded. Mention has been made above (p. 13) of a trial for sorcery against the king, and there was recognition that the destructive weapon of *ḥkꜣ* was morally neutral, and could be used for evil purposes. Medical treatises contain recipes to "drive out *ḥkꜣ* from the body" of afflicted patients,[80] and late wisdom literature warned of the seriousness of casting spells.

pꜣ nt ỉr nꜣy⸗f ḥky ỉw⸗w šm n-ỉm⸗f
As for the one who performs his magical spells, they go into him.[81]

79. For the text, see Volten 1945, pp. 75 and 78 (§P 136–37). For translations, see Gardiner 1914, pp. 34–35 and Lichtheim 1973, p. 106. An overly narrow interpretation of this passage appears in Drioton 1927a, p. 133.

80. See Pap. Ebers §§165–74, 182, and 733, in Wreszinski 1913, pp. 44–45, 48, and 180; and Pap. Hearst §§36, 54, and 159, in idem 1912, pp. 8, vii, and 37 (respectively) and Reisner 1905, pls. 3/6, 4/6, and 11/1. These remedies are republished with further parallels in von Deines, Grapow, and Westendorf 1958, pp. 117–18, 146–53, 266, and 287 and Grapow 1958, pp. 204–06, 256–69, 456–57, and 494–95.

81. A "proverbial" statement in Pap. Spiegelberg (Petubast), col. 11/21–22. Spiegelberg (1910, pp. 26–27, and 43*, no. 283) translated *ḥqy* as "snare," but the writing determinative fits "magic," unlike his suggested parallels in Pap. Krall, cols. 16/32 (cited as P 29), 17/11, and 17/14 (cited as Q 10 and Q 13) which have a "strong-arm" determinative. Moreover, his translation "He who lays a trap comes into it" requires that the antecedent of the plural *ỉw⸗w* be the singular *pꜣ* rather than the logical plural *nꜣ ḥqy.w*. The correct translation is given in Borghouts 1970, p. 232. A more exact parallel suggested by Spiegelberg in Pap. Insinger, col. 15/19 is an additional, previously unrecognized writing of "magic" in a negative context: *ḥḏ pꜣ ḥqy r-ḫꜣꜥ pꜣ ntr ḥr pꜣ tꜣ n pꜣ sꜣbꜣ rwš⸗f ḫr hrw*, "Money is the enchantment which God placed on earth for the impious, that he might worry daily." For previous treatments of this passage, see Lexa 1926, p. 49 and Lichtheim 1980, p. 197. A doubtful parallel warning against magic has been seen in the inscription on Statue Base Louvre 2540, edited in Drioton 1928, with further textual discussion in Vernus 1985. The inscription of the lady *Tꜣ-šr.t-Mn* is addressed to "all who come to seek every secret (of) the scorpion" (*ỉỉ nb wḫꜣ ỉmn nb wḥꜥỉ.t*) in the temple of Coptos, and thus probably derives from a private healing statue dedicated in the Coptite temple. The conclusion of the address describes the omniscience and retributive power of Re: "He who does good, He (= Re) does

The Coffin Texts speak directly of the "evil magic" (*ḥkȝ ḏw*) of underworld demons and sorcerers which the deceased refuses to obey.[82] It should be noted, however, that such hostile *ḥkȝ* is termed "evil" from the specific perspective of the deceased who hopes to escape it, and does not constitute "black magic" in any general, moral sense.[83] In the Book of the Dead, the threat to the deceased can be posed by the god Heka himself together with "the thousand violent ones who are beside him."[84] These are divine guardians to be overcome, but not the inherently evil "devils" of Christian myth.

Even the gods could be threatened by this force which they are said to fear. Ptolemaic offering rituals include a purifying incantation against the poisoning of their food by sorcery.[85] The demon Apophis, who is destroyed by *ḥkȝ* (and Heka), nonetheless possesses his own, albeit ineffectual *ḥkȝ* which he marshals against Re:

---

good to him; he who does evil, He does the like to him." Drioton interprets this as a warning against a perceived scribal tendency to subordinate all religion to the practice of magic (1928, p. 54), and his interpretation is modified in Traunecker 1983, pp. 76–77, where the text is interpreted to mean that only the righteous pilgrim will be cured by the statue's magical spells. The discussion of righteousness refers not to the pilgrims, however, but to the statue's donor. The statue's praise of Re is made only after an appeal to visitors to praise the donor as a "noble spirit in her town, who did what the heart of her god desired" (*šps.t m njw.t=s ir ȝb ib n nṯr=s*). The concluding pious remarks about Re seem designed to bolster this assertion of the donor's piety, and thus assure the desired gesture of favor from temple visitors—which was the underlying reason for the statue's erection. No suggestion of hostility to "magic" should be implied—especially on a statue which would have been covered in "magical" formulae and intended (by the donor!) to provide "magical" aid to those suffering from scorpion and snake bite. On the contrary, it is the erection of the curing statue with its "magical" formula that is praised here as that which "the heart of her god desired," and which proves the donor worthy of being a "noble soul of her town." For her benefaction she expects to receive praise from the temple visitors, and blessings from Re who rewards good deeds with goodness. Drioton (1927b) had previously sought to find evidence of a conflict between cult and magic within a spell on a similar Ptolemaic statue base in the Indjandjian collection. As with the Louvre text, however, the supposed conflict derives from a textual misinterpretation. A standard threat to halt cult offerings if the poison continues to circulate is mistranslated as a declaration of the relative ineffectiveness of cultic versus magical healing.

82. See de Buck 1938, p. 54d (spell 87): *n sḏm=y n ḥkȝw nb ḏw*; and cf. de Buck 1935, pp. 372b–c and 398b (spell 75); de Buck 1938, pp. 53g (spell 87) and 54i and m (spell 88); de Buck 1954, p. 224e (spell 407); and de Buck 1956, p. 132n (spell 535). For hostile magic, see also the "Dream Book" of Pap. Chester Beatty 3, col. 7/18: "(If a man see himself in a dream) being bitten by a dog—BAD; (it means) a cleaving fast to him of magic" (Gardiner 1935, vol. 1, p. 16).

83. Compare Griffiths 1975, p. 50: "It could scarcely be claimed that Egyptian thought distinguishes between good and bad magic in a moral sense; the dichotomy is achieved rather by a process of association. As Seth-Typhon becomes a sort of Satan, his magical powers are regarded as evil. Isis too can rebuke and punish ..."

84. BD spell 146w, §15, in Allen 1974, p. 136.

85. Goyon 1970, especially pp. 278–79. Compare also the protective rite of Pap. Salt 825 that "overturns magic" (*pnʿ ḥkȝ.w*) hostile to the dormant Osiris; Derchain 1965, pp. 139 and 7* and pls. 5–6 (cols. 5/10–6/1).

His utterance (*ḏꜣỉs*), his magic (*ḥkꜣ*), and his spells (*ꜣḫw*) are caused to withdraw.[86]

Re may be threatened by earthly sorcery as well. In the "Book of the Heavenly Cow," he withdraws into the heavens in flight from magicians "who act as they desire against the entire land using the magic that is in their bodies."[87] Similarly, in the tale of "Isis and the Name of Re," he refuses to divulge his true name since "I hid it in my body when I was born to prevent the power of any male or female magician coming to be against me."[88] One theological response to such fears was to insist on the deity's immunity to hostile magic. In the Coffin Texts, Shu declares:

I do not obey Magic, for I came into being before him.[89]

At Medamud, the local divine bull is praised in similar terms:

There is no prescription against him in the collections of writings.
There is no magic against him in the written word.[90]

Such statements find their counterpart in the Hellenistic aretalogies of Isis, who proclaimed "I overcome Fate; Fate obeys me."[91] Despite these claims to immunity, threats against the gods, the course of the solar bark, and even the existence of creation are commonplace in preserved Egyptian magical spells, reflecting a belief in the inexorable power of *ḥkꜣ* to which both gods and men are subject.[92]

86. See Faulkner 1933, p. 74 (col. 29/19). Similarly, cols. 24/3 and 10, 27/13 and 18, 28/1 and 5, 28/7, 29/12 and 13, 30/3, and 31/5; and see BD spell 15 A 5, §S3, in Allen 1974, p. 19 and 1949. See also n. 156, below.

87. Hornung 1982, pp. 21 and 45.

88. See Pleyte and Rossi 1869–76, pl. 132/11–12 and Wilson 1969b, pp. 12–13.

89. De Buck 1935, p. 372b–c (spell 75), discussed by te Velde 1970, pp. 182–83. Although te Velde considers this a limited controversy between priests of Shu and Re-Atum, the following examples (not noted by te Velde) from Medamud and the aretalogies indicate a wider theological problem of reconciling henotheism with the coercive force of magic.

90. Drioton 1927a, pp. 38/13 and 40. Compare also the Ptolemaic anti-scorpion charm in Drioton 1927b, pp. 134–35, which proclaims Selket's power over Heka: "Selket the great, the lady who binds Heka when he adores Re at his rising" (ll. 9–10).

91. See Grant 1953, p. 133 and Nock 1961, pp. 139 and 100ff. The association of Magic and Fate (*Šꜣy*) as "cause and effect" is natural, and the two appear together in the "Enthronement of Osiris" scenes. For these, see below, n. 113.

92. See Grapow 1911, pp. 48–54 and Sauneron 1951, pp. 11–21.

Productive and destructive, the force of magic animates and permeates the cosmos, resident in the word, in the bodies of gods and men, and in the plants and stones of earth.[93] Despite the Western tendency to identify magic as "supernatural," it is clear that *ḥkꜣ/Ḥkꜣ* does not stand apart from the created order in Egyptian thought. Its appearance is not "prenatural," but marks the beginning of "nature."[94] Heka has not only *given* life to the gods (Coffin Texts spell 261); he *gives* life to them (Coffin Texts spell 641). If Heka is immanent in the cosmos it is because the creating divinity is immanent in him. In "The Book of the Heavenly Cow" Re states this relationship unambiguously. Discussing spells (*rꜣ.w*), Re declares:

mk Ḥkꜣw im ḏs=f mk ir ʿm sw mk wi

Behold, Heka himself is in them. As for him who ingests ("knows") them, there am I.[95]

The association of Heka and Re is further defined in the "*ba*-theology" of the same text, in which Re declares Magic to be his "external manifestation" or *ba*-spirit.[96]

> I am the one who made heaven and who established [it] in order to place the *ba*s of the gods within it. I shall be with them for eternity which time begets. My *ba* is Magic (*ḥkꜣw*). It is older than it (*scil.* "time") ... The *ba* of Re is in Magic (*ḥkꜣw*) throughout the entire land.[97]

The text continues with a ritual to be said by a man "that he might make his protection by magic."

93. For *ḥkꜣ* in the body of gods and men, see *inter alia* Hornung 1982, pp. 21–22, 27, 45 (l. 225), and 47 (l. 288); Pap. BM 10188, col. 30/13, in Faulkner 1933, p. 78 and 1938, p. 43; and CT spell 454 in de Buck 1954, p. 325 and passim. For the notion of magical "properties" resident within matter, see Gardiner 1922, p. 266b and Pap. Salt 825, cols. 1/1–5/9 in Derchain 1965, pp. 1*–6* (text) and 137–38 (translation). Borghouts' 1980 attempt (cols. 1139–40), to equate Egyptian and Zande conceptions is discussed above, pp. 11–12. Contrary to the statements of Borghouts, *loc. cit.*, magic in Egypt is viewed always as a *force* (like "life" or "strength") which is consumed and which permeates the body, but never as a tangible, material "substance" (like Zande *mangu*). The same objections apply to the statements of Sauneron 1962b, pp. 260–61. Borghouts (1987a, p. 35) now repeats his opinion with reference to magic being eaten, smelled, etc. Magical power may certainly be made to permeate a tangible object and thus be manipulated in these ways (see *Chapter 3*, below), but this does not mean that magic is itself inherently tangible.

94. The term "prenatural" is te Velde's (1970, p. 176). In any case, Egyptian concepts of "nature" do not correspond to Western counterparts; cf. the term for "all, totality," *ntt iwtt*, "that which is and that which is not" (*Wb* 2: 354/10).

95. Hornung 1982, pp. 20 and 44 (ll. 218–20).

96. For the *ba*-spirit, see Žabkar 1968 and the references cited in Hornung 1982, p. 69, n. 189.

97. Hornung 1982, pp. 26–27 and 46–47 (ll. 275–86). The translation of the final clause involves an interpolation of the texts of Seti I and Ramses VI (Hornung ibid., pp. 27, l. 286 and 70, n. 196).

> I am that pure Magician (*Ḥkꜣw*) who is in the mouth (or "utterance") and body of Re ... On your face, enemy of Re! I am his *ba*, the Magician (*Ḥkꜣw*).[98]

Elsewhere, Re may be provided with as many as seven *bas*, but even there may be found *bꜣ Ḥkꜣ*, "the *ba*, Heka."[99] In a Berlin hymn which assigns the role of creator to Ptah, Heka correspondingly appears as the *ba* of that deity:

> Everyone trembles when his *ba* comes into being, Magic (*ḥkꜣ*) who has power over the gods.[100]

In later periods this relationship is expressed differently, with Heka designated as the *ka*-spirit ("double, vital essence") of Re. Thus, in Papyrus BM 10188 (col. 27/5–6), the sun god declares: *kꜣ=y pw ḥkꜣw*, "Magic is my *ka*."[101] This conception seems to have become popular, and was by no means restricted to priestly speculation, for the title "*ka* of Re" accompanies several depictions of the god on the publicly displayed "healing statue" of Djedhor.[102] On the walls of the Greco-Roman temples of Dendera, Edfu, Kom Ombo, and Philae, Heka appears as one of the fourteen *kas* of Re.[103] The accompanying inscriptions, though "conventional," nevertheless convey clearly the role of the god in later theology.[104] Presented to Hathor of Dendera by the king, Heka arrives "bearing his spells (*ꜣḫw*) and his magic (*ḥkꜣ*) mingled in his body. His words are efficacious, his dignity flourishes in the hearts of men."[105] Significantly, Hathor receives Heka in her quality of "Great of Magic among the gods."[106] At Edfu, the king escorts before Horus "Heka who performs magic (*ḥkꜣ*), with his magic spread out before you. He has made your magic. He has caused that the respect of you and the fear of you be mingled in every body."[107] As in the Coffin Texts

98. Hornung ibid., pp. 27 and 47 (ll. 287–95).

99. Shorter 1938, pp. 60, 69, and pl. 5.

100. Wolf 1929, pp. 40–41, ll. 8–9 (col. 11/7), cited incorrectly in te Velde 1970, p. 182, n. 44.

101. Faulkner 1933, p. 61 (col. 27/5–6). Faulkner (1937b, p. 172), however, mistranslates this as "it was the very essence of magic." Compare also col. 32/4: "O Heka, *ka* of Re," in idem 1933, p. 87 and 1938, p. 46.

102. Jelínková-Reymond 1956, pp. 24–25 and Daressy 1919a, pp. 132, 142, and 143 (versus Jelínková-Reymond's copy on p. 25).

103. See Dümichen 1981, pls. 133 (= 189) and 156 (Dendera), 157–58 (Edfu), and 162 (Philae); de Morgan 1909, p. 186; Chassinat 1928, p. 99 and 1933, p. 115 (= Dümichen, pls. 157–58); Junker 1958, pp. 95–96 (fig. 49) and 98 and 100 (fig. 51 = Dümichen, pl. 162); and Porter and Moss 1939, pp. 60 (= Dümichen, pl. 156), 78 (= Dümichen, pls. 133 and 189), 122 (= Dümichen, pls. 157–58), and 215 (= Dümichen, pl. 162). These are discussed in Gardiner 1915, pp. 258–60.

104. The scenes are dismissed as "conventional" in Gardiner 1915, p. 259 and te Velde 1970, p. 179.

105. Dümichen 1981, pls. 133 and 189 and see Gardiner 1915, p. 259.

106. Dümichen 1981, pls. 133 and 189.

107. Dümichen 1981, pl. 158 (middle text = Chassinat 1928 p. 99, no. vii; right hand text = Chassinat 1933, p. 115, no. xii).

of the previous millennium, Heka remains the conduit of magical creativity and protection from Re to the local gods.

Heka's association with the *ka* derives from this earlier period, however, for in Coffin Texts spell 261 Heka styles himself "Lord of *ka*s," and in spell 648 it is stressed that "his myriad of *ka*-spirits is within his mouth." In fact, his name itself may indicate the origin of the relationship. Although later theorists at Esna derived his name by "folk etymology" from *ḥ(ꜣ.t)-kꜣ(.t)*, "first work" in reference to his preeminent position in the order of creation, te Velde has suggested that the name stems from *ḥwỉ-kꜣ*, "He who consecrates (literally "strikes") the *ka*."[108] Seeming confirmation of this etymology is found in a variant of Coffin Texts spell 26l, which states that Heka (here identified with the deceased) *ḥwỉ kꜣ.w⸗f*, "consecrates his (*scil.* the creator deity's) *ka*s."[109] Illustrations of this consecration are found in the royal birth scenes of the New Kingdom and later in which Heka is shown presenting the new-born king and his *ka* to their creator.[110] Similarly, at Edfu the god Shu is said to dedicate (*ḥwỉ*) every good thing to Atum, "since he has become Heka."[111]

Thus may be explained the method of Heka's effectiveness. At the stroke of a word, Magic penetrates the *ka* or "vital essence" of any element in creation and invests it with power, either generative or destructive. The notion of power is central to the role of Heka, and becomes the very emblem of his name. Attested as early as the Twentieth Dynasty, the sign  or  (*pḥty*), meaning "strength/power," frequently replaces the phonetic spellings of the god's name.[112] Although an alternate emblem has been suggested for

108. For the Esna etymology, see Sauneron 1962b, p. 212. For te Velde's suggestion, see 1970, pp. 179–80.

109. De Buck 1947, p. 385c. Borghouts 1987a, pp. 33–34, prefers to translate *ḥwỉ* as "drive" to avoid nuances of creative action by Heka.

110. For the role of Heka in the divine birth of the king, see Brunner 1986, pp. 139 (= pl. 13) and 161 (= pl. 15); Naville 1896, vol. 2, pls. 53 (= Brunner, pl. 18) and 55 (= Brunner, pl. 19); Gardiner 1915, pp. 260–61; and te Velde 1970, pp. 178–79. His role is equally prominent in the jubilee rituals of royal rebirth (Uphill 1965, pp. 370 and 376). The traditional prominence of "magic" was retained even by the iconoclastic Akhenaton; see the jubilee hymn in Spalinger 1988: "Hail to you O king Neferkheprure ... who has seized the magic of Horus" (col. 2, Spalinger's translation ibid., p. 30, ignores the writing of "Horus" visible in fig. 16). In later periods, Heka has the same function in the derivative scenes of the birth chapels ("mammisis") which depict the birth of the child deity of the local triad (Daumas 1958, pp. 464–65 and 472–76 and Junker and Winter 1965, pp. 104–07).

111. See Blackman 1945, pp. 59 and 65, n. 35; discussed also in te Velde 1970, p. 179.

112. Gardiner 1973, p. 464, Sign-list F 22. For this writing of *ḥkꜣ*, see *Wb* 3: 176, upper right; Dawson 1938, p. 128; idem 1945, p. 105; and te Velde 1970, pp. 183–84. The writing may be attested as early as the Middle Kingdom in a personal name *Ḥkꜣ*(?) (Ranke 1935, p. 256, no. 22 [S. Louvre C 45]). Perhaps related to this spelling is the occasional depiction of Heka as a sphinx (de Wit n.d., pp. 213–14).

Heka, written  , *"revered one," this proves to be an editor's error for  .[113] So widespread does this usage become, that in Ptolemaic hieroglyphs the image of Heka with the *pḥty*-sign atop his head may serve as a writing of the word *nṯr*, "god," reflecting an understanding of the gods as sources of magical power.[114] The ultimate source of this power depicted in the god's name is, of course, the creating deity, whose name is also equated with Magic. In Papyrus BM 10188 (col. 28/22) Re-Atum states: *rn=y pw ḥkꜣ.w*, "Magic is my name."[115]

The god so honored in Egyptian theology should not be dismissed as simply a colorless "personification" of abstract magical power, for Heka received a public cult as well. As noted above, prophets of the god (*ḥm-nṯr Ḥkꜣ*) are attested as early as the Old Kingdom.[116] A "Mansion of Heka,"  (*Ḥw.t-Ḥkꜣ*) was associated with Heliopolis, and Heka is given special veneration in the Memphite necropolis, appearing on the "Sphinx Stela" of Tuthmosis IV as "The Elder Magician of the Sacred Place of the Primordial Beginning."[117] In the New Kingdom tomb of *ꜣInḥr-ḫꜥw*, Heka is found together with Hu, Re, and other deities as a donor in the standard *ḥtp-di͗-nysw.t* funerary prayer.[118] During the Libyan

113. Badawi 1956, p. 171 and pl. XI. The traces are almost invisible on the plate, and Badawi (p. 170) notes that the inscriptions are in a poor state of preservation and difficult to read. Although Badawi does not recognize this deity as Heka, the scene is the standard "Enthronement of Osiris" which regularly includes—as here—an anthropomorphic Heka standing behind Osiris and holding serpent staves crossed over his chest. Parallel representations are found in Budge 1912, pl. 108 and p. 81; Montet 1947, pl. 24; Daressy 1909, pls. 44 (and p. 104), 48 (and p. 127), and 56 (and p. 187); and Piankoff and Rambova 1957, papyrus 10. General discussions of the motif are found in Dawson 1938, p. 128 and Piankoff and Rambova 1957, pp. 59–61. A further, unrecognized depiction of Heka within the tomb scenes of crown prince Sheshonq is labeled 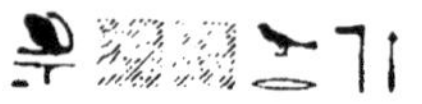 (Badawi 1956, p. 170 and pl. XI and above, n. 74).

114. See *Wb* 2: 358 and *Wb* 3: 4 (right column), under "sportive writings"; and for an example at Edfu, see Alliot 1949, p. 431 (in re. Rochemonteix et al. 1984–87, p. 369/4). For Dendera examples, see Junker 1903, pp. 5–8 (especially pp. 7–8).

115. Faulkner 1933, p. 70; idem 1938, p. 41; and te Velde 1970, p. 182.

116. See n. 62, above. There is no substantiation for Gardiner's expressed opinion (1915, p. 262) that these titles "display nothing more than a devotion to magical arts" and do not indicate a cult of the god. Later examples of *ḥm-nṯr Ḥkꜣ* may be found in S. Cairo JdE 85647 published in Bakir 1943; and cf. Sethe 1904, p. 164/8: *ḥm-nṯr ḫnm.t n Ḥkꜣ pꜣ ḫrd*, "prophet of the nurse (= Sakhmet?) of Heka the child" (Ptolemaic).

117. For "The Mansion of Heka" at Heliopolis associated with the spouse of Re, *ꜣIwsꜥꜣs*, see Gardiner 1915, p. 256. For Heka on the Sphinx Stela, see above, n. 77 and Zivie 1976, pp. 332–33.

118. See Bruyère 1930, p. 158.

period, the influence of Heka is particularly strong in the Letopolite and Andropolite nomes north of Memphis in the western Delta. As a recipient of fields, he appears on donation stelae from Kom Firin and Kom el-Hisn, and his name has been found on a block from Amria near lake Mareotis.[119] It is perhaps significant that this is the very region in which Old Kingdom funerary estates were dedicated to the god.[120] Personal names compounded with Heka proliferate in the Late Period, with *Pꜣ-ti-Ḥkꜣ*, "He-whom-Heka-has-given"; *Ḥkꜣ*, "Heka"; *Ḥkꜣ-m-ḥꜣ.t*, "Heka-is-at-the-fore"; *Ḥkꜣ-m-sꜣ⸗f*, "Heka-is-his-protection"; and *Ḥkꜣ-tꜣy⸗f-nḫt*, "Heka-is-his-strength," et cetera.[121] In the Greco-Roman periods, Heka is one of the chief deities at Esna. His festival of Hathor 22 was marked by a procession of the god's image through the fields to encourage growth after the inundation, with a triumphal return as a victorious king.[122]

Much has been made of Heka's appearance within differing local triads, being equated with Nefertum or Geb, and made the son of Ptah, Khnum-Re, or Sobek.[123] This has even been considered by te Velde and Kákosy to indicate a lessening of his status, a trivializing of his position into that of the "ordinary" child divinity.[124] Nonetheless, in each of his various cult sites, and despite varying identifications with local gods, Heka's function remains consistent. Wherever Heka is venerated, he is represented as the eldest child of the creating divinity. At Heliopolis this creator is Re-Atum, at Memphis, Ptah, in the west Delta, Sobek-Re, and at Esna, Khnum-Re. Far from being demoted, the theology of Heka has so far permeated local cults that he has supplanted the original younger members of regional triads. Thus may he appear as *Ḥkꜣ-pꜣ-ẖrd*, "Heka the child" with the consorts of these local creators (Sakhmet, Neith, Tefnut), or seated upon an opening lotus as the solar infant "who opens his two eyes that the two lands might see."[125]

119. See Spiegelberg 1920b, pp. 57–58 and pl. V; Bakir 1943 (Kom Firin); de Meulenaere 1964, pp. 170–71; Yoyotte 1961, pp. 143–44 (§§30 and 32) and 146; Schott 1930a, p. 107, n. 2; and Kees 1930. At Armant, Heka the child is said to "exact tribute from the land of Libya (*Ṯmḥ*)" (Lepsius 1972–73, Abteilung IV, pl. 63c [second seated child god from left]).

120. See the comments by Jacquet-Gordon 1962, p. 99.

121. Ranke 1935, pp. 125 (no. 19) and 256 (nos. 21–27) and cf. Björkman 1974. Personal names compounded with *ḥkꜣ* are also attested in the Old (*Ḥkꜣ⸗f*, "His magic") and Middle Kingdoms (*Ḥkꜣ⸗y*, "My magic," and *Ḥkꜣ*[?], "Heka"; Ranke 1935, p. 256 [nos. 21, 27, and 22, respectively]).

122. See Sauneron 1962b, pp. 29–35.

123. For the varying associations, see Gardiner 1915, pp. 256–57; Bonnet 1952, p. 302; te Velde 1970, p. 186; Kákosy 1977, cols. 1109–10; and Sauneron 1962b, pp. 21 and 23, n. b.

124. Te Velde 1970, p. 186; Kákosy 1977, cols. 1109–10; and cf. Baines 1985, p. 124.

125. For the quote, see n. 74, above. For Heka upon the lotus at Esna, see te Velde 1970, pl. 31b.

The undisputed prominence of Heka/heka within orthodox Egyptian theology necessarily provokes skepticism about the supposed incompatibility of "religion" and "magic." In his initial study of the god Heka, Gardiner was even led to deny the existence of any such distinction:

> That Magic should have been regarded as an attribute of a deity, and *a fortiori* as itself a deity, destroys at one blow the theories of those who discern a fundamental distinction between what is religious and what is magical.[126]

Despite this theoretical pronouncement, however, Gardiner and other scholars continued to make this distinction in practice, since the categories were traditional and the terminology commonplace.[127]

126. Gardiner 1915, p. 262.

127. See below, *Chapter 2*, p. 70, n. 316.

CHAPTER 2

THE VOCABULARY OF MAGIC

> … a spell—which is merely the setting in motion of a force as natural as any other, but operating primarily in a region beyond the ken of the mortal who makes use of the force.
>
> George MacDonald 1981, p. 131

ꜣḫw

Having established that magic—as *ḥkꜣ*—constitutes a pivotal, and by no means "artificial" category in *Egyptian* thought,[128] we must consider related phrases and synonyms in order to discover the perceived range and nature of this force. Among the most important of these associated terms is *ꜣḫw*, , surviving into Old Coptic as Hϩ, and translated previously (p. 24) in a Ptolemaic text from Dendera as "spells."[129] The verb *ꜣḫ*, the root of this term, may mean either "to be effective" or "to be bright," and derivatives of both nuances are common.[130] In the case of *ꜣḫw*, "spells," the literal meaning is presumably "effective things," but a pun on the alternate meaning "bright" may be found in the "Book of Amduat," in which it is said:

ḫpr n mdw⸗ṯn šsp n ḥkꜣw⸗ṯn
May your words occur; may your magic shine.[131]

A case has recently been made by Borghouts for a sharp delineation in meaning between *ḥkꜣ* and *ꜣḫw*, with the latter alone being a "self-sufficient creative power."[132] Restricted to the divine sphere, *ꜣḫw* "may substitute another element (even a 'void') and thus have an apotropaic function too."[133] In contrast, *ḥkꜣ* "only blots out impediments to a desired result, and in selectively doing so may arrive at the same results as *ꜣḫw*."[134] Borghouts' theory derives directly from the comments of Chabas in 1868, in which he distinguished *ꜣḫw*, "benefaction" (*bonté*) from other magical notions of "repelling" in what

128. Contrary to te Velde 1970, p. 186, who applies to magic Lévi-Strauss' terminology "*unité artificielle*" (an artificial concept existing only in the minds of researchers).

129. For *ꜣḫw*, "spells," see *Wb* 1: 15/6–8. For Hϩ, see Westendorf 1965–77, p. 503 and Osing 1976b, vol. 1, p. 92 and vol. 2, p. 569, n. 446. The word may also survive as ⲁϩ, in Griffith and Thompson 1904, p. 67 and 1909, p. 116 (col. 9/5): "Your name is Magic(?)."

130. For the verb *ꜣḫ* and its derivatives, see *Wb* 1: 13–18 and 33. The question of the root meaning of *ꜣḫ* has been much discussed (Englund 1978; the review by Friedman 1982; idem 1985a; idem 1985b; and Assmann 1984a, pp. 108–12).

131. See Hornung 1963, vol. 1, p. 81 and vol. 2, p. 98; discussed by te Velde 1970, pp. 176–77. Literally, "A coming to be for your words; a shining for your magic."

132. Borghouts 1980, col. 1139. This argument is expanded in idem 1987a, pp. 29–46.

133. Borghouts 1980, col. 1139. Borghouts 1987a, p. 37: "We may speculate that what actually happens is, that *ꜣḫw* simply substitutes itself for the opponents of the sun god."

134. Borghouts 1980, col. 1139. Compare, however, Borghouts 1987a, p. 37: "Pressing the interpretation a little more, one might put it that the use of *ꜣḫ.w blots out* other entities" (emphasis added, RKR). Borghouts' intentions are better expressed by the graph on p. 41.

has since become known as the "Standard Text A" of the stelae of Horus-on-the-crocodiles.[135] These proposed distinctions are readily proved false. From the prior discussion of the role of Heka in the act of creation, it should be obvious that *ḥkꜣ* cannot be restricted to a purely "negative" function. The description of creation in Papyrus BM 10188, col. 28/22 is explicit and conclusive:

in.n=y rꜣ=y ḏs=y rn=y pw ḥkꜣw
I brought forth my spell myself. Magic (*ḥkꜣw*) is my name.[136]

The deity Heka possesses both *ḥkꜣ* and *ꜣḫw* "mingled in his body," and the two terms occur frequently in parallel usage.[137] Thus, in another description of the creation in Papyrus BM 10188, the creator describes the same act by using a verbal derivative of *ꜣḫw*: *ꜣḫ.n=y m ib=y*, "I made spells in my heart."[138] In the "Litany of Re," the separation of heaven and earth—accomplished elsewhere by *ḥkꜣ*—is attributed to *ꜣḫw*.[139] Re is praised as:

Unique one who raised the earth through his *ꜣḫw*.[140]

The creative power of both *ḥkꜣ* and *ꜣḫw* enables Re to sail without water or hauling in the seventh hour of the Amduat: "It is by means of the magic (*ḥkꜣw*) of Isis and the Elder Magician and by the spells (*ꜣḫw*) on the mouth of this god (Re) himself that he travels."[141] Te Velde has even argued that both *ḥkꜣ* and *ꜣḫw* are found as expressions of general

135. Chabas 1868, p. 103, n. 5. For text A, see below, n. 144.

136. Faulkner 1933, p. 70 and 1938, p. 41.

137. For *ḥkꜣ* and *ꜣḫw* in the body of Heka, see above, p. 24 The parallel usage of these terms is noted by te Velde 1970, pp. 176–77 and by Kákosy 1977, col. 1109. Borghouts 1980, col. 1139, considers this "deceptive" and in 1987a, p. 31, "disconcerting."

138. Faulkner 1933, p. 60 (col. 26/23) and cf. idem 1937b, pp. 172 and 181, who translates "I considered(?) in my heart." The same passage is found in col. 28/24, in Faulkner 1933, p. 70 and idem 1938, p. 41. The best published translation is that of Budge 1910, p. 14: "I made use of magical words of power in my heart." Perhaps literally "I was effective in my heart," the phraseology is clearly a pun on the creation by *ꜣḫw* in the heart of the deity discussed *inter alia* by Borghouts (1980, col. 1139). For *ꜣḫw* in the heart, see n. 156, below. For a parallel verbal use of *ꜣḫ*, "to make spells," see below, pp. 40–41 and n. 184. *ꜣḫ* is also used to describe the creation at Esna, where the newly created gods say to Neith: "How effective (*ꜣḫ sp*-2) is all that which came forth from your heart" (Sauneron 1968, p. 30 [no. 206/3 {text}] and 1962b, p. 257 [translation]). Similarly, Neith announces "Let us reckon 4 spells (*ꜣḫw*) that we might make clear what is in our bodies" (Sauneron 1968, p. 30 [no. 206/5 {text}] and 1962b, p. 259 [translation], and below, p. 44).

139. For *ḥkꜣ* as the force which separated heaven and earth, see above, nn. 72–75.

140. Hornung 1975, p. 75; idem 1976, p. 71 (§66); and Piankoff 1964, p. 27.

141. Hornung 1963, vol. 1, p. 118 and vol. 2, p. 125.

artistic creativity as well.[142] It should be noted that Borghouts himself acknowledges an example in which Isis is transformed by means of unquestionably "positive" *ḥkꜣ*.

wn.in=s ḥr šnty m ḥkꜣ=s iw=s ir.t ḫpr.w=s m w'(.t) šri(.t) nfr.t m ḥ'.w=s
Then she conjured by means of her magic, and she made her transformation into a young girl with a beautiful body.[143]

The most damaging evidence for the theories of Chabas and Borghouts is forthcoming from the very text which Chabas analyzed in 1868. The widely disseminated text A of the cippi of Horus contains the following statements placed in the mouth of the reciter:

šd.n=y m ḥkꜣw=k dd.n=y m ꜣḫw=k ... sḫpr n=y qfꜣ.w=k m ḥkꜣ=k
I have recited by means of your magic (*ḥkꜣw*); I have spoken by means of your spells (*ꜣḫw*) ... Create for me your prestige by means of your magic (*ḥkꜣ*).[144]

142. Te Velde 1970, p. 185. For *ḥkꜣ*, see line 7 of S. Louvre C 14 of a sculptor who states: "As for every *ḥkꜣ*, I was equipped (*'pr*) with it." For an overview of differing interpretations of this passage, see Barta 1970, pp. 78–91. Barta considers this ritual, not artistic, magic. For *ꜣḫw*, see Pap. Prisse, l. 56 ("The Instructions of Ptahhotep"): "There is no artist who has command of his *ꜣḫw*." For this text, see Žába 1956, p. 20 and Barta 1970, p. 82. Borghouts 1980, cols. 1142 and 1149, n. 82, denies this link with "inspiration." But, see below, p. 38.

143. Gardiner 1932, p. 44, "Horus and Seth," (Pap. Chester Beatty 1) col. 6/4–5. The text is cited in Borghouts 1980, col. 1147, n. 22 and in idem 1987a, p. 40, where an attempt is made to explain "this apparent contradiction": "Since *ḥkꜣ.w* is the type of magic allowed to mankind, it is perhaps the dominant anthropocentric view of this text on the divine world that influences the use of this term. Alternatively, Isis' use of it may signify that she wishes to prevent anything from coming between herself and the vision she wishes to call up with Seth. In other words, *ḥkꜣ.w* forms the protective 'aura' around her changing appearances. These are brought about by her creative act which in theological terms would be based on *ꜣḫw*. But for all its mythological consistency, this is not a theological text but a folk-tale. To expect subtleties of this kind is perhaps asking a bit too much." Borghouts' analysis has several deficiencies: it implies—wrongly—that *ḥkꜣ* is not a theological term, it devalues the common use of this force by the gods (especially Isis), it assumes that the unmentioned *ꜣḫ.w* must play a role in the act of creative magic; and it dismisses the example as aberrant because of "the social dimension of this terminology." The example is by no means aberrant, and is paralleled in Pap. Sallier IV (BM 10184), col. 3/5: *wn-in Ḏḥwty ḥr ir.t ḫpr.w=f m ḥkꜣ smn sw m tpty*, "Then Thoth made its transformation by magic, establishing it (Isis' head) on the Isis cow" (Budge 1923, p. 35 and pl. 90). A third instance of this cliché appears in the funerary Pap. BM 10194, col. 2/12 (a theological context as defined by Borghouts 1987a, p. 31), as signaled by Caminos 1987, pp. 156 and 152 (incorrectly cited as Pap. BM 10241 in Borghouts 1987a, p. 46, n. 55).

144. Daressy 1903, pp. 2 (S. Cairo 9401, ll. 2–3 and 10–11), 7–8 (S. Cairo 9402, § 2, ll. 2–3 and 10–11) and passim; and cf. Sander-Hansen 1956, pp. 51 and 53, ll. 106–07 and 121–22; and Jelínková-Reymond 1956, pp. 57 and 61 (l. 120), who, however, translates the final phrase "J'ai créé ton aspect par ta puissance magique." In a synthetic translation of the varying versions of this spell, Borghouts (1978, pp. 83–85, no. 123) renders the final phrase similarly: "I have created awe of you through your magic" (p. 84). However, cf. the Ramesside variant in von Bergmann 1886, p. vii and pl. V (l. 9): *sḫpr=k qfꜣw=[k] {m?} ḥkꜣ.w=k siqr=k ꜣḫw*, "May you create [your] prestige {by means of ?} your magic, may you perfect spells." For *sḫpr* with *Ḥkꜣ*, see also de Morgan 1895, p. 186, no. 245 and Dümichen 1981, p. 158.

Here *ḥkꜣ* is expressly said to have the ability "to create" (*sḫpr*), and *ꜣḫw*—though possessed by the deity—is not restricted to the divine sphere, but is directly manipulated by the human reciter. That the reciter claims elsewhere to be associated with various deities in no way diminishes the value of this evidence, for such identifications are routine in virtually all magical spells, regardless of whether they concern *ḥkꜣ* or *ꜣḫw*.[145]

Similarly, no distinction may be found in the use of *ḥkꜣ* or *ꜣḫw* as a destructive force. Examples of parallel usage are widespread and unmistakable in their implications. A few will suffice. For simplicity, *ḥkꜣ* is translated as "magic" and *ꜣḫw* as "spells":

ḥm tw Ỉtm m ꜣḫw tp-rꜣ.w=sn sḏm=k ḥkꜣ=y
May Atum repel you (Apep) with the spells of their mouths when you hear my magic.[146]

sꜥm=s ỉm=k m ḥkꜣw tp-rꜣ=sn
It has swallowed you by means of the magic of their mouths.[147]

ḥkꜣ=sn ꜥq=sn ỉm=k ꜣḫ=sn ḫpr=sn r=k
Their magic enters into you (Apep), their spells come to be against you.[148]

sḫtm tw ỉmy.w wỉꜣ=f m wỉꜣ=f m ꜣḫw n tp-rꜣ=sn m ḥkꜣw ỉmy.w ẖ.t=sn
Those in his (Re's) bark destroy you in his bark with the spells of their utterances, with the magic in their bodies.[149]

ꜣs.t ... sḫmt sp.w šd-ḫrw m ꜣḫw rꜣ=s
Isis ... who repels the deeds of the enchanters by the spells of her mouth.[150]

ꜣḫw Ḏḥwty ḥr msnḥ ḥr=w sd r ḏꜣḏꜣ ỉm=sn pḥd m s.t=sn
The spells of Thoth twist about their faces tail to head among them, they being struck down in their places.[151]

ỉr.n=y mk.t ḥꜥ.w=k m ḥkꜣ=y m ꜣḫw tp-rꜣ=y
I (*scil.* the king) have made the protection of your limbs by means of my magic, by the spells on my mouth.[152]

145. See *inter alia*, Lexa 1925, vol. 1, pp. 56–58. For priests using *ꜣḫw* in the role of gods, see also Assmann 1984a, pp. 109 and 112.

146. Faulkner 1933, p. 77 (col. 30/6). The last clause is translated as a separate sentence "May you hear my magic" in idem 1938, p. 43.

147. Faulkner 1933, p. 80 (col. 30/21–22) and 1938, p. 44.

148. Faulkner 1933, p. 79 (col. 30/18–19) and 1938, p. 44.

149. Faulkner 1933, p. 76 (col. 29/26–27) and 1938, p. 43.

150. Moret 1931, pp. 739–40 (S. Louvre C 286, l. 14) and Lichtheim 1976, p. 83. On *šd-ḫrw*, see below, p. 45 and n. 210.

151. The Epigraphic Survey 1932, pl. 82, l. 30.

152. Ramses IV to Onuris in his Abydos Stela, ll. 25–26. Similarly to Sakhmet in ll. 27–28 (Korostovtsev 1947, pp. 159 and 163–64 and Kitchen 1983b, p. 24/11 and 14).

Such parallelism is by no means "deceptive" but fundamental, and the mental abstractions which Borghouts devises to account for them (creation of a void, etc.) render his distinctions absolutely meaningless.[153] Conclusive proof—should any further be needed—is found in "The Rite for Repelling the Angry One," in which the Middle Egyptian statement "who repels the angry one with his spells (*ꜣḫw*)" is translated into Late Egyptian as "he drives back the angry one with his magic (*ḥkꜣ*)."[154]

The precise relation of *ꜣḫw* to *ḥkꜣ* is obviously difficult to specify. Both may be *tp-rꜣ*, "on the mouth," and thus spoken; both may be in the body, and thus thought. As a title "sorceress," *ꜣḫ.t* is found in place of the expected *ḥkꜣy.t*, "magician" as an epithet of Isis and the uraeus serpent.[155] *ꜣḫw* may be possessed by evil characters as well. Of Apep it is said:

nn ꜣḫw n ib=k iw (= r) s.t=f
The spells of your heart are not in their place (i.e., "not right, functioning").[156]

In the Metternich Stela, Isis conjoins the terms in what may allude to the best explanation of their ultimate relationship:

ink ꜣs.t ntr.t nb(.t) ḥkꜣ ir ḥkꜣ ꜣḫ ḏd mnḫ mdw
I am Isis the goddess, the possessor of magic, who performs magic, effective of speech, excellent of words.[157]

Expressing the notion of "effectiveness," *ꜣḫ* serves as an attribute of magical speech; as the noun *ꜣḫw*, it embodies that attribute in a literary synonym for the basic term *ḥkꜣ*. The quality of "effectiveness" is thus seen as fundamental to magic, and the equation is often

153. The term "deceptive" is that of Borghouts 1980, col. 1139. His explanation of "deceptively" destructive aspects of *ꜣḫw* as the creation of non-creation (void) to negate creation is contorted in the extreme, and yields no practical distinction between *ḥkꜣ* and *ꜣḫw*.

154. See Schott 1929, p. 103/5–8; noted also by Klasens 1952, p. 77 and te Velde 1970, p. 177. Borghouts (1987a, p. 32) cites this instance and adds a further example of interchange between the terms, noting that "this looks rather discouraging" for his proposed distinction between them.

155. For Isis as *ꜣḫ.t*, "sorceress," see Klasens 1952, p. 77 (in re. Metternich Stela l. 75, in which Horus is addressed as *sꜣ ꜣḫ.t*, "son of the sorceress") and Moret 1931, pp. 741–42. Moret translates *ꜣḫ.t* as *l'inspirée*. For the uraeus, see Erman 1911, pp. 35, 37, and 48–49 (cols. 9/3 and 17/1). Although Erman translates "shining one," the parallel invocation of the serpent as *wr-ḥkꜣw* favors "sorceress."

156. Faulkner 1933, p. 77 (col. 30/4) and 1938, p. 43. See also n. 86, above, and n. 219, below. For the idiom "to be in place" = "to be right," cf. Pap. Berlin P. 8869, l. 5: *ḫt m s.t*, "Everything is fine," in Smither 1942, pp. 16–19. *ꜣḫw* is attributed to other evil snakes as well (Hornung 1982, pp. 18–19 and 44, l. 208).

157. Sander-Hansen 1956, pp. 38 (text) and 41, l. 59 (translation) and cf. Klasens 1952, pp. 16 (text) and 53 (translation).

emphasized by textual statements that spells, amulets, and rites are "*ꜣḫ*-effective for the one who does them."[158]

MAGIC AS SPEECH, PROPERTY, AND RITE

The preceding statement of Isis is also of value for its clear declaration of the tripartite nature of magic, being viewed as an inherent quality or property to be "possessed," an activity or rite to be "performed," and as words or spells to be "spoken." Interestingly, to each of these aspects corresponds an element in the Egyptian creation myths: the spoken evocation of the cosmos, the physical separation of heaven and earth, and the origin of man as the tears of the sun god.[159] The intrinsic association of magic and word is noted above (p. 17, n. 71), and lies at the heart of modern Egyptology's obsession with the spell as the *sine qua non* of magic. This almost exclusive interest in the spoken and written spell is quite understandable in view of the many Egyptian statements which also stress this aspect of *ḥkꜣ*. Thus Thoth, the god of writing, is regularly qualified as "excellent of magic" (*mnḫ ḥkꜣ*) in his capacity as "Lord of hieroglyphs" (*nb mdw-nṯr*).[160] Similarly, *ḥkꜣ* may be directly identified with the spoken word. Spells are specifically labeled as "god's words" (*mdw-nṯr*),[161] and in the "Apophis Book," the reciter warns the demon: "Retire, turn back at this magic which has come forth from my mouth for Pharaoh!"[162] Depictions of the god Heka are also instructive. As a *ka* of Re, he is described at Dendera as "excellent of words," a quality which he bestows upon the local deity Hathor, who is in consequence

158. For examples, see below, nn. 202 and 203. The translation of *ꜣḫ* as "effective" is certain in these standard recommendations; compare the Demotic equivalent using *ỉr šw*, "to be valuable/useful/effective" in the London and Leiden Magical Pap., col. 29/30: "It is effective for a youth, and it is effective for you yourself alone"; in Griffith and Thompson 1904, pp. 168–69. The understanding of *ꜣḫ* as a qualifying synonym of the basic notion of *ḥkꜣ* obviates the awkward dichotomy posed between the terms by Borghouts, and readily explains both their parallel usage and the rarer occurrence of *ꜣḫ*. Thus one must not infer too much from the absence of the latter term, contra Borghouts 1987a, pp. 32–33 (regarding "The Instructions for King Merikare," see above, n. 79).

159. For these creation myths, see above, n. 73.

160. Papyrus BM 10188, col. 33/17–18: *ꜣI mnḫ ḥkꜣ nb mdw-nṯr*, in Faulkner 1933, p. 93 and 1938, p. 53. The relation of Thoth to magic is discussed in detail in Boylan 1979, pp. 124–35. His titles include *wr ḥkꜣ*, "great of magic" (p. 184); *siꜣ m ḥkꜣ*, "wise in magic" (p. 125); *nb ḥkꜣ*, "Lord of magic" (p. 189); *hb mnḫ ḥkꜣ*, "Ibis excellent of magic" (p. 191); *šꜣꜥ ti.t nḫb ḥkꜣw*, "who first fashioned signs and wrote magic" (p. 198); and *mk.n ꜣḫw=f ms sw*, "whose spells protected the one who bore him" (p. 186).

161. In the phrase introducing the rubric: *ḏd mdw-nṯr (ḥr)*, "divine words to be said over ..."; see the Harris Magical Pap., cols. 6/8 (text I) and 9/12 (text V), in Lange 1927, pp. 51 and 80 and Sauneron 1970, pp. 10 and 12 (l. 5).

162. Papyrus BM 10188, col. 24/17–18, in Faulkner 1933, p. 50 and 1937b, pp. 169–70.

"great of magic."[163] In this scene, Heka is accompanied by a feminine equivalent of the *ka*, the *ḥmws.t* () *Ḥkꜣ*, whose inscriptions—though rather bland—are nonetheless significant in that Hathor receives her gifts as "Seshat (the goddess of writing), ... who copies [texts ...]."[164] At Edfu, Heka presents to Horus "his magic spread out (*pgwt*) before" the god.[165] Both the term "spread out" (used mainly for the unrolling of papyrus scrolls) and the depiction of Heka bearing writing determinatives on his tray make obvious the association with writing (see fig. 1). The accompanying *ḥmws.t Ḥkꜣ* complements this impression. Carrying the scribal equipment which is the hieroglyph for the word "writing," she is described as follows:

ḥmws.t Ḥkꜣ nb ꜣḫw ḥ(r) sš=s ỉmy.w rꜣ=s sꜣḫ=s sns.w=k sr=s nfr.w=k dỉ=s qbḥ.w=k gnḫ m ỉb.w

> The *ḥmws.t* of Heka, possessor of spells (*ꜣḫw*), bearing her writings which are in her mouth. She has caused worship of you (Horus) to be effective (*sꜣḫ*). She has prophesied your good fortune. She has caused that your mercy be fixed in hearts.[166]

Not only does this inscription stress the importance of writing, but it also settles the disputed question of whether oracles should be considered within the context of Egyptian magic.[167] Here they are expressly claimed to fall within the sphere of Heka, a claim

163. Dümichen 1981, pls. 133 and 189 (= Porter and Moss 1939, p. 78).

164. Dümichen 1981, pls. 134 and 189 (= Porter and Moss 1939, p. 78). The text states: "He (Nero) has brought to you (Hathor) the *ḥmws.t* of Heka. Abundant is her radiance and great is her love for humanity; she has granted her mercy for those on earth; fear of her circulates throughout eternity." For *ḥmws.t*, see *Wb* 3: 95/7–8 and 177/4 and Gardiner 1915, pp. 259–60. Heka is paired with Seshat "Great of Magic" on the architrave of the Osiris chamber at Dendera (Lepsius 1972–73, Abteilung IV, p. 58a). For proposed shamanistic associations of Seshat and magic, see Helck 1984, p. 107.

165. Dümichen 1981, pl. 158 (with two variant texts = Porter and Moss 1939, pp. 122 and 132). For the Pylon exemplar (= Dümichen 1981, p. 158 right), see also Chassinat 1933, p. 115/7–9 (no. xii). For figure 1 (= Dümichen 1981, p. 158 left), see also Chassinat 1928, p. 99/4–6 (no. vii) and pl. LXVI.

166. Dümichen 1981, p. 158; Chassinat 1928, p. 99/7–9 (no. viii) and pl. LXVI.

167. Explicit confirmation of this is also found in the Esna litany to Heka, in Sauneron 1982, pp. 31–32. Heka is praised as *nb šm.w nb bỉꜣ sr ḫpr.w*, "Lord of oracles, lord of revelations, who foretells what will happen." The "oracular" significance of the latter epithets *nb bỉꜣ sr ḫpr.w* has been questioned in some instances by Graefe (1979), who prefers a solar interpretation "lord of wondrous appearance, announcing dawn" (reference courtesy E. Wente). His reservations cannot apply here, however, as the epithets are directly appended to *nb šm.w*, "lord of oracles." Sauneron mistranslates *šm.w*,  as "magic formulas." For the previously unidentified *šm* > Coptic ϣHM, see Crum 1939, p. 564a, Westendorf 1965–77, p. 314, Černý 1976, p. 242; Vycichl 1983, pp. 262–63; and, contra Crum 1939, p. 570a, add ϣMNOYϥЄ, "good news." Compare *sr nfr*, in n. 166, preceding. A further unrecognized instance of the term appears in the autobiography of the astrologer Harkhebi, whose

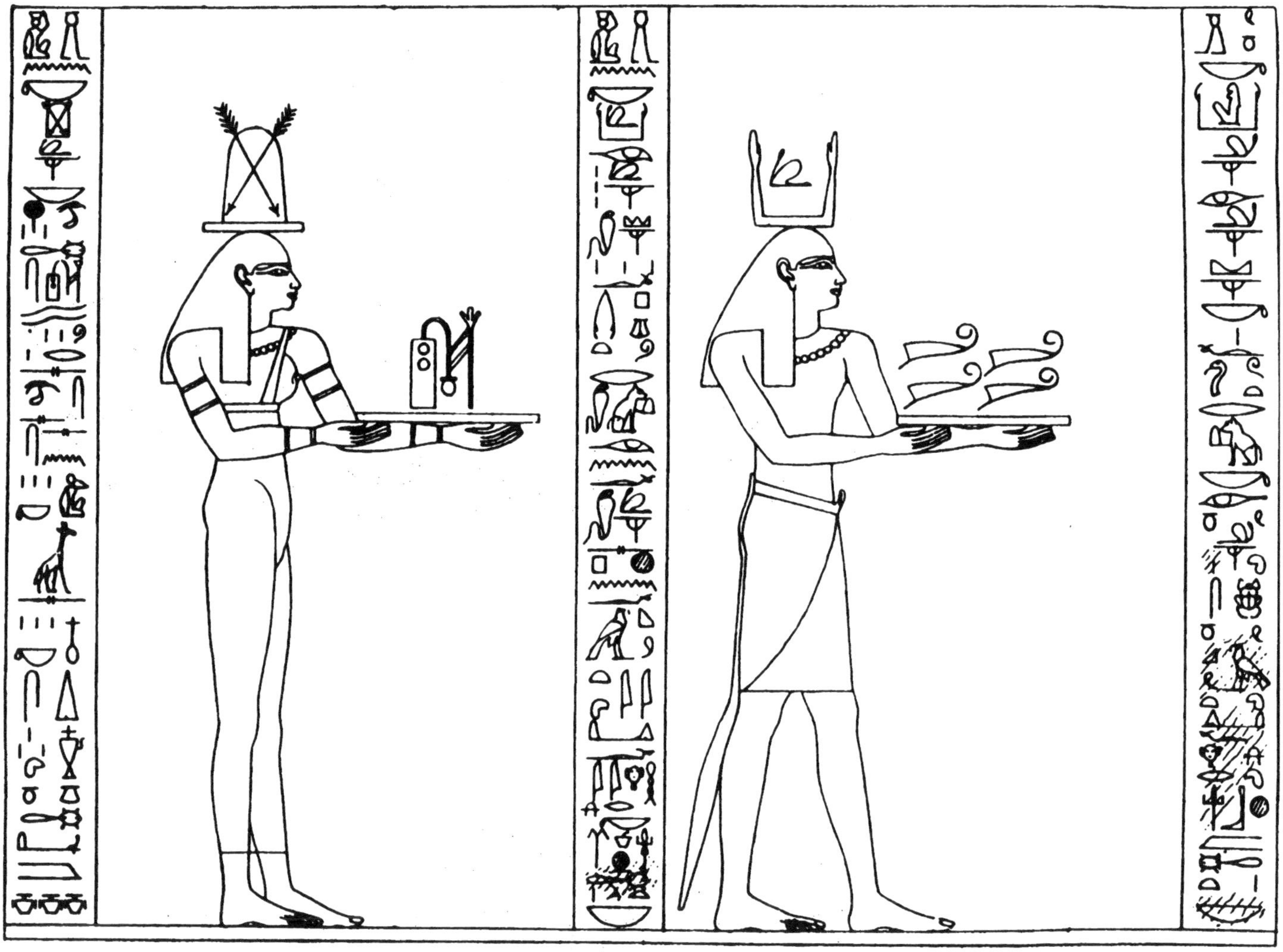

Figure 1. Heka and His *ḥmws.t*, from the Outer Wall of the Edfu Pylon (after Dümichen 1981, pl. CLVIII).

abilities to interpret the heavens included "diagnosing their wind(s) and their omens" ((?)). The phrase is untranslated in Daressy 1916, pp. 2–3, but wrongly explained as "knowing their conjunctions (*ẖnm*) and their phases (*gsgs*)," in Neugebauer and Parker 1969, p. 215; followed by Derchain 1989, p. 79. The word is attested in Demotic in the London and Leiden Magical Pap., cols. 18/9 and 11/2: *šm r pꜣy ḥm-ẖl my pẖr=f pꜣ wyn*, "Inspire this youth; let him enchant the light" (Griffith and Thompson 1904, pp. 118–19 and Erichsen 1954a, p. 508). The word is written and (unetymologically, from *šmw*, "summer"). In the form , the term is combined with *sr*, "to foretell" in Pap. Louvre 2380 vo., col. 1/8: *sr n=s šm pꜣ nt-ỉw=s (r) ḫpr*, "foretell for her a sign (of) what will happen" (R. Williams 1976, pp. 268–69 [misunderstood by the editor]). An additional instance (courtesy R. Jasnow) is found in Pap. BM 10238, ll. 2–3, in Revillout 1888, p. 4 (untranslated) and pl. 6: *ỉ-ỉr=f gm pꜣ šm pꜣ mḫrr n wꜥ sṯy*, "In dung (*sṯy* > ⲤⲞⲦ Crum 1972, p. 359a; Černý 1976, p. 164; Westendorf 1965–77, p. 199) he found the omen ( ) of the scarab." This body of evidence directly disproves Borghouts 1980, col. 1144: "(Divination) cannot be classified as m(agic) in its Egyptian context." No clearer Egyptian context could be provided. Compare also Sauneron 1982, p. 34: "Heka who protects the multitudes by the revelations of his oracles" (*nḏty ꜥšꜣ.w r biꜣ.t=f*). For *biꜣ.t* as "oracle," see Posener 1963a. For *šm*, see also p. 202 and n. 931, below.

confirmed by a passage in Papyrus Chester Beatty 4 which has been all but ignored in studies of magic. The theme of the author is the superiority of written literature as a memorial in preference to children and tombs. In verso 3, ll. 7–11, he develops this theme with reference to prophecy:

> The sages who prophesied (*sr*) ill fortune, that which came forth from their mouths happened, being found in statements written in their books ... They concealed their magic (*ḥkꜣw*) from the entire world, (though) read in a book of instruction. They are gone; their name is forgotten. It is writing which causes them to be remembered.[168]

Since the works of the sages mentioned in this passage are known, and contain nothing which could be considered spells or enchantments, the term "magic" (*ḥkꜣw*) must refer to the written prophecies themselves, or to the notion of "artistic creativity" in the very act of literary composition.[169] This link with writing is apparent even in the signs which compose *ḥkꜣ*. At Philae, the formation of Heka's name with multiple writing determinatives parallels his depiction both here and at Edfu: , and it should not be forgotten that the word *ḥkꜣ* itself is often spelled with the so-called "man-with-hand-to-mouth" determinative () indicating speech.[170]

Nonetheless, speech alone cannot be considered the totality of *ḥkꜣ*. A variation in the "Apophis Book" on the frequent idiom *ḏd m ḥkꜣ*, "say as magic" adds *ḫft rdỉ ꜥꜣpp ỉw* (= *r*) *sḏ.t*, "while putting Apep on the fire."[171] The ritual as well as the spell is crucial for the success of magic. Moreover, in the "Apophis Book" it is specified that the fire must be of bryony (*ḫsꜣw*).[172] Specific ingredients, by virtue of inner properties, are equally essential.

168. Gardiner 1935, vol. 1, p. 39 and vol. 2, pl. 19. Overlooked by the works cited above, in n. 59, this passage is obliquely discussed with relation to magic in Posener 1956, pp. 33–35. Posener is concerned only with the role of one author, Neferty, as a lector priest, and does not mention the presence of *ḥkꜣ* in the text. This example of *sr ỉy.t* (with evil determinative) cannot be solar, and was missed by Graefe 1979 (see the preceding n. 167).

169. For "artistic creativity" as a function of *ḥkꜣ*, see above, pp. 31–32 and n. 142.

170. For Heka at Philae, see Dümichen 1981, pl. 162 (= Porter and Moss 1939, p. 215) and Junker 1958, pp. 95–96, 98, and 100 (= Dümichen 1981, pl. 162). As at Edfu, Heka is shown bearing writing determinatives on his tray. For the spelling of *ḥkꜣ*, see *Wb* 3: 175–77.

171. Papyrus BM 10188, col. 23/1, in Faulkner 1933, p. 45 and 1937b, p. 168. For the idiom *ḏd m ḥkꜣ*, see Pap. Ebers, §356, in Wreszinski 1913, p. 101; von Deines, Grapow, and Westendorf 1958, pp. 50–51; and Grapow 1958, pp. 86–87; and see Pap. Westcar, cols. 6/8 and 12, in Sethe 1983, p. 28/1, 5–6 and Lichtheim 1973, p. 217.

172. Papyrus BM 10188, cols. 23/10, 26/4, and 29/15, in Faulkner 1933, pp. 46, 56, and 73; 1937b, pp. 168 and 171; and 1938, p. 42. Bryony is similarly required in the anti-Apep ritual at Esna (Sauneron 1962b, p. 25). See also the rite in Schott 1956, p. 185. An oblique reference to this usage is perhaps to be found in CT spell 311 (de Buck 1951, p. 67). For *ḫsꜣw* as bryony, see Dawson 1934, p. 45. The poisonous, acrid nature of the plant accounts for its use here.

A practical application of this magic by substance is found in Papyrus Berlin P. 8769, a Demotic text of Roman date used for amulets or dream-interpretation.[173] Corresponding to each variety of stone mentioned is a prediction for its possessor:

ỉny mꜣʿ.t r Pr-ʿꜣ r ỉr n=f sḥn-nfr
Pearl—Pharaoh will make good fortune for him.[174]

ỉny Prs ỉw=f r mwt n tkr
Stone of Persia—He will die soon.[175]

mstmy r pꜣy=f ʿnḫ nfr.ṯ m-sꜣ bn wr
Lead sulfide (galena)—His life will be pleasant after great misfortune.[176]

ỉny sš ỉw=f ỉr nb n mt nfr.t ỉw=f rḫ sḥm.t r wn mtw=s hy
Alabaster—He will be the possessor of favor; he will know (sexually) a woman who has a husband.[177]

Perhaps nowhere is this "doctrine" of properties better explained than in Papyrus Salt 825, whose disputed "magical" nature is mentioned above (pp. 6–7).

> Horus cried. The water fell from his eye to the earth and it grew. That is how dry myrrh came to be. Geb was sad on account of it. Blood fell from his nose to the ground and it grew. That is how pines came to be and resins came to be from their fluid. Then Shu and Tefnut cried exceedingly. The water from their eyes fell to the ground and it grew. That is how incense came to be.[178]

These materials—myrrh, resin, and incense—are then used in the preparation of a figure of the god Osiris, imparting to it their divine nature.[179] Directly descended from this concept of properties is the "plant aretalogy" in PGM IV, ll. 2967–3006, which professes to describe an Egyptian ritual for harvesting plants for ceremonial use.[180] Although written in Greek

173. Spiegelberg (1902, p. 29 [discussion without transliteration or translation] and pl. 98) takes it to be an amulet papyrus. The suggestion that it was used for dream interpretation was made by von Oefele (1904, p. 120).

174. Column 1/5.

175. Column 1/8.

176. Column 2/2.

177. Column 2/4; cf. Col. 1/9–10: *ỉny sš m-ỉr tỉ šm=f m-sꜣ sḥm.t r wn mtw=s hy / b-ỉr[=w] tỉ ʿḥʿ=f ỉrm=s*, "Alabaster—Don't let him go after a woman who has a husband; He is not allowed to stand with her." For *šm m-sꜣ*, cf. *ỉy m-sꜣ* in Smither 1941, pp. 131–32.

178. Column 2/1–5, in Derchain 1965, pp. 1*–2* (text) and 137 (translation). Similar ontological myths are found in cols. 1/1–5/9 (see above, n. 93). For a general discussion of this theme, see Aufrère 1982–83 and Barta 1980.

179. Derchain 1965, pp. 17*–18* (text) and 143–44 (translation).

180. Preisendanz 1928, pp. 168–71 (= Betz 1986, p. 95).

(with the substitution of Greek equivalents for certain Egyptian deities), the stated Egyptian origin of the ritual is not in doubt, and a comparison with Papyrus Salt 825 is striking. Having purified the chosen herb with pine resin and incense, the practitioner invokes it as follows:

> ... You are the dew of all the gods, you are the heart of Hermes (= Thoth), you are the seed of the primordial gods, you are the eye of Helios (= Re) ... your flowers are the Eye of Horus, your seed is Pan's (= Min's) seed ...[181]

As in Papyrus Salt 825, the plant is equated with the fluid or body of a deity (or deities) from whom it derives its efficacy: "Your roots come from the depths, but your powers are in the heart of Hermes (= Thoth)."[182] It is this indwelling divine power that the magician hopes to tap. Both preceding and following the invocation (ἐπίκλησις) in PGM IV is the πρᾶξις, or rite, which forms the final element in magical "practice," unifying spell and matter.[183]

Into these three aspects—magic by word, by rite, or by material—may also be divided most native Egyptian terminology (hieroglyphic/hieratic, Demotic, and Coptic) associated with the art of *ḥkꜣ*. Not surprisingly, the terms indicating magic by speech are particularly numerous, words for "spell" being of necessity direct expressions of speech. Thus such general terms as *mdw*, , "word"; *rꜣ*, , "speech"; and *ḏd*, , "statement" often assume magical connotations, exemplified by their direct juxtaposition with *ḥkꜣw* and *ꜣḫ* in "Text A" of the Horus cippi:

ḏd.n=y m rꜣ=k šd.n=y m ḥkꜣw=k ḏd.n=y m ḏd=k ꜣḫ.n=y m ꜣḫw=k
šn.n=y m mdw=k (var. *šd=k*) *qmꜣ.n=k m ḥkꜣw pwy ỉmy rꜣ=k*

181. Preisendanz 1928, ll. 2982–85 and 2994–96. The technique of listing identifications between divine and human (or, as here, plant) body parts is a commonplace in all Egyptian funerary, magical, and religious literature. The basic study on this technique of "lists" is Massart 1959. Compare Dawson 1931, pp. 26–27 ("Protection of Parts of the Body by the Gods"); Borghouts 1970, p. 19; Wildung 1977a, p. 175; and Hornung 1975, pp. 209–15 and 1976, pp. 87–88 (= Piankoff 1964, pp. 38–39). Examples in the Coffin Texts alone include spells 280, 292, 531, 682, 705, 761, 822, 945, 953, and 979. The implications of this technique have been misinterpreted as an indication that the Egyptians did not view the body systematically, but only as a "Gliederpuppe," or collection of independent limbs to be treated independently (Ritner 1989c, critique of Brunner-Traut 1988).

182. Preisendanz 1928, pp. 168–69 (ll. 2992–94).

183. In contrast, Festugière 1932, pp. 284–89, divides magical practice in the PGM into invocation and rite only, subordinating the role of indwelling "properties." For Festugière, (pp. 294–303) the "power" of such objects derives from the invocations and rites that infuse the materials with force (δύναμις) and spirit (πνεῦμα). Such power is, however, often declared to be pre-existent and "natural" in specific objects and need not be implanted by the magician. Instruments are certainly "charged" by rite and spell, but they are also strengthened by the application of innately divine material.

> I have spoken (*ḏd*) by means of your spell (*rꜣ*), I have recited (*šd*) by means of your magic (*ḥkꜣw*), I have spoken (*ḏd*) by means of your statement (*ḏd*), I have made spells (*ꜣḫ*) by means of your spells (*ꜣḫw*), I have enchanted (*šn*) by means of your words (*mdw*) (var. "recitation," *šd*) which you created by means of this magic (*ḥkꜣw*) which is in your mouth.[184]

Here the notions expressed by *ḏd*, *rꜣ*, *šd*, *ꜣḫ*, *šn*, and *mdw* are not only paralleled by *ḥkꜣw*, but are said to *derive directly from* the *ḥkꜣw* in the god's mouth. Regarding *ḏd* and *mdw*, little more need be said, their magical nature being discussed above in reference to the proficiency in sorcery of Isis and Thoth. It should be noted, however, that conjoined as *ḏd mdw*, , "words to be said" (> ^{B}ϪⲈⲘⲦⲀⲨ, "to recite magic") the terms conclude most magical recitations, serving to introduce the directions for the accompanying rite. Despite this fixed idiomatic usage, the phrase is by no means limited to purely "magical" practice (as traditionally defined), and appears commonly as the introduction to both ritual responses by deities on temple walls and to cultic recitation.[185] It is perhaps significant that this simple phrase, often encountered yet rarely analyzed, occurs in just those environments in which the traditional distinction between magic and religion is the most tenuous.

Similar in usage is *rꜣ*, , derived from the word for "mouth" and employed both as a general term for "spell" and as a section heading "chapter" for temple and funerary ritual recitation. Thus a god may be praised for "his spells of magic" (*rꜣ.w⸗f n ḥkꜣ*);[186] a lector priest who reads the temple liturgy boasts that he "knows his spell" (*rḫ rꜣ⸗f*);[187] temple cult may include "spells of incense" (*rꜣ n sntr*),[188] the temple library of Edfu describes its

184. Though this is the commonly accepted translation, an often ignored variant in a Ramesside papyrus in Vienna clearly interprets the otherwise ambiguous *sḏm.n⸗f-* forms as augmented imperatives (*r/ỉ-sḏm*) plus dative (*n⸗y*): "Hail to you Horus, come forth from Osiris, born of Isis, recite (*r-šd*) for me by means of your magic, speak (*ỉ-ḏd*) for me by means of [your statement]" (von Bergmann 1886, p. vii and pl. V, l. 3). The augmented imperatives are not noted by von Bergmann or Borghouts (1978, p. 84 [no. 123]). For the basic bibliography, see n. 144, above.

185. See *Wb* 5: 625–26. For ϪⲈⲘⲦⲀⲨ, "to recite magic," see Crum 1939, p. 196a; Westendorf 1965–77, p. 424; and Spiegelberg 1924, p. 160.

186. For *rꜣ*, see *Wb* 2: 391–92; for a god whose spells are filled with magic, see *Wb Beleg.* 2: 579, §18.

187. E.g., Sethe 1933, p. 122, l.13: *ỉnk ꜣḫ ỉqr ꜥpr ḫry-ḥb.t rḫ rꜣ⸗f*, "I am an excellent equipped blessed spirit, a lector priest who knows his spell." See also Edel 1945, pp. 19–21. For *ḥkꜣ* in these biographical texts, see ibid., pp. 22–26.

188. See Gardiner 1952, p. 16 and pl. 6 (l. 69). This use of *rꜣ* clearly implies ritual action as well as speech.

holdings as books, instructions, laws, and "Chapters for averting the Evil Eye" (*rꜣ.w nw ẖsf ỉr-bn.t*);[189] mortuary literature is divided into "chapters" (*rꜣ.w*);[190] and the funerary offering ritual contrasts "glorifications" (*sꜣẖ.w*) with "spells" (*rꜣ.w*).[191] It is obvious, however, that the distinction between "chapters" and "spells" is an entirely artificial one not reflected in the Egyptian term. Both the Edfu and mortuary "chapters" could as easily—and more properly—be translated "spells." As with *ḏd mdw*, the usage of *rꜣ* is restricted to ritual and magical contexts.[192] Secular literature does not use the term to mark section divisions. The only exception to this distinction in secular and ritual terminology seems to be the word *ḥw.t*, , "stanza" (literally "house"), which is used in poetry as well as in the Pyramid Texts and the "Apophis Ritual" of Papyrus BM 10188.[193]

Closely related to *rꜣ* are two derivatives: *tp-rꜣ*, , "utterance" (> Coptic ⲦⲀⲠⲢⲞ, "mouth") and *ḥm.t-rꜣ*, , "spell" (> Old Coptic ϨⲘⲎⲢ, "spell").[194] The literal meaning of the first phrase, "(what-is-)on-the-mouth," is fully functional and often gives rise to ambiguity in translation. Thus such common expressions as *ꜣẖ.w tp-rꜣ⸗k* and *ḥkꜣ tp-rꜣ⸗k* may be rendered as either "spells/magic of your utterances" or "spells/magic on your

189. See Chassinat 1928, p. 351 (text); H. Brugsch 1871, p. 44 (translation); and idem 1891, p. 156. In 1871, Brugsch translates *ỉr-bn.t* as "that which brings bad luck"; in 1891, he suggests that this is a medical text. A simpler explanation is to take *ỉr-bn.t* as a writing of *ỉr.(t)-bn.t*, "Evil Eye"; cf. *Wb* 1: 107/5. This interpretation is now confirmed by the publication of a chapel at Dendera provided with carved extracts from this book, in which Thoth protects the temple from the "Evil Eye" (Cauville 1989, pp. 51–56). For a general discussion of the Edfu library, see Wessetzky 1984b.

190. See *Wb* 2: 391/20, and Book of the Dead, Coffin Texts, passim.

191. See *Wb* 2: 391/19, and *Wb Beleg.* 2: 579, §19, TT 82 (Amenemhat): *ḏd⸗sn sꜣẖ.w rꜣw ʿšꜣ.w n NN*, "They say glorifications and many spells to/for NN."

192. The terms are conjoined in the expression *ḏd mdw ḏd m rꜣ*, 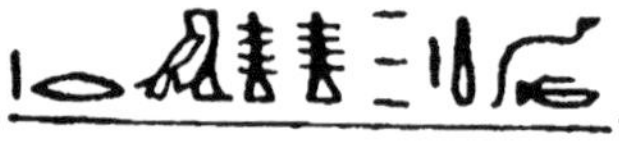, "to be recited in continuation of the spell," in Pap. BM 10188, col. 24/8 (Faulkner 1933, p. 49; idem 1937b, p. 177; and *Wb* 5: 629/9).

193. For *ḥw.t* in Pap. BM 10188, see col. 24/21: "Second stanza of overthrowing Apep the enemy of Re," in Faulkner 1933, p. 51 and 1937b, p. 170; and col. 29/16: "Stanza of conjuring their names" (*ḥw.t ḥkꜣw rn⸗sn*), in Faulkner 1933, p. 74 and 1938, p. 42. For the term in the Pyramid Texts and literature, see *Wb* 3: 6/1–5; Gardiner 1931, p. 27; Blackman 1938; and BD spell 172 §S2–9, in Allen 1974, p. 179. The term also appears in Demotic in the oracular "Demotic Chronicle," col. 2/7 and passim, in Spiegelberg 1914, pp. 10 (unread) and 96–97 (no. 340); and in the funerary text Pap. BM 10507, col. 4/1, 3, 18, and passim, in Mark Smith 1987, pp. 80 and 174.

194. For *tp-rꜣ*, see *Wb* 5: 287/4–16; Crum 1939, p. 432b; and Černý 1976, p. 192. For *ḥm.t-rꜣ*, see *Wb* 3: 85/1–2; Černý 1976, p. 284; Westendorf 1965–77, p. 373; and Crum 1942, pp. 25 and 28, l. 11. An unambiguous use of *tp-rꜣ* as "spell" is found in Schott 1929, p. 57/23: *tp-rꜣ⸗y r⸗f m tm* (var. *m nbỉ.t*), "My spell is against him as a knife (var. "as fire")."

mouth." For examples, see above, p. 33. Similarly, the second term *ḥm.t-rꜣ*, literally "craft of the mouth," is also subject to two interpretations, being used most commonly to mean simply "etc."[195]

Associated with *ḏd*, *mdw*, and *rꜣ* in the cippus text above are the terms *šnỉ* and *šd*. Regularly translated "to enchant, conjure, or exorcise," *šnỉ*, , derives from an extended use of a common verb meaning "to ask" or "to recite."[196] Given the identical writing of the two verbs, there seems no reason to postulate differing verbal stems, and Anthes may be correct in tracing the root to the word *šnỉ*, "to bind" or "to surround."[197] Derivatives of *šnỉ* itself include *šnw*, "conjurer," *šn.t*, "conjuration," and the Late Egyptian variant *šnty*, "to conjure."[198] The frequently apotropaic usage of the term is marked. Thus, within at least five passages in the "Apophis Book," Apep and his confederates are "exorcised" (*šnty*) from the shrine of Re.[199] An inscription at Medamud specifies that such "conjurations" (*šnw*) formed part of the "divine books" or liturgical texts "which protect the Ennead."[200] Nonetheless, as with *ḥkꜣ*, the term *šnỉ* or *šnty* may have positive overtones as well. In the tale of "Horus and Seth," Isis disguises herself from Seth through *šnty m ḥkꜣ*, "conjuring by magic."

wn.ỉn=s ḥr šnty m ḥkꜣ=s ỉw=s ỉr.t ḫpr.w=s m wʿ(.t) šrỉ(.t) nfr.t m ḥʿ.w=s
Then she conjured by means of her magic, and she made her transformation into a young girl with a beautiful body.[201]

Similarly, passages referring to the simple "recitation" of a ritual need have no hostile nuance.

195. For *ḥm.t-rꜣ* as "etc.," see, for example, Pap. BM 10188, cols. 28/15 and 32/6, 11, and 12, in Faulkner 1933, pp. 68, 87–88; idem 1937b, p. 174; and idem 1938, p. 46. A general discussion of the term appears in Borghouts 1970, p. 55, n. 51. As a term for "spell," the phrase was already in use during the Middle Kingdom (Erman 1901, pp. 14–15 [text D, col. 2/6] and 50 [text V, vo. 6] and cf. p. 34 [text M, col. 8/5–6] where the phrase means "etc." following a list of enemies: "dead men, dead women, etc.") Thissen (1987) argues that the term *ḥm.wt-rꜣ* (with the nuance of "magical spells") underlies the name "Ambres" (Αμβρης), which is given by Horapollo as the title of a holy book possessed by the Egyptian sacred scribes.

196. See *Wb* 4: 496/2–6: "to enchant" and 496/9–17: "to ask/say," especially 496/17: "to recite a magic book."

197. See Anthes 1961; followed by Goedicke 1984, pp. 97–98. Anthes' hesitation (p. 88) is unfounded, however, regarding the unity of the verbs "to enchant" (*šnỉ*) and "to ask/say" (*šnỉ*).

198. See *Wb* 4: 496/7: *šnw*, "conjurer"; 496/8–12: *šn.t*, "conjuration"; and 518: *šnty*, "to conjure."

199. See Pap. BM 10188, cols. 24/1, 27/22, 28/12, 29/10, 30/7, and 30/20, in Faulkner 1933, passim.

200. Drioton 1926, p. 42, no. 97, l. 3.

201. Gardiner 1932, p. 44, "Horus and Seth," col. 6/4–5; see above, n. 143. For other examples of *šnt m ḥkꜣ*, see below, n. 215.

It is effective (*ꜣḫ*) for a man who makes conjuration (*šnty*) for himself with this book before this noble god.[202]

As for the recitation (*šnw*) of this rite (*n.t-ꜥ*), it is effective (*ꜣḫ*) for Osiris, it is effective for the one who recites (*šnty*) it.[203]

A highly questionable relative of this term is the *šn-nṯr*(?), "god-inquirer" read by de Cenival in the Demotic Papyrus Louvre E 3266, line 8, which concerns the transference of ownership of a one-third share of temple revenue.[204]

Parallel to *šni͗*, the term *šd*, "to enchant," , also represents a specialized nuance of a basic word meaning "to recite."[205] As with virtually all of the terminology discussed thus far, the use of the term extends to both magical and ritual contexts. Thus, for example, the "magical" use of *šd* in the Horus cippus above is complemented by its appearance in the temple texts of Edfu:

ḥry-ḥb tp ḏbꜣ m ḫkr.w⸗f ḥr šd () *rꜣ.w n pr r-ḥꜣ*

The chief lector priest outfitted with his adornments recites the spells of appearance (literally "going outside").[206]

At Esna, the term *šd* is selected by the creatrix Neith to describe her spoken evocation of the cosmos:

> Let us devise 4 spells (*ꜣḫw*) that we might clarify what is in our bodies (= "our thoughts");
> let us recite (*šd*) our utterances (*tp-rꜣ⸗w*) so that we might know it all today.[207]

Not only may the word reflect divine speech, but as a title "Reciter/Enchanter" it appears both as a divine name and epithet. Although misidentified for over a century with a homophonous, but differently written word meaning "savior," *Šd* serves as the name of the central healing deity on the magical cippi, either alone or compounded as "Horus-Shed" ("Horus-the-Enchanter").[208] The feminine equivalent of this epithet, *tꜣ šty.t*, is applied to

202. See Faulkner 1933, p. 57 (col. 26/7) and 1937b, p. 171.

203. Papyrus MMA 35.9.21, col. 18/3–4, unpublished, hand copy kindly supplied by K. Baer. Compare Schott 1929, p. 61, ll. 17 and 20 and Goyon 1969, pp. 64–65, where *šd* replaces *šn* in a similar statement. A parallel to the MMA text is found in Goyon 1967, pp. 95 and 141 (l. 5: *šnty*).

204. De Cenival 1972b, pp. 25, 43, 63 (n. 88), and pl. 11. She compares Pap. BM 10622, l. 12: **šn-nṯr* read by H. Thompson 1940, p. 78 (n. 9); but this has now been reread as *ẖ.t-nṯr*, "ghost" (Zauzich 1976).

205. See *Wb* 4: 563–64, especially 564/12–16.

206. See Chassinat 1930, p. 30/1–4 (text) and Alliot 1949, pp. 509–10.

207. See Sauneron 1968, p. 30 (no. 206/5) (text) and 1962b, pp. 259–61 (translation).

208. See Ritner 1986a, pp. 103–04 and 106 and 1989b, pp. 109–11.

Isis in hieroglyphic script on cippi (adjacent to the hieroglyphic *Ḥr-Šd*) and in Demotic in the London and Leiden Magical Papyrus and elsewhere.[209] The curative powers of the deity derive from his or her skill in reciting magical spells to curse, and thus repel, the poison of scorpions and other animals. Cursing seems equally implied in the term for enemy *šd-ḫrw*, "disturber," perhaps literally "one who enchants with the voice."[210]

This nuance of cursing, inherent in both *šnỉ* and *šd*, is most directly expressed by the verb *sḥwr*, , (> Coptic ⲥⲁϩⲟⲩ) "to curse," literally "to cause to be wretched" (causative *s* + *ḥwrw*, "wretched/weak").[211] Used by both gods and men, the word possesses a range of meaning which parallels that of the English "curse," extending to mundane oaths of displeasure as well as to the destructive force of "hexes." A comparison of the word's appearance in the "Instructions of ʿOnchsheshonqy" makes this clear:

bꜣk ỉw b-ỉr⸗w mẖy.ṯ⸗f nꜣ-ʿ sḥw n ḥꜣṯ⸗f
As for a servant who is not beaten, great is the cursing in his heart.[212]

m-ỉr ḥms n ʿ.wy ỉw⸗f sḥwr n-tr.t pꜣ nṯr b-ỉr tꜣy⸗f wt.t sṯ r-ỉr⸗k
Don't dwell in a house (or "place") cursed by god lest his wrath rebound against you.[213]

While the former example has only connotations of "despising," the latter is of relevance for the study of *ḥkꜣ*.[214] Presumably operating by magical force, *sḥwr* is not infrequently paired with *ḥkꜣ*:

209. For *ꜣs.t tꜣ šty.t*, see Wilkinson 1878, vol. 3, opposite p. 152 (cippus), and Griffith and Thompson 1909, p. 83, no. 880. These and other examples are fully discussed in the articles cited in the preceding note. Cf. also the parallel between "Isis *wr.t ḥkꜣ.w* who knows her spell (*rꜣ*), who protects Horus with her effective word (*ꜣḫ.t*)" (Rochemonteix et al. 1984–87, p. 233), and "Isis the mother (*Tmꜣ.t*) who enchanted (*šd*) Horus in his nest" (ibid., p. 240); signaled in Cauville 1987, p. 47.

210. See *Wb* 4: 566/3–9 and Moret 1931, pp. 739–40 and 746–47, where the term describes the activity of the enemies of Osiris in general and that of Seth in particular. Moret (p. 740) translates *šd-ḫrw* as "ceux qui incantent des cris." An alternate understanding of the term may be implied in Schott 1929, p. 7 (l. 17), where the determinatives of this epithet of Seth suggest "He who extracts villainy," 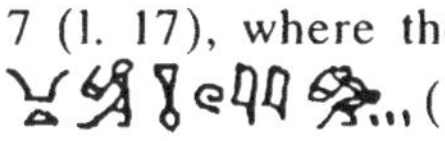 (ibid., p. 6, "who sowed enmity").

211. See *Wb* 4: 213/4–5 and Erichsen 1954a, p. 445 for *sḥwr*, *sḥwy*; Crum 1939, p. 387a; Westendorf 1965–77, pp. 214–15; Černý 1976, p. 175; and Vycichl 1983, pp. 206–07 for ⲥⲁϩⲟⲩ. For *ḥwrw*, see *Wb* 3: 55–56 and (?) 149/5 (*ḥrwr*).

212. Papyrus BM 10508, col. 7/18, in Glanville 1955, pp. 20–21.

213. Papyrus BM 10508, col. 27/14, in Glanville, ibid., pp. 60–61. The passage was mistranslated by Glanville; see now Lichtheim 1980, p. 180.

214. For the significance of cursing in magical texts and rites, see Posener 1977, pp. 503–04 and below, n. 632.

ḥkꜣ n Ḏḥwty mn m ḥꜥw⸗tn sḫwrỉ tn ꜣs.t
The magic of Thoth is fixed in your limbs; Isis curses you.[215]

A similar kinship is found in the Demotic "Prophecy of the Lamb," in which prophecies of misfortune—shown above (p. 38) to be within the sphere of *ḥkꜣ*—are described as "curses" (*sḫwy.w*), and the misfortune itself is seen as "the curse which Pre made."[216]

Less frequent parallels to the former connotation of cursing include *wꜥꜣ*, , (var.? *wꜣr*),[217] and the root of *sḫwr* itself, *ḫwrw*, , used either as a verb or as an adjective in such phrases as *ṯs ḫwrw*, "evil utterance."[218] Like *mdw*, this last term *ṯs*, "utterance,"  (> Late *ḏꜣỉs*, 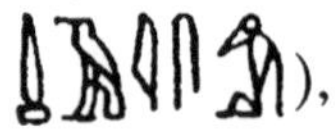), may acquire magical connotations. In the "Apophis Book," the "utterance" (*ḏꜣỉs* var. *ṯsỉs*) of the monster is repelled together with his "magic" (*ḥkꜣ*) and "spells" (*ꜣḫw*).[219] At Philae, the king is *ꜣḫ rꜣ nfr ḏꜣỉs sḥtp nṯr.w m mdw⸗f*, "Effective/magical of spells, good of utterance, who pacifies the gods with his words."[220] At Edfu, the term is twice applied to Nephthys, who is qualified as one "who sanctifies her siblings who came forth before her with the utterances (*ḏꜣỉs.w*) and the spells (*ꜣḫw*) on her mouth (*tp-rꜣ⸗s*)."[221] Paralleling *ḥkꜣ* itself, the term is hypostasized as the seven so-called "sages" of the primordial *Mḥ.t-wr.t* cow to represent

215. Wooden Tablet BM 20775, ll. 1–2, in Vittmann 1984a, pp. 165–67 and pl. 5. A similar association appears in the "Anti-Seth" ritual in Schott 1929, pp. 27/10–29/6, in which Re, Thoth, and Isis curse Seth with their magic. The terms used are *sḫwr* and *šnt*: "You (Re) have cursed (*sḫwr*) him with your own mouth ... The great god has conjured (*šnt*) him with his own mouth ... Thoth has conjured (*šnt*) him with his magic (*ḥkꜣw*) as has the Great One of Magic (Isis) with her utterance (*tp-rꜣ*)."

216. See Pap. Vienna D 10000, col. 2/19: *mnq pꜣ hyb nꜣ sḫwy.w r-r⸗w ḏr.w*, "The lamb finished all the curses against them"; and col. 3/12: *tw.s pꜣ sḫwy r-ỉr [Pꜣ]-Rꜥ (n) Kmy*, "Behold the curse which Pre made against Egypt," in Zauzich 1983, pp. 165–74 and pl. 2. See also cols. 2/4 and 2/14.

217. See *Wb* 1: 279/14–17 and Erichsen 1954a, p. 82: *ḏ wꜥ*, "to curse" > ϫⲓⲟⲩⲁ, "to speak blasphemy," Crum 1939, p. 468b. See also *wꜣ* and *wꜣwꜣ*, in *Wb* 1: 244/10–13 and 249/12–15 (> ? *wꜣr*, see 252/12); and cf. Osing 1976a, pp. 151–52 and Baer 1965. For an example of this usage, see Schott 1929, p. 57/20: *ỉw⸗y r dỉ.t pḫr wꜣw* (var. *wꜣwꜣ*) *r ỉr s*, "I shall cause a curse to circulate against the one who did it."

218. See *Wb* 3: 55–56; for *ṯs ḫwrw*, see 56/2.

219. For *ṯs*, see *Wb* 5: 403/10–21 and for *ḏꜣỉs*, see *Wb* 5: 521–22 and Dévaud 1912, pp. 127–29. Reymond (1969, p. 139) translates *ḏꜣỉs* as "learned spells" in the compound *nỉs ḏꜣỉsw*, "recite spells." For the "utterance" of Apep in Pap. BM 10188, col. 29/19; see Faulkner 1933, p. 74 and 1938, p. 42. Similarly, in col. 31/8 it is said of Apep: *nn ḫpr ṯsỉs⸗k*, "Your utterance will not occur" (Faulkner 1933, p. 82 and 1938, p. 45).

220. See *Wb Beleg.* 5: 94 §522,1 in re. Philae (1582), photograph 207.

221. See Rochemonteix et al. 1984–87, p. 73 (text); Husson 1977, pp. 62–64 (translation); and Blackman and Fairman 1941, pp. 404–05, §13 (= Rochemonteix et al. 1984–87, pp. 15–16, §40).

the seven creative words or "utterances" which brought the world into being.[222] These utterances are attested as early as Coffin Texts spell 407, the "spell of the 7 utterances of *Mḥ.t-wr.t*" (*rꜣ n ṯs.wt 7 nw Mḥ.t-wr.t*) and in Coffin Texts spell 691 (and its descendant Book of the Dead spell 71) where they have been occasionally misinterpreted as the similarly written word "knots."[223] The identification as "utterances" is certain, however, as the texts consist of seven responses to or by the creator on behalf of the deceased. In the Ptolemaic period, texts from Dendera, Edfu, and Esna provide more detailed information on the *ḏꜣis.w*, , who appear as hawk-headed associates of Thoth in his role as magician.[224] The *ḏꜣis.w* themselves may appear in the act of recitation with scroll in hand.[225] The most informative text is from Esna where the creation of the *ḏꜣis.w* closely follows that of Thoth and Neith's cult center, Sais:

> Then the seven utterances (*ḏꜣis.w*) came forth from her mouth. They became seven gods. That which she said as the name of the utterances (*ḏꜣis.w*) became the name of hieroglyphs ("god's-words") and as the name of Sais. The seven utterances (*ḏꜣis.w*) became the protection (*sꜣ*) of *Mḥ.t-wr.t* in every place in which she went.[226]

The link between these "utterances" and *ḥkꜣ* is emphasized further in the name of the second *ḏꜣis*: 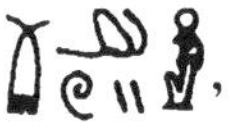, which may be read either "equipped with magic" (*ʿpr ḥkꜣ*) or "equipped behind" (*ʿpr pḥwy*).[227] Even in the latter case a pun could well be intended on "magic," since similar visual and verbal puns are often made on the spelling of *ḥkꜣ* with .[228]

222. For examples, see Rochemonteix et al. 1984–87, pp. 295–96 (and pl. XXIXa); Chassinat 1928, p. 315 (and pl. LXXX); and idem 1929b, pl. CCCXXII. For discussion, see Chassinat 1894, pp. 106–08. These are taken by Sauneron 1962b, p. 269, to represent "the active elements of the deity's words." This interpretation is followed by Husson 1977, pp. 62–64 and Meeks 1980, p. 443, no. 77.5143.

223. For CT spell 407, see de Buck 1954, pp. 212–24 (= Lacau 1904, pp. 64–67 [text]) and Faulkner 1977, pp. 58–59. Similar spells include 406 and 408. For CT spell 691, see de Buck 1956, pp. 322–24 and Faulkner 1977, pp. 256–57. In all cases, Faulkner translates *ṯs* as "knot." For BD spell 71, see Allen 1974, p. 64, who translates the word as "counselors." See also Naville 1886, vol. 1, pl. LXXXIII, l. 16.

224. See Chassinat 1894, p. 107 and Sauneron 1962b, p. 269.

225. See Chassinat 1894, p. 108.

226. Sauneron 1968, p. 33 (no. 206/12–13) (text) and 1962b, pp. 268–69 (translation).

227. See Chassinat 1928, p. 315 (no. 2°) and pl. LXXX (no. 6). The text is translated in Ibrahim 1975, p. 47, as "well-equipped behind." The name of the first *ḏꜣis*, *Nfr ḥꜣ.t*, could be translated "Good before," which would strengthen Ibrahim's translation. He has, however, translated this as "Good of heart," which is also possible. Puns could easily be intended on both "heart" and "magic" with "first" and "after," since the *ḏꜣis.w* are divinized magical concepts which arose first in the "heart" and came forth "after" as spoken magic. For the common idiom *ʿpr m ḥkꜣ*, "equipped with magic," cf. n. 142, above.

228. For puns on *ḥkꜣ* and *pḥwy*, "back" (where the god is in the back of the solar bark), see Dawson 1945, p. 105. The phonetic complements *-wy* need not invalidate a punning reference to *ḥkꜣ*; compare the writings with the phonetic complements *-ty*, punning on *pḥty*, "strength," in Dawson 1938, p. 128.

Remaining words which associate magic with the spoken word include *ḥsw-m-mw*, and its variants *ḥsw*, and *sḥs-m-mw*, "water spell" (literally "chanting in the water"), found in the Coffin Texts, the "Story of the Herdsman," and the Harris Magical Papyrus.[229] It is noteworthy that literary, funerary, and "magical" texts agree in their terminology for this magical act. The relation of the term *ḏꜥl-mt*, "gathering of words/spell" with the spoken word is obvious.[230] Somewhat less so are a variety of terms used in magical contexts to mean "to repel/exorcise": *ꜥn*, *rk*, *stwhꜣ*, and *šnꜥ*.[231] The most frequent word for "exorcising" a spirit or demon is *sḫr*, literally "to cause to fall" (like the English "to lay" a ghost), which is not restricted to vocal magic, but is applied equally to physical acts of magic.[232] An example of its strictly oral use is found in the second Setna story, in which the hero reads aloud a "book of exorcising spirits" (*mḏy n sḫr iḫy*) after a visit to the underworld.[233] A questionable example of spoken magic is the rite *sꜥšꜣ*, perhaps meaning "to magnify/glorify," which has been taken to be a protective magical ritual.[234] As

229. For *ḥsw*, "chants/songs," see Goedicke 1970, especially p. 246, l. 13; and for interpretation, see Kaplony 1969; idem 1970; Altenmüller 1973; and Gilula 1978. An additional example is in Pap. Leiden I 350, col. 3/18, where Amon is praised as "a water charm" (Gardiner 1905, pp. 28–30). For *ḥsw-m-mw*, see CT spell 836 l, in de Buck 1961, p. 36 and Faulkner 1978, p. 23. For *sḥs-m-mw*, see Lange 1927, pp. 53–55 (col. 6/10). The origin of the term is clearly the verb *ḥsi*, "to sing," as is stipulated by the title of the papyrus: *rꜣ.w nfr.w n ḥsi nty sḫri pꜣ mḥi*, "Good spells to sing to drive away the swimming one (*scil.* crocodile)" (Lange 1927, p. 12 and Ogdon 1989, p. 59). No root is given in *Wb* 3: 160/2.

230. See Griffith and Thompson 1904, pp. 72–73 (col. 9/24) and 76–77 (col. 10/8) and Erichsen 1954a, p. 685, *s.v.* *ḏlꜥ*, "to gather/record."

231. For *ꜥn*, see *Wb* 1: 189/1–2; for *rk*, see *Wb* 2: 458/5 (probably the unrecognized ancestor of *lg*, *lk*, "to stop/repel," in Erichsen 1954a, p. 264); for *stwhꜣ*, see *Wb* 4: 334/11–13 (a causative of *twhꜣ*, "to turn back," in *Wb* 5: 255/5); for *šnꜥ*, see *Wb* 4: 504/6–8 and 13. The terms *stwhꜣ* and *rk* are used as synonyms in the Harris Magical Pap., col. 11/3, in Lange 1927, p. 92 (ll. 7–8): "I am equipped with the good scroll which Re placed in my hand *nty stwhꜣ mꜣi.w rk rmṯ .w nty stwhꜣ rmṯ.w rk mꜣi.w* (which repels lions and repulses men, which repels men and repulses lions)."

232. See *Wb* 4: 257/3–15 and 258/3, especially 257/9–11. For the physical act of "felling," see the "Apophis Book," 24/21: "The Second Stanza of felling (*sḫr*) Apep the enemy of Re," which concludes with the instructions to make wax figures and then *sḫr m mꜥbꜣ m ds*, "fell with harpoon and with knife," (col. 26/4) in Faulkner 1933, pp. 51 and 56. For numerous other examples, see Faulkner, ibid., passim.

233. Setna II, col. 2/26, in Griffith 1985, pp. 160–61.

234. For *sꜥšꜣ* as a ritual, see *Wb* 4: 55/19 = Pap. BM 10188, cols. 3/23 and 9/13 ("The Songs of Isis and Nephthys"), in Faulkner 1933, pp. 7 and 17, and idem 1936, pp. 122, 124, and 126; and for discussion,

the term is followed by *ḏd-mdw*, it is presumably vocal in nature.[235] A suggested term for "enchanter" in Ostracon Bodleian 846, 2: **ʿš-wby*, *"one-who-recites-on-behalf-of-(someone)," which was thought to be the origin of the Coptic ⲁϣⲉⲃⲉⲛ, "enchanter," has now been reread out of existence, and a Semitic origin for the Coptic term accepted.[236] Of the various terms which display the vocal nature of magic, none is perhaps so telling as the common verb *mdw*, , "to speak," which as *mdw r*, "to speak against," may mean "to curse," and which becomes a standard Coptic word for "enchanter" in the compound ⲣⲉϥⲙⲟⲩⲧⲉ ("a man who speaks").[237] All of these phrases and synonyms are gathered in table 1 (see p. 50).

Magic by ingredient or essence is equally well represented in the Egyptian vocabulary. Most such terms pertain either to objects and potions which are made up of individual magical "elements" or to amulets which by design and/or material convey magical force. For the latter, the basic term is *sꜣ*, , "amulet/talisman," an extended usage of the identically written word for "protection."[238] A corresponding extension of meaning occurs

p. 134. Faulkner translates *sʿšꜣ* as "protective rite," but the term may mean only "worship/praise"; compare the identically written presumed verbal root "to magnify/glorify," in *Wb* 4: 54–55 > *sʿšʿ* (Erichsen 1954a, p. 492) > Coptic ϣⲟⲩϣⲟⲩ (Crum 1939, p. 604a and Černý 1976, p. 259: "to boast/pride [oneself]"). For the derivative of this word meaning "chapel" ("place of adoration"), see Ritner 1984a, p. 177. Faulkner's translation is based on the nuance "to drive off," ascribed to the term in *Wb* 4: 55/11–13, and that of "police" ("one who drives off") in *Wb* 4: 55/14–18. The latter term appears in Naville 1892, pl. 20, applied to dwarfs in procession with lector priests (*ḥry-ḥb*), and was translated "police" (Aufseher) in Spiegelberg 1920b, p. 60. A translation "praiser" might be equally permissible, though the nuance of "police" is elsewhere clear; see now Andreu 1987. The rite *sʿšꜣ* appears also in Pap. Vienna 6319, cols. 4/31 and 3/22, where it was understood by the editor as the verb "to magnify" with a special technical meaning "to give magical protection" (Reymond 1977, p. 88, n. b).

235. In Pap. BM 10188, col. 3/23, the term is followed by "words said by the two long-haired ones" (women impersonating Isis and Nephthys) and in col. 9/13 by the phrase "without seeing, without hearing. Words said by the lector priest." Recitations then follow in both examples. Compare, however, Faulkner 1936, p. 134, who takes the phrase as "a kind of stage-direction indicating an act external to the actual recitations."

236. For the supposed title, see Wångstedt 1981, pp. 24–25. The "term" **ʿš-wby* has now been reread for the forthcoming *Chicago Demotic Dictionary* as two independent words in the phrase *ʿš wby*, "to call to." For the origin of Coptic ⲁϣⲉⲃⲉⲛ, see Černý 1976, pp. 15–16.

237. For *mdw r*, "to curse" ("speak against"), see Pap. BM 10188, col. 32/11: "It is Re who shuts for him (the king) every mouth which speaks against Pharaoh with every evil word," in Faulkner 1933, p. 88 and 1938, p. 46. See also Schott 1930c, pp. 36–39, 41, and especially 38, n. 1 for additional references. For ⲣⲉϥⲙⲟⲩⲧⲉ, "enchanter" and its derivatives, see Crum 1939, p. 192a.

238. See *Wb* 3: 414–15, especially 415/12–17; Erichsen 1954a, p. 403. An explicit correlation between amulets and *ḥkꜣ* is found in a "pectoral-offering scene" at Kom Ombo in which the officiating king is qualified as *nb ḥkꜣ.w*, "lord of magic," the amulets as *ḥkꜣ.w ꞽItm*, "the magic of Atum," and the recipient Khonsu as *mnḫ ḥkꜣ*, "excellent of magic" (Graefe 1979, pp. 72–75).

Table 1. Magic by Speech.

Transliteration	*Coptic**	*Translation*	*Reference*
ꜣḫw	> ⲏϩ	"spells"	*Wb* 1: 15/6–8 and *KHwb* 503
ꜥn		"to repel"	*Wb* 1: 189/1–2
wꜥꜣ	> ϫⲓⲟⲩⲁ	"to curse"	*Wb* 1: 279/14–17; *Glossar*** 82; and Crum 1939, p. 468b
mdw	> ⲙⲟⲩⲧⲉ	"to speak/enchant"	*Wb* 2: 179/2ff.; *Glossar* 184; and Crum 1939, p. 192a
mdw	> ⲙⲧⲁⲩ	"(magical) word"	*Wb* 2: 180/6 and Crum 1939, p. 196a
rꜣ		"spell"	*Wb* 2: 391–92 and *Glossar* 240
rk > lg		"to repel"	*Wb* 2: 485/5 and *Glossar* 264
ḥm.t-rꜣ	> ϩⲙⲏⲣ	"spell"	*Wb* 3: 85/1–2 and *KHwb* 373
ḥkꜣ(w)	> ϩⲓⲕ	"magic"	*Wb* 3: 175–77; *Glossar* 333–34; and Crum 1939, p. 661a
ḥsw		"water-charm"	*Wb* 3: 160/2
ḥsw-m-mw		"water-charm"	*Wb* 3: 160/2
sꜥšꜣ		"protective adoration(?)"	*Wb* 4: 55/19
sḥwr	> ⲥⲁϩⲟⲩ	"to curse"	*Wb* 4: 213/4–5; *Glossar* 445; and Crum 1939, p. 387a
sḥs-m-mw		"water-charm"	*Wb* 4: 220/22
sẖr		"to exorcise"	*Wb* 4: 257/9–11
stwhꜣ		"to repel"	*Wb* 4: 334/11–14
šnỉ	> ϣⲓⲛⲉ	"to conjure/enchant"	*Wb* 4: 496/2–6 and Crum 1939, p. 570a
šn.t		"conjuration"	*Wb* 4: 496/8–12
šnꜥ		"to repel"	*Wb* 4: 504/6–8 and 13
šntỉ		"to conjure/enchant"	*Wb* 4: 518
šd		"to enchant"	*Wb* 4: 563–64 and *Glossar* 529
tp-rꜣ		"(magical) utterance"	*Wb* 5: 287/4–16
ṯs		"(magical) utterance"	*Wb* 5: 403/10–21
ḏꜣỉs		"(magical) utterance"	*Wb* 5: 521–22
ḏꜥl-mt		"word gathering/spell"	*Glossar* 685
ḏd	> ϫⲱ	"to say/recite (magic)"	*Wb* 5: 621/12–16 and *KHwb* 413
ḏd-mdw	> ϫⲉⲙⲧⲁⲩ	"(magical) words to be said"	*Wb* 5: 625–26; *Glossar* 691; Crum 1939, p. 196a; and *KHwb* 424

*Coptic derivatives given only when they retain the magical nuance.

***Glossar* = Erichsen 1954a.

in the synonym *wḏꜣ*, "security," found paired with *sꜣ* in the "bilingual" funerary text Papyrus Rhind I. Translated into Demotic as *sꜣ.(w)*, , the hieroglyphic *wḏꜣ.w*-amulets, , are qualified as "being of every precious stone" (*m ꜥꜣ.t nb.t šps*).[239] The significance of such stones for the efficacy of amulets is demonstrated above, pp. 38–40, and there remains to be noted only the often complex interaction between the material and the very name and function of a talisman. Thus the "papyrus column" amulet, , (*wꜣḏ*) is made of a green (*wꜣḏ*) stone and embodies the concept "to flourish" (*wꜣḏ*).[240] Individual varieties of amulets—with corresponding names—abound. While the name of some is compounded with *sꜣ* (*sꜣ-rnp.t*, "protection/amulet of the year"; *sꜣ.w-n-pꜣ-sḥtp-Sḫmı͗*, "amulets for the pacification of Sakhmet"; *sꜣ-n-ꜥnḫ*, "amulet for life"), many have simple names expressing either their function or benefit: *ꜣw.t-ı͗b*, "joy," *swꜣḏ.t*, "that which causes to flourish."[241] A selection of these amulet names may be found in table 2 (see p. 52).

The amuletic specialist or "curandero" who prescribes and applies amulets is a *sꜣw*, , meaning simultaneously "protector," "guardian," and "amulet-man."[242] The

239. Papyrus Rhind I, 8 d 2 h 3, in Möller 1913, pp. 38–39 and 50, no. 328. For *wḏꜣ.w*, which may refer to either amulets or spells, see *Wb* 1: 401/10–12. A variant of this term is perhaps to be found in Pap. Ramesseum 3, col. B/31, written (*w*)*ḏꜣw* (von Deines and Westendorf 1962, p. 995; followed by Meeks 1981, p. 437, no. 78.4865; versus Borghouts 1978, p. 43, no. 69, who translates "fortified places"). For the pairing of *sꜣ* and *wḏꜣ*, cf. Pap. Insinger, col. 24/4–5: "Don't despise a small amulet in its time of seeking it. As for an amulet (*sꜣ*) without evil in it, its possessor is safe (*wḏꜣ*) before it (*scil.* evil)" (Lichtheim 1980, p. 204). For *wḏꜣ* as the general term for amulet in the Greco-Roman periods, see Graefe 1979, pp. 71–77.

240. See Allen 1974, p. 156, Spell 160: "Spell for the papyrus amulet (*wꜣḏ*) of green feldspar ... If it (the *wꜣḏ*-amulet) stays sound (*wḏꜣ*) then I stay sound (*wḏꜣ*)." For the text, see Naville 1886, vol. 1, pl. CLXXXIII. For similar puns on *wꜣḏ* and *wḏꜣ*, see BD spell 167, in Allen 1974, p. 162 and Naville 1886, vol. 1: pl. CLXXXVI. See also Pap. Ebers §385 in Wreszinski 1913, p. 108: "Come malachite (*wꜣḏ*)! Come malachite! Come vigor (*wꜣḏ*)! Come vigor! ... To be recited over malachite pounded up with honey." For the papyrus amulet, see also CT Spells 106 and 135 (de Buck 1938, pp. 117 and 160). An explicit statement on the relation between green stone, papyrus, and growth (all written *wyṯ* < *wꜣḏ*) is to be found in the Demotic "Mythus" tale, col. 6/3–25, in Spiegelberg 1917a, pp. 22–23.

241. See Spiegelberg 1917a, pp. 22–23, col. 6/8 (*nꜣ sꜣ.w n pꜣ sḥtp Sḫmı͗*), pp. 28–29, col. 9/13 (*sꜣ rnp.t*). For *sꜣ-n-ꜥnḫ*, see Möller 1913, pp. 50–51 (Pap. Rhind I 11 d 9 h 9) and Spiegelberg 1917a, pp. 44–45, col. 18/4–5. For *ꜣw.t-ı͗b*, see *Wb* 1: 4/20 and Reymond 1969, p. 31. For *swꜣḏ.t*, see *Wb* 4: 65/11. A general list of amulet names is found in Pap. MacGregor (Capart 1908) and in Petrie 1972, pl. 48. See further Meeks 1976; Posener 1980, p. 89 and pls. 64–64a (no. 1637); and Shorter 1935, pp. 171–76.

242. *Wb* 3: 415/18. For discussion, see Gardiner 1917. For examples, see Ward 1982, pp. 146, no. 1254 (*sꜣw*) and 147, no. 1261 (*sꜣw-Srq.t*); and cf. p. 136, no. 1170 (*ḫrp-Srq.t*). A possible pun on this title in a divine context is found in Pap. BM 10188, col. 24/4–5, in which Apep is said to be broken (*sꜣw*) by "those who break up illness (*sꜣw mr.w*)" (Faulkner 1933, p. 49 and 1937b, pp. 169 and 177). A translation "guard (against)" may be preferable for *sꜣ*.

Table 2. Magic by Property—A Selection.[1]

Name	*Suggested Meaning*	*Type*	*Source*
ꜣw.t-ỉb	("joy")	pectoral amulet	*Wb* 1: 4/20
ỉmn.t	("she-who-is-hidden")	vulture amulet	*Wb* 1: 85/7
ỉr.t-byn.t	("evil eye")	term for Evil Eye	*Wb* 1: 107/5 and Crum 1939, p. 39b
ʿbb	("winged solar scarab")	scarab amulet	*Wb* 1: 178/11
ʿnḫ-mrr	("living and loving")	scarab amulet	*Wb* 1: 203/10 and compare 204/7–8
wꜣḏ	("flourishing")	papyrus amulet	*Wb* 1: 264/10
wḏꜣ.t	("the sound eye")	eye amulet	*Wb* 1: 402/2 and *Glossar* * 108
wḏꜣw	("health")	general term for amulet	*Wb* 1: 401/10
pḫr.t	("that which contains")	basic term for potion or recipe	*Wb* 1: 549/1–12; *Glossar* 139; and Crum 1939, p. 282b
mnhp	("for mounting")	aphrodisiac	*Wb* 2: 82/18
mnqby.t	("cooling/refreshing")	serpent-headed amulet[2]	*Wb* 2: 91/2
mqn	(?)	amulet(?)	*Wb* 2: 159/2
nh.t	("bulwark/protection")	protective drink	*Wb* 2: 282/1
nh.t	("bulwark/protection")	amulet	*Wb* 2: 282/2
nh.t	("bulwark/protection")	magical book	*Wb* 2: 282/3
nhy	("bulwark/protection")	magical book/amulet	*Wb* 2: 282/4
nṯry	("divine")	magical cord	*Wb* 2: 365/17
nḏ-rꜣ	("advisor")	heart amulet	*Wb* 2: 372/7
ḥmw.t-sꜣ	("craft of amulets")	term for bewitchment	*Wb* 3: 85/3
ḫns	("going about")	double-headed amulet	*Wb* 3: 300/5
sꜣ	("amulet")	basic term for amulet	*Wb* 3: 414–15 and *Glossar* 403
siꜣ.t	("bandaged one"?)	bird amulet	*Wb* 4: 29/10
sʿḥ-ḥr-pʿ.t	("human-faced mummy")	mummy amulet	*Wb* 4: 52/16
swꜣḏ.t	("she who invigorates")	Thoueris amulet	*Wb* 4: 65/11
tỉ.t	("symbol")	Isis knot	*Wb* 5: 238/4
ḏd	("endurance, stability")	pillar amulet	*Wb* 5: 627/3

* *Glossar* = Erichsen 1954a

1. For general lists of amulets, see above, n. 241.

2. Variants: *mnqry.t* *Wb* 2: 91/5 and *mqr.t* *Wb* 2: 159/7.

activity of such individuals at court is attested by the title *sꜣ-bỉty*, , "amulet-man of the King of Lower Egypt," who appears together with "courtiers in charge of magic" (*smr.w ḥry.w ḥkꜣ*).[243] In an official capacity, the *sꜣw-Srq.t*, "amulet-man of Selket, the scorpion goddess" (seemingly otherwise known as the *ẖrp-Srq.t*, "controller of Selket"), is found accompanying mining expeditions to treat the ever-present problem of scorpion bites.[244] The Ebers papyrus includes the *sꜣw* together with "doctors" (*swnw*) and "priests of Sakhmet" (*wʿb Sẖm.t*) in a list of medical practitioners who might be expected to apply a "hands on" method of examining patients:

> ... when any doctor, priest of Sakhmet or amulet-man places his hands or fingers on any head, on any back of the head, on any hands, on any chest ("place of the heart"), on any arms, or on any feet, then he places them on the heart, for its vessels belong to all its limbs.[245]

In keeping with the amoral nature of Egyptian magic, however, the "charmer" and his "charms" could be hostile as well. Medical and "magical" texts contain recipes to avert the effects of "the craft of amulets."[246] The pairing of the "amulet-man" and "doctor" in Papyrus Ebers, both as professional colleagues and—in the case of negative sorcery—professional opponents, underscores the intimate relation between medicine and magic, whose connecting, religious link is embodied in the presence of the priest of Sakhmet (the goddess of plague and disease).

243. See the royal jubilee rituals in Naville 1892, pl. VIII, nos. 22–23 and Gardiner 1917, p. 41. The "amulet-man of the King of Lower Egypt" is certainly accompanied by a corresponding "amulet-man of the King of Upper Egypt," *[sꜣw]-nysw.t* as suggested by Gardiner. Scribes of the House of Life also appear among these officials (see below, pp. 220–22, 230, and 232) in company with a chief lector priest and "supervisors of magic" (*ḥry.w-ḥkꜣ*; see Naville 1892, pls. X, no. 5 and XIII, no. 1). For the prominent role of court magicians in the royal jubilee, see Spalinger 1988, pp. 29–33 and Uphill 1965, pp. 370 and 376.

244. See *Wb* 4: 415/19 and Gardiner 1917, pp. 33–44 (*ẖrp-Srq.t*) and 44 (*sꜣw-Srq.t*). Von Känel collects the attestations of these offices in 1984, pp. 284–305. The prominence of these healers may account for the declaration of Selket's ability to bind Heka (Drioton 1927b, pp. 134–35). See above, n. 90.

245. Wreszinski 1913, p. 205 §854 (col. 99/2–3).

246. For *ḥm.t-sꜣ.w* in a negative context, see Pap. Ebers §733 (col. 88/13) "Prescription to expel the craft of charms," in Wreszinzki 1913, p. 180. This usage is paralleled in Pap. Ebers by recipe §165 "to expel magic (*ḥkꜣ*) from the body" (see n. 80, above). Compare also the injunction in Erman 1901, p. 39 (spell P vo., col. 2/5): "Be spat out, oh charms!" (*šp=k sꜣ.w pw*).

The link between medicine, magic, and religion is immediately evident in the basic term for "magical potion": *pẖr.t*,  (var. 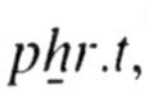), "recipe/prescription."[247] Used as the standard term for any medical concoction, *pẖr.t* may be applied indiscriminately to medical or magical recipes. Thus, in the ninth case of the Edwin Smith Surgical Papyrus which concerns a fractured skull, the term is applied to a compress of broken ostrich shell used for reasons of "sympathetic magic," due to "the resemblance of the frontal bone to a segment of the shell."[248] The association of this "prescription" with magic cannot be questioned, for directly following the description of the remedy is a spell (*ḏd.t m ḥkȝw ḥr pẖr.t tn*, "that which is said as magic over this prescription") to activate its curative powers.[249] In the New Kingdom, the term is found with clearly negative overtones in the "harim conspiracy" papyrus (Papyrus Rollin) which contains an accusation of the making of *pẖr.wt n di͗ gnn ʿ.t n rmṯ*, "potions for laming human limbs."[250] In Demotic, the word is a commonplace of the magical papyri, appearing as "a remedy for a donkey's not moving," "a potion for causing a woman to love you," etc.[251] The magical nuance of *pẖr.t* survives into Coptic, where as S ⲡⲁϩⲣⲉ, B ⲫⲁϧⲣⲓ it may mean either "medical remedy" or "magical potion."[252] The latter use is unmistakable in a Bohairic version of Galatians 5:20:

247. See *Wb* 1: 549/1-12 and Erichsen 1954a, p. 139. For the association of *ḥkȝ* and *pẖr.t*, see Pap. Insinger, col. 31/22: *i͗-i͗r sȝ.w ḥyk.w ḫpr pẖr.w n nm*, "Through whom do amulet and magic become remedies?"; discussed in Volten 1942, pp. 43–44. For the ritual use of the term, see Golénischeff 1927, p. 128 (Pap. Cairo 58027, col. 4/1), where it designates a list of ingredients for a secret oil of the scriptorium (*pr-ʿnḫ*) used in the rite of "protecting the bedroom" (*sȝ-ḥnk.t* improperly transcribed by the editor, see Jankuhn 1972, p. 142).

248. See Breasted 1930, pp. 217–24. The quotation is on p. 217. An Old Kingdom date for this papyrus is suggested in Westendorf 1966b, pp. 10–11.

249. Breasted 1930, pp. 219–20.

250. Papyrus Rollin, l. 1 and cf. Pap. Lee, col. 2/1. For the hieratic text, see Devéria 1867, pl. 5, and p. 410. The hieratic *pẖr.wt*,  was miscopied *rmṯ*, 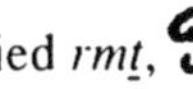, "people" by Pleyte 1868, pl. 16 and p. 25, and specifically corrected by Devéria 1867, p. 410, n. 2. Nonetheless, editors have persisted in repeating Pleyte's reading (while citing Devéria's hand copy!; see Breasted 1906, vol. 4, p. 220; Goedicke 1963, pp. 72–76; and Kitchen 1983a, p. 361/1). The correction is again made by Posener 1976a, p. 435 and 1976b, p.147.

251. E.g., Pap. BM 10588, cols. 7/12: *pẖr.t r tm i͗r ʿȝ m ʿš*, and 8/1: *pẖr.t n ti͗ i͗r s[ḥm].t mry.ṯ=k* (Bell, Nock, and Thompson 1933, p. 13 and Ritner 1986a, pp. 99–100). See also Griffith and Thompson 1904, pp. 34–35 (col. 3/20): A recipe (*pẖr.t*) for enchanting the vessel quickly"; and pp. 36–37 (col. 3/22): A recipe (*pẖr.t*) to bring the gods in by force."

252. See Crum 1939, p. 282b; Westendorf 1965–77, p. 157; Černý 1976, p. 131; and Vycichl 1983, p. 167b.

ⲘⲈⲦⲢⲈϤϮⲪⲀϨⲢⲒⲚϨⲒⲔ, "sorcery" (literally "the practice of giving potions of magic").[253] The Egyptian use of *pẖr.t* directly parallels that of the Greek word which it translates: φαρμακεία, "pharmacy" > "poisoning/sorcery," which as ⲪⲀⲢⲘⲀⲄⲒⲀ is adopted into the Coptic vocabulary as a synonym for native words meaning "poisoning," "enchantment," or "witchcraft."[254]

The term *pẖr.t* has religious overtones as well, being used to describe the funerary preparation of the dead through the ritually enhanced application of sacred oils, amulets, and unguents by the embalming priests (*wt*). In a Demotic papyrus of the Ptolemaic period, a guild of a competing class of funerary priests, the coachytes (*wꜣḥ mw*, "water-pourers"), agrees not to encroach upon the privileges of these embalmers, deciding *r tm ḥwy pẖr.t r mwt n pꜣy=n ʿ.wy*, "not to put remedies (embalming materials) on the dead in our workshop ("house")."[255] That the term was one of general currency is shown by a corresponding embalmer's agreement: *mtw=y mnq=f n pẖr.t mtw=y ti=s n-tr.t pꜣy=k wꜣḥ-mw*, "and I shall complete it (the mummy) with embalming materials, and I shall give it into the hand of your coachyte."[256] These "remedies" for the dead find their divine counterpart in Sokar, "the golden remedy (*pẖr.t*) in the temples."[257] The deity of inertness, Sokar contains within himself the seed of regeneration. As the recipient of the dead, he constitutes the apex of the "medical history" of any man: the remedies of life (ordinary *pẖr.t*), the remedies of death (embalming *pẖr.t*), and the remedy of rebirth (Sokar as *pẖr.t*).

253. *ⲠⲒϪⲰⲘ ⲚⲦⲈ ϮⲀⲒⲀⲐⲎⲔⲎ ⲘⲂⲈⲢⲒ* [The Book of the New Testament] 1934, p. 418 and Crum 1939, p. 176b, *s.v.* ⲘⲚⲦ-. The phrase is paralleled in Sahidic in the homily of Theophilos on the cross, published in Rossi 1887, p. 66 (col. 172): ⲘⲚⲦⲢⲈϤⲢⲠⲀϨⲢⲈ ⲚϨⲒⲔ. See also Orlandi 1980, pp. 44–45: ϤⲤⲞⲞⲨⲚ ϨⲰⲰϤ ⲚⲘⲠⲀϨⲢⲈ ⲚⲚϨⲒⲔ ⲚⲚⲈⲬⲢⲈⲒⲤⲦⲒⲀⲚⲞⲤ, "He himself knows the magical potions of the Christians." See also n. 55, above.

254. Liddell, Scott, and Jones 1940, p. 1917a. For ⲪⲀⲢⲘⲀⲄⲒⲀ in a Coptic text, see Kuhn 1960, vol. 1, p. 52, and vol. 2, p. 48. ⲪⲀⲢⲘⲀⲄⲒⲀ is coupled with the term ⲢⲈϤⲘⲞⲨⲦⲈ, "enchanter."

255. Papyrus Berlin P. 3115, col. D/3 in de Cenival 1972a, pp. 126 and 128, n. 3, 1.

256. Papyrus BM 10077, cols. A/8 and B/8 in Reich 1914, pls. 11–12. The word *pẖr.t* is misread *tꜣ.w*, "offering bread" on pp. 39–40. For further references to *pẖr.t* as "embalming materials," see *Wb* 1: 549/12 (= Pap. Bulaq 7, col. D/1 and Pap. Bulaq 3, col. 7/14). Compare also the funerary Pap. BM 10507, col. 2/14: *nfr=y n nꜣy=y pẖr.w ʿn=y n pꜣy=y šny*, "I am well through my remedies; I have returned (recovered) from my sickness"; in Mark Smith 1987, pp. 37 and 70.

257. Papyrus BM 10188, col. 18/5 in Faulkner 1933, p. 35 and 1937a, pp. 12 and 14. Neither Faulkner nor *Wb* 1: 549/13 understand the import of this epithet which is left untranslated. Goyon, who publishes the parallel text Pap. Louvre I. 3079 in 1968, pp. 65 and 70–71, translates the epithet without comment or justification as "swathed in gold." This last translation is echoed in Cauville 1983, p. 139 and 1987, p. 160. See further, p. 59 and n. 273, below. The epithet may also appear in Pap. Leiden I 384 vo., col. I*/12ff. in J. H. Johnson 1975, pp. 34–35.

This use of the identical word "remedy" for the treatment of both the living and the dead attests to the unmistakable continuum in Egyptian thought between medicine and religion. Indeed, the title most closely approximating the English "doctor," *swnw*, 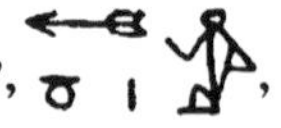, may be applied as well to the embalming priest, and is translated into Greek as ταριχευτής, "embalmer."[258] It is in this capacity that the archetypal embalmer, the deity Anubis, receives the epithet *pꜣ wr swnw*, "the chief physician."[259] The concomitant magical aspects of medicine are similarly granted divine patronage in the person of *Ḥr-swnw-nfr*, "Horus the good doctor," whose words (*mdw*) "repel death," whose utterances (*tp-rꜣ*) "cure scorpion bite," and whose magic (*ḥkꜣ*) "pacifies inflammation."[260] Honored in Letopolis as "chief physician in the house of Re,"[261] Horus the doctor is indistinguishable from "Horus the Reciter" (*Ḥr-Šd*), whose role in the curing of scorpion bite has been discussed above. This conception of deity as doctor is by no means restricted to Anubis and Horus; Amon, Isis, Imhotep, et al., are invoked for remedies, and the Demotic Papyrus Insinger (col. 18/23) goes so far as to identify deity and remedy: "A daily remedy is to prevent disease by having the greatness of god in your heart."[262] The frequent appearance of deities and magic in the treatment of illness derives from an Egyptian conception of disease as "the stroke (*s.t-ꜥ*, 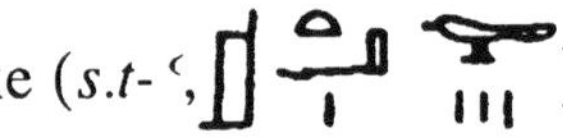) of a god, of a goddess, of a dead man, or of a dead woman."[263]

258. For the embalmer as *swnw*, see Pap. Berlin P. 3115, col. C/10–11 in de Cenival 1972a, pp. 118–19 and 123, n. 10, 1: "let no man at all bring an embalmer (*swnw*) into the guild of Amenope but only a coachyte." So also in Pap. BM 10074, l. 3 in Reich 1914, pp. 43–47 (§III/2) and pl. 7: *tꜣ swn(.t)*, "the female coachyte"; and cf. idem 1910, p. 258. For *swnw* = ταριχευτής, see Erichsen 1954a, p. 415 and Vergote 1959, pp. 123–24.

259. See Griffith and Thompson 1904, pp. 28–29 and 1909, p. 72, no. 721 (col. 2/18).

260. Spiegelberg 1922 (O. Strassburg H. 111 = Pap. Turin Pleyte and Rossi 124, l. 4); Borghouts 1978, p. 75, no. 103 and 1987b, p. 260 (Pap. Turin 1993). The divine name *Ḥr-swnw-nfr* appears in a Demotic inscription on pot Brooklyn acc. no. 16.589, l. 1 (manuscript by George R. Hughes [Brooklyn Museum, in press]). For the variant *Ḥr-swnw-ḥtp-nṯr*, "Horus the physician who pacifies the god," see Drioton 1939, p. 73 (Ramses III prophylactic statue, right side, l. 11); Gardiner 1935, vol. 1, pp. 56–57 and vol. 2, pl. 33 (Pap. Chester Beatty 7, cols. 1/7–2/5); and van de Walle 1967, p. 24 (O. Brussels E 3209, l. 11). As a personal name, *Ḥr-pꜣ-swnw* is found in Demotic in Pap. BM 1201 (Reich 1910, p. 258).

261. Spiegelberg 1922, p. 70, n. 2.

262. For Amon as *swnw* who cures "without remedies," see Pap. Leiden I 350, stanza 70, in Wilson 1969a, p. 369; Gardiner 1905, pp. 28–30; and Zandee 1948, pp. 54–55 and pl. 3 (col. 3/14). For Isis, see, e.g., O. Ḥor 28, ll. 15–16: "Her lady Isis makes a remedy (*pḫry.t*) for the Queen," in Ray 1976, pp. 97–98. For Imhotep and incubation dreams, see Pap. Leiden I 384 vo., col. 1*/4: "Let him say to me a fitting remedy (*pḫr.t*)," and passim, in J. H. Johnson 1975, pp. 34–37. For Pap. Insinger, col. 18/23, see Lexa 1926, pp. 59–60 and Lichtheim 1980, p. 200. For god as remedy, cf. nn. 247 and 257, above.

263. For *s.t-ꜥ*, see *Wb* 1: 157/5 and cf. *Wb* 4: 495/4 *šnw s.t-ꜥ*, "sickness of a stroke/hand." For examples, see Pap. Hearst, col. 5/10, 12, 14 and passim in Reisner 1905, p. 17 (*ỉs.t-ꜥ*) and pl. 5. For the rather literal meaning of this term, compare the death of Osiris by the physical "blow, hand" (ꜥ) of Seth in CT spell

Just such a stroke may be implied in "The Instructions for King Merikare" as the "blow" (*ꜥ*, ) for which magic is the divine antidote.[264] In any case, the preparation and administration of remedies unites not only the triad of priest, magician, and physician, but also that of spell, material, and rite. Thus even the application and removal of bandages and the measurement of drugs may become a ritual accompanied by the recitation of spells.[265]

ENCIRCLING

The suggested root of the word for remedy, *pẖr.t*, is the verb *pẖr*, 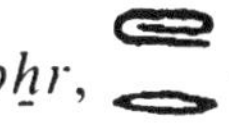, "to go around/encircle," whose own magical connotation "to enchant" may lie at the heart of that of *pẖr.t*: "that which encircles/contains/controls" > "that which enchants/protects/ potion."[266] As an example of Egyptian terminology expressing magic by rite, *pẖr* exhibits a long and complex development which well repays study. The magical ritual of "encircling" (*dbn*, *pẖr*) for purification is almost coeval with Egyptian civilization itself, being attested

---

681 (de Buck 1956, p. 306) and in Pap. BM 10188, cols. 1/27 and 14/26 (*s.t-ꜥ*). For the latter examples, see Faulkner 1933, pp. 3 and 27 and 1936, pp. 123 and 130. For a similar conception in Mesopotamian medicine (the "hand of a ghost" or "touch" of a deity), see Biggs 1980–83.

264. See above, p. 20 and n. 79.

265. See, for example, Borghouts 1978, pp. 44–49 (nos. 71–81). For a thorough analysis of the ritual for the removal of a bandage (idem 1978, no. 81), see van Dijk 1979–80. General discussions of the role of the Egyptian pharmacist are found in Jonckheere 1955.

266. See *Wb* 1: 544–47 and cf. Griffith and Thompson 1904, pp. 34–35 (col. 3/20) "Recipe (*pẖr.t*) for enchanting (*pẖr*) the vessel quickly." For the suggested link between *pẖr* and *pẖr.t*, see Osing 1976b, vol. 1, p. 124. Similar notions of "encircling" > "enchanting" are current in Egyptian thought; compare *šn*, above, p. 43 and n. 197, and the image of the ouroboros, discussed in Ritner 1984b, pp. 219–20. The notion of circling for protection is common; cf. the protective function of *ḥꜣ*, "around" in the standard (and archaic) expression *sꜣ ꜥnḫ ḥꜣ NN*, "May the protection of life be around NN" and variants, in *Wb* 3: 9/15–17 and Gardiner 1903, pp. 334–36. Specific examples of protective circles of magic include CT spell 342 (de Buck 1951, p. 347): "magic encloses (*šnn*) its settlements." As noted by Faulkner 1973, p. 277, n. 6, this containment is "presumably in a protective sense." The encircling arms of the personified Western Desert serve a similar purpose: "With my arms having encircled (*pẖr*) you forever and ever, truly I shall be the protection (*sꜣ*) of your flesh" (Davies and Gardiner 1915, p. 48 and pl. 10). See also the text of Nephthys on the door of the third shrine of Tutankhamun: "I have encircled you (*pẖr.n⸗y ḥꜣ⸗k*); you are not weary; these limbs of yours are not weak," in Piankoff and Rambova 1955, p. 72 and pl. 72 (related to BD spell 151 c §S1, in Allen 1974, p. 148). Compare also Derchain 1965, pp. 16*, 143, and pls. 14–15 (cols. 14/11–15/1): "... the flame surrounding (*pẖr*) him as his protection/amulet (*sꜣ*)." This pervasive, protective nuance of encircling is implied (or punned upon) in a spell from the Metternich Stela (l. 203) in which the cry of Nephthys brings aid to the injured Horus by encircling (*pẖr*) the swamp where the god lies stricken (Sander-Hansen 1956, pp. 64 and 71).

from the earliest archaic funerary rituals to the temple ceremonies of the Greco-Roman periods. Thus, a Thirteenth Dynasty text believed to derive from an original of the Third Dynasty contains several references to the funerary procession "circulating around the mastaba four times."[267] Over a millennium later, Ptolemy IX is the recipient of a similar rite of "circulating around four times" in the "purgatorium" at Edfu.[268] It is a testament to the longevity of Egyptian rituals that even the vessels (*dšr.t*) associated with this rite remain unchanged.[269]

Comparable rituals of circumambulation comprise both public, cultic ceremonies and private, "magical" ones.[270] In particular, the royal coronation ritual included such a "procession about the desert" (*dbn ḥ3s.t*) and a "circumambulation of the walls" (*pḫr ḥ3 ỉnb.w*) to delimit the "sacred space" of the kingdom, and a repetition of this encirclement

267. See Gardiner 1955a, pp. 9–17 (Pap. Ramesseum E, col. 74, broken examples in 14a and 27). This text uses the synonym *dbn*, "to circulate." For the antiquity of the concept, compare the use of *s3 ḥ3*, "protection around" as the name of a royal chapel in the archaic period, discussed in Roth 1991, pp. 86 and 164–69. Indisputable ritual circumambulations are described in the Pyramid Texts; see for example, PT spell 659 (§1866): "Take these white teeth of yours in a bowl, go around them with an arrow in this their name of arrow," in Sethe 1910, pp. 454–55 (text); Faulkner 1969, p. 271 (translation); Ritner 1991, pp. 211–12; and cf. also n. 297, below.

268. See Chassinat 1928, pp. 336–38 and cf. Mallet 1909, p. 75: *pḫr ḥ3 sp 4 m dšr.t 4 nt mw*, "go about four times with four jugs of water." For the idiom *pḫr ḥ3 r sp 4*, see *Wb* 1: 545/12–13. Notable also is the purification ceremony enacted by Tuthmosis III at the dedication of an enclosure wall at Heliopolis, in Sethe 1907, p. 832. The king is depicted bearing four jugs of water and is said to go around four times (*pḫr ḥ3 sp 4*) (l. 9), forming a ritual counterpart to the "surrounding" (*pḫr*) of the temple by the enclosure wall (l. 13).

269. Compare Chassinat 1928, p. 338 and Gardiner 1955a, p. 16 (frag. c).

270. The term *pḫr* commonly designates temple processions; cf. *pḫr ḥm=s m ḥb*, "Her Majesty (*scil.* Hathor) goes about in festival," in Chassinat 1932, p. 26 (l. 13) and Alliot 1954, p. 449, n. 3. See also the terminology of oracular processions: "[the procession] went about (*pḫr*) the hall on its two sides"; in Sethe 1930b, p. 158/8 (Tuthmosis III election by Amon, l. 6); and "You go about (*pḫr*) in the fashion of my words"; in Drioton 1926, p. 44, no. 100 (words of a Roman emperor in the oracle of the Bull of Medamud). The term *pḫr* serves also to designate the ritualized inspection route of the pyramid complex of Neferirkare (Posener-Kriéger 1968, pp. 114 and 117). The implied nuance is uncertain in the dream book Pap. Chester Beatty 3, col. 2/5: (If a man see himself in a dream while) "his [towns]folk circulate [around him]; [Good]; it means [...]" (Gardiner 1935, vol. 1, p. 11 and vol. 2, pl. 5). For ritual burial circuits, see the reenactments of funerary ship processions in the New Kingdom, discussed in Davies and Gardiner 1915, pp. 52–53 and pl. 11 and Norman de Garis Davies 1973, p. 84 and pl. 79 (*pḫr m ḫsft / pḫr m ḥd r tp mw*). Compare also the funerary spell written *around* the shrine of Osiris, the "Presider over the West" in BD spell Pleyte 174, §T; in Allen 1974, p. 223.

occurred at the *ḥb-sd* jubilee festival.[271] Similarly, the popular *dwꜣ-nṯry* festival of Sokar on the 25th–26th days of the month Choiakh involved a procession of the god and his followers *pẖr=f inb.w*, "while he goes around the walls" of Memphis.[272] Indeed, this *pẖr* of Sokar is the object of a pun in his above-mentioned epithet "golden remedy (*pẖr.t*) in the temples," which occurs at the beginning of the hymn recited at the outset of this very procession.[273] Cultic encirclement appears as well in the Ptolemaic ritual of "Protecting the House" (*sꜣ-pr*) of the sacred falcon venerated in Edfu, involving the surrounding of the

271. See Sethe 1928a, pp. 129 and 133 §28d, and see also pp. 192, 194, 254, 137, and 238. For the circumambulation of the walls, see the coronation ritual of Hatshepsut in Sethe 1930c, pp. 261/6, and 262/8: *smꜣ-tꜣ pẖr ḥꜣ inb.w*, "uniting the land, going around the walls"; and compare the references to *Wb* 1: 546/1. General discussion is found in Wilkinson 1985, pp. 46–51. Similar rituals of "going around the walls" are discussed in Gardiner 1903, pp. 334–36 and Lauer 1931, pp. 354–55. For the concept of "sacred space," see Eliade 1959, pp. 20–65. An elucidation of the concept in Egyptian terms appears in PT spells 366 and 454. With regard to the coronation procession (*pẖr*), the king is said to be "great and enclosing" (*dbn, šn*; PT spell 366 §629), and to embrace all gods, lands, and possessions (PT spell 454 §847). For these, see Sethe 1908, pp. 339–40 and 471–72 and Faulkner 1969, pp. 120–21 and 151. On the jubilee race, see Kees 1912; idem 1915, pp. 64–69; and Uphill 1965; and for the retention of this ritual action by Akhenaton, see Uphill 1963. For a Ptolemaic equation of the *ḥb-sd* race with the encirclement of sacred territory (*sḫ.t*, "field," *iꜣ.t*, "mound"), see Kees 1915, pp. 68–69 and Chassinat 1931, p. 288 (*iṯi ḥp.t*). Although Kees (1915, pp. 68–69) considers the Ptolemaic scribes to have been "confused and incorrect" in their equation of this rite with that of the *pẖrr sḫ.t*, "going about a field" or *ḥnk sḫ.t*, "offering a field," the essential significance of these rites is identical. What the procession encloses is transferred to its lord (god or king). The ultimate fusion of these rites appears in the agrarian festival of Heka at Esna, in which the god, honored as a rejuvenated king, encircles the fields to restore their vitality (Sauneron 1968, p. 282 [no. 340, 6] and 1962b, pp. 33–35: *ir ḥb m pẖr iꜣ.t tn*, "perform the festival in circling this mound"). Perhaps related to this coronation *pẖr* is the expression for heir *pẖr-ns.t*, "he who goes about the throne" (*Wb* 1: 547/13–16). See also the processional route indicated in Goyon 1972, p. 35.

272. See Keimer 1933, especially pp. 54–56; Hari 1985, p. 49 and pl. 35 (l. 143); and Gaballa and Kitchen 1969, especially p. 52. For the route, see Goyon 1978a, pp. 415–38. See also the funerary wish *di=sn pẖr=k inb.w r-ḥnꜥ Skr*, "May you be allowed to go around the walls with Sokar," in Barta 1968, p. 181 (§262). Compare also the ceremonial driving of oxen and donkeys around the walls mentioned in the tomb of Kheruef: "Four times they go around the walls on this day of erecting the august *ḏd*-pillar for Ptah-Sokar-Osiris (var. "which is in the *Šty.t*-shrine")"; in Helck 1958a, p. 1864/11–14 and The Epigraphic Survey 1980, p. 66 and pls. 61 and 63. A similar ritual "running around the field four times" for Sokar is attested at Abydos (David 1973, p. 176).

273. For the epithet, see above, n. 257 and for the date of the recitation, see Faulkner 1937a, p. 12. The pun has not been previously recognized.

temple by torches and the "bedchamber" of the god by tamarisk twigs.[274] Nuances of encircling are elaborated within the accompanying recitation to include allusions to the coronation "encirclement as boundary," to the ouroboros "encirclement as protection," and to the simple "going around" as an enactment of free, unhindered movement.[275] Closely related to other late "encirclement" rituals (such as the *sꜣ-ḥnk.t*, "protection of the bedroom"), this rite's origin is probably to be found in a private ritual of Middle Kingdom date for the preservation of a house against the dangers of the new year.[276] The second of several incantations against the disease-bringing "pest of the year" preserved in Papyrus Edwin Smith concludes with the instructions:

> *ḏd mdw ỉn s ẖt ds m ʿ=f pr=f r-rwty pẖr=f pr=f n mwt.n=f n ỉꜣd.t rnp.t*
> Words to be said by a man with a stick of *ds*-wood in his hand while he goes outside, going around his house. He cannot die by the pest of the year.[277]

274. See Jankuhn 1972, pp. 21, 23–24, 26, 31, and 66. An unrecognized reference to this or a similar rite may appear in Pap. BM 10188, col. 13/14: "They (*scil.* Isis and Nephthys) place protection (*sꜣ*) about his temple." See Faulkner 1933, p. 24. Compare also Faulkner 1958, pp. 30* and 13 (col. 19/10): "Nut who lights the torch (*stꜣ tkꜣ*) and makes the protection of the house" (*sꜣw-pr* translated "protection" by ed.), and the related(?) torch ritual in BD spell 137B, in Naville 1886, vol. 1, pl. CLI and Allen 1974, p. 115. The term reappears in the "Book of Hours" in col. 25/6 and was translated "The Door(?) of the House" by Faulkner (1958, pp. 40* and 17). Parallel rites of encircling for protection appear also in Coptic magic (Worrell 1929–30, pp. 258 [around bed] and 259–61 [around house]).

275. The ritual encircling is given a divine prototype: "It is the protection of Horus whose heart is glad, whose voice is justified after he went around (*pẖr* *ḥꜣ*) the gods on that day of his being assigned to his inheritance" (Jankuhn 1972, p. 31). "It is the protection of Him who bends the knee in the Great Mansion, who goes about (*pẖr*) surrounded (*dbn*) in his protective serpent" (ibid., p. 66). For the image of the enclosing ouroboros serpent, see above, n. 266. The previously unexplained Ptolemaic writing of *pẖr*, with (literally *r-tp* = "*r* atop/superscript [*r*]") probably derives from the writing , whose superscript *r* is itself a back formation from the hieratic *pẖr*-sign: (*Wb* 1: 544; cf. Möller 1909b, p. 47, no. 526 [*pẖr*] and p. 8, no. 91 [*r*]). This back formation from hieratic may date from the Middle Kingdom (Ranke 1935, p. 136, no. 6 [*Pẖrr* read *Pẖr*]).

276. For the origin of the Ptolemaic ritual in the private rite, see Jankuhn 1972, pp. 5–9. For the ritual of *sꜣ-ḥnk.t*, see ibid., pp. 142–43, n. 91 and Golénischeff 1927, pp. 114–31, especially 125–26 (Pap. Cairo 58027, col. 3/11–14); and cf. Goyon 1971, pp. 154–59 and Ritner 1990, pp. 25–41.

277. Breasted 1930, pp. 478, 502 (col. 18/15–16), and cf. 504 (col. 20/5–8). For a suggested Old Kingdom date for this papyrus, see above, n. 248. A curiously similar practice is dictated by modern Texas folklore: "Walk around the house barefooted in the first snow of the season and you will stay healthy all winter" (Davis and Gillis 1989, p. 64). Contrast the ancient Mesopotamian rite for home protection which dictates the encircling not of the house, but of the images of potential enemies, in Meier 1941–44, p. 151: "The flour circle of Nidaba, the charm of the great gods, have I laid round about you."

A literary echo of this ceremony is perhaps to be recognized in the actions of the heroine of Papyrus Westcar, Rudjedet, who "makes a circuit of the room" in which she hears preternatural music.[278] At Edfu, all of these nuances of *pẖr* are found again in the temple dedication ritual of "giving a house to its lord," in which the king and priests go about the temple, simultaneously purifying the site, delimiting its sacred/cosmic space, and protecting it from external, demonic forces.[279] Derived directly from such consecration rituals, though returned to private use, is the βοτανήαρσις (plant-harvesting rite, see above, pp. 39–40) of Egyptian origin preserved in the corpus of Greek magical papyri, in which the magician goes about (περιφέρω) the selected plant three times while fumigating it with pine resin.[280]

The magical nuance of the verb *pẖr*, implicit in earlier usage, becomes explicit in the Demotic verb *pẖr*, , "to enchant" > Coptic ᴮⲫⲁϧⲉⲣ.[281] In the first Setna tale, the term is used to describe the enchanting of heaven, the underworld, the mountains, and the seas so that the magician "finds out all that which the birds of the sky, the fish of the deep and the animals say."[282] A direct parallel is found in the "Fable of Sight and Hearing" ("I enchant the sky so that I may listen to that which is in it"), and one would readily accept the editor's suggestion of a further parallel in Papyrus Vienna 6636 (*[p]r=y pẖl nwny.t [...]*, "I go forth to enchant the underworld") were it not for the determinative () of *pẖl*, which suggests the verb of motion "to go about (the underworld)."[283] Less trivial than it may appear at first sight, the ambiguity of this example is paralleled elsewhere, and implies that the notions of "encircling" and "enchanting" are still fully melded—differing determinatives notwithstanding. Thus within an oracular statement in the "Demotic Chronicle" (col. 2/11) the moon is said to *pẖrꜣ*, 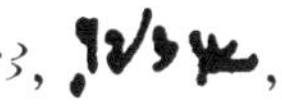, the depths and the king to "go around (*ỉr nꜣ qty*)

278. Papyrus Westcar, col. 12/3: *wn-ỉn=s ḥr dbn tꜣ ꜥ.t*. For the text, see de Buck 1970, p. 87. A translation and additional bibliography may be found in Lichtheim 1973, pp. 215–22.

279. De Wit 1961, p. 94 and cf. pp. 60, 92, 282, and 284.

280. PGM IV, ll. 2967–3006. For bibliography, see above, n. 181. Although this rite is of Egyptian origin, similar (related?) processions are known from classical and early Christian sources (Pax 1957).

281. See Erichsen 1954a, p. 139; Crum 1939, p. 282b; Westendorf 1965–77, pp. 157 and 533; and Černý 1976, p. 131.

282. See Griffith 1985, pp. 20–21 and 25 (cols. 3/13–14, 3/35–36, and 4/1) and Lichtheim 1980, pp. 128 and 130–31.

283. For the fable, see Pap. Leiden I 384, col. 14/3, in Spiegelberg 1917a, pp. 36–37 and Tait 1976, pp. 38 (translation) and 49 (text). For Pap. Vienna 6636 (col. 1/x+5), see Reymond 1977, pp. 118–19, but ignore this author's fanciful mystifications which include translating *pẖl* variously as "essence" (p. 35), "charm" (p. 122), and "to endow with the knowledge of" (p. 121). Her primary translation of *pr=y pẖl nwny.t* opts for "to reveal the charm of the primeval waters" (pp. 118–19). For *nwny.t* as Nut, see Mark Smith 1977, p. 129.

the entire land."[284] Parallelism would indicate that *pẖrꜣ* be translated "to go around," but the determinative is that of "to enchant"; probably both nuances are intended.

The "magical" examples of Setna et al. take on even greater significance when it is realized that they reflect the culmination of an ancient *topos* describing the control of the universe by the sun god, who is variously said to "go about" (*pẖr*) and "rule" (*ḥqꜣ*) the earth, heaven, and underworld.[285] From the evidence of the Demotic texts, the two terms may be synonymous—Re rules by enclosing and enchanting. In fact, a Demotic version of a much-copied solar hymn replaces the hieroglyphic "walking-legs" determinative of "to go around" with the "man-with-hand-to-mouth" determinative of "to enchant."[286] Rather than being an error on the part of the copyist, this may instead reflect a clarification (or later re-interpretation) of the ancient text.

Forming a divine counterpart to the coronation procession about the walls and desert, the circuit of Re both delineates the universe and establishes his sovereignty over it. In the course of the development of Egyptian theology, participation in this cosmic circuit had been extended to the king (already in the Pyramid Texts), and the privilege was ultimately claimed by the blessed dead (Book of the Dead) in funerary texts which had as their stated goal the subjugation of the universe to the needs of the deceased.[287] From the very nature

284. Spiegelberg 1914, pp. 10 and 15, especially 15, n. 1 (col. 2/11). Compare BD spell Pleyte 168 §S54 in which the lunar Osiris encircles the Two Lands and thus (as king) controls "their lands, their cities, and their nomes," in Allen 1974, p. 220.

285. For the *topos*, see *inter alia*, the solar hymn examined in Mark Smith 1977. For an example with *ḥqꜣ*, see Donadoni 1973, p. 56, l. 1. Compare also CT spell 1016 (de Buck 1961, p. 235) in which the eye of the god "goes about (*pẖr n-ḥꜣ*) the enemy," with "The Instruction of Amenemope" (Pap. BM 10474), col. 17/10: "His (*scil.* the god's) eyes encircle the lands" (*ỉw ỉr.t=f pẖr tꜣ.w*); in Budge 1923, pl. 9 and Lichtheim 1976, p. 156. Amon's encircling of lands and people is stressed in Pap. Leiden I 350, col. 2/19–20, in Zandee 1948, pp. 32–34 and pl. 2. The equation of encircling and controlling is explicit in BD spell 185 A §S4: "What the disk has circled is under his supervision"; in Allen 1974, p. 204. Thus should be explained the prominent mention of the divine circuit throughout the funerary literature, including CT spells 818 (de Buck 1961, p. 17) and 960 (de Buck 1961, p. 178), and BD spells 15 A5 §S2; 62b §S; 70 §S2; [78 §S1]; 79 §S1; 108 §S3; [119 §S2–3]; 130b §S5–6; 133 §S1; 136B b §S; 145 dyn. 21 w §S4; 147 a §S2; [147 b §S2]; 147 g §S2; 148 dyn. 18 a §S3; 153 §S3; 178 s §S; [181 d §S1]; 192 §S3; Pleyte 168 §S54; and Pleyte 173 §P1, in Allen 1974, passim.

286. Ostracon Naville 11, in Mark Smith 1977, p. 124 (the text was formerly identified as O. Hess). Smith takes the writing as a simple error without examining the lexical complexity of *pẖr*.

287. For the king as participant in the cosmic cycle, see *inter alia*, "the cannibal hymn" (PT spell §406c), in Sethe 1908, p. 212 and Faulkner 1969, pp. 81–82: "He has gone about (*dbn*) the two entire heavens, he has encircled (*pẖr*) the two banks." Speleers gathers additional references to circumambulation (*pẖr*) in 1935, p. 315. Similar claims made by non-royal deceased appear throughout the Book of the Dead; for example, BD spell 38A: "I have made my circuit (*pẖr*) to the *Ḥnḥn*-bark of Khepri"; in Naville 1886, vol. 2, p. 103 (and cf. p. 106, BD spell 38B) and Allen 1974, p. 45. Compare also BD spell 132:

of these texts, whose "magical" attributes are noted above, one could reasonably expect that the nuance of "magical control" had always been inherent, though orthographically indistinct, in the references to "cosmic circuits." Explicit confirmation of this suspicion is possible only for the latest representatives of this genre, made evident by Demotic orthography and by a pun on both aspects of *pẖr* found in Papyrus Louvre E 3452. Earliest of the Demotic funerary texts, the papyrus contains transformation spells in which the deceased becomes a "dog enchanted in all his limbs" (*ỉwỉw pẖr m ʿtwe=f nb*) that "his *ba* go about as a dog on earth and the underworld daily" (*pẖr sp 2 by=f m ỉwỉw šme by=f m ỉwỉw ỉḥ tꜣ twꜣ.t m ẖr-hrw*).[288]

It is within the context of these funerary texts that one must understand the formula which is recited in Setna I "to enchant heaven, the underworld," et cetera. Providing not merely the logical origin of the formula's terminology, the funerary corpus constitutes as well the only antecedent for the spell's purpose. The implications of this relationship are clear; Setna's spells *are funerary spells* used with equal facility by the living, and the *pẖr* involved is *not simply figurative*, but—as in the case of the mortuary literature from which it derives—represents a fusion of the magician with the god Re in his circuit. The likelihood of such an assertion is confirmed by the accompanying formula in Setna. Designed for seeing the bark of Re in heaven from both the underworld and the earth, the spell is expressly stated to be of use for both living and dead, corresponds directly to Book of the Dead spells 133–34, and contains *within itself* the means for effecting a circuit of

"Spell for letting a man return (*pẖr*) to see his house (on earth)," in Naville 1886, vol. 2, p. 342 and Allen 1974, p. 108. Further illustrative examples include BD spells 178 f §S2 (deceased circles like Re); 179b §S3 (gods circle in train of deceased); 149 e §S2 (Lunar Eye of Horus circles for deceased), etc.

288. Mark Smith 1979, col. 7/6–8. The punning references to *pẖr* are unnoticed by Smith.

heaven, the underworld, and the earth.[289] Thus even in these seemingly extended uses of *pẖr* as "enchant," Demotic terminology constitutes no break with earlier usage, and retains the fundamental association with "encircling."[290]

The "control" conveyed by this act of encircling may be hostile as well, as is evident from Coffin Texts spell 114 where the deceased escapes execution by declaring: "I am not encircled! I am not enclosed!"[291] Though the deceased is encircled in the Book of the Dead, he may escape by divine aid: "The spell (*rꜣ*) of his (*scil.* Osiris') enemies is around (*ḥꜣ*) me, but I have been illumined since you have illumined my face."[292] Papyrus Chester Beatty 8, a "Book for Banishing an Enemy," warns: "Take care of this book ... Do not let

289. For the second spell in Setna I, see Griffith 1985, pp. 20–21 and 25 (cols. 3/14–15, 3/36–37, and 4/1–3) and Lichtheim 1980, pp. 128–31. "If you recite the second formula, whether you are in the underworld or whether you are in your form on earth also, you will see Pre rising in heaven with his Ennead and the moon in its form of rising" (3/14–15). The additional passages stipulate that the reciter sees also the stars in the sky and the fish in the deep. The envisioned circuit thus includes both heaven and the lower ocean. The comparable BD spells 133–34 "Roll for initiating the blessed one," are found in Naville 1886, vol. 2, pp. 343–46 and Allen 1974, pp. 108–10. The accompanying directions, which are explicitly designed for a living "initiate" ("do not use for anyone except yourself"), include the preparation of a bowl painted with an image of the solar bark. Filling the bowls with water or oil may have enhanced their use in scrying; BD spell 134 recommends that the image of the person to be visualized in the solar boat should be anointed with oil. Unrecognized evidence for the actual practice of this rite is forthcoming from the tomb of *Ṯ-n-n(ꜣ)-hb.w* (Bresciani, Pernigotti, and Silvis 1977, pp. 73–75, and pl. 27). A similar bowl, misinterpreted as a terracotta hypocephalus and suggested to be of Greco-Roman date, appears in Maspero 1902, p. 285. The bowl contains registers of deities drawn in meal and plaster "délayés dans de l'eau." A rite for seeing the bark of Re appears also in the Demotic London and Leiden Magical Pap., col. 27 (Griffith and Thompson 1904, pp. 156–63). For the question of the use of funerary spells by the living, compare Gilula 1978 and Wente 1982. For further examples of bowl magic, see below, *Chapter 5*, nn. 1017 and 1020.

290. The example of *pẖr*, "to enchant" in Tait 1976 (see n. 283, above) could easily represent a pun upon the original nuance of "to go about," as the speaker is a bird who could literally "go about/enchant the sky" to listen to what is in it. Demotic orthography simply makes explicit a magical nuance *equally present* in earlier usage. This is particularly clear in the London and Leiden Magical Pap., in which hieratic writings 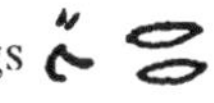 and 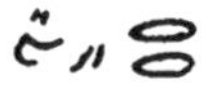 alternate with Demotic 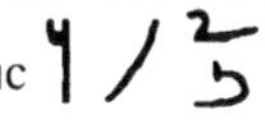 and 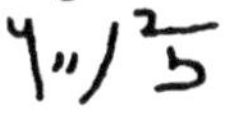 in identical contexts and often within the same spell (Griffith and Thompson 1909, p. 32, no. 318 and 1904, pp. 34–35 [col. 3/20: *pẖr.t n pẖr pꜣ hne n gtg*, "Recipe for enchanting the vessel quickly"] and 166–67 [col. 29/11: *my pẖr pꜣ ꜥlw*, "Enchant the youth!"]). Despite the hieratic walking legs determinative, these examples must represent the extended meaning "to enchant."

291. De Buck 1938, p. 132; Faulkner 1973, p. 108. The verbs of encircling are *dbn* and *šny*.

292. BD spell 168B, MMA 35.9.19 §d S4 (OIM photo 38038), in Allen 1974, p. 174. The "enemies" are determined as feminine (with final *.t*). This hostile encirclement is to be contrasted with the text's immediately previous proclamation (§d S3) by the son(?) of Nut: "I have surrounded (*pẖr.n=y ḥꜣ*) my brother; surrounding (*pẖr=y ḥꜣ*) my brother Osiris NN."

another encircle/control (*pẖr*) it! "[293] The magical implications of the act are readily apparent in a series of statements regarding Seth, who figures as both sorcerer and victim. Thus the "dramatic Ramesseum papyrus" re-enacts the murder of Osiris at the hands of the confederates of Seth by ritually encircling a figure of the slain god with goats.[294] Conversely, the avenger of Osiris threatens in the "Anti-Seth Book":

ỉw=y r dỉ.t pẖr wꜣw (var. *wꜣwꜣ*) *r ỉr s*
I shall cause a curse to circulate against the one who did it.[295]

Just such an "encirclement" of the powers of Seth by the avenging Horus is attested, though previously unrecognized, in Coffin Texts spell 16:

ỉw pẖr.n=f sḫm.w Stẖ m-ḥꜣ.w sḫm.w=f
He (*scil.* Horus) controlled (*pẖr*) the powers of Seth in addition to his own powers.[296]

An earlier reference to this act is presumably to be found in the "encircling of Horus" invoked in Pyramid Texts spell 509.[297] Coming "full circle," Seth appears again as an "encircler" in his beneficent role as the protector of the solar bark from the chaos monster Apophis. Addressing the monster, Seth declares in Book of the Dead spell 108:

293. Verso 7/7, in Gardiner 1935, vol. 1, p. 74 and vol. 2, pl. 46. The rubric warns further that the book is to be recited by the chief lector priest.

294. Sethe 1928a, pp. 223 and 225, n. 119e. Additional instances of potentially hostile encirclement are found in Tablet BM 20775 and Pap. Leiden I 384 vo., cols. 2/14 and 2/26–27. In the former, potential enemies of the wearer of the amulet are told (ll. 7–8): *nn pẖr=tn Ḫꜣp-nb=s*, "You will not go about the necropolis *Ḫꜣp-nb=s*" (Vittmann 1984a, pp. 165–67). In the Leiden magical papyrus, a spell to cause a woman to hate a man twice includes the phrase *ṯ nꜣ (?) qt n*, "take the circuit of" to express the mastery of a demon over the woman's emotions. For the phrase, cf. ϫⲓ ⲕⲟⲧⲥ in Crum 1939, p. 127b. The phrase is untranslated in J. H. Johnson 1975, pp. 42–43.

295. Schott 1929, p. 57/20 and cf. n. 217, above.

296. See de Buck 1935, pp. 48d–49a and Faulkner 1973, p. 10. Faulkner translates the passage: "The powers of Seth served him in addition to his own powers," with *pẖr n* taken as "go about for = serve." However, the required verbal form is the past narrative *ỉw sḏm.n=f* and not *ỉw sḏm=f* plus dative, cf. the following §49b: *ỉw rdỉ.n n=f ỉṯ=f*, "His father gave to him." No variant has the required *ỉw pẖr.n n=f sḫm.w* for Faulkner's translation, which also violates the required sense of the passage in which Horus "has removed the movements of the one (Seth) who slew his father" (de Buck 1935, p. 52a). Faulkner notes (1973, p. 10, n. 7), that his translation produces "a most unexpected phenomenon."

297. See PT spell §1122, in Sethe 1910, p. 128 and Faulkner 1969, pp. 184–85. Faulkner (p. 185, n. 3) suggests that the *pẖrw.t* of Horus "may refer to his walking round and round his father's body affixing the funeral wrappings." The ritual could refer to the coronation rite (see above, n. 271). A clear use of hostile encircling in the Pyramid Texts is found in spell 255: "the flame in my eye encompasses (*pẖr*) you" (Sethe 1908, p. 160 and Faulkner 1969, p. 66). Compare also spell 251, §269 "circuit of the warlike faces" in Sethe 1908, p. 146 and Faulkner 1969, p. 62.

> I am the Great One of Magic (*ḥkꜣ*), the son of Nut. My magic (*ḥkꜣ*) has been given to me against you ... I have encircled/enchanted (*pẖr*) the sky, while you are rubbed out (var. "in bonds").[298]

This clear association of the terms *pẖr* and *ḥkꜣ* argues persuasively that the author of the text was fully cognizant of the "magical implications" of the former. Moreover, foreshadowing the Demotic examples of "enchanting the sky" for knowledge, the spell was designed to enable the practitioner to "know the souls of the West."[299]

If the magical aspects of the theme of "encircling heaven, the underworld, and earth" are often ambiguous, those of the idiom "encircling the heart," (*pẖr ỉb/ḥꜣt*), are not. Attested at least as early as the Eighteenth Dynasty, the idiom is applied to the qualities of an individual (god, king, or man) that are able to "captivate" the minds of mankind. Thus, a New Kingdom hymn to Osiris declares: *ỉꜣm.t=f pẖr.n=s ỉb.w*, "His grace has enchanted hearts."[300] Similarly, in the Ptolemaic temple at Edfu, it is the fear of the king which "circulates within hearts" (*pẖr m ḥꜣt*).[301] In a Demotic astrological handbook, the same ability is conceded to a propitiously born individual: *[ỉw=f r] pẖr ḥꜣt (n) rmt*, "He shall enchant the heart of men."[302] Such "bewitchment" need not imply actual magical activity, but, like its English counterpart "enchantment," depends upon the imagery of such activity for its impact. It is a figurative use of the nuance "to enchant," which is itself an extended use of the verb "to go about." An example of such a "heart-enchantment" is

298. See Naville 1886, vol. 2, p. 245 and Allen 1974, pp. 85–86.

299. See Naville 1886, vol. 2, p. 245 and Allen 1974, p. 85.

300. See Moret 1931, pp. 725–50, especially p. 746. For the idiom, see *Wb* 1: 544/14–545/3; Metternich Stela ll. 176–77; and Schott 1929, p. 13/1. The phrase is also attested at Edfu as the name of the goddess of the first of Pharmouthi: , "She who enchants hearts" (Cauville and Devauchelle 1985, p. 53 [paired with Re]). Compare also , *Nb.t-dbn*, "Lady of encircling," in ibid., p. 61 (13 Mesore, paired with Re) and , *Pẖr.t-mr.t*, "She who encircles the desert," in ibid., p. 53 (11 Pharmouthi). With these goddesses, cf. the epithet of Hathor, *pẖr=s tꜣ.wy*, "She encircles the two lands" at Dendera (*Pẖr.t*, "The city of the one who encircles"), in Gauthier 1925, p. 150. A pun on the common idiom of "encircling hearts" is found in Hari 1985, p. 51 and pl. 37 (l. 175): "When he (*scil.* Osiris) hears (the cry of Isis and Nephthys), *pẖr ỉb=f n=sn* his heart goes about for them." Whereas in the Louvre Osiris hymn noted above it is the god's qualities which encircle hearts, here it is the god's heart which turns in circles.

301. See Chassinat 1931, p. 293/12. See also ibid., p. 289/11: *nr=f pẖr.t m ỉb.w*, "His terror circulates in hearts"; and p. 294: *šfy.t=k pẖr.t m ỉb=sn*, "Respect of you circulates in their hearts."

302. Papyrus Berlin P. 8345, col. 4/21 in Spiegelberg 1902, p. 28 (discussion without transliteration or translation) and pl. 97. The text is now republished in Hughes 1986, pp. 55, 58, and 68.

forthcoming from the Demotic "Mythus" tale, in which the entreaties and parables related by Thoth to convince a recalcitrant goddess are labeled succinctly *nꜣ [šm].w n pḫr-ḥꜣt*, "the small heart-enchantments."[303] Nonetheless, it should be remembered that any speech delivered by Thoth could be considered *ipso facto* a genuine vocal spell by virtue of his role as "Excellent One of Magic" and "Lord of Divine Words."[304] A specifically literal use of the phrase occurs in an Old Coptic spell from the great magical papyrus of Paris, in which the magician declares: ⲉⲓⲉ ⲡⲉⲉ̀ⲣ ⲉ̀ⲉⲧⲏⲥ, "I will enchant her heart."[305] Underscoring the original association of "enchanting hearts" with actual magic, Heka announces to the king at his coronation: *spḫr=y ḥkꜣ.w=k m ỉb.w*, "I have caused your magic to circulate in hearts."[306] With the causative verb *spḫr*, , our investigation of the tripartite nature of Egyptian magic concludes as it began, for the verb means not only "to cause to circulate," but also "to copy" texts, and puns upon the association of magic and word.[307]

A DEFINITION OF MAGIC

As is evident from the foregoing, rather prolonged discussion of *pḫr*, the physical act of "encircling" underlies an elaborate complex of magical conceptions which culminate in the adoption of the term as an expression for "enchanting." The terminology and significance of a simple rite of circumambulation (*pḫr*) to "contain" or coerce has been extended both to an application of ingredients (*pḫr.t*) which "contains" disease, and to words which "encircle" the heart (*pḫr-ḥꜣt*) and thoughts of men. The results obtained from this single example of "magic by rite" suffice to suggest a new methodology for the study of Egyptian magic, for it demonstrates that the *practical mechanics* of magic may provide a focus not only for the pertinent materials (magic by essence) and attendant spells (magic by word) of any magical procedure, but also for the fundamental meaning of the procedure itself. It is in the rite—and not the spell—that the essence of Egyptian magic is to be sought. By

303. Spiegelberg 1917a, pp. 30–31 and 133, no. 278 (col. 10/1).

304. See above, p. 35 and n. 160.

305. See Erman 1883, p. 106 (text) and Griffith 1900, p. 93.

306. See Chassinat 1928, p. 337. Compare also the text of the *ḥmws.t-Ḥkꜣ* at Dendera: "fear of her circulates throughout eternity"; for bibliography, see above, n. 164. For other connections between Heka and hearts, see above, nn. 105 and 166.

307. See *Wb* 4: 106. Compare the remarks associated with Seshat, the goddess of writing and magic in Cauville and Devauchelle 1985, p. 41/9–10: "Seshat the great, the lady of writing, great of magic, foremost of the library, who causes your annals to circulate forever ...," and Chassinat 1931, p. 288, in which Seshat states: "your command circulates in the land." The parallelism with *pḫr m ḥꜣt* is obvious.

virtue of its ready accessibility to observation in contemporary cultures, such a "ritual-oriented" approach to magic has long been utilized in anthropology; so much so, in fact, that it has been necessary to defend the magical significance of the spell.[308] In Egyptian studies, on the contrary, the often laconic references to magical procedures within rubrics attached to verbose and mythologically ornate spells have both subordinated the importance of these procedures and hindered their study. Indeed, Egyptian magical rites have been characterized as commonplace, and their study dismissed as unrewarding.[309] Nonetheless, as evidenced by the analysis of *pẖr*, sufficient information survives to provide insights by no means trivial. Nor is the supposed "universality" of Egyptian ritual grounds for disregard. Thus, although ritual encirclement is well documented in many cultures, the centrality of the rite in Egyptian magic is striking, and its uses and terminology uniquely Egyptian.[310] In any case, it is the viewpoint of the Egyptian practitioner, and not that of the comparative historian, which determines the significance of the rite. That the rite was of fundamental significance to the success of Egyptian magic is evident not merely by the presence of specified directions in rubrics and depictions in literary, religious, medical, and even historical texts, but also by the very turns of phrase which the Egyptian employed to describe magic. Thus in addition to the simple *ỉr ḥkꜣ*, "doing magic," there are found such expressions as *sp*, "spell" (literally "deed"); *sp n sẖ*, "deed of a scribe/magical act"; *ỉr sp*, "spell making"; *ỉr mḏꜣ.t*, "perform a magical book/rite"; and *ṯ-ỉwy.t*, "taking security/ exercising magical control."[311] Such terms are not, of course, restricted to instances of

308. See the *apologia* in Tambiah 1968, p. 175: "the orthodox anthropological approach devalued the role of words in ritual which was seen as stereotyped behaviour consisting of a sequence of non-verbal acts and manipulation of objects"; and cf. the discussion of rites in idem 1973.

309. See the remarks of Sauneron 1966, pp. 32, 34–36, and 42: "Peut-on parler du *matériel* du magicien? Il est, il faut le reconnaître, des plus réduits, et se ramène à un petit nombre d'éléments ..." (p. 36); "Les formules, cela est évident, constituent l'élément principal de toute action magique" (p. 42). Compare also the comments of Malinowski (1948, p. 51): "Follow one rite, study one spell, grasp the principles of magical belief, art and sociology in one case, and you will know not only all the acts of the tribe, but, adding a variant here and there, you will be able to settle as a magical practitioner in any part of the world yet fortunate enough to have faith in that desirable art."

310. For circumambulation in Greco-Roman and Christian magic, see above, n. 280; for Coptic uses, see above, n. 274. Mesopotamian examples appear in J. and A. Westenholz 1977, pp. 203 and 214–15; the motif was already well documented in R. C. Thompson 1971, pp. lviii and passim.

311. For *ỉr ḥkꜣ*, see *Wb* 3: 176/7, above p. 20, and the Coptic descendant above, p. 14 and n. 52. For *sp*,  and its compounds, see *Wb* 3: 439/5 and Erichsen 1954a, p. 425 (*sp-n-ḥyq, sp-n-sẖ*). Examples are found in Griffith and Thompson 1904, pp. 86–87 (col. 11/26: *sp-n-sẖ*); in Setna II, cols. 6/13, 6/15, 6/17, 6/30, and 7/4 (*sp-n-ḥyq sẖ*) and 6/16 (*sp-n-ḥyq-n-sẖ*) and 6/32 (*sp-n-sẖ*) in Griffith 1985, pp. 196–205. For *ỉr-spy*, "spell making," see Ray 1976, pp. 61–62 and 64–65 (O. Ḥor 16, l. 7 and O. Ḥor 17A, l. 10). Compare also ibid., pp. 67, 71, and 72, n. x (O. Ḥor 18 vo., l. 2): *Ḏḥwty nb sp.w*, "Thoth Lord of

"magic by rite" any more than the English phrase "magical practice" which subsumes magic by speech, amulet, or potion. They are, however, indicative of a fundamental understanding of magic as "a thing done"—not simply "a thing said" or "a thing possessed." As the only member of the "magical triad" broad enough to include the other two, magic by rite is the logical point of departure for an investigation of the range and significance of Egyptian *ḥkꜣ*. By focusing upon the magical act rather than the spoken spell, the investigator avoids the subjective ambiguities discussed above in *Chapter 1*, and is able to formulate an objective criterion for judging the "magical" nature of any given act.

For the purpose of this study, any activity which seeks to obtain its goal by methods outside the simple laws of cause and effect will be considered "magical" in the *Western* sense. To what extent this "working definition" of magic conforms to the *Egyptian* understanding of *ḥkꜣ* will, it is hoped, become clearer in the course of investigation. Just such an approach to Egyptian *ḥkꜣ* was suggested in 1925 by Lexa, who added a significant *caveat*: Western and Egyptian conceptions of magical actions will not always conform, for certain acts which seem dependent upon the law of causality to one culture may be viewed as "magical" by another.[312] Thus, a remedy for graying hair which incorporates the blood of a black bull could reflect a "primitive" understanding of blood as the carrier and transmitter of the animal's qualities, while another culture might see in the act only "magic

spells." Unrecognized examples are found in ibid., pp. 67–68 (O. Ḥor 18, l. 11): *spw⸗s*, "its spell" (versus ed., "its remainder"); and in Nur el Din 1974, pp. 266–67 and 652 (O. Leiden 334, l. 1): *n ỉr ꜥꜣyꜥ n spe nt-ỉw⸗w ỉr⸗f*, "For making *ꜥꜣyꜥ* by spell which is to be used." Both of these examples could represent hostile sorcery since the former switches from praises to curses at *sp*, and the latter seems to contain a recipe for inflicting the *ꜥꜣyꜥ*-disease/possession (*Wb* 1: 167/2–4; Westendorf 1966a, pp. 128–54; and idem 1970, pp. 145–51). Alternatively, however, the phrase *ỉr ꜥꜣyꜥ n spe* could mean "attempting (a cure for) *ꜥꜣyꜥ* by spell" (Ritner 1990, p. 33, n. 28). With *sp-n-sẖ* should be contrasted the expression for magic in Setna I, col. 4/23: *wp.t n sẖ nfr*, "the work of a good scribe," in Griffith 1985, pp. 114–15. Further unrecognized examples of *sp.w*, "spells" (translated "deeds") appear in Faulkner 1958, pp. 29* and 13 (col. 18/12): "Isis Lady of spells" (cf. col. 18/13: "Isis who pacifies the gods with what she says") and pp. 31* and 14 (col. 19/25): "Nephthys excellent of spells." For *ỉr mḏꜣ.t*, see *Wb* 2: 187/19. For *ṯ-ỉwy.t*, see Erichsen 1954a, p. 23 and Crum 1939, p. 62b: ϫⲓ-ⲉⲟⲩⲱ, ϭⲓ-ⲗⲟⲩⲱ. Examples appear in Griffith and Thompson 1904, pp. 144–45 (col. 23/7 in a hostile sense); Setna I, col. 4/32: *ḏmꜥ.w n ṯ-ỉwy.t*, "books of taking security" (defensive) and Setna II, col. 2/27: *ꜥš sẖ nt ṯ-ỉwy.t*, "recite spells of taking security" (neutral) in Griffith 1985, pp. 118–19 and 160–61. The term also appears in the literary Pap. Spiegelberg (Petubast), col. 2/22 in a confrontation over the diadems of Amon, in Spiegelberg 1910, pp. 16, 17, and 4*. Clearly hostile use of the term occurs in Pap. Insinger, col. 32/14: "He (*scil*. God) created life and death before him for the torment(?) (*ṯ-ỉwy.t*) of the impious man" (Lichtheim 1980, p. 211).

312. Lexa 1925, vol. 1, pp. 15–18, especially p. 17 for the definition of magic.

by contagion."[313] In actual practice, however, such instances are quite few and in no way vitiate the unparalleled usefulness of *activity* as the diagnostic of magic.

Opposition to Lexa's definition of magic was forthcoming in a review by Roeder who, noting that magic could be analyzed in a narrow or wider sense, found that Lexa's "overly broad" definition inflated the scope of magic in Egyptian culture "which knew nothing of the law of causality."[314] Moreover, Roeder professed regret that this definition, by stressing action, did not concentrate on the "fundamental conceptions" of magic.[315] Such objections provide their own rebuttal, for if one is to study the "fundamental conceptions" of Egyptian magic *it may be done only by looking at magic in its widest possible sense*. To arbitrarily exclude aspects of magic from discussion because "it is fully in accordance with the practice of Egyptologists"[316] in no way provides insight into the fundamental nature of magic and severely *and artificially* limits the scope of investigation. There can be no "wide" and "narrow" magic. Nor does the concentration upon action in any way exclude the possibility of grasping these fundamentals, as is clear from the analysis of *pḫr*. Whether the Egyptians consciously recognized a "law of normal causality" is open to dispute.[317] Despite the statement of Lexa to the contrary, no Egyptian term corresponding to "natural forces" can be identified.[318] One Egyptian term which has been suggested to apply to both "the (ordinary) force of nature" and the force of *ḥkꜣ* is *hp*, the word for "custom" or "law."[319] In the two Demotic Setna stories (as well as in an unpublished Berlin papyrus) the word appears in the combination *hp n sẖ* ("a *hp* of writing") as an expression for a written spell.[320] Although Nims has sought to explain this usage as indicating "customary"

313. See Lexa 1925, p. 16, for his discussion of spells 29 and 30 from Pap. Ebers. With his analysis should be compared the comments of Frazer 1971, pp. 17–18 and 37 on Hindu and Greek parallels.

314. Roeder 1928, p. 197.

315. Roeder, ibid., p. 197.

316. The statement is from Gardiner 1922, p. 263a. Like Roeder, Gardiner recognized a broad and narrow approach to magic. Unlike his contemporary, however, Gardiner (in his "broader" view) even insisted upon the essential unity of magic and religion. Nevertheless, he bowed to "custom" and excluded from his study rites for the dead and for the gods.

317. See the remarks of Gardiner 1922, p. 262, who suggests that the distinction between magical and ordinary actions was never consciously made.

318. Lexa 1925, vol. 1, p. 17, suggests that *nḫt.w*, *nḫt.t*, or *wsr.w* describe natural law. Rather, all these terms mean simply "strength" or "power" (*Wb* 1: 362–63 and 2: 317).

319. See *Wb* 2: 488–89; Erichsen 1954a, pp. 274–75; and Nims 1948, pp. 243–60.

320. For Setna I, see Griffith 1985, pp. 92–93 (col. 3/12–14), 102–03 (col. 3/35–36), and 104–05 (cols. 3/40, 4/2). For Setna II, see ibid., pp. 196–97 (col. 6/15). The term is found in a similar context in Pap. Berlin 30023 (+23725+15675), an unpublished Demotic literary text to be published by Zauzich, which records the activities of the magician *Ḥr* son of *Pꜣ-wnš*. In line 13, the magician animates a ship of

Egyptian magic as opposed to foreign enchantment, the original explanation by Griffith as "written formula" ("a pattern of writing") seems preferable.[321] Recently, Reymond has published a Vienna papyrus in which she found evidence of Heka as the controller of a **Pr-ḥp*, which she translated as "House of Natural Law" and associated with the terminology in the Setna tales. By implication, magic and ordinary natural force would be undifferentiated by the Egyptians.[322] However, the reading *Ḥkꜣ* is far from clear, and the supposed **Pr-ḥp*, 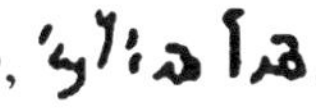, is in actuality *pr-ʿnḫ*, "scriptorium."[323] The relation of *ḥkꜣ* to *ordinary* nature thus remains to be specified. As noted above, *ḥkꜣ* is certainly a part of the natural *cosmic* order. It would not seem, however, to be part of the *normal mundane* order. The effects of *ḥkꜣ* are not "supernatural"; they are "supernormal" or "extraordinary."

The implications of Lexa's definition of magic have yet to be realized, and to date no treatment of Egyptian magic (including that of Lexa) has concentrated primarily upon the actual practice of the magician. As a result, the instructions which accompany spells in the so-called "rubrics" with their vignettes and lists of materials, instruments, and ritual actions remain largely uninvestigated. Fifty years after Lexa's recognition of the importance of rubrics for the identification of magic, Morenz urged a study of them to settle the question of the "magical" nature of funerary texts and their potential use by the living; his *desideratum* is still unfulfilled.[324] The present study seeks not only to correct this deficiency (compare the discussion of Setna's use of funerary spells, above, pp. 61–64), but to

---

wax by *hp-n-sḫ*, "magical formula." For a synopsis of this text, see Zauzich 1978, p. 36. The Demotic tale is paralleled by an Aramaic translation in Cowley 1923, pp. 179–82, no. 71, republished by B. Porten 1986, p. 16 ("The Tale of Ḥor son of Pawenesh").

321. Nims 1948, p. 245. Contra Nims, ibid., p. 245, nn. 22 and 23, the Egyptian magician Ḥor is specifically described as using a *hp-n-sḫ* only once (col. 6/15, *not* cols. 6/14 or 6/20). Elsewhere, both he and the Nubian use simply *ḥyq*. See col. 5/17, and cf. col. 5/13 in which the book of Thoth used by Ḥor is called *tꜣ mḏy n ḥyq*, "the book of magic," in Griffith 1985, pp. 186–87. The term *ḥyq/ḥkꜣ* requires no modifier to mark it as Egyptian. Nims was correct, however, in recognizing that the nuance of "custom" in the term *hp*, 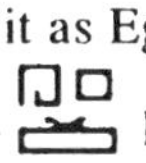 probably provides the explanation for its use in these passages. As the meaning "law" of *hp* derives from the nuance of "customary patterns" of activity, so *hp-n-sḫ* should reflect a customary written pattern, or "formula." It is interesting to note that recently published Egyptian "law codes" are formulated strictly according to the notion of "pattern" (Mattha and Hughes 1975, p. 22 and passim: "If a man does X ... here is the pattern of the petition (etc.) which he shall make"). The similarity of legal and magical phraseology is also notable in Greek papyri (Levi 1975).

322. Reymond 1977, pp. 153 and 200 (Pap. Vienna D. 6614, l. 2). For her idiosyncratic discussion of *hp* as "natural law," see pp. 137 and 153. Reymond's interpretation is repeated in idem 1983.

323. The writing of the supposed *Pr-ḥp* is easily shown to be *pr-ʿnḫ* (Erichsen 1954a, p. 63).

324. Morenz 1975, p. 201: "Es besteht in den sogenannten "Nachschriften," die viele der Texte abschlissen ... Eine auf Sammlung des errichbaren Materials beruhende Darstellung kann hier nicht vorgelegt werden; sie bleibt ein recht dringendes Desiderat."

confront systematically the wider question of the interpenetration of magic, religion, and medicine. Rubrics, complemented by tomb and temple scenes, surviving artifacts, and literary and historical documents form the raw materials. Clearly, it would be impossible to analyze all magical methods in a single study; only a selection of the most representative can be dealt with here. Nonetheless, these will suffice to demonstrate the utility of the method.

This approach to Egyptian magic has, like "behaviorism" in social psychology, the advantage of simplicity; clearly indicated behavior—not intuited mental attitude—provides the focus. As a result, the continuity of any given genre of magic is easily traced (e.g., encirclement for purification), as is the impact of one genre upon another (medical upon funerary magic, curses upon love charms). Unlike behaviorism, however, this study must also seek to understand the connections between word (the spell) and act (the rite) and object (magical material). Ultimately, the deferred question of the identity of the magician and his social role must be considered.

CHAPTER 3

SPITTING, LICKING, AND SWALLOWING

... whom Thoth himself has taught, and into whose mouth Seshat has spat

Stela Cairo JdE 46200
Palette Berlin 7798

One day St. Automona di Meris, seeing a young novice yawning, suddenly spat into her mouth, and *that* without malice or thought of mischief. Some ninety hours afterwards the said novice brought into the world the Blessed St. Elizabeth Bathilde, who, by dint of skipping, changed her sex at the age of forty and became a man.

Ronald Firbank, *Valmouth*

C'est son père tout craché.

French idiom

He is the spitting image of his father.

English idiom

The oral dimension of Egyptian magic so prominent within native terminology extends well beyond the simple recitation of spells to include ritualized usage of the common bodily actions of spitting, licking, and swallowing. Each of these actions has a long history within the practice of Western magic and folklore, and all have been ritualized in other cultures as well, both ancient and modern. Similarity of practice, however, may mask a variety of interpretation and intent, and even within a single culture any one magical technique may function in disparate ways. Such is certainly the case with the techniques discussed here, for all are "bivalent" in Egyptian practice, being used to transfer powers whether healing or harmful.

SPITTING AND SPITTLE

Of these three ritual acts, the best known—and most thoroughly discussed—is the technique of magical spitting.[325] The conspicuous position accorded to spitting in Egyptian myth and ritual is commensurate with the surprisingly rich vocabulary pertaining to "spit" and "spittle" in the Egyptian language, comprising well over twenty words and expressions: *ꜣb.t*, *ꜣš/i̓š*, *i̓šš*, *i̓šd(d)*, *ꜥꜥ*, *bst*, *bšy*, *pꜣy/pꜥy*, *pꜥg*, *psḫ/pḫs*, *psg/pgs*, *fꜣḫ* (?), *mw*, *mwy.t-rꜣ*, *nby*, *nẖ(ẖ)/nẖnẖ/nš(n)(š)*, *rdi̓ r tꜣ*, *hmh*, *ḫr*, *ẖꜥꜥ*, *sty*, *šp*, *qꜣꜥ*, *qys*, *tf*, *tfn*, *dp/tp*, and *ḏꜣk*.[326] While some of these terms may properly indicate related actions and nouns ("pour/flow out," "vomit," "saliva," etc.), the lexical (and cultural) significance of the concept is nonetheless clear, and is underscored by the standard selection of a spitting mouth () as the hieroglyphic determinative for words signifying fluids of any variety, as well as "flow," "pour," "spit," "gush," "vomit," and even "kiss."[327] As determinative or logogram, the sign

325. Zibelius 1984a and 1984b. Comparative studies and discussions are found in *CAD*, vol. 7, pp. 139–41, s.v. *imtu* (Mesopotamian); Goetze 1969, p. 347 § iii.10–end (Hittite); Morton Smith 1978, pp. 128 and 204 (biblical); Aune 1980, pp. 1534 and 1537 (Mark 7:31–36, Mark 8:22–26, and John 9:11–41); Nicholson 1897 (Greek and Roman); Tavenner 1916, preface and pp. 35, 40, 41, 49, 58, 71, 75, 106, 108, 110–11 (Greek and Roman); Elsworthy 1958, pp. 412–23 (European and African); and Evans-Pritchard 1937, p. 116 (Zande).

326. See the list gathered in *Wb* 6 (Deutsch-aegyptisches Wörterverzeichnis), p. 144; adding *ꜥꜥ* (*Wb* 1: 169/1–2); *pꜣy/pꜥy* (Erichsen 1954a, p. 130); *pꜥg* (*Wb* 1: 504/15); *fꜣḫ* (?) (CT spell 681 = de Buck 1956, p. 307); *sty* < *sṯi̓* (Erichsen 1954a, p. 475); *šp* (*Wb* 4: 443–44); *ẖꜥꜥ* (*Wb* 3: 364/9); *dp* (*Wb* 5: 445/12); and *ḏꜣk* (Erichsen 1954a, p. 673). For *psḫ/pḫs* > *psg/pgs*; see Vikentiev 1943, pp. 130–31 and Roquet 1980, p. 80. For *ꜣb.t*, see de Buck 1938, p. 32. For *ḫr*, see Faulkner 1937b, p. 181. For *bst*, *ntt*, *nẖnẖ*, and *tfn*, see de Wit 1956, pp. 111–16.

327. See de Wit, ibid., pp. 111–16; Grdseloff 1952, pp. 482–84; and Ritner 1986a, pp. 98–99. Undoubtedly, the presence of this determinative with rare or unknown words has resulted in an artificial inflation in the number of words tentatively translated "to spit/spittle." For the Old Kingdom forms of this sign, see the variants in Edel 1955, p. 190 (§429), and note the overlap with the ideogram  for "washing/purifying the mouth" (*ꜥb-rꜣ*) discussed in de Meulenaere 1981, pp. 87–89.

thus complements and overlaps the use of the pot with flowing water () associated with words indicating "wash," "purity," "inundation," et cetera. So common was the hieroglyphic sign of the spitting mouth that it was chosen to represent the basic letter "p" (<*p*‘*y*) in late and enigmatic writings.[328]

CREATION BY SPITTLE

Well known from the Heliopolitan creation myth in which the sun god's spittle forms the primordial pair of Shu (air) and Tefnut (moisture), the act of spitting occurs repeatedly in mythological and ritual contexts as an expression of generative force. Gods, kings, demons, animals, plants, materials, and even the earth itself may be viewed as the product of spitting.[329]

O you whom the Pregnant One spat (*nšnš*) forth ...[330]

O Atum-Khepri ... you spat out (*ỉšš*) Shu, you expectorated (*tfn*) Tefnut.[331]

Atum spat (*ỉšš*) me out as the spittle (*ỉšš*) of his mouth together with my sister Tefnut.[332]

Raise yourself Re ... spit out (*bš*) the day.[333]

His name is 'One who spits out (*bš*) the Inundation.'[334]

328. Less frequently, the sign may substitute for *m*, *ỉw*, or *tfn*; see de Wit 1956, pp. 111–16.

329. Examples are gathered in Zibelius 1984b, pp. 403–04 and 406–07 (considered "figurative" usages of the concept). Generative spitting is frequently encountered; in hymns from the Hibis temple alone, Amon is said to have spit out winds, lions, and gods (Norman de Garis Davies 1953, pls. 31, ll. 6 and 10, and 32, l. 8).

330. PT spell 222, §205a, in Sethe 1908, p. 118 (cf. §199a). The reference is to Seth.

331. PT spell 600, §1652, in Sethe 1910, p. 373. Additional examples in the Pyramid Texts include spells 34 (§26c–d); 237 (§241); 241 (§246); 455 (§850a); 660 (§1871a); and 669 (§1965a).

332. CT spell 76 in de Buck 1938, pp. 3–4 and Faulkner 1973, p. 77. CT references include spell 75, (de Buck 1935, p. 354, most versions); spell 77: "He created orgasm and fluid {of his mouth} fell from his mouth. He spat me out as Shu together with Tefnut who came forth after me," in de Buck 1938, p. 18 and Faulkner 1973, p. 80; spell 78: "father of expectorating the Chaos-gods," in de Buck 1938, p. 22 and Faulkner 1973, p. 82, n. 15; and spell 80: "I am Everlasting, who fashioned the Chaos-gods, reproduced(?) by the spittle of Atum which issued from his mouth when he used his hand; his saliva(?) will be made to fall to the earth," in de Buck 1938, pp. 31–32; and Faulkner 1973, p. 83.

333. CT spell 1029, in de Buck 1961, p. 254.

334. CT spell 1076, in de Buck 1961, p. 346 and Faulkner 1978, p. 146. For further examples, cf. *inter alia*, CT spells 905, 942, 946, and 951 (though these last two references to the "rod which spits out [on?] the plebs" are coupled with a mention of restraining the masses, and may entail a hostile rather than a generative nuance of spitting; cf. CT spell 469 for the rod of Orion by which the deceased "spits on/out" the great ones).

My {semen} is more effective than his (*scil.* Re's) spittle (*h̠*ʿʿ).[335]

You are the one who spat out (*q*ʿ) the secret, the thought which entered into his heart.[336]

The most noted "magical" application of the creative power of spittle is found within Papyrus Turin 1993 and variants, "The Legend of Isis and the Secret Name of Re," a spell designed to heal scorpion stings.[337] Within this recited *historiola*,[338] Isis fashions a serpent from clay and animates it by means of the spittle which drooled from the senile sun god's slackening mouth. The practical directions for using the spell involve not spitting but licking, and are discussed below.

The creative power of spittle as envisioned in these Egyptian tales finds numerous parallels, ranging from Akkadian creation mythology[339] to contemporary English and French expressions describing a child as the "spitting image" of its parent. In tacit deference to the Freudian theory of dislocation/displacement, this generative aspect of spitting has been explained as deriving from a psychological pairing of spittle with semen and mouth with vulva.[340] Within Egyptian thought, the parallelism of semen and saliva is confirmed by the myths of Shu and Tefnut, who are variously described as begotten from Atum by spitting or by masturbation.

It was I who created excitement with my fist; I copulated with my hand;
I let fall from my own mouth. I spat forth as Shu; I expectorated as Tefnut.[341]

The same pairing seems evident in Book of the Dead spell 110, quoted above, where—if correctly reconstructed—the deceased contrasts the fertility of his semen with the spittle of Re. The suggested "equivalence" of mouth and vulva is less certain in Egyptian speculation, however, for if the irregular birth of Seth from "the Pregnant One" may be described in terms of spitting,[342] the conception of Shu and Tefnut takes place not in the mouth but in the hand:

335. BD spell 110 §a5, S1, in Allen 1974, p. 88 and Naville 1886, vol. 2, p. 254.

336. Drioton 1926, p. 103, §230/7.

337. Pleyte and Rossi 1869, pls. 131–33, especially 132, ll. 2–4; for further references and translations, see Wilson 1969b; Borghouts 1987b; Ferrero 1987; and Piantelli 1987.

338. A short mythical tale or extract serving as a precedent to activate or legitimate a spell. The standard use of these mythic elements further undermines attempts to separate "religion" from "magic," and it is interesting to note that Wilson (1969b) classes this section of Pap. Turin 1993 under "mythology" (pp. 3–34) rather than "magic" (pp. 325–30).

339. Zibelius 1984b, p. 400.

340. Zibelius ibid., p. 403, following Zandee 1972, p. 151.

341. Papyrus Bremner-Rhind, cols. 26/24–27/1 (Faulkner 1933, p. 60 and 1937b, p. 172). Compare also cols. 28/27–29/1: "My desire came to me in my hand, ejaculate (ʿȝʿ) fell from my mouth. I spat forth as Shu; I expectorated as Tefnut," in Faulkner 1933, p. 71 and 1938, p. 41.

342. PT spell 222, §205a, in Sethe 1908, p. 118. Cf. PT spell 669, §1965.

> Atum says: 'This is that which came forth from my lips and what I spat into my hand which was a vulva. Shu, Tefnut, *Ka*, Vulva.'[343]

The featured role of the hand as vulva is here intended to complement its function in Atum's creation of Shu and Tefnut by masturbation; in both, the hand is seen as playing the feminine role.[344] A parallel concept has been noted in the Mayan tales of the *Popol Vuh*.[345] Psychoanalytic theory notwithstanding, supposed Egyptian equations of mouth and vulva rest primarily on mistranslations in which the ejection of saliva/semen *from* (*m*) the mouth is interpreted as ejection *into* the mouth.[346]

343. Frankfort, de Buck, and Gunn 1933, vol. 1, p. 86 and vol. 2, pl. 85, l. 41, and cf. l. 40: "Then his hands became a vulva." See also Vikentiev 1943, pp. 130–31.

344. "He married his fist, since there was yet no woman" (Pap. Leiden I 350, col. 5/2–3), in Zandee 1948, p. 92. Thus the title "God's hand" is applied to various goddesses as well as the priestess of Amon at Luxor associated with rituals of the primordial creation (*Wb* 5: 585/1–6; see Leclant 1977, cols. 813–15). The feminine gender of the word for "hand" (*ḏr.t*) may have strengthened this concept. These symbolic associations are seemingly overlooked in Sourdive 1984. For the association of the hand of healing statues with the "hand of Amon," see Kákosy 1987, p. 180.

345. Vikentiev 1943, pp. 130–31; Tedlock 1985, pp. 114–15: "And then the bone (*scil.* "skull") spit out its saliva, which landed squarely in the hand of the maiden ... Right away something was generated in her belly, from the saliva alone, and this was the generation of Hunahpu and Xbalanque." See also p. 114: "His son is like his saliva, his spittle."

346. Zandee 1972, p. 151, (tacitly reversing his own interpretation in 1948, pp. 69 and 92) objects to the traditional understanding of Atum's creative gestures as complementary, insisting that the god first ejaculated into his own mouth, and only then spit out the divine twins Shu and Tefnut. Unnoted by Zandee, the same suggestion was long anticipated by Budge 1904, vol. 1, pp. 297 and 310, and vol. 2, p. 17. This interpretation derives from the phrase *ḫr m rꜣ*, which the authors understand as "fall into the mouth" in CT spell 77 (de Buck 1938, p. 18a–e): "when he created orgasm, when the 'Chosen' (= 'semen') fell into his mouth"; and Pap. Bremner-Rhind, cols. 28/27–29/1: "My desire came in my hand, semen fell into my mouth." Although *ḫr m* may have this nuance, in both cases "fall from" is the better translation since it is also syntactically acceptable and yields a typical (and expected) reference to Atum's creation by spittle. The description of spittle "falling from" Atum's mouth parallels other mentions of Atum's spittle "coming from his mouth" (*pr m rꜣ=f*); cf. CT spell 80 (de Buck 1938, p. 31). A variant of CT spell 77 specifies that the fluid which falls from the god's mouth is "of his mouth," a clear reference to oral saliva—not injected semen; cf. the "spittle of his mouth" in CT spell 76. The term *stp* in CT spell 77 should be understood as "spittle" rather than "Chosen/semen"; see *Wb* 4: 357/15: "drip," and the unrecognized example in Urk. 6: "He (Seth) has spat into the sea of the *Ḥtm.t*-cow"; Schott 1929, pp. 22–23, l. 20, mistranslated "versiegen(?)." Further proof, if any be needed, is afforded by the determinative of "fall" in the parallel passage in Pap. Bremner-Rhind, col. 27/1, which displays a spitting mouth, not an ejaculating penis. For standard translations of these passages, see nn. 332 and 341, above. Zandee's citation (1972, p. 151, n. 91) of the unrelated CT spell 576 ("Semen is in my mouth"; de Buck 1956, p. 191e) demonstrates only the known link between semen and saliva; it proves no relationship between mouth and vulva. Zandee's interpretation is repeated in his study of CT spell 77 (1973, pp. 71–72).

Notions of "dislocation" seem equally irrelevant in the Egyptian pairing of semen and spittle. The ejection of bodily fluids is obviously common to both, and it is *as bodily fluids* that the pairing of semen and spittle most likely arose. The perceived bond is thus not an exclusive relationship, but shared among all bodily emissions. Divinity was felt to reside within the creator, and was therefore inherent in the god's tissues and fluids. Examples of mythological creation by semen or saliva should be understood no differently from tales of the creation of mankind from the creator's tears, the goddess Sakhmet from his eye, plants and minerals from divine sweat, blood, et cetera.[347] In each instance, the cast off portion of the god's body retains divine power and may engender new life. Traditional theory would categorize such a concept as "magic by contagion"[348] or "synecdochism,"[349] the rationale for both the veneration of relics and the inclusion of personal effects (ουσια) in magical rites.[350]

SPITTLE AS REMEDY

Surely deriving from this same rationale is the ritual use of spittle in the transmission of healing and blessing.[351] This is perhaps clearest in texts of purification, in which saliva serves as a medium to convey the invigorating power, and thus the "blessing" or skill of a god:

> My purification is the purification of the spittle which issued from the mouth of Re-Atum.[352]

347. For the origin of mankind in the tears of Re, see Hornung 1982, pp. 3 (§30, text), 38 (translation), and 54, n. 26 (CT references); for the origin of Sakhmet/Hathor, see ibid., pp. 4–6 (§§45–60, text) and 38–39 (translation). For the products of divine sweat, blood, tears, and spittle, see Derchain 1965, pp. 137 (cols. 1/1–3/4) and 1*–3*, and above, pp. 39–40 (Pap. Salt 825 and PGM IV, ll. 2967–3006). None of these creative acts entails a corresponding "vulva symbol." Similar divine powers are ascribed to the efflux (*rḏw*) of Osiris throughout the mortuary literature, and the notion of divine body parts underlies their standard equation with injured human (and animal) counterparts in mortuary and healing spells (Massart 1959; Dawson 1931, pp. 26–27 ["Protection of Parts of the Body by the Gods"]; and Sourdive 1984, pp. 391–401). Zibelius (1984b, pp. 403–04) would explain the power of creative words on the same basis as "verbal bodily emissions."

348. See above, p. 9.

349. *Pars par toto*; "the belief or practice in which a part of an object or person is taken as equivalent to the whole, so that anything done to, or by means of, the part is held to take effect upon, or have the effect of, the whole"; *Oxford English Dictionary* (1933, vol. 10, p. 381).

350. See below, pp. 210, n. 971 and 224–25, nn. 1043–44.

351. Contra Zibelius (1984b, p. 401), who suggests that the destructive aspect of spittle is primary, with healing aspects being only the use of one destructive force to repel another destructive force. Such an interpretation cannot be reconciled with the use of spittle in creation and blessing where no destructive element is involved. Though the principle of "venom versus venom" certainly plays a role in repelling poisons, etc., it is not the primary rationale for all applications of "healing spittle."

352. CT spell 527, in de Buck 1956, p. 119 and Faulkner 1977, p. 152.

I salve your body with the water of your mouth.[353]

NN ... whom Thoth himself has taught, and into whose mouth Seshat (the goddess of writing) has spat.[354]

Fill your mouth with the water [of the pool?], pour it on my head together with the one who is at my hand; make me prosper, make him prosper.[355]

The power transmitted by such purifications may also cure and resuscitate. Examples of "medical" spitting are common throughout the funerary literature, being used within mythological contexts to cure baldness and weak vision,[356] injuries of the shoulders, arms and legs, wounds from animal bites, and even instilling breath in a newborn child.[357] Within these texts, the use of curative spittle is not limited to the primary gods, but may be applied to—and by—the divinized deceased.

May you spit on the face of Horus for him so that you may remove the injury which is upon him.[358]

The king will sit beside you, O Osiris, the king will spit on your scalp, O Osiris. He will not let it be ill, the king will not let it be bald, according to the king's daily speech/spell at the half-monthly festival and monthly festival.[359]

353. Ritual for a divine falcon, in Jankuhn 1972, p. 24 (oil equated with spittle).

354. S. Cairo JdE 46200 (Edfu) and Palette Berlin 7798, both of Second Intermediate Period date, in Polotsky 1971, p. 319. The passage on the Berlin palette is misunderstood in Goedicke 1988. Compare also BD spell 145w §S3: "I have come as a spitting scribe," in Allen 1974, p. 133.

355. Invocation of a scarab in a spell for a lamp divination, Pap. London and Leiden, col. 9/30, in Griffith and Thompson 1904, p. 73.

356. Baldness (of Horus or Osiris) and bleariness (of Re) are references to the waning moon and eclipsed sun respectively (PT spells 324 and 684 [festivals of full and new moon], and spells 1033, 1089, and 1113 [Re's solar eye wounded by Apep]).

357. CT spell 770: "Horus has spat," in a spell "to cause a child to breathe," in de Buck 1956, p. 405 and Faulkner 1977, p. 301.

358. PT spell 215, §142a, in Sethe 1908, p. 83 and Faulkner 1969, p. 42. Compare also the Abydos stela of Ramses IV, l. 20 (Kitchen 1983b, p. 24/2): "O Horus, I have spit on your eye after it was taken by its conqueror," in Korostovtsev 1947, p. 163.

359. PT spell 684, §2055 (and 2056, substituting Horus for Osiris), in Sethe 1910, pp. 498–99 and Faulkner 1969, p. 294. Compare also PT spell 324, §521a, discussed below; CT spell 133, in de Buck 1938, p. 158 and Faulkner 1973, p. 116: "I have spat on the scalp of *Sw* in order to heal it"; CT spell 139, in de Buck 1938, p. 173 and Faulkner 1973, p. 119: "I have spat on him whose name is *Nn-ἰssw* in order to heal him"; and CT spell 667, in de Buck 1956, p. 296 and Faulkner 1977, p. 239: "He spits on the scalp."

I have come that I may spit on the head and arm, cool the scalp
and ease the leg of the ailing great god.[360]

I make firm the heads, vertebrae, and necks of the gods, I spit on their shoulders.[361]

I am one whom Apep detests, since I know how to spit on your (*scil.* Re's) wounds;
I see, for I am one who spits on wounds which will heal.[362]

When his (*scil.* Re's) eye was sick as a result of having been weeping
for its mate, then Thoth would spit upon it.[363]

I have appeased Suty with the spittle of the Earth-God, and blood from Geb's marrow.[364]

NN, may you spit on your elbows, your hand, your foot ...[365]

The association of such spitting with *ḥkꜣ* is expressly stated in Pyramid Texts spell 324, a dialogue between the deceased king and an underworld doorkeeper. In response to the king's request for admittance since he has come to Horus with curative hair-spittle, the doorkeeper complies: "May you cool him with magic (*ḥkꜣ*)."[366] The use of spittle as a remedy may well be generalized from "rational" observation and experience, however, deriving from the instinctive habit of licking wounds and the weak antibacterial properties of saliva.[367]

360. CT spell 164, in de Buck 1947, p. 4 and Faulkner 1977, p. 142. See also CT spell 610 (scalp and backbone) and 622 (head, hair, arms, legs), in de Buck 1956, pp. 224 and 237 and Faulkner 1977, pp. 198 and 205.

361. CT spell 818, in de Buck 1961, p. 17 and Faulkner 1978, p. 9. Compare also the Abydos stela of Ramses IV, l. 18 (Kitchen 1983b, p. 23/14): "I have become a companion of Thoth in writing on the day of spitting at his shoulder," in Korostovtsev 1947, pp. 162–63; interpreted as a scribal initiation rite in Zibelius 1984b, pp. 402–03.

362. CT spell 1113, in de Buck 1961, p. 444 and Faulkner 1978, p. 162. Further references to healing the wounds of Apep by spittle are found in CT spell 1033, in de Buck 1961, p. 273 and Faulkner 1978, p. 129; and spell 1089, in de Buck 1961, p. 370a and Faulkner 1978, p. 150.

363. BD spell 17 §S11, in Allen 1974, p. 29. Compare BD spell 136B §S3, in ibid., p. 112. Spitting on the injured shank of Re is mentioned in BD spell 102 c, in ibid., p. 84, and his wounds by Apep are thus healed in BD spell 147e §S, in ibid., p. 138.

364. BD spell 96 §S, a spell for being associated with Thoth, in Allen 1974, p. 77. The text alludes to the healing by Thoth of Seth's injured testicles; the mention of Geb's marrow refers to the ancient belief that semen originated in the bone marrow (La Barre 1985, p. 3 and passim). The same conception underlies the disputed mention of the "marrow of Hermes" in the love spell PGM CIX (Griffiths 1977 and Betz 1986, p. 312).

365. Klakowicz 1980, pp. 36–37, col. c, l. x+1.

366. PT spell 324 §521a, in Sethe 1908, p. 266 and Faulkner 1969, p. 103. The king states: "Tell my name here to Horus, for I have come with hair-spittle for this hair of his which is ill [at the beginning of] months and which is bald at the beginning of half-months."

367. Zibelius 1984b, p. 399.

Within the conventionally designated "medical" texts, spittle is encountered far less frequently. In Papyrus Ebers recipe 499, col. 69/3–5, "Another (spell) for conjuring a burn on the first occasion (= initial treatment?)," the god Horus is said to be burnt on the desert, with water to extinguish the fire being present in the reciter's mouth. Actual treatment, however, involves an application of mother's milk rather than spittle.[368] A late dynastic treatise detailing therapy for serpent bite prescribes spitting in twenty-one "emetics" (*sbš.w*) designed to "open the throat" of a patient with constricted breathing.[369] A representative example is found in col. 3/9: "Emetic for the bite of a black-tailed cobra, likewise any snake: onion $\frac{1}{8}$ measure, beer $\frac{1}{16}$ and $\frac{1}{64}$ measure, northern salt $\frac{1}{64}$ measure. Grind, swallow, spit out, for four days."[370] Spitting as a means of administering medicines is found in the Demotic gynecological compilation, Papyrus Berlin P. 13602, l. 6, in which various roots are selected, "and then you spit their juice at her face with your mouth."[371]

Though found in "magical" texts, more typical examples of curative spitting are logically obvious in their motivation: the spitting out of venom[372] and the expelling of bones caught in the throat.[373] From the former notion derives the medical treatment of *wḫdw*-disease in Papyrus Ebers recipe 131, in which the corruptive agent is urged to be spat forth from the body, while the practitioner spits on the patient's infected limb.[374] Direct use of spittle reappears in a Saite Demotic spell against scorpion sting inscribed in the Wadi Hammamat. In this "spell for enchanting scorpion (sting)," a series of exorcising

368. Wreszinski 1913, p. 131; von Deines, Grapow, and Westendorf 1958, p. 215; and Grapow 1958, p. 373. The specified milk of a "woman who has borne a male child" is a reference to Isis, the mother of the god Horus invoked in the *historiola*. Milk is here paired with spittle as yet another divine bodily fluid capable of transmitting curative powers. For this "drug" and its continued medical history, see Dawson 1932, pp. 12–15 ("A Strange Drug").

369. Papyrus Brooklyn 47.218.48+45 (Sauneron 1989, pp. 234 [index, s.v. *pgs*] and 186 [discussion]).

370. Sauneron 1989, p. 66. A similar use of expectorated beer (*psg, bš*) underlies an emetic process to soothe the stomach (Borghouts 1970, pp. 27 [col. 13/5, spells 24–25] and 134, n. 311).

371. Erichsen 1954b, pp. 368–69.

372. This goal is probably also envisioned in the "emetics" of the Brooklyn serpent treatise, noted above. See the incantation in Sauneron 1989, pp. 108–09 (col. 5/12): "I have caused that its venom go forth to the ground." For other typical examples, see Borghouts 1978, pp. 51–83 and 91–97 ("Be spat/Break out!"); Koenig 1982, pp. 286–89; Griffith and Thompson 1904, pp. 122–23 (col. 19/2–5), and cf. pp. 124–25 (col. 19/16). Of particular interest is the exhortation of a Vatican papyrus and parallels: "Come out in spit, come in sweat, come into the face of any bird that you might enter into them" (Massart 1957, p. 180 [ro. 7, 6–7]).

373. Griffith and Thompson 1904, pp. 124–27 (col. 19/21–32) and Roccati 1970, p. 36 (Pap. Turin 54003, vo. 15–18).

374. Column 30/6–17, in Wreszinski 1913, pp. 35–36; von Deines, Grapow, and Westendorf 1958, p. 14; and Grapow 1958, pp. 24–25.

incantations is followed by the directions: "You should recite them to your finger while it is moistened with spittle. Then you should seal the opening of the wound with it (*scil.* "the spittle")."[375]

If notions of inherent divine power and the natural qualities of saliva each played a role in the ritualization of spitting, these last remedies suggest a further meaning for the act, made clearer in Pyramid Texts spell 455.

> O ... see the purification of my father this king as one purified with *zmn* and with natron, the saliva which issued from the mouth of Horus, the spittle which issued from the mouth of Seth, wherewith Horus is purified, wherewith the evil which was on him, which Seth did against him, is cast out on the ground; wherewith Seth is purified, wherewith the evil which was on him, which Horus did against him, is cast out on the ground ...[376]

Here, spittle not only conveys purification and healing, but further conducts corrupting evil away from the body, washing it off harmlessly onto the ground. Spitting thus constitutes a ritual washing, the basic meaning of "purification" (*w῾b*) in Egyptian speech and practice.[377] The same notion may be one factor implied in the medicinal spitting directed against *wḫdw* and scorpion venom.

SPITTLE AS CORRUPTION, CURSE, AND WEAPON

In its description of the pathogenic substance *wḫdw*, , Papyrus Ebers recipe 131 provides an unambiguous reference to the most common Egyptian interpretation of spitting and spittle. In this and other sources, the purulent agency responsible for disease, aging, and death is depicted as a by-product of unexpelled bodily waste, a source of decay originating in decay.[378] Medical treatments therefore standardly entailed purges and emetics to rid the body of such waste, and the recited spell of Ebers 131 envisioned the same result, for *wḫdw* "which has come forth from excrement" was commanded: "Be spat out! Be vomited out! *Perish just as you came into being*!"[379] In company with feces and vomit, spittle is here seen as a form of bodily excrement, a source and carrier of corruption and filth. Its potential role in disease is specified in Papyrus Ebers recipe 855b: "As for the

375. Vittmann 1984b; with further commentary in Ritner 1986a, pp. 105–06; Zauzich 1985; and Vittmann 1989.

376. PT spell 455 §§848–51, in Sethe 1908, pp. 472–74 and Faulkner 1969, p. 151.

377. For examples of ritual washing, see Pap. Leiden I 348, col. 13/2–3, in which honey, poured into a bowl inscribed with a spell, is used to wash the patient (Borghouts 1970, p. 26, spell 23) and Pap. Ramesseum 16, col. 17/2–3, said by a man while washing in the morning (Gardiner 1955, p. 16 and pl. 55). In both cases, the fluid is charged by the spell, whether written or spoken. For the technique, see also Heerma van Voss 1984, p. 31.

378. Full discussion of *wḫdw* appears in Steuer 1948 and Steuer and Saunders 1959.

379. Column 30/16.

condition termed 'His heart is flooded.' It is saliva; all his limbs are feeble."[380] While saliva was considered the sensory medium for taste,[381] food having the "taste of saliva" could be construed as a sign of impending death.[382] Dripping spittle was felt to characterize both illness and the infirmity of old age,[383] and embalming materials were employed to remove this source of decay from the corpse:

> I have brought to you *bd*-natron, a ball of incense and *ḥsmn*-natron that I may do away with the spittle of your mouths therewith. I have come to do away with the evil that is in your hearts.[384]

A late echo of this nuance is perhaps to be seen in a fourth century love spell preserved in Old Coptic, in which the accumulation of saliva is an omen of the victim's mental and physical distress.[385]

Although the concept of spittle as waste and corruption would seem diametrically opposed to its function in blessing and healing, both concepts have natural correlatives,[386] and positive and negative nuances may appear together. Coffin Texts spell 667, designed to ensure proper food supply for the deceased in the underworld, proclaims:

> The detestation of NN is efflux, and NN will not eat what NN's lips spew out ... having flown among his brethren the gods who are in the horizon, he spits on the scalp ... he gives breath to him whose throat is constricted.[387]

This spell is but a variant of the well-known incantations against the eating of dung in an "upside-down" underworld,[388] a particularly Egyptian expression of universal fears and taboos regarding discharged bodily "impurities."[389]

380. Column 99/17–18, in Wreszinski 1913, p. 206; von Deines, Grapow, and Westendorf 1958, p. 5; and Grapow 1958, p. 8.

381. "The Instruction of Amenemope," col. 23/13–16, noted in Zibelius 1984b, p. 400.

382. Papyrus Vandier, col. 1/4 ("The beer tasted like saliva. ... He could not sleep; His clothes would not adhere to him."), in Posener 1985, p. 40.

383. For illness, see Klasens 1952, pp. 54 and 84 (M 170); for old age, see Pap. Turin 1993, discussed above.

384. BD spell 79, §S2, in Allen 1974, p. 69 (addressed to the council of gods, but the funerary implications are clear). Compare BD spell 105, §S1, in ibid., p. 84 (addressed to one's own spirit): "I have brought to you *bd*-natron and incense, that I may purify you therewith, that I may purify your saliva therewith."

385. PGM IV, ll. 131–33 (Preisendanz 1928, pp. 74–75 and Betz 1986, p. 40): "If a large amount of saliva forms in your mouth as you speak, understand that she is distressed."

386. Any natural anti-bacterial properties of saliva are offset by the commonly recognized role of spittle in the transmission of disease.

387. CT spell 667, in de Buck 1956, pp. 295–96 and Faulkner 1977, p. 239.

388. Kadish 1979.

389. The basic anthropological study is Douglas 1966; cited in Kadish 1979, p. 217 and Zibelius 1984b, p. 399.

Such negative connotations translate easily into expressions and acts of derision and cursing.[390] Derogatory usage is clear in the Pyramid Texts:

> If the god *Ḫnty-ʾIr.ty* comes in his evil coming, do not open your arms to him, but let there be said to him this name: 'Spittle.'[391]

Within such spells, these taunts are designed not merely to insult the recipient, but to repel him forcibly. There is thus little distinction between (psychological) insult and (magical) curse. As "impure" spittle is viewed to be inherently dangerous, so the act of spitting may be hostile and magically threatening. It is significant that Seth and Apep, the principal adversaries of the gods, were both engendered by spitting,[392] and may pose their threat in the same manner. It is in his capacity of god of rain and "Spewer" (*ʾIššy*)[393] that Seth is especially noted for his evil spitting, from which Osiris is protected, and by which the sea was rendered brackish:

> As for the Lord of Storm, it is forbidden(?) Seth to spit, when he carries you.[394]

> The Great Ennead has protected you, they have put Seth under you on your behalf that he may be burdened with you, they have warded off his "evil influence" (*ꜣꜥ*) which he spat out against you.[395]

> He (*scil.* "Seth") has spat into the sea of the *Ḥtm.t*-cow.[396]

Magical associations of hostile spitting found an obvious natural counterpart in the ejected venom of serpents, scorpions, insects, and other creatures. This link certainly

390. Examples of spitting as a form of social insult are well discussed in Zibelius 1984b, pp. 405–06, including references to "The Instructions of ʿOnchsheshonqy" (col. 11/10), Siut Tomb 3, "Horus and Seth" (col. 12/4), and "Sinuhe" (§B 40). See also Helck 1969, pp. 29–31: "Those anointed with my myrrh spat before me" ("Instructions of Amenemhat I").

391. PT spell 534, §1270a–b, in Sethe 1910, p. 216 and Faulkner 1969, p. 201.

392. Te Velde 1977, p. 104. Seth is spat out by the pregnant Nut (PT spell 222, §205), while Apep derived from the spittle of Neith (reminiscent of the serpent in Pap. Turin 1993 formed from the spittle of Re [Sauneron 1962b, p. 265]).

393. Te Velde 1977, p. 85.

394. PT spell 247, §261a–b, in Sethe 1908, p. 143 and Griffiths 1960, p. 10 (misidentified as §1261a–b). The final passage dictating Seth's subservient punishment is misinterpreted in Faulkner 1969, p. 60, as indicating that Horus will raise up Osiris.

395. PT spell 593, §1628a–c, in Sethe 1910, p. 361 and Faulkner 1969, pp. 243–44. Seth's spittle is also directed against Horus (Griffiths 1960, p. 45).

396. From a list of Seth's transgressions in Urk. 6 (Schott 1929, pp. 22–23, l. 20 [mistranslated "dried up{?} the sea"]). For *stp* "spit," see de Buck 1938, p. 18 and *Wb* 4: 357/15 "drip." This action is probably the origin of Plutarch's disputed statement that the saline sea was considered "the spit of Typhon"; for the statement and previous analysis, see Griffiths 1970, pp. 167–69 and 421–22.

underlies the consistent use of spitting phraseology and ritual in anti-venom spells from their earliest through their latest instances. Previously mentioned examples of spitting against scorpion sting and the monstrous Apep serpent form part of this long tradition.

O spittle which has come to naught ... O monster lie down![397]

O you expectoration of a wall, you vomit of a brick, what comes out of your mouth is turned back against yourself.[398]

Babi stands up, having met *Ḫnty-ḫm*. Down/halt spittle![399]

May you be spat upon; fall, turn back, turn over![400]

A man shall say this spell over a louse from his head; he shall place it on his knee, spitting until a fly comes to snatch it. [401]

In these early recitations, a progression of techniques is clear: the offending creature is derided as excrement, its expectorated venom is said to recoil upon itself,[402] and the victim may ultimately "counter attack" with spittle of his own. "Hostile spittle" is thus not exclusively evil, but, as in the last instance, can function positively as a defensive or offensive weapon. The clearest expression of the dual nature of "venom spitting" is embodied in the symbol of the uraeus, through which the powers of the feared serpent are made to serve the gods, the king, and mankind.[403] The dichotomy became proverbial, reflecting contemporary ritual:

One rejoices at the Uraeus; One spits upon Apep.[404]

In similar manner, the hostile spitting of Seth is turned against Apep at the prow of the solar bark,[405] and the actions of both may be countered by defensive spitting. Thus Osiris,

397. PT spell 237, §241, in Sethe 1908, p. 134 and Faulkner 1969, p. 56.

398. PT spell 241, §246, in Sethe 1908, p. 136 and Faulkner 1969, p. 57.

399. PT spell 278, §419, in Sethe 1908, p. 218 and Faulkner 1969, p. 85. The uncertain passage is translated by Faulkner as "whom the spittle protects(?)," but the verb *hn* would seem an early attestation of terms meaning "bow down" or "stop" (*Wb* 2: 492/6–7 and 494). The serpent (Babi) that is rearing to strike is made non-threatening.

400. PT spell 385, §678a, in Sethe 1908, p. 369 and Faulkner 1969, p.127.

401. CT spell 98, in de Buck 1938, p. 94 and Faulkner 1973, p. 97.

402. Thus a serpent may be said to be "cursed with its own mouth" (Sander-Hansen 1937, p. 140, ll. 470–72). For the typical terminology of anti-serpent spells, see Ogdon 1989.

403. For the uraeus and its role in magic, see Ritner 1990.

404. "The Instruction of Amenemope," col. 10/19–20 (Lichtheim 1976, p. 153).

405. Te Velde 1977, pp. 99–108.

Isis, and Nephthys each assume the role of "Spitter," while this aspect of Osiris was even accorded local prominence in his cult center , "Spit-town."[406] Funerary texts assign these protective roles to the deceased:

> I have warded off Seth for you, I have spat on his confederacy for you.[407]
>
> I am the spitter at the prow of the bark. I have come to provide protection for Osiris.[408]
>
> I have repulsed Apep; I have spat on the wound.[409]

The fate of Apep, Seth, and cohorts is explained concisely by a Demotic proverb:

> He who spits at heaven—it is on him that it falls.[410]

Heaven's revenge was not confined to mythology, but enacted literally on a daily basis. Accompanying the apotropaic techniques of trampling, stabbing, and burning (with which it was often equated),[411] spitting figures prominently in both the recitations and praxis of late

406. To my knowledge, these epithets have not been gathered or studied. "Osiris as Spitter" (*Wsỉr m psg/pgꜣs*) appears within a list of the god's names in BD spell 142, §S1, in Allen 1974, p. 118 and cf. ibid., §S2, translated with hesitation as "Osiris in the House of Re's Spittle." This unidentified cult site is named *Psg* or *Psg-Rꜥ*; for attestations, see *Wb* 1: 555/16; Budge 1912, pl. 41, col. 2/8; Gauthier 1925, pp. 47, 152, and 154; and Gardiner 1947, vol. 2, pp. 76*–77*. As recognized by Gardiner, the name properly signifies "Spit-Town" or "Spit of the Mouth-Town." An allusion to a mythological event probably associated with the site is found in the ritual against Seth in Urk. 6: "A falcon enduring of beauty on the night of purification through the power of(?) Spit-town (*m sḫm Pgs*)." The final phrase is understood as "in (the town of) *Sḫm-Pgs*" in Schott 1929, pp. 142–43, ll. 10–11. Coffins from the royal caches provide examples of Isis and Nephthys as spitters protecting or healing Osiris (Daressy 1909, p. 87 and pl. 40, middle right ["Isis the Spitter, Mistress of the West"]; p. 187 and pl. 56, middle right ["Isis the Spitter"]; and p. 112 and pl. 45 [Isis and Nephthys lament Osiris with 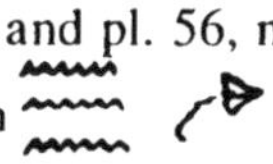 above their outstretched hands]). The epithet "Spitter" is written with the ideogram of the spitting mouth. Although it is possible to read this sign as the copula *pw* (de Wit 1956, p. 116), such an interpretation is grammatically unnecessary, and unlikely in the context. The spittle of Isis is invoked in Pap. Ebers recipe 499, noted above, and both Isis and Nephthys are said to spit on Seth: "Shu sticks his spear in you, the two sisters spit on you"; Schott 1929, pp. 130–31, ll. 17–18. Isis' role as spitter of venom is personified as *ꜣs.t-Ḥddy.t*, "Isis-Scorpion," for whom see Goyon 1978b.

407. CT spell 315, in de Buck 1951, p. 97k and Faulkner 1973, p. 237.

408. BD spell 146w, §S9, in Allen 1974, p. 136. The protective gestures against Apep and Seth are here conflated.

409. Sander-Hansen 1937, p. 48, l. 96, combining—by implication—both protective and curative spitting. For a further use of spitting imagery with Apep, cf. "I have caused the *nkỉw*-serpent to vomit what he had swallowed," in Urk. 6, 97/9 and Pap. Bulaq 17, cols. 3/7–4/1 (Schott 1929, pp. 96–97).

410. "The Instructions of ʿOnchsheshonqy," col. 11/10 (Lichtheim 1980, p. 168, correcting Glanville 1955, pp. 28–29).

411. Reflecting the common notion of "fire-spitting" serpents (and thus gods and demons); see Urk. 6, 51/7 (Eye of Horus versus Seth): "Spit fire among his limbs"; 57/22 (Nut versus Seth): "My spittle is

temple execrations directed against the two demons and their associates.[412] As a form of "venom against venom," this ceremonial spitting ensured the "social death"[413] of its victim:

> His name will not be in the mouth of the people. It will not be remembered in the heart of the gods. He will be spat upon each time that he is remembered.[414]

Given the cultic significance accorded such "destructive" spitting throughout these rituals, it might at first seem inappropriate that mentions of the sun-god's "creative" spitting are also present, and even stressed in two "Books of Knowing the Transformations of Re and of Overthrowing Apep."[415] The rationale for such mentions may well be based on the need to evoke a mythological "primal time" (*in illo tempore*), and thereby ensure "re-creation" out of chaos and divine triumph over demons.[416] The inclusions also provide further insight into the workings of "magical" spitting, for if no contradiction seems implied, it is because "spitting" is primarily neither positive nor negative, but only "power-laden."[417] Saliva is not itself the blessing or curse, but only its conveyer or medium. In execration ritual, saliva is infused with the spoken curse, which spitting directs upon the victim's image. Declarations of the "creative" power of spittle do not contradict its

---

against him as fire"; and Pap. Bremner-Rhind, col. 31/14 (Ennead versus Apep): "They spit their flame into your eye." Compare also the suggested derivation of ⲡⲓ (< *pʿw*) "fire" from *pʿi* "spit" in Westendorf 1965–77, p. 530. It is significant that ritual spitting often occurs while the image of the victim is on fire: Urk. 6, 5/18 and Pap. Bremner-Rhind, cols. 23/12 and 24/19ff. This is to reinforce the burning, not extinguish it; contrast the insult popular in contemporary Texas: "I wouldn't spit on him if he were on fire!"

412. In the anti-Seth rituals of Urk. 6, hostile spitting is invoked within the recitations in Schott 1929, pp. 51/7, 51/11, 57/22, 97/9, and 131/18. Actual spitting ("four times" or "many times") is performed in ibid., pp. 5/13 and 5/18, with complete spitting rites in 41/2–43/7 and 53/2–59/16. Comparable Pap. Bremner-Rhind rites versus Apep use spitting imagery in cols. 22/2–5 (full rite), 23/1–4, 24/18–19, 26/11–12, 26/17, 26/20, 27/23, 28/4, 28/15, 30/2–4, 31/14, and 32/3, in Faulkner 1933, passim. Participatory spitting appears further in cols. 23/11–12, 26/3, and 28/16–17. Compare also the remarks against Apep at Edfu in Chassinat 1928, p. 342/8. This practice is not a late development; see the proverb of Amenemope (10/20), noted above, and the phraseology of ll. 18, 24, and 26–27 of the healing statue of Ramses III from Almazah, in Drioton 1939; idem 1957; and Kitchen 1983a, pp. 261–68.

413. Zibelius 1984b, p. 405.

414. Papyrus Bremner-Rhind, col. 27/23. So also col. 26/17: "Be spat on, rebel ... may you be spat on whenever you are remembered"; and Urk. 6, 51/11 (Eye of Horus versus Seth): "Your spittle is against him. He is not perceived."

415. See Schott 1929, pp. 96–97, l. 21 ("You have spat forth yourself as a falcon"). Pap. Bremner-Rhind examples (detailing the creation of Shu and Tefnut) are contained throughout the two books, cols. 26/21–28/20 and 28/20–29/16, in Faulkner 1933, pp. 59–74.

416. Eliade 1971, pp. 17–21 and passim.

417. Contra Zibelius 1984b, p. 401. While some spitting terms have only negative nuances (*šp*), most are neutral and are used in both creative and destructive contexts (*išš*, *tf*, etc.).

"hostile" cultic usage; they establish the effectiveness of the vehicle later used against the demon. Such a concept of "activated" spittle certainly motivated the praxis of the Wadi Hammamat scorpion spell: "You should recite [the spell] to your finger while it is moistened with spittle. Then you should seal the opening of the wound with it."[418] The saliva is here "charged" by the words which pass over it, and thus empowered to heal. Comparable procedures are not rare in Egyptian magic. In the "Book of the Heavenly Cow," the speaker's justification is guaranteed by painting an image of the goddess Maat on his tongue. Spoken words passing over the tongue are consequently infused with truth.[419] Water poured over the inscribed spells of healing statues is similarly "impregnated" by contact. The patient who drinks the water from the statue's basin thereby obtains the curative force of the unspoken texts.[420] Carved spells imbue the water of healing basins just as spoken spells imbue the saliva of the mouth.

BLOWING

Before passing to review the survival of magical spitting within Coptic sources, mention should be made of the late "subset" of this technique, the spitting not of saliva, but of air. The envisioned mechanics of "expectorated breath" are identical to those of spittle. Thus, in a third century Demotic prescription for curing gout, the topical application of unguents is supplemented:

> In addition to this, you should blow (*nyf*) at him with your mouth.[421]

This manner of treatment was perhaps more common than present textual evidence suggests, since the second century author Celsus notes that Egyptian magicians "drive demons out of men and blow away diseases."[422] A fourth century spell attributed to the Egyptian magician Pibechis does recommend the use of blowing in exorcisms, but the text

418. See above, n. 375.

419. Hornung 1982, pp. 25 and 46, ll. 259–60 and cf. Heerma van Voss 1984, pp. 25–26. The reciter is thereby rendered "pure of tongue"; for the idiom, cf. BD spell 178, §f S1, in Allen 1974, p. 187. Compare also the practice of painting the Sound Eye of Horus on the mummy's face in CT spell 936, in de Buck 1961, p. 138j–k and Faulkner 1978, p. 71. Alternatively, the act of painting Maat on the tongue could imply the *consumption* of the goddess to produce the same result. Compare CT spell 1017: "I have eaten Maat, I have swallowed Magic (*ḥkꜣ*)"; in de Buck 1961, p. 238d–e and Faulkner 1978, p. 118. See further under "magical swallowing," below.

420. For discussion and references, see the discussion of "magical swallowing," below, n. 518.

421. Demotic Magical Pap. of London and Leiden vo., col. 8/7–8, in Griffith and Thompson 1904, p. 181 and Betz 1986, p. 244.

422. Quoted from Origen, *Contra Celsum*, 1. 68. For the reference and New Testament parallels, see Morton Smith 1978, pp. 112–13. Smith suggests an Egyptian origin for the biblical practice (pp. 48 and 58).

is preserved in Greek, and the imagery is Hebraic.[423] Though early parallels for such practices are lacking, the Egyptian association of breath and spittle is of long standing. As noted above, the air god Shu was the first product of the creator's spittle, and Amon is expressly said to have "spat out the wind (*ṯ3w*)."[424] The notion of transferring invigorating breath is a commonplace in offering rituals, which promise the donor the "breath of life" (*ṯ3w ꜥnḫ*),[425] and funerary texts recognize the same technique, particularly emphasized in variants of the late "Books of Breathing":

> O *ba*, breathing upon his feet, he begins to go in peace over every land.[426]

The treatment here envisioned for the resuscitated corpse would later be applied to the gout-stricken patient.

CONTINUITY AND CHRISTIANIZATION

Neither Roman sanctions nor conversion to Christianity resulted in the suppression of traditional magical techniques.[427] Numerous papyri inscribed in Demotic and Greek testify to the endurance of Egyptian practice during the Roman and Christian centuries,[428] and previously quoted examples furnish ample demonstration of the survival of native concepts regarding the magical applications of spittle. The circulation of such texts in Greek translation, and the wanderings of magicians themselves, exported Egyptian notions throughout the Mediterranean, where pre-existing local conceptions will have been influenced or strengthened. The common presence of "saliva magic" in surrounding areas makes any evaluation of influence difficult, however, and thus it is unclear whether

423. PGM IV, ll. 3080–85, in Preisendanz 1928, pp. 172–73; Betz 1986, p. 97; and Morton Smith 1978, p. 113.

424. See above, n. 329.

425. *Wb* 5: 352/18–24 and note the corresponding "breath of death," on p. 352/25–26. Medical treatises (especially Pap. Ebers §§854–56) show that the breaths of life and death were felt to enter the body (through the ears) and circulate with the blood. See the references in von Deines and Westendorf 1962, pp. 964–65.

426. Pap. Louvre E 3452, col. 9/8, in Mark Smith 1979, p. 145.

427. See *Chapter 6*, below.

428. For sources and discussion, see Betz 1986. The texts represent only a fraction of what once must have existed, since many magical books were burned during Christian pogroms (though quoted figures are probably exaggerated for propaganda purposes; see Morton Smith 1978, p. 94 and Barns 1964).

Egyptian concepts affected the Alexandrian miracle of the Roman emperor Vespasian, who cured a blind man by spitting in the suppliant's eye.[429]

In the same way, Egyptian practice will have coincided with certain healing miracles of Jesus, though the direct influence of Egyptian methodology has been strongly suggested.[430] With the Christianization of Egypt, ancient concepts were adapted to the new faith, and Coptic literature provides many examples of spittle used to curse, heal, and bless. In contrast to New Testament ritual, Old Testament references stressed the negative associations of spittle, which was seen as a symbol of madness (1 Kings 21:13) and worthlessness (Isaiah 40:15), and as a source or transmitter of impurity (Leviticus 15:8). Such common negative associations reappear in Coptic extra-biblical literature, where spitting is typically linked with raging men, camels, and demons,[431] and the practice is condemned for defiling ritual purity:

> [Priests] shall not put sandals on their feet when they go
> into the church, nor shall they spit in the sanctuary.[432]

This very prohibition motivated the thirtieth wonder of the Arabic "Life of Saint Pisentius," in which a careless priest is struck dead for spitting before the altar. The priest had unwittingly struck the wing of one of the invisible cherubim, and the angel retaliated by inflicting paralysis and death.[433] Spitting at pagan deities is altogether another matter, however, and Samuel of Kalamun is praised for spitting at the rising sun during the religious services of his Berber master.[434]

429. The difficulty is made almost insurmountable by mutual influence in ritual matters extending back for millennia. For the incident with Vespasian, see Morenz 1975, pp. 551–60 ("Vespasian, Heiland der Kranken. Persönliche Frömmigkeit im antiken Herrscherkult?"). Spitting to cure eye injury has traditional precedent in Egypt, following Thoth's cure of the Eye of Horus (PT spell 214, §141d–42d); see above n. 358. As noted in the second satire of Persius, spitting was also a common Roman practice to repel the Evil Eye; for further Roman sources and discussion, see n. 325, above.

430. For the miracles in which Jesus cures blindness and dumbness by spitting on the eyes and tongue, see Aune 1980, pp. 1534 and 1537 (Mark 7:31–36, Mark 8:22–26, and John 9:11–41), and for Egyptian influence, see Morton Smith 1978, pp. 48 and 58.

431. A brother is spat upon and beaten in D. W. Johnson 1980, vol. 1, p. 17 (text) and vol. 2, p. 13 (translation) (§3, 7). For poison-spitting demons, see Alcock 1983, p. 103 and cf. the possessed camel in ibid., pp. 14, ll. 14 and 89. For general references to spittle, see the examples gathered in Crum 1939, pp. 286b (ⲡⲁϭⲥⲉ), 453a (ⲧⲁϥ), and 796b (ϫⲓϩ).

432. Appendix §24,1 in Kuhn 1960, vol. 1, p. 69 (text) and vol. 2, p. 64 (translation). The prohibition of sandals corresponds to Greco-Roman, not Egyptian, injunctions.

433. O'Leary 1930, pp. 411–17.

434. Alcock 1983, pp. 91–93. Compare the parallels cited in Crum 1939, p. 286b (ⲛⲉϫ ⲡⲟϭⲥⲉ ⲛ̄ⲥⲁⲡⲣⲏ). The saint was barred from further attendance.

Despite such negative connotations of spitting, the old notion of healing saliva remained, given new justification by the miracles of Jesus. Evoking earlier praise of Thoth, one text declares that "the spittle in His mouth is healing salve,"[435] while a spell for exorcism invokes Gabriel by "the spit that came forth from the Father's mouth and became a well of water of life."[436] One of the more repellent episodes in Coptic hagiography finds its motivation precisely in the pointed contrast between common notions of spittle as corruption and magical concepts of curative saliva. The final days of the archimandrite Apollo produced the following "mystery of the faith":

> He fell into a great illness when his inward parts were stricken, and thereafter he continued to spit blood and phlegm for the rest of his days. So he was sick in this fashion, but his sickness was also a healing for others. For while he was sitting one day speaking with believers who had come to him to be blessed by him, there was one among them, too, who was suffering from a sickness. O that spittle that issued from the saint's mouth! O the sickness that became the healer of another's sickness! For the sickness constrained our father to expectorate such things. It is holy spittle, one might say. At once when it dropped upon the ground, the sick man took it in perfect hope and swallowed it. And suddenly the grace of faith became the healing of the believer through that holy spittle. And so the man was healed.[437]

The nadir of this technique is found in the Ethiopic life of Takla Ḥawāryāt, in which the saint lunges forward to consume an expectorated piece of communion bread, which transmits healing as "the body of Christ."[438] In all such tales, holy spittle now functions as a "bodily relic," deriving its power from divinity inherent in the saintly figure. The same notions of indwelling divinity had sanctified the fluids of the ancient gods, but the veneration of human saints made such materials more accessible. Comparable wonders are obtained by consuming dirt from the saint's feet or water used to wash his corpse,[439] and even by salving bodily sores with the pulp of saints freshly ground between millstones.[440]

435. Pierpont Morgan Ms. vol. 43, p. 218, cited in Crum 1939, p. 286b (ⲡⲁϭⲥⲉ).

436. Kropp 1930–31, vol. 1, p. 75 and vol. 2, p. 188 (16/20).

437. See Kuhn 1978, vol. 1, cols. 35/15–36/1 (text) and vol. 2, p. 27 (translation; §19). I have removed the word "almost" from Kuhn's translation of ⲥⲭⲉⲇⲱⲛ, "roughly speaking, one might say." The author does indeed call the spittle "holy."

438. Conti Rossini 1910, pp. 73–74 and cf. Praetorius 1911, p. 782.

439. Kuhn 1978, vol. 1, p. 29 and vol. 2, p. 22 (§16: dirt from saint's feet put on bread) and idem 1978, vol. 1, p. 37 and vol. 2, p. 28 (§20: water from corpse put into common cistern). See also the "Tales of Apa Daniel," in which water used to wash a saint's feet is subsequently placed on the heads and faces of the faithful and cures blindness; Mallon 1926, pp. 66–67 (reference courtesy Terry Wilfong).

440. Reymond and Barns 1973, pp. 124 and 219–20.

Healing saliva survived the change to Islam as well, since the ancient technique was used by the prophet Mohammed to transmit his *baraka* or "blessing," a practice continued by the Moslem holy men of North Africa.[441] The tenacity of the belief is also seen in modern proverbs circulating among the Copts, in which the drying out of saliva is an indication that god has withdrawn his blessing.[442]

The history of magical spitting in Egypt has been shown to be both long and intricate, entailing notions varying from creation, blessing, healing, and washing, to venom, cursing, decay, and death. The existence of similar beliefs in foreign cultures in no way invalidates the significance of the concept within Egyptian thought,[443] and the complexity of native phenomena has been little illuminated by the reductionistic categories of "folk medicine," "homeopathic" or "contagious" magic.[444] Nor should these spitting practices be classed as subreligious "superstition," since in each case they are direct expressions of orthodox theological concepts, following the precedents of religious leaders—whether gods, kings, emperors, or prophets.

LICKING

If spitting serves as an all but universal ritual practice, the related technique of licking is more rarely encountered. In Egyptian magical methodology, the term "licking" (*nsb*, 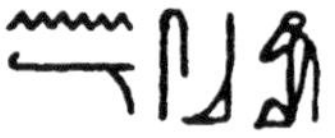)[445] is accorded seemingly unique status, appearing commonly as a technical expression for spell manipulation. In so far as the action is but a variant of spitting in the physical transfer of saliva, the underlying "mechanics" should be understood similarly. Like spitting, also, the practice may encompass a variety of meanings, ranging from curative to cursing. Egyptian references to "magical licking" have received little scholarly attention, however, and a survey of examples is thus necessary to establish the traditional patterns.[446]

Funerary literature again provides the most plentiful source for this magical technique, which serves a variety of purposes already in the Pyramid Texts. In the offering rituals of

441. Zibelius 1984b, p. 400.

442. Wissa Wassef 1971, p. 250.

443. Compare n. 309, above. One might as well abandon the study of Egyptian grammar or architecture on the basis of the commonality of verbs and columns.

444. E.g., Faulkner 1969, p. 295 and cf. Frazer 1910, pp. 57 and 201.

445. *Wb* 2: 334/11–14. Examples from the funerary literature are mistakenly translated "swallow" (*Wb* 2: 334/11), a related, but not identical, notion.

446. A brief mention of the process appears in Heerma van Voss 1984, p. 32.

Pyramid Texts spells 166 and 181 and Coffin Texts spell 936 (restored), the deceased king is presented two bowls of zizyphus-fruit, qualified as the "Eye of Horus which they have licked."[447] Faulkner has suggested that the unspecified "they" refers to "the followers of Seth,"[448] and "licking" would thus represent a form of injury to Horus's eye, perpetrated by Seth and his cohorts. While such negative usage of licking is attested and is discussed below, it would seem that these passages refer instead to the healing of Horus's eye by the gods, so that the king is presented with the "Sound Eye of Horus." Elsewhere, the restoration of the eye is attributed to the curative force of divine saliva, and "licking" would here parallel "spitting" as a "medico-magical" technique.[449] As previously noted, the "magical" transfer of health or blessing by saliva reflects such "naturally" observable phenomena as the licking of wounds. As a magical technique, licking represents a ritualized extension of such instinctive acts.

Natural observation certainly underlies the licking imagery associated with the cow goddess Hathor. Like a cow with her calf,[450] the goddess "licks Horus whom she has borne,"[451] and bestows her blessing on Hatshepsut at Deir el-Bahari in the same manner: "kissing your hand, licking your limbs, endowing your Majesty with life and dominion."[452] The goddess' kiss in the form of a lick charges the recipient with renewed life:

> I kiss your hand, I lick your limbs with my pleasant tongue which has come forth from my mouth, you being born daily on the hands of your father Amon.[453]

This blessing of Hathor may be extended to the deceased in funerary contexts; a vignette from the Book of the Dead of *Ṯ3-nfr* depicts the goddess licking the man's hand to ensure his rebirth.[454] The healing kiss of Hathor is still evoked at the Ptolemaic temple of Edfu, where the goddess appears before Horus: "She has licked the injury that is in your

447. PT spell 166, §98c and spell 181, §104b, in Faulkner 1969, pp. 31 and 34. CT spell 936, in de Buck 1961, p. 141 and Faulkner 1978, p. 74.

448. Faulkner 1969, p. 31.

449. For Thoth and others spitting to cure the Eye of Horus, see n. 358, above.

450. For the use of *nsb*, "lick" with cattle, see *Wb* 2: 334/12–13. For similar licking imagery in Mesopotamian magic, see J. and A. Westenholz 1977, p. 215: "Then the ewe licked (... lit. "took good care of") her lamb."

451. Sethe 1930c, p. 239, l. 5.

452. Ibid., p. 239, ll. 7–9 and see also p. 236, ll. 13–15: "kissing the hand, the divine limbs are licked, the king is endowed with life and dominion." For this connection of kissing with licking, compare the similar link between the terms of kissing and spitting (*pʿy*), above, n. 327. For kissing as a means of contact with texts, see Heerma van Voss 1984, pp. 26–29.

453. Sethe 1930c, p. 238, ll. 1–4.

454. Erichsen and Schott 1954, pl. 2.

body."[455] A contrasting concept associated with the Apis bull survives in the Greek legends of the astronomer Eudoxus of Knidos, a pupil of Plato who subsequently traveled to Egypt to study with the native clergy (fourth century B.C.). When his cloak was licked by the Apis, Eudoxus was informed by the priests that his fame would be great, but that his life would be short.[456] He had, in effect, acquired certain qualities of Osiris, transmitted by the god's earthly representative, the Apis.

Therapeutic licking is performed by human practitioners as well. In Coffin Texts spell 81, the practitioner identifies himself with the god Shu to ensure that his "flesh is alive," and his limbs "nourished." The spell is recited over images of the Ogdoad painted on the hand in yellow pigment and Nubian ochre "to be licked off every day very early."[457] In his translation of this text, Faulkner is perplexed by the wording, since "it seems unlikely that the hands of the deceased are to be ochred."[458] Moreover, he modifies the translation of "licked" to "rinsed(?)," since "it does not seem at all probable that actual licking was intended."[459] There is, however, nothing unusual about this spell, which accords with practice common in the non-funerary "magical" literature. Like much of the supposedly "funerary" corpus, this text was certainly devised for use by the living, and its directions should be understood literally.[460] Daily licking of the hand restores the ritualist's flesh, and echoes the mythological passage in the spell wherein Shu boasts that the sun god Atum "kissed me every day." Such a solar blessing may be expressly equated with licking, as in Coffin Texts spell 1053: "I am the Lord of the Horizon, and the daily flame licks me."[461] Variants state "Khepri shines and licks me," reinforcing the association of solar "licking" with the rays of early dawn.[462]

455. Rochemonteix et al. 1984–87, p. 588.

456. References are collected in Lindsay 1971, pp. 87–88. In a poem, Diogenes relates: "No chattering tongue for Apis did Nature devise; but standing sideways there, it licked his cloak and plainly thus foretold: You will die soon"; ibid., p. 88. The Apis bull of Osiris and the Hathor cow of the West are linked by their common funerary associations. The "blessing" of Eudoxus may have ensured a future life at the expense of the present one.

457. De Buck 1938, p. 44 and Faulkner 1973, p. 87.

458. Faulkner 1973, p. 87, n. 4.

459. Ibid., p. 87, n. 5. Rinsing, washing, or wiping would have exactly the opposite effect, as is discussed below, n. 496.

460. Compare CT spell 100, designed to send the practitioner's soul to appear before a man, "to be recited over an image of the Foremost of the Westerners and to be inscribed on his (*scil.* the practitioner's) hand"; in de Buck 1938, pp. 96–97 and Faulkner 1973, p. 98.

461. Faulkner 1978, p. 138.

462. Ibid., p. 138, n. 6. Khepri, of course, is the image of the early morning sun.

Non-funerary applications of curative licking were certainly in use by the Middle Kingdom. Papyrus Turin 54003, an early Twelfth Dynasty manuscript containing older spells from the First Intermediate Period, includes among its ophthalmological recipes the following:

> My eyes are opened by the Great One; My eyes are opened by the Opener; The Eyes [of Hathor] are opened in the House of the Statue; The Eyes of Hathor are opened in the [House of] Gold, that she might look at that red [...]-animal(?) when he opens his mouth, when he opens his jaws(?), when he looks at that pupil of gold, faience, quartz, and carnelian which flourishes (literally 'grows') on the eye of the majesty of Ptah. When Isis bent over it, she licked it; When I bent over my eye, I licked it. From this my face, from this my eye, I dispelled the blow of a god, goddess, dead man, or dead woman. Dispelled is the obscurity, being thoroughly stripped away. As Shu has licked what was done to him, so Maat(?) has licked what was done to her. To be said by a man as he puts water into his eyes.[463]

Emulating divine prototypes, the human reciter restores his injured vision by figuratively "licking" his own eye through the administration of "eyedrops." Such an eye cure by licking supports the similar interpretation of Pyramid Texts spell 166 and 181, discussed above. From the end of the Middle Kingdom, a literal example of protective licking appears within the collection of priestly papyri discovered beneath the Ramesseum (late Twelfth Dynasty to Thirteenth Dynasty). The rubric of the fragmentary Papyrus Ramesseum 14 stipulates: "This spell is [to be written] on ... fresh ... It should be licked off (*nsb*) by a man."[464]

The therapeutic licking of spells and images drawn on the hand continues in Ramesside magical manuals. The best-known example accompanies the anti-scorpion spell of Papyrus Turin 1993, "The Legend of Isis and the Secret Name of Re,"[465] This extensive spell concludes:

> Words to be recited over an image of Atum and of Horus-of-Praise, a figure of Isis, and an image of Horus, drawn (on) the hand of the sufferer and licked off by the man; do likewise on a strip of fine linen, placed on the sufferer at his throat. Its plant is scorpion plant. Or ground up with beer or wine, it is drunk by the man who has a scorpion sting. It is what kills the poison—truly effective, (proved) a million times.[466]

463. Verso 2–8. Parallel *sḏm.n=f* clauses lacking adjuncts are here taken as wechsel-clauses. For the difficulties of this text, and a variant translation, see the edition in Roccati 1970, pp. 31–33.

464. Gardiner 1955b, p. 15 and pl. 46 (vo. 3–4).

465. See above, n. 337.

466. Pleyte and Rossi 1869–76, pls. 77+31, ll. 2–5. At least four other exemplars of the spell's incantation are known: HO 2; HO 3, 2; O. Deir el-Medineh 1263; and Pap. Chester Beatty 11, which preserves passages of the same rubric in the fragmentary cols. 3/12–4/2. For bibliography, see Wilson 1969b, p. 12. Wilson, ibid., p. 14, translates the third sentence from the end, *sym pw sym wḥʿ.t*, as "It is the way of caring for a scorpion poison." For "scorpion plant," cf. σκορπιοειδής, "scorpion-wort (so called because of the likeness of its seed to a scorpion's tail)"; in Liddell, Scott, and Jones 1940, pp. 1614–15.

The power of the spell is brought into contact with the patient in various ways: direct application as an amulet to "open" the throat,[467] and either licking or drinking the text to ingest its efficacy. Such "consumption" of written spells is discussed in greater detail below.

Even where complemented by notions of "swallowing," however, the curative function of licking probably still finds its basis in the simple licking of wounds. This is expressed clearly within a third century Demotic remedy for wound treatment, which yet retains the old methodology. Papyrus London and Leiden, col. 20, ll. 1–27, a spell to cure scorpion sting, begins with an *historiola* directed to the wound itself, detailing the injury of Anubis and his subsequent cure by Isis. In the mythological recitation, Isis instructs Anubis:

> Lick from your tongue to your heart and vise versa, up to the edges of the wound! Lick to the edges of the wound up to the limits of your strength! What you shall lick, you shall swallow. Do not spit it out on the ground, for your tongue is the tongue of Shay (Fate); your tongue is that of Atum.[468]

The spells' directions then instruct the practitioner regarding his own wound: "And you should immediately lick it with your tongue while it is bleeding."[469] The patient, assimilated to Anubis, is thus depicted as a dog licking his wounds. The spell concludes with the topical application of enchanted oil. The two incantations which bracket the spell are each designed to "charge" fluids with curative power: the flowing blood that is lapped and the oil that is applied. As in Papyrus Turin 1993, the healing spell is rendered tangible, and administered both internally and externally.

A further significant feature which links this spell to Papyrus Turin 1993 and the yet earlier Coffin Texts spell 81 is the specific mention of the god Atum, whose kiss, lick, or tongue is invoked within each recitation. Such mentions are clearly motivated by the mythological significance of the god's creative saliva. By association with this creator deity, the lick bestowed by the practitioner acquires generative force, exactly paralleling the use of "healing spittle."

As spittle may be both "healing" and "corruptive," so licking may also acquire hostile or dangerous overtones. In "The Cannibal Hymn" of the Pyramid Texts (spells 273–74), the king is said to be "disgusted when he licks the emetics which are in the Red Crown."[470]

467. Compare the snake venom remedies to "open the throat" and thus prevent constriction of breathing, discussed in Sauneron 1989, pp. 179 and 186.

468. Griffith and Thompson 1904, pp. 130–31 (col. 20/10–13); J. H. Johnson 1986d, p. 228. The term for "lick" is *lkḥ* > ⲗⲱϫϩ (Erichsen 1954a, p. 264).

469. Griffith and Thompson 1904, pp. 130–31 (col. 20/14); J. H. Johnson 1986d, p. 228.

470. PT spell §411a, in Sethe 1908, p. 214. Faulkner (1969, pp. 82 and 84, n. 24) does not translate *sbš.w*, "emetics."

The hymn poses a contrast between the repellent licking of the emetics, and the resultant joyful possession of their power. The importance of emetics (*sbš.w*) as snake venom remedies is noted above. Here licking is again related to swallowing,[471] but with hostile intent; the king consumes the emetics of the crown just as he devours the hearts and lungs of the gods.

Snake remedies provide yet a further link between negative instances of spitting, licking, and swallowing. In the recitation against serpents of Pyramid Texts spell 228, it is stated: "it has swallowed for itself that which it has licked." Though this passage has been justly described as obscure,[472] it would seem that the term licking is used here to describe the method by which a serpent emits its venom, paralleling the common use of "spitting" imagery found elsewhere in the Pyramid Texts.[473] As in these other spells, the intent of the recitation is to make the venom recoil upon the snake itself,[474] so that the hostile reptile is forced to "swallow for itself" the poison that it has ejected by licking.

This interpretation is confirmed by a Middle Kingdom spell against the Rerek-serpent carved on a stone box in the Louvre (inv. E 25485).[475] Within the spell, the serpent is directly addressed as: "licker who has come forth from the cavern! You have swallowed the eye of Re, you have licked the eye of Baba."[476] As the serpent is later styled the "son of Baba" (literally "hole-inhabitant"?),[477] the reptile is thus told that he has attacked his own father while attacking Re.[478] An ironic echo of this legend may survive in the late Papyrus Jumilhac, in which Baba attempts to slander Thoth by declaring that "it is Thoth who has taken what belonged to Re, who has eaten Re, his abomination. He has licked what came forth from him."[479]

471. As recognized by *Wb* 2: 334/11. The magical force of the emetics is next described as being in the king's belly. Faulkner 1969, p. 84, n. 25, misattributes this force to the "hearts" mentioned in §410c.

472. Borghouts 1984, p. 704, n. 5.

473. See nn. 397–400, above. "Licking" is not infrequently associated with serpents; compare the Greek usage of λιχμάω, in Liddell, Scott, and Jones 1940, p. 1055a.

474. See n. 402, above.

475. Borghouts 1984, pp. 704–16.

476. Ibid., pp. 703–04. The reference to swallowing and licking the eyes of Re and Baba is later repeated in the spell (p. 705).

477. Ibid., p. 705, n. 14. The rearing snake is addressed as Bab(a)i in PT spell 385, §678a; see n. 399, above.

478. Borghouts ibid., p. 709, attempts to pair Re and Baba as positive luminary deities.

479. Vandier (1961, p. 128, col. 16/12–13) provides a differing translation. The false accusation of eating a portion of Re is expressed by a euphemistic circumlocution, inserting the phrase "the enemies of" before the god's name (Posener 1969, p. 35); for the continued use of this formula, see Quack 1989. Vandier, following a suggestion of Posener, read the word "enemies" as "repast/food" (p. 195, n. 534).

In the Coffin Texts and the Book of the Dead, hostile licking of spells appears as a threat to the deceased:

> As for any god, goddess, spirit, dead man, or dead woman, who shall lick off his spell against me today, he shall fall to the execution blocks, to the magic that is in my body, the terrible flames that are in my mouth.[480]

> Food offerings are all around me through the "Effective Eye" that licks/burns up (*nsb*) any male or female dead who shall come opposing me.[481]

> Back, O (crocodile) who is in the West, for there is a *nʿw*-serpent in this my belly. I shall not be given to you; you shall not lick off my spell.[482]

> As for any god or dead man who shall lick off his spell in my presence on this day, he shall fall to the depths.[483]

Such underworld references play upon the associations of licking with both serpents and "tongues of fire"; the notions are conjoined in the persons of fire-licking serpent guardian genii.[484] Protective use of hostile licking is also notable in this religious literature. In the later "Glorifications of Osiris," the deceased is told:

> Your tongue has been assembled as the One who guides the Two Lands, so that it might lick against (*nsb r*) your enemies.[485]

480. CT spell 277, in de Buck 1951, p. 19. Faulkner 1973, pp. 208 and 209, n. 8 understands *nsw.ty.fy rꜣ=f* as "open(?) his mouth." The writing with *ns*, "tongue" suggests a defective spelling of *nsb*, "lick" as in BD spell 149, discussed below.

481. CT spell 316, in de Buck 1951, p. 107 and see Faulkner 1973, pp. 239–40 (who reads *ꜣḫ.t nsbs*). Contra Faulkner, the text should be understood as *ꜣḫ.t nsb=s* (Zandee 1960, p. 137). The verb "lick" is provided with a brazier determinative.

482. BD spell 32, Twenty-first Dynasty, b §S1, in Allen 1974, p. 43. "Lick off my spell" signifies "lick off a spell against me." This spell is designed to repel four crocodiles who come to steal a man's heart and magic, and it repeats the same invocation for the crocodiles of the East and South. The crocodile of the North presumably cannot lick off a spell since he is said to be "wiped" dry.

483. BD spell 149 e, §S2 (Allen 1974, p. 143).

484. Frequently *nsb* has the nuance of "burning" (*Wb* 2: 334/17–18 and Zandee 1960, p. 137). For "licking" guardians, see *Wb* 2: 334/16 and 19, with reference to "Licker," a name of the second underworld portal in BD spell 146 b §S, mistranslated "Wailer," in Allen 1974, p. 134. For the text, see Naville 1886, vol. 2, p. 370, § 5. See also Chassinat 1929a, p. 128 (ll. 12–13) and 1960, pl. LXXXVIII: *Nsbty*, "Licker," a serpent-headed deity whose name incorporates a brazier determinative.

485. Papyrus MMA 35.9.21, col. 20/1, unpublished, hand-copy courtesy of K. Baer. The text is a variant of the "Fourth Book of the Glorifications of Osiris" as categorized by Goyon 1967. In the parallel passage in Pap. Louvre 3079, col. 110/34, Goyon (ibid., p. 98) translates the terms *nsb r* as "darts forth," suggesting serpent imagery.

Probably associated with this hostile technique is the apotropaic gesture of sticking out the tongue, found at all periods with the protective deity Bes, and labeled a derisive act (*qʿns*) in Greco-Roman temple texts.[486]

Magical uses of licking continue unabated in native texts of the Greco-Roman eras, appearing in both the Demotic and Greek language magical compilations. A Demotic example of curative licking is already cited above, and a further instance appears within a revelation ritual (*pḥ-nṯr*) designed to elicit a direct vision of the healing god Imhotep. In Papyrus Louvre E 3229, col. 7, the god is summoned by the traditional method of licking a formula inscribed on the hand (l. 10).[487] The text then instructs the ritualist:

> You should open your mouth to the ground in a cry saying: [...] 'The Sound Eye, the Sound Eye is what I ate.' You should open your mouth to it in order to lick it (or 'when he has licked'). Awake at dawn. You should say: 'Horus is my name. I am Horus the triumphant.'[488]

The surrounding context is fragmentary, and varying interpretations of the ritual scenario are possible. Nonetheless, the recited spell does allude to the injury and restoration of the Sound Eye of the god Horus, who is proclaimed "triumphant" at its conclusion. Given the bivalent qualities of ceremonial licking and swallowing, however, it is unclear whether "eating" the Sound Eye is to be seen as a hostile reenactment of its injury, or as a positive reference to ingesting its efficacy.[489] Correspondingly, licking could be either the physical enactment of the proclaimed consumption, or a remedy for it.

The ritual employment of licking is found in several of the Egyptian magical manuals preserved in the Greek language, and is but one of many indications of the inherently

486. See *Wb* 5: 7/14–15 and the corresponding *Wb Beleg.* 5: 2 (Kom Ombo and Thebes). The idiom properly suggests "spitting" (*qʿ*) with the tongue.

487. J. H. Johnson 1977, p. 73 and 1986e, p. 329. Though the passage is broken, the reference to licking is clear, and the feminine antecedent should refer to "your hand," mentioned in the same line. The text is to be written with myrrh ink.

488. Column 7/11–13 in J. H. Johnson 1977, pp. 73–74 and 1986e, p. 329. The word "lick" (*nsb*) is partially broken in l. 12, but certain. Less certain is the translation of the final clause in the line, which is written *ỉw ns[b]=f* and understood by the editor as a writing of *r nsb=f*, "in order to lick it." Within the sentence, however, the pronouns translated "it" do not agree in gender; the mouth is opened to an object with a feminine antecedent (*r-r=s*), while the pronoun following "lick" is masculine (*f*). The antecedents may be the "hand" (fem.) and "head" (masc.) mentioned in the adjacent broken passages.

489. Compare the "negative" and "positive" consumption of the Eye in CT spell 935: "O NN, I give to you the lesser Eye of Horus, of which Seth ate. O NN, I give to you the Eye of Horus by which your mouth is opened. The pupil that is in the Eye of Horus, eat it. O NN, I give to you the Eye of Horus and you will not be ill(?)"; in de Buck 1961, p. 136 and Faulkner 1978, p. 70.

traditional Egyptian basis of most PGM (*Papyri Graecae Magicae*) ritual.[490] In PGM IV, the so-called "Mithras Liturgy," a spell for a direct revelation incorporates the old mechanism of licking an inscribed magical name so that its power is absorbed.

> Write on a leaf of the persea tree the eight lettered name, as given below. And having kept yourself pure for 3 days in advance, come at morning to face the sunrise; lick off the leaf while you show it to the sun, and then he [the sun god] will listen to you attentively ... Now this is the name: "IEE OO IAI." Lick this up so that you may be protected.[491]

As in Coffin Texts spell 81, approximately two and one half millennia earlier, the licking is performed before the rising sun to elicit the god's favor. Another revelation text in PGM VII expressly combines the related actions of licking and swallowing to achieve the same purpose.

> Write the name in myrrh ink on two male eggs. Regarding one, you are to cleanse yourself thoroughly; then lick off the name, break it, and throw it away. Hold the other in your partially open right hand and show it to the sun at dawn ... Then speak the formula 7 times, crack the egg open, and swallow its contents.[492]

Recalling Ramesside practice in Papyrus Turin 1993, licking and swallowing are here associated as complementary means of internalizing divine force.

In PGM XIII (Papyrus Leiden I 395), the traditional methodology occurs in no fewer than five procedures, entailing the licking of inscribed natron plaques, gold lamellae, and leaves. Three of these instances are found in textual variants of the revelation spell known as "The Eighth Book of Moses," a composition otherwise dependent upon contemporary Egyptian temple cosmologies.[493]

490. Licking is occasionally accorded magical force in Greece; two similar mythological examples are mentioned in Halliday 1967, p. 83 (snakes lick the ears of future prophets, who thereby obtain the ability to understand the language of birds). For the relationship between the Greek and native Egyptian spells, see Ritner 1995.

491. Licking appears in ll. 785 and 789 (Preisendanz 1928, pp. 98–100 and M. W. Meyer 1986, p. 53). The inscription of a sacred name on the persea leaf recalls Thoth's use of the leaves of the *ished*-tree, often identified with the persea, for inscribing the names of kings.

492. The mention of licking is found in l. 522 (Preisendanz 1931, p. 24; and H. Martin 1986, p. 132). The term "male eggs" signifies eggs which will hatch a male offspring (see the discussion by H. Martin ibid., p. 132).

493. Sauneron 1959, pp. 43–44; 1961, pp. 43–48; and 1962b, pp. 268–69. The rite also takes place within an initiation tent (ll. 98, 210, 566, and 652). For the use of tents (as recreations of the sky vault in rites for visions), see BD spells 148 (Twenty-first dynasty) §P7 and 190 §P7, in Allen 1974, pp. 141 and 214 (for initiation) and cf. E. Brugsch 1889. The tent is labeled an "unexplained residuum" of a mystery rite by Morton Smith 1986, p. 174, n. 24. Contra O'Neil 1986, p. 72, no mention of a tent is found in PGM IV, ll. 1949–50, where the term σκῆνος signifies "corpse."

> Have present a mixing bowl containing milk of a black cow and wine not mixed with sea water, for this is the beginning and end. Then, having written the (text of) the stela on the two faces of the natron plaque, lick off the one side, and pouring upon the other, wash it off into the mixing bowl ... Then, before you drink off the milk and wine, say over it this petition.[494]

This standard combination of licking and swallowing a soluble inscription figures prominently in all three versions; there is no need to assume, with Morton Smith, that the techniques are a later insertion.[495] The contrasting symbolism of washing is resumed in a

494. PGM XIII, ll. 128–36. The prohibition of sea water derives from its association with Seth, as noted above. The three versions of "The Eighth Book of Moses" comprise: Text A, ll. 1–230 (licking in l. 132, in Preisendanz 1931, p. 93 and Morton Smith 1986, p. 175); Text B, ll. 343–618 (licking in l. 434, in Preisendanz 1931, p. 109 and Morton Smith 1986, p. 184); and Text C, ll. 646–734 (licking in l. 690, in Preisendanz 1931, p. 118 and Morton Smith 1986, p. 188).

495. Morton Smith 1984. Smith's hypothetical source criticism appears on pp. 687–88. Despite abridgments or reordering of sections, the texts yield a largely consistent ritual order for the licking procedure: recitation of the natron stela (A: ll. 54 and 127; B: ll. 424–25; C: l. 684); licking (A: l. 132; B: l. 435; C: l. 690); washing off the text (A: ll. 132–33; B: ll. 435–36; C: ll. 690–91); petitioning [the intercessor gods of hour and day] (A: ll. 54–55 and 136; B: ll. 424–25 and 440; C: l. 695); drinking the dissolved spell (A: l. 135; B: l. 441; C: l. 694); reclining on a mat (A: l. 136; C: l. 696); and reciting the "Hermetic" spell (A: ll. 138ff.; B: ll. 442ff.; C: ll. 697ff.). Smith's list of textual inconsistencies between the variants (Betz 1986, p. 184, n. 90) conflates the petition of the hour gods with the Hermetic spell. Smith (1984, p. 687) is disturbed by the appearance of the angel intercessor toward the conclusion of B, following the deferred description of the invocation to be written on the natron stela: "to have an angel come at the end of the first invocation and anticipate the god's revelation is structurally anticlimactic and only to be explained by the supposition that there was an earlier, simpler form which used only one invocation, after which, without any licking, drinking, or repetition, the revelation would occur." Despite Smith's discomfort with such an "anticlimax," the appearance of divine intermediaries prior to the main revelation is well attested; compare Pap. London and Leiden, cols. 1/1–3/35, using Anubis (J. H. Johnson 1986c, pp. 195–200). Nor does the deferred placement of the natron text imply that it was originally only a terminal, spoken spell. Its proper position within the ritual is clearly stated (ll. 424–25 and 430), and similar deferral of technical subsections is common in magical texts; cf. the ritual of Pap. London and Leiden, col. 5/1–33 (J. H. Johnson 1986c, pp. 201–03), which appends both its initial invocation and its ointment recipe. Smith's suggestion of an original, simplified version is a non sequitur. Given the great antiquity of the magical techniques of licking and swallowing, it is hardly accurate to suggest that "when the notion came in that the magician must get the prayer inside him before he could utter it, the original form was changed ..." (Smith 1984, pp. 687–88). This notion had "come in" long before "The Eighth Book of Moses" was ever composed.

later prayer, in which the divinity is requested to "wash off from me the evils of fate."[496] An appended revelation procedure for protection and power again recalls Papyrus Turin 1993 in its pairing of amulet and licking.

> It is to the suns (*scil.* dawn, midday, and sunset) of the thirteenth day of the month that one should complete this initiation of the gold lamella, which is licked off and over which one recites: 'IAIA ...' At the initiation, this is said six times with everything else. One writes the 7 vowels on the gold lamella for licking off, and the 7 vowels on the silver one for the phylactery.[497]

A final example in the papyrus occurs in a spell to repel fear and anger, and entails the standard solar blessing and amulet.

> Take a laurel leaf, and write the characters on it thus. Having shown it to the sun, say: 'I call on you ...' When you have said this three times, lick off the leaf, and keep the lamella with you.[498]

The choice of laurel leaf betrays Greek cultural influence, but the procedure is otherwise canonically Egyptian.

This native procedure has now been followed through three millennia, from the Pyramid Texts through the Roman era, and its patterns of ceremonial employment are clear. Where licking serves primarily to transfer saliva, it is but a variant of ritual spitting, and may be construed as a blessing, a cure, or a curse. Where licking serves primarily as a means of consumption, however, it is but a variant of ritual swallowing, employed either to ingest divine force, or to devour hostile figures.

SWALLOWING

The rationale for the technique of magical swallowing is intuitively obvious, being derived by analogic reasoning from the mundane act of eating. Seen strictly from the perspective of actions, there are no distinctions among the simple "physical" swallowing of

496. Text B, l. 613 and cf. Text C, l. 713, in Preisendanz 1931, pp. 116 and 119 and Morton Smith 1986, pp. 187 and 189. Washing (to repel a trait) is here the functional opposite of licking (to absorb a trait). With this technique of "removal" by washing, compare the wiping off of a spell or image drawn on the hand to terminate a vision in two dream oracles of Bes: PGM VII, ll. 222–49 and VIII, ll. 64–110, in Preisendanz 1931, pp. 10 and 50; Grese 1986a, pp. 122–23; and idem 1986b, pp. 147–48. To initiate such a revelation, one might instead lick the image, as in Pap. Louvre E 3229, col. 7, discussed above. For the contrast between licking and wiping, see BD spell 32, Twenty-first Dynasty, b §S1, in Allen 1974, p. 43 (the crocodile of the North cannot lick off a spell, since it has been wiped dry).

497. References to licking are found in ll. 889–90 and 897, in Preisendanz 1931, p. 126 and Morton Smith 1986, p. 192.

498. Licking is mentioned in l. 1051, in Preisendanz 1931, p. 130 and Morton Smith 1986, p. 195. The inscription on the lamella includes the mention of "Ptah, O Health" (transcribed from Egyptian as PHTHA PHOOZA).

food for nourishment, the "medical" swallowing of dates, minerals, or prescriptions, and the "magical" swallowing of enchanted water or dissolved ink. Consumption entails the absorption of an object and the acquisition of its benefits or traits. Alternatively, the act can serve a principally hostile function, whereby "to devour" signifies "to destroy"—though even here the concept of acquiring power may be retained. The technique is interesting not for its explanation, but for its development.[499]

The bond between eating and ritual swallowing is made explicit throughout the offering rituals of the Pyramid Texts, where foodstuffs are often identified with the stolen Eye of Horus. By the implied swallowing of proffered bread, dates, wine, et cetera, the Eye is internalized and thus restored to the recipient's body.[500] A similar notion of "consuming" Horus perhaps underlies Pyramid Texts spell 504:

> If he (*scil.* Re) is pleased with me, he will be pleased with Horus who is on his tongue(?);
> If he is pleased with Horus who is on his tongue(?), he will be pleased with me.[501]

The most famous expression of this general concept appears in the elaborate "Cannibal Hymn" (Pyramid Texts spells 273–74).[502]

> The King is one who eats men and lives on the gods ...
> The King eats their magic, swallows their spirits:
> Their big ones are for his morning meal,
> Their middle ones are for his evening meal,
> Their little ones are for his night meal, ...
> He has smashed bones and marrow,
> He has seized the hearts of the gods, ...
> The King feeds on the lungs of the wise,
> and likes to live on hearts and their magic.[503]

499. See the summary of "magical swallowing" in Ritner 1989b, pp. 106–08 and the brief remarks on ritual "drinking" and "eating" in Heerma van Voss 1984, pp. 31 and 33.

500. E.g., PT spells 43, 46, 51, 53, etc. Such rituals may be the ultimate inspiration for the Demotic recitation of Pap. Louvre E 3229, cited above, p. 99 and n. 488, in which the practitioner "eats" the Eye of Horus and thus becomes "Horus the triumphant." Other rituals in the Pyramid Texts equate the food offering with the fluid of Osiris, milk of Isis, teeth of Horus, etc. In all such cases, the food transfers to the king the numinous qualities of its divine analog. The same technique could benefit hostile forces as well, and in PT spell 57K (§40+11) the king is told to thwart the designs of Seth: "take to yourself the Eye of Horus to prevent it from being consumed" (Faulkner 1969, p. 12).

501. Sethe 1910, p. 101 (§1088b–c); see Faulkner 1969, p. 180. Compare, however, the different interpretation suggested for an image of Maat painted on the tongue, above, p. 88 and n. 419. The translation of PT spell 504 here follows Faulkner, but the reference to *ns*, "tongue," if correct, is surely a pun on *ns*, "throne" mentioned earlier (with proper determinative) in the same spell (Sethe 1901, p. 99 [§1086c]).

502. See above, n. 470.

503. Sethe 1908, pp. 209–14 (§§400–10). For translations of the larger spell, see Faulkner 1969, pp. 80–84; Lichtheim 1972, pp. 36–38, and Altenmüller 1977.

The image recurs throughout the recitations of the Coffin Texts [504] and influences the praxeis of these spells as well. Thus while in spell 612 the reciter may declare that "I have swallowed the seven uraei,"[505] in spell 341 the rubric dictates the literal swallowing of seven Eyes of Horus:

> This spell is to be spoken over seven sketched Sound Eyes,
> dissolved in beer and natron and drunk by a man.[506]

By this technique, the practitioner directly fulfills the standard claims of having "swallowed *ḥkꜣ*," "filled the body with *ḥkꜣ*," or—in one instance—"flooded the body with *ḥkꜣ*."[507] In the same corpus of spells appears perhaps the first instance of an increasingly common idiom expressly linking consumption with acquired familiarity, in which the terms "to taste/taste" (*dp/dp.t*) assume the nuance "to experience/experience": "It goes well with every god of whom I have experience (literally "whom I have tasted")."[508]

In the subsequent New Kingdom spells of the Book of the Dead, the imagery of "eating" and "swallowing" remains prominent, though the accompanying rubrics lack

504. References to swallowing and devouring (magic, gods, and demons) are pervasive, appearing *inter alia* in CT spells 30, 33–35, 36, 37, 239, 241, 650, 689, 1017 (magic eaten and drunk), 248 ("I eat the gods"), 275 (Ennead swallowed), 285 ([as Sobek] "I eat the Great One"), 342 (hostile crocodile threatens to devour magic), 573 (cannibal hymn: "To Eat the Magicians, All of Them"), 839 (Seth eaten as bull), and 863 (dead swallowed). See Speleers 1947, p. 178, note to CT spell 30, §90b.

505. De Buck 1956, p. 225k and Faulkner 1977, p. 199.

506. De Buck 1951, p. 345g–i and Faulkner 1973, p. 276.

507. For claims of the consumption of magic, see the examples in n. 504, above. The notion of bodies "filled with magic" is found already in PT spell 273, §397b: "(The King) is one who eats their entrails, those who come with their bodies filled with magic"; Sethe 1908, p. 207. The reference to "flooding" the body with *ḥkꜣ* appears in CT spell 650; de Buck 1956, p. 272h and Faulkner 1977, p. 225. Not unreasonably, Faulkner takes the writing of *mḥ* with water determinative as an error for the common *mḥ*, "to fill." However, the scribe may well have intended exactly what he wrote (if only as a pun on the stereotyped phrase), as is shown both by the rubric to spell 341 and by references which equate "filling" with drinking: "I have filled my body with *ḥkꜣ*, I have quenched my thirst with it"; CT spell 239, in de Buck 1947, p. 321e–f and Faulkner 1973, p. 188 (identical statement in CT spells 30, 33, 36, and 37). For the contrast between these conceptions and Zande *mangu* or so-called "witchcraft," see n. 93 in *Chapter 1*, above.

508. CT spell 316, in de Buck 1951, p. 108i (and cf. p. 108e) and Faulkner 1973, pp. 239–40, with nn. 30 and 33. For the idiom, see *Wb* 5: 445/7–9 and Klasens 1952, pp. 19 (§M 68) and 78 (Spell 1, §b2, in a "magical" context against scorpion bite: "She has tasted/experienced [the effects of] her utterance"). Contra Klasens, the idiom need not always be unfavorable, as is shown by CT spell 316. An unrecognized example is found in the "Satire on the Trades" (*Dwꜣ-Ḫty*), §6, 1: "I mention to you likewise the mason; painful is his experience {usually translated "loins"}" (Helck 1970, pp. 59 and 63 and Lichtheim 1973, p. 187). The same phrase appears in §7 (Helck 1970, pp. 78 and 82–83).

specific references to ritual consumption.[509] Nonetheless, the mention of swallowing gods "as a potion for death" directly reflects contemporary medical practice, in which prescriptions and fluids were first "charged" with divine force by spells and then swallowed by the patient.[510] The best known example of such a recitation is the generic "Spell for Drinking a Remedy" found near the beginning of the Ebers Papyrus:

> Come, remedy! Come, that which dispels what is in this my heart and in these my limbs! Magic (*ḥkꜣ*) has power over a remedy, and vise-versa! Do you remember that Horus was taken together with Seth to the great palace of Heliopolis when one negotiated regarding the testicles of Seth with Horus? Thus he will be healthy like one who is on earth; he does all that he desires like one who is there (*scil.* 'in the underworld'). Recite when drinking a remedy. Truly effective—(proved) millions of times.[511]

The same practice has already been noted in the ritual of the rather literary Papyrus Turin 1993, in which scorpion poison is neutralized by reciting a lengthy *historiola* over drawn images and scorpion plant, ground up with beer or wine and drunk by the victim.[512] The motif enters literature directly in the "Tale of the Two Brothers," wherein the protagonist Bata is miraculously revived when his excised and desiccated heart swallows water and is in turn swallowed by the lifeless hero. These miracles by which Bata "took in" (literally "swallowed") the condition of life were themselves preceded by miracles whereby the hero's brother "took in" or "comprehended" (literally "swallowed") Bata's lifeless condition.[513] The pun is legitimate, for—in a semantic recognition of a magical principle—

509. Compare BD spells 125, §S1; 125b, §§S 4 and 13; 125c, §S2–3 ("sipping Maat"); 133a, §S2; 134, §S; 153, §S3; 179b, §S3; and 181e, §S2 (NN eats gods and men).

510. See BD spell 153B, b §S (NN swallows god as potion/remedy for death), in Budge 1899, pl. 43a, ll. 12–13; Allen 1974, p. 153; and garbled in Naville 1886, vol. 1, pl. CLXXVIII, ll. 12–13. The term for "remedy" is *sẖbw*, literally "what is swallowed" (*Wb* 4: 269/6), from *sẖb*, "to swallow" (*Wb* 4: 268–69). For its medical applications, see von Deines and Westendorf 1962, pp. 793–94. The divine force of this potion is graphically stated at the conclusion of the section (ll. 18–19): "I have eaten Shu, I have swallowed Shu, I have defecated Shu." Examples of oral remedies activated by spells are gathered by Grapow 1955, pp. 13–21. Selected translations appear in Borghouts 1978, pp. 45–47 (nos. 72, 73, 75, and 76). Examples are numerous, and many more probably await publication; compare O. Turin 57380, seemingly a spell over beer, in López 1982, pp. 26–27 and pls. 118–18a (vo. 2).

511. Column 2, ll. 1–6 (recipe 3) (Grapow 1958, p. 534). A recent translation appears in Borghouts 1978, p. 45 (no. 72).

512. Pleyte and Rossi 1869–76, pls. 77+31, ll. 4–5. See above nn. 337 and 466.

513. Compare Pap. D'Orbiney, cols. 8/6 and 14/1–3, in Gardiner 1932, pp. 18 and 23–24 and Lichtheim 1976, pp. 206 and 208–09. Magical swallowing constitutes a primary motif within this tale. At its conclusion, Bata is again reborn by this technique when the king's favorite becomes pregnant with the hero after swallowing a chip of wood—paralleling the "pregnancy" of Seth in the tale of "Horus and Seth." See Gardiner 1932, pp. 28 ("Two Brothers," col. 18/14–15) and 52–53 ("Horus and Seth," col. 11/11–12).

the verb "to swallow" (*ꜥꜣm*, ) has come to mean "to know."[514] By the Coptic period, this verb (as ⲉⲓⲙⲉ) had effectively supplanted the traditional verb of "knowing" (*rḫ*).[515] If the magical connotations of "swallowing" are both obvious and widely invoked, this yet constitutes a specifically Egyptian development, standing in marked contrast to English and American usage, in which "gullibility" or "swallowing" signifies not intimate knowledge, but foolish belief.

While the equation of "swallowing" and "knowing" may be present in the Book of the Dead,[516] it is certainly in evidence in the royal "Book of the Heavenly Cow," which pairs the verbs *rḫ* and *ꜥꜣm* in parallel phrases when the sun god Re warns against the potential power of magicians "using the magic (*ḥkꜣ.w*) which is in their bodies":

> Moreover, guard against those magicians who know (*rḫ*) their spells, since the god Heka is in them himself. Now as for the one who ingests/knows (*ꜥꜣm*) him, I am there.[517]

From the New Kingdom also derive the earliest attestations of a new genre of curative and apotropaic stelae, the so-called "cippi" depicting "The Enchanter" Shed or Horus (-Shed) vanquishing the terrors of the river and desert as embodied by crocodiles, snakes, scorpions, lions, and gazelles.[518] Often styled "Horus on the Crocodiles" after their most common feature, these stelae may be traced from the Eighteenth Dynasty through the Roman era, with survivals among Byzantine Christian amulets as well.[519] Typically, these stelae depict the youthful god Horus standing atop (and thus trampling)[520] two or more crocodiles, while firmly grasping in each hand an assortment of noxious animals suspended

514. Compare *Wb* 1: 183–84: "to swallow" and 184/4 and 16–21: "to know."

515. Crum 1939, p. 77b; Westendorf 1965–77, p. 49; Černý 1976, pp. 46–47; Vycichl 1983, pp. 62–63, questions the relationship without justification.

516. See the demon "Knower of Stelae," whose name is restored in the late "Ancient Egyptian Book of Hours" col. 33/19 (Faulkner 1958, pp. 23 and 53*) on the basis of BD spell 125b, S4: "The Swallower/Knower of Shadows who has come forth from the cavern" (Allen 1974, p. 98).

517. See verses 218–20 in Hornung 1982, pp. 20 (text) and 44 (translated differently). See also above, p. 23 and n. 95, and below, pp. 202–03 and n. 938. For the suggested New Kingdom date of this text, see Hornung 1982, pp. 79–81.

518. The basic studies are Lacau 1921–22; Daressy 1903; Kákosy 1980a; and Traunecker 1983. Further bibliography and discussion appear in Ritner 1989b; Kákosy 1980b; idem 1987; Quaegebeur 1987; Satzinger 1987; Sternberg-el-Hotabi 1989; and Hodjash and Berlev 1982, pp. 244–74 (excellent bibliography, pp. 244–45). For the Sethian significance of the desert animals, see below, *Chapter 4*, nn. 583 and 743. See also nn. 135 and 144, above, and 685, below.

519. For late survivals, see the references in Ritner 1989b, p. 114.

520. For the significance of the motif, see the discussion of "trampling," in *Chapter 4*, below, pp. 119–36.

harmlessly by the tail.[521] As the god tramples, inverts, and throttles these hostile forces, he is surrounded by a cadre of supporting deities, and a canonical series of engraved texts. The popularity of the stelae extended from court to commoner, with larger examples erected before temple compounds as public benefactions for the cure of animal bite. Such community stelae were often incorporated within "healing statues" that depicted a cippus clasped by the donor, whose image was virtually blanketed with protective spells. Despite the standard presence of these curative texts, the primary method of utilizing the stelae and statues involved not reading, but ingested water. Water poured over the stela or statue absorbed the efficacy of the spells and images and was subsequently drunk by the sufferer. Smaller, portable cippi may have been immersed in bowls of water, but larger healing statues and stelae were provided with shallow basins to collect this curative water, and similar receptacles are indicated at a healing shrine at Karnak by the remains of inset basins, conduits, and jars.[522] This association is particularly obvious on a little-known cippus example in Cairo, carved directly on the side of a stone vase, [523] while the texts of the Tyszkiewickz healing statue in the Louvre explicitly designate the patient as "this man who drinks this water."[524] The water's restorative function may well be twofold on donated stelae—serving both as medicine for the patient and as a libation for the spirit of the donor.[525]

Late association of consumption with knowledge extends well beyond the common use of cippi. Thus, the theological proclamations of the coffin of Ankhnesneferibre, daughter of Psammetichus II and God's Wife of Amon, include an address to deified "Perception" (Sia) as "the Great Swallower."[526] Demotic references to the technique of magical swallowing are among the most significant attestations of this long-standing native practice. The semantic pairing of "eating" and "knowing" surfaces even in a legal document of the Ptolemaic period,[527] and from the same era derives the most explicit Egyptian description of the magical procedure. In the tale of Setna I, a revived mummy details the means by which written spells were made effective for the illiterate:

521. Compare CT spell 885: "The snake is in my hand and cannot bite me"; de Buck 1961, p. 97 and Faulkner 1978, p. 49.

522. See Lacau 1921–22, pp. 189–209; Traunecker 1983, pp. 74–75; and Sternberg-el-Hotabi 1987, p. 28.

523. Cairo Museum 18490, in von Bissing 1907, pp. 97–98 and pl. 3; Daressy 1893, p. 38 (no. LIX); and Gauthier 1916, p. 75 (no. XXXVII). The inscription is dated to the reign of Psammetichus I.

524. Lefebvre 1931, pp. 89–96.

525. Satzinger 1987, pp. 189–204.

526. Sander-Hansen 1937, p. 49, ll. 98–99 (*Si3 twt ʿm3 wr*).

527. See Pap. Cairo 30647, l. 6, in Sethe and Partsch 1920, p. 9: "Comprehend/learn my acceptance" (*wnm t3y=y mt n šp*, literally "Eat my speech of accepting").

> I read another formula of writing ... though I cannot write. I was speaking with regard to my elder brother Naneferkaptah, who is a good scribe and a very wise man. He caused that a new sheet of papyrus be brought before him. He wrote down every word that was on the papyrus, completely. He burned it with fire; he dissolved it with water. He recognized that it had dissolved; he drank it and he knew that which was in it.[528]

In the succeeding Roman era, the second tale of Setna revives the terminology of the Coffin Texts by describing a powerful Nubian magician as "swallowing magic."[529] Actual swallowing of "magical potions" remained a commonplace, and specific recipes for such philters are found throughout the Demotic magical corpus.[530]

The same praxis is adopted in Egyptian magical texts redacted in the Greek language. Coupled with ritual licking, the methodology has already been noted in PGM VII (third to fourth centuries) and in recurrent variants throughout PGM XIII (fourth century).[531] As an independent action in the latter papyrus, the eating of drawn figures constitutes a preliminary "initiation" (*scil.* "intimate knowledge and control") of the ruling decans who determine the success of the larger procedure:

528. Griffith 1985, pp. 104–06 (col. 4/1–4) and Lichtheim 1980, p. 131. Both Griffith and Lichtheim mistranslate "He filled/soaked it with beer" for "He filled/burned it with fire" (*mḥ=f s m sty*). For the text, see Spiegelberg 1906, pl. 45, col. 4/4.

529. Setna II, col. 6/5, in Griffith 1985, pp. 194–95 and Lichtheim 1980, p. 148. Griffith, followed by Lichtheim, ignores the traditional phraseology and translates *ỉw=f ʿm m ḥyq* as "he being crammed with magic." Like the older "Tale of the Two Brothers," this story combines puns on "swallowing magic" with references to miraculous portents produced by items to be swallowed (beer, wine). The incident is related by, but not of, Setna's son, Si-Osire; one must correct the attribution in Ritner 1989b, p. 107.

530. Compare the potions using a divinized (drowned) shrewmouse in Pap. London and Leiden, col. 13/11–12 and 19–20 (poison), 17–19 (love philter), a divinized hawk in col. 13/21–22, and an elaborate love spell in col. 15/1–23, in Griffith and Thompson 1904, pp. 94–97 and 104–07. Representative healing potions are found in col. 19/10–40, in Griffith and Thompson, ibid., pp. 124–29.

531. Compare nn. 492–95, above. Swallowing occurs in PGM VII, l. 527 (Preisendanz 1931, p. 24 and H. Martin 1986, p. 132). The variants in PGM XIII appear in ll. 133–35, 432–41, and 690–94 in Preisendanz 1931, pp. 93, 109, and 118–19 and Morton Smith 1986, pp. 175, 184, and 188. See also the references in Fowden 1986, p. 60, n. 48.

> You will be initiated to them thusly. Make three figures from fine flour: one bull-faced, one goat-faced, one ram-faced, each standing atop a celestial sphere, having an Egyptian flail. And when you have censed them, eat them while saying the spell for the gods of the hours ... and you will have been initiated to them.[532]

In the subsequent century, PGM CI (fifth century) conjures by the power of the blood drunk by Seth,[533] while the yet later PGM C (fifth to sixth centuries) continues the traditional practice of dissolving spells (ἀπόλυσον), while invoking the newly-fashionable name of Christ.[534]

The Mosaic adultery curse in Numbers 5:11–31 had already given early Christians a legal precedent for ritual use of liquids charged with the force of a spell.[535] Ascribed to God's commands to Moses, this test of female fidelity was sworn over an earthenware bowl filled with clean "water of contention," in which had been dissolved one-tenth of an *ephah* (< Egyptian *oipe*-measure) of barley meal ("the grain-offering of jealousy"), sacred dust from the Tabernacle floor, and the ink-written words of a curse washed from a scroll by a priest:

> The priest shall write these curses on a scroll and wash them off into the water of contention; he shall make the woman drink the water that brings out the truth, and the water shall enter her body.[536]

Should the swearer prove adulterous, the ingested curse is activated, and illicit pregnancy is terminated by miscarriage or untimely birth. While this procedure seems most at home among Egyptian practices conventionally termed "magical," its canonization within Hebrew scripture well illustrates the arbitrary and capricious nature of the "religion" versus "magic" dichotomy. Had this orthodox ritual been recorded in any other context, it would

532. PGM XIII, ll. 31–37, in Preisendanz 1931, p. 89 and Morton Smith 1986, p. 173. The notion—like the technique—of initiation is here purely Egyptian, corresponding to the meanings and uses of the native concept *bs*, *Wb* 1: 473–74. The papyrus contains other examples of swallowing for magical effect. Ritualized "tasting" of sacrifices appears in ll. 376–79, in Preisendanz 1931, p. 107 and Morton Smith 1986, p. 182. A philter is detailed in ll. 319–20, in Preisendanz 1931, p. 103 and Morton Smith 1986, p. 181.

533. The designation PGM CI follows Betz 1986, pp. 307–08. For the exhortation "by the blood that the great god Iothath took" (ll. 20ff.) see Betz 1986, p. 308; Wortmann 1968a, pp. 85–102; and the full discussion in idem 1968b, pp. 227–30.

534. The designation PGM C follows Betz 1986, p. 307, where the significance of the word "dissolve" is not understood (n. 4). The original edition appears in Wortmann 1968a, pp. 102–04 (text 5), where an apt comparison is made with the technique of the Horus cippi (p. 103).

535. The adultery curse has been studied in detail by Brichto 1975, pp. 55–70 and Frymer-Kensky 1984, pp. 11–26 (references courtesy Martha Roth).

536. Numbers 5:23–24.

unquestionably be dismissed as "magic" antithetical to "religious" convention.[537] In both orthodox and "magical" contexts, the consumption of sanctified fluids becomes a standard feature of Coptic religious practice; particularly graphic examples of swallowed phlegm and bath water are quoted above.[538] Enchanted cups[539] designed to instill divine praise form a surreptitious counterpart to the sacrament of the mass—which itself evokes the consumption of deity once canonical in the Pyramid Texts. Heterodox Christianity was no less influenced by the ancient technique, and the Gnostic *topos* of "drinking down knowledge" clearly reflects the Egyptian conception here traced from its earliest sources.[540] The technique easily survived the Arabic conquest as well, and continues to the present in the common folk custom of drinking curative powder scraped from ancient temple walls.[541]

537. The obvious affiliation of this "ordeal" with general concepts of "magic" necessitated the remarks of Brichto (1975, p. 65), who defends this law from the accusation of "magic" because the ultimate actor is said to be God. The ultimate actor of all Egyptian "magic" is similarly God (Heka). Frymer-Kensky (1984, p. 25) also attempts to impart a moral basis to this ritual, yet concedes that the potion of Numbers 5 should be classified among "ritual, symbolic or 'magical' actions which effectuate the oath."

538. See nn. 437–40, above.

539. E.g., London Ms. Or. 6794, in Kropp 1930–31, vol. 2, pp. 104–09.

540. See Fowden 1986, p. 60, n. 48 (with further bibliography).

541. See Traunecker 1987. This practice of gouging walls and reliefs for curative powder is attested from dynastic times to the present.

CHAPTER 4

IMAGES AND INTERMEDIARIES

Witchcraft by a Picture

I fixe mine eyes on thine, and there
Pitty my picture burning in thine eye,
My picture drown'd in a transparent teare,
When I looke lower I espie;
Hadst thou the wicked skill
By pictures made and mard, to kill,
How many wayes mightst thou perform thy will?

But now I have drunke thy sweet salt teares,
And though thou poure more I'll depart;
My picture vanish'd, vanish feares,
That I can be endamag'd by that art;

Though thou retaine of mee
One picture more, yet that will bee,
Being in thine owne heart, from all malice free.

John Donne

Sister Helen

"Why did you melt your waxen man,
Sister Helen?
To-day is the third since you began."

• • •

"Oh the waxen knave was plump to-day,
Sister Helen;
How like dead folk he has dropped away!"

Dante Gabriel Rossetti

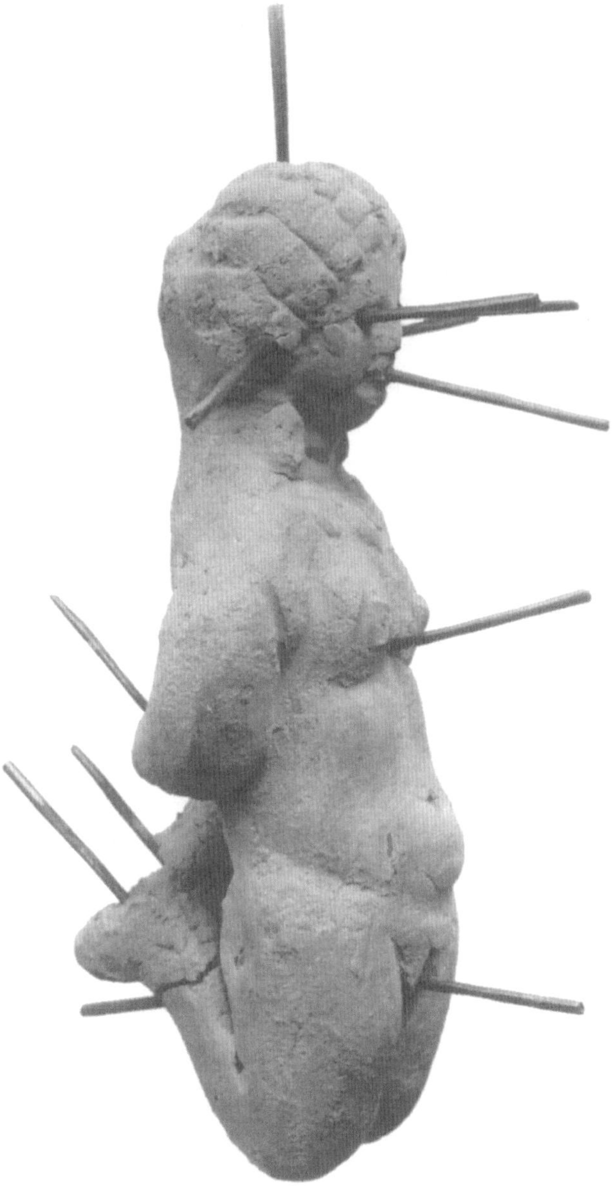

Figure 2. Roman Period Clay Figurine (Louvre inv. E 27145).

No discussion of the rites of magic can fail to consider what is perhaps its most universally recognized practice: the manipulation of images. Readily familiar as a mainstay of medieval European sorcery (and numerous Hollywood movies), the ubiquitous "voodoo doll"[542] provides a perfect embodiment of our working definition of magic as action which ignores the ordinary laws of "cause and effect." The principles of the act are well known and intuitively obvious; punishment inflicted upon the doll (by pins, etc.)

542. The popular association of the "voodoo doll" with Haiti is actually erroneous; see W. Davis 1985, p. 208.

produces an analogous result upon the victim with whom it is identified (by attached personal effects, name, etc.). The existence of an identical practice in Egypt is documented by numerous examples, the most striking of which is a clay figurine in the Louvre of a bound female pierced by thirteen nails (see fig. 2) which was found near Antinoopolis in a clay vase with an inscribed lead plate, or lamella.[543] Both the figure and its accompanying Greek inscription correspond directly to a procedure described in the great magical papyrus preserved in the Bibliothèque Nationale of Paris (PGM IV, ll. 296–466) in which the magician is instructed as follows:

> Take wax {or clay} from a potter's wheel and make two figures, a male and a female. Make the male in the form of Ares, fully armed, holding a sword in his left hand and threatening to plunge it into the right side of her neck. And make her with her arms behind her back and down on her knees. And you are to attach the 'personal effects' (ουσια) to her head or neck ... And take thirteen copper needles and stick one in the brain while saying, 'I am piercing your brain, NN'; and stick 2 in the ears and 2 in the eyes and 1 in the mouth and 2 in the midriff and 1 in the hands and 2 in the sexual organs and 2 in the soles, saying each time, 'I am piercing such and such a member of her, NN, so that she may remember no one but me, NN, alone.'[544]

Despite the Greek language of the text, the intrusive appearance of Ares, and the Roman date (third to fourth centuries) of both papyrus and figurine, the rite here described is not of Greek origin, but instead represents the culmination of an indigenous Egyptian tradition whose origins are contemporary with the creation of Egyptian civilization itself. The posture and material of the female figurine, and even the detailed attitude of the missing Ares figure, attest to the millennia old tradition from which they derive. To trace the development of this tradition, and the position of the Louvre figurine within it, one must first examine the techniques not of private but of royal magic, attested from the earliest remains of ancient Egypt.

THE BOUND PRISONER MOTIF

In a predynastic royal tomb of Gerzean date (ca. 3400–3200 B.C.) at Hierakonpolis (modern Kom el-Aḥmar) was discovered a wall painting whose wide-ranging subject matter provides the first examples of numerous artistic themes which were to become canonical throughout the remainder of Egyptian history. Among these images to be standardized is the representation of a victorious ruler in the act of striking a series of

543. Louvre inv. E 27145 (du Bourguet 1975, pp. 255–57 and 1980, pp. 225–38 and pls. 34–38).

544. PGM IV, ll. 295–329 (Preisendanz 1928, pp. 82–83). The accompanying text is published in Kambitsis 1976, pp. 213–23 and pls. 30–31.

a

b 

c 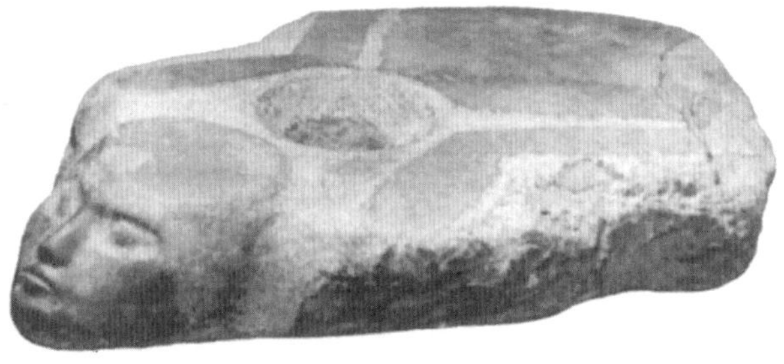

Figure 3. (*a*) Hierakonpolis Wall Painting, Scene of Smiting Kneeling Bound Prisoners (after Kantor 1974, p. 252, fig. 213b); (*b*) White Quartz Figure of Bound Prisoner with Drill Hole in Neck (Archaic Period, from Abydos; after H. W. Müller 1964, fig. A55, and Basel Museum 1978, fig. 99b); and (*c*) Door Socket in Form of Bound Prisoner from Hierakonpolis.

kneeling, bound captives (see fig. 3a).[545] With hands secured behind their backs and necks linked by rope, these captives are paralleled by similar representations on roughly contemporary votive cosmetic palettes, ivory cylinders, and maceheads.[546] It is highly significant that all of these images were found within the religious context of temple and tomb, and appear on every genre of "luxury item" donated to the gods in predynastic Egypt. The reason for their appearance is not difficult to discover, and is explicitly presented on the famous Narmer palette of Dynasty "0" from the temple precinct of Hierakonpolis.[547] On the "recto" of this palette, as the standing king grasps his kneeling enemy by the hair and raises his mace to strike, he faces the falcon god Horus who stands atop an anthropomorphic symbol of the defeated territory with its head tethered by a rope held in the god's claw. In both posture and meaning, the acts of king and god are identical. The victory of the king, as the god's representative on earth, is *ipso facto* the victory of the god. Conversely, the political opponents of the king are transgressors against the god, demonic agents of chaos and death in an unending holy war. The king's sacrifice of the kneeling captive, like the palette which records it, is offered to the god not to commemorate the conquest, but to perpetuate it. Rendered tangible and permanent in stone, the image was designed not simply to reflect, but to create reality, guaranteeing by "sympathetic magic" the victory of the state and the gods. So pervasive was this image to become, that the exterior walls of virtually every Egyptian temple were provided with a rendition of the scene, which rapidly acquired more of a ritual than an historical validity.[548] The fully developed motif is exemplified by the great pylon of Medinet Habu, on which Ramses III sacrifices prisoners before Amon, while the base line upon which both stand is composed of a series of anthropomorphic symbols of foreign lands, which are crushed underfoot by king and god alike in imitation of Horus on the Narmer palette.[549] Forming a

545. For a bibliography of the wall painting, a discussion of its date, and the importance of its themes, see Kantor 1974, pp. 251–52; adding Kaiser 1958, pp. 183–92 and Kemp 1973, pp. 36–43. For the bound captives, see Kantor 1974, p. 252 and fig. 213b.

546. For examples, compare the "Bull" and "Battlefield" palettes in Ridley 1973, pp. 37–42 and Kantor 1974, pp. 249–50 and fig. 212a. For ivory cylinders, see Quibell 1900, p. 7 and pl. 15. On maceheads, prisoners appear in groups joined at the neck by rope in Quibell, ibid., p. 7 and pl. 12 (fig. 4), and individually as a kneeling, bound figure on the Narmer macehead in Quibell, ibid., pl. 26B and Ridley 1973, p. 68. On an "archaic" period celt from Saqqara, see Weigall 1907, p. 43.

547. See Quibell 1900, pl. 29 and Ridley 1973, pp. 47–53.

548. See the remarks of Gardiner (1961, pp. 56–57) on the fictional reuse of battle scenes. The development of "smiting scenes" has been much discussed (see Hall 1986; idem 1983; Anthes 1930; Schulman 1988, pp. 8–115, and the bibliographic synopsis in Wildung 1977b). For the theoretical basis of the royal act and its liturgical nature, see Hornung 1966 and Derchain 1962a.

549. See The Epigraphic Survey 1932, pl. 101.

"protective bulwark" for both the temple and the cosmos which it represented, the sacrificial triumph is performed directly by the god Horus himself at the Ptolemaic temple of Edfu.[550] The latest example extant is from Esna, and depicts the Roman emperor Titus (A.D. 79–81) in the role of pharaoh.[551] Within two centuries, the conqueror was to be cast as Ares, and the kneeling, bound prisoner as the Louvre figurine.

The transmission of this omnipresent motif from carved relief to figurine by no means represents an innovation of Roman times, however. From the earliest temple sector in Abydos, and dated to the First or Second Dynasty, derive two small stone figurines in a Lucerne collection which depict kneeling prisoners with their hands bound behind their backs.[552] On one of these carvings (A 55), the neck is drilled to permit the captive to be suspended from a string (see fig. 3b). The figure is thus a three-dimensional rendering of the image found on the Hierakonpolis wall-painting and the predynastic palettes, being designed to enable the possessor to have his enemy physically by the throat.[553] That the use of such statuettes was not isolated is shown by the discovery at Hierakonpolis of a similar figure in glazed pottery of equal date.[554] As in the case of the palettes, these were presumably votive objects for the benefit of god and king.

Designed more specifically for royal benefit are the numerous stone statues of prisoners discovered within the funerary complex of Pepi I.[555] Clearly distinguished by their physiognomy as Nubians, Libyans, or Asiatics, the statues do not represent individual enemies, but serve instead as symbols of the neighbors, and thus traditional enemies, of Egypt. Greatly enlarged in scale from their predynastic predecessors, these Old Kingdom statues of waist height form an *architectural* element of the royal funerary temple.[556] Their

550. See Derchain 1961, pp. 47–49.

551. Porter and Moss 1939, p. 117. For the longer continuity of the motif in sculpture and terracotta, see Hall 1983 and the references in Wildung 1977b, cols. 16–17.

552. See H. W. Müller 1964, p. 38, figs. A 54 and A 55, and Basel Museum 1978, figs. 99a and 99b.

553. Compare the depiction of enemies symbolized as *rḫy.t*-birds hung by the neck on the Narmer macehead in Quibell 1900, pl. 26C (fig. 1); and the Old Kingdom clay figures discussed in Osing 1976a, p. 156 and pl. 5.

554. See Quibell 1900, p. 8 and pls. 21 (figs. 2–3) and 22 (fig. 3).

555. See Lauer and Leclant 1969, pp. 55–62; Lauer 1969–70, pp. 37–45 and pls. 1–3; and Leclant 1979, p. 8 and pls. 16–17.

556. The architectural role of the statues is discussed in Lauer 1969–70, pp. 43 and Bothmer 1982, pp. 27–39. For further examples from the Old Kingdom, see Lansing 1947, pp. 149–52 (Sixth Dynasty) and Hayes 1990, vol. 1, pp. 113–16. Such statues are attested as early as the Fifth Dynasty at the pyramid complexes of Niuserre and Unas (Hayes ibid., vol. 1, p. 115), and small wooden examples have now been discovered at the Abusir temple of Neferefre (Verner 1985, pp. 145–52).

religious significance derives simply from the fact of their existence—as concrete expressions of foreign subjugation.[557]

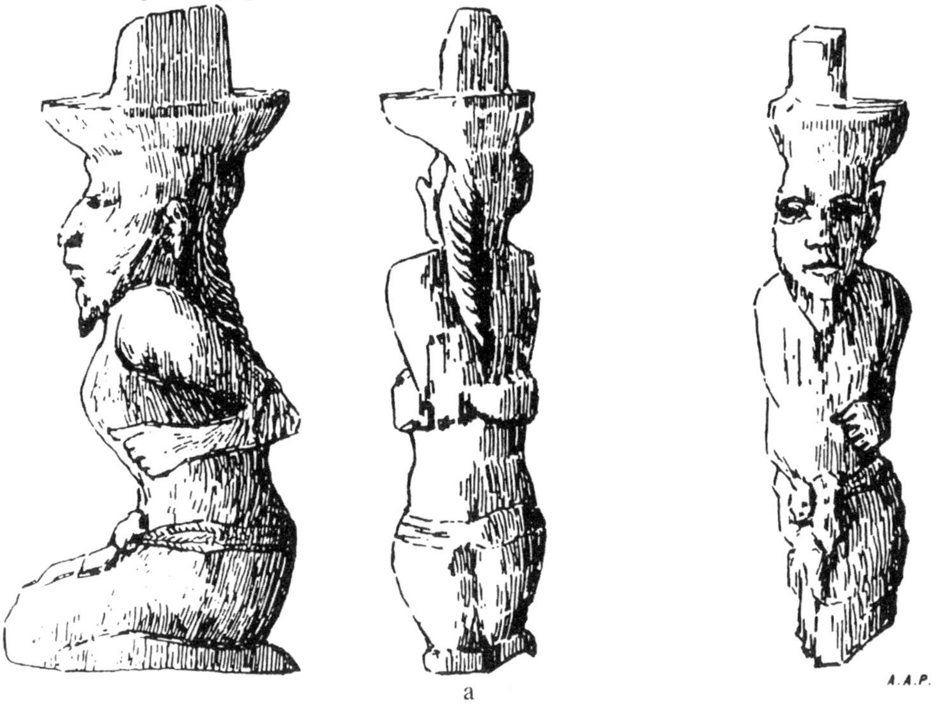

a

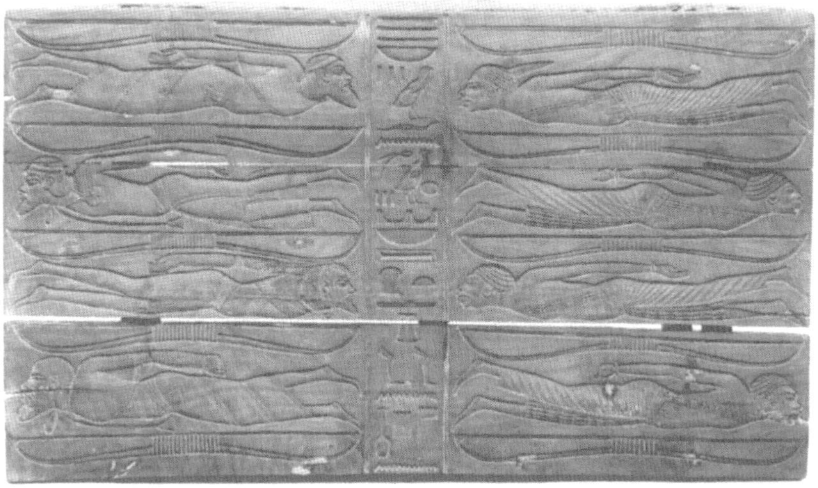

b

Figure 4. (a) Chair Support in Form of Bound Prisoner from Hierakonpolis (after Quibell 1900, pl. 11) and (b) Splayed Details of Tutankhamun's Footstool.

The same conception underlies a parallel development of the use of such figures not as free standing statues, but as "decorative" elements in a larger composition or construction which emphasizes their subservient role. The origin of this motif may be traced to the

557. Suggestions that the statues were ritually smashed have been refuted by Lauer 1969–70, pp. 37–45. For likely Old Kingdom mutilations, see Tefnin 1991.

design of a door socket found in situ in the First Dynasty temple at Hierakonpolis (see fig. 3c). Representing a prostrate captive with his arms tied firmly behind his back at the elbows, the door socket supports the peg of the door leaf by a hole bored into the middle of the prisoner's back.[558] The motif of the simple "voodoo doll" has here become architecturally ritualized. With peg for pin, the figure is pierced not once but eternally; for with every motion of the door leaf, the peg is ground deeper into the back of the hapless prisoner. The complement to this representation is found in a description of a door socket in hell, written in the second Demotic romance of Setna Khamuas. Within an episode often compared to the parable of Dives and Lazarus, the heroes visit the underworld to witness the outcome of the funerals of a poor and a wealthy man. On entering the fifth portal of the netherworld, the heroes find that "the pivot of the door of the fifth hall was fixed in the right eye of a man who was pleading and lamenting loudly."[559] The recipient of this fate was the wealthy man, whose impious acts on earth qualify him as an enemy of the gods, and the counterpart of the terrestrial enemy of gods and king depicted in the First Dynasty door socket.

> They found his misdeeds more numerous than the good deeds which he had done on earth. It was ordered to imprison him in the netherworld. He is [the man whom you saw] with the pivot of the door of the netherworld fixed in his right eye, so that it opens and shuts on his eye, and his mouth is open in great lamentation.[560]

Separated by over three millennia and bracketing virtually the entirety of Egyptian history, these two representations are all but identical in outward form. The fundamental difference between them is the result of a gradual, internal religious modification, whereby the ethical misdeeds of an individual have come to outweigh the political misdeeds of a foreign enemy.[561] The ethically recast imagery of the Setna tale was in turn influential and is still invoked in ninth century Coptic stories of the miscreant Symmachus: "The tormentor

558. University Museum Philadelphia, no. E 3959 (Gunn 1934, pp. 9, 12–13 and pls. 6–7; Quibell 1900, p. 6 and pl. 3; and Pritchard 1954, pp. 234 and 338, fig. 750). Two more such sockets in the collection of the University College London are signaled by Quibell 1900, p. 6.

559. Setna II, 2/3 (Lichtheim 1980, p. 140).

560. Setna II, 13–15 (Lichtheim 1980, p. 141).

561. Quibell 1900, p. 6, suggests that similar threats against evil doers are found in the Book of the Dead, and he is followed by Zandee 1960, p. 299. However, neither Quibell nor Zandee provide examples of such punishment—despite the extremely thorough examination of underworld tortures by the latter. Although no clear examples are known to me from the Book of the Dead, a previously unrecognized example may be found in CT spell 1132 (de Buck 1961, p. 474), a description of an underworld gate in the "Book of the Two Ways": "A gate which has fire in front and is hidden behind, in which there is a man who is bound." For translations of the passage, see Faulkner 1978, p. 170 and Lesko 1972, p. 25. For bound prisoners beneath the scale of judgment, see Barguet 1961, pp. 7–10.

answered and said: 'When I die, may the pupil of my right eye be set under the hinge of the gate of Hell.'"[562]

TRAMPLING UNDERFOOT

The perpetual subservience of bound captives, so graphically expressed in the Hierakonpolis door socket, becomes a generalized motif for the decoration of a wide variety of structural supports. Contemporary with the door socket, and deriving from the same temple precinct, is an ivory figure of a kneeling bound captive which served as the foot of a ceremonial chair (see fig. 4a).[563] The chair's occupant would thus rest upon the back of the prisoner exactly as the god Horus had perched atop the conquered enemy on the Narmer palette. Two Second Dynasty statues of an enthroned figure of king Khasekhemwy from the same site reveal an elaboration of this theme. Running along the base of the statues, below the feet and chair of the king, a sprawling jumble of enemies is carved lying prostrate in slaughter, crushed beneath the feet of the monarch.[564] The trampling underfoot of the enemy, depicted unambiguously here, becomes a permanent feature of Egyptian royal seated (and striding) statues—with a slight modification. Replacing the literal images of the vanquished enemies is a series of Nine Bows, the symbols of the traditional foes of Egypt, carved as if protruding from beneath the feet of the ruler.[565] In conformity with the divine prototype of the image, statues of the king as Osiris may display the same feature.[566] Figures of trussed captives (often tied to the symbol of the unification of Upper and Lower Egypt) continue to appear, however, upon

562. From the "Martyrdom of Shenoufe and his Brethren" (118 vii. 24–25); Reymond and Barns 1973, pp. 102 and 202. The passage is paralleled in the "Martyrdom of Epima" (folio 46 vo.; see Mina 1937, pp. 26 and 71, with n. 4).

563. Quibell 1900, p. 7 and pl. 11. For older discussion, see Capart 1904, pp. 166–67 and 190–91.

564. Quibell 1900, pls. 39–40. For discussion, see Junker 1955, pp. 162–75, with which compare Nelson 1931, pp. 12–21.

565. The motif appears at least as early as the Third Dynasty on statuary of Djoser (Firth 1926, p. 99 and pl. 1A). For later examples, compare Borchardt 1925, pp. 5 (386), 7 (389), and 33 (429) and Legrain 1906, pls. 2, 4, 8, 14, 17, 29, and 49. A general discussion of the motif appears in Uphill 1967, pp. 393–420; for further bibliography, see Wildung 1977c and Valbelle 1990.

566. Borchardt 1925, p. 33 (429).

ornate royal thrones, podiums, hassocks, and statue bases of the New Kingdom.[567] The decoration of the wooden footstool of Tutankhamun consists exclusively of such prisoners and bows,.outstretched to receive the royal tread (see fig. 4b).[568] The logical extension of this practice is reached in the decoration of the same king's sandals, the soles of which depict the traditional bows and abject enemies whom Tutankhamun would crush underfoot with every step (see fig. 6a).[569] The king's cane, with its handle in the form of two recurved captives, provided an accompaniment to the design of the sandals, allowing the ruler visually to throttle and trample his foes simultaneously (see fig. 5).[570] In the Roman period, such designs on sandals would reappear, painted on the bottom of the cartonnage footboards of mummies to ensure the victory of the deceased over his potential enemies in

567. For examples of bound prisoners on thrones and podiums, see the representations in Radwan 1969, pls. 11–12 and 15; Metzger 1985, vol. 2, pls. 18 (fig. 111), 19 (fig. 117), 20 (figs. 125–27 as *rḫy.t*), 23 (figs. 162–63), 25 (fig. 176), 29 (fig. 195), 32 (figs. 231–32), 33 (figs. 234–36), and 34 (figs. 237–39); compare the inlays in Hayes 1990, vol. 2, p. 318. Royal throne rooms feature captives on dais, pavement, and podium stairs (Hayes 1937, pp. 12–13; Fisher 1917, pp. 218 and 221, fig. 82; and O'Connor and Silverman 1979, p. 25, fig. 36). Actual bases preserved at Karnak are discussed in Habachi 1938, pp. 69–70 (= Porter and Moss 1972, p. 59) and Legrain 1917, p. 27 (= Porter and Moss 1972, p. 43, no. 149). For the hassock of Tutankhamun, see Carter 1933, pl. 69 and Bosse-Griffiths 1975, p. 117 and pl. 17. For statue bases, see Wildung 1973, pp. 108–16 and Scheurleer 1984, pp. 73–74. Small faience images of prisoners (inlays from furniture?) have also been recovered from Amarna (Petrie et al. 1974, pl. 17, fig. 292 and Samson 1978, p. 88 and pl. 6). Wooden figures of a lion and prisoner (from a model chair?) derive from a late New Kingdom private burial at Saqqara; Quibell 1908, p. 79 and pl. 35 (fig. 3).

568. For the footstool of Tutankhamun, see Desroches-Noblecourt 1963, pp. 51 and 296. This footstool is paralleled by representations of those of Amenhotep II and III in Metzger 1985, vol. 1, pp. 91–93 and vol. 2, pl. 40 (figs. 272–73).

569. See Edwards 1976b, unnumbered plate; el Mallakh and Brackman 1978, p. 297, fig. 151.

570. For the canes with their Asiatic and Nubian figures, see Desroches-Noblecourt 1963, pp. 82 and 298; el Mallakh and Brackman 1978, p. 296, figs. 1148–49.

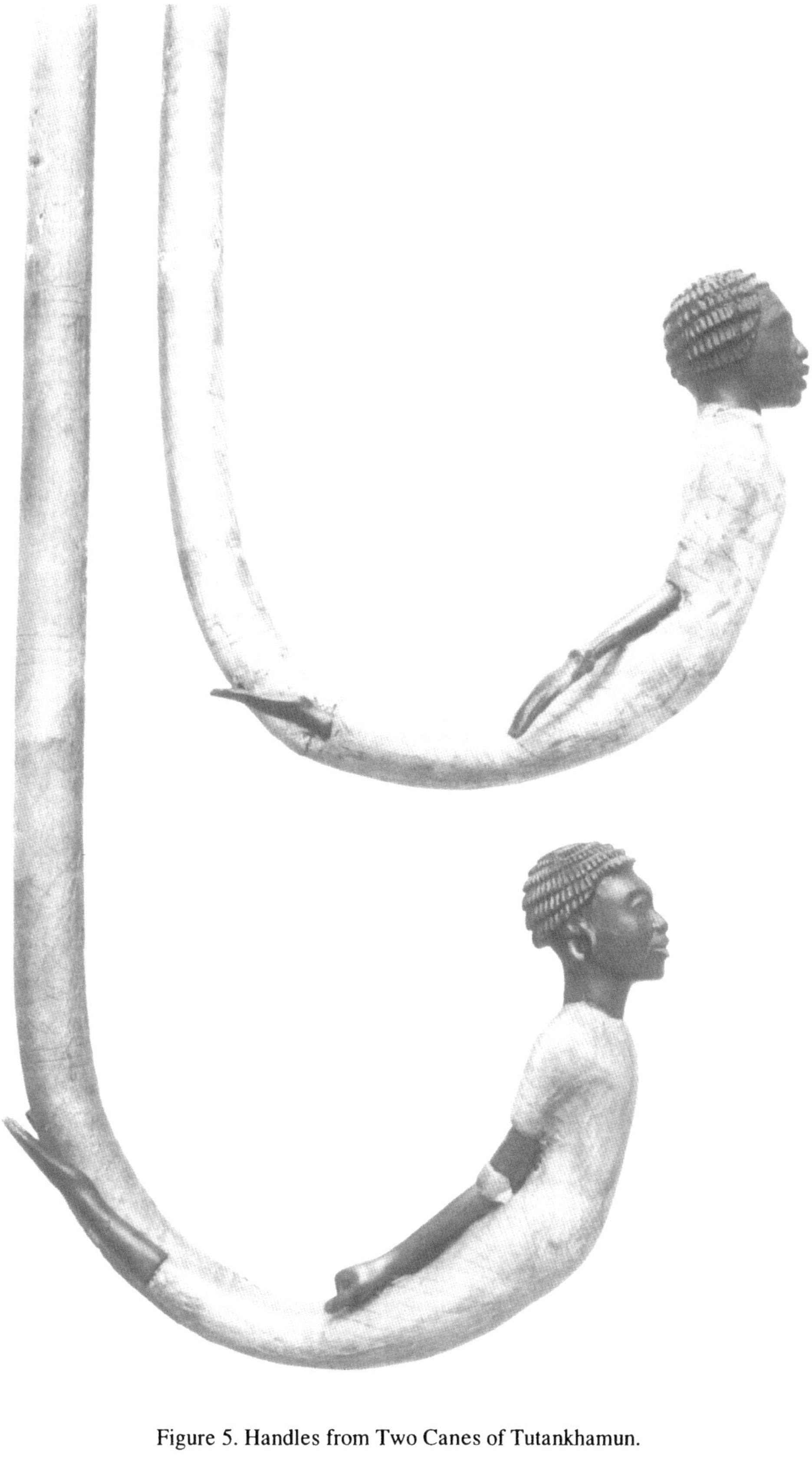

Figure 5. Handles from Two Canes of Tutankhamun.

this world and the next (see fig. 6b).[571] These Roman examples attest to the durability of the "magico-religious" component of the motif, and suggest that its force was felt even where the image might seem to serve largely decorative purposes. Thus should probably be explained the heads of captives on the base of an unguent jar from the tomb of Tutankhamun (see fig. 9), or the use of a prostrate figure as a handle on the lid of a stone box of Sheshonq III.[572]

Among the more unusual representations of the motif is its appearance upon the linchpins of the chariot wheels of Ramses II in the form of an Asiatic head bitten by a lion,

571. Simpson 1973, pp. 50–54; idem 1972a, pp. 113–22; Brovarski 1987, pp. 74–75 (MFA 1971.217); Edgar 1905, pp. 78 (Cairo 33220) and 81 (Cairo 33219); Rühlmann 1971, pp. 61–84; Siliotti 1985, pp. 205–06, no. 14 (Museo Archeologico del Palazzo Reale, Venice); and Corcoran 1988, pp. 106–16 (in response to the thesis version of the present work). Two unpublished, thin wooden "sandals" found in the debris of the western high gate at Medinet Habu may be the earliest examples of the series (see here fig. 7 [reference courtesy John Larson]). Registered as Cairo Museum 59738 and given field notation MH 31: 28 (January 31, 1932), the sandals are painted on their upper sides with bound prisoners and the Nine Bows drawn in red ink. Remains of mummy linen still adhered to the upper side of the left sole. Lacking archaeological context, stylistic dating is necessary and would suggest a late New Kingdom date. In the excavation "Teilungsliste," Hölscher even suggested that the sandals might derive from the mummy of Ramses III! Further validating such images are the Book of the Dead spells copied on Late Period coffins that promise the subjugation of enemies beneath the sandals of the deceased; compare Rowe 1938, pp. 183–84 (= BD spell 151b, §S3). Contra Corcoran 1988, pp. 111–12, the physical placement of these spells elsewhere on the coffin does not invalidate their importance for the inspiration or continued depiction of the motif. This developing iconography belies the general opinion that in the Roman period "ornamentation of the mummy-cases gives evidence that the religious symbolism was 'misunderstood and its significance forgotten'"; H. I. Bell 1953, p. 64, quoting G. Elliot Smith and Warren R. Dawson. The hostile nuance of trampling, implicit in the placing of a name or image on a sandal, is still current and provocative. In 1989, two thousand protesters in Dhaka, Bangladesh, rioted during two days of protest against Canadian-based Beta Shoe Co. for marketing rubber slippers bearing a logo resembling the Arabic characters for Allah. Walking on the slippers was felt to constitute blasphemy against Islam (*Chicago Tribune*, Sunday, June 25, 1989, Section 1, p. 5).

572. For the jar of Tutankhamun, see Edwards 1976a, pp. 124–25. For the box of Sheshonq III, see Weill 1914, pp. 93–94. Compare also the carved figure of a prisoner beneath the cartouches of Osorkon II on a balance beam, in Barguet 1961, pp. 7–10.

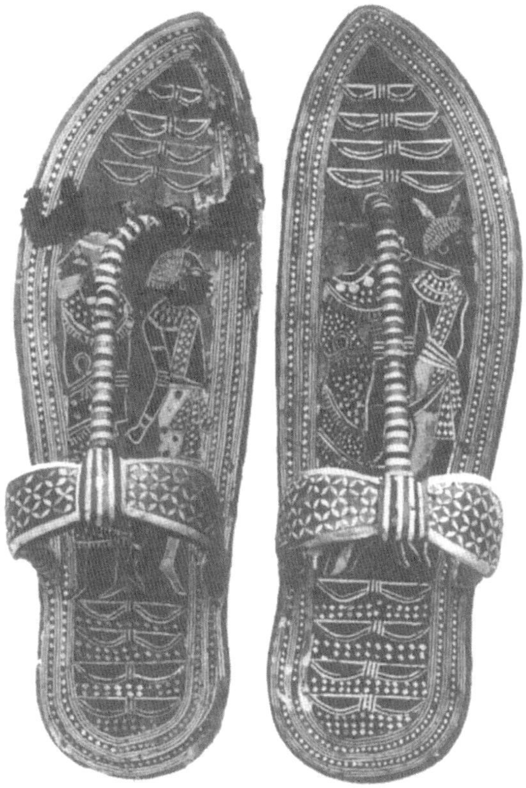

a

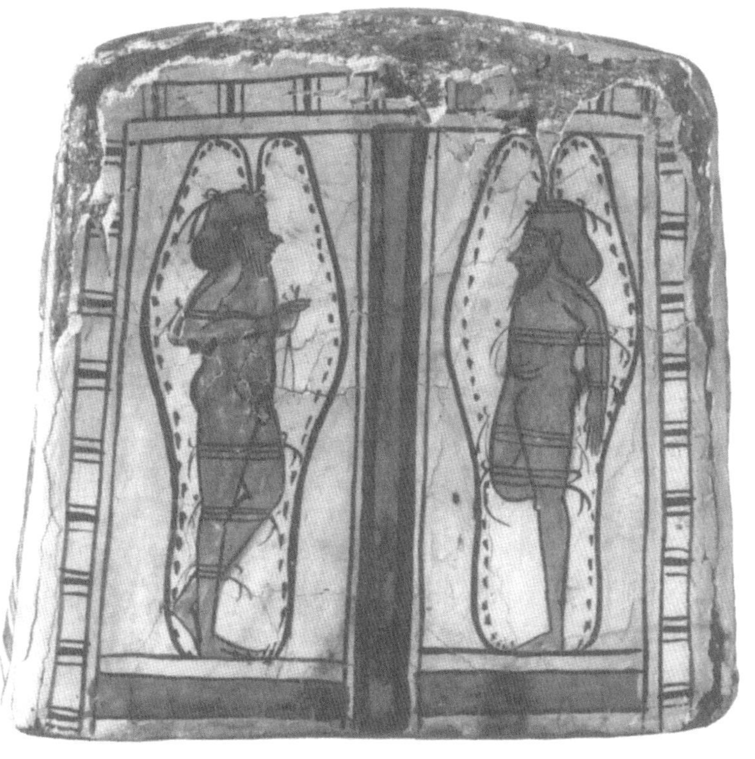

b

Figure 6. (*a*) Sandals of Tutankhamun and (*b*) Roman Period Mummy Footcase with Prisoners Beneath Soles.

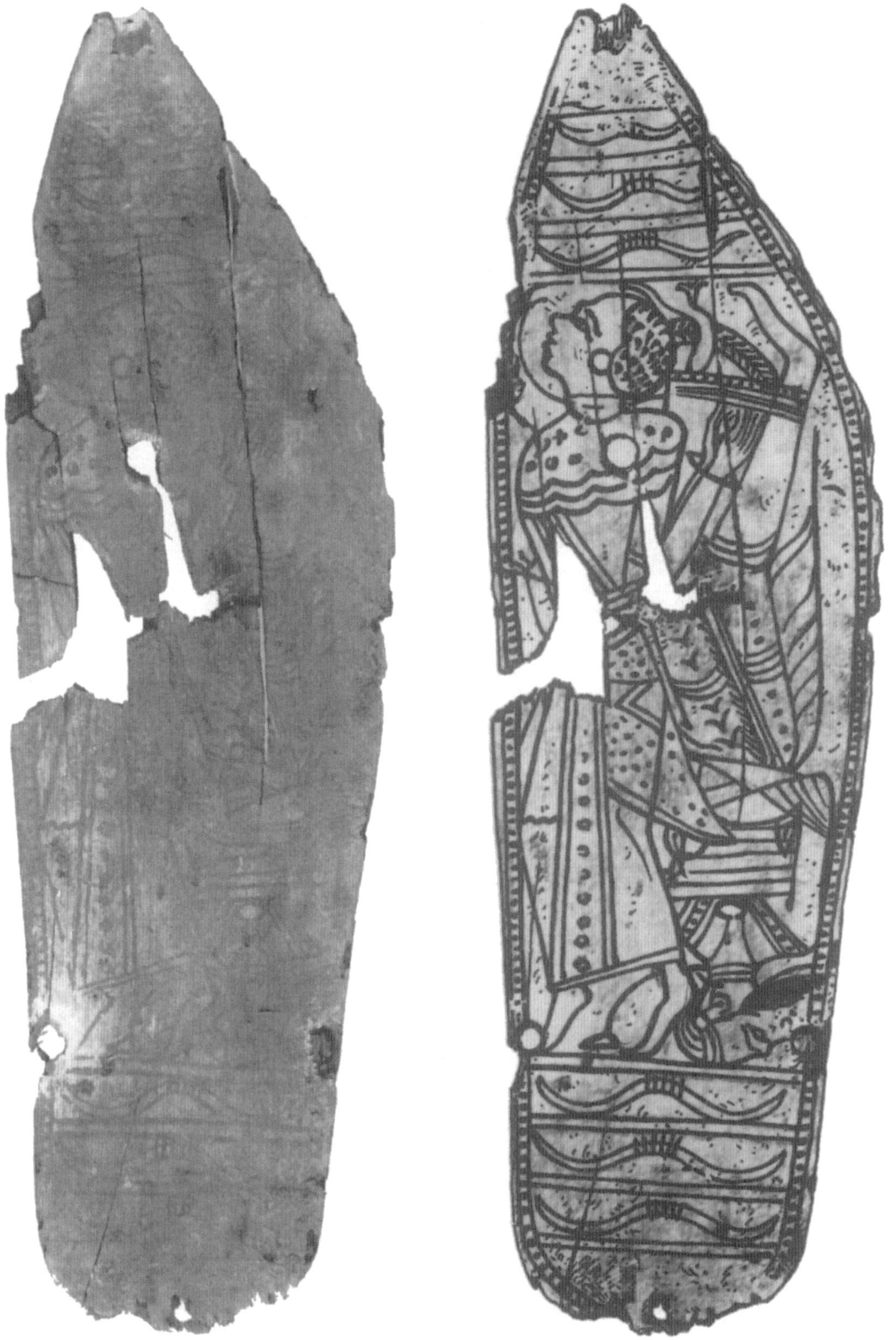

Figure 7. Photograph and Line Drawing of Wooden Mummy Sandal (Right Foot) from Medinet Habu with Prisoners Beneath Sole (Cairo 59738, Late New Kingdom?)

a symbol of the king (see fig. 10a).[573] Caught by its beard in the spokes of the wheel and mauled by the royal beast, the pin prefigures the fate of the royal enemy. The state chariot of Tutankhamun was also provided with images of prisoners on the curved terminals of its yoke (see fig. 10b).[574] When tugged, the reins which passed through the yoke restrained not only the horses, but these figures as well. Similarly inventive is the use of enemy heads as the stops for the oars on the bark of Amon depicted on the reliefs of the valley festival at Karnak.[575] With every stroke, the oarsmen would knock the enemies in the side of the head. A truly "baroque" development of the motif appears in the design of the first palace of Ramses III at Medinet Habu. Extending beneath and beyond the "window of appearance" of the king, a row of sculpted prisoners' heads forms the base line for the window itself, two flanking reliefs of the king leading captives to the window, and two larger reliefs of Ramses in the act of smiting foreign enemies (see fig. 11a).[576] The cumulative effect produced by these representations was, in the words of their excavator, "self-explanatory."[577] When Ramses stood in the window to receive audiences, he necessarily trod underfoot the stone heads carved beneath his feet—forming a living counterpart to the flanking triumphal reliefs. The identity of symbolic relief and physical

573. On reliefs from the forecourt of the Seti temple at Abydos and from Medinet Habu; for these and other examples, see Ellis 1966, pp. 41–48. Ellis, however, fails to recognize either the magical function of the design at Medinet Habu or the components of the design itself, which he describes as two "teddy-bears" (p. 43). Further examples appear now in The Epigraphic Survey 1986, pls. 2, 6, 9, 10, 23, 27, 28 (= p. 88), 29, 33, and 35 (= p. 107). The only extant examples of such pins are tentatively identified and discussed in Ritner 1986b, pp. 53–56, an equation denied by Littauer and Crouwel 1987, pp. 57–61, whose argumentation rests largely on extraneous foreign practices and questions of impracticality (for *ceremonial* chariots, compare the "impractical" gilt ceremonial shields of Tutankhamun). The image of the royal lion/sphinx devouring a prisoner is a commonplace of Egyptian art, compare the Ramesside statues published by Hamza 1930, pp. 46–51; see the discussion in Rühlmann 1964, pp. 651–58 and pls. 1–7 and de Wit n.d., pp. 16–36. It is from this political/cosmological viewpoint—and not from a theory of ancient racism—that one should also understand the faience vessel of a Nubian eaten by a crocodile published in Metzler and Hoffmann 1977, pp. 5–20.

574. Carter 1927, pp. 304–05 (pl. 41) and Littauer and Crouwel 1985, pls. 23–24. The iconography of the royal chariot is necessarily associated with the bound or slain prisoner motif (Desroches-Noblecourt 1963, pp. 91 and 298) and compare the decoration of a buckle of Tutankhamun that depicts the king's chariot resting on a base of prisoners with a further captive tethered on a rope in Edwards 1976a, pp. 106–07.

575. See Schott 1955, pp. 96–99. For comparable smiting scenes performed by kings (and Nefertiti) depicted on royal barges, see Redford 1975, pp. 11, 13 (n. 13) and pl. Vb; and compare the scenes discussed in Grimm 1987.

576. See Hölscher 1932, p. 24 and pl. 3 and 1941, p. 40 and pl. 3. The use of carved heads as a base line appears as early as the Third Dynasty, and Old Kingdom examples may have been reused as late as the Twenty-first or Twenty-second Dynasties (see Bothmer 1982, pp. 27–39).

577. Hölscher 1932, p. 24.

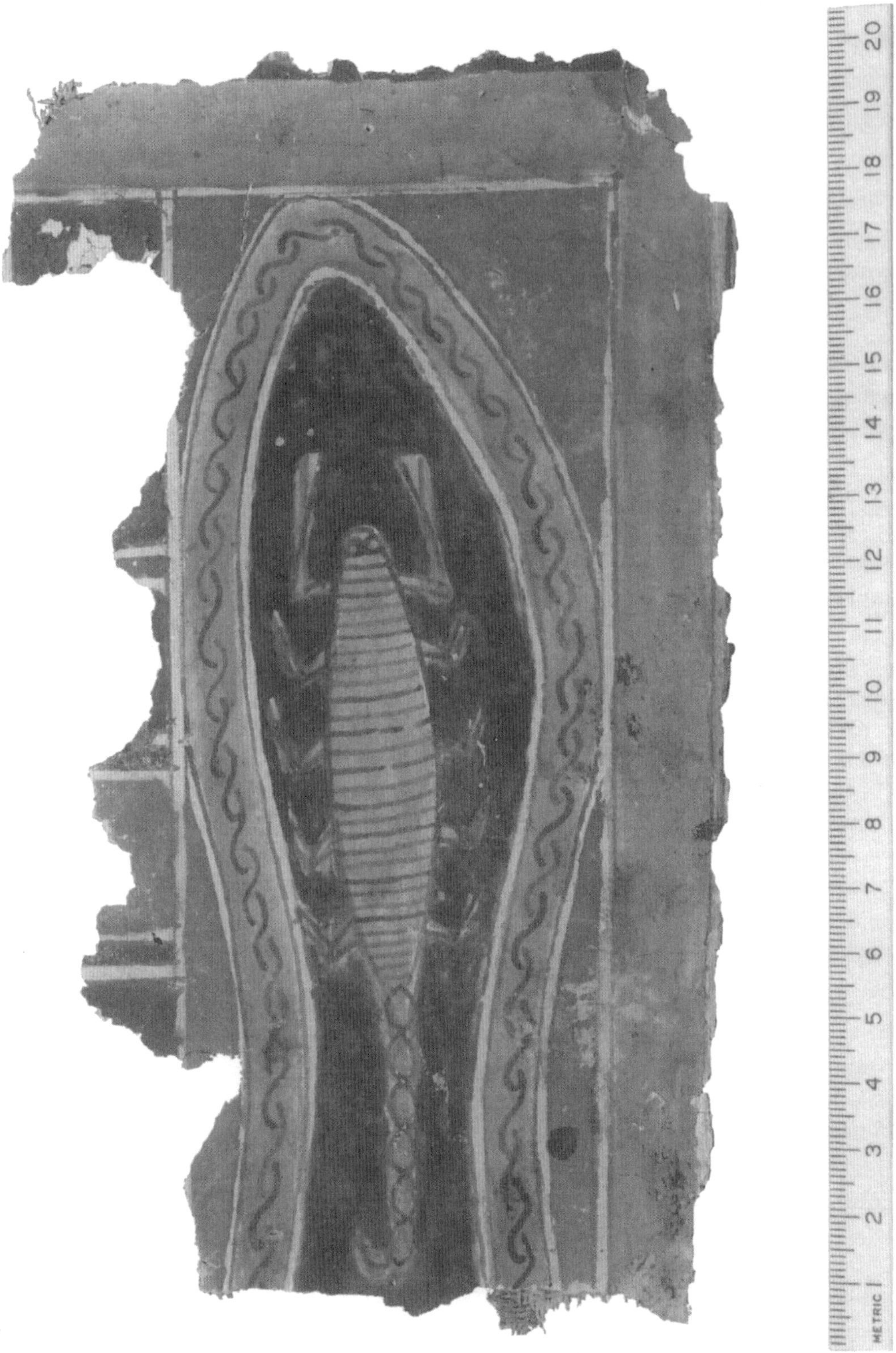

Figure 8. Cartonnage Portion of Mummy Footcase with Scorpions Crushed Beneath Feet (Oriental Institute Museum no. 4784, Dendera, Ptolemaic?).

enactment is underscored by the common base line of heads, crushed by both living king and carved image alike. These three-dimensional enemy heads, themselves the descendants of the free-standing prisoner statues of the Old Kingdom, thus provide the architectural setting for the fusion of the two traditional techniques of ritual conquest—the static symbolism of relief known from the Narmer palette and the pylon facades, and the "inherent kinetics" of the Hierakonpolis door socket, footstools, et cetera. Architectural setting provides yet a third, unnoted dimension to the symbolism, for the placement of the window at head height establishes the king directly above his audience as well.[578] As the king and his image are equated by standing above the base line, so the audience and the carved prisoners must correspond by lying beneath that line. From a distance, the visual impression—and concomitant symbolism—of the king atop his audience would be unmistakable. Developing simultaneously with the motif of the bound prisoner, the theme of the subservient *Egyptian* population, symbolized as *rḫy.t*-birds (), had been used in conjunction with the former in the decoration of throne, dais and statue bases, windows of appearance, et cetera.[579] At Medinet Habu, the king was quite literally *Ḥr ḥr tp rḫy.t*, "Horus atop ('on the heads of') the masses."[580] Although ornate, the Medinet Habu palace window is by no means unique. Sculpted heads of captives appear beneath the windows in the high gate at the same site, and bound prisoners, often in the form of glazed tiles, served a similar function in the royal windows of many kings.[581] A small sculpture in Cairo of Horus standing atop two human heads provides the expected divine counterpart (see fig. 11b).[582] The image of the triumphant Horus treading foes beneath his feet becomes

578. Hölscher 1941, p. 40, remarks that the window was "about a man's height above the court pavement," but he fails to recognize the significance of this feature.

579. Gardiner Sign-list G 24. For the identification of the *rḫy.t*-peoples, see Clère 1958, pp. 43–44, who suggests that the image originally designated hostile Egyptians of the Delta margins in predynastic art. Koenig 1990, p. 115, following Favard-Meeks, assumes that this remained the only significance of the image—an overly strictured interpretation given the later elaboration and distribution of the theme. For "subjugated" examples, see nn. 553 and 567, above; and for palace decoration, see Riefstahl 1968, p. 48 and the sources in n. 581, below. It should be noted that the enemies on many predynastic objects (the Narmer palette, for instance) were in fact Egyptians.

580. For this epithet of the king, see Helck 1958a, p. 1927/9.

581. For the heads at the high gate, see Hölscher 1941, p. 40; The Epigraphic Survey 1970, pls. 611 and 613; and compare the remarks in Badawy 1969, p. 18. For bound prisoners beneath windows of appearance, see *inter alia*, Kaiser 1967, p. 64 and fig. 723 (figured ostracon); H. W. Müller 1964, pl. 1 and pp. 99–101 (tile); Hayes 1990, vol. 2, pp. 334–37 (tiles); idem 1937; and G. T. Martin 1979, pp. 33–35.

582. Daressy 1906, p. 160 and pl. 34. The figure is paralleled on the plate by images of Horus atop an antelope and a crocodile, two animals of Seth. There is no justification for the suggestion by Wildung that this statuette might belong to a tradition different from that of the Medinet Habu sculptures, contra idem 1973, p. 114, n. 35.

standardized on the cippi of "Horus on the Crocodiles," in which guise the motif remains influential until Byzantine times.[583]

The ultimate significance of this widespread motif of the "subservient captive" can be appreciated only by viewing the phenomenon as a whole. Such an examination reveals at once that the motif is not an element of *popular* or *folk* decoration generally current on common wares or utensils.[584] Rather, it is confined to the ornamentation of state and

583. For the stelae of "Horus on the Crocodiles," see above, *Chapter 3*, nn. 518–19, and below, p. 207, n. 956. For the hostile, Sethian nature of the crocodiles and other wild animals on these cippi, see below, n. 743. The traditional understanding of these animals as defeated and trampled enemies has been questioned by Quaegebeur 1984, pp. 131–43, repeated in summary in 1987, p. 187. Quaegebeur would view these dangerous animals as emissaries or assistants of the superior deity, ultimately positive in nature. The primary notion of such images, however, is to express the deity's *mastery* over the beasts—regardless of whether the animals' aggression is felt to be directed "inward" against the god or "outward" toward other noxious forces. The animal is shown to be subject/subservient to the god, whether as assistant or opponent. In either case, the iconologic notion remains "superposition = control." The distinction between "assistant" and "opponent" need not be as great as posed, since the primary magical method of neutralizing serpents, et cetera, is to make their attack recoil upon themselves ("evil to turn away evil"), with force directed "inward" rebounded "outward." When snakes are directed against snakes, opponents are made to function as allies, and "assistant" means only "subjected opponent." The cobra is first and foremost a dangerous animal; its dangerous force may be controlled and thus directed by a god—only thus is it beneficent. The image of a god walking on ("controlling") a uraeus is therefore not so surprising, contra Quaegebeur 1984, p. 136. By the same rationale, Horus' scorpion wife *Tꜣ-Bṯ.t*, or Isis *Ḥddy.t*, can subjugate and repel scorpions; their function is to restrain or destroy their own "emblematic" animal. This does not make the scorpion a "good" animal, merely a "subjugated" one. Contra Quaegebeur ibid., p. 143, the myths of Horus establish clearly that such "trampled" animals were a genuine threat to the deity. Horus' triumphant depiction on cippi as "master of the animals" (a posture attested from Pre-Dynastic times in the Asiatic-inspired Gebel el Arak knife handle) shows his ability to throttle his helpless enemies in his hands, while reducing his crocodile opponents to subservience "beneath his feet," as in common Egyptian idioms explicitly quoted on cippi: "Every male and female serpent, every snake, every lion, every crocodile is under the feet of this god" (Whitehouse 1990–91, p. 5). There need be no great contrast here with images of Bes atop frogs as symbols of fertility (Quaegebeur 1984, pp. 140–42, fig. 17). In both cases the deity controls and directs the force which the animal incarnates. On this question, compare the disputed case of Tutu and the disease demons, in Ritner 1989b, pp. 111–12. Further confirmation of the traditional assessment of the trampled animals is afforded by an unpublished fragment of Ptolemaic (?) mummy cartonnage deriving from Dendera (EEF 1897–98), OIM no. 4784 (see here fig. 8). Half of the bottom of a footcase, the cartonnage depicts a scorpion crushed beneath the sole of the mummy's sandal, a representation directly comparable to late footcases provided with bound prisoners in identical position (see above, n. 571). The equation of hostile prisoner and scorpion is thus obvious—both are trod beneath the sandals of the victorious deceased.

584. Being neither used by the general populace nor displayed chiefly for their benefit—contra Hayes 1990, vol. 1, p. 113, who suggests that it provided "a naïve sense of satisfaction and security." Many of these images (the sandal soles, for example) would have been invisible to all but the king (and the gods); they could hardly qualify as propaganda. Publicly displayed examples of the prisoner motif (on

Figure 9. Cosmetic Jar of Tutankhamun, Symbolizing the Role of Pharaoh: At Summit, Recumbent Lion Personifying the Monarch, Identified by Cartouche; Beneath, the King as Lion Defeats Wild Animals, Symbols of Foreign Enemies; At Bottom, the Heads of Foreign Prisoners.

---

temple walls, processional ships, chariots, et cetera) certainly will have provided a sense of security to the Egyptian onlooker, but contra Corcoran 1988, p. 111, *this was not their primary, theological function.* Even for such public rituals, the intended *chief* beneficiaries of this "propaganda" were the gods. Bound prisoners are not a typical decorative theme on common pottery, mirrors, cosmetic items, et cetera, but their use is restricted to royal, votive, and religious contexts. Thus, while captives may appear on the "mummy sandals" of deceased (and ritually divinized) private individuals, they would not have appeared on the sandals used by such individuals in daily life. The funerary context also explains the presence of the motif on model chair(?) fragments from a private tomb at Saqqara; Quibell 1908, p. 79 and pl. 35, no. 3.

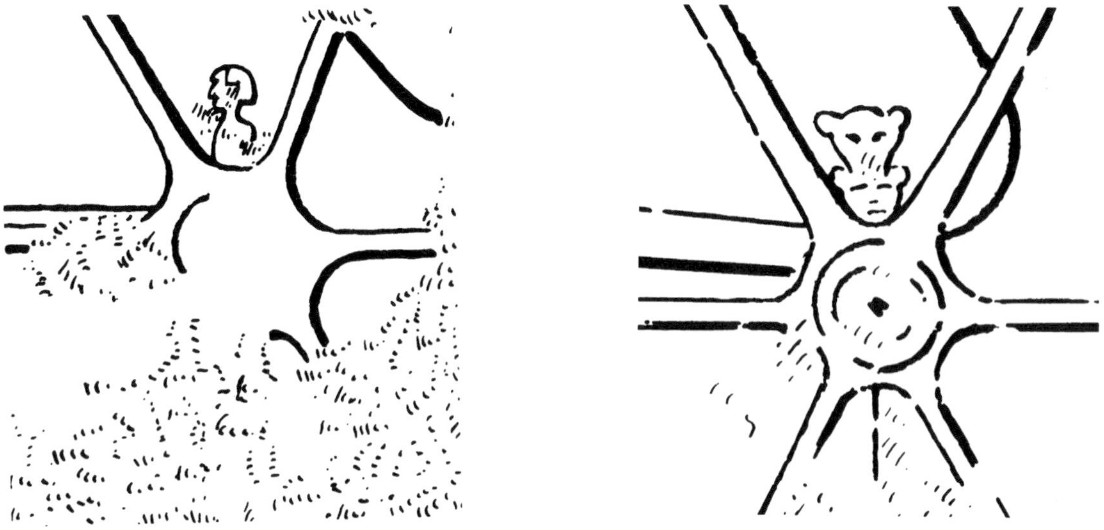

a

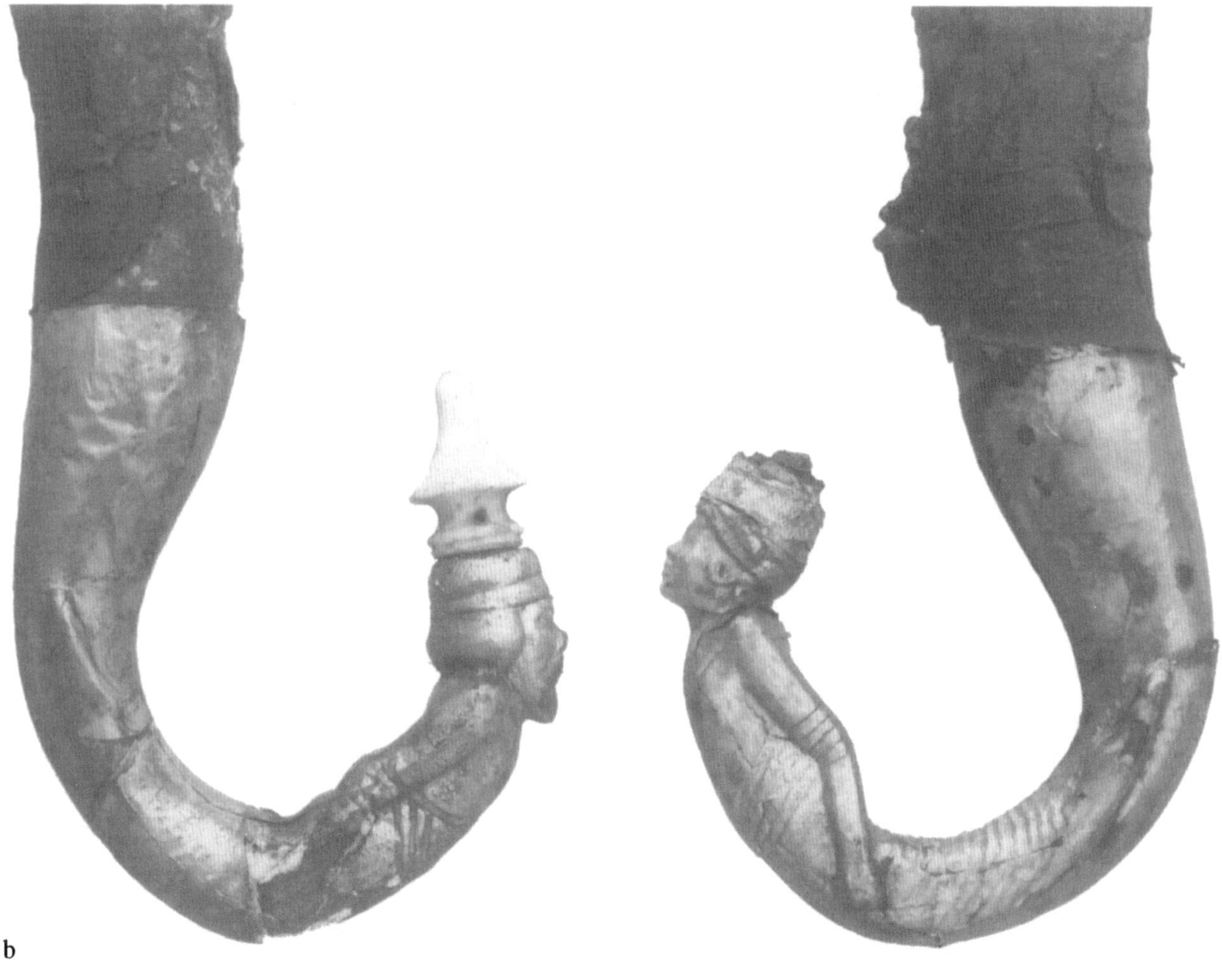

b

Figure 10. (*a*) Linchpins from Chariot Wheels on Reliefs of Ramses III at Medinet Habu (after The Epigraphic Survey 1930, pls. 17 and 31); on the Right, the Royal Lion Bites the Head of a Foreigner, Miscopied with Animal Ears (as a "teddy bear"); and (*b*) Chariot Yoke Terminals as Prisoners.

especially royal property.[585] In fact, the symbol of the bound captive would have been confronted by the king at every moment of his ceremonial duties: on the handles of his cosmetic jars, the soles of his sandals, the handles of his canes, the spokes of his chariot, the base of his footstool, throne, dais, and window. In each case, the incorporation of the image as handle or support requires that it be grasped or crushed. Like the Hierakonpolis door socket, the inherent use of the object produces the symbolic result. Simply by making a state appearance, the king becomes a passive actor in the ritual destruction of the enemies of Egypt.

What artistic and archaeological evidence suggests, textual evidence confirms. Although the earliest inscribed example of the "subjugated prisoner" motif, the Narmer palette, fails to label the central scene, one might reasonably expect that the Egyptian descriptive term would have comprised a verb of striking (*sqr*, *ḥwỉ*, etc.)—especially since the native expression for captive, *sqr-ʿnḫ*, meant literally "one who is stricken yet living."[586] In fact, however, that does not often appear to have been the case. When descriptive labels do accompany these scenes, the action is generally termed *ptpt*, "trampling," even where the visual suggestion of trampling is secondary, or even non-existent.[587] On the Narmer palette as elsewhere, the *fundamental* significance of the image and rite lies not in the action of the king, but in that of the god Horus which the king evokes. Quite simply, the motif of the prisoner, like that of the *rḫy.t*, makes concrete the "superiority" of the victor as "Horus atop the masses." Physical elevation produces political, social, and cosmic domination.[588] So inextricably mixed are the notions of

585. The distinction is confused by Hayes 1990, vol. 2, pp. 337–38, who improperly contrasts Ramesside examples of this hostile ritual motif with earlier, (non-ritual) peaceful scenes of foreigners as an index of Egypt's worsening foreign relations. Genuinely comparable imagery, like the Hierakonpolis door socket, statue bases of all periods, and the Tutankhamun objects, disproves Hayes' suggested contrast. Ramesside imagery may differ in quantity, but not in nature.

586. *Wb* 4: 307/12–19.

587. *Wb* 1: 563/9–16. For an example with the literal depiction of trampling, see the throne of Tuthmosis IV: *ptpt ḫꜣs.t nb*, "trampling all foreign lands," in Pritchard 1954, p. 138, fig. 393. Extended uses of the term for non-literal trampling scenes appear in Saʿad 1970, p. 191, *ptpt* [*w*]*r.w* (?), "trampling chiefs"; and The Epigraphic Survey 1932, pl. 101, *ptpt wr.w nw ḫꜣs.t nb*, "trampling the chiefs of all the foreign lands." Examples of "striking" do occur, however; cf. the tag *ḥwỉ ḥkꜣ-ḫꜣs.wt*, "striking the rulers of foreign lands" (Amenhotep II), in Helck 1955b, p. 1333, l. 13. Later tags also describe the scene as *smꜣ sbỉ*, "slaughtering enemies" (Yoyotte 1980–81, p. 34 and Junker 1910a, p. 70).

588. Thus the inscription on a phylactery against the dangers of travel begins: "All waters, foreign lands, mountains, and all waters in them are beneath the feet of Horus the son of Isis" (Daressy 1903, p. 37). By the same method the deceased may triumph over the force of life itself; compare the depiction on the inner footboard of a Middle Kingdom coffin of two *ʿnḫ*-signs with the inscription: *ʿnḫ.wy r tꜣ ḫr rd.wy⸗k(y)*, "the two symbols of life are on the ground beneath your feet," and the actual use of such *ankhs* beneath the corpse in the funerary purification ceremony, in Grdseloff 1941, pp. 30 and 32–33.

"above," "superiority," "chief," etc. in the Egyptian language, that even the two hieroglyphs which compose the phrase "atop,"  are given mythological significance, being interpreted as "Horus atop Seth."[589] Similar in inspiration was the late reinterpretation of the signs composing the "Golden Horus" name of the king  as "Horus atop the Ombite" (a title of Seth).[590] In the Oryx Nome, the equation of the tutelary animal with Seth produced both a modified writing of the name of the district with a Horus falcon atop the back of the oryx , and a new name for the Horus priest in the chief city of Hebenu: "He who is on his back."[591] As in the case of "encircling," a simple physical action has acquired a non-literal, ritual nuance. Prominent throughout Egyptian religious literature, this ritual aspect is already in evidence in the Pyramid Texts, where it serves as both a counterpart and an explanation for traditional designs on thrones, footstools, sandals, et cetera.

Geb has put his sandal on the head of your foe, who flinches from you.[592]

Horus has laid hold of Seth, and has set him under you in your behalf so that he may lift you up and quake beneath you.[593]

Horus has stretched out for you your foe under you.[594]

Horus has caused Thoth to bring your foe to you, he has set you on his (*scil.* the foe's) back that he may not thwart you; take your place upon him, go up and sit on him, do not let him escape from you.[595]

589. See Myśliwiec 1972; *ḥr tp*.

590. See Gardiner 1973, p. 73, who notes that the phrase is translated on the Rosetta Stone as ἀντιπάλον ὑπέρτερος "superior to his foes."

591. See Montet 1961, pp. 157–59; Gardiner 1947, vol. 2, p. 92*; and cf. de Meulenaere 1967, pp. 21–29, especially 24–25, who disputes the usual reading, but not the translation, of this title. Compare also the Ptolemaic hieroglyphs of Horus atop bulls, crocodiles, and the oryx, read variously *Wnty*, *Dwnty*, and *Ḥry-sꜣ*, in Fairman 1935, p. 31 and Blackman and Fairman 1943, pp. 30–31.

592. PT spell 356, §578, in Faulkner 1969, p. 114; for the text, see Sethe 1908, p. 301.

593. PT spell 356, §581, in Faulkner 1969, p. 114; for the text, see Sethe 1908, p. 304.

594. PT spell 371, §650, in Faulkner 1969, p. 123; for the text, see Sethe 1908, p. 356.

595. PT spell 372, §§651–52, in Faulkner 1969, p. 123; for the text, see Sethe 1908, p. 357. These are only a small selection of the examples in the Pyramid Texts.

a

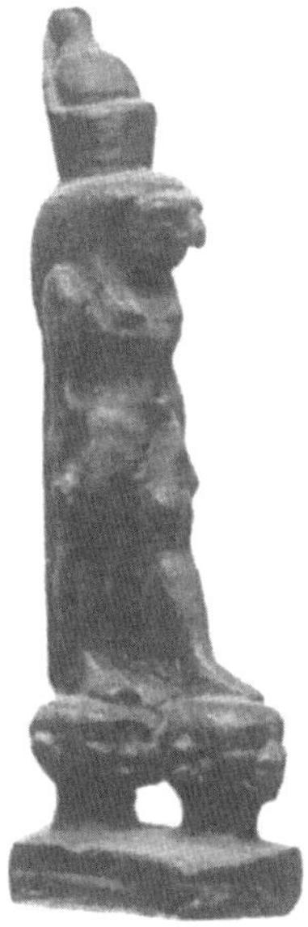

b

Figure 11. (*a*) Reconstructed Drawing of Window of Appearance of First Palace at Medinet Habu (after Hölscher 1932, pl. 3) and (*b*) Statuette of Horus Atop Human Heads (Cairo 38.616; after Daressy 1906, pl. 34).

Ritual subjugation of divine, royal, and personal enemies reappears in the Coffin Texts.[596] So standardized has the imagery become, that the enemy may be said to be "under the sandals" of Horus even when the latter is not in anthropomorphic, but falcon form.[597] The Book of the Dead continues this verbal subjugation and couples it with ritual practice. Within an exemplar of spell 168, a description of the gods of the caverns in the netherworld, the enemies of the deceased are consigned beneath the feet of Osiris, conforming to the placement of the spell itself:

> ... (as for) one who harms him, he is put under thy feet forever. To be used on the [corner] under the feet of Osiris the lord of eternity.[598]

The accompanying texts on the footstools of Tutankhamun are no less explicit, exclaiming "All lands and every secret Phoenician are under the feet of this good god," or simply "Every foreign land is under your sandals."[599] A millennium later, the phraseology is unchanged in a Demotic petition to a Ptolemaic ruler (*mtw=w tỉ nꜣy=f sꜣb ẖr rt=f*, "Let his enemies be put under his feet"),[600] while contemporary temple rituals for the destruction of Apophis, Seth, and foreign enemies dictate the trampling underfoot (*dgꜣs*, *dgdg*, or *sỉn m rt*) of images of these demonic forces.[601] The "magical" component of this activity is unmistakable, and when the motif recurs in the Demotic magical papyrus of London and Leiden, adapted for the practitioner rather than the Pharaoh, the gods, or the private tomb owner, there can be no question of any real substantive difference:

596. For examples, see CT spells 148, 745, 761, 835, 839, 946, and compare 960 in which the enemy (Seth) is kicked.

597. In CT spell 148, a spell to assume falcon shape. See Faulkner 1973, p. 126; and the comments in Griffiths 1960, p. 53. For the text, see de Buck 1938, pp. 224–25. This terminology is all the more striking by comparison with CT spell 149, "Becoming a human falcon," in which the practitioner has his foe "with my talons" as he "alights" upon the enemy's spine (Faulkner 1973, p. 127 and de Buck 1938, pp. 236–40).

598. BD spell 168B, Pap. MMA 35.9.19, b §S17, in Allen 1974, p. 172. The directions are to be performed by the ritual priest, see §S19. For enemies beneath the feet of Osiris, see n. 566, above.

599. See el Mallakh and Brackman 1978, pls. 82 and 121–23.

600. Ray 1976, pp. 26 (text 3 vo., ll. 3–4), 37 (text 7, ll. 8–9), and 170 (text 60, ll. 4–5). A similar sentiment is found in the "Instructions of ʿOnchsheshonqy" (col. 3/4–5): "Nut the great, the mother, the great goddess, will place the foreign lands of all the earth beneath the feet of Pharaoh entirely" (Lichtheim 1980, p. 162 and Glanville 1955, p. 9 [differing translations]). Compare the contemporary stereotyped temple inscriptions in Mallet 1909, pp. 82 and 96: "the (nine) bows are united under your sandals."

601. See Pap. Bremner-Rhind, cols. 22/5–9, 23/4–5, 23/12, 26/4, 27/18, 28/3, 28/4, 28/16, and 29/14–15, in Faulkner 1933, 1936, 1937a, 1937b, and 1938 (*sỉn m rt*); Schott 1929, p. 5 (col. 43/9–21: *dgꜣs*); and Chassinat 1930, pp. 132/3–134/9; Alliot 1954, pp. 521 and 525; and Sauneron 1962b, p. 25, n. b (*dgdg*).

[I am ...] of earth by name, under the soles [of] whose [feet] the gods of Egypt are placed.[602]

The various manifestations of the motif in the Greek language PGM are further evidence for the dependence of these texts upon the Egyptian milieu in which they were composed. Thus, a curse requires that the enemy's name be inscribed on a lead plate put under the sole of the left foot of the magician.[603] An invocation to Seth for the same purpose concludes: "Enslave NN to NN and cause him to come under my feet."[604] The significance of the act is expressed succinctly in a further curse: "As these holy names are trampled down, so too is NN, my oppressor."[605]

The influence of the "prisoner motif" was felt not only by Greeks, but by the Meroitic inheritors of Pharaonic culture. Ironically, Hellenistic Meroe freely adopted the image of the Nine Bows and bound prisoners placed under the royal throne which had formerly symbolized its own subservience.[606] Free-standing statues and applied throne decorations of prisoners also appear, recalling the archaic and Old Kingdom prototypes from which the motif had originally developed (see fig. 12a, b).[607] Meroitic adaptations of the motif reveal innovations as well. Sacrificial animals were adorned with bells engraved with images of bound prisoners, struck repeatedly by the clapper as the animal was led to slaughter.[608] Pierced by a nail, small plaques of enemies were fixed beneath temple flag staffs, crushed beneath the post like the Hierakonpolis door socket some thirty centuries earlier.[609]

602. Griffith and Thompson 1904, p. 2 (col. 1/24).

603. Preisendanz 1931, pp. 40–41 (PGM VII, ll. 925–39 [= Betz 1986, pp. 142–43]).

604. Preisendanz 1931, p. 42 (PGM VII, ll. 965–68 [= Betz 1986, p. 143]).

605. Preisendanz 1931, p. 53 (PGM X, ll. 36–50 [= Betz 1986, p. 150]).

606. For the Nine Bows on thrones and footstools, see Lepsius 1972–73, Abteilung V, pls. 25, 35, 37, 46, 50, and 51. For prisoners, see ibid., pls. 27, 30, and 32; Tomandl 1986, pp. 63–72; Hofmann and Tomandl 1986a, pp. 101–11; idem 1986b, pp. 115–19; and Kendall 1982, p. 56. Murals depicting bound prisoners on footrests have been identified at the "Augustus Temple" at Meroe, otherwise notable for its execration features: the bronze sculpted head of Augustus buried outside its threshold and the (defleshed) skull inserted in the painted wall (Shinnie and Bradley 1981). For Meroitic adaptations in relief of the traditional smiting scene, see Hall 1986, pp. 44–47 and figs. 88–90. Cushite use of the Egyptian motif is already found in the Second Intermediate Period on fortress seals in Lower Nubia (B. Williams 1985, p. 45).

607. Wenig 1978, pp. 218–19 (figs. 139–40; fig. 140 = Khartoum, Sudan National Museum 24397).

608. Hermann 1966 and Kendall 1982, pp. 53–55 (enemies include the contemporary Romans). The execration nature of the bells is obviously strengthened by their placement on sacrificial animals, whose fate prefigures that of the represented enemies.

609. Kendall 1982, pp. 55–56 (second century B.C. to second century A.D.). Like Egyptian execration figurines, the pierced bronze plaques are inscribed with individual names and ethnic designations. The practice may well derive from lost Egyptian prototypes.

a

b

Figure 12. (*a*) Meroitic Statue of Bound Prisoner from Argo Island (Khartoum, Sudan National Museum 24397; after Wenig 1978, p. 219, fig. 140) and (*b*) Prisoner Figures from Steps of Throne Base at Meroe (after Tomandl 1986, p. 68).

At the end of this iconographic tradition is the Louvre figurine of the female lover depicted as a bound prisoner. Yet while the "prisoner motif" contributed the imagery for the figure, it is to a different tradition that one must look for its manipulation, and for the transition of the image from royal to private magic.

THE EXECRATION TEXTS

If the magical aspect of the "prisoner motif" and its related imagery is largely passive in nature, dependent upon either the mere existence or the "inherent kinetics" of the design itself, there remains yet a second use of prisoner figurines in which active, ritual manipulation is unmistakable: as supports for the so-called "execration texts." First noted on some 289 pottery fragments by Schäfer and Sethe in 1925,[610] these cursing formulae inscribed on pots and figurines now number in excess of 1,000 exemplars, and are attested from the Old Kingdom through the Late Period.[611] Although the texts vary widely in complexity, ranging from individual figures to elaborate assemblages, their unity of purpose and general similarity of technique have defined them as a corpus. Unlike the "prisoner motif" which presents only generalized images of foreigners, the execration texts are quite specific in their intended victims.[612] For by the addition of names, the pot or figurine becomes a substitute image of those victims, an Egyptian counterpart to the "voodoo doll" (see fig. 13a). The coupling of name and prisoner image thus effected directly parallels standard practice in the hieroglyphic script as well, where enemy names may receive a "bound prisoner" determinative 𓀏 (Gardiner Sign-list A 13).[613] While the use of a figurine as a substitute image is obvious to the modern researcher, the symbolism

610. Sethe 1926 (Berlin P. 14501–14606).

611. A general listing is found in Posener 1975a and 1987, pp. 2–6. To these references should be added the London and Hanover figures published in Munro 1972 and Ritner 1989a; the Balat figurine discussed in Posener-Kriéger 1982, p. 384 and pl. 70b; Giddy 1983, p. 107; Grimal 1983, p. 111; idem 1985 (with critical remarks by Posener 1987, p. 6, n. 6); Galerie Nefer 1992, p. 33 (number 34); and two unpublished stone figurines in the Milwaukee Public Museum. Aside from Sethe's initial study, basic publications of the material are found principally in the work of Posener. In addition to his two studies just cited, see Posener 1939a, 1939b, 1940, 1958, 1963b, 1966, 1971, 1974, 1975b, 1976a, 1977, and 1984. Other pertinent studies of the material include: Daressy 1901, p. 98 (Cairo 25376); Reisner 1913, p. 62; Montet 1928; Lansing 1933, pp. 23–25; Edgerton 1940, p. 492, n. 44; Junker 1947, pp. 30–38 and pls. 6–7; Helck 1971, pp. 44–67; Vila 1973; idem 1963; Abu Bakr and Osing 1973; Osing 1976a; Heimer 1981; Koenig 1987a; and idem 1990. It is important to note that not all execration figurines are provided with text, and the stress here laid on *named* figurines should not devalue the many *uninscribed* images probably linked to their victim by oral recitations. For a selection of these, see Petrie 1902, p. 26 (no. 39) and pl. 53 (clay torso with arms bent behind back, from the temenos of the Osiris temple at Abydos, "early dynasties"); Petrie, Griffith, and Murray 1888, p. 73, §70 and pl. 40, nos. 8–13 (thirty to forty limestone figures, Saite); Schoske and Wildung 1985, pp. 83 (no. 65, prone limestone figure of a tied Nubian, Nineteenth Dynasty) and 162–63 (at least six broken clay figures of Asiatics, Ptolemaic period).

612. An intermediate position between the specificity of the execration texts and the generality of the "prisoner motif" is found in the Ramesside Statue Base Cairo 755 with prisoner heads labeled "chief of vile Mitanni" and "chief of vile Cush," in Borchardt 1930, pp. 75–76 and Wildung 1973, pp. 112–13. Where the current ruler was unknown, the execration texts followed this same pattern. Compare also the personified captive cities, found *inter alia* at Medinet Habu; see above, n. 549.

613. Gardiner 1973, p. 443. The sign regularly determines expressions for "enemy," and by extension may be applied to names of hostile persons. For examples from execration figures, see Posener 1984, p. 613 and pl. 1; 1976a, p. 442; and 1987, pp. 15–16 and 55.

a b c

Figure 13. (*a*) Execration Figurine from Brussels (inv. E 7442); (*b*) Execration Figurine from Saite Fortress at Defennah (after Petrie 1972, pl. 5); and (*c*) Clay Imprint of Execration Figure with Knife Bisecting Neck (New Kingdom, Giza; after Posener 1958, p. 256 [with addition of knife from pls. XXVI–XXVII]).

of pottery as human substitutes would have been no less so to the Egyptians whose creator deity Khnum fashioned mankind on a potter's wheel.[614]

614. This activity of Khnum is best reflected in the "great hymn" at Esna (see Sauneron 1968, pp. 130–34, no. 250/6–21; idem 1962b, pp. 94–107; and Lichtheim 1980, pp. 111–15). Compare also the possibly Egyptian-inspired wisdom text of Ben Sira: "Like clay in the hand of a potter, To be moulded as he

The earliest preserved texts, four Giza deposits from the reign of Pepi II, follow no single format.[615] Two of these deposits include a large shattered clay figure inscribed with differing prototypes of a "rebellion formula" which was to be standardized only in the Middle Kingdom:

> [Every rebel of this land, all people, all patricians, all commoners (*rḫy.t*), all males], all eunuchs, all women, every chieftain, [every Nubian, every strongman, every messenger], every confederate, every ally of every land who will rebel in *Wꜣwꜣt*, *Zꜣṯw*, *ʾIrṯt*, *ʾIꜣm*, *ʾIꜣnḫ*, *Mꜣsỉt*, and *Kꜣ*(*ꜣw*), who will rebel or who will plot by saying plots or by speaking anything evil against Upper Egypt or Lower Egypt forever.[616]

> Every Nubian who will rebel in *ʾIrṯt*, *Wꜣwꜣt*, *Zꜣṯw*, *ʾIꜣm*, *Kꜣꜣw*, *ʾIꜣnḫ*, *Mꜣsỉt* *Mḏꜣ*, and *Mtrtỉ*, who will rebel or who will make plots, or who will plot, or who will say anything evil.[617]

Augmenting these general designations of threatening Egyptians and Nubians are many smaller clay figurines bearing individual Egyptian and Nubian names. Also associated with the deposit containing the first of these texts was an uninscribed clay statuette, broken and incomplete. The remaining deposits consisted only of individually labeled figurines, and the use of such images without the "rebellion formula" continues into the Middle Kingdom, while from the New Kingdom on this pattern alone is typically attested. Despite the variation in content (extending also to the number of smaller figurines), all four of these deposits are nonetheless intimately associated by date (three within the space of two months), handwriting (seemingly only two scribes for four deposits), and by the recurrence of identical names throughout.[618] All were interred in the Giza cemetery, most enclosed in jugs docketed with the regnal year and a personal name.[619]

---

chooses, So are men in the hand of their maker," in Lichtheim 1983, p. 142. In magic, the concept clearly underlies a Ramesside cursing spell which identifies an enemy as a lump of clay, malleable and helpless in the hand of the magician (Shorter 1936). The Egyptian association of clay with mankind is also reflected in an episode in Pap. Vandier, in which the magician molds clay (*qd ʿmʿ.t*) to form a subservient man of earth (*rmṯ n sꜣṯw*) or "golem" (see Posener 1985, pp. 31–32 [col. 5]). These examples directly disprove the contention of Derchain 1981, p. 46a (end of first paragraph: "il ne semble pas que le mythe du modelage ait mené à une association particulière de l'homme et de la glèbe."

615. See Junker 1947, pp. 30–38; Abu Bakr and Osing 1973, pp. 97–133; and Osing 1976a, pp. 133–85.

616. Text in Osing 1976a, pp. 153–54, updating text and discussion in Abu Bakr and Osing 1973, pp. 117–30.

617. Text and discussion in Osing 1976a, pp. 146–53.

618. For the interrelated dates of the deposits, see Osing 1976a, p. 155; for paleography, see p. 170 and for names, see pp. 158–64 and the comments on 155.

619. The conditions of discovery of one of the deposits is unrecorded, but it may be presumed that it too was interred within a jug, see the comments of Osing 1976a, p. 134.

In the more elaborate examples of the Middle Kingdom,[620] a series of unbaked pottery vessels or schematically modeled figures of prisoners (in clay, limestone, alabaster, wood, or wax) is inscribed with a formulaic list of the names and parentage of contemporary Nubian, Asiatic, and Libyan princes with mention of their retainers, soldiers, messengers and countrymen "who may rebel, who may plot, who may fight, who may think of fighting, or who may think of rebelling on this entire earth."[621] This "rebellion formula" reappears in the following section concerned with potentially hostile classes of Egyptians, and to this section a list of the names of such individuals is appended. Completing the later pattern is an enumeration of generally threatening forces, including evil speech, slander, plots, strife, nightmares,[622] et cetera. Whereas previous sections defend against political or military threat, these concluding designations serve to ward against magical assault, perhaps in anticipation of similar execration magic by Egypt's foes.[623]

In any individual find, the entire sequence of foreigners, Egyptians, and forces may appear in multiple copies by different scribes, and, like the Old Kingdom (and New Kingdom) examples, the resulting assemblage is most often interred within a traditional necropolis. Although there is great variation in the manner in which the texts may be

620. The texts of the Middle Kingdom assemblages show progressive development from Old Kingdom prototypes, providing internal evidence for their chronological sequence: the Cairo alabaster figurines (Sesostris I), the Mirgissa deposit (Amenemhat II–Sesostris II), the Berlin bowls (mid Twelfth Dynasty), and the Saqqara figures (end of Twelfth Dynasty). For the respective dates, see the table in Posener 1987, p. 14, with the minor corrections in Koenig 1990, p. 102, n. 8.

621. From the Berlin bowls; for a translation of the general pattern of these texts, see Sethe 1926, pp. 72–73 and Wilson 1969c. The alabaster figures in Cairo (JdE 63955–59) display a slightly different ordering of the texts, being intermediate in development between the Giza and Berlin finds (from Helwan?, dating to Sesostris I; see Posener 1987, pp. 17–56). Only these Cairo exemplars include a section devoted to the geographic areas of Egypt; ibid., pp. 38–40. For the Mirgissa texts, see Koenig 1990.

622. Literally "evil dreams in evil sleep"; for this improved reading, see Posener 1966, pp. 283.

623. See the remarks of Vila 1973, p. 627. The complete text of this section has been provided for the Berlin and Mirgissa finds (see Sethe 1926, pp. 69–72 and Koenig 1990, pp. 116–17). For the Egyptian fear of foreign magic, compare the remarks of Amenhotep II to his viceroy in Nubia: "Do not be merciful to the Nubians at all. Guard yourself against their people and their magicians," in Helck 1955a, p. 25. The perception of a Nubian magical threat is still in evidence in the Roman period, see the second Setna tale in Lichtheim 1980, pp. 138–51. Actual adoption of Egyptian execration techniques by the Hebrews (Amos 1:2–2:16) has been suggested in Bentzen 1950; followed by West 1971, p. 244; but denied by Weiss 1969. For this question, see the obvious execration rite of the broken pottery in Jeremiah 19:1–11 (noted also in Koenig 1990, p. 101): "Thus said the Lord, 'Go, buy a potter's earthen flask, and take some of the elders of the people and some of the senior priests, and go out to the valley of the son of Hinnom at the entry of the Potsherd Gate, and proclaim there the words that I tell you' ... Then you shall break the flask in the sight of the men who shall go with you, and shall say to them, 'Thus says the Lord of hosts: So will I break this people and this city, as one breaks a potter's vessel, so that it can never be mended.'"

copied, with sections contained on individual pieces or spread across several pots or figures, so standardized are the texts themselves that restorations of lacunae are fairly easy, both within a single find and—allowing for foreign regnal changes—from one find to another.[624] To produce such an assemblage would require a canonical textual schema, distributed most likely from a single source, a staff of trained scribes, and detailed, current records of the names and parentage of rulers from even small localities well beyond Egypt's borders.[625] Clearly, only the state could meet these requirements.[626] Thus, despite their typically rather undistinguished find spot in or beside private graves, the elaborate execration formulae would seem not private but state productions, obviously designed to suppress revolt at home and abroad.

This straightforward scenario may be a bit too simplistic, however, and Posener in particular has suggested a greater degree of participation by private individuals or localities in the drafting of the list of condemned Egyptians, who are usually qualified by the term *mwt* (dead man) or *mwt.t* (dead woman).[627] These terms, he insists, must be taken literally, and the texts should constitute the *damnatio memoriae* of deceased—and possibly executed—local criminals. It should be noted, however, that the term *sqr* "stricken one/prisoner" is applied prospectively to foreign soldiers who have not been captured,[628] and the form of the figurines themselves constitutes a "wish fulfillment" projected upon the

624. See the discussions by Sethe 1926, pp. 7–13 and 18ff.; Posener 1940, pp. 20–24; and Koenig 1987a, p. 306.

625. The desire to ensure that the records were kept current is reflected by the updating of the names of rulers and states (Sethe 1926, pp. 42, 62, and 70; Posener 1940, pp. 24–25; idem 1976a, pp. 438–39; idem 1987, p. 18; and Koenig 1990, p. 104, textual note d [successive heirs of *Kꜣꜣ*]).

626. Compare the remarks of Posener 1966, p. 284, n. 1; noted in Koenig 1987a, p. 306 and idem 1990, p. 102. The central figures of the Mirgissa deposit were made of limestone, not local to the area and thus presumably sent by the royal chancellery. Posener suggests that these figures were dispatched already inscribed to serve as a model for the other textual copies at the site.

627. Versus Sethe 1926, pp. 62–69 (followed by Wilson 1969c, p. 329), who was unaware of the feminine examples and interpreted *mwt* as the optative form of the verb "to die," yielding the translation "Let NN die." Posener's re-interpretation of the term as a noun was first advanced hesitantly in 1939b, p. 46 and more forcefully in 1958, pp. 265–70. For the question of local input in these rites, see ibid., p. 269 and Posener 1976a, pp. 439–40. Egyptians not described as "dead" occur in the Giza texts discussed in Abu Bakr and Osing 1973, pp. 129–30; the alabaster figures in Posener 1987, pp. 55–56 and compare the Cairo "tablets" discussed in Posener 1976a, p. 439. See also below, p. 184 and n. 856.

628. For the reading *sqr* (phonetic spelling), see Posener 1966, p. 283 and 1940, pp. 26–28 versus van de Walle 1940, pp. 108–09, who accepts a variant reading *ḥnk*, "trusted ones," for the Berlin texts (following Sethe 1926, pp. 15–16). The anticipatory use of the term *sqr* is acknowledged by Posener himself (1977, pp. 504–05). Such usage is perfectly in accord with standard Egyptian practice; compare the common application of the word *ẖsy*, "wretched/defeated," to the names of Cush, Khatti, etc. (*Wb* 3: 399/11).

associated individuals.[629] The term "deceased" could be similarly anticipatory,[630] and the related Bremner-Rhind ritual specifically includes enemies of both king and practitioner "whether dead or alive."[631] Private influence is probable also in those finds consisting *only* of Egyptian names on individual figures. Lacking the "rebellion formula" (and thus any clear indication of state interest), these figures may nonetheless retain the term *mwt*, and are subjected to the same treatment as figures in ostensible state productions. Despite the implication of a private impetus for these deposits, they have been analyzed as forming a unity with the Egyptian section, whose social implications are discussed below.

BINDING

Aside from the one certain and one possible use of wishful terminology, the execration lists contain nothing which, in itself, could be called magical, serving merely to identify the individual, nation, or force with the inscribed pot or figure.[632] The desired magical effect of these assemblages must thus derive *not from the text*, but from the *ritual* to which they were subjected.[633] Just what might constitute this ritual has been the subject of some dispute.

629. See the remarks of Posener 1974, p. 400: "Couleur et attitude portent malheur aux victimes, elles constitutent un préenvoûtement." The phrase is echoed in Koenig 1987a, p. 302.

630. The "dead man" determinative (Gardiner Sign-list A 14) after foreign names on the Berlin bowls (Sethe 1926, p. 19) has the same implications.

631. See col. 26/2: "Now make for yourself every enemy of Re, every enemy of Pharaoh, dead or alive, together with every accused one in his heart" (Faulkner 1933, pp. 56 and 1937b, p. 171); and col. 28/17–18: "Then inscribe for yourself these names of all male and female enemies whom your heart fears as the enemies of Pharaoh, whether dead or alive" (Faulkner 1933, p. 69 and 1937b, p. 175).

632. Notably, no verbs of cursing appear anywhere in the standard text, producing an extended list whose significance is clear only from its context on prisoner figurines or broken pottery. Compare the remarks of Sethe 1926, pp. 19–20 (discounting his example of *mwt*, "Let NN die"). Posener 1987, p. 1, n. 2, thus insists that the common designation "execration text" is inappropriate, accepting only the term "proscription." However, some cursing elements do occur, such as the selection of red ink and enemy determinatives, and the prospective use of *sqr* (and possibly *mwt*) just mentioned. The Cairo alabaster figures follow the names of Nubian princes with insults to produce the pattern: "NN, against whom one says, 'Is there anyone attached to him?' (var. 'Are you an adversary,' 'Bull born of a [female ape],' 'Calf,' etc.)" (Posener 1987, pp. 20–31 and 1977, pp. 503–04). Mud tablets from Lisht also qualify the intended enemies as "separated from" (*wꜣ r*) former names and titles (Hayes 1955, pp. 57–58 and Vernus 1974, pp. 121–23). Such derogatory epithets are not simple expressions of pique, but known cursing techniques—as acknowledged by Posener 1987, p. 21: "le ridicule tue."

633. Contra Posener 1975b, p. 407, who emphasizes the spell with reference to the late execration ritual against Seth (Schott 1929); similarly in Posener 1974, p. 401, where the operative force is said to be psychological rather than magical: "L'effet recherché est obtenu non par un moyen surnaturel, mais de façon indirecte en atteignant l'imagination, par une sorte de contrainte psychologique." One might well wonder how the "contrainte psychologique" of an act carried out in an Egyptian graveyard would affect a chieftain in a hilltop village in Palestine, a tent in Libya, or a hut in Nubia.

With regard to the figures, at least, one obvious constituent was bondage, for in addition to the summary indication of tied limbs on representations in alabaster and wood,[634] clay exemplars from Giza and Saqqara reveal holes for binding or suspension with cords.[635] Such images parallel the archaic prisoner figurine from Abydos discussed above (p. 116), and provide but the first of many correspondences between the execration rite and tortures enacted on earth, in the netherworld, and in temple cult and private enchantment.[636] As the tangible counterpart to the "surrounding" (*šnỉ*) and "encircling" (*pẖr*) so prominent in the Egyptian vocabulary of magic, physical binding is correspondingly "bivalent,"[637] signifying

634. For the design of alabaster figures, see the discussion in Heimer 1981 and Posener 1987, pp. 7–10; for wooden images, see Reisner 1913, p. 62 and Posener 1984. A selection of bound execration figures from the archaic(?) through the Roman periods appears in Petrie 1972, p. 19 (no. 60, a–d) and pl. 5.

635. For Old Kingdom examples, see Junker 1947, pp. 32–34; Abu Bakr and Osing 1973, p. 98; and Osing 1976a, p. 156 and pl. 51. Carbonized traces of cord still adhered to some Saqqara examples (Posener 1940, pp. 18–19).

636. For binding, see Zandee 1960, pp. 78–81, 125–33 and 338; BD spells passim, especially 180, §S8 (Allen 1974, p. 191); the "Apophis Book," cols. 22/17–20, 26/3, 28/16, 29/14, 29/20, 31/25, and 32/47–53, in Faulkner 1933, passim; the "Anti-Seth Book," in Schott 1929, pp. 5/15 and 37/13–39/22; idem 1956, pp. 185–86; Bell, Nock, and Thompson 1933, p. 12; and Gardiner 1951.

637. A concise discussion of the significance of binding derived largely from German folklore appears in Morenz 1958, with which cf. the entirely "cross-cultural" interpretation of Petrie 1972, p. 29. While such interpretations of shared symbols are broadly correct, they cannot elucidate the *specific* range of meaning *within individual societies*. Thus, in contrast to the German "Bindezauber," the French "nouer l'aiguillette à quelqu'un," the Greek κατάδεσις, and the Latin "ligatio" (see Kropp 1930–31, vol. 3, p. 199) or even "religio," Egyptian terminology generalized the notion of "surrounding" in preference to that of "binding." The distinction is of some significance as a reminder that even such common cross-cultural magical phenomena as "magical knots" are evaluated and understood differently by differing cultures (as is magic itself) and should be analyzed *in cultural context*. Contrast the "culturally-specific" analysis of "sealing" in Ritner 1984b, pp. 209–21. "Binding" as an expression for "magic" is rarely used in Egyptian texts. The term *ṯs.t* in the late Pap. Salt 825 has been translated "conjuration" by Derchain, but only the literal nuance of "knot" (as "phylactery") may be intended: "(a rite) that overthrows magic (*ḥkꜣ.w*), ties/firms knots, fixes knots, and subjugates the entire world" (cols. 5/10–6/1; see Derchain 1965, pp. 139, 7*, and pls. 5–6). Amuletic knots are used throughout this rite; Derchain, ibid., pp. 140 (cols. 7/9, 8/1, and 8/5) and 143 (col. 15/6). A single, highly uncertain Demotic example of "binding" (*mrỉ.t*) as a technical term for "magic" has been suggested in Spiegelberg 1917a, pp. 34–35 (col. 12/13) and p. 144 (no. 330). Coptic use of binding terminology is more common but may derive from Greek precedent, see ⲘⲞⲨⲢ, "binding magic" as a type of spell in Crum 1939, p. 181b, and cf. ⲢⲈϤⲘⲞⲨⲢ, ⲘⲚⲦⲢⲈϤⲘⲞⲨⲢ, and ϬⲒⲚⲘⲞⲨⲢ, in ibid., p. 182a. Preserved binding spells in Coptic include Ms. Oriental Institute 13767 (Stefanski 1939), Pap. Heidelberg 1682 (Bilabel 1934, pp. 393–96), and Parchment Strasbourg 135 (Crum 1922, pp. 541–42 and Kropp 1930–31, vol. 2, p. 228).

either protection (as magical knots[638]) or hostile restraint.[639] Obviously, it is the latter nuance of constriction which is depicted in the prisoner motif and enacted on the execration figurines, and this is expressed unambiguously in the ritual binding recommended for the prototype of the Louvre female figurine. While tying each knot, the magician is to call out: "Abrasax, hold her fast!"[640]

BREAKING THE RED POTS

No such figurines were associated with the first identified texts, the Berlin bowls, which consisted exclusively of shattered and generally inscribed red clay vessels.[641] Sethe concluded that the vessels had been ceremonially broken, and he linked the execration rite with that of "Breaking the Red Vases" (*sḏ dšr.w*) attested in Pyramid Texts spell 244.[642]

> Hail, [Osiris NN,] this is the Eye of Horus. Take it so that you may be strong and that he may be terrified of you—Break the red vases.[643]

The determinative of the word "break," , in the Merenre version of this spell implies the use of a mortar and pestle, and Schott has suggested that it is this pestle which the verse

638. The protective aspect of binding (*ṯs*) and knots (*ṯs.t*) derives from the nuance of "joining/coming together" both in acts of creation and as protection from threatened dissolution. Thus the same word *ṯs* is used when semen "comes together" in conception (*Wb* 5: 398/3–5), Atum punningly "joins together" his fist at the world's creation by masturbation (Pap. Bremner-Rhind, col. 28/22), a deity "comes together" in the egg (CT spell 938 and *Wb* 5: 398/1), Isis "joins" the severed limbs of Osiris, and the deceased "knits together" his own limbs (*Wb* 5: 397/15–20). Embodied in the royal cartouche (see Gardiner 1973, p. 74), the positive significance of knots is metaphorically applied to the red crown in CT spell 684: "it ties up life for me" (see Faulkner 1977, p. 250 = de Buck 1956, p. 314). For a discussion of the root meaning of *ṯs* as "to congeal/make firm/solidify," see Roquet 1984, pp. 355–85.

639. In medicine, such hostile knots appear less as "bonds" than as "obstacles" to poisons and disease; see Gardiner 1922, p. 266b; *Wb* 1: 348/8 *wḥꜥ ṯss.t*, "to loose what is knotted" = "to remove difficulties"; and, for examples, see Borghouts 1978, p. 24. The same conception probably underlies the untying of knots to facilitate pregnancy in Pap. Westcar, col. 10/2 (Staehelin 1970 and compare Bonner 1950, p. 93; versus Borghouts 1970, p. 156 and Goedicke 1985, p. 21, n. 9).

640. Preisendanz 1928, pp. 82–83 (PGM IV, l. 332); Betz 1986, p. 44. Compare also PGM V, ll. 325–45, in Preisendanz 1928, pp. 192–93 and Betz 1986, p. 106. For late associations of binding with love magic, see also Michaïlides 1966, pp. 71–72.

641. The use of an enclosing(?) jar (unrecognized by Sethe) is suggested by the presence of a clay jar seal (Sethe 1926, p. 5; uninscribed sherds are noted on p. 7).

642. Sethe 1926, p. 20. For discussion, see also Posener 1974, pp. 397–99 and Lüddeckens 1943, pp. 12–14. For the red vessels, see also *Wb* 5: 493/3–11. An excellent overview of the ritual "breaking of the red vases" is now found in van Dijk 1986, cols. 1389–96.

643. PT spell 244, §249, in Faulkner 1969, p. 58; for the text, see Sethe 1908, p. 137. See also the discussion in Sethe 1935a, pp. 232–34.

identifies with the Eye of Horus.[644] The process of smashing by pestle is termed *sḥm* in Egyptian,[645] and it is tempting to recognize an implied pun on this word with the homophonous *sḥm*, "to drive back/cause to retreat," although clear examples of this word play are not found until the Late Period.[646]

The ritual of the red vases is well attested from burial practices, and it figures prominently in an archaic mortuary liturgy in which the mastaba is encircled by the funeral party, among whom are the *ẖry.w dšr.w*, "Bearers of the Red Pots."[647] As this liturgy represents an adaptation of royal ritual for a private tomb owner, so it is not surprising to find the rite similarly adapted in the reliefs and inscriptions of private tombs. On the Fifth Dynasty coffin of *NN-ẖft-kꜣ* from Deshasheh it forms part of the conclusion of the standard schedule of mortuary offerings, bracketed by the fundamental rites of "reversion of divine offerings" (*wḏb ḥtp-nṯr*), "pouring cool water" (*sṯỉ qbḥ*), and "burning incense" (*sḏ.t snṯr*).[648] A similar schedule of offerings painted in a Sixth Dynasty burial chamber at Meir associates the rite with that of "removing the footprints" (*ỉn.t-rd*), the cultic sweeping of the ground at the completion of temple or funerary offerings,[649] and this pairing is repeated in inscriptions and relief decoration from the contemporary tomb of Mereruka at Saqqara.[650] The red vessels reappear in the frieze of purification utensils on Middle Kingdom coffins,[651] and spell 926 of the Coffin Texts echoes the Fifth Dynasty offering list in a direct address to the deceased:

> Wash yourself, sit down at the meal, put your hands on it; divert the god's offerings, break the red pots, give cold water, purify the offering-tables ... fire and incense are for NN ...[652]

The association of the "breaking of the red vases" with the funerary offering meal was already implied in the Pyramid Texts of Unas, where the spell containing the rite follows others designed to provide the king with offerings (spell 199), libations (spell 32), and

644. Schott 1928, p. 101. The Unas version of the spell uses as a determinative a prone, broken pot: .

645. *Wb* 4: 215/9ff.; Wreszinski 1926, p. 2, fig. 2; and compare Sethe 1926, p. 20.

646. For *sḥm*, "to repel," see *Wb* 4: 215/2–7. For *sḥm*, "to repel" written for *sḥm*, "to break/ pound up," see *Wb* 4: 215/8.

647. See Gardiner 1955a, p. 16. See also above, p. 58 (nn. 267 and 269).

648. Petrie 1898, pl. 29, the inside left panel, bottom row, third text from right end.

649. Blackman 1924, pp. 50–51 and pl. 18. For the *ỉn.t-rd* rite, see also Nelson 1949 and Altenmüller 1971.

650. Duell 1938a, pl. 67 (chamber A8) and see Sethe 1928b, p. 102, contra the doubt expressed by Borchardt 1929, p. 16, n. 2.

651. See Grdseloff 1941, pp. 26 and 30.

652. Faulkner 1978, p. 66 (= de Buck 1961, p. 128j).

incense (spells 25 and 200).[653] Its clear affiliation in private texts with the concluding ceremonies of that meal suggests that the red pots were those that were actually used in the offering and broken at its termination.[654] The ceremony would thus appear to be an inherent part of early Egyptian funerary practice, and the durability of the underlying concept is demonstrated by the reappearance of a similar custom performed beside funerary offering booths in the New Kingdom.[655] The vitality of the practice in the New Kingdom is confirmed by the first incorporation of the ritual into the divine liturgy. At the Luxor temple, Amenhotep III performs the ceremony before Amon-Re by striking two of these pots together.[656] The use of such red vessels (*dšr.w*) continues into the Ptolemaic period, where—as in the archaic liturgy—they are carried about the site to be purified.[657]

While the sources explicitly linking the "Breaking of the Red Vases" with offering meals are strangely silent about the significance of the act, the earliest reference to the rite in the Pyramid Texts is quite specific; breaking the red vases inflicts terror upon one's enemies.[658] The aggressive nature of the ritual is reinforced by the simultaneous butchering of a bull in the slaughterhouse of the pyramid temple.[659] The pairing was fundamental, and, relocated before the private tomb, the sacrifice accompanies New Kingdom performances as well.[660] The breaking of the vessels corresponds to the sectioning of the bull, and in a subsequent libation, the strewn water was perhaps equated

653. See Blackman 1924, pp. 50–51.

654. See Blackman, ibid., p. 51.

655. See Borchardt 1929; Norman de Garis Davies 1925, p. 48; and idem 1948, pl. 25 (bottom right) and p. 36 (misidentified as sprinkling offerings on the road). Similar scenes appear in the tomb of Horemhab at Saqqara (G. T. Martin 1989, p. 101, n. 4 and pls. 118–23 and van Dijk 1986, cols. 1391–96). An intact deposit of broken vessels from such a funerary meal appears in G. T. Martin 1985, pp. 3 and 47–48. The relationship of this rite to that of the Pyramid Texts (and execration texts) was denied by Sethe as quoted in Borchardt 1929, p. 16, n. 8, because the earlier ritual seems to have been accomplished by pestle, whereas the New Kingdom examples show vessels simply thrown to the ground. However, the discovery by Moret of an example of *sd dšr.w* performed by smashing two vessels together shows that it is not the method of breaking, but the breaking itself which is the basis of the rite. Compare the remarks of Lüddeckens 1943, p. 14 and Posener 1974, p. 398.

656. See Moret 1938.

657. See Chassinat 1928, p. 338 (and above, p. 58, n. 268) and Mallet 1909, p. 75.

658. The importance of "emic" analysis for ritual acts is underscored by a deceptive parallel to New Kingdom burial customs in modern Haiti, where the funeral of a voodoo initiate is accompanied by the breaking of a clay jar (*canari*) to release the soul of the deceased. Far from frightening enemies, the rite marks the most propitious moment for enemies to snare the defenseless spirit (W. Davis 1985, pp. 182 and 269).

659. Altenmüller 1972, pp. 98–100 and van Dijk 1986, cols. 1392–96.

660. Van Dijk ibid., col. 1393.

with the animal's blood.[661] Both bull and pot are substitute figures for the enemy, repulsed and dismembered.

RED

The hostile overtones of the ritual are at once evident in the specified color of the pottery itself, for the negative "Sethian" associations of the color red are well known.[662] The customary color of demonic figures (Seth, Apophis, etc.) in wax or clay, red is also the preferred color for ink used to write the names of such demons and enemies.[663] The two uses are combined in the execration texts, where both substitute figure (pot or clay figurine) and identifying inscription are often red.[664] A further link between this color and the execration texts may reside in an Old Kingdom title which Edel has read *sẖ*

661. See van Dijk ibid., col. 1393 and Altenmüller 1972, pp. 99–100 and compare pp. 92–93. In the New Kingdom, the Old Kingdom libation is paralleled by the emptying of the vessels prior to breaking.

662. Compare Pap. MMA 35.9.21, col. 29/9–10: "Back, Seth, haughty, red-haired, ruddy complexioned" (*ḥȝ=k Stš qȝ ḥr dšr.t fʿy mrš ỉnm*), in Goyon 1975, p. 381. Underworld demons are similarly qualified as "red one," "red-haired," "red-eyed," and even "with red eyelashes"; see BD spells 145p, §S; 146p; 148, §S2–3, and Pleyte 166, §S 2, in Allen 1974, pp. 132, 135, 139, and 215; Fairman 1974, p. 94; and Erichsen 1954a, p. 658. For red-haired men as "Sethian," see Gardiner 1935, vol. 1, pp. 10 and 20–21. As an adjective, "red" is often a synonym to "evil"; compare *Wb* 5: 488/4. The evil connotations of the color can also be stressed by the determinatives of the word "red" (*dšr*) itself; see the use of the "evil-bird," (Gardiner Sign-list G 37) and "dying-man," (Gardiner Sign-list A 14) determinatives in *Wb* 5: 488. Similarly, late writings of the word with the Oxyrhynchus fish (Gardiner Sign-list K 4; *Wb* 5: 488, usual value *ẖȝ*), although derived from the "red fish" (*Wb* 5: 492/10–11) may evoke a visual pun on the word for corpse (*ẖȝ .t*); see the following n. 663. For a general discussion of the color, see Griffiths 1972 and Lefebvre 1949. The link between the vases and the god Seth was first suggested with hesitation by Sethe 1928b, p. 102 and followed by Lüddeckens 1943, p. 13, n. 1.

663. Red wax figures of Apophis are ritually destroyed in the "Apophis Book" (Faulkner 1933, pp. 46 [col. 23/6–7] and 59 [col. 26/20]). Faulkner 1937b, pp. 168 and 172, confuses the word "red" with "corpse" and translates "waxen body"; for this confusion, cf. the preceding note. Ramesside examples appear in the magical Pap. Chester Beatty 7, col. 5/5 (red snake pierced by black knives), and among the vignettes on the verso (serpent pierced with knives, whole image brushed over with red; see Gardiner 1935, vol. 2, pls. 34, 38, and 38a). Similar figures of Seth appear in the "Anti-Seth Book," see Schott 1929, pp. 4–5 (l. 6) and 36–37 (l. 2). An image of Seth as a red wax hippopotamus (inscribed with enemy names) was used in conjunction with a red goat and ox in ceremonies at Edfu (Alliot 1954, pp. 521 and 524 [= Chassinat 1930, pp. 132–34]). The hippo figure was adopted in a dream sending spell in the PGM (see Preisendanz 1931, p. 103 [= PGM XIII, l. 309]). For the use of red ink in rubrics and the avoidance of the color for gods' names, see Posener 1949 and Faulkner 1937b, pp. 166–67 and n. 1. The avoidance of the color in beneficial magic is maintained in Demotic spells and derivatively in the PGM; compare the requirement that divinatory lamps be "without a slip of red lead" (*ỉwṯ prš* = ἀμίλτωτος), in Griffith and Thompson 1904, pp. 44–45, n. to 5/4. The violent connotations of the color are not, however, restricted to ancient Egypt, cf. Sheridan's *The Rivals*, Act 3, scene 4: "I must be in a rage ... Come here's pen and paper. I would that the ink were red!"

664. For the use of red ink in the execration inscriptions, see the remarks of Posener 1958, p. 257.

dšr-šnw, "scribe of redheads" and interpreted as the designation of the clerk responsible for recording the "Sethian" individuals whose names comprise the Egyptian section of the execration lists.[665] If the notion of "red hair" (as either a genuine physical characteristic or a figurative expression[666] for "Seth-like/Typhonic") could be firmly associated with the enemies of the execration texts, it would provide a ready explanation for the peculiar tradition recorded by Diodorus (I.88) concerning the ancient sacrifice of red-haired men.[667] Unquestionably, however, the most peculiar speculation in this regard derives from the recent determination by French scientists that the original hair coloration of Ramses II was red, leading to the suggestion that the grandiose achievements of this monarch resulted primarily from a desire to compensate for this physical "defect."[668]

BREAKING

The hostile overtones implicit in the color red are made explicit by the act of breaking. From the earliest periods of Egyptian history the breaking of grave goods had constituted "killing" the objects to assimilate them to their deceased owner. [669] More pertinent to the malevolent intent of the execration ritual is the widespread practice of defacing extant images of enemies to produce a *damnatio memoriae* which rendered the depiction "magically" useless, and whose effect could be felt in the underworld as a "second death."[670] Royal, ecclesiastical, and personal in motivation, the practice is best exemplified by the well-known destruction of images of Hatshepsut by Tuthmosis III, of the god Amon by Akhenaton, of Akhenaton by Horemhab, of the Cushites by the succeeding Saite

665. Edel 1970, pp. 39–41 and Borchardt 1937, pp. 8 (1316) and 24–25 (1353). For red hair as a Sethian diagnostic trait, see n. 662, above. "Redheads" might refer not to "Sethian" persons, but to demons; compare *Wb* 5: 439/13 and Faulkner 1958, pp. 25, 38, and 56* (col. 35/13): "The souls of the red-haired ones."

666. Compare the use of "red-faced" (*dšr ḥr*) and "red-hearted" (*dšr ib*) as expressions for "angry"; *Wb* 5: 490/4–6; and the modern American counterpart "seeing red," and French "voir rouge."

667. Diodorus would either misrepresent execration ceremonies as actual human sacrifice or record actual sacrifice which was replaced by the execration rite. See also the remarks of Plutarch in Griffiths 1970, p. 165. A thorough analysis of this tradition and the possibility of human sacrifice in Egypt is found in Yoyotte 1980–81. But compare also nn. 755 and 795, below.

668. Desroches-Noblecourt 1985, p. 390: "... he encouraged his people to look on his distinguishing red hair as an expression of divinity presented as a blessing from his forbears ... who had no doubt been the family's first 'carrot-tops'!"

669. See Grinsell 1961, especially pp. 480–82; idem 1973; A. Hassan 1976, pp. 122–27; and compare the dismantled and buried "enigmatic object" discussed in Hafeez Abd el ʿAl 1977, p. 117; Lehner and Lacovara 1985, pp. 169–74; and Grimm 1987, pp. 202–06. Similar practice in the worship of Hathor probably derives from the funerary associations of that goddess (Kertesz 1976, pp. 134–36).

670. For the practice, see Davies and Gardiner 1915, pp. 19–21 and 39 and Drioton 1952.

dynasty, of the god Seth by the late priesthood, and by the mutilation of figures in private tombs of all periods.[671] Though intensified, Coptic and Islamic destruction of "pagan" images merely follows the traditional technique.

As an obvious expression of destruction, breaking appears in the Pyramid Texts not only in the ritual of the red vases, but also in a spell to supplant a divine scribe:

> Scribe, scribe, smash your palette, break your pens, tear up your rolls! Oh Re, expel him from his place and set me in his place.[672]

Although this text might seem straightforward without symbolic nuance, its Coffin Texts descendant suggests that the opposite is true. Spell 425, a "spell for driving away a vulture," addresses:

> ... you two vultures who are on the booths of the Potter! I have come to you that I may break your water-pots and smash your inkwells, for a path is prepared for me to the place where the great god is.[673]

From parallel spells 667 and 688, it appears that these vultures are hostile underworld emissaries who must be repulsed from the offerings of the deceased:

> ... your dues are faeces, and NN will not give you this which he brings into the Island of Fire (the island of the sun god).[674]

The mention of the booths of the Potter and the smashing of the water-pots as a preliminary act in the procession to the underworld cannot but recall the ritual "breaking of the red pots"—especially the New Kingdom attestations performed at booths beside funerary processions—and the chosen enemy, the vulture, is an obvious threat to the food and corpse of the deceased. It is difficult to resist the conclusion that these Coffin and Pyramid Texts spells actually pertain to the rite, and that the unidentified enemy (or at least *an* enemy) repelled from offering meals by breaking the serving vessels was the vulture.

Whether or not this identification is correct, the ritual nature of "breaking" in the Coffin Texts is clear. To render an enemy harmless, eyes, fingers, staffs, teeth, oars, knives, shields, and even potter's wheels are broken.[675] The most blatant reference to the ritual

671. For such intentional breakage of statuary and relief, see Gardiner 1961, pp. 182–83, 187, 228, and 360; Hari 1984; and for the persecution of Seth, see te Velde 1977, pp. 144ff.

672. PT spell 476, §953–55, in Faulkner 1969, p. 164.

673. CT spell 425, in Faulkner 1977, p. 70 (= de Buck 1954, pp. 269–70).

674. CT spell 667, in Faulkner 1977, p. 239 (= de Buck 1956, pp. 295–96); and compare CT spell 688, in Faulkner 1977, p. 253 (= de Buck 1956, p. 318). Alternatively, the spell may read "which he brings *from* the Island of Fire," if the island is to be identified with Egypt or the necropolis (Grieshammer 1977).

675. Compare CT spells 698, 836, 882, 885, 888, 891, 1021, 1099, and passim.

power of breaking appears in spell 571, in which the equal pairing of spell and rite is notable:

> If something be said over the waters, or if something be broken over the Nile, this mansion of mine among the waters will be thrown down ...[676]

The hostile aspect of breaking continues unchanged in the Book of the Dead, where, for example, the deceased likens himself to a bird whose "egg has not been broken,"[677] and a ritual shattering of a green block of faience may re-enact the dismemberment of Osiris at the hands of Seth.[678] Seth and Apophis experience the same fate in temple cult, in which wax figures of the demons are pounded (like the Berlin red bowls) after being bound, trampled, spit upon, stabbed, burned, and boiled in urine.[679]

Presumably influenced by such ritual practices, the *topos* of breaking passes into popular expressions. Thus by the Middle Kingdom, the serpent Apophis is characterized as "He of the broken *ka*s" (*ḥḏ-kꜣ .w*).[680] In the second Semna stela of Sesostris III, the king belittles his Nubian opponents as "wretches, broken of hands and hearts."[681] The imagery

676. CT spell 571, in Faulkner 1977, p. 173 (= de Buck 1956, p. 173).

677. BD spell 85b, §S3, in Allen 1974, p. 73.

678. In BD spell 125c, §S6, the deceased shatters a block of green faience which he has previously buried and mourned and then throws the fragments into a lake (Allen 1974, p. 100). If the block represents Osiris, the ritual breaking would re-enact the cutting up of the corpse of that god by Seth and its subsequent dispersal. The elements of this initiatory rite, though enigmatic, seem to relate to the Osiris cycle: 1) rejoicing in the land of Phoenicia (cf. the finding of Osiris in Byblos, in Griffiths 1970, p. 141); 2) the severed haunch representing the leg of Seth which struck Osiris; 3) the water in which Osiris was drowned (cf. te Velde 1977, pp. 84–91); and 4) the torch for repelling Seth (Griffiths 1958, pp. 5–7). The associations of Osiris with green and faience are numerous; compare his epithets "Green-head" (*wꜣḏ-tp*) in Pap. Harkness, col. 4/31, published without translation in Logan 1976, pp. 156–57; and "He who lives by means of (literally "eats of") gold and faience" in the tale of "Horus and Seth," col. 14/8: *wnm m nwb ḥr tḥn.t*, in Gardiner 1931, pl. 14; clarified in BD spell 17b, §S5 (Allen 1974, p. 31). For general discussions of Osiris and green, see also Raven 1978–79, pp. 263–66 and 282 and Baines 1972, p. 290, n. 1. An Osirian interpretation of this spell is also accepted in Lichtheim 1976, p. 132, n. 12.

679. See the "Apophis Book," col. 23/10, in Faulkner 1933, p. 46 and 1937b, pp. 168 and 176; and compare an unpublished magical ostracon in the Oriental Institute collection, O. OIM 19120: "said over an image of Apep, made in [wax (?) ...] put on a fire, ground smooth (*nḏ-sn ʿʿ*) ...." For Seth, see below, n. 684. The procedures in these rituals find a Mesopotamian counterpart in the rite *Maqlû*; see below, n. 729.

680. See Kees 1924, p. 70 (Eleventh Dynasty, CT spells 378 and 381 = de Buck 1954, pp. 41, 42, and 44). Faulkner 1977, pp. 12–13, does not recognize this phrase as the name of the conjured serpent, ignoring the seated god determinative in de Buck 1954, p. 42d (text B1C).

681. Line 13 (with a parallel at Uronarti; see Fischer 1973). The association of this expression with the execration rite would be even stronger if the word read by Fischer as "hands" is to be reinterpreted as

at once recalls the actual breaking in the execration rite and may well derive from it.[682] The Chester Beatty "Dream Book" of the New Kingdom incorporates this execration technique within its collection of hostile symbolism: "(If a man see himself in a dream) breaking a vessel with his feet—BAD; it means fighting."[683] Idiom and rite are combined in the "Anti-Seth Book" of the Late Period which dictates the destruction of wax figures of Seth and his confederates while proclaiming that "the Breaker of Millions has broken their hearts."[684] The adoption of execration terminology is nowhere more striking than in the stereotyped and widely-disseminated stelae of "Horus on the Crocodiles." Used popularly as amulets against animal bite, the stelae petition the gods to seal the mouths of lions, crocodiles, snakes, and scorpions:

> Make them for me as the pebbles of the desert, as the potsherds along the street.[685]

Such a reduction of enemies to harmless potsherds is, of course, exactly what the ritual of the red vases had accomplished—quite literally—since its first appearance in the Pyramid Texts. A similar conception may underlie the use of ostraca in private curses from the New

---

the "broken pot" determinative, as in W. V. Davies 1976. Further figurative uses of the verb "to break" (*sḏ*) are found in *Wb* 4: 374/17–24 and *Wb* 3: 419/8–10 (*sꜣw*).

682. It is interesting to note that the appearance of this expression at the Nubian forts of Semna and Uronarti is in accord with the Middle Kingdom enactment of execration rites at such sites; compare the remains from Uronarti and Mirgissa discussed in Vila 1973 and 1963; with Dunham 1967, pp. 54 (no. 29-1-159), 160–62, and pls. 31C–E and 32A–B.

683. Papyrus Chester Beatty 3, col. 10/9, in Gardiner 1935, vol. 1, p. 19 and vol. 2, pl. 8. See also the prognostication for the followers of Seth: "[He will engender(?) dis]putes so as to break vessels, destruction(?) ... [...]"; col. 11/17, in ibid., vol. 1, p. 20 and vol. 2, pl. 8.

684. See Schott 1929, p. 55/11 and compare the "Apophis Book," col. 24/4–5 and 6 (Faulkner 1933, p. 49), as translated by Faulkner 1937b, p. 169: "You have been broken by those who break up ills." This translation is uncertain, however, and the word "break" (*sꜣw*) could be translated as "guard/restrain" (*Wb* 3: 416–17 or 419/4–11).

685. Standard Text A, attested from the New Kingdom through the Greco-Roman eras. See Daressy 1903, pp. 2, 8, 13, and 19; Lange 1927, pp. 33 (ll. 27–28), 34, and 38, (spell G, col. 4/8); and Sander-Hansen 1956, pp. 53–54 (l. 119); and for a Coptic descendant, see Kropp 1930–31, vol. 2, p. 68 (Pap. Rylands 104). The common and innocuous nature of pottery led to its selection as an Egyptian expression for the general notion "things" (*ḫn.w* "pots" > "things"; compare English and German "stuff/Stoff"); see *Wb* 3: 107/11 and Hayes 1955, pl. XIV (text B vo., ll. 3 and 5). Although potsherds were a major constituent of ancient garbage and a ready symbol of death, the special significance of broken pottery in the Egyptian execration rite leaves little doubt about the intended magical allusion in this text, itself an execration of hostile animals. For the imagery in Mesopotamia, compare Kramer 1969a, p. 459: "Its people, not potsherds, filled its sides"; and 1969b, p. 618: "Ur is shattered by the weapon like a (potter's) vessel." Magical allusions appear as well, cf. Lambert 1957–58, pp. 292 (no. 39): "[They have made images of me and li]ke a broken pot they placed them in a well"; 294 (no. 75) and 299 (no. 42) "Smash them (*scil.* images of witches) like a pot!"

Kingdom through the Greco-Roman periods[686] and is clearly the basis of the "death by potsherd" listed among the seventy potential causes of death nullified by Osiris in an oracular papyrus in Turin.[687]

Three millennia after the initial evidence of the Pyramid Texts, a third century papyrus from Oxyrhynchus provides perhaps the final echoes of the rite, preserved not in Egyptian but Greek. The papyrus contains the fragments of "The Potter's Prophecy," an apocalyptic tale translated from Demotic that foretells the foreign conquest of Egypt and its ultimate salvation. The motivation for the prophecy is the impious seizure of the titular potter, a divine representative, and the breaking of his pots.[688] Here the traditional destruction of foreign enemies by the breaking of pots has taken an ironic turn, for in this text it is the Egyptians themselves who have abrogated justice and become strangers to the gods. As a result, they bring about their own destruction by unwittingly re-enacting the ancient ceremony.[689]

Although the Berlin bowls showed unmistakable signs of intentional breakage,[690] later discoveries of execration figurines seemed to reveal only accidental damage and led to a

686. E.g., the curse in O. Gardiner 49 (= HO 7, 1), with a vignette in which the magician(?) holds a small object (the ostracon?) before Renenutet and Nepri (Černý and Gardiner 1957, p. 2). For the use of ostraca in Demotic and Greek spells, see J. H. Johnson 1975, p. 41 and Preisendanz 1931, p. 171 (PGM XXXVI, ll. 256–64 = Betz 1986, p. 275) plucked from the crossroads as in the imagery of the Horus cippi; and Betz 1986, pp. 282 (PGM XLVI, ll. 4–8), and 321 (PGM CXXIV)—for which see the discussion in Maltomini 1979, p. 103. For the presence of ostraca (in contrast to pots subsequently broken) in the Mirgissa deposit, see below, p. 153.

687. Papyrus Turin 1995+1996 vo. (Dawson 1931, pp. 23–25, especially p. 24 [no. 43], superseding Chabas 1909, pp. 55–56 [no. 46, translated "poste périlleux"]). Dawson failed to understand the reference to execration magic: "Some of these potential agents of death seem quite innocuous: how a potsherd, for instance, ... can be the cause of death is not evident. The reading of the word rendered «potsherd» seems quite unambiguous, unless it be a textual corruption of some totally different word" (p. 24). A fuller translation of this decree by Osiris appears in Borghouts 1978, pp. 4–6 (no. 9). For the current inventory number of this text, see Borghouts 1987b, p. 262; contra idem 1978, p. 119 (no. 9), where it is identified as Pap. Turin 1993 [23].

688. Although the actual reference to the breaking of the pots is restored, the preserved context justifies the restoration. The pots are snatched (σπασάμενοι, l. 15) from an oven which is later described as "desolate" (ἐρημωθήσεται, l. 56). For the text, see Lobel and Roberts 1954, pp. 89–99. For the reconstruction of text and story, see Koenen 1968, especially pp. 183, 185, 196/15–16, 197 (n. to l. 25), and 207/54–57; 1970; and 1984. The relation of the events in the frame story of the prophecy to the ritual "breaking of the red vases" has not been previously recognized.

689. An echo of the rite may have survived into modern times; cf. the modern Arabic expression *bitiksar ʾulla waraah*, "You break a pot behind him," meaning "good riddance!" said of an unwelcome guest after his departure (personal communication, Everett Rowson).

690. Sethe 1926, p. 20.

re-interpretation of the rite, stressing not breaking but burial.[691] The resulting controversy over the question of intentional versus accidental damage affected even the interpretation of broken prisoner statues from Old Kingdom funerary complexes,[692] and still excites comment in the publication of execration figurines.[693] Such controversy is now anachronistic, however, for with the discovery in 1962 of an intact deposit of execration texts on pots and figurines at the Nubian fortress of Mirgissa,[694] it is clear that the rite comprised both breaking and burial.

THE MIRGISSA DEPOSIT

Roughly contemporary with the Berlin bowls (mid Twelfth Dynasty),[695] the Mirgissa deposit directly parallels both the material and the text of this earlier find. But while the Berlin collection, purchased from a Luxor dealer, was incomplete and without context, the in situ Mirgissa assemblage has revealed a rite far richer in both the quantity and complexity of its elements. For the "deposit" actually comprises four separate but related interments involving 197 broken inscribed red vases (and ostraca)—as compared with 80 in Berlin—in addition to 437 broken uninscribed red vases, 346 assorted mud figures, 3 limestone prisoner figurines with the head of a fourth, and the remains of a human

691. Posener (1940, pp. 19–20) noted that the breakage of the Brussels figurines was accidental. But in 1939b, p. 45, he suggested that the burial of figurines constituted a parallel ceremony to that of the breaking of the red vases. Both breaking and burial were features of the Giza ritual (Osing 1976a, p. 156 [figures broken prior to deposition in pot and burial]).

692. Ritual breaking of these figures was suggested by Jéquier 1940, pp. 26–29 but denied by Lauer 1969–70, pp. 42–43 and Lauer and Leclant 1969. See now Verner 1985, p. 149.

693. See the remarks of Heimer 1981, p. 137, "... les rites d'envoûtement n'impliquaient ni le bris, ni la mutilation de tels objets, mais seulement leur enfouissement."

694. See Vila 1963; idem 1973; Posener 1966; Koenig 1987a; and idem 1990.

695. Judging by paleography and onomastica; for the date of the deposit, see Posener 1966, p. 279 and Koenig 1990, p. 102. The Mirgissa find is dated slightly anterior to the Berlin bowls, being thus contemporary with the construction of the fortress.

sacrifice.[696] Comparable to a foundation deposit,[697] though probably interred well after the erection of the fortress in an official act of consecration,[698] the Mirgissa assemblage had provided a magical safeguard for the inhabitants of the adjacent second cataract fortress. By virtue of its undisturbed condition, it provides the modern scholar with the most detailed evidence for actual ritual practice associated with the "breaking of the red vases." Its very complexity, however, militates against its being considered the *representative* deposit for execration rites in general. For while scattered finds from the comparable sites of Uronarti and Shelfak could corroborate the existence of a similar, standardized rite for the Nubian fortresses of the Middle Kingdom,[699] intact deposits within Egypt from the Old, Middle, and New Kingdoms are manifestly not identical,[700] and the Saite descendant of the Mirgissa rite, at the fortress of Defennah, consisted only of some thirty to forty limestone prisoner figurines, buried and often broken (see fig. 13b).[701] Nonetheless, many of the elements of the Mirgissa deposit recur in differing combinations within the less complex variations of the rite, and it is as an index against which to compare these variations that the Mirgissa assemblage is most valuable.

Situated some 600 meters from the fortress itself, the deposit lay within a small sandy depression beside a granite outcrop well removed from the normal thoroughfares of the fort and its adjacent town. Vila, the discoverer and excavator of the deposit, has attempted to explain its placement by suggesting that the Egyptians adhered to a hypothetical list of

696. The revised tabulation of pots and figures appears in Vila 1973, p. 630.

697. The magical intent of these ancestors to modern cornerstones is clearly demonstrated in the deposit of clay disks recovered from the Middle Kingdom Nubian fortresses of Kuban, Buhen, Areika, and Uronarti (contemporary with the Mirgissa assemblage) which depict Egyptian soldiers leading bound (Nubian) enemies (Säve-Söderbergh 1941, pp. 132–35 and Posener 1958, p. 254). Although, Posener (ibid.) doubts that there could be "une relation quelconque avec les figures d'envoûtement," the identity of purpose in the two rites is obvious: the eternization of the destruction and subjugation of Egypt's enemies. For subsequent Nubian adaptations of such seal types (reversing the ethnicity of captor and captive) during their tenure of these fortresses in the Second Intermediate Period, see B. Williams 1985, p. 45.

698. For the relatively late installation of the deposit, see Vila 1973, p. 634.

699. See Vila 1973, pp. 638–39, in regard to Dunham 1967, pp. 54 (no. 29-1-159), 160–62, and pls. 31C–E, 32A–B, 39, and 64C.

700. See the overview in Posener 1975a. Plaques recently suggested to be of New Kingdom date are uncharacteristically provided with a "Nubian formula" (Galerie Nefer 1992, p. 33 [no. 34, untranslated, but legible]).

701. See Petrie, Griffith, and Murray 1888, p. 73, §70 and pl. 40, nos. 8–13: "... they are all represented as having the legs bent back from the knees, and the ankles and elbows bound together." Petrie identified the images as "draughtmen" for playing games in the sand. One figure is reproduced in Petrie 1972, p. 19 (no. 60, c 2) and pl. 5. See also the additional references in Posener 1987, p. 4.

requirements which only this site would have fulfilled: isolation from the disruptive factors of traffic, protection against natural erosion, and burial in sand.[702] While the first two *desiderata* are logical enough as practical considerations for the preservation of the deposit, the preference for burial in sand—despite the ready abundance of granite strata and trained stone-cutters[703]—detracts from this protection and must be explained on other grounds. Although unrecognized by Vila, the significance of the sand is not far to seek, deriving not from practical but from religious considerations.

SAND

By virtue of its early appearance from the receding flood waters, sand was intimately associated with the creation of the Egyptian cosmos,[704] and hence with all creative acts. As a purifying substance, sand is thus used in the foundations (and foundation deposits) of temples and sanctuaries,[705] is ritually strewn during processions of the gods[706] and private magical rites,[707] is offered to deities,[708] and even serves in the composition of divine

702. See Vila 1963, p. 140 and 1973, p. 628.

703. Compare the remarks of Vila 1963, p. 140.

704. Perhaps thus should be explained the festival of Amon, "from the first to second month of summer for the sand in the river," for which a wine delivery is recorded in O. Ashmolean 543; see Wångstedt 1965–66, pp. 41–43. A brief overview of the Egyptian use of sand is found in K. Martin 1984, cols. 378–79.

705. See Spencer 1979, pp. 132–37 and Bissing and Kees 1922, pp. 9–10. For sand as the foundation of the "House of Life," see Derchain 1965, pp. 49 (n. 4), 139, and 8* (col. 6/9–10). See also Rochemonteix et al. 1984–87, p. 173/11–15 and Alliot 1954, p. 514: "The sand on their sanctuary will not be cleared away," to which should be compared the threat in Griffith and Thompson 1904, pp. 142–43 (col. 21/35–36): "Send ... to the sand of the foundation that it may be scattered without wind." The crucial term "foundation" (*snyṯ* < *snty*) has not been previously translated. For sand as the cover of foundation deposits, see Weinstein 1973, pp. 420–23 and 434.

706. See *Wb* 3: 290/17 for the festival of *ḫnp šʿ*, "sprinkling sand." See also the statements of the coachytes who sprinkle "dust" (κονίαν καταστρωννύειν) in the "Hermias Prozess," in Wilcken 1935, p. 71; recognized as the ritual act of "preparing a road" in Foucart 1924, pp. 17–19.

707. See Griffith and Thompson 1904, pp. 76–77 (col. 10/10): "You sprinkle it (the chamber) with clean sand brought from the inundation." See also Setna I, 3/28 and 30, in Lichtheim 1980, p. 130.

708. For the rite of offering sand (*wšꜣ šʿ*, "strewing sand"), see David 1973, pp. 71 and 74 (in foundation rites) and 103 (identified with the Eye of Horus, and used to heal the god's eye); Moret 1902, pp. 200–02; and Chassinat 1932, p. 105 (*ḥnk šʿ*). See also CT spell 112: "I present to you sand from the Gate of Khemennu," in Faulkner 1973, p. 106 and de Buck 1938, p. 128.

figures[709] and as a platform for magical images,[710] lamps,[711] bowls,[712] and the embalming of the Apis bull.[713] In funerary contexts, sand is a basic requirement in tomb construction (used for filling the tomb shaft) and is early ritualized as an obvious symbol of the desert necropolis.[714] Negatively, sand is an omnipresent weapon for the blinding of enemies,[715] and as such is feared by the deceased[716] and used to repel demons.[717] In funerary texts from royal and private tombs (Pyramid Texts,[718] Amduat,[719] etc.) a sand pellet or pebble replaces the figure of an enemy used as a determinative, a conceit perhaps deriving from the association of Seth and his confederates with the desert,[720] and obviously related to the desire expressed in the Horus cippi to reduce one's enemies to "the pebbles of the desert."[721] From such associations, the sand used as a base for temples, statues, et cetera,

709. Sand and dough comprise the Osiris figures detailed in Pap. Salt 825 (Derchain 1965, pp. 143 and 17*, col. 16/2–3 and Beinlich 1984, pp. 272–74); for actual examples, see Raven 1982. Perhaps associated with the ritual fabrication of these figures is the festival *sḏ.t-šʿ*, "dough and sand" mentioned in the famous biography of Khnumhotep (*Wb* 4: 569/6).

710. See the Demotic Pap. Louvre E. 3229, ll. 4–6: "Afterwards you (spread) pure sand and you make a layer of sand under it (a mummy of Osiris) ... You set up the image on the layer of sand," in J. H. Johnson 1977, pp. 68–69 and 81. See also Griffith and Thompson 1904, pp. 136–37 (col. 21/14).

711. See Griffith and Thompson, ibid., pp. 44–45 (col. 5/6).

712. See Griffith and Thompson, ibid., pp. 100–01 (col. 14/19).

713. See Spiegelberg 1920a, pp. 7 and 20 (pls. 10/1 and 13/17).

714. See the rubric of CT spell 111: "To be spoken over sand of the temple of Anubis, it being placed about him. This means burial in the West," in Faulkner 1973, p. 106 and de Buck 1938, p. 126. This spell to guarantee burial clearly precedes death and is a further example of a Coffin Texts spell used prospectively—presumably by the reciter on his own behalf. With this spell compare BD spell 151, §f, in Allen 1974, p. 149: "It is I who catch the sand to choke the hidden place (the tomb) and repel him who would repel it to the flame of the desert."

715. See Spiegelberg 1917a, pp. 44–47, cols. 17/31 and 18/8–9, for the strewing of sand (*šʿš šʿ*) in the face of a lion, but contrast the use of sand to heal the eye of the god in n. 708, above.

716. See BD spell 169e, §S, in Allen 1974, p. 176 (= CT spell 23, in de Buck 1935, pp. 70b–71a): "Sand shall not be put on your face."

717. See O. Deir el-Medineh 1640 vo., ll. x+3–4: "And they filled their (sickness demons) eyes with sand ... to prevent the limbs of NN born of NN from being gnawed," in Posener 1980, p. 90 and pls. 66–66a.

718. See Gardiner 1973, p. 490 (Sign-list N 33) and for general discussion, see Lacau 1914, pp. 63–64.

719. Compare Hornung 1963, vol. 1, pp. 181, 188, and 191.

720. For this well-known association, see *inter alia*, Griffiths 1960, pp. 71, 98, and 145. Compare also the threatening "sandbanks" of Apophis in the underworld, *Wb* 5: 402/3–4. The desert affiliation passes directly into Coptic treatments of Satan, though with obvious biblical precedent in the temptation of Jesus in the Judean wilderness, see *inter alia*, Alcock 1983, pp. 87 and 111.

721. See above, p. 151 and n. 685.

may come to symbolize the prostrate enemy of the "prisoner motif," trampled beneath the sacred objects.[722] Not only whole figures of enemies are replaced by sand, but also sections of them. Thus the intentional mutilation of potentially threatening hieroglyphic images (snakes, lions, men, etc.) found on occasion in burial chambers may be accomplished by carving the sign in halves with grains of sand between them: , effectively preventing their reunification.[723] This method of destruction is repeated in the first Demotic romance of Setna Khamuas, when the hero defeats the self-regenerating "eternal snake" only by placing sand between its severed sections.[724] While all of these nuances may have contributed to the selection of a sandy burial for the Mirgissa execration texts—the use of sand as a cosmic foundation, the significance of sand in burial, its crippling effect in the face of the figurines, the transformation of the enemy to a harmless pebble, and the rendering permanent of magical dismemberment—it is the final nuance which seems most directly significant for the ritual shattering of foreign enemies.

INCINERATION

As deduced from the excavation, the scenario of the Mirgissa ritual began with the digging of an oval pit 68 cm deep in the form of a truncated cone (increasing in diameter from 100 to 200 cm). Into this pit were placed five unbroken crucibles of dried mud, duplicates of the crucible used for copper smelting which Petrie had recovered from the turquoise mines at Serabît el Khâdem.[725] Although the significance of these objects at Mirgissa has yet to be noted, there can be little doubt but that they represent the "furnace of the coppersmiths" (*mn.t n.t ḥmty.w* var. *wꜣwꜣ*, "furnace") specifically stipulated by the

722. While New Kingdom rituals equate sand with the Eye of Horus (see above n. 708), the Ptolemaic ritual adds also the notion of defeated enemies (Chassinat 1932, p. 105 [text without translation]): "Offering sand. Recitation: Sand is for you; I have elevated to your face the Eye of Horus in offering to your *ka*, so that you might have power over the misery in Heliopolis after you have punished the confederates of the hippo (Seth)."

723. For these mutilations, see Lacau 1914 and Lexa 1925, vol. 3, pl. 71. The grains of sand may indicate the separate burial of the two halves.

724. Setna I, col. 3/33, in Lichtheim 1980, p. 130. Compare also the proverb in "The Instructions of ʿOnchsheshonqy," col. 11/8: "Don't kill a snake and leave its tail"; Lichtheim 1980, p. 168 and Glanville 1955, pp. 28–29. For the notion that a severed snake can reassemble itself, cf. modern Texas folklore: "A joint snake in times of danger breaks into joints, rejoining himself when the danger is past"; Davis and Gillis 1989, p. 38.

725. See Vila 1973, pp. 630, n. 14 and 635 (for the intact deposit of the furnaces) and 1963, p. 156 (§D, 9, identified as "grands récipients verseurs"); for the crucible at Serabît el Khâdem, see Petrie 1906, pp. 51–52, 162, and fig. 161. See further Davey 1985.

"Apophis Book" for the incineration of wax figures of enemies.[726] The ritual burning of such figures, as a cultic analog to executions on earth[727] and in the underworld,[728] is a commonplace of temple practice,[729] and permanent furnaces attached to temples for this purpose have been excavated at Tanis and possibly at Bubastis.[730] A similar motivation should explain the unique use of *baked* clay plaques in a New Kingdom execration rite from Giza, despite objections by their editor that the figures were fired before being inscribed, and thus could not sympathetically effect the victim.[731] Magical practice does not begin only with the finished image; no less significant for the identification of image and object are the materials and procedures used in the *preparation* of figures.[732] Once identified with the fired plaques, the victims of the Giza rite are "sympathetically" burned nonetheless—not as incinerated inscribed figures, but as inscribed incinerated figures. Magically speaking, the effect is the same.[733] In private magic, burning is similarly used for torturing substitute figures of individuals to be mastered, and in the Greco-Roman and Coptic periods the heating element of public baths (ὑποκαύστρα) substitutes for the temple

726. Column 26/4: "Fell with the spear or knife, place on the fire in the furnace of the coppersmith." See Faulkner 1933, p. 56 and 1937b, p. 171. For *wꜣwꜣ*, see cols. 24/15, 25/6, and 26/18.

727. For executions by burning, see the examples collected by Posener 1985, pp. 32–33 and see below, p. 160, n. 743 and p. 170, n. 791.

728. See Zandee 1960, pp. 133–46; adding the Demotic attestation in Griffith 1972, vol. 3, pp. 110 and 250 (Pap. Rylands IX, col. 22/7): "He is for the furnace of Osiris in the Place of Darkness(?)."

729. For the burning of enemy images in the New Kingdom, see Grimm 1988. For later practice, see the "Apophis Book," cols. 22/22, 22/24, 23/7, 23/10–11, 23/19, 24/15, 26/4, 26/18, 26/20, 28/20, et cetera, in Faulkner 1933, passim, and the "Anti-Seth ritual" in Schott 1929, pp. 5, 9/8, 13/8, 17/6, 49/19–51/21, and 65/7–8. Further examples appear in Chassinat 1931, p. 235; idem 1960, pl. 150; idem 1934b, pls. 585–86; Alliot 1946, pp. 60–62; and Goyon 1969, pp. 62–65. Cf. also the sacrificial immolation of *ḫt-ḫꜣwy*, mistakenly identified as a ceremony of "firewalking" in Wainwright 1932, pp. 164–67 and Caminos 1958, pp. 48–51 (where the sacrificial nature is made obvious by the burning of goats, the symbolic enemies of Osiris [p. 79, n. 492]). For Mesopotamian parallels, see Meier 1937; idem 1966; Lambert 1957–58; and Abusch 1974. Ugaritic parallels are noted in Rüterswörden 1976.

730. The furnace at Tanis is unmistakable, with clay images of bound prisoners at the cardinal points (Yoyotte 1973, p. 85). A furnace at Bubastis for "amulets and ushebtis" may have served a similar role (Vachala 1976).

731. Posener 1958, p. 255.

732. Compare the discussion of the magical properties of plants and minerals used in such figures, and the significance (and restrictions) on the use of the color red, above, pp. 39–40 and 147–48.

733. Compare(?) the prohibition of fired wax in PGM IV, ll. 2378 and 2945; Preisendanz 1928, pp. 146–47 and 166–67.

furnace or ritual crucible.[734] At Mirgissa, the number of crucibles corresponds directly to the number of sections of the execration texts, with one each for the Asiatics, Nubians, Libyans, Egyptians, and evil things. Perhaps associated with this ritual burning are the ashes found in various levels of the central deposit and the remains of melted red wax found beside the skull of the sacrificial victim.[735]

The central rite entailed, of course, the breaking of the red pots. From the fracture markings on the reconstructed vessels, it is clear that Sethe's original suggestion was correct, and that the pots were broken by percussion with a striker, perhaps the stone spheroid found near the top of the central deposit.[736] Both inscribed and uninscribed red pots were broken, with the latter predominating (at the ratio of one inscribed sherd to ten uninscribed sherds at the bottom, one to twenty at the top). The preponderance of uninscribed vessels should not be dismissed as simply "filler," for it is their presence which firmly links the execration rite with the "breaking of the red pots" performed in funeral and temple ceremony.[737] Although the only enemies that the fortress would have been likely to face were Nubians, the entire execration formula was nonetheless systematically copied by several scribes, with a complete series apportioned over as many as four vessels.[738] Some preference does seem to have been shown to the Nubian section, however, for it is the only text currently identified at all levels of the deposit.[739]

FIGURINES

At seven regular intervals, the stream of broken pottery was interrupted by the casting into the pit of a standard collection of mud figures comprising a severed human head or

734. This is especially common in spells of love compulsion or separation (see Bell, Nock, and Thompson 1933, p. 23 [cooking a lizard] and J. H. Johnson 1975, pp. 38–41). For the use of the bathhouse furnace in Demotic, Greek, and Coptic texts, compare J. H. Johnson ibid., pp. 44–45 (col. 1/13); Preisendanz 1928, pp. 24–25 (PGM II, ll. 48–49); idem 1931, pp. 21 (PGM VII, l. 469), 165 (PGM XXXVI, l. 75), and 176 (PGM XXXVIII, l. 3); and Kropp 1930–31, vol. 1, pp. 51–52 and vol. 2, p. 32 (K 25, 38: ⲧⲱⲕⲉ ⲛ̄ⲧⲥⲓⲉⲓⲁⲩⲛⲉ), and compare vol. 1, p. 61 and vol. 2, p. 47 (M 95, requiring water from a bath for a curse). Excavated examples from the spring at Bath are discussed in Cunliffe 1983, p. 20. Perhaps from these immolations derive the "bath demons" in Roman folklore (see Bonner 1932 and Alcock 1982).

735. For the ashes, see the remarks of Vila 1973, pp. 629 and 637 (who notes the possibility of ritual incineration, but fails to link this with the crucibles) and 1963, p. 144. For the red wax (beeswax dyed with red ochre), see idem 1973, p. 631, n.15.

736. See Vila 1973, p. 637, replacing the comments in 1963, p. 149. The spheroid had certainly been used in crushing the red ochre used to dye the wax mentioned above, for one face was stained with ochre.

737. For uninscribed fragments in the Berlin corpus, see above, n. 641.

738. See Posener 1966, pp. 280–81.

739. See Vila 1973, pp. 632–33 (fig. 1).

foot, a headless torso of a bound prisoner, a blinded human eye, a domestic animal (probably a cow, and possibly mutilated), a reptile (crocodile?), six or seven papyrus or reed skiffs intentionally broken, twelve flying geese, and various unidentified geometric forms (lenticular, conical, and flat).[740] Though still uninterpreted, the significance of the identified objects is clear, for they constitute the destruction of the enemy himself (head, torso, foot, and blinded eye[741]), his herd (cow), and his methods of passing by the fortress (foot, boats). The resultant destructions correspond precisely to the very purpose of the Nubian fortresses as expressed by Sesostris III: "to prevent any Nubian from passing it downstream or overland or by boat, (also) any herds of Nubians."[742]

The figures of wild animals (reptiles, geese) are equally explicable as well-known symbols of the demonic forces of chaos believed to threaten the Egyptian cosmos *through the medium of foreign enemies.*[743] The relationship between wild animals and foreign enemies is thus an intimate one in Egyptian symbolism (both may personify disease[744]), and the two images are regularly coupled in ritual scenes of hunting, trampling, and

740. See Vila 1973, pp. 635–36 and 1963, pp. 156–59.

741. The identification of these eight figures as human eyes lacking pupils is made in Vila 1973, p. 632, but incorrectly cited in n. 29; compare idem 1963, p. 159g and fig. 17, no. 3. If correctly interpreted, compare the blinding of enemies by sand in nn. 715–17, above. The figures may, however, be representations of bows. As many of the mud figures were reduced to powder by the impact and weight of the sherds, it would be quite possible that one more of this type had existed, and that they symbolized Egypt's traditional enemies, the "Nine Bows."

742. The first Semna Stela of Sesostris III (see Breasted 1906, vol. 1, §652). The translation is from Gardiner 1961, p. 135.

743. See above, p. 115 (enemies as demonic) and *Chapter 2*, p. 65 (goats surround Osiris); and compare n. 663 (hippo, goat, and ox as Sethian symbols) and pp. 146–47 (bull sacrifice paired with breaking of red pots). A brief discussion and bibliographical synopsis is found in Wildung 1977c. The transformation of the confederates of Seth into animals is stated directly in the "Legend of the Winged Disk": "Now the foes descended into the water and became crocodiles and hippopotami," in Fairman 1935, p. 29. Elsewhere, the demons become snakes, birds, fish, lions, etc. See Kees 1942; Fairman 1974, p. 95 (snakes); Derchain 1962b, pp. 23–36; and Griffiths 1960, pp. 102–03. These demons also assumed human form as opponents of the kingdom: "Their forms came to be as humans within Heliopolis, with the children of their children up to today" (Schott 1929, pp. 64–65, ll. 3–6). For the equation of wild animals with the political enemies of the king, see Malinine 1934; Schott 1956, pp. 184–85; and Caminos 1958, pp. 48–51, in which sacrificed enemies are "carried like goats on the night of the feast of the Evening Sacrifice on which braziers are kindled." Compare also the pairing of theriomorphic confederates of Apophis with "all the (human) enemies of Pharaoh" in the "Apophis Book" (cols. 32/6–12 and 32/13–33/18), in Faulkner 1933, pp. 87–93 and 1938, pp. 46 and 52–53, and the plaque, presumably designed for an execration rite, depicting Seth and an Asiatic bound back to back at a stake in Michaïlides 1968, p. 82 (here fig. 19a, p. 212, below). The authenticity of this piece is not questioned in the otherwise critical review by Bingen 1969, p. 163.

744. See the examples gathered in Sørensen 1984, pp. 13–14 (nn. 40–41).

offering.[745] The presence of both in the Mirgissa deposit confirms the theological/magical orthodoxy of the rite, and the use of flying geese as symbols of the Nubian threat is particularly interesting as it is directly paralleled in the second Demotic tale of Setna Khamuas in which a Nubian sorcerer and his mother assume precisely that form to evade capture by the Egyptians.[746] Completing the inventory of mud figures, two isolated models of an ax and a brick recall similar figures from foundation deposits.[747] Explanation may also be possible for the unidentified "lenticular" objects if these are to be associated with the clay balls (*bnn.t*) thrown to repel Seth, Apophis, and foreign enemies in temple ritual.[748] Of the activity at the central deposit little more can be noted, except to remark that even the number of repetitions of casting the mud figures into the pit was not without meaning, for the significance of seven as the "number of efficacy" in Egyptian theology and "magico-religious" ritual is unmistakable.[749]

Eleven meters from the central deposit was found the second standard component of the execration ritual: the buried figurines of four bound prisoners, corresponding to the four

745. For discussion, see Junker 1955; with which compare Nelson 1931, pp. 12–21. For ritual hunting, compare also Alliot 1946. For the trampling of animals as a parallel to the "prisoner motif," see nn. 582 and 591, above; and the standard cippus depictions of Horus on the Crocodiles discussed above, nn. 518–19 and 583.

746. See Lichtheim 1980, pp. 149–50.

747. See Vila 1973, p. 637 and 1963, p. 159. For parallels from foundation deposits, see Weinstein 1973, pp. 60, 96–99 (axes), 419–21 (bricks), and passim. The ax could, of course, refer specifically to the destruction of the conjured enemies.

748. For this rite, see Goyon 1975, pp. 349–99; Parker, Leclant, and Goyon 1979, pp. 61–65; Ziegler 1979, pp. 437–39; adding Raven 1982, p. 24. A suggested link between this ritual and the Mirgissa finds is now suggested also by Koenig 1987a, p. 311, n. 10.

749. The number seven figures prominently in Egyptian theology in the seven Hathors who decree fate, the seven creative utterances who begat fate (*ṯs*, var. *ḏꜣἰs*, discussed above, pp. 46–47), the seven uraei who guard Re, the seven gates of the underworld palace of Osiris, the seven horns of the goddess of writing, et cetera. Perhaps influenced by these associations with deities of creation and authority, the number abounds in religious and magical literature from the Pyramid Texts through the Coptic period. In the Coffin Texts alone, the number appears in spells 164, 398, 401, 406–09, 479, 612, 662, 691, 695, 729, 744, 772, 997, 1011, 1027, et cetera. Steadily increasing in importance, the symbolism of the number seven acquires cosmopolitan influence in the Hellenistic period from the seven vowels (Greek) and seven planets (Mesopotamian); for which see the references in Ritner 1984b, p. 218. For general discussions of the number, see Dawson 1927; Sethe 1916, pp. 33–37; Kees 1980, pp. 158–59; Derchain 1974, pp. 7–8; and Posener 1985, p. 23.

cardinal points.[750] Recovered from a shallow grave (22 cm deep), three inscribed limestone figures and the head of a fourth all showed signs of intentional blows to the top of the skull which had been administered *prior to the painting of the statuettes' hair*.[751] This mutilation must thus be considered an integral part of the fabrication of the figures, which thereby become tangible images of the "stricken ones" (*sqr.w*) conjured in the accompanying texts. Corresponding injuries on Brussels figurines, pierced by three holes in the crown of the head, probably attest to a similar practice at Saqqara.[752] At Mirgissa, yet further ritual striking must have occurred, for although the group was undisturbed, one of the figurines was found reduced to small fragments. This suspicion is confirmed by the Old Kingdom deposits from Giza in which the clay figures were shattered before their burial in jars.[753] The single head may derive from a similar destruction prior to burial, or (like the mud head in the central pit?) allude to the sacrificed Nubian, whose severed skull constitutes the major component of the third deposit.[754]

HUMAN SACRIFICE

It is the content of this third deposit which yields the most curious and unexpected element of the Mirgissa find, for it provides the first indisputable evidence for the practice

750. By virtue of its association with the cardinal directions, four is the most common symbol of "completeness" in Egyptian numerological symbolism and ritual repetition (Sethe 1916, pp. 31–33). For the common ritual use of four enemy figurines, see the examples discussed in Parker, Leclant, and Goyon 1979, pp. 61–65. Although four is the expected number of figures, an illegal excavation at Helwan(?) produced five alabaster examples later acquired by the Cairo Museum (see Posener 1939a, pp. 313–17; and the complete publication in idem 1987). Though the five figures could correspond to the sections of the execration litany, Posener posits the original existence of a sixth for symmetry (1939a, p. 314). The preserved figures contain duplicate copies of all but the first (Nubian) section, which might have been copied on a lost, sixth statuette.

751. Vila 1973, p. 631 and 1963, p. 147. With this "mutilation in production" compare the argument for magical significance in the use of clay images fired prior to being inscribed, advanced above, p. 158.

752. Posener (1940, p. 19) notes that the careful placement of the holes argues against their being the result of later blows. However, he does not recognize that these could still represent intentional mutilation, and he theorizes instead that they might have been filled with hair, feathers, or knives. Of these suggestions, the last (itself a form of intentional mutilation) is the most likely, see below, p. 166.

753. See the comments of Osing 1976a, p. 156.

754. Versus the suggestion by Vila 1973, p. 638, that the head might be "the conventional sign" for commanding the decapitation of a real prisoner (an Egyptian counterpart to the ring of Herod in Wilde's *Salome*). One would expect that the rite had made use of four originally complete figurines; see n. 750, above, and now Koenig 1990, p. 101. The use of "severed" sculpted heads within the execration rites may have Old Kingdom antecedents in the so-called "reserve heads" that typically show disfigurement (Tefnin 1991).

of human sacrifice in classical ancient Egypt.[755] Interred about four meters from the central deposit, a skull rested upside down on one half of a broken pottery cup, its mandible missing and its upper jaw flush with the surface.[756] About the skull were found small traces of beeswax dyed with red ochre, presumably the remnants of melted figurines.[757] Although the cup which had probably once held the skull seemed naturally broken, perhaps as a result of burial, an intentionally shattered piece of inscribed red pottery 15 cm to the southeast clearly affiliated the find with the ritual of the central deposit. Lying a further 5 cm from this broken pottery was a flint blade, the traditional ceremonial knife for ritual slaughter.[758] That the skull derived from a ritual sacrifice cannot be denied, as it was the initial discovery of a nearby decapitated and disarticulated skeleton which had led to the find of the execration assemblage.[759] Clearly, the head had belonged to the adjacent body, which appeared less buried than discarded. Examination of the fragile remains suggested a Nubian origin for the sacrificed individual—a human counterpart to the broken enemy figurines.[760]

KNIVES

The close correspondence between the destruction of such substitute images and the Mirgissa sacrifice is underscored by the design of clay figurines from Giza (Old Kingdom) and Saqqara (late Middle Kingdom) whose rudimentary modeling suggests the depiction of

755. This example resolves the issue, but is only briefly mentioned in the basic study by Yoyotte 1980–81, p. 58. See also above, p. 158, n. 727 and p. 160, n. 743. For the possibility of a comparable execration sacrifice at Meroe, compare Shinnie and Bradley 1981, p. 167 (a defleshed skull lacking its mandible placed in a temple wall).

756. Vila 1963, pp. 146–47 and 145, fig. 6; idem 1973, p. 631; and Koenig 1987a, p. 309 (fig. 4).

757. Vila 1973, p. 631, n. 15.

758. The use of flint (*ds*, cf. *Wb* 5: 485–86) for knives dates from Egyptian prehistory, providing the basic Egyptian term for knife (*ds*, literally "flint object," cf. *Wb* 5: 486), and thus attaining traditional and sacred status. In the Book of the Dead, for example, it is specifically used against the enemies of the gods; see BD spell 172, §S5, in Allen 1974, p. 180: "(your) nails like knives of flint against the faces of them that do these (things) against thee." Similarly, the "Apophis Book" stipulates that images of Apep be struck with knives of flint, compare Faulkner 1933, pp. 44–45 and 56 (cols. 22/20–23 and 26/4) and 1937b, pp. 168 and 171 (the significance of flint is ignored by Faulkner, who translates only "knives"). Flint knives are used as well in the cultic sacrifice of the oryx, like foreign enemies a symbol of Seth (see above, p. 132; see also Rochemonteix et al. 1984–87, p. 77/13–14 and Derchain 1962b, pp. 58/7 and 59). A divine pedigree for the weapon appears in Pap. Salt 825: "A knife of flint from eastern Beḥdet is brought. It came forth from Ra to repel his enemies by means of it" (Derchain 1965, pp. 139 and 7* [col. 6/5]). In light of this evidence, it is difficult to accept Vila's suggestion (1973, p. 638) that the flint blade was used only after a more merciful death by strangulation.

759. Vila 1973, pp. 628–29 and 631.

760. Vila ibid., pp. 637–38.

decapitated prisoners.[761] More forceful depiction of this symbolic execution appears on a series of clay seal impressions which constitute an execration rite of the New Kingdom. Stamped with an image of a bleeding prisoner, the inscribed clay imprints are bisected at the neck by a knife drawn in red ink (see fig. 13c).[762] The use of actual knives has been postulated for the Middle Kingdom figures in Brussels, whose pierced heads may have once been fitted with small daggers.[763] From the same period, a formula to repel snakes in a Turin papyrus recommends the recitation of a spell "over clay with a circle of knives in it."[764] Transfixed by knives, such images of enemies and hostile creatures owe their ultimate origin not to ritual, but to the apotropaic mutilation of hieroglyphs in the Pyramid Texts, where potentially harmful signs are incapacitated by incomplete or bisected carving (discussed above, p. 157).[765] The same rationale has been suggested for Old Kingdom representations of Seth, whose tail appears as an arrow piercing his hindquarters (see fig. 14a),[766] and the intention is certain in images of crocodiles with heads struck by arrows in carvings of the First Intermediate Period and the Middle Kingdom (see fig. 14b).[767]

761. See Junker 1947, p. 34; Abu Bakr and Osing 1973, p. 98; and Posener 1987, p. 10.

762. See Posener 1958, pp. 257–58.

763. See Posener 1940, p. 19; and compare above, p. 162.

764. Roccati 1970, p. 26 (l. 16): *ḏd mdw ḥr sin šny dm.t im=s*. In ll. 13–14, the clay is said to be "of Isis." *Contra* Sørensen 1984, p. 12, the knives are not the teeth of the snake "rendered harmless in the clay," and the association of Isis with clay is not "otherwise unknown." Rather, the spell anticipates the events of the later-attested anti-snake spell "Isis and the name of Re," in which Isis molds a snake of earth and Re's spittle (Pap. Turin Pleyte and Rossi, pls. 131/11–133/14, 133/31, and 77/1–5); for editions and translations, see the sources cited in n. 337, above. This clay serpent is "detoxified" by Isis when Re reveals to her his secret name. As in this later spell, the clay in Pap. Turin 54003 should represent the serpent modeled by (and subject to) Isis. Encircled and pierced, the clay—and thus the serpent—is destroyed.

765. See Lacau 1914. A beheaded serpent appears in CT spell 493 (= de Buck 1956, p. 74). The various methods of mutilation grouped together in Lexa 1925, vol. 3, pl. 71, fig. 162b, are from differing historical periods. Incomplete carving may also appear in a private tomb of the Old Kingdom, see the crocodile carved without legs in the tomb of Khuenankh, in Quibell 1902, p. 258; suggested by Gilliam 1983. Isolated examples of bisected carving appear even in the Greco-Roman periods, compare Sauneron 1982, p. 151, no. 187 (demon carved in halves).

766. See Borchardt 1909 and the discussion of te Velde 1977, pp. 16–17. Further Old Kingdom examples appear in Piankoff 1969, pls. 62 (l. 54) and 67 (l. 111) (reference courtesy Henry G. Fischer).

767. On the nome standard of Dendera (see Fischer 1961, pp. 59–60 [First Intermediate Period] and Spiegelberg 1901, pp. 101–02 [in a Middle Kingdom stela at Leiden]). Spiegelberg's explanation of the magical significance of the arrow accords perfectly with the development of magical mutilation, and should be accepted despite Fischer's uncertainty. With these depictions should be compared the contemporary Brussels figurines also pierced in the head. See also the late carving at the temple of Dendera of the crocodile on the nome standard clearly pierced with arrows, in Mariette 1873, pl. 33, top right (with which cf. the snake pierced by a knife on pl. 34, top middle).

Appearing also in the Middle Kingdom is the first common use of the image of a knife for such mutilations: .[768] By the New Kingdom, these sketched knives are used not only on the execration seals noted above, but are affixed in multiples on images of Apep both in mythological scenes and, following the practice of the Pyramid Texts, when used as a hieroglyph (see figs. 14c and 14d).[769] In the Late Period, determinatives of both Seth and Apep are regularly mutilated (see figs. 14e and 14f),[770] and at Dendera the mythological execution of Seth follows the now traditional pattern (see fig. 14g).[771] Repeatedly stabbed, such images of Apophis, and later Seth, derive from the merger of symbol and rite. Reflecting the multiple wounds inflicted on figures of these demons in the regular performance of temple cult,[772] they are at once apotropaic design and textual vignette illustrating written cultic incantations: "A knife is fixed in his head before Re daily."[773] The quite obvious significance of the imagery survives well into the Roman period, when it reappears on an amulet against the "Evil Eye," shown pierced by a knife and two arrows (see fig. 14h).[774]

768. See Gardiner 1973, p. 457 (Sign-list D 57 used *inter alia* as the determinative of words for "mutilation") and Möller 1909a, p. 11 (no. 123, Twelfth Dynasty). Note also the seemingly contemporary origin of the expression *h̲ry dm.t* (*Wb* 5: 450/16–18), "sufferer," literally, "he who is under the knife," first attested in Griffith 1898, p. 13 (prescription 2, l. 51). For the standard use of the phrase in later magico-medical texts, see Jelínková-Reymond 1956, p. 15, n. 1.

769. Not only the practice, but the motivation of the Pyramid Texts is imitated in these New Kingdom mutilations which occur *within tombs.* For Apep thus slain in mythological scenes, see Hornung 1963, vol. 1: unnumbered plate of the seventh hour (see fig. 14c, below, p. 167) and vol. 2, p. 132. For knives in images of Apophis used as a determinative; see The Epigraphic Survey 1980, pp. 70–71 and pls. 20 (l. 8), 73, and 76 (l. 3; here as fig. 14d, below, p. 167) and Helck 1958a, p. 1850, ll. 6 and 10. A serpent determinative (for *ḏdfy.t*) is similarly stabbed on a Ramesside ostracon in Gardiner and Černý 1957, pl. 3, 2 (line 3), though its contemporary textual parallel in Pap. Turin Pleyte and Rossi, pl. 131/13, is uninjured. Ramesside examples appear also in the magical Pap. Chester Beatty 7, col. 5/5 and among the vignettes on the verso (Gardiner 1935, vol. 2, pls. 34, 38, and 38a).

770. For Apep, compare Möller 1909b, p. 23, no. 249 and 1912, p. 23 (Pap. Bremner-Rhind, passim). Similar representations of Seth appear in Pap. Bremner-Rhind, cols. 2/10, 2/17, 5/2, 7/3,13/23, and 23/14–15, in Faulkner 1933, passim and in the ritual texts in Schott 1929, passim. Seth and Apophis are both carved with knives at the temple of Hibis (Norman de Garis Davies 1953, pl. 20, North Wall [Seth] and pl. 25 [Apophis]).

771. See Mariette 1873, pl. 56a (= Porter and Moss 1939, p. 98, no. 58). The scene is a vignette for the tenth hour of the "Mystery of Osiris in Khoiak"; for the text, see Junker 1910b, p. 122.

772. See the "Apophis Book" cols. 22/20, 26/4, 29/20, etc., in Faulkner 1933, passim; Schott 1929, pp. 5 and 47/17–49/17; and the "Play of Horus," with its ritual harpooning of a hippopotamus image prior to the slicing of a hippopotamus cake, in Fairman 1974. Given the customs of Egyptian art, the numerous knives may represent only one knife, repeatedly used.

773. Faulkner 1933, p. 64 (col. 27/20–21) and compare p. 74 (col. 29/20).

774. Delatte and Derchain 1964, pp. 72–73.

Translated from the two dimensions of papyrus and relief to the three dimensions of actual practice on small figurines, these clusters of knives find a ready equivalent in the common needle or nail, obvious "miniature knives."[775] As a method of "killing" images, repeated nail blows are attested as early as the Second Intermediate Period,[776] and needles or nails may have already served as "knives" on the Middle Kingdom figures in Brussels noted above. Directly paralleling contemporary temple imagery, this method is adopted by private magic in the Greco-Roman periods, appearing in both Demotic and Greek language execration spells—and the infamous Louvre figurine.[777] The material specified for the composition of these nails is either copper, used by Isis and Horus against Seth, or iron, a mineral associated in Egyptian sources with Seth and the weapon which he used against Apophis.[778] The selection of these minerals in private texts is quite purposeful, using

775. The practice is quite familiar in the West; compare the ubiquitous European parallels discussed by the antiquarian Elsworthy 1958, pp. 53–58 and 84–85. Such familiarity can be misleading, however, and the Egyptian understanding of even this common magical technique should not be taken for granted without careful examination of *Egyptian evidence*. Parallel practice in differing cultures may disguise the most contrary of meanings; contrast the Coptic amulet for the protection of a house (seventh–eighth centuries) published in Wortmann 1968, p. 107. In the form of a *tabula ansata*, the amulet bears the inscription "One is God, the helper of Julios," and is pierced with eighteen nail holes (not used for attachment). The nails were certainly not intended to "kill" the amulet; they seem to form a κλίμα "incline," a standard device for reducing sickness. See Betz 1986, p. 3 and passim. Similarly deviant from the expected norm are the "nail fetishes" (*nkisi*) of the Kongo peoples of Africa. These wooden spirit figures with compartments for "medical" substances are pierced by numerous nails and blades to *enhance* their power, not to slay them. First recorded in 1818, these figures may have been influenced by Christian icons of the suffering Christ and saints (particularly St. Sebastian); for discussion, see Gillon 1984, pp. 283–85 and de Heusch 1968, pp. 77ff.

776. A cultic plaque of king Neferhotep of the Thirteenth Dynasty was "killed by nail imprints" (Bietak 1981, p. 273 and pl. 35b).

777. A Demotic spell for compelling a demon uses a three-lobed pod of garlic pierced by three iron needles (Griffith and Thompson 1904, pp. 66–67 [col. 8/17]). For Meroitic use of nails to pierce inscribed bronze figures, see Kendall 1982, pp. 55–56. An Old Coptic example ⲒⲂⲦ' ⲚⲂⲈⲚⲒⲠⲈ, appears in Preisendanz 1928, pp. 72–73 (PGM IV, l. 110). In Greek, examples are found in ibid., pp. 82–83 (copper; = PGM IV, ll. 296ff., corresponding to the Louvre figurine, see above, p. 113), 166–67 (= PGM IV, ll. 2943–50), et cetera, and perhaps in Maltomini 1979, pp. 94–112.

778. For the slaying of Seth by copper/bronze, see Lichtheim 1976, pp. 218–19; *Wb* 1: 437/10 (reading *ḥmty*); Blackman and Fairman 1943, p. 10 = Fairman 1974, p. 89. Compare also two small bronze representations of the spear of Horus, affixed in the back of a crocodilian Seth, in Schoske and Wildung 1985, pp. 132–33 (nos. 114–15). For Seth and iron, see Sethe 1908, p. 8; Faulkner 1969, p. 4 (PT spell 21); Otto 1960, vol. 1, p. 107 and vol. 2, pp. 106–07; te Velde 1977, pp. 86–91; Faulkner 1933, p. 62 (col. 27/9); and Griffiths 1970, pp. 217 and 522–24, quoting Manetho: "They still call … iron 'the bone of Typhon'." The significance of selected metals in the PGM is discussed in Hopfner 1974, pp. 353–64 (§§596–612), but one must now substitute "copper" (*ḥmty*) for "iron" (*bἰꜣ*) in the passage quoted from Pap. Sallier IV on p. 354.

"magic by substance" to ensure that the fate of the magician's victim is equated with that of the underworld demons.

Figure 14. (*a*) Seth with Tail Designed as Arrow in Flanks (after Fischer 1961, p. 60); (*b*) Crocodile with Head Pierced by Arrow, on Standard of Sixth Upper Egyptian Nome (after Fischer 1961, p. 59); (*c*) Apep Stabbed with Knives, from Amduat Scene of Seventh Hour (after Hornung 1963, vol. 1, plate to seventh hour); (*d*) Snake Determinative in Name of Apep, Pierced by Knives (after The Epigraphic Survey 1980, pl. 76); (*e*) Snake Determinative in Name of Apep, Pierced by Knives (after Faulkner 1933, p. 43 [col. 22/9]); (*f*) Seth Determinative Pierced by Knives (after Schott 1929, p. 15 [Pap. BM 10252]); (*g*) Seth Bound and Stabbed before Osiris at Dendera (after Mariette 1873, pl. 56a); (*h*) Evil Eye Pierced by Knife and Two Arrows (after Delatte and Derchain 1964, p. 72).

DECAPITATION AND REVERSAL

The need to assure netherworldly repercussions for earthly practice motivated the Mirgissa sacrifice as well, for the fate of the Nubian victim—beheaded and overturned—incorporates two of the most feared underworld punishments allotted to enemies of the gods. Decapitation (*ḥsq*,) appears as a constant threat by demons in the Coffin Texts, and the deceased thus styles himself prophylactically "the living one who knits on heads, who makes necks firm," while the Book of the Dead provides a safeguarding "Spell for a Secret Head" so that "thy head can never be taken from thee."[779] The fear of "going upside down" (*sḫd*,)—entailing the reversal of bodily functions and the forced consumption of excrement and urine—is especially prominent in the Coffin Texts, themselves roughly contemporary with the Mirgissa deposit, and this posture reappears in the royal funerary compositions of the New Kingdom in which it is reserved for depictions of the damned in Hell.[780] These later texts are of particular interest for the study of the Mirgissa execration rite as they also combine directly the tortures of decapitation and reversal. Thus in the Book of Caverns, the deceased king proclaims:

> Oh beheaded ones, without their heads, foremost of the place of destruction!
> Oh fallen ones, without their *bas*, foremost of the place of destruction!
> Oh overturned ones, fettered ones, foremost of the place of destruction!
> Oh overturned ones, bloody ones deprived of hearts, foremost of the place of destruction!
> Oh enemies of the ruler of the underworld, Osiris Foremost of the West,
> behold I have commanded you to destruction! I have assigned you to non-existence![781]

The accompanying illustration in the tomb of Ramses VI corresponds exactly to this description, showing decapitated bodies and severed heads as well as enemies falling and upside down—all in sets of four, paralleling the four limestone figures in the second

779. Spell 80, in Faulkner 1973, p. 84 (de Buck 1938, p. 37) and BD spell 151, in Allen 1974, pp. 147–48 (quote on p. 148). For the threat of beheading, see Zandee 1960, pp. 16–17 and 226 and Hornung 1968, pp. 18–19 and pl. 3. Textual references to the practice are uniformly negative, contra the recent suggestions of Wright 1979, p. 353. For the suggested use of "reserve heads" as "decapitated" images in Old Kingdom execration rites, see Tefnin 1992.

780. For reversal, see Zandee 1960, pp. 73–78; Hornung 1968, pp. 15, 16, and 29; and Kadish 1979, pp. 209ff. The upside down depiction of a Hittite prince pulled from the water in the Kadesh victory reliefs of Ramses II probably puns on this standard posture of tortured spirits; for the scene, see Kuentz 1928, pl. 40. For a cross-cultural analysis of the significance of being upside down, see J. Z. Smith 1978, pp. 147–71 and compare the treatment accorded European "witch bottles" in Merrifield 1987, pp. 168, 175, and 189. Reversal of enemy names appears in Pap. Chester Beatty 8, col. 4/10 in Gardiner 1935, vol. 1, p. 68. A crocodile (symbolic of Seth) is overturned on a plaque discussed in Daressy 1912. For overturning as an expression for negating hostile magic, cf. the phrase *pnʿ ḥkꜣ.w* in the protective rite of Pap. Salt 825; Derchain 1965, pp. 139, 7*, and pls. 5–6 (cols. 5/10–6/1).

781. Piankoff 1944, p. 13 and pls. 24–25 and compare 1942a, p. 11 and pl. 9.

Mirgissa deposit.[782] The association of these punishments is equally evident in the eleventh hour of the Book of Amduat ("What is in the Underworld"), when the opponents of Re and Osiris are ritually slaughtered at the command of Horus:

> The majesty of this god issues commands to cut up ... the corpses of the enemies and the bodies of the dead, the upside down ones who are hindered from moving.[783]

> Your heads are cut off. You cannot come into being, for you are upside down.[784]

Nor is the similarity exhausted by the pairing of these punishments, for the netherworldly Amduat rite reproduces the execration ritual's burning of the severed enemies (substituting deceased spirits for wax figurines), and duplicates even the location of the act, with destruction and burial in sandy pits (*ḥ3d*) in the desert.[785] In fact, so closely does the Amduat rite evoke the ceremony at Mirgissa that in essence they are identical, comprising the incineration, decapitation, dismemberment, overturning, and burial of enemy figures. Only the form of the victims—not their identities—distinguishes the two rites, with simulacra (pots or figurines) on earth replaced by spirits in the underworld.[786] Common to both is the human corpse, condemned in the netherworld by Horus, and in Mirgissa by Horus' earthly incarnation, the pharaoh. The implications of this similarity are clear: the ritual destruction envisioned in the text of Amduat must derive from genuine earthly

782. Piankoff 1942a, pl. 10.

783. See Hornung 1963, vol. 1, pp. 188–91 and vol. 2, pp. 180–83 (quote in vol. 1, p. 188 and vol. 2, p. 180). Compare the recitation in the Late Period ritual quoted in Schott 1956, p. 187: "Ihre Köpfe dort sind kopfüber und rücklings—umgekehrt anordnen—Sie gehen nicht."

784. Hornung 1963, vol. 1, p. 189 and vol. 2, p. 181. Beheading appears also in the seventh hour, see ibid., vol. 1, unnumbered plate.

785. Hornung, ibid., vol. 2, pp. 180 and 65 and 1968, pp. 21–29 and pls. 2 and 5 (burning), and p. 23 (pit). Note that the four goddesses who direct the destruction, one of whom is named "She-who-is-over-her-sand," all wear the symbol for desert atop their heads. With these deities compare the four goddesses in Ziegler 1979; adding Raven 1982, p. 24.

786. Minor variations exist as well. By virtue of the greater number of victims, the Amduat scene shows six pits with whole bodies reversed and the severed heads upright. With only one sacrifice at Mirgissa, one pit is sufficient and the head must be both severed and reversed.

ceremonies similar, if not identical, to the execration ritual.[787] The royal funerary texts are thus in reality neither exclusively royal nor funerary, but derive—at least in part—from state rituals performed by the priesthood in public[788] for earthly benefit.[789] The influence of such ritual upon the iconography of the damned continues into the Late Period. In Papyrus Jumilhac, Seth is depicted upside down in a pit beneath the throne of Osiris, a demonic counterpart to the human enemies of the royal tombs and the Mirgissa sacrifice (see fig. 15a).[790]

The dependence of underworld tortures upon the execration rite is logical enough, as both are primarily symbolic performances. Nonetheless, it should not be forgotten that the execration rite is itself derivative of actual public executions whose capital punishments it re-enacts. Decapitation is already attested in the predynastic Narmer palette, and references to public incineration are increasingly frequent in later Egyptian history.[791] "Overturning" appears in the biography of the Eighteenth Dynasty vizier Rekhmire, who declares that he "caused the liars and thieves(?) to be upside down."[792] From context, it is unclear whether this describes a genuine torture or is a derived metaphor paralleling the English

787. A vestige of this ritual origin is perhaps to be noted in the description of the divine executioners "who perform *ṯmsw*, 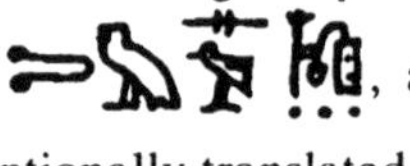, among the enemies of Osiris"; Hornung 1963, vol. 1, p. 191. Although conventionally translated "slaughter" in the religious texts to which it is generally confined, *ṯmsw* means literally "redness" (especially in reference to hostile red ink, see *Wb* 5: 370/2–6) and readily evokes the ancient ritual of the red vases. As a reference to the magical red ink of this and similar rites, *ṯmsw* may be the Egyptian term for "ritual execration" rather than a rare expression for "slaughter." For related nuances of *ṯms* as "evil," "crime," "injustice," or "punishment," see Lefebvre 1949, pp. 74–75; Zandee 1960, pp. 292–93; Goyon 1972, p. 123 (§345); and Sander-Hansen 1937, p. 58 (l. 133): "She is not reckoned (to) the Book of *ṯmsw* (execration list?)." Alternatively, Gardiner has suggested that this writing may serve as the antecedent of the Coptic ⲦⲰⲘⲤ, "to bury" (1925, p. 74).

788. The site of the ceremony at Mirgissa was in direct view of the occupied fortress, and the rite could thus not have been performed secretly; see the remarks of Vila 1973, pp. 634–35.

789. For the adaptation of the "royal funerary literature" from earthly rites, see Wente 1982, pp. 161–79. The apparent relationship of the Amduat ritual with Middle Kingdom practice provides further evidence for maintaining the traditional dating of these "underworld texts" to the Middle Kingdom or First Intermediate Period; for the controversy, see Wente ibid., pp. 175–76 and the rejoinder in Hornung 1980, p. 9.

790. Vandier 1961, vignette 10 = te Velde 1977, pl. 6/1. Compare Piankoff 1942b, pl. 9 and p. 61.

791. In the literary Pap. Westcar, execution by burning is attributed to the Third Dynasty (Simpson, Faulkner, and Wente 1973, p. 18, col. 4/9–10); in official statements it appears at least as early as the Thirteenth Dynasty; see Randall-MacIver, Mace, and Griffith 1902, p. 93 and pl. 29/6: "whoever shall be found within these stelae except a priest in the execution of his duty shall be burnt." For later examples, see Posener 1985, pp. 32–33.

792. Gardiner 1925, pp. 70–71, who does not make the restoration of *ṯ3* [*y*].*w*, "thieves"; compare *Wb* 5: 350/2–10.

"overthrow." No such uncertainty obscures the fate of the seven Asiatic captives slain in the succeeding reign by king Amenhotep II: "they being placed head downwards at the prow of His Majesty's ship."[793] The posture is not accidental; as in the execration and funerary rites it signifies—and creates—the "overthrow" of the enemy and his "every evil word, every evil plot, every evil fight,"[794] et cetera. Performed after the death of the enemies, the act of overturning is here of magical and symbolic significance, a "backformation" from ritual onto public execution.[795] At Meroe, ritual and execution may again be conjoined in a political reversal of the earlier Egyptian rite at Mirgissa. Embedded within a temple wall, a defleshed and jawless skull lay behind a mural of bound prisoners, while a bronze head severed from a statue of Augustus was buried before the threshold.[796] This reciprocity of imagery between execution and execration finds a distant echo in the praxis of a fifth century Greek magical papyrus which effects a curse by placing a pierced wax figurine upside down in a pot of water.[797] At Mirgissa, the interdependence of rite and execution is expressed concretely—by the corpse of the human sacrifice.

793. Amada Stela, l. 17; see Helck 1955b, p. 1297 and Černý 1967, pls. 3 and 7; translation in Gardiner 1961, p. 199.

794. Compare Sethe 1926, pp. 71–72.

795. The suggestion of ritual motivation in this act is strengthened both by the fact that the king himself performed the execution, and by the mention of the king's having made "execration figures" (*rs.t*) of his enemies (l. 5, on which see below, p. 187). The passage (ll. 16–17) describing the slaying of the chieftains is grammatically ambiguous, and subject to two interpretations: *ỉỉ.n ḥm=f m ꜣw.t-ỉb n ỉt=f ꜤImn smꜣ.n=f pꜣ wr.w 7 m ḥḏ=f ḏs=f*, "Joyfully, His majesty came to his father Amon *after he had slain* the 7 chieftains with his own mace" (*smꜣ.n=f* as circumstantial), or "Joyfully, His majesty came to his father Amon. With his own mace he slew the 7 chieftains" (*smꜣ.n=f* as emphatic). The second interpretation seems preferable, producing a poetic parallel structure (two emphatic clauses) and explaining the seven victims as sacrifices before Amon in Thebes (cf. Breasted 1906, p. 313, though doubted by Yoyotte 1980–81, p. 37, n. 29). However, the first translation has been generally adopted, though it removes the reason for the king's return to Amon and would require that the victims' corpses had been hung from the royal ship for the entire journey back from Lebanon. As six bodies were subsequently suspended from the walls of Thebes and a seventh dispatched to Napata, one might wonder just what would have remained to display after such a journey. In fact, reliefs substantiate the display of *living* prisoners, probably destined for subsequent execution, suspended from ships in wooden cages (Karnak second pylon, reign of Tutankhamun; see Grimm 1987). For standard translations of the Amada passage, see Helck 1961, p. 31 and Cumming 1982, p. 27. For a similar sacrifice performed by Osorkon II at Thebes, see Caminos 1958, pp. 48–51. The ritual aspect of a comparable execution within a literary tale is noted in Posener 1985, p. 33: "La peine capitale se trouve ainsi ritualisée, les condamnés étant traités comme les victimes animales sacrifiées dans les temples."

796. Shinnie and Bradley 1981, p. 167. Directed against Roman Egypt (among other enemies), the components of the ritual protection of the temple thus include decapitated human remains, a captured and decapitated image of the enemy ruler (Augustus), and painted imagery to eternize foreign subjection.

797. See Maltomini 1979, pp. 98 and 112 and Betz 1986, p. 321.

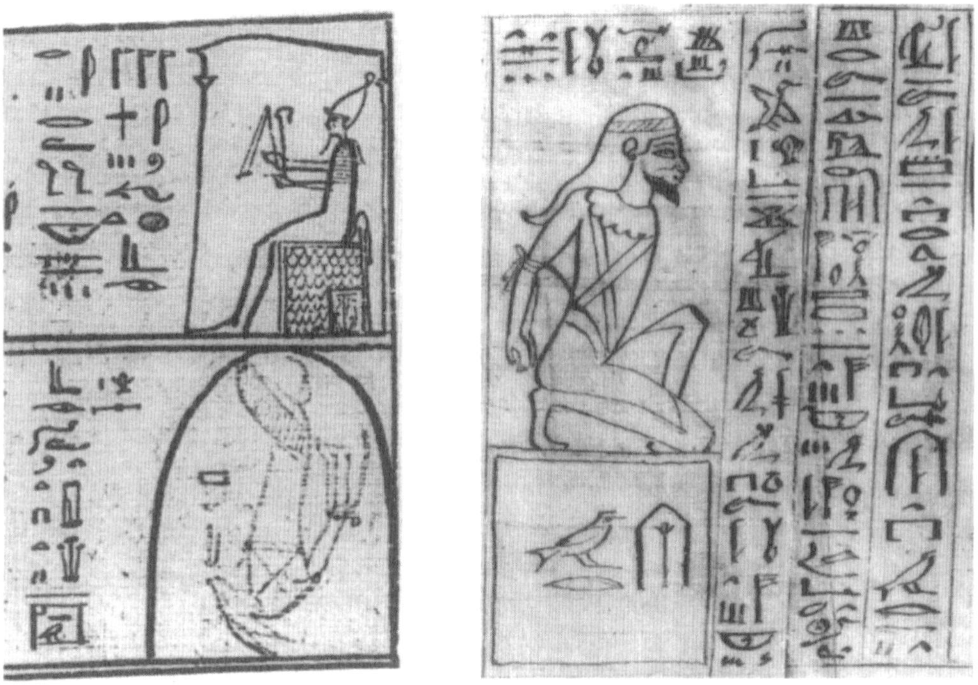

a b

Figure 15. (*a*) Seth Bound and Inverted in Pit beneath Osiris (Pap. Jumilhac, after Vandier 1961, vignette 10) and (*b*) *Nkỉw-mnt*—"The Vanquished One at the Stake" (after Śliwa 1973, fig. 1, facing p. 8).

BURIAL

The final element of the Mirgissa assemblage consists only of this corpse, carelessly buried and largely ignored by its discoverer in his analysis of the execration rite.[798] The significance of the corpse should not be too easily dismissed, however, for the major unifying characteristic of execration figures when found in situ has been their location in traditional cemeteries.[799] At the virgin site of Mirgissa, no such local cemetery had existed; by the interment of the Nubian sacrifice an *ad hoc* burial ground was created. If the importance of burial in the rite is as great as its proponents have claimed,[800] this requirement alone may have necessitated the human sacrifice. Be that as it may, the overriding significance of burial in the ceremony is unmistakable, for despite the prominence of dismemberment, burning, and other tortures, it is burial alone which unites the entire corpus of execration figures, whether inscribed or uninscribed, intact or

798. Vila 1973, pp. 628–29 and 631.

799. See the comments in Junker 1947, p. 38 and in Osing 1976a, p. 156. Of the execration figures with certain provenience, only one has come from a village rather than a necropolis site: a fragmentary figure inscribed in red found in the fill between two Old Kingdom levels at Balat (Posener-Kriéger 1982, p. 384 and pl. 70B; Giddy 1983, p. 107; Grimal 1983, p. 111; and idem 1985).

800. Best expressed in Posener 1939a, pp. 316–17.

mutilated.[801] The same criterion may serve to identify an archaic wooden statuette in Boston as the earliest execration figure. Said to derive from the First Dynasty royal tombs at Abydos, the fragmentary Boston statuette is thus to be distinguished from the various figurines of the "prisoner motif" recovered from the temple precinct at that site.[802]

Justification for the importance of burial has been based on neither royal nor temple sources, however, but on the rubric of Coffin Texts spell 37, a spell for vindication against personal enemies:

> To be spoken over a figure of the foe made of wax and inscribed with the name of that foe on his breast with the bone(?) of a synodontis fish: To be put in the ground in the abode of Osiris (*scil.* 'graveyard').[803]

What has not been noticed is that the entire spell is of relevance for the execration rite. Arguably a funerary adaptation of a common, "private" cursing ritual,[804] the spell utilizes a standard Egyptian pattern of attributing impious acts and statements to one's enemies:

> See, that foe etc., who is among men and gods and the inhabitants of the necropolis, has come to break your house, to ruin your gate ...
>
> O Osiris, see that foe who is among men and who is in the necropolis has come, having joined with Seth ... he has said that your wounds are hidden, he has said: 'Sore be the pains of your suffering which are on you.' ... May you break and overthrow your foes and set them under your sandals.[805]

801. Compare also the two, presumably ritual, burials at the "Augustus Temple" at Meroe comprising a human skull and a severed bronze head from a statue of Augustus; Shinnie and Bradley 1981, p. 167.

802. For the statuette and its suggested identification as a kneeling prisoner, see W. S. Smith 1967. Smith does not, however, associate the sculpture with the execration figurines.

803. Faulkner 1973, p. 28 (= de Buck 1935, p. 157). Noted by Posener 1939a, p. 316. Although "the foe" could be equated with Seth, the identification is not specific and is certainly not restricted to Seth. As a spell against personal enemies, this text should be compared with the "Apophis Book," col. 28/16–18, see below, p. 184. There is no justification for Posener's suggestion (1987, p. 11) that the burial of a figure of wax (rather than of clay) is "évidemment un usage impropre."

804. Only the phrase, "he having departed from(?) his companions upon earth" (Faulkner 1973, p. 28 = de Buck 1935, pp. 153–54), requires a funerary setting and may be an interpolation. The translation of the phrase is uncertain, however, as most versions have "laugh at" rather than "depart from."

805. Faulkner 1973, p. 28 (= de Buck 1935, pp. 154–56). For this common pattern, compare CT spells 656 (Faulkner 1977, p. 228 = de Buck 1956, pp. 277–78) and 837 (Faulkner 1978, p. 24 = de Buck 1961, p. 37) where the technique is attempted (without success) by Seth. Seth is himself the recipient of the process in Schott 1929, pp. 18–23 and his son Maga is likewise treated in Pap. Harris Magical, col. 9/5–13, in Lange 1927, pp. 80–81. The motif continues unchanged into the Egyptian papyri in Greek language, compare Preisendanz 1928, pp. 33–39 (PGM III, ll. 1–164) and 154–59 (PGM IV, ll. 2622–2707); idem 1931, pp. 27–28 (PGM VII, ll. 593–619) and 167–68 (PGM XXXVI, ll. 134–60); and passim. This is also the explanation for the alleged ritual cannibalism discussed in Brashear 1979, pp. 269–71 (NN is to be replaced by the name of the conjured victim). See further my comments in Betz 1986, p. 83, n. 314.

Assimilated to the enemies of the gods, the foe is equally subjected to the breaking and felling of the state rite, if only by the simplified mechanism of the spoken curse. The use of "etc." (*ḥm.t-r3*) after the mention of "foe" allows for the insertion of the name of the conjured enemy in the curse, and it is this personal enemy whose inscribed figure is buried. If the enemy, though "among men," is also "in the necropolis," it is because the burial of the ritual figurine has put him there.[806]

While the act of breaking or piercing has been shown to constitute a ritual "killing" of objects that they may be associated with the dead, the burial of such objects is an even more obvious method for producing this association. Its practice at funerals in all periods of Egyptian civilization is and was so commonly recognized that any ritual burial necessarily evoked this funerary context,[807] with the dispatching of the buried object to the realm of the dead. That this is no less true for human images than for the more commonly offered foodstuffs or other grave goods is expressly shown in Coffin Texts spell 103, which is designed to send one's own soul from the earth to the underworld and is recited "over an image of clay(?) ... [The name of] the man is to be placed upon it in the ground." [808] In the execration texts, the same result is produced, albeit with hostile intent.

The actual depiction of this result appears in the "mythological papyri," where dispatched foreign prisoners are bound beneath the throne of Osiris,[809] and the essence of the ritual is embodied in the netherworld creature *Nkỉw-mnt*, "The Vanquished One at the Stake," a god shown as a bound foreign captive whose existence repels evil (see fig. 15b).[810] The obvious association of this figure with the execration rite is underscored by his

806. Such phrases also allow for the possibility that the foe might be a god, demon, or dead man; see the standard recitation of potentially threatening beings in CT spells 47, 455, 585, etc.

807. This seems true even for agricultural rituals of plowing and planting; compare the "hacking of the earth" (*ḫbs-t3*, *Wb* 3: 256/1–7) performed at the sowing season for Sokar, god of the dead, discussed in Kees 1980, pp. 94–95; Gaballa and Kitchen 1969, pp. 22–23; and Griffiths 1960, pp. 61–62 (construed as the burial of the blood of Seth's confederates). For the ritual in funerary literature, compare CT spell 146, in Faulkner 1973, p. 124 (= de Buck 1938, pp. 202–03) and BD spells 12, §S and 178b, §S, in Allen 1974, pp. 11 and 186. Planting is ritualized as burial in the "corn Osiris" figures, impregnated with seeds and interred (see Raven 1982).

808. Faulkner 1973, p. 101 (= de Buck 1938, p. 110). Both the content and rubric of the spell again suggest its origin in earthly practice, contra the suggestion of Faulkner 1973, p. 101, n. 1. For further ritual burials of enemies, see Gardiner 1935, vol. 1, p. 68 (Pap. Chester Beatty 8, cols. 4/5–5/3); Schott 1956; and particularly idem 1930c, in which one buries (*ṯms*) a wax or clay figure of a royal enemy under an execution site together with a papyrus sheet inscribed in fresh ink with the enemy's name and those of his father and mother (p. 41). For *ṯms* > Coptic ⲦⲰⲘⲤ, "to bury," see Schott 1956; p. 187 and n. 787, above.

809. See Piankoff and Rambova 1957, pp. 58–59, fig. 44.

810. See Śliwa 1973, who does not, however, associate the figure with the execration rite.

epithet *pr m i͗mḥ.t*, "who has come forth from the abyss," an unmistakable reference to the ceremonial burial in a sandy pit.

This notion of burial is enforced by the occasional use of clay coffins to enclose execration figurines,[811] and the coffining of divine, state, and personal enemies recurs within the cultic "Apophis Book."[812] More often, however, the same effect was created by placing the figurines and texts within a large jar, a practice attested in the more complex assemblages from the Old to the New Kingdoms.[813] The use of jars as coffins is well known from the so-called "Canopic jars," and is actually employed for burials of children and adults (as "slipper-coffins"[814]), continuing into the Late Period as the "coffin of choice" for embalmed sacred ibises.[815] The significance of the practice for the execration ceremony is illustrated clearly in Coffin Texts spell 1016:

> Oh you who are hateful ... I put my hands on the jar in the bounds of which you sit;
> it descends before you.[816]

The hostile interment of personal enemies which is described in this spell finds its cultic analog in Papyrus Salt 825, whose "magical" nature has been the subject of much

811. As noted, for example, by Lansing (1933, pp. 23–25) at Lisht and by Posener (1939b, p. 41) and Capart (1940, p. 8) for certain Brussels figurines from Saqqara; see also the thorough listing in Posener 1987, pp. 3 (Saqqara and Lisht) and 5 (Tura[?] and Wasta or Atfiḥ).

812. Faulkner 1933, pp. 68–69 and 73 (cols. 28/16–18 and 29/14); 1937b, pp. 174–75 and 185; and 1938, p. 42. With the discovery of actual figurines inside coffins, Faulkner's uncertainty regarding the translation of *ḫn*, 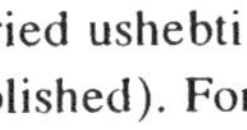, "box(?)" need no longer be retained. The spelling is but a late variant of the common word "chest" (*hn* in *Wb* 2: 491/16–17) used from the Old Kingdom as an expression for "coffin"; compare the euphemistic *hn n ꜥnḫ.w*, "chest of the living," in the inscription of Weni; Sethe 1933, p. 106/15. The Pap. Bremner-Rhind examples of *ḫn* are misread *ṯs.t* in *Wb* 5: 408/15 (= *Wb Beleg*. 5: 61).

813. See *inter alia*, Junker 1947, pp. 30–32; Abu Bakr and Osing 1973, p. 97 and pl. 31 (Old Kingdom); and Posener 1987, p. 5 (Elephantine, Middle Kingdom?). For the New Kingdom, see Posener 1958. Jars also enclosed buried ushebti figures in the Ramesside cemetery at Bubastis (excavated by Zagazig University, unpublished). For the suggested presence of a sealed jar in the Berlin corpus, see above, n. 641.

814. See Kuchman 1977–78.

815. Compare the phrase "one god one pot" (*ḏny.t* < *Wb* 5: 575/11) in Ray 1976, pp. 76 (n. h) and 78 (O. Ḥor 19 vo., l. 8), 83 (O. Ḥor 20, l. 18), and 86 (O. Ḥor 22, l. 14). For earlier funerary uses of the same type of vessel, see Ogdon 1986.

816. Faulkner 1978, p. 116 (= de Buck 1961, p. 235), translates "it descends to your faces"; but see *Wb* 3: 128–29. Compare also CT spell 545, in Faulkner 1977, p. 160 (= de Buck 1956, p. 139): "I am this one whom you protected from the *djinn* (*bqꜣ*) who is in his jar"; and CT spell 999, in Faulkner 1978, p. 105 (= de Buck 1961, p. 216): "Hail to you Re, in this city of yours ... when you put female images(?) in a jar in it."

discussion.[817] There can be little dispute, however, concerning the temple affiliation of the papyrus, for it contains a ritual to protect the sacred temple scriptorium, the "House of Life." The rite "overturns charms" (*ḥkꜣw*) and "subjugates (*rtḥ*) the entire universe" by methods drawn directly from the standard execration repertoire: the incineration of bound wax figures of political and demonic enemies felled with a flint knife and enclosed within a jar.[818] The vignette depicting this destruction is labeled appositely "The male enemy and female enemy in the vile jug (*ds*)"[819] (see fig. 16a), and a schematic drawing of the jug itself appears with an apotropaic tag: "May you have power over rebels" (see fig. 16b).[820] Within the jug is an enigmatic inscription. Unread by the editor of the papyrus, the conclusion of the text is nonetheless clear: "go round about it" (*pẖr ḥꜣ=f*).[821] The hostile encirclement (*pẖr*) thus enacted serves to re-enforce the constrictive nuance of binding and burial. The jar itself is the actor, physically "going round about" its victims. Not simply a utilitarian container of magical material, the jar is a direct participant in the execration process. The prominence of the jug in Papyrus Salt 825 has clear implications for the related dynastic occurrences; it also provides the textual correspondent of the jar burials associated with the Louvre figurine and other "Greek" spells of domination.[822]

Burial maintains its prominence as a magical technique in private ritual of the Greco-Roman (and Coptic[823]) eras, appearing in both Demotic and Greek spells for compelling

817. See above, pp. 6–7.

818. Derchain 1965, pp. 139 and 7*. With its dismembered, burned, and encased wax figures, the ceremony for the "House of Life" (like the underworld torture in the "Book of Amduat") readily reveals its origin in the execration rite, of which it is but a variation. The preservation of a small limestone plaque with identical imagery suggests that the scriptorium ritual may have produced its own variations, stressing the burial rather than the burning of images (see above, n. 743 and below, p. 212, here fig. 19a).

819. Derchain ibid., pp. 145 and 22*. Derchain's hesitation over the translation "jar" is unwarranted.

820. Derchain ibid., pp. 144 and 21*. A comparable jug is used (without hostile implications) for the entombment of an Osiris figure (p. 25*).

821. Derchain ibid., pp. 144 and 21*. The first line should read *pḏ.t šʿd smꜣ*, perhaps to be understood as "the bowman, slaughtered and bound(?)." Could *smꜣ*, "to unify"(?) be a reference to the tying of prisoners to the unification symbol (*smꜣ*), or to the act of burial (*smꜣ-tꜣ*)?

822. For the jar enclosing the Louvre figure, see du Bourguet 1980, p. 228 and pls. 34–35. For further examples, see Wortmann 1968a, pp. 85ff.; Maltomini 1979, pp. 98 and 112; and Betz 1986, pp. 309 and 321. The use of a red jar to enclose a magical text buried under the floor of a Coptic monk's cave is noted in Kropp 1930–31, vol. 1, p. 50 (text XIII) and cf. Crum 1934, p. 197 (love spell): "Draw the figure on the bottom of the new pot."

823. Compare the burial of a wax figure in a foundation ritual in Kropp 1930–31, vol. 1, p. 52 and vol. 2, p. 33 (§K 47–51) and the discovery of a buried magical text noted in ibid., vol. 1, p. 50.

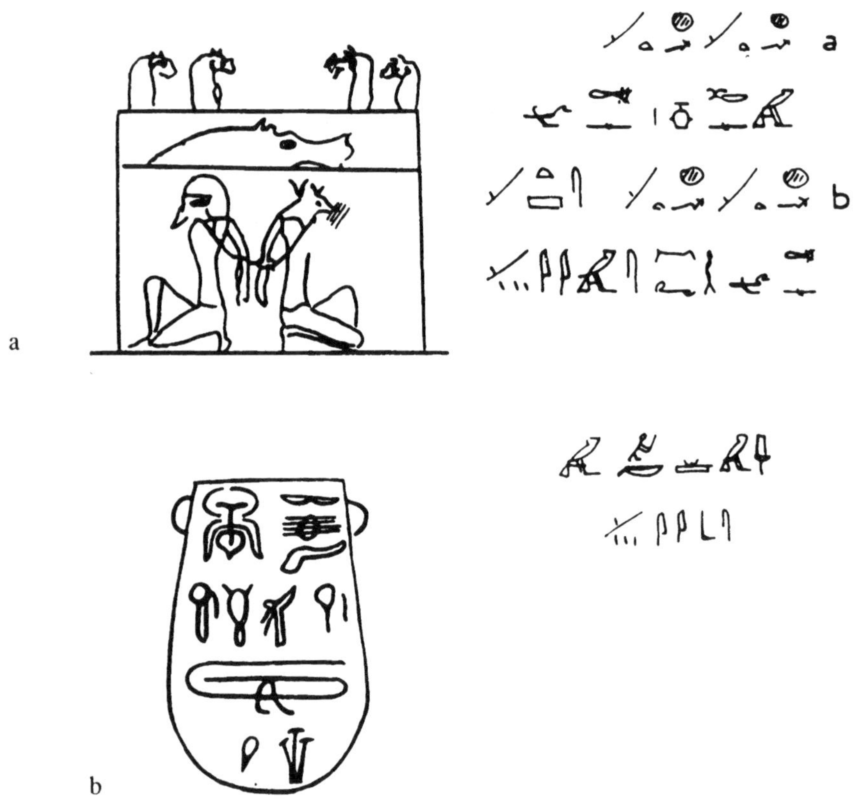

Figure 16. (*a*) Vignette Showing Destruction of Political and Divine Enemies "in vile jug" (after Derchain 1965, p. 22*) and (*b*) Vignette of Jug with Enigmatic Inscription Ending "Go Round About It" (after Derchain 1965, p. 21*).

love[824] or producing separation and hatred.[825] The seeming contradiction between two such opposite results produced by the same means is more apparent than real, as the true underlying goal of these procedures is the same: *control over the emotions and actions of the victim.* The "love" engendered by these methods is thus little different from the "hate" similarly produced, for both represent the submission of the will of the victim to the power of the magician. Like the victims of the execration texts, the would-be lover becomes an

824. See Bell, Nock, and Thompson 1933, p. 13 (col. 8/2 and 5, burial of a wax figure of Osiris) and Griffith and Thompson 1904, pp. 92–93 (col. 12/31, burial of a fish assimilated to Osiris by ritual drowning), and pp. 104–05 (col. 15/2, use of "barley buried in the tomb of a dead man"—a clear reference to the "corn Osiris"; for which see Raven 1982). Greek examples include Edgar 1925; PGM IV, ll. 2943–66 in Preisendanz 1928, pp. 166–67 and Betz 1986, p. 94; and PGM CI, in Wortmann 1968a, pp. 85–102 and Betz 1986, p. 307–09.

825. See J. H. Johnson 1975, pp. 38–39 (col. 4/13). For Greek texts, see PGM V, ll. 304–69, in Preisendanz 1928, pp. 190–93 and Betz 1986, pp. 106–07 (grave or unused well); PGM IV, ll. 2215–17, in Preisendanz 1928, pp. 140–41 and Betz 1986, p. 77; and passim.

emotional prisoner unable to "rebel, plot, fight, talk of fighting, or talk of rebelling" against the practitioner:

> Bind her for all the time of my life and help force her, NN, to be serviceable to me, NN, and let her not frolic away from me for even one hour of life.[826]

> When he stands, you shall not allow him to stand; when he sits, you shall not allow him to sit; when he sleeps, you shall not allow him to sleep, but let him seek after me from village to village, from city to city, from field to field, from country to country, until he comes to me, and becomes subject beneath my feet.[827]

These late spells for coercing love and fear are simply a translation into the concerns of the private sphere of the political coersions of the state execration rite and the cosmic coersions of demons in temple rites.[828] They are not, however, of importance solely as the final representatives of the execration tradition, for it is in their more explicit directions for use that a key is found to clarify the role of burial in earlier state and temple practice.

These instructions reveal that cemetery burial produces an association not simply with death, but with the dead. Charms, lamellae, and complex assemblages are to be interred in extant tombs, and written spells are placed on the corpse itself (often inserted in the mouth of the mummy), or even inscribed on a bone extracted from the cadaver.[829] The spells address the spirit of the corpse directly:

826. PGM IV, ll. 380–83, in Preisendanz 1928, pp. 84–85 and Betz 1986, p. 45.

827. Smither 1939, pp. 173–74. For the subjugation "beneath the feet," see above, pp. 119–36.

828. The result of such rituals and spells—whether temple, state, or private—is *respect and fear*, qualities united in the Egyptian concepts *šfy.t* or *qfꜣ.t*, traditionally translated "respect/prestige"; for the association of fear with these terms, see *Wb* 4: 457/12, 15, 17; and *Wb* 5: 31–32. For an indicative example, see "The Instructions of ʿOnchsheshonqy" col. 10/4: "It is when a crocodile surfaces that fear of it (its respect) is measured," in Lichtheim 1980, p. 167. Magic (*ḥkꜣ*) is specifically stated to produce this quality at the destruction of evil forces on the Horus cippi: *sḫpr n=y qfꜣ.w=k n ḥkꜣ.w=k*, "create for me your respect/fear by your magic," see above n. 144. By contrast, private spells for "praise and love" (*ḥs-mr.t*) are less violent; see Griffith and Thompson 1904, pp. 68–71 (col. 9/12 and 18), 82–85 (col. 11/9 and 17), 96–97 (col. 13/21); Bell, Nock, and Thompson 1933, p. 12 (col. 7/1–5); and J. H. Johnson 1977, pp. 62 and 70 (col. 4/17), which, however, combines *ḥs-mr.t* and *šfy.t*. Compare also the salutatory "prayer" for *ḥs-mr.t* in Pap. Oxford Griffith 13, l. 8, in Bresciani 1975, pp. 12–13 and pl. 4.

829. PGM, passim and Wortmann 1968a, pp. 57–80. See, for example, the instructions for the prototype of the Louvre assemblage in PGM IV, ll. 330ff., in Preisendanz 1928, pp. 82–83 and Betz 1986, p. 44. The assemblage is buried beside a grave as the magician recites: "And arouse yourself for me, whoever you are, whether male or female." For a representative Coptic example, see Rémondon 1953, pp. 157–61 (especially l. 4, discussed on p. 160). With these practices should be compared a love charm inscribed in hieroglyphs on a figure representing a deceased woman, in Drioton 1942: "Raise yourself, bind him whom I see that he might copulate (*smꜣ*, "join") with me. I do obeisance before you." For texts inserted in the mouth of the mummy, see the following n. 830 and PGM LXIV, in Preisendanz 1931, p. 197. Demotic examples include Pap. London and Leiden vo., col. 17, in Griffith

> Arouse yourself for me, daimon of the dead, ... fulfill what has been inscribed and inserted in your mouth ... As long as the divine mystery (the spell) remains within you, do not allow Karosa ... to think of her [own] husband ...[830]

Although the practice of depositing similar cursing tablets (*defixiones*) or phylacteries in tombs and wells[831] is later attested throughout the Greco-Roman world, appearing in Athens, Rome, and even in the Burgundian region of France[832] (with tablets found occasionally in the mouths of corpses[833]), the origin of this Hellenistic commonplace seems

---

and Thompson 1904, pp. 190–91 and probably Pap. Louvre E 3229, col. 2/25–27, in J. H. Johnson 1977, pp. 60 and 68. The presence of a Demotic curse on a "mummy tag" probably reflects a similar (though unrecognized) attempt to join spell and corpse, since these tags were usually tied to the mummy. For the tag, see Edgerton 1936, pp. 77–79. For a Coptic example of an inserted lead tablet, see Kurth, Thissen, and Weber 1980b, pp. 109–12 and the review in Vittmann 1982, pp. 126–27. For the use of bones, see PGM IV, l. 1886 in Preisendanz 1928, pp. 130–31 and Betz 1976, p. 71; and PGM CXXIV, in Maltomini 1979, pp. 98 and 106 and Betz 1986, p. 321. For Coptic examples of cursing spells inscribed on bones, see Pellegrini 1907, pp. 156–59 (no. 21) and (in red ink) Drescher 1948. Re-editions of these spells have been prepared by myself for the Coptic Magical Papyri Project of the Institute for Antiquity and Christianity, Claremont. Curses are also deposited in tombs in Mesopotamia, see *CAD*, vol. 11/1, p. 206a, s.v. *nâlu*, §d: "you (pl.) have placed figures of me with a dead man, you have placed figures of me in the lap of a dead man ... ."

830. See PGM XIXa, in Preisendanz 1931, p. 142 and Betz 1986, pp. 256–57.

831. As passages to the underworld; for the obvious association, compare the modern popular author Gorey 1983, unnumbered page: "The way to Hell is down a Well."

832. The classic studies of the *defixiones* are Wünsch 1898 and Audollent 1904. The Egyptian iconography ("Sethian") and background of these texts is already recognized in these formative studies. For more recent examples and bibliography, see Jordan 1975 and 1985, especially pp. 165–67 for the burial of these tablets in older tombs. Jordan, however, fails to understand the reason for the presence of these tablets in tombs, assuming (pp. 165–66) that they had served the tomb owners as amulets in life and were buried "as a treasured possession." On the contrary, the tablets found in tombs were deposited as a magical act on the behalf of living individuals well after the original burial, and never belonged to the tomb owner. The Egyptian element of the spell in the Vigna Codini tablet is discussed in Griffiths 1985. For an example from Autun in Burgundy, see Marcillet-Jaubert 1979. The (unrecognized) Egyptian origin of even this text is made manifest in the magical phrase ⲔⲞⲘⲠⲰⲐ (ibid., p. 185), garbled on the tablet from ⲔⲞⲘⲪⲰⲐ (ibid., p. 186), and deriving from the ⲔⲞⲘ ⲪⲦⲞ of Crum 1939, p. 109a and Černý 1976, p. 59 < *qmꜣ* (*pꜣ*) *tꜣ*, "earth creator" (var. ⲔⲘⲠⲦⲞ, in PGM LX; ⲔⲞⲘⲦⲰ, in Demotic Pap. London and Leiden, col. 7/6). A thorough discussion of this epithet appears in Thissen 1991, pp. 300–02. Egyptian influence on certain *defixiones* is now denied by Faraone 1985, p. 153, on the basis of their date (end of the fifth century B.C.). As should be clear, however, Egyptian antecedents long precede even these first Greek texts.

833. See Jordan 1985, p. 167. Again, Jordan is unaware of the Egyptian and PGM parallels (styling the placement "unique"), and thus doubts the excavation report unjustly.

not Greek but Egyptian, deriving directly from the ancient native custom of private "letters to the dead."[834]

LETTERS TO THE DEAD

Attested from the Old Kingdom, these letters invoke the aid of the deceased in matters of health, fertility, fortune, and justice. The spirit may be petitioned in its own right as an "effective spirit" or *ꜣḫ* (a term related to the *ꜣḫ.w*, "spells" over which the deceased has mastery), reflecting the Egyptian belief in the power of the dead to influence persons and events:[835]

Please become a spirit (*ꜣḫ*) for me [before] my eyes that
I may see you fighting on my behalf in a dream.[836]

More pertinent to the Greco-Roman examples of curses and love charms, the angered or neglected *ꜣḫ* is able to possess and destroy a human victim.[837] Thus to ensure the hostility of the deceased recipient to the deposited victim, late Greek texts often specify that malevolent spells be placed in the tombs of those who died untimely or violent deaths, the

834. The basic study is Gardiner and Sethe 1928 (for the relation to the *defixiones*, see p. 10). Further examples appear in Gardiner 1930; Schott 1930b; Simpson 1970; Goedicke 1972; and Wente 1975–76. An overview is provided in Grieshammer 1975. For a PGM parallel, see PGM LI, ll. 1–27 (with my appended note), in Betz 1986, p. 283. The relationship between Greek, Coptic, and earlier Egyptian letters to the dead was denied by Drescher (1948, p. 275, n. 4) through a misreading of Gardiner and Sethe.

835. See Maxims 50–52 of the "Wisdom of Ani," in Suys 1935, pp. 84–89 (Text B, beginning with *ḥtp*) and Volten 1937, p. 55: "Pacify a spirit (*ꜣḫ*) by doing what he desires, being pure for him from his abominations that you might be safe from his many afflictions. His are all destructions. The head of cattle taken in the fields; it is he who has acted likewise. As for every loss in the threshing floor or in the field, one also says: 'The spirit (*ꜣḫ*)!' When he places disturbance in a household, and the heart is turned back, they all pray (*Wb* 2: 294/7) to him also."

836. See Wente 1975–76, p. 597.

837. See the Bentresh Stela in Lichtheim 1980, pp. 90–94: "He found Bentresh to be possessed by a spirit (*ꜣḫ*); he found him to be an enemy whom one could fight" (p. 92) and compare Pap. Harkness, col. 2/37, in Logan 1976, pp. 152–53 (photo and hand copy without transliteration or translation): *nn ḥq=w ṯ.t sḫ ḥyk rmt ḫꜣs.t*, "A magical writing of a dead man shall not capture you" (= Pap. BM 10507, col. 10/14; Mark Smith 1987, p. 49). See also Berlin and Cairo bowls, in Gardiner and Sethe 1928, p. 7. For the source of illness as "the stroke of a dead man or dead woman," see above, pp. 56–57. The hostile nuance of *ꜣḫ* continues in Coptic; see the Bohairic term for magician, ϥⲁⲣⲡⲉⲣ-ⲓϩ, "One who loosens demons (*ꜣḫ*)," in Westendorf 1965–77, p. 152. For similar Mesopotamian beliefs concerning the untimely or disgruntled dead, see *CAD*, vol. 4, p. 399b, s.v. *eṭemmu*, and Tsukimoto 1985, pp. 146–54.

ἄωρος or βιαιοθάνατος, who could be presumed to be jealous and vengeful.[838] Although this practice cannot be confirmed for most dynastic deposits, it does accord nicely with the situation at Mirgissa, where the state rite is clearly accompanied by a corpse "untimely and violently" slain.

Alternatively, the spirit may be summoned to act as an intermediary with the infernal tribunal for similar purposes, and thus the tomb becomes a receptacle for petitions to the underworld, styled "the noble (mail)-box of Osiris" (*tꜣ ꜥfd špsy n Wsir*) in hieratic[839] and the "(deposit)-box" (πύξις) in the Greek language texts.[840] From this conception derive the numerous Demotic and Greek petitions for vengeance directed to deities and recovered from cemeteries.[841] It is this format which appears in the "love" spell accompanying the Louvre assemblage (invoking the divinized Antinous), where it is combined with an appeal to the prematurely dead.[842] The explicit requirement that late personal spells of execration

838. See PGM IV, l. 2885; PGM CI; PGM CVII; and passim in Betz 1986, pp. 92, 307–09, 311, and passim. For discussion and bibliography, see Daniel 1975, pp. 255–57. The explanation for this preference is provided by the Egyptian priest Chaeremon (first century A.D.), as exerpted by Porphyry: "... a bad and irrational soul which tried to depart the body after having been detached from it by violence yet stays near to it (because the souls of men who die by violence also keep themselves near to the body—a fact which should prevent one from committing suicide) ... Hence many souls are seen to lament and the souls of the unburied adhere to the bodies, souls which are abused by sorcerers for their own service, pressing them by retaining the body or part of it." For the passage, see van der Horst 1984, p. 37 (= Porphyry, *De Abstentia* 2.47).

839. HO 80, l. 1, in Černý and Gardiner 1957, p. 22 and pls. 80–80a.

840. PGM XV, l. 17, in Preisendanz 1931, p. 134 and Betz 1986, p. 251. Less likely, the term could mean "tablet" in this context (so Preisendanz, see Liddell, Scott, and Jones 1940, p. 1554b), referring to a spell inscribed on wood rather than to the tomb where it was placed.

841. Demotic examples are published in Hughes 1958 (especially pp. 4–5 for the best discussion of the phenomenon); 1968; and 1969. Derivative Greek examples appear throughout the PGM (invoking Seth, Anubis, etc.); see also Pap. Oxyrhynchus XLI.2976 (petition to Thoueris), in Browne et al. 1972, p. 71.

842. The spell is directed to various underworld deities (Pluto, Persephone, Adonis, Hermes-Thoth, Anubis, "the son of Ptah"), but special prominence is given to the spirit of the dead Antinous. The identification of the νεκύδαιμον 'Αντίνοε with Antinous the favorite of Hadrian was first recognized by du Bourguet (1975, p. 256), though he recanted this position in 1980 (p. 227) following the denial by Kambitsis (1976, p. 217, n. 1). Kambitsis prefers to identify this Antinous with an otherwise unnamed, prematurely deceased Egyptian in whose tomb the assemblage was placed. The original identification is correct, however, since 1) the placement in graves of letters to deities is an attested practice, exemplified by this spell with regard to Pluto et cetera, 2) the divine Antinous was associated with the underworld (as an aspect of Osiris) and was himself "prematurely deceased" so that he is in proper company with Pluto et al. and is particularly appropriate for these spells, 3) the prematurely dead are distinguished from the more exalted Antinous whom they are to assist, and most importantly 4) Antinous is invoked *by name*, unlike the invariable practice in the PGM where the deceased recipient is unnamed so that the spell might be generally applicable. It is just this general character which most clearly distinguishes these spells from the traditional "letters to the dead."

be buried in older tombs thus utilizes the traditional mechanism of "letters to the dead" to ensure the aid of the spirit as an agent or intermediary. The identical placement of earlier state execration rites in or beside extant private tombs must reflect the same intent.

Indications that this is so appear already on the Old Kingdom execration deposits from Giza, which each bear the name of a private individual, determined by the "seated noble" hieroglyph  (Gardiner Sign-list A 50) usually reserved for the revered dead.[843] Although these individuals have been considered "dedicators" of the deposit or agents associated with its delivery,[844] the determinative of their names suggests that they are deceased,[845] and the "name" of one of them is otherwise unattested as a personal name, though it serves as the fundamental title of the blessed dead: *ꜣḫ-ỉqr*, "Excellent Spirit."[846] While no more verifiable than earlier speculation, the suspicion is nonetheless tempting that these individuals should be identified as the intended recipients of the jugs, deceased intermediaries between earth and the underworld.[847]

The similarity of technique between the "letters to the dead" and the state execration ritual extends also to the use of inscribed red bowls and vases.[848] When used as "letters," these bowls may once have held food offerings for the deceased recipients.[849] The

843. The names, inscribed on the enclosing jars, are without title and preceded only by the date of the deposit. See Junker 1947, pp. 31–32: *Ḫtmỉ* (reread in Abu Bakr and Osing 1973, p. 133, n. 132); Abu Bakr and Osing 1973, pp. 131–33: *Ms*; and Osing 1976a, pp. 154–55: *ꜣḫ-ỉqr*.

844. Abu Bakr and Osing 1973, p. 133.

845. Acknowledged by Abu Bakr and Osing ibid., p. 133.

846. *Wb* 1: 16/3. See the comments of Osing 1976a, p. 155, and for the title and its significance, see Demarée 1983.

847. In no case, however, were these deposits found in tombs of similarly named individuals, and the association of certain deposits with any specific tomb is unclear (Abu Bakr and Osing 1973, p. 127). Burial in the graveyard alone would have to serve as the method of contact (as in CT spell 37, discussed above). But see the comments in Junker 1947, pp. 31 and 38. If "Excellent Spirit" is only a title, any tomb would have sufficed for that deposit, paralleling the indiscriminate placement of deposits in the Demotic and Greek spells.

848. See the discussion in Gardiner and Sethe 1928, pp. 9–12 on the Qaw, Ḥû, Berlin, Cairo, Oxford, and Moscow bowls; and compare the use of bowls inscribed with protective spells in funerary contexts: BD spells Pleyte 167–69, in Allen 1974, p. 216. The use of bowls is a characteristic feature of the "letters to the dead," and the custom may have spread, under Egyptian influence, to Crete, Palestine, and Mesopotamia, serving as the origin of the Aramaic and Mandaean "incantation bowls" (see C. H. Gordon 1969). For recent discussion of these incantation bowls, see Naveh and Shaked 1985, pp. 13ff. Like the Egyptian letters, the incantation bowls are often found in cemeteries (ibid., pp. 15–16), but they are usually found inverted. Their origin is suggested to be Mesopotamian in McCullough 1967, pp. xii–xv.

849. Gardiner and Sethe 1928, pp. 9–12.

execration bowls can also be understood as proffering a gift to the deceased—the victim inscribed on the bowl, delivered over to "the hand of a dead man or a dead woman."[850] The fundamental unity of the two practices is demonstrated by a late love spell from Oxyrhynchus (third to fourth centuries).[851] Inscribed on a pot, the Oxyrhynchus spell was buried in the necropolis, and invokes the resident spirit of the dead for its effect. In format and purpose, it is both a "letter to the dead" and a "private execration rite" directly comparable to the contemporary Louvre assemblage with its tortured figure. Taken together, the Louvre and Oxyrhynchus love spells display the same interchange of bowl and figurine already noted in the state rite of the Middle Kingdom.

Designed as a prisoner, bound, pierced, enclosed, and entombed with the dead, the Louvre figurine may now be seen to derive its "magical mechanics" from a purely Egyptian milieu.[852] Its constituent elements have been traced from Egyptian prehistory to the Christian era, appearing indiscriminately in royal, temple, and private contexts. The interdependence of these contexts is particularly striking given the long-standing attempt to isolate private ritual as "magic." With regard to "execration magic," however, any attempt to dissociate private from state and temple technique is clearly suspect. Nor can private rite be dismissed as "derivative" or "debased." On the contrary, the apparent affiliation of the state rite to the private custom of "letters to the dead" necessarily raises the question of the degree of influence exerted by *private* custom on public ceremony and challenges the relevance of maintaining strict distinctions between private and public rites.

PRIVATE VERSUS STATE MAGIC

Indeed, the fundamental identity of private and state "execration magic" has already been tacitly recognized by commentators who have explained the significance of the latter by reference to the private Coffin Texts spell 37. The question of private use of the execration format is even more pertinent in the many finds of small sets of buried figurines inscribed not with the "execration formula" but with individual names.[853] Best understood as the evidence of personal vendettas (and thus the direct ancestors of the Louvre

850. Perhaps derived from such offerings (or a parody of them) is the placement on a bowl of the severed skull at Mirgissa.

851. Wortmann 1968a, pp. 80–84 (text 3).

852. Contra du Bourguet 1980, p. 234.

853. For examples, see the overview in Posener 1975a and 1984, p. 615, n. 6. For the difficulty of distinguishing "private" figurines from "public" ones, see the comments on private sorcery in Posener 1976a, pp. 438–40; especially p. 438: "Il s'en trouve peut-être parmi les pièces isolées, mais elles ne se laissent pas reconnaître."

figurine), these smaller groupings are nonetheless equivalent in meaning and method to the more elaborate state production, differing only in scope. Traditional attempts to distinguish personal magic from state religion must of necessity be frustrated in such cases as these, where practice is identical and only the notion of "private versus state" remains as a distinguishing criterion. Even this criterion becomes unclear in the Egyptian section of the official ritual where private and state concerns may overlap,[854] and it disappears entirely in the state ritual of the execration of Apophis, which enjoins the practitioner to destroy not only the image of Apophis and the enemies of pharaoh, but also one's own personal foes:

> This spell is said over Apep drawn on a new papyrus with fresh ink and placed within a coffin ... Then inscribe for yourself these names of all male and female enemies whom your heart fears as every enemy of pharaoh whether dead or alive, the name of their fathers, the name of their mothers, the name of (their) children; (to be placed) within a coffin, to be made (also) in wax, to be placed on the fire after the name of Apep.[855]

This unity of public and private practice may have been present in the earliest execration rites if the personal names on the jars of the Pepi II deposits are to be understood as the donors of the ritual. Though performed primarily on behalf of the monarch, the execration could easily have included personal enemies of the donors among the intermingled Egyptians and foreigners—exactly as is stipulated by the later "Apophis Book."[856] Potential trespassers against the funerary estate of Amenhotep son of Hapu are threatened with just such a fate, with their names being added to the list of the condemned in the rite against Apep: "They are for the knife on the day of destruction; Let them be termed *Nkỉw* ("The Vanquished One," a name of Apep)."[857]

854. See Posener 1958, p. 269.

855. Faulkner 1933, pp. 68–69 (col. 28/16–18) and 1937b, pp. 174–75. Compare the rubrics of cols. 26/2–7 that urge the actor: "Now make for yourself every enemy of Re, every enemy of Pharaoh, dead or alive, together with every accused one in his heart." Faulkner (1937b, pp. 177 and 179) failed to understand the writing of "Now make for yourself" (*ỉs ỉr n≡k*) using the pupil, *0*, for the verb "to make" (cols. 24/19 and 22; 26/2, 9, and 12; 27/3 and 12; and 28/14 and 18–19); see also Posener 1987, p. 7, n. 3. The basic compatibility of temple and private ritual is underscored by the use of the Bremner-Rhind papyrus itself. Though intended for a temple library, the papyrus ultimately served as a private funerary text. For this and similar adaptations, see Schott 1956, pp. 181ff.

856. None of the Egyptians is termed *mwt*, "deceased," and thus all could be living enemies of the king or donor (see Abu Bakr and Osing 1973, pp. 129–30).

857. See Varille 1968, pp. 71 and 73–74 (l. 11). For *Nkỉw* (= *nỉk*, *Wb* 2: 205/14–16), cf. *Nkỉw-mn.t*, above, pp. 174–75.

Terminology provides yet another point of intersection between state and private ritual in the generally unrecognized expression for "execration figures": .[858] Traditionally read *_ṯs.t_ or *_ṯstyw_ and translated "destruction" or "enemy,"[859] the collective noun appears within a representative magical context in the "Apophis Book," where it designates the drawn figures of the enemies ritually felled and burned: "The drawings of the execration figures ( ) which are made on a new sheet of papyrus."[860] Within this larger category, individual figures may also be indicated by the more commonplace , *twt* (*w*), "image," or the generic terms for "enemy," *ḫfty* and *sbỉ*.[861] In comparable rituals against Seth, though single figurines of the deity are styled *twt n Stš m sqrỉ-ʿnḫ*, "an image of Seth as a prisoner,"[862] collectively they are said to be pierced or bound "in/as ,"[863] and Seth is informed that "every form of yours and every name of yours is made into daily before Re and before the Ennead."[864] The significance of *_ṯs.t_ as "modeled figurines" is unmistakable in the instructions for the ceremony to protect the House of Life:

> Now as for wax, it is made into enemies (*sbỉ.w*) specifically to slaughter his name and to prevent his *ba* from leaving the place of execution. As for wax, one makes execration figures ( ) with it to destroy his name.[865]

858. A version of this discussion of terminology now appears in Ritner 1989a.

859. So *Wb* 5: 408/12–15 and 409/1–2.

860. Papyrus BM 10188, col. 32/43 in Faulkner 1933, p. 91 and 1938, pp. 52 and 53 (n. to col. 32/43 [translated "enemies"]).

861. For *twtw*, see *Wb* 5: 255–56 and Pap. Bremner-Rhind, col. 32/46, 51, and 53, in Faulkner 1933, pp. 91–92 and 1938, pp. 52–53. *twtw* is also used for the figurines in CT spells 37 (de Buck 1935, p. 156, §h) and 103 (de Buck 1938, p. 110, §l), discussed above, pp. 173–74. For *ḫfty* and *sbỉ*, see Posener 1987, p. 7.

862. "The Rite of Overthrowing Seth and his Confederates," in Schott 1929, pp. 36–37, l. 3 and compare pp. 4–5, l. 6: "One brings an image (*twt*) of Seth in red wax" (Louvre version); "Now make for yourself an image (*twt*) of Seth in wax" (BM version).

863. "The Rite for Repelling the Angry One," in Schott 1929, pp. 76–77, ll. 4–5: "His enemies are pierced in/as *_ṯs.t_" (Middle Egyptian version); "His enemies are bound in/as *_ṯs.t_" (Late Egyptian version). Schott, p. 76 (and n. b), translates "in heaps."

864. Papyrus MMA 35.9.21, col. 30/4–5, in Goyon 1975, pp. 384–85, who suggests (p. 384, n. 6) a relationship between the term and *ḥtm*, "to destroy" (*Wb* 3: 197/10–12).

865. Papyrus Salt 825, col. 5/4, in Derchain 1965, pp. 5*–6*, 138, and 162, n. 48 (read *nṯstyw*).

No less clear is the usage within Papyrus Jumilhac, which warns of war and sedition "if one does not decapitate enemy figures () in the divine presence, in wax, new papyrus, acacia, or *ḥmꜣ*-wood, according to all the prescriptions of the ritual."[866]

Frequently encountered in the temple texts of the Greco-Roman periods, the word and its variant  (read **nṯstyw*) have been studied at Edfu by Blackman and Fairman, who translate both **ṯs.t* and **nṯstyw* as "companies," "hordes," or "heaps" of enemies.[867] Though overlooked, the inherent *ritual context* of these terms is often apparent from the captions, statements, and epithets in which they occur. Thus, on the thirteenth column of the Edfu forecourt, the ceremony of "Putting the  on the flame" is illustrated with a vignette which shows the king holding small prisoners by a tether over a brazier before Osiris.[868] On the east wall of the temple library, the chief lector priest (*ḫry-ḥb ḥry-tp*) is depicted in the act of skewering nine figurines on a lance before the king. The title of the ritual reads "Overthrowing the enemies of the king daily as  (and) as the Nine Bows."[869] The most common use of these words, however, is in standardized epithets and addresses in which enemies are said to be gathered together, burned, or trampled beneath the feet of the god or king *m *ṯs.t* or *m *nṯstyw*.[870] In each of these instances, the statement alludes directly to known cultic practice with prisoner figurines, and the crucial passage would best be translated "as execration figures," and not simply "in hordes." Thus the promise of Hathor to present to the king those who rebel against him "as execration

866. Vandier 1961, pp. 130 (col. 18/9–11) and 204, n. 634 (read *ṯs.t*). The ritual to which allusion is made corresponds closely to that prescribed in Schott 1929, pp. 5–6, with Seth-figures in wax, drawn on a new blank papyrus with fresh ink, or carved of acacia or *ḥmꜣ* wood.

867. Blackman and Fairman 1941, pp. 415–16, §58.

868. Chassinat 1930, p. 293/6 (= idem 1960, pl. CXXXIV).

869. Chassinat 1928, p. 349/3 (= ibid., pl. LXXXII). The destruction of figures of royal enemies by the priest is flanked by a comparable scene of the king spearing Apep as a turtle before Re-Horachty.

870. Blackman and Fairman 1941, p. 415. Such epithets are found in divine hymns in papyri and on stelae as well; compare the Amon hymn in Pap. Berlin P. 3056, col. 2/4–5, *tỉtỉ ḫfty.w=k m *ṯs.t*, "to trample your enemies as execration figures," in Königlichen Museen zu Berlin 1905, pl. 28 and the Osiris hymn in S. Louvre C 286, l. 10, "firm of heart when he tramples execration figures," in de Buck 1970, p. 111/4 and Moret 1931, pp. 737 and 738–39, n. 41.

figures" is quite comprehensible within the ritual of "Slaying Apep,"[871] which actually used such images and which is labeled elsewhere: "Slaying the of Apep."[872]

If the interpretation of **ṯs.t* requires re-evaluation, so does the reading of the term itself. No certain phonetic spellings of **ṯs.t* are known,[873] and the logogram (, var.) used to write the word is ambiguous, often serving for , with the reading *rs*.[874] Moreover, a comparable word *rs.t* is known, spelled with the latter logogram and in a context identical to that of the supposed **ṯs.t* of the late religious texts. In the Amada Stela of Amenophis II, the king is said to have "made as his enemies, (and) the Nine Bows likewise."[875] The parallelism is obvious between this phrase and the Edfu ritual of "Overthrowing the enemies of the king daily as execration figures (and) as the Nine Bows." In both cases, the term for "enemy figure" should be identical and thus read *rs.t*. Further, the unmistakable ritual context of the Edfu example strongly favors a similar ceremonial interpretation for the Amada parallel. Both should reflect the standard "smiting scene" depicted on temple

871. Chassinat 1932, p. 157/11 (within a rite of *smꜣ ꜥꜣpp*). Blackman and Fairman 1941, p. 415, misinterpret the *m* ("as") before **ṯs.t* as a unique variant spelling of **nṯstyw*.

872. Chassinat 1932, p. 100/8: *smꜣ *ṯstyw nw ꜥꜣpp*. This tag is directly paralleled at Bab el Abd; see the *Beleg.* to *Wb* 5: 409/2. Further examples of stereotyped expressions with **ṯs.t* or **nṯstyw* within Apep rituals appear in Chassinat 1931, p. 333/7 and 1932, p. 201/3. Examples are also common within rites directed against Seth; compare Chassinat 1929a, p. 375/9; the title of Horus "who pierces the hippopotamus as execration figure," in Rochemonteix et al. 1984–87, p. 292/10 and Ibrahim 1975, pp. 57–58. For the actual use of an execration figure of Seth in hippopotamus form (of cake); see Fairman 1974, pp. 111 and 113–14.

873. All examples cited in the Belegstellen to *Wb* 5: 408–09 are logographic except for 409/1 (= Rochemonteix et al. 1984–87, p. 69/5–6) which is carved without the *ṯs* hieroglyph ( ) and may represent a separate word. The writing is modified in the *Wb* to accord with other examples (with a *ṯs* hieroglyph substituted for the *wḏ* sign, Gardiner Sign-list V 25:), but was unchanged in the re-edition of *Edfou* 1. For the rereading of *Wb* 5: 408/15 as *ḥn*, "chest/ coffin," see above, p. 175, n. 812.

874. Gardiner 1973, pp. 512 (Sign-list T 13) and 521 (Sign-list U 40). The hieratic forms of *rs* ( ) and *ṯs* (, , , or) are frequently conflated; cf. Möller 1909a, pp. 56 (*rs*, no. 588) and 38 (*wṯs*, no. 405); 1909b, pp. 53 and 36; and 1912, pp. 57 and 39. For the confusion between and , see also Faulkner 1935, p. 51.

875. Amada stela, l. 5 (*rs.t m ḫfty.w* for the later *ḫfty.w m rs.t*). For the text and translations, see Kuentz 1925, pp. 9 and 36 (read *rs.t* and translated "surprise attack"); Helck 1955b, p. 1291/10; and idem 1961, p. 30 (translated "slaughter"); followed by Cumming 1982, p. 26. The relation between the Amada passage and the term from magical texts was first signaled by Faulkner 1938, p. 53, n. to 32/43 (translated "enemies").

walls, in which the destruction of substitute figures had replaced the sacrifice of human prisoners.[876]

This reading and interpretation of *rs.t* is confirmed by the stela of an artist (S. Louvre C 14) who boasts of his ability to depict such "smiting scenes," knowing "how to make frightened the face of the ."[877] The phonetic spelling of *rs.t* suggests a literal translation "those who are guarded";[878] the late variant with initial *n* would signify "One/Those belonging to" that group.[879] If correctly analyzed, the designation *rs.t* may have been applied primarily to those foreign princes and individuals placed on the execration lists, and only secondarily to the figurines themselves. Such an interpretation accords better with other occurrences of the term where the translation "figurines" seems excluded, but affiliation to the execration ritual is not.[880] Despite the uncertainty regarding

876. The slain enemies of the Narmer palette were presumably replaced by figurines in later enactments, such as that depicted at Medinet Habu. For these "smiting scenes," see above, pp. 115–16. For the substitution of figurines for human victims, see Yoyotte 1980–81. Such substitutions are paralleled within the funerary cult, in which subsidiary burials of slain retainers are replaced by statues, models, and ultimately by ushebtis. The hostile character of the original rite was not forgotten, however, and reappears in the Book of the Dead where ushebtis are likened to prisoners in compulsory service; see Pleyte 166, §4, in Allen 1974, p. 216: "(But for) Osiris N., all of these were his slaves while he was on earth. It was he who brought them as rebels(?) to his city."

877. Line 10 (= *Wb* 2: 452/16). For the text, bibliography, and previous translations, see Barta 1970, pp. 14 and 104–18. The ritual significance of these prisoner scenes may be implied as well in the accompanying references to depictions of trapped(?) birds and hunted hippopotami.

878. Derived from *rs*, "to watch/guard," *Wb* 2: 449–51.

879. Reading *ny* (var. *ny.w*)-*rs.t* with the nisbe adjective (*Wb* 2: 196–97).

880. See the stela of Horus, chancellor of Sesostris I, who praises the king as *ỉn ḏr.w rs.t Nḥs.wt*, "one who reaches the utmost frontiers of the Nubian *rs.t*,"  (ll. 2–3), in Rowe 1939, pp. 189–90. Rowe notes the feminine ending of *Nḥs.wt*, but he does not recognize the attributive use of the word (as an adjective modifying *rs.t*) and translates: "who reaches the utmost frontiers of the Reset and [of] the blacks" (p. 190). The phrase "Nubian *rs.t*" could indicate all those Nubian territories and kingdoms known to the Egyptians in the execration lists. A similar implication can be argued for the term in the speech of the god Dedun to Tuthmosis III at Semna, in Sethe 1930b, pp. 200/17–201/1 (ll. 7–8): "[I have] placed [fear of you] in the lands of the *rs.t* (), and terror of you in the bodies of those who had been ignorant (of it)." The creation of such fear was, of course, the specific goal of the execration rite. An example from the Late Period appears in Goyon 1972, p. 123, §345 (col. 20/9): *ḫsf kꜣ rs.t* () translated "Then the *rs.t* will say 'Destroy?'" Goyon considered the alphabetic spelling to be an error, styling the term a "mot embarrassant" (p. 123). See also the name of a netherworld demon *Ḥsf rs.t*, "He who destroys the *rs.t* ()," in Faulkner 1958, pp. 24, 38 (n. to 35/2), and 55* (col. 35/2). Faulkner, (p.

the root meaning of the term, there can be little doubt that it ultimately came to signify "execration figures" in royal, temple, and private ritual. The most convincing proof of this assertion is provided by a group of unrecognized figurines from a private collection in London. Depicting a man, woman, and child, three crude clay images are best interpreted as the artifacts of a ritual of execration directed against a family. Inscribed in black ink below the clasped hands of the female figurine is the identifying label , *rs.t* (see fig. 17).[881]

As neither terminology nor technique separate public from private ritual sorcery, so a comparison of the potential *efficacy* of the two practices yields no discernible distinction. Contrary to modern preconceptions of magic as impotent fraud, the question of magical effectiveness is a genuine issue within societies which accept (and fear) the possibility of its success. Within such societies, hostile sorcery or "witchcraft" is often highly successful, resulting in a lethal wasting sickness (dubbed "voodoo death" by anthropologists).[882] Within Egypt, private no less than public rites were believed to manipulate the genuine

---

38, n. to col. 35/2) further suggests that *rs.t* should be read in a damaged passage in the Ikhernofret stela describing the ritual combat enacted for Osiris (S. Berlin 1204, 18): "I repelled the  from the *nšm.t*-bark; I felled the foes of Osiris." If correct, this example could easily signify "execration figures" slain in a mock battle. The passage has elsewhere been read *ḫrwy.w*,  or *sbỉ.w*, , "enemies"; for the text and translations, see Lichtheim 1973, pp. 123–25, adding Volten 1942, p. 21, n. 1; Simpson 1973, pl. 1; and Anthes 1974.

881. The figures are in the collection of Mr. Michael Rice; a parallel is in the Kestner Museum in Hanover. For the images, see Munro 1972 and the analysis in Ritner 1989a. The statuettes had been attributed to the Predynastic Period on the basis of the crudity of the work (Munro 1972, p. 28, notes that the faces resemble hamsters more than humans), but execration figures of all periods are invariably crude, and workmanship cannot be used to determine date. Thus Posener (1958, p. 255) speaks of this shoddy workmanship as "une vieille tradition, car les figurines d'envoûtement sont presque toujours mal façonnées." Ironically, these unidentified figures were published together with an obvious prisoner figurine of a bound female (Kestner Museum 1926.200, also crudely modeled and thus misidentified as a foreign product), a prototype of the Roman period Louvre figurine. Like the two parallels cited from the British Museum (Munro 1972, p. 29, BM 56914 and 56928), this female figurine is identical in meaning (if not in modeling) to the "hamster-faced" images; it does not represent "ein ganz anderes Motiv" (contra Munro 1972, p. 28). For the female figurines, see Posener 1987, p. 6, n. 4.

882. For evidence of the phenomenon and a suggested medical/psychological explanation as "shock," see Cannon 1942.

force of *ḥkꜣ*,[883] and both could dictate prolonged suffering for a human victim: "If this spell is recited against any enemy of NN, evil will happen to him for seven days."[884]

What then is the relationship between private and public ritual magic?

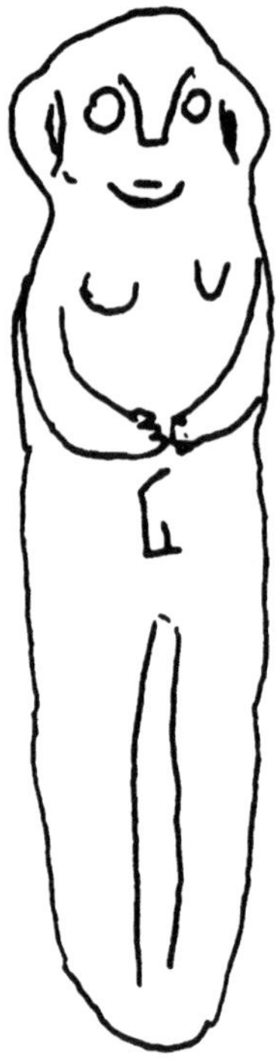

Figure 17. Execration Figure Labeled *rs.t* (after Ritner 1989a, fig. 1).

883. See the theological pronouncements of the "Book of the Heavenly Cow" (above, p. 23) and compare the fears inherent in the oracular amuletic decrees (below, p. 216). For the potential success of sorcery within the harim conspiracy under Ramses III, see below, n. 897.

884. From the "Rite for Repelling the Angry One (*scil.* Seth)," a temple rite adapted for private use, in Schott 1929, p. 61, ll. 17–18.

CHAPTER 5

PRIESTS AND PRACTITIONERS

He is a good scribe and a very wise man.
Setna I, col. 4/3

THE HARIM CONSPIRACY

The solution to the question of the difference between royal and private execration ritual is perhaps best illustrated by the single certain instance in which the use of magic by king and commoner was anciently felt to be in direct conflict—the "Harim Conspiracy" during the turbulent reign of Ramses III (ca. 1182–1151 B.C.).[885] With the compliance of stewards, inspectors, and certain women of the harim, and with the aid of a general, a troop commander in Nubia, a priest, a magician, and other functionaries, a certain queen Tiye plotted unsuccessfully to murder the reigning monarch and place her son Pentawere upon the throne. The partially preserved trial records of their failed attempt document the indictment of twenty-eight men and an undetermined number of women, and the execution or enforced suicide of all but five (four of whom were mutilated by the loss of nose and ears). They also constitute the only evidence of a trial or accusation for sorcery known from ancient Egypt. Having failed to designate either a "Great Royal Wife" or a crown prince, Pharaoh Ramses himself had provided the necessary preconditions for the conspiracy.[886] Interestingly, these prerequisites appear to correspond closely to those anticipated by the current anthropological model for witchcraft accusations, in which the determining factors are social instability and the absence of defined channels of power.[887] The pertinent sections of the conspiracy records are as follows:

885. The primary sources are Papyri Lee, Rollin, Rifaud, and the Turin "Judicial Papyrus." The precise date of the plot within the reign of Ramses III is unknown. For editions and discussion, see Devéria 1865, 1866, and 1867; Pleyte 1868; Newberry 1899, pp. 19–22 and pls. II–III; Breasted 1906, vol. 4, pp. 208–21; Lexa 1925, vol. 2, pp. 116–17; de Buck 1937; Sauneron and Yoyotte 1952; Gardiner 1961, pp. 289–92; Goedicke 1963; Vernus 1974; Posener 1976a; Weber 1977, cols. 989–91; Groll 1982, pp. 78–87; Kitchen 1983a, pp. 360–66; and Koenig 1989. Compare also nn. 46 and 250, above.

886. See the remarks of Weber 1977, col. 989 and Gardiner 1961, p. 291.

887. See Douglas 1970, p. xxxv: "Where social interaction is intense and ill defined, there we may expect to find witchcraft beliefs"; and Brown 1970, p. 21: "Late Roman society was dominated by the problem of the conflict between change and stability in a traditional society. It is here that we find a situation which has been observed both to foster sorcery accusations and to offer scope for resort to sorcery." The Egypt of Ramses III represented a similar traditional society in transformation. Beset by foreign invasion, political instability, and work strikes at home, and the loss of colonial possessions abroad, the Twentieth Dynasty marks the end of the New Kingdom and the cultural self-satisfaction that had characterized it. Unlike later European (or American) "witchcraft" accusations, however, there seems little reason to doubt the reality of the crime or the veracity of the court proceedings. The techniques of hostile magic involved were commonplace, and the accused were precisely the individuals with access to, and familiarity with, the necessary rituals.

PAPYRUS ROLLIN

[...] He began[888] to make writings of magic (*ḥkȝw*)[889] for exorcising[890] (and) for disturbing, (and he began)[891] to make some gods of wax[892] (and) some potions

888. For *ḫpr ḥr* + infinitive, "to begin to do something," see *Wb* 3: 264/18–19. For the nuance of continuity, see Capart, Gardiner, and van de Walle 1936, pp. 175 (n. i) and 176, who translate the phrase "contracted the habit"; Erman 1933, pp. 273–74, §§569–71; Korostovtsev 1973, pp. 194–95; and Collier 1986, especially p. 18. The translation, "it happened because," offered by Goedicke 1963, pp. 72–73, derives from a conflation of *íw=f ḫpr ḥr* + infinitive and *íw=f ḫpr* + circumstantial to produce an "impersonal reference to a past event." Only Goedicke's examples of the latter construction yield an impersonal "it happened that." For this common idiom in the conspiracy trial papyri, see also the remarks of Koenig 1989, p. 56, n. i.

889. Contra Goedicke 1963, p. 73, the phrase *ír sš.w*, "to make writings," is not the least ambiguous, nor is it "unlikely that the culprit was accused of composing magic writings," since "magic" (*ḥkȝ*) is specifically mentioned. Utterly groundless is Goedicke's perverse attempt to debase the meaning of *ḥkȝ* to "that non-supernatural sense in which 'bewitch' is used in modern times, with the implication of causing confusion." His uneasiness (pp. 74–75) over the conspirators' use of magic in a situation "too risky" for the "uncertain outcome" of sorcery betrays a modern Western perspective quite alien to ancient Egypt. There is no reason to doubt that the conspirators—or their victims—felt "a high degree of confidence in the efficacy of Egyptian magic" (p. 75).

890. The term is the *stwhȝ*, "to exorcise/avert" ("bannen") of *Wb* 4: 334/11–13, a causative of *twhȝ*, "to turn back" (*Wb* 5: 255/5). The verb appears primarily in "magical" contexts, found here as well as in Pap. Lee, col. 1/5, used of men, and in the Harris Magical Pap. (cols. 10/4, 10, and 11/3), where it is used equally against threatening animals and men; see Lange 1927, pp. 84–87 (Spell X, ll. 14 and 35), 92, and 94 (Spell Y, ll. 7–8): "I am entrusted with the good scroll which Re placed in my hand, which averts (*stȝhȝw* < *stwhȝ*) lions and stops (*rȝkȝ*) men, which averts (*stwhȝ*) men and stops (*rȝkȝ*) lions." The previously unidentified *rȝkȝ* (Lange, ibid., p. 96) should be the antecedent of Demotic *lg*, "to stop (misfortune, etc.)"; see Erichsen 1954a, p. 264. An extended use may appear in Pap. Anastasi I, col. 15/2, where the king is described as a raging lion to be pacified; see Gardiner 1964, pp. 54 and 17* and (courtesy K. Baer) compare *rk* in the Harsiyotef stela, ll. 103 and 107, in Schäfer 1905, pp. 130–31 and Grimal 1981b, pp. 55–56 and 85 (translated "defeat"). Although Goedicke (1963, p. 74) recognizes that the term *stwhȝ* is "peculiar to magic literature," his bias requires that it "undoubtedly does not refer to an 'act of magic' although the figure of speech might seem to imply it." His translation of *stwhȝ* as "to cause unintentional inactivity" has little to recommend it.

891. Contra Goedicke 1963, pp. 74(b) and 76(d), *ḥr ír* does continue the earlier *ḫpr ḥr ír*, since not only the writings, but the waxen gods and potions, were delivered to *Pȝ-bȝkí-kȝmn*.

892. The only possible implication of this phrase is that wax statuettes of deities were fabricated for magical purposes. Numerous examples of wax figures are known; see Raven 1983, adding the unpublished example from the tale of *Ḥr sȝ Pȝ-wnš*, above, n. 320. For execration figures, see below, p. 199. No credence can be given to Goedicke's ludicrous twisting of this passage to mean "'priests', i.e. 'godly ones'" were "made into wax," i.e., malleable, "amenable to one's plans," in 1963, pp. 74–75; see the curt dismissal by Raven 1983, pp. 9–10.

(*pḫr.wt*)[893] for laming the limbs of people. They were placed in the hand of *Pꜣ-bꜣkỉ-kꜣmn*,[894] whom Pre did not allow to be majordomo,[895] and the other great enemies, saying: 'Let them approach,'[896] and they let them approach. Now after he allowed the ones who did the evil to enter—which he did but which Pre did not allow him to be successful in it[897]— he was examined, and truth was found in every crime and every evil which his heart had found fit[898] to do, (namely) that truth was in them, and that he did them all with the other great enemies like him,[899] and they were great crimes worthy of death, the great abominations of the land, which he had done. Now when he realized the great crimes worthy of death which he had done, he killed himself.

893. For the reading *pḫr.wt*, "potions," and not *rmṯ.w*, "people," see above, p. 54 and n. 250, and Posener 1976a, p. 435 and 1976b, p. 147.

894. As a magical *damnatio memoriae*, the name has been intentionally deformed from "The servant of Amon" to "The blind servant"; for this phenomenon, see Posener 1946. For Demotic parallels, see Griffith 1909a and 1909b.

895. The terminology falsifies the actual state of affairs, and is equally an act of *damnatio memoriae*, intended to deprive the victim of any underworldly benefits accruing from his earthly status; see Vernus 1974; Koenig 1989, pp. 53–54 (ll. 1 and 6); and compare the execration practice noted in Posener 1977, p. 511 and above, n. 632.

896. I.e., "bring them inside."

897. As this phrase is also formulaic for magical purposes, the relative success of the conspiracy is open to question; see Vernus 1974, p. 123. Goedicke's translation, "(oh) that Rēᶜ had not allowed that he grow up" (1963, pp. 72 and 76, n. f), substitutes a non-existent negative optative *bw-pw* for the standard negative past and mistranslates *r(w)d*, "to succeed" as *rd*, "to grow," (pp. 72 and 77, n. k) despite the presence of the distinctive determinative of *rwd* (*Wb* 2: 410–12). His inference that the offender was young, and probably to be identified with Prince Pentawere, can thus be dismissed.

898. For the "pregnant" sense of *gmỉ*, "to find (fit/worthy)," see Gardiner 1935, vol. 1, pp. 41 (n. 11) and 47 (n. 1) and Caminos 1954, p. 84.

899. *mỉ-qd=f* or "in his position," see the Leiden "Letter to the Dead," vo. 37, in Gardiner and Sethe 1928, p. 9 (translated "like me") and pl. 8. Breasted 1906, vol. 4, pp. 220–21, translates the phrase here and in Pap. Lee as "all (together)."

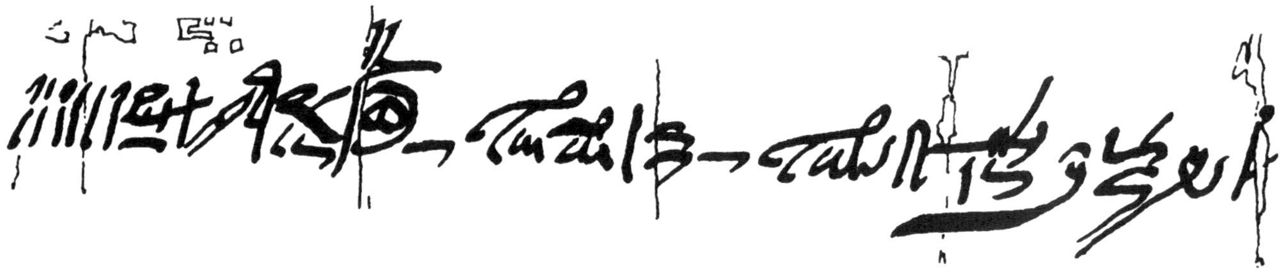

Figure 18. Royal Ownership of Execration Scrolls Indicated in Pap. Lee 1, 3 (after Devéria 1867, pl. VI).

PAPYRUS LEE, COLUMN 1

[... was made to swear an oath] of the Lord, l.p.h. of undertaking fealty,[900] swearing(?) at every [time ... saying, 'I have not given] any [magical roll] of the place in which I am to anyone on earth.' But when *Pn-ḥwy-bỉn*,[901] who was overseer of cattle said to him, 'Give to me a roll for giving to me terror and respect,'[902] he gave to him a writing of the

900. An oath "for establishing what must be respected," see Baer 1964. An alternate interpretation "fettering what is impure" is suggested in Hornung 1979, p. 93 and 1980, p. 101, n.1; and compare idem 1963, vol. 2, p. 163, n. 5. Following *sḏfꜣ-try.t*, Kitchen (1983a, p. 361/13) copies [*nb*].*w*, "all/entire," the sense of which is unclear in this passage.

901. "He of evil Huy," see above, n. 894.

902. For the fundamental association of "magic," "terror" (*nrw*), and "respect" (*šfy.t*), see above, nn. 301 and 828.

scrolls(?)[903] of *Wsr-Mꜣꜥ.t-Rꜥ-mry-ỉmn* (Ramses III), l.p.h., the great god, his lord, and he began to petition god[904] (for the) derangement(?)[905] of the people, and he penetrated the

903. The hieratic signs are (see fig. 18, p. 195), and have been variously read and transcribed, owing to confusion over the hieratic equivalents of the letters *n* and *ꜥ*, and the ideograms or determinatives *sš* and *ḫt*. See Möller 1909b, p. 30, no. 331 (*n*, >); p. 8, no. 99 (*ꜥ*, >); p. 47, no. 522 (*sš*, >); and p. 24, no. 269 (*ḫt*, >). Devéria (1867, p. 404, n. 4) transcribed only a final , translating the word as "book." Newberry (1899, pp. 20–21) read **rꜣ-ꜥ*, , and his translation "library(?)," was adopted by Lexa (1925, vol. 1, p. 126 and vol. 2, p. 116): "(un grimoire de) la bibliothèque." *Wb* 2: 395/2–3 and 3: 477/11 transcribed the hieratic as **rꜣ-ꜥ-sš.w*, , signifying "bookrolls" or "documents," and this has been followed by Kitchen (1983a, p. 362/2) and Groll (1982, p. 83, n. 7). Breasted (1906, vol. 4, p. 220, §455) translated the whole phrase (with the preceding *sš n*, "writing of") as "magical roll," and was followed by Wilson (1951, p. 269). Goedicke (1963, p. 81), read the signs as **rn.w*, , "names," which he translated with the preceding *sš n* as "(piece) of writing of the (royal) names," i.e., "royal letter-head paper"! Goedicke's fanciful translation derives from a thoroughly misguided attempt to deny the role of magic in the conspiracy and may be readily disregarded; see above, n. 889. An unambiguous use of **rꜣ-ꜥ-sš* as "(magic) scroll" appears in the Harris Magical Pap., col. 11/2 (= spell Y, 5) in Lange 1927, pp. 92, 94, and 96: "I am entrusted with the good scroll ( ) which Re placed in my hand, which averts (*stwḥꜣ*) lions and stops (*rꜣkꜣ*) men, which averts (*stwḥꜣ*) men and stops (*rꜣkꜣ*) lions." The identical context of the term in the Harris and the Lee papyri is striking; in both papyri the word describes magical texts designed to "avert" or "exorcise" (*stwḥꜣ*). A further example may be forthcoming from a notation on Pap. Geneva MAH 15274 vo., col. 4/2, if the reference to a transferred **rꜣ-ꜥ-sš* indicates the papyrus collection of anti-poison spells on which the docket itself is copied (Massart 1957, p. 183 and pl. 38; Kitchen 1983b, p. 144/12). Massart (1957, p. 183) translates simply "writing materials." That the term can be used simply for "documents" is clear from Pap. Ambras, l. 9, which summarizes the "total of the papyrus rolls which were in the jar, nine documents ( )"; see Peet 1930, p. 181 and pl. 38. Further examples are gathered in Eyre 1984, p. 198, n. h. For this disputed group, Posener (1976a, p. 436) adopted the reading **rꜣ-ꜥ* (with writing and wood determinatives), which he translated as "chests" or "coffers (for papyrus)" without further proof. Posener's unstated evidence is easily reconstructed from examples formerly understood as "writing materials." Thus, in the Ramesside "Journals" of the Theban necropolis, year 3, col. 4/3–4, a is mentioned in conjunction with two "chests" (*ꜥfdy*): "We gave two chests to the two fanbearers and one **rꜣ-ꜥ* (?)" (translated by the editors as "writing equipment[?]"); see Botti and Peet 1928, pp. 51–52 and pl. 56. Similarly, in Pap. Chester Beatty 5, col. 7/8, a scribe's equipment is described as his palette (*gsti*) and his , emended by the editor to , and translated "writing materials"; see Gardiner 1935, vol. 1, p. 48 and vol. 2, pl. 25. The translation "writing set" appears also in Caminos 1954, pp. 477–78 (Pap. Turin C, col. 2/2, read **rꜣ-ꜥ-sš*). All of these examples would be understood by Eyre (1984) as "writings." In the absence of consensus, a new

side(?)[906] of the harim and this other great deep place.[907] And he began to make inscribed people of wax[908] in order to cause that they be taken inside by the hand of the agent I(d)rimi for the exorcising (*stwhꜣ*)[909] of the one crew and the enchanting[910] (*ḥkꜣw*) of the others, to take a few words[911] inside and to bring the others out. Now when he was

---

reading and interpretation may be proposed for this critical term. An alternate reading **rꜣ-ʿ-ḫt*, , "(written) weaponry" (cf. *Wb* 2: 394/12–395/1) is also possible and would fit the threatening nature of the documents; cf. the hieroglyphic example of a book title from the temple library at Edfu in Chassinat 1928, p. 351 (= Porter and Moss 1939, p. 135, §97) and H. Brugsch 1871, p. 44: , "the (ritual) book of all writings of weaponry," (translated by Brugsch: "das Buch von den Schriften allen zum Arbeiten"). Here *ḫt* cannot be a determinative, and the phrase cannot mean "chests." Notably, the mention of this book follows immediately after that containing the rite *rtḥ pʿt*, , "subjugating the populace," which also made use of wax figures to exorcise evil; see below, p. 209.

904. *pḥ-nṯr*, literally, "to reach god." The use of *pḥ*, "to arrive/reach" in the nuance of "petition" is directly paralleled by that of *spr*, "to arrive/petition/complain" (*Wb* 4: 102–04). For the term *pḥ-nṯr*, see below, pp. 214–20. Goedicke (1963, p. 78) translated the sentence: "And it happened because of (the feast of) the Arrival of the God," by which he understands the conspiracy to have occurred during the "Feast of the Valley" (pp. 81–84). This central feature of Goedicke's historical reconstruction is, however, untenable. A *pḥ-nṯr* need have no relation with Amon even in Thebes, is not restricted to major festivals but could be done privately, and is not the "Arrival (of the) God" but rather "arriving (to the) God."

905. For the meaning of *syḥ*, , see *Wb* 4: 40/4, which suggests a connection with Coptic ⲥⲓϩⲉ, "to be removed/displaced" (Crum 1939, p. 379b; Černý 1976, p. 172; and Vycichl 1983, p. 204a), derived from *sḥꜣ*, "to turn back." The Bohairic form ⲥⲓϩⲓ means "to be deranged" (Westendorf 1965–77, p. 210). Goedicke (1963, p. 84) translated "excitement, rapture," taking the word as a causative of *ʿḥ*, "to capture" (*Wb* 1: 213/18). Groll (1982, p. 83) translates "fit of madness."

906. *riꜣ.t*, or(?) translate "room," as in Demotic; see Erichsen 1954a, p. 241 (*ry.t* > ⲣⲓ). The term should not mean the "side (approach)," as postulated by Goedicke (1963, p. 86).

907. For *mḏ.t*, "depth/thickness," see Carter and Gardiner 1917, pp. 137–38; Hayes 1942, pp. 21 and 22, n. 115; and Simpson 1963, pp. 76–77. The notion of horizontal depth implicit in the term *mḏ.t* is here strengthened by the use of the verb *pḥ*, "to penetrate." Goedicke's translation "high," (1963, pp. 78 and 85) is unacceptable and his attempted identification of the site with the high gate of Medinet Habu is thus excluded. Similarly, in the Demotic Pap. London and Leiden, col. 29/6–7, the term is used to indicate depth in contrast to width (*wsḫ.t*): "Open to me the heaven in its width and depth"; contra Griffith and Thompson (1904, p. 167) who translate: "in its breadth and height."

908. Contra Goedicke (1963, p. 78): "It happened because the people were made into wax"; see above, n. 892. For examples of the use of wax captive figures in execration magic, see below, p. 199.

909. For the term, see above, n. 890.

910. Contra Goedicke (1963, p. 78) who mistranslates *ḥkꜣw nꜣ k.t-ḫ.w* as "the others deceived."

911. Incorrect determinatives vitiate Goedicke's attempt (1963, pp. 78 and 89) to convert *mdw.t*, "words" into *mdw.ti*, "talker" (*Wb* 2: 182/6) with an unattested nuance of "conspirator."

examined concerning them, truth was found in every crime and every evil which his heart had found fit to do, (namely) that truth was in them, and that he did them all with the other great enemies whom every god and goddess abominate like him. And there were done to him the great punishments of death which the gods said: 'Do them to him.'

PAPYRUS LEE, COLUMN 2

[...] ... [...] on the basket, and he went off [...] his hand lame. Now as for [every crime and every evil which he did, he was examined concerning] them, truth was found in every crime and every evil which his heart had found to do (namely) that truth was [in them, and that he did them all with the other] great enemies whom every god and goddess abominate like him, and they were great crimes worthy of death, the great abominations of [the land, which he had done. Now when he[912] realized the] great crimes worthy of death which he had done, he killed himself. Now when the officials who were in charge of him realized that he had killed himself [... abomination(?) of][913] Pre like him, which the hieroglyphic writings say: 'Do it to him!'

From these fragmentary records, certain facts are clear. In the course of the plot, several conspirators had made use of written magical spells (*sẖ.w n ḥkꜣw*), inscribed wax figurines, and potions[914] to "exorcise" (*stwhꜣ*), "disturb" (*sẖnn*), "lame" (*dỉ.t gnn*), and "enchant" (*ḥkꜣw*). The inclusion of inscribed figurines immediately suggests a connection with the "royal" execration ritual designed for identical purposes. Such a possibility is all the more likely since the source of this magical information was the king's own library. Court records state unambiguously that the unknown defendant of Papyrus Lee, column 1, had provided the criminal *Pn-ḥwy-bỉn* with a royal text, despite his oath to the contrary.[915] It is thus absolutely excluded that the "great crimes worthy of death, the great abominations of the land" are to be equated with the practice of sorcery *per se*, since both the

912. Restoration following Kitchen 1983a, p. 363/5; differently in Newberry 1899, p. 22.

913. Kitchen (1983a, p. 363/7–8) restores: "[with the other great criminals, the complete abomination of] Pre"; following (but slightly differing from) Newberry (1899, p. 22). Such a restoration, however, does not yield a complete sentence, and the text clearly ends at this point. The missing phrase must have supplied the officials' reactions and probably contained a reference to "the great punishments of death" as the antecedent to the final phrase "which the hieroglyphic writings say: 'Do it to him!'"; compare Pap. Lee, col. 1/7, in Kitchen 1983a, p. 362/12–13.

914. This combination of written spell, manipulated figures, and magic by ingredient conforms directly to the tripartite nature of magic as previously analyzed.

915. On this point, see Baer 1964 and Posener 1976a, p. 436.

ownership of the texts in question, and their use *for royal benefit* were certainly legal.[916] Obviously, the "great capital crime" consisted of complicity in the attempt on the life of the king. Whether this was accomplished by magic or by physical force was irrelevant; assassination by sword would hardly have been more acceptable. Comparable to a sword, magic was a weapon for the Egyptians,[917] and the legality of its usage was dependent upon the identity of the intended victim. The records of the Harim Conspiracy thus reveal a condemnation of sorcery *against the king*, not a condemnation of sorcery itself.

The truth of this statement is evident from a comparable use of execration technique in seemingly identical circumstances not by the conspirators, but by agents of the king. Evidence for this harim conspiracy is forthcoming from the "Instructions of Amenemhat I," ostensibly dictated by the ghost of that assassinated monarch to his son and co-regent, Sesostris I. In the course of the Instruction, Amenemhat describes those who plotted his murder:

> It was he who ate my bread who raised troops. He to whom I had given my hands created terror by means of it. He who was dressed in my linen viewed me as fodder. He who was anointed with my myrrh spat before me ... Had women ever previously marshaled troops? Are rebels bred within the palace?[918]

The identity of one conspirator may be provided by a series of five alabaster execration plaques now in the Cairo Museum.[919] Said to derive from Helwan, the plaques were part of an assemblage which included a broken prisoner figurine of clay covered with a long (and now illegible) inscription. In addition, the find contained six sheets of wax which had been inscribed before being folded or rolled to form a torso to which wax arms and legs were added. The resulting six wax figures had the appearance of captives, and are the obvious counterparts to the "men of wax" used in the conspiracy against Ramses III. As these figures have not been unrolled, their texts, like that of the illegible clay figure, remain unknown. The five alabaster plaques, however, bear a variant of the standard "execration

916. Contra Posener 1976a, p. 437: "Il n'est pas précisé que ces pratiques de sorcellerie n'étaient pas répréhensibles en soi, mais le devenaient par l'usage qui en était fait. La technique et son utilisation forment un tout et constituent de «grands crimes passibles de la peine capitale»." Were this true, much of the priesthood throughout the country would have been guilty of capital crimes on a daily basis.

917. For *ḥkꜣ.w* as weaponry (*ꜥḥꜣ.w*), see the "Instructions for King Merikare," discussed above, p. 20 and n. 79.

918. For the text, see Helck 1969, pp. 26–31 (§4) and 61–67 (§9). For translations and commentary, see Wilson 1969d, especially p. 419, n. 11 and Lichtheim 1973, pp. 135–39, especially 137. For the likely identity of the plotters, see the remarks of Posener 1956, p. 84.

919. See the full publication in Posener 1987, with the condemned Egyptians on pp. 55–56. Earlier studies are Posener 1939b, p. 43 and 1939a, p. 315 (JdE 63955–59); for the assemblage, see idem 1976a, pp. 440–42 and 1987, pp. 10–11 and pl. 3.

formula" whose final Egyptian section comprises two names. The first of these is "the deceased Intefiker," whose parents are Intefiker and Satsisobek.[920] The elder Intefiker can be identified,[921] and was none other than the vizier of the murdered Amenemhat I. That the vizier and his family fell from grace is clear not only from these texts, where all of their names are determined by the hieroglyph for "enemy,"[922] but also by the willful destruction anciently inflicted upon images of the vizier in the Theban tomb belonging to his family.[923] The reason for the suppression of Intefiker is unknown, as is its date. Until recently, it had been assumed that the career of the vizier spanned at least from the tenth year of Amenemhat I (attested by graffiti from Korosko in Nubia) to the seventeenth year of Sesostris I (suggested by Papyrus Reisner II, dated to year 17 of an unnamed king), a period of more than thirty years.[924] However, recent analysis suggests that the evidence linking "year 17" to Sesostris I is unsupported, and that the date could refer instead to the reign of Amenemhat I.[925] Thus there is no longer any proof that Intefiker's career survived the transition of reigns,[926] and, consequently, there is every reason to suspect that the *damnatio memoriae* inflicted on himself and his son was connected with the purge of officials implicated in the successful assassination of Amenemhat. The connivance of the

920. The second name is Senwosret, son of Iams(?); no designation for "deceased" precedes this name; Posener 1987, pp. 55–56.

921. The name Satsisobek is otherwise attested only in TT 60, where the name belongs to the wife of the vizier Intefiker. For the identification of the family, see Posener 1976a, p. 441 and the brief remarks in 1987, p. 55.

922. Posener 1976a, p. 442 and 1987, p. 55 and pls. 4–5.

923. For the destruction of TT 60 (of Senet, mother? of Intefiker the vizier), see Davies, Gardiner, and Davies 1925a, pp. 5 (deliberate burning) and 6–7 (erasure of Intefiker throughout). Contra Gardiner (p. 5), the presence of graffiti from the Eighteenth Dynasty praising the tomb decoration need not imply that the burning took place later than that period. Ancient antiquarians may have been attracted to ruins no less than their modern counterparts; compare the activities of Khaemwese, discussed in Gomaà 1973. Posener (1976a, p. 441) is suspicious of linking the erasures of Intefiker the vizier with the mention of his son on the execration plaques. However, both father and son are defamed on the plaques (p. 442), and both could have been involved in the harim conspiracy.

924. Posener 1976a, pp. 441–42.

925. See the discussion in Simpson 1969, pp. 10–11.

926. The appearance of an erased Intefiker before Sesostris I in TT 60 (Davies, Gardiner, and Davies 1925a, p. 13) need not prove that the vizier functioned during the independent reign of that monarch. Of course, the discovery of the vizier's complicity—if such were the case—might not have been made immediately, and he could have continued to act as vizier for an unknown length of time.

vizier in such a plot was probably not without precedent; Amenemhat I had himself been the vizier of the preceding king Nebtawyre Montuhotep, whose fate is unknown.[927]

Yet another example of a harim conspiracy combated by execration rites appears to be represented by the famous Berlin red pots, the first discovered exemplars of the genre. Now dated to the reign of Sesostris III or later, the Berlin texts are notable for the presence in the Egyptian section of "names characteristic of the 12th dynasty royal family" and "functionaries of women who seem to be princesses or queens."[928] Despite the absence of definite corroborating evidence, the ritual cursing of these deceased(?)[929] royal ladies and their retainers almost certainly derives from the suppression of a conspiracy originating in the harim, and the texts have been suggested by van Seters to illustrate the discordant historical context decried in the literary "Admonitions of Ipuwer."[930] Although the correlation is far from certain, one passage from the "Admonitions" is of particular pertinence for the discussion of the "Harim Conspiracy" and the "private" use of execration ritual:

927. See the remarks of Gardiner 1961, p. 125 and Posener 1956, p. 51. A peaceful transition is suggested in von Beckerath 1965.

928. Wilson 1969c, p. 329, n. 15.

929. See above, pp. 141–42, especially n. 627. Following the original edition of Sethe, Wilson (1969c, p. 329) translates "May NN die." Whereas the interpretation of Sethe and Wilson construes the texts as the work of the conspirators (designed to effect a coup), the retranslation "deceased" suggests instead that they are the product of royal agents (as does the presence of the African, Asiatic, and Libyan sections) dictated after the failure of a plot. The very fact that such confusion of authorship is possible underscores the fundamental unity of method utilized by conspirator and king alike.

930. Van Seters 1964, p. 22 and 1966, p. 120. Van Seters notes the similar fear of Asiatics, Nubians, and Libyans in the "Execration Texts" and the "Admonitions," and for the hypothetical harim conspiracy he compares such passages as "Admonitions," col. 7/2–4: "A few lawless men have ventured to despoil the land of kingship. Men have ventured to rebel against the uraeus ..." Although the texts display similar anxieties, these lists of potential enemies are standard at all periods of Egyptian history, and it is hazardous to assume a specific relation. The attempt to link both the "Execration Texts" and the "Admonitions" to the Second Intermediate Period is unconvincing, as much of van Seters' argument depends upon the now-discredited theory of a peaceful absorption of Egypt by the Hyksos.

> Indeed, magical spells (*ḥkꜣ.w*) are divulged; oracles (*šm.w*)[931] and spells of seeking(?) (*sẖn.w*)[932] are made dangerous (*snḥꜣ*) because they are remembered by men.[933]

The rare term *snḥꜣ*, , here translated "made dangerous," means literally "to make rough."[934] As recognized by Gardiner, the editor of the "Admonitions," the word in this passage is susceptible to two quite opposite interpretations, signifying either that—by repetition—spells were made "threatening" (through uncontrolled usage) or "frustrated" (diminished in efficacy by overuse).[935] After reflection, Gardiner opted for the latter interpretation. There is, however, no evidence that the power of *ḥkꜣ* (or the force of oracles) can be lessened by repeated usage, and the retention of traditional spells (whose antiquity was felt to *enhance*, not exhaust their efficacy) argues convincingly against such a possibility.[936] Nor can the mere "recalling of magic" be inimical in itself, as is proved by the existence of spells "to remember magic" (*sḫꜣ.t ḥkꜣw*).[937]

Rather, the dissemination of *ḥkꜣ* could become a threat to the realm of Pharaoh as it had to that of the sun god Re in primordial time:

> Moreover, guard against those magicians who know their spells, since the god Heka is in them himself. Now as for the one who ingests him, I (*scil.* Re) am there.

931. Versus Gardiner (1969, p. 48) who suggested that both *šm* and *sẖn* were types of incantations named for their beginning word (as *hꜣ-snḏ*, *Wb* 2: 471/12 and "Hail Mary," "Our Father," etc.). The terms are untranslated in *Wb* 4: 467/13. For *šm*, "oracle," see above, n. 167.

932. Or "spells of meeting/uniting." A hapax; for the root, see *Wb* 3: 468–70. The range of meanings for *sẖn* is later extended to include the concepts "chance" and "(astrological) conjunctions" (Erichsen 1954a, p. 455), though these meanings are unlikely here.

933. "Admonitions," col. 6/6–7, in Gardiner 1969, pp. 47–48.

934. A causative of *nḥꜣ*, "rough/roughness," (*Wb* 2: 290–91: "wild/terrible") used of eyes (*Wb* 2: 290/19), dry stone (*Wb* 2: 291/1), raw copper (*Wb* 2: 291/2), etc.; for the term, see Lloyd 1975, pp. 59–66 and Hornung 1963, vol. 2, p. 133.

935. See the discussion in Gardiner 1969, p. 48, implicitly followed by te Velde 1986, pp. 255–56, who translates the term "worthless."

936. Compare also the common recommendation which concludes magical spells: "Found truly effective a million times!" (*Wb* 4: 542/14–15). Pedigrees attesting to the great antiquity of spells and recipes are often encountered; see *inter alia* Pap. Ebers §419 (col. 63/4–6), §468 (col. 66/15–18), §856 (col. 103/1–2); BD spells 64, 130, 134, 137A, 148, 151e §T2, Pleyte 167; and Pap. BM 10059, §25 (col. 8/8–9/4, in Borghouts 1978, pp. 35–36, §53). The use of such pedigrees continues into Greco-Egyptian magic, see PGM XXIVa, in Betz 1986, p. 264; Brashear 1979, p. 266; and compare Iamblichus, *De Mysteriis*, viii. 5 (1966).

937. CT spell 657, in de Buck 1956, p. 278 and Faulkner 1977, p. 228.

> ... I commend them to your son Osiris. Keep watch over their children and cause the hearts of their elders there to forget their magical power (*ꜣḫw*), they who act as they desire against the entire land using their magic (*ḥkꜣ.w*) which is in their bodies.[938]

Attempts to safeguard this power of magic (as a *ba* of Re[939]) should be seen in light of other restrictions on access to sacred knowledge, such as the exclusion of foreigners from temples ("No Phoenician should approach it, no Greek enter it, no Bedouin tread it, its magic [*ḥkꜣ*] should not be seen within it"),[940] the "House of Life" or sacred scriptorium,[941] and the ownership of ritual books (*ba*s of Re),[942] as well as the warnings for secrecy found in rubrics to funerary spells ("Roll for understanding the words of the House of Life ... to be used ... without the rabble's knowledge," "You shall use it without letting anyone see it except your true close friend and the ritual priest ... not a slave who has come from abroad," etc.),[943] and even in incantations against crocodiles:

> First spell of enchanting all that is in the water, concerning which the chief lector priests (*ḥry-tp*)[944] say: 'Do not reveal it to others.' A veritable secret of the House of Life.[945]

938. "The Book of the Heavenly Cow," verses 218–25, in Hornung 1982, pp. 20–21 (text) and 44–45 (translated differently). See also above, p. 23, n. 95 and p. 106, n. 517.

939. See above, pp. 23–24.

940. Chassinat 1952, pp. 60/10–61/2, in regard to the temple crypt. For further examples, see ibid., p. 54/6–8 (vs. Asiatics, Bedouins, and Greeks) and compare 97/4 (hide from those who come from outside). See also Esna inscription 197, l. 20 (on precautions before the Opet feast), in Sauneron 1968, p. 12: "Do not permit any Asiatic to enter the temple whether he be old or young." For discussion, see Junker 1959.

941. See Pap. Salt 825, col. 7/5, in Derchain 1965, pp. 9*, 140, and 168, §83: "An Asiatic may not enter into this House of Life, he may not see it."

942. Compare Pap. BM 10188, colophon 33–38, in Faulkner 1933, p. 34 and 1937a, pp. 10–11: "As for any man of any foreign land, whether a negro of Cush or a Syrian, who will carry off this book and take it away from me—their corpse shall not be buried; they shall not receive cool water; one shall not offer incense to them; their name shall not be remembered anywhere on earth; they shall not see the rays of the solar disk." For ritual texts as *bꜣ.w Rꜥ*, see *Wb* 1: 414/1.

943. Compare BD spells 101, §P2 (not reveal to rabble); 115, §S2 (not reveal mysteries); 116, §S1 (not reveal mysteries); 133b, §S (not reveal mysteries) and T3 (not reveal to son or father); 136, §T 3 (use only for oneself); 137A, §§T8 and 16 (use only for oneself); 144, §T6 (not let anyone see); 147, §T3 (use only for oneself); 148, Twenty-first Dynasty, §§P4 and 6 (only to ritual priest and bosom friend, not to foreign slave or rabble); 161, §§T2–4 (no outsider, rabble, father, mother); 162, §T5 (not to anyone); 190, §§P4, 6, and 8 (only to ritual priest and bosom friend, not to foreign slave or rabble); and Pleyte 167c, §T2 (use only for oneself).

944. Lange (1927, p. 55) translates "superiors," by which he understands the "controlling and thus discerning classes of the people." For *ḥry-tp*, "chief (lector priest)/magician," see below, pp. 220ff.

945. Papyrus Harris Magical, col. 6/10 (§K, 1–4), in Lange 1927, pp. 53–54.

Restricted access to such powerful spells was intended to preserve the privilege of the elite (gods, kings, priests), and lessen the threat of misuse.[946] It is the loss of this privilege—with the concomitant threat of revolt—which is bemoaned in the "Admonitions." As noted by Gardiner:

> This passage affords the direct proof that in Egypt magic, as such, was by no means regarded as a forbidden art. It was only when magic was used for illegal purposes, as in the case described by the *Lee-Rollin* papyri, that it became punishable; in such instances it was the end, not the means, that incurred the penalties of the law.[947]

Using identical methods—and identical texts—royal and private magic are here distinguished exclusively by self interest. Even this distinction grows evanescent once it is realized that the "categories" themselves are only illusory, for there are no truly "royal" or "private" magical spells in ancient Egypt, only *priestly* spells used for royal or private benefit. Of necessity, the ability to compose, copy, or recite such spells was limited to the king, the priests, and the scribes who alone comprised the approximately one percent of the population able to read or write.[948] Neither king nor commoner freely composed written spells or rites; the former did not[949] and the latter could not. Rather, as exemplified by the warnings for secrecy quoted above, the composition and preservation of magical incantations (as well as hymns, rituals, and even medical potions) was the prerogative of the "House of Life,"  (*pr-ʿnḫ*),

946. Contrast the praise given ancient authors in Pap. Chester Beatty 4, vo. 3/9–10, in Gardiner 1935, vol. 1, p. 39: "They hid their magic from the masses. It is read in their Instructions," with the punishment accorded to Setna, who "had no occupation on earth but to unroll the book (of Thoth) and read from it to everyone" (col. 4/38 in Lichtheim 1980, p. 133).

947. Gardiner 1969, p. 47.

948. See Baines and Eyre 1983; Baines 1983; and te Velde 1986. For literacy as a fundamental requirement for priesthood in the Late Period, see Sauneron 1962a and Fairman 1958, p. 87, n. d. Sacerdotal authorship of magical texts continues unabated throughout later Egyptian history, contra Sadek 1971, who unjustifiably characterizes later magical papyri as "most often the work of not very literate commoners" (p. 113); for full discussion, see Ritner 1995.

949. For the non-scribal role of the literate king, see Baines and Eyre 1983, pp. 77–81. The priests concerned with magical spells on behalf of the king (*sš mḏꜣ.t nṯr n nb tꜣ.wy*, "scribe of the divine book of the Lord of the Two Lands") are discussed in Wessetzky 1984a. The non-royal composition of even such "royal" texts as the Pyramid Texts is evident from obvious insertions, cf. PT spell 467: "I have not opposed the king," in Faulkner 1969, p. 156 and n. 6 ("I" explained as "the successor to the throne?"). A similar transition from the private to the royal sphere is suggested for the anti-serpent spell in Altenmüller 1979, attested in papyri, on private statuary, and on the curative statue of Ramses III at Almazah (spell VI); see Drioton 1939 and 1957. In all cases, however, the spell was surely a scriptorium product, and the Almazah statue represents a royal benefaction *for public benefit*. Any transition is simply a question of patronage (the hazy distinction between temple and king); neither authors nor audience has changed.

the sacred scriptorium attached to temples throughout the country.[950] Thus, there need be little surprise that "spells" and "hymns" so often overlap,[951] since they were composed by the same sacerdotal group and derive from the same theology. A similar rationale should be held to account for the apparent relationship previously noted between the "private" execration ritual of Coffin Texts spell 37 and the "royal" execration (and Amduat) texts (above, pp. 168–70 and 173–74). Identical in practice and purpose, such spells share priestly authorship as well, differing only in application. In fact, the general limitation on literacy severely circumscribes the whole notion of "private magic" in ancient Egypt. Leaving funerary compositions aside, the "private" ownership of magical books was

950. The basic study remains Gardiner 1938: "It is in the 𓉐𓋹𓉐 that medical and religious books were written and it was there that all questions relating to such learned matters were settled" (p. 159); "... magical spells intended for the use of the living came within the scope of the House of Life" (p. 164); "No doubt the Books of the Dead ... were characteristic products of the House of Life" (p. 178). For magic, see further, pp. 164–68, noting especially the title recorded on p. 166: *ḫrp ḥry.w ḥkꜣ m pr-ˁnḫ*, "leader of the masters of magic in the House of Life." For the "Apophis Book" as a "secret book of the House of Life" (Pap. Bremner-Rhind, col. 29/16), see p. 169. For medical ointments, see p. 178. For the priestly rank of "scribes of the House of Life," see p. 170. For the association of the scriptorium with temples, see pp. 173 and 177. More recent studies of the institution include Weber 1980; Koenig 1989, pp. 55–56; Habachi and Ghalioungui 1971; and Derchain 1965, pp. 48–61 and 96–108.

951. See above, *Chapter 1*, pp. 6–7.

largely limited to priests who obtained the rolls from temple libraries[952] or scriptoria.[953] The known exceptions to this rule include only the scribally-educated among the royal tomb-builders at Deir el-Medineh,[954] and this distinction undoubtedly resulted from their

952. For the magical holdings of such libraries (*pr-mḏꜣ.t*) attached to temples, compare the Edfu list published in Chassinat 1928, p. 351 (= Porter and Moss 1939, p. 135, §97), translated in H. Brugsch 1871, pp. 43–45, and discussed in Wessetzky 1984b and Derchain 1965, pp. 58–61. For the suggested existence of collections of spells against scorpion sting at the temple of Hor-Khenty-Khety at Athribis, see Jelínková-Reymond 1956, pp. 132–33, especially 132, n. 6. Diodorus Siculus 1933, vol. 1, pp. 172–73 (1.49.3) records that the temple library of the Ramesseum was designated ψυχῆς ἰατρεῖον, "Healing Place of the Soul." The Egyptian temple origin of the Demotic spells and most—if not all—of the PGM collections is discussed at length in Ritner 1995. The bulk of the Demotic and PGM "grimoires" probably derives from a single Theban temple archive acquired by Anastasi in the early nineteenth century (subsequently dispersed through auctions of his collection).

953. Aside from the Ramesseum magician's collection (see below, pp. 222ff.), the evidence for such "borrowings" all dates from the Late Period. This proprietary attitude toward temple property is indicative of the late, hereditary priesthood which regularly derived its income and status from the exploitation of temple assets. For the phenomenon, compare J. H. Johnson 1986b. Among the magical temple papyri appropriated for "private" use by priests are the "Apophis Book" (Pap. Bremner-Rhind) copied by the god's father and prophet Nesmin (who adapted as well the liturgical "glorifications" of Pap. BM 10208 and 10209); the Osirian rituals of Pap. MMA L 23.79.3 modified for the priest Imhotep; the rituals against Seth (Schott 1929) which include Pap. Louvre E 3129 belonging to the god's father Pasherenmin; Pap. BM 10252 adapted for the god's father Pawerem; and the prophylactic Pap. BM 10288 also modified for the god's father Pawerem. See Faulkner 1933, pp. 32–34; idem 1937a, pp. 10–11; Haikal 1972; Goyon 1969, p. 26, n. 3; Schott 1929, pp. 2–3; and Caminos 1972, pp. 205–24. Literate priestly redactors are certainly responsible for the "private" adaptation of the originally royal protective rites published in Sauneron 1970a. Access to royal ritual papyri would have been impossible for "commoners with little refined knowledge of the current cults and a frequently confused sense of mythology"; contra Sadek 1971, p. 114. A temple origin is certain for the Metternich stela (copied by the god's father Nestem "after he had found it removed from the domain of Osiris Mnevis"), and other "healing statues"; see Borghouts 1978, p. 71, §95 and Jelínková-Reymond 1956, pp. 4–6 (for dedicator as chief doorman of the temple of Hor-Khenty-Khety at Athribis) and 132–33 (for texts copied from temple rolls, the *bꜣ.w R ꜥ*). For such adaptations, see also n. 855, above. For the question of the "private" magical practitioner, see below, pp. 211–12 and 220ff.

954. Thus the "Dream Book" and other magical rolls from the Chester Beatty collection were the property of the scribes Amennakhte and Keniherkhepeshef, and the latter copied (though he did not compose) spells against demons and ghosts. It is notable, however, that Pap. Chester Beatty 8 is said to have been a temple text: "This writing was found in the library, (in a) room of the temple" (col. 4/3); see Gardiner 1935, vol. 1, p. 68 and compare vol. 1, p. 74 (vo. 7/7): "to be recited by the chief lector priest." For the ownership of magical texts at Deir el-Medineh, see Gardiner ibid., vol. 1, pp. 8 and 26; Černý 1973, pp. 334–36; and Pestman 1982. For the copies of Keniherkhepeshef, see Edwards 1968 and Koenig 1981. The attribution of these copies is made certain by distinctive paleography; other preserved charms from Deir el-Medineh may be the work of specialized "magicians" within the community, and need not have been copied by their intended beneficiary—for example, Pap. Deir el-Medineh 36, published by Sauneron (1970b). Clear evidence of the circulation of magical papyri among the scribes of Deir el-Medineh is afforded by the dockets on the verso of Pap. Geneva MAH

unique, cloistered lifestyle which required that the workers act as their own priests.[955] Admittedly, memorized incantations against crocodiles, snakes, infant disease, et cetera, may have circulated among the population at large, but the theological basis of even these "popular" spells suggests transmission from a priestly source.[956]

The priest, of course, was not immune to influence from the general popular culture, as is illustrated by the suggested impact of "letters to the dead" on execration ritual (above, pp. 180–83). Nevertheless, such influence in no way minimizes the central role of the priest as redactor of the execration rite in all its various manifestations, which include not only those intended for "private" or "royal" benefit, but numerous temple execration rites[957] which entail the destruction of figures for the benefit of the gods and the cosmos:

15274, which record the "giving of spells for extracting poison"; see vo. 2/1–6, vo. 6/1–3, and possibly vo. 4/2 (reference to a delivered **r3-ʿ-sš*), in Massart 1957, pp. 182–83 and pl. 38 and Kitchen 1983b, pp. 133–34 and 144. The transferred spell may be the anti-scorpion remedy copied in vo. 5; Massart 1957, pp. 183–84 and pl. 37.

955. For the priestly role of the workmen, see Bierbrier 1982, p. 96: " With such a multiplicity of divinities and temples, the community might be thought to have required a large number of priests to serve its needs. This was not, however, the case. The workmen themselves acted as their own priests and performed all the sacred rituals for their gods." So also Valbelle (1985, pp. 328–31), who notes the mingling of religious acts at the site: "En effet, la distinction entre les pratiques communes et les pratiques individuelles paraît souvent assez floue" (p. 330).

956. Compare the examples of "fording spells" from tombs of the Old Kingdom, in the "Story of the Herdsman," in PT spell 240, in CT spell 836, and in the Harris Magical Papyrus. Though these have often been described as "common knowledge" (thus Goedicke 1970, p. 252), it is notable that the example in the "Story of the Herdsman" is said to be recited (*šd*) by the *knowledgeable ones* (*rḫ.w-ḫ.t*, literally, "knowers of things") of the herdsmen" (ll. 12–13). For this term meaning "magician," see below, pp. 229–31. This nuance of specialized knowledge even for spells of daily life appears also in the Harris Magical Pap., which specifies the "water spell" as "a veritable secret of the House of Life," whose completed amulet alone may be entrusted simply to "a man at the prow of the boat," see n. 945, above. The theological complexity of these spells in Old Kingdom tombs has been investigated by Kaplony (1969 and 1970) and Altenmüller (1973). For further bibliography, see above, p. 48, n. 229, adding Borghouts 1978, p. 83 (no. 122); Ogdon 1982 and 1979; G. Meyer 1990; and compare the funerary parallels in Zandee 1975–76; and PT spell 240: "The oxherd is Horus when he treads" (in Faulkner 1969, p. 57). See also below, pp. 225–31. Common spells against scorpion and snake bite were certainly priestly creations, carved on cippi of Horus and on "healing statues" dedicated by priests or the king. Individuals neither read nor memorized these spells, but instead drank a water offering poured over the carved surface. See *inter alia* Lacau 1921–22; Drioton 1939; and Traunecker 1983. Spells for childhood illnesses are similarly specialized knowledge; where the practitioner is indicated, he is a *ḥry-ḥb*, or "lector-priest," whose magical function is discussed below, pp. 220ff. See Erman 1901, pp. 25–26 (Pap. Berlin P. 3027, col. 6/5, broken, but certain). There is no proof for Erman's suggestion (p. 4) that the spells were recited by mothers in the harim; compare the *ḥk3y n k3p*, 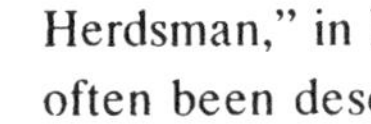, "magician of the nursery," noted in Gardiner 1917, p. 32.

957. An overview of these rites is found in Schoske 1986, who follows the traditional distinction of "official" versus "private" enactments. To the former should be added the rituals in Grimm 1987 and 1988.

basic purification rites,[958] the Apophis ritual,[959] the rite against Seth,[960] the rites of Sokar-Osiris,[961] the "Play of Horus"[962] and other execrations at Edfu,[963] the ritual for protecting the bark of Osiris,[964] offering rites at Kom Ombo,[965] the Anubis ritual of Papyrus

958. See the execration ritual enacted at Piye's entrance into the shrine at Heliopolis, in Grimal 1981a, pp. 36* and 131: "Coming in procession to the estate of Re; entering into the temple in praise, with lector priests giving thanks and repelling the rebels (literally, "those who were overturned") against the king; carrying out the rites of the robing room … ."

959. Papyrus Bremner-Rhind, cols. 22–33; for discussion and bibliography, see below, pp. 210–11, additional references in *Index of Texts and Objects Cited*.

960. Schott 1929; for discussion, see additional references in *Index of Texts and Objects Cited* under Pap. Louvre E 3129. One makes a figure of Seth made of red wax, acacia or *ḥmꜣ*-wood, with its name carved on its breast and inscribed on a new sheet of papyrus with fresh ink. The figure is then bound (with a tendon of a red cow), spat upon, trampled, pierced, and cut (p. 5). The same procedure (pp. 37/3–59/16) is performed on a figure of a bound captive, who may be assimilated to one's personal enemy (p. 61/17–18). Reference to the text appears in the Edfu book list, see H. Brugsch 1871, p. 44 and above, n. 903. A further reference to this rite may be preserved in Plutarch, *De Iside et Osiride*, 30.362 F (see Griffiths 1970, pp. 164–65 and 411–12), which speaks of sacrificial cakes with the image of an ass tied by rope.

961. Figurines of enemies are placed on a brazier, see Goyon 1978a. For the text, see Chassinat 1930, p. 293 = idem 1960, pl. 134. This execration rite derives from what may have been in the Middle Kingdom a mock battle within a liturgical enactment of the Osiris myth; compare the statements of the priest Ikhernofret: "I repulsed the attackers of the *neshmet*-bark, I felled the foes of Osiris," in Sethe 1983, p. 70 (ll. 12–13 and cf. 17–18), translated with bibliography in Lichtheim 1973, pp. 123–25. For the relation of this "drama" to the Edfu rite, see Gaballa and Kitchen 1969, p. 24.

962. See Fairman 1974 and Blackman and Fairman 1942, 1943, and 1944. For the text, see Chassinat 1931, pp. 60–90; 1960, pls. 146–48; and 1934a, pls. 494–514. The sacrifice of a prisoner figurine by the king (enacted by a priestly representative) is paralleled by the sacrifice of Seth in the form of a hippopotamus-shaped cake by the chief lector priest; see Fairman 1974, pp. 111–18 (= Chassinat 1960, pl. 146, bottom middle and 1931, pp. 86–87 [prisoner figure] and 87–90 [Seth cake]). The parallelism is reinforced by calling Seth "a Nubian," see Fairman 1974, p. 111. The relationship of this rite to the "breaking of the red vases" is noted in Blackman and Fairman 1942, pp. 37–38.

963. E.g., the rituals depicted on the interior walls of the temple library. On the east wall, a lector priest pierces nine prisoner figures (the "Nine Bows") on a lance; see Chassinat 1928, p. 349 and pl. 82 and Capart 1940, p. 7. On the west wall, four enemy figures are successively stabbed while being burnt before Horus; see Chassinat 1928, pp. 346–47 and pl. 82 and Derchain 1965, pp. 59–60 (misidentified as Chassinat 1929b, pl. 82). With the latter rite, compare the burning of four enemy figures slain with a flint knife before Horus and Hathor in Chassinat 1930, pp. 142–45 and 1960, pl. 118.

964. Goyon 1969, first attested in TT 7 (reign of Ramses II) at Deir el-Medineh, then in the adapted temple rolls Pap. Louvre N 3219 and Pap. BM 10252 (= Schott 1929) and Pap. MMA L 23.79.3; for these texts, see above, n. 953. The text appears also at Dendera, see Chassinat 1894, pp. 108–15. Within the rite, a wax figure of Seth is bound, snared in a fishing net, cut to pieces and burnt in a fire of bryony.

965. The rear wall of the adyton features a relief of offerings complete with a small bound prisoner figurine; see de Morgan 1909, p. 291 (no. 938) and Gutbub 1978, especially figs. 144 and 149.

Jumilhac,[966] and—notably—the rite to protect the sacred scriptorium itself.[967] More elaborate variants include the rituals of *rtḥ pꜥt*, , "subjugating humanity," in which figures of enemies are snared in a net before incineration,[968] and *dgdg rm.w*, "trampling fish," in which four fish are labeled with the names of state enemies and then trampled, burned, and discarded.[969] These rites appear together with the apotropaic casting of balls and the slaughter of a red goat and ox, various geese, and wax figures of a hippopotamus

966. Vandier 1961, p. 130 (col. 18/9–10): "Si on ne décapite pas l'ennemi qu'on a devant soi, (qu'il soit modelé) en cire, (dessiné) sur un papyrus vierge, ou (sculpté) en bois d'acacia ou en bois de *ḥmꜣ*, suivant toutes les prescriptions du rituel, les habitants du désert se révolteront contre l'Égypte, et il se produira la guerre et la rébellion dans le pays tout entier; on n'obéira plus au roi dans son palais, et le pays sera privé de défenseurs." See also above, p. 170 and n. 790.

967. Papyrus Salt 825; for discussion and bibliography, see above, pp. 6–7, 163, and 175–76.

968. Spells are recited "while repelling the attack of the four enemies whose names are written on their chests with fresh ink and who are placed on the brazier." See Alliot 1946, pp. 57–118 (= Chassinat 1931, p. 235; idem 1960, pls. 145 and 150; idem 1934, pls. 585–86; and Sauneron 1975, pp. 163–66, no. 531). The fundamental unity of this rite with the "breaking of the red pots" and other execration rites is discussed in Alliot 1946, pp. 106ff. Compare also the ritual protection of the bark of Osiris, in which a wax figure of Seth is similarly caught in a net, above, n. 964. Reference to the text appears in the Edfu book list, see H. Brugsch 1871, p. 44 (book of "*Rotḥ*?"), and above, n. 903. A further reference to the rite may appear in the mention of *ḫnr ḫft.w*, "restraining enemies," in Faulkner 1951, pp. 48 (ll. 6–7), 49, and 50 (n. k): "swift of hand in restraining enemies in the District of Offerings." Both *ḫnr* and *rtḥ* mean literally "to restrain," and both may be written with the same ideogram (⟵—, *Wb* 2: 460 and 3: 296). Within a liturgical context, the passage suggests an enactment like that of Ikhernofret (n. 961, above). See also the scriptorium rite of Pap. Salt 825, above, pp. 175–76.

969. The complete ritual (termed *ḥwi rm.w*, "striking fish") is given at Esna. At each of the four directional gates of the temple, priests smite a fish which has a name of a demonic enemy of the king and cosmos (Apep, "Evil of Character," Baba) written with fresh ink on a new papyrus sheet affixed to its mouth with wax. The fish, now become these enemies, are thrown into a fire of fenugreek and bryony as the "Book of Overthrowing Apep" is read. The charred remains are cast into a canal by the priests of Sakhmet. See Sauneron 1962b, pp. 24–25, n. b and 1968, pp. 15–16, no. 199. The relation of this rite to that of *rtḥ pꜥt* is noted in idem 1975, p. 164, n. c. For the rite at Edfu, see the following note. The notations of the festival calendar at Kom Ombo record that the rite was performed there for five days: "Epiphi 19: Causing this god to appear in his beautiful festival called 'trampling fish'; reaching the upper court; trampling fish by this god; performing his rites; doing likewise until day 23, making 5 days; resting in his sanctuary." For the text and translation, see de Morgan 1909, p. 52 (no. 596), ll. 14–15; idem 1895, p. 314 (no. 424), l. 9 (dated incorrectly to Epiphi 10); and Alliot 1954, p. 527, n. 2. An allusion to the rite appears on a sketch for a Ptolemaic door inscription from the Faiyum, in which Sobek is said to have created the waterways(?) and the Mediterranean "in order to catch confederacies of enemies as fish"; see Winter 1967, pp. 68–72. A reminiscence of this ritual in the works of Apuleius and Plutarch is discussed in Derchain and Hubaux 1958 and Griffiths 1970, pp. 64, 126–27, and 279 (Plutarch, *De Iside et Osiride*, 7.353 D).

and crocodiles in the fourteen-day Festival of Beḥdet at Edfu,[970] where their symbolic interpretation is clearly stated:

> To know the interpretation of the trampling of the fish. They are the enemies who are in the water. As for these balls, they are the corpses of Napata. As for these *gby.w*-geese who are in these nets, they are the souls of the dead. As for these fans of dom-palm, they are their hair.[971]

The affiliation of this complex ceremony to the earlier "breaking of the red pots" is underscored by the processional route of the festival, for though the execration itself now takes place at the House of Life (as in Papyrus Salt 825), the procession first visited the burial-ground of Edfu—recalling the necropolis setting of the ancient ritual.[972] A simplified version of this ceremony appears in Papyrus BM 10081, in which one slays birds and fish, while burning on a fire of bryony a wax image of Seth placed in a fish skin.[973] The existence of yet further variants stressing burial rather than burning is attested by the unearthing of small limestone plaques, carved with bound images of Seth associated with prisoners, inverted crocodiles, pierced serpents and turtles (see figs. 19a and 19b).[974]

In one fashion or another, such rites were performed daily in temples throughout Egypt, so that—in the words of Posener—"l'envoûtement fut, de tout temps, une véritable institution."[975] The crucial importance of this "magical" act for Egyptian "religion" can be seen not only from the numerous manifestations of the rite, but by its transmission from

970. See Alliot 1954, pp. 520–27, 529–30, and 533 and Fairman 1954, pp. 197–98 (= Chassinat 1928, pp. 132/3–134/9).

971. The rites are performed by the prophets, god's fathers, and scribes of the divine books. See Alliot 1954, pp. 521, 525, and 527. The balls, *bnn.w* (translated "evils" on p. 525), should be identified with the four balls used in the rite discussed in Goyon 1975; idem 1979, pp. 61–65 and pl. 25; and Ziegler 1979. The reference to the "hair" of the enemy is interesting, as locks of hair have been found in these balls, see Crompton 1916, p. 128 and pl. 16. For the possible presence of such balls at Mirgissa, see above, p. 161. Alliot 1954, pp. 525 and 527, failed to recognize either the term for geese (*Wb* 5: 164/5) or nets (*Wb* 5: 555/2 and 4). The political significance of this cursing of Meroitic Napata is discussed in Vernus 1978. For the symbolism of fish and geese as enemies, see above, pp. 160–61. The ritual burning of fans painted with enemy figures is attested in the Eighteenth Dynasty (Hatshepsut, Chapelle Rouge); see Grimm 1988, especially p. 212 (though the Edfu parallel is not noted). The New Kingdom ritual is performed by a god's father and god's wife, in the company of other priests.

972. See Fairman 1954, pp. 197–98.

973. Schott 1956. The papyrus includes as well a "royal" rite, see idem 1930c, in which one buries (*ṯms*) a wax or clay figure of a royal enemy under an execution site together with a papyrus sheet inscribed in fresh ink with the enemy's name and that of his father and mother (p. 41).

974. Michaïlides 1968, p. 82, fig. 9 (see above, n. 743) and Daressy 1912. With these plaques, compare the figures in Derchain 1965, pp. 22*–23*.

975. Posener 1958, p. 270.

temple to private concerns, particularly clear in the evolution of the "Apophis ritual." Best known from the late variants in the "Apophis Book" of Papyrus Bremner-Rhind, the ritual is nonetheless of much earlier date (Middle Kingdom?).[976] It rapidly acquires the character of a cultural institution, with participation in the rite extended to "private individuals" for both funerary and daily life concerns by the New Kingdom,[977] before becoming an all-purpose apotropaic temple ritual in the Late Period.[978] The dissemination

976. The recognition of variant Apep rites is evident from Pap. Bremner-Rhind itself, which includes several. Such recognition is also implicit in the section designations "a book" rather than "the book" for repelling Apep; see Lorton 1977. For the suggested Middle Kingdom origin, see Posener 1975b, p. 406. CT spell 414 (de Buck 1954, pp. 244–48) constitutes a spell for "Driving Apep from the bark of Re," and may attest to the existence of a form of the rite at this period.

977. Contra Lexa 1925, vol. 1, p. 126, who views the temple rite as a secondary development from "popular charms of the Middle Kingdom"—specifically CT spell 37 (see p. 105), whose "priestly" rather than "popular" nature is noted above, p. 205. For private funerary use of the rite, see BD spell 7, addressing Apep as a wax execration figure: "O one of wax ..."; in Allen 1974, p. 9. An illustration of this performance is found in Shorter 1937. Textual parallels to the "Apophis Book" in Pap. Bremner-Rhind appear in later funerary texts, cf. the inscriptions of Sheshonk, the majordomo of the divine votaress Ankhnesneferibre, in Roccati 1973, pp. 26–27. Private performance of the ritual in the course of worship is evidenced by the "Book of Gates." Addressed by Re as "those who adore (me) and repulse Apophis from me," a group of individuals in the underworld are labeled "Those who worshipped Re upon earth, who enchanted Apophis, who made offerings and who censed the gods"; see Piankoff and Rambova 1954, p. 144 (first division, upper register) and compare also Hornung 1980, pp. 92–96. Similar performance is attested at Deir el-Medineh in Pap. Chester Beatty 8, vo. 7/4, a spell "privately" owned by workmen in the village: "I have fought for you against your Apophis," in Gardiner 1935, vol. 1, p. 74 and vol. 2, pl. 46. The intersection of royal and private conjurations of Apep in the Ramesside period is represented by a spell against snakes which parallels the Bremner-Rhind papyrus and which is found on a healing statue erected for *public benefit* by Ramses III; see Drioton 1939, pp. 78–82; idem 1957, pp. 63–65; and Altenmüller 1979. An unpublished Ramesside ostracon in the Oriental Institute Museum (O. OIM 19120) may represent a private copy of a similar spell: "said over an image of Apep made in [wax?], put on fire, ground fine ..." For later enactments of the rite, see Abdallah 1984, pp. 69–70 (ll. 5–6): "I [enchante]d the confederates of the evil snake, overthrowing the disaffected, the abomination of the *Nšm.t*-bark, he being given over to the flame, the knife fixed in his head." From the same dynasty, a curse against potential violators of a decree for the divinized Amenhotep, son of Hapu associates these "enemies" with those slain in the ritual destruction of Apep: "May he (*scil.* Amon) put them on the brazier of the king on the day of his anger, let his uraeus vomit fire atop their heads to destroy their flesh; may it eat their bodies so that they become like Apep on the morning of the opening of the year (*wp-rnp.t*) ... They are for the knife on the day of destruction; Let them be termed *Nkỉw*" ("The Vanquished One," a name of Apep); see Varille 1968, pp. 71 and 73–74 (ll. 8–11). A reference to the popular performance of the rite perhaps underlies the gnomic remark in the "Instruction of Amenemope" (col. 10/20): "One spits upon Apep"; see Lichtheim 1976, p. 153.

978. See Chassinat 1930, p. 79; Sauneron 1962b, p. 25; de Morgan 1909, p. 52 (no. 596), ll. 11–12; and Drioton 1926, pp. 46–47: "One recites the 'Book of Overthrowing Apep' on this day." The rite may also have been used in the funerary ceremony of the Apis bull; see the ritual *sḥrỉ*, "Repelling" (of Apep or Seth?) in Spiegelberg 1920a, p. 21.

a b

Figure 19. (*a*) Plaque with Seth and Prisoner Bound to Stake (after Michaïlides 1968, p. 82, fig. 9) and (*b*) Detail of Plaque with Kneeling, Bound Seth (after Daressy 1912, p. 143, fig. 2).

of the rite is paralleled by the fate of the "Apophis Book" itself. Compiled for a temple, the papyrus ultimately became the private property of a priest.[979] In the Roman Period, the ritual yet survived as a spell against snakes; in a Greek papyrus, a palm branch is broken so that the serpent, identified with Apep, might split in half like its mutilated counterparts in the Pyramid Texts of the second and third millennia B.C.[980]

As the redactor, compiler, and custodian of this "institution," the priest played a pivotal role in its transmission as well. In the case of the "harim conspiracy" under Ramses III, such priestly involvement is easily documented and has long been recognized, for three of the conspirators were "scribes of the House of Life," a fourth was a "chief lector priest" or professional magician (see below, pp. 220ff), and a fifth was an overseer of priests of the goddess Sakhmet.[981] The last personage in particular appears to have played a significant

979. See above, n. 953.

980. Preisendanz 1931, p. 101 (PGM XII, ll. 260–64) and Betz 1986, p. 180. The magician recites seven times: "Stop, for you are Apophis ('Αφυφις)." This Greek rendering of *ꜥꜣpp* invalidates Gardiner's claim (1935, vol. 1, p. 30, n. 4) that the only authentic translation for the name of the serpent is "Apopis" ('Απoπις).

981. The Turin Judicial Pap., col. 5/5: "The great criminal Messui, who was a scribe of the House of Life, the great criminal Prekamenef, who was a magician (*ḥry-tp*), the great criminal Iyroy, who was overseer of the priests of Sakhmet ... the great criminal Shadmesdjer, who was a scribe of the House of Life." For the text and discussion, see Kitchen 1983a, p. 358; de Buck 1937, pp. 156 and 163, n. u; Posener 1976a, p. 437; and Gardiner 1938, p. 161, no. 13. A further scribe of the House of Life (*Nmtt*/*Msḏr* ?) appears as a conspirator in the newly published Pap. Rifaud E/1–2; see Koenig 1989, pp. 53 and 55–56, n. e. Perhaps this *Msḏr* (?) should be identified with the Shadmesdjer of the Turin Judicial Papyrus.

role in the conspiracy. Possibly mentioned no less than five times in the indictments recorded in Papyrus Rifaud,[982] Iyroy is also known from the funeral monuments of his family at Khatâʿna-Qantîr, where his name was sporadically erased in *damnatio memoriae* for his role in the conspiracy.[983] Styled both "chief lector priest"[984] and "overseer of priests of Sakhmet," Iyroy held authority in the House of Life affiliated with the Bubastite temple of Sakhmet, the goddess of both healing and destruction. In such a capacity he would have had easy access to hostile spells,[985] and it is notable that amid the indictments of an "overseer of priests of Sakhmet" in Papyrus Rifaud there is a possible mention of a "sacred book of the House of Life."[986] If correctly read, it is tempting to associate this book with the royal "roll for giving terror and respect" of Papyrus Lee, column 1, which was improperly given to the conspirator *Pn-ḥwy-bỉn*.[987] In both instances, consultation of the book led to an audience with a deity.[988] In Papyrus Lee, this consultation, styled *pḥ-nṯr*, was clearly

982. The context in Pap. Rifaud is necessarily unclear, owing to the preservation of this text only in a hand copy dating from 1834–36. For the complete text, see Sauneron and Yoyotte 1952 and Kitchen 1983a, pp. 363–66. The possible mentions of Iyroy are in Pap. Rifaud A/4 (= Kitchen 1983a, p. 364/7), A/6 (= Kitchen 1983a, p. 364/12), B/4 (= Kitchen 1983a, p. 365/13), B/5 (= Kitchen 1983a, p. 365/14), and C/6–7 (= Kitchen 1983a, p. 366/13–14). A newly-discovered hand copy of a further portion of this lost collection (Pap. Rifaud E) has now been edited by Koenig (1989), who identifies Iyroy's(?) co-conspirator in A/6 and B/4 with the scribe of the House of Life *Nmtt/Msḏr* (?) of E/1 (pp. 54–55).

983. Habachi and Ghalioungui 1971, pp. 61–67, updating Habachi 1954, pp. 493–97.

984. For the significance of Iyroy as *ḥry-tp*, see Quaegebeur 1985, p. 168.

985. For the destructive aspects of the goddess Sakhmet and the role of her priests in channeling her anger, see Hoenes 1976, pp. 35–42 (role of priests) and 42–66 (fury of goddess) and Germond 1981, pp. 286–304 (fury of goddess) and 304–09 (role of priests). The role of this priest in the performance of the *dgdg rm.w* execration rite is mentioned above, n. 969. See also Koenig 1989, pp. 55–56.

986. Papyrus Rifaud C/4 (Kitchen 1983a, p. 366/9): *mḏꜣ.t-nṯr* (?) *pr-ʿnḫ*.

987. Note also the charge in Pap. Rifaud: *ỉw=f ḫpr ḥr pnʿ nꜣ mk.w*, "He began to overthrow the protections(?)" (A/5 and A/6 = Kitchen 1983a, p. 364/9–10, 14). If properly identified, the term *mk.(t)*, "protection" may be significant, as it is especially used to indicate "magical protection"; see *Wb* 2: 160/22. Less likely, the term could be the *mk.w* "rewards" discussed in Janssen 1975, pp. 489ff. (to be connected with the "numerous benefactions" of the king mentioned in A/2 and 3). For *pnʿ*, "to overthrow" used in regard to words and texts, see Théodoridès 1967; and for its use in "overthrowing magic" (*pnʿ ḥkꜣ.w*), see Derchain 1965, pp. 139, 7*, and pls. 5–6 (cols. 5/10–6/1).

988. Compare Pap. Rifaud C/3–4 (Kitchen 1983a, p. 366/7–11): "[...] Pre to the place whose name is unknown, which was built by king *Wsr-mꜣʿ.t-Rʿ-mry-ꜣImn* the great god, the father(?) of king(?) [...] sacred book(?) of the House of Life [...] and he (the conspirator) entered (or "went") before him (the god). The god [...] his father [...] and he began to [...]." Further correspondence of the two papyri may exist if "the place whose name is unknown" can be equated with the "other great deep place" penetrated by conspirators in Pap. Lee. Cf. also B/3 and C/5 ("He gave to him some like them") with Pap. Rollin, ll. 1–2 ("He began to make some gods of wax and some potions ... given into the hand of *Pꜣ-bꜣkỉ-kꜣmn*").

enacted for nefarious ends, and the whole oracular process affords an unparalleled view of the links between "priestly" and "private" rite, "religion" and "magic."

THE *pḥ-nṯr*

Because of its appearance within a context of hostile spells and manipulated figurines, the term *pḥ-nṯr* () has been considered a technical expression of sorcery, being rendered by Breasted: "to employ the magical powers of a god."[989] Recent study, however, has shown that the *pḥ-nṯr* is by no means restricted to clandestine or hostile ritual, but is instead the standard expression for an oracular consultation of a divine statue.[990] The literal meaning of *pḥ-nṯr*, "to reach god,"[991] should be compared with that of the cognate term *spr*, "to petition (a deity)," whose basic meaning is similarly "to approach."[992] This use of *pḥ*, with the nuance "to petition" appears already in the "Complaints of Khakheperresoneb" from the Middle Kingdom: *n gr.n ỉb pḥ*, "A petitioned heart does not keep silent."[993] The *pḥ-nṯr* is thus a direct confrontation and communication with the deity, an oracular divine audience.

Oracular consultations, first attested in the New Kingdom, become a normative feature of Egyptian life in the Ramesside period and later as officially sanctioned tribunals for obtaining justice, fully equivalent to "secular" courts of law.[994] Not merely legal, the *pḥ-nṯr* is the arbiter of legality. Thus, in the attendance lists of the necropolis records from year nine of Ramses IX, the worker Qenna is reported absent *r pḥ pꜣ nṯr*, "in order to petition the god,"[995] and under Pinudjem II, the granary chief Djehutymose recorded at Karnak

989. Breasted 1906, vol. 4, p. 221. Cf. Lexa 1925, vol. 2, p. 116: "faire usage de la force divine."

990. See Kruchten 1985; idem 1986, pp. 63–65 and 329–32; and J. H. Johnson 1977, pp. 90–91; correcting the readings $^{\emptyset}$*wḫe* or $^{\emptyset}$*wḥꜣ-nṯr*, proposed in Griffith and Thompson 1909, p. 22, no. 220; Erichsen 1954a, p. 99; and Bresciani 1987, pp. 318–20.

991. The transitive meaning of *pḥ* is clear from Pap. Turin 2072/142 vo. 6; see Kruchten 1985, p. 9. One must thus modify the suggested translation "god's arrival" in J. H. Johnson 1977, pp. 90–91.

992. *Wb* 4: 102–04. The two terms are used in parallel in the oracular text of Pinudjem II. For *spr m-bꜣḥ*, "to consult," see ll. 10, 11, 13, 15, etc., in Kruchten 1985, pp. 40–41. For a similar use of *spr* in an oracular consultation, see Černý 1962, p. 45.

993. Verso 6; for the text, see Gardiner 1969, pp. 108–09 and pl. 18. The nuance is not discussed by Gardiner. Compare also the translation in Lichtheim 1973, p. 148: "A heart addressed must not be silent."

994. See Černý 1962. Egyptian courts were never, of course, purely secular in the modern sense; compare the priestly judges of the Late Period distinguished by their amulet of the goddess of truth, Maat, discussed in Möller 1920.

995. Papyrus Turin 2072/142, vo. 6, in Allam 1973, vol. 1, pl. 129 (= Kitchen 1983b, p. 632/10–11) and see Kruchten 1985, pp. 12–13.

several judgments in his behalf decided by *sḫʿ in nṯr ʿ3 m pḥ-nṯr*, "appearance by this great god (*scil.* Amon) in a *pḥ-nṯr*."[996] The significance of the term for public oracles may still be echoed in the early Demotic Papyrus Rylands IX, where Amon is said to have "reached" (*pḥ*) certain defaced tablets before "nodding" assent.[997] "The Instructions of ʿOnchsheshonqy" provide a further Demotic instance of Ptolemaic date:

> You should ask three wise men about an individual matter if it is important enough for a *pḥ-nṯr* of the great god.[998]

Intrinsically "private"—eliciting answers, revelations, and aid for purely personal concerns—the oracular procedure was no less sacerdotal, being generally administered by priests within the context of public temple festivals. Priestly authorship is even specified for the solitary, secretive performances of the ritual in Demotic papyri of Roman date which utilize lamps, bowls, and incubation to produce divine audiences through visions and dreams.[999] The mention of a lamp (*ẖbs*) in connection with the consultation by the necropolis worker Qenna suggests the existence of similar, approved usage in Ramesside Egypt.[1000] If so, a formula for a *pḥ-nṯr* may have been contained in the royal "roll for giving terror and respect" whose theft preceded the consultation in Papyrus Lee.[1001]

Though incontrovertibly "legal" and "religious," such consultations were nonetheless of a "magical" nature as well. The affiliation of oracles to the power of *ḥk3* has already been noted, and as "Lord of oracles, Lord of revelations, who predicts what will happen," the

996. Line 14 of the inscription; for the text, see Kruchten 1985 and 1986, pp. 63–65 and 329–32.

997. Column 24/1–2; see Griffith 1972, vol. 2, pl. 41 and vol. 3, pp. 110 and 251. Here it would be the god and not the consultant who "arrives," strengthening the case for the translation "god's arrival." For the oracular use of *hn*, "to nod," see Černý 1962, pp. 44–45.

998. Column 8/6; for the recognition of the term *pḥ-nṯr*, see Thissen 1984, pp. 21 (passage translated differently) and 71.

999. See the Magical Pap. London and Leiden, col. 8/12, attributed to a priest of Cusae, in Griffith and Thompson 1904, p. 65 and Betz 1986, p. 209. Compare also cols. 1/1(?) and 18/7, attributed to a physician of Oxyrhynchus, in Griffith and Thompson 1904, pp. 21 and 119 and Betz 1986, pp. 195 and 225.

1000. See the remarks of Kruchten 1985, pp. 12–13. From its laconic mention in the attendance roster, this divine audience was assuredly legal—regardless of whether it was privately or publicly performed. Earlier instances of direct revelation by vision or incubation are known, see Helck 1969, pp. 9 and 13 (*wp-m3ʿ.t*); Wente 1975–76; Assmann 1978; Otto 1971; but compare Philips 1986. Direct shamanistic visions may have been a central feature of the earliest Egyptian religion, see Helck 1984.

1001. As priests were implicated in the harim conspiracy under Ramses III, the *pḥ-nṯr* of Pap. Lee could have been performed secretly in a temple with cult images rather than in a private context with incubation or lamps.

magical deity Heka is himself the patron of the process.[1002] Indeed, the "enigmatic" spelling of the god's name with the *pḥ*-sign () produces a rebus *pḥ-nṯr* which may not be entirely unintentional.[1003]

As the force of *ḥkꜣ* is morally neutral, so direct petitioning of the god may serve hostile purposes (as in Papyrus Lee) or produce unfavorable results. It is particularly fitting that such eventualities, termed *pḥ-n-nṯr bỉn*, "an evil petitioning of god," were combated by magical protection in the form of oracular amuletic decrees granted by the gods and dispensed by the temples. In one such decree, Thoth declares:

> I shall nullify every evil *pḥ-n-nṯr*, every evil upset(?), and every evil thing which has been done to NN the son of NN, the son of NN, my excellent servant; I shall make them recoil on those who did them, and I shall make them recoil on those who said 'do them.' I shall never allow them to have magical power (*ꜣḫw*) over him throughout his whole lifetime.[1004]

Here the oracular process of the *pḥ-nṯr* is clearly said to be capable of inflicting hostile magic (termed *ꜣḫw*[1005]) which could be countered by correspondingly magical means. Mention of civil redress is conspicuously absent, for, as has been noted, the petitioning of deities for personal ends was inherently legal, with both hostile and beneficent oracles deriving from the *same sanctioned temple rite*—and potentially the same gods.[1006] The perceived willingness of the consulted deity to provide either is consistent with a fundamental Egyptian belief in divine ambivalence, susceptible to threat and constrained

1002. Sauneron 1982, pp. 31–32. For the association of magic and oracles, see above, pp. 7, 36–38, and 202. A textual misreading led Naville to qualify Amon, Mut, and Khonsu: *m nb nfr n pḥ-nṯr*, "le maître (la maîtresse) bienfaisant(e)" of the *pḥ-nṯr* (misinterpreted as "la barque Neterpeh") in the oracular text of Djehutymose at Karnak; see Naville 1883, p. 4. The reading is actually *m ḥb=f* (var. *=s*) *nfr n pḥ-nṯr*, "in his/her beautiful festival of the divine audience"; see Kruchten 1986, pp. 116–17.

1003. See above, n. 112. The writing with the *pḥ*-sign and the oracular *pḥ-nṯr* both arise in the New Kingdom, and were it not for the occasional honorific transposition of the *nṯr*-hieroglyph before *pḥ*, the writing would be perfectly acceptable as a spelling of *ḥkꜣ*, "to enchant."

1004. Papyrus BM 10587, ll. 90–98 (Twenty-second or Twenty-third Dynasty); see Edwards 1960, vol. 1, p. 39, n. 61, where the term *pḥ-n-nṯr* is translated "divine visitation(?)" and vol. 2, pl. 13. Written oracles were worn in cylindrical cases as phylacteries; see Edwards 1960, vol. 1, pp. xviii–xix; adding examples in Ray 1972; Ogden 1973; idem 1974; and compare (?) Wenig 1978, p. 194, no. 114 and Galerie Nefer 1987, p. 33, no. 50 (unrecognized top to such a case?).

1005. See above, pp. 30–35. For the hostile use of *ꜣḫw* by male and female magicians in these texts, see also Edwards 1960, vol. 1, p. 54, n. 47. It should be noted that these decrees specifically envision the manipulation of *ꜣḫw* by *human* practitioners, directly disproving the theory advanced by Borghouts 1987a.

1006. Compare the Ramesside petitioning of a series of statues of the same god (Amon) in hopes of a favorable verdict, discussed in Černý 1962, pp. 40–41.

by magic in both cult and private ritual.[1007] From this Egyptian view, it was not the conspirators who actually "deranged" the royal attendants of Ramses III, but the gods themselves, made subject to the power of *ḥkꜣ* encoded in the temple rite. At once private and priestly, the *pḥ-nṯr* epitomizes the Egyptian melding of the force of *ḥkꜣ* within the legally sanctioned practices of religion.

This situation is drastically altered with the conquest of Egypt by Rome, which had long viewed foreign religions with undisguised suspicion and hostility, often terming them "superstitious" or "magical" rather than "religious." The term "magic" is itself indicative of this xenophobia; derived from the Zoroastrian religion of the Magi, *magia* had come to signify fraudulent trickery or demonic sorcery.[1008] As such, it was pronounced illegal within the boundaries of Roman control for the duration of the empire, with edicts promulgated by Augustus, Tiberius, Claudius, Nero, Vitellius, Vespasian, Domitian, Marcus Aurelius, Constantine, Constantius, Valentinian, and Theodosius.[1009]

The Egyptian approach to foreign religions and "magic" could hardly have been more different. No Egyptian word for "superstition" exists, and foreign practices were respected or feared rather than derided.[1010] In fact, no term for "religion" exists either, the closest Egyptian approximation being *šms* (*nṯr*), "to serve (god)."[1011] In the course of such service, the Egyptian would have regularly performed legal acts which he would have termed *ḥkꜣ*. To Roman eyes, these acts of *ḥkꜣ* must have constituted *magia*. Before the defeat of Cleopatra, Egyptian practices in particular were often stigmatized as unfit for Roman citizens, and attempts to expel Egyptian cults from Rome were frequent and futile,

1007. This ambivalence is seen most readily in the personality of Sakhmet, for whose cult see above, n. 985. For the standard practice of threatening the gods, see above, n. 92.

1008. For references, see above, pp. 4 and 9. Although this conception was first developed in Greece, the Ptolemaic rulers of Egypt responded quite differently to native religion. No laws disparaged Egyptian practice, and it is particularly notable that immigrant Greeks not only adopted Egyptian worship, but are well represented among the clients of surviving Egyptian "magical" papyri as well; see Artemesia of PGM XL, in Preisendanz 1931, pp. 177–78 and Wilcken 1927, pp. 97–104.

1009. For an overview of this legislation, see Parássoglou 1976, pp. 262–63.

1010. For Egyptian fear of foreign magic, see above, nn. 321 and 623. The same fear is evidenced by the amuletic decree cited above, which not only protected against the *pḥ-n-nṯr bỉn*, but warded off equally Syrian, Egyptian, Bedouin, Libyan, and Nubian magic (Pap. BM 10587, ll. 71–75), in Edwards 1960, vol. 1, p. 38 and vol. 2, pl. 13. For such fears, see also Erman 1901, p. 14 (spell D, directed against Asiatic and Nubian women) and Koenig 1987b, on the role of Nubia in Egyptian magical texts.

1011. See *Wb* 4: 483–84. Morenz 1984, p. 22, suggested the comparable expression *ỉr ỉḫ.t*, "to perform ritual acts" (see below, n. 1063). A later approximation is found in *wšt*, "to greet" > ⲟⲩⲱϣⲧ, "to worship"; see Erichsen 1954a, p. 102; Crum 1939, p. 504a; Černý 1976, p. 221; Westendorf 1965–77, p. 283; and Vycichl 1983, p. 240b.

occurring in 59, 58, 53, and 48 B.C.[1012] Once Egypt was subject to Roman law, it was inevitable that Roman prejudice would clash with Egyptian practice. The most direct expression of this cultural conflict is found in a decree of Q. Aemilius Saturninus, prefect of Egypt under Septimius Severus in A.D. 199:

> [Since I have come across many people] who consider themselves to be beguiled by the means of divination [I quickly considered it necessary,] in order that no danger should ensue upon their foolishness, clearly herein to enjoin all people to abstain from this hazardous (or "misleading") superstition. Therefore, let no man through oracles, that is, by means of written documents supposedly granted in the presence of the deity, nor by means of the procession of cult images or suchlike charlatanry, pretend to have knowledge of the supernatural, or profess to know the obscurity of future events. Nor let any man put himself at the disposal of those who inquire about this nor answer in any way whatsoever. If any person is detected adhering to this profession, let him be sure that he will be handed over for capital punishment ...[1013]

Apparently promulgated only within Egypt, this prohibition of oracles encompassed the suppression of both the *pḥ-nṯr* and amuletic decrees which are at once dismissed as nonreligious "charlatanry"—despite their accepted role in later Egyptian religion! As in Rome itself, the prohibition was unsuccessful, for in 359 an Egyptian oracle (of Bes at Abydos) again troubled Roman authority, prompting Constantius to decree a general abolition of oracles throughout the empire.[1014] Coptic evidence shows that even this attempt was without success.[1015]

Nonetheless, official Roman condemnation of these activities did produce a significant change. What had constituted public religion was now driven underground, becoming exclusively private practice.[1016] Though of priestly origin, all Demotic examples of the *pḥ-nṯr* (as well as the related Greek σύστασις and αὐτόπτος) are for private use only, performed secretly in secluded quarters.[1017] *Only now* could the practice be termed

1012. See Cumont 1956, p. 81.

1013. Papyrus Yale inv. 299, translation adapted from: Rea 1977 and Horsley 1981, pp. 47–51. For the text, see also Parássoglou 1976 and Lewis 1977.

1014. Ammianus Marcellinus 1971, pp. 535–43 (xix.12, 3–16). See also Piankoff 1958–60.

1015. Černý 1962, pp. 47–48 (seventh to eighth centuries). One should also contrast the famous oracles of the Coptic monk John of Lycopolis, deemed "legal"—since Christian—by the Byzantine emperors, with the illegal oracles of other local "seers"; MacMullen 1984, pp. 77 and 152, n. 15.

1016. The need for secrecy led also to the development of a cipher in which to write magical manuals; see Griffith and Thompson 1904, pp. 8–9; idem 1909, pp. 105–12; and J. H. Johnson 1977, p. 93.

1017. Demotic examples appear in Pap. Louvre E 3229, cols. 6/6, 11, 26, and 7/13 and in the Demotic Magical Pap. of London and Leiden, cols. 4/3, 8/12, 27/29, and 28/32–33. For discussion and

"magic" in the Western sense (i.e., "illegal" and "private") and then *only from the Roman perspective*. Egyptian reaction to the Roman prohibition is epitomized in the second century Greek tale of Thessalos, a physician from Asia Minor who traveled to Egypt in search of secret botanical cures. [1018] Having befriended priests in Thebes, Thessalos asked them if anything remained of Egyptian magical power (τι τῆς μαγικῆς ἐνεργείας) to conduct an audience with the gods or the dead. Although most appeared scandalized (φερόντων) by the question, an old priest agreed to conduct the rite with the aid of a bowl filled with water. After preparations and fasting, Thessalos was led to a secluded room—perhaps within a temple[1019]—where in a vision he confronted Aesclepius/Imhotep who answered his questions. The techniques of this procedure (bowl,[1020] fasting, seclusion) accord perfectly with those in contemporary "private" Demotic (and Greek) papyri. Fear of Roman punishment for *magia* may have made the priests wary[1021] and the rite secretive, but the *pḥ-nṯr* experienced by Thessalos was still administered by an Egyptian *priest* as a

identification, see J. H. Johnson 1977, pp. 90–91; contra Erichsen 1954a, p. 99, which suggests ᴓ*wḫꜣ-ntr*, following the tentative reading *wḫe* proposed in Griffith and Thompson 1909, p. 22, no. 220. This discredited reading is still defended—without reference to unambiguous hieroglyphic equivalents—in Bresciani 1987, pp. 318–20. For the affiliated Greek examples, see Preisendanz 1931, pp. 14–30 and passim; Betz 1986, pp. 10–18 and passim; and Cunen 1960 (= PGM V, ll. 1–52). See also the Coptic "bowl-inquiry," ϣⲉⲛϩⲓⲛ, in Crum 1939, p. 685b. The practice continues in medieval Arabic and European tradition, see Lefébure 1902 and for (related?) African usage, see S. Davis 1955.

1018. Festugière 1939; Nock 1961, pp. 108–09; J. Z. Smith 1978, pp. 172–89; and Segal 1981, pp. 371–72.

1019. The term is οἰκός, which (like the word *ʿ.wy* found in corresponding Demotic rites) may signify either a sacred or profane room. For the Greek term, see Festugière 1939, pp. 61–62, n. 21 versus J. Z. Smith 1978, p. 180.

1020. For Demotic examples of bowl magic, see above, nn. 289 and 1017. The practice may be represented already in Middle Kingdom statuary that depicts individuals bending over a large vat or bowl—unless these figures are to be associated with brewing; see Capart 1944. Compare also the "Alexander Romance" of Pseudo-Callisthenes, in Wolohojian 1969, p. 23: "[Nectonebo] went to his palace alone, took a basin, and, isolating himself, worked this sorcery of the basin. He poured spring water into his basin, and with his hands created ships and men from wax, and set the men upon the ships and put them into the basin." The Egyptian element in this tale is striking; similar manipulations of model ships and wax men are recorded of the Egyptian magicians *Sỉ-Wsỉr* and *Ḥr sꜣ Pꜣ-wnš*, see above, n. 320.

1021. Traditionally, the priests' initial shock at the question of Thessalos has been interpreted in light of Roman prohibitions of magic, which entailed capital punishment for both performer and teacher. J. Z. Smith (1978, p. 179), however, has argued that it is rather an indication of their disbelief in the efficacy of magical power. This reinterpretation is unconvincing, given 1) the centrality of *ḥkꜣ* to Egyptian religion even in the latest periods (which would entail priests professing disbelief in the religion which they serve), 2) the severity of Roman punishment for magic, and 3) the fact that Thessalos was a stranger to the priests, and a foreign Greek stranger at that. The most likely interpretation would be that the priests were unwilling to risk capital punishment for imparting secret (and sacred) knowledge to a foreigner who could not be trusted, and who should be excluded from such knowledge in any case.

religious rite.[1022] Despite imperial sanctions, Egyptian and Roman conceptions of "magic" did not merge until the Coptic period when Christian hostility stigmatized all pagan practices—Roman as well as Egyptian—with the derogatory *magia*. Stripped of its ancient theological significance, Coptic ϩⲓⲕ was now reduced to the same strictured range of meaning.[1023]

THE IDENTITY OF THE MAGICIAN

The foregoing analysis of the *pḥ-nṯr* reveals the intersection of religion and magic not merely in practice, but in practitioner, for as the priest was the author and compiler of magical spells and rites, so he was also the performer and "magician." The role of the Egyptian priest as magician has long been recognized, especially for the 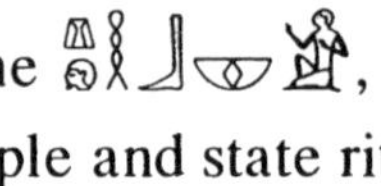, *ḫry-ḥb. (t)*, or "lector priest" who recited incantations and hymns during temple and state ritual, as well as during private apotropaic magic and funerary rites.[1024] The "chief lector priest," or *ḫry-ḥb ḫry-tp*, , was particularly associated with magical practices, and abridged to *ḫry-tp*, the title becomes the basic Late Egyptian and (as *ḫry-tb*, 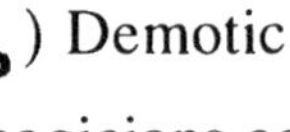) Demotic word for magician,[1025] transcribed in an Assyrian list of priests, doctors, and magicians as

1022. Contra J. Z. Smith's attempt (1978, pp. 180ff.) to describe the epiphany in the Thessalos tale as a reversal of the traditional priestly/temple context in favor of "temporary sacrality sanctified by a magician's power" (p. 182). The rite may well have taken place in a temple, and the magician responsible for the vision was definitely *not* Thessalos, but the traditional Egyptian priest trained in traditional temple practice. Compare also the temple-sponsored incubation vision of Aesclepius/Imhotep recorded in Pap. Oxyrhynchus XI.1381 (equally second century), translated in Grant 1953, pp. 124–27.

1023. I.e., fraudulent trickery or demonic sorcery. Whereas *ḥkꜣ* had been the duty and privilege of gods and priests, its Coptic descendant ϩⲓⲕ is never acknowledged by Christ or saints. Instead, the term is applied to pagans and heretics; see above, p. 14. A similar fate befell astrology, adopted in Egypt (from Mesopotamia; see Parker 1959) as a priestly science (under the care of the *ỉmy-wnw.t*), and subsequently proscribed by Roman and Christian law.

1024. The full writing of the title is *ḫry-ḥꜣb.t* and signifies literally "he who carries the festival scroll"; see Sethe 1934. For general discussion, see Otto 1975; Gardiner 1917; idem 1947, vol. 1, pp. 55*–58* (no. 129); and Sauneron 1966, pp. 33–34. For examples of the role of the lector priest in magic, see above, p. 203, n. 944; p. 207, n. 956; and p. 213, n. 984. On the basis of archaic features in the "Opening of the Mouth" ritual, Helck (1984) has suggested that the earliest Egyptian magician was the *s(t)m*-priest, who functioned by shamanistic dream trance and adopted the leopard skin dress for animal transformations in the spirit world. Only as ritual became codified through writing was the inspired shaman replaced by the literate lector priest, whose office was in turn subjected to bureaucratic reorganization and hierarchical ranking.

1025. The title is attested from the Old Kingdom, and may have acquired specific magical significance at this earlier period, compare the titles of magicians in Pap. Westcar, discussed in n. 1031, below. For

ḫarṭibi[1026] and translated as Akkadian *āšipu* (magician-priest) in the diplomatic correspondence between Ramses II and the Hittite court.[1027] Phonetically rendered as *ḥarṭumîm*, the term is adopted in Hebrew to designate the magicians of pharaoh (and of Babylon) in the tales of Joseph, Moses, and Daniel.[1028] In execration ritual, the chief lector priest is accompanied by the *ꜥḥꜣw-ꜥ*, , or "fighter" priest,[1029] and—presumably—it is to these functionaries that are addressed the ritual instructions in the second person found in papyri and on temple walls.[1030]

In literature from the Old Kingdom through the Greco-Roman periods, the priestly qualifications of the magician protagonist are almost invariably specified, being indicated

---

Late Egyptian (Harris Magical Pap.), see Gardiner 1938, pp. 164–65 (no. 24). Recent attempts to reorder the transliteration as *ḥry-tp ḥry-ḥb.t* are unconvincing; compare Ward 1982, p. 126. A general discussion of the Demotic writing and attestations is found in Spiegelberg 1925, pp. 4–7; supplanting idem 1917b, p. 31, n. 1. See also Erichsen 1954a, pp. 321–22. The relation of *ḥry-tp* to *ḥry-ḥb* is questioned by Spiegelberg 1925, pp. 6–7, but see Quaegebeur 1985, pp. 163–65. The full form *ḥr-ḥb.w ḥr-ỉtm*, "chief lector priests" () is found in Demotic in reference to embalmer priests associated with the royal burial in Pap. Krall, 8(= G)/13–14: "their chief lector priests who go into the embalming house," in Spiegelberg 1910, pp. 48–49, misread *ḥr-ḥb syn*(?) "lector priests and doctors(?)"; Stricker 1954, p. 52, translated "sacred scribes (and) xxx"; and Bresciani 1964, pp. 42–43, translated "embalmers and magicians." See the discussion in Quaegebeur 1985, pp. 166–67, though Quaegebeur's uncertainty regarding the reading *tm* is unwarranted. For the role of the *ḥr-ḥb* as embalmer, see the bibliography in n. 1024, above, and Glanville 1939, pp. xxii (n.1) and 15–17.

1026. See Gardiner 1938, p. 165 (no. 24) and Edel 1976, p. 56.

1027. Edel, ibid., pp. 53–63 (discussion) and 68–69 (text and translation). For an example of an Egyptian chief lector priest sent as emissary to foreign lands, see Habachi 1954, p. 498 (*Ṯnry*). For the functions of the *āšipu*, see *CAD*, vol. 1/2, pp. 431–35 and Ritter 1965.

1028. Quaegebeur 1985, pp. 162–72 and 364–65.

1029. *Wb* 1: 216/7 (and cf. 216/8–9 *ꜥḥꜣ wr* var. *wr ꜥḥꜣ*, "great fighter priest"). For examples, see Pap. Bremner-Rhind, col. 22/22 (the ritual executioner who cuts up the model of Apep), in Faulkner 1933, p. 45 and 1937b, p. 168; Daressy 1919b, p. 184 (l. 5: *ꜥḥꜣ-ꜥ* of *Ṯm*, the lion of Horus). Compare also Pap. MMA 35.9.21, cols. 17/6, 18/10, 31/5, and 38/15 for the title *ḥm ꜥḥꜣ sw*, , "the priest who fights him (*scil.* Apep or Seth)"; titles unpublished, text copies courtesy of Klaus Baer. A possible reference to this title is found in Pap. Chester Beatty 8, vo. 7/4: "I have fought (*ꜥḥꜣ*) for you against your Apophis," in Gardiner 1935, vol. 1, p. 74 and vol. 2, pl. 46.

1030. The duties of the "fighter-priest" in the Apophis rite are apparently those specified in the rubrics: "Make for *yourself* (*ỉs ỉr n=k* not understood by Faulkner 1937b, pp. 177 and 179; cf. cols. 24/19, 24/22, 26/3, etc., the pupil *0* for *ỉr*) every enemy of Re and every enemy of pharaoh either dead or alive and every accused one in his heart." With these ritual instructions in the second person in papyri one should compare the Edfu inscriptions published in Alliot 1954, pp. 521 and 524 (= Chassinat 1930, pp. 132–34): "Engrave (a red wax hippo) with the names of the enemies in *your* heart, then *you* bring [...] 2 crocodiles ..."; "Do everything *you* know against them in the presence of this god."

as either "chief lector priest" or "scribe of the House of Life." [1031] The close affiliation of these terms is reflected in the fate of *ḥarṭumîm* in the Old Testament story of Joseph. Derived from the Egyptian "chief lector priest" (*ḥry-tp*), this title was translated into Greek as τοὺς ἐξητὰς, "the interpreters (of dreams)," only to be rendered by Coptic redactors as ⲤⲪⲢⲀⲚϢ, "scribe of the House of Life" (*sẖ n pr-ꜥnḫ*).[1032] From the latter designation derive also the simple references to magicians as "good scribes" (*sẖ nfr*) and magical acts as "deeds of a (good) scribe" (*wp.t n sẖ nfr*, *sp n sẖ*).[1033]

The direct priestly affiliation of magicians is highly significant, and strongly suggests that itinerant magicians did not exist in ancient Egypt.[1034] Even the most likely candidate, the *ḫrp Srkt* or "scorpion charmer," was undoubtedly schooled in the House of Life, and was not infrequently a trained physician (*swnw*).[1035] The best evidence for the profession of magician derives from the discovery of a Middle Kingdom magician's box beneath the

1031. Compare the Old Kingdom magicians of Pap. Westcar, *Wbꜣ-ỉnr* and *Ḏꜣḏꜣ-m-ꜥnḫ*, both chief lector priests; bibliography and translation in Lichtheim 1973, pp. 215–22. Although a third magician, *Ḏdỉ*, is only said to be a commoner (*nḏs*, col. 7/2), he nonetheless possesses books and perhaps students (*ẖrd.w*, col. 8/3–4) which strongly suggests priestly training and status—especially in the Old Kingdom when literacy was severely limited. The hero of the late hieratic Pap. Vandier, the magician *Mry-Rꜥ*, is both a scribe and chief lector priest (see Posener 1985, pp. 16–17). The late equivalence of the lector priest and sacred scribe (*sẖ mḏꜣ.t nṯr*, "scribe of the divine book") is discussed in Otto 1975, col. 941 and compare Alliot 1954, p. 518. For Demotic literature, see Spiegelberg 1917b, pp. 30–33 (*Ḥn-n=w* whose title *ḥry-tb* is misread *mḥ-tb*, p. 31, n. 1); idem 1910, pp. 37 and 70–71 (no. 497) a *ḥry-tb* priest involved with an oracle in Pap. Ricci 5, x+3; idem 1912, pp. 8, 14–15, and 25 (no. 3) for the *ḥry-tb Ḥy-Ḥr*; and Griffith 1985, pp. 182–83 (especially p. 182, n. to l. 3) and passim for the *ḥry-tb* (mistranslated "librarian?") *Ḥr* son of *Pꜣ-nḥse* in Setna II, cols. 5/3, 5, 10–11 (*ḥr-tb n Pr-ꜥꜣ*, "chief lector of Pharaoh," pp. 184–85), 18, and 6/4. "Scribes of the House of Life" appear in Setna II, col. 6/7–8, and the protagonist *Sỉ-Wsỉr* is trained in the House of Life (col. 1/11–13), in Griffith 1985, pp. 194–95 and 146–47. In the tale of Setna I, both Setna and *Nꜣ-nfr-kꜣ-Ptḥ* are royal children, trained to read writings of the House of Life (Griffith, ibid., pp. 90–91, 118–21, etc.), and Setna was additionally High Priest of Ptah in Memphis (see Griffith, ibid., pp. 1–12 and Gomaà 1973). An uncertain example of an untitled royal magician may appear in Spiegelberg 1932a.

1032. Genesis 41:8 and 24. This etymology of Bohairic ⲤⲪⲢⲀⲚϢ was first proposed by Gunn 1917. A variant suggestion by Černý 1964 (< *sbꜣ n pr-ꜥnḫ*, "teacher of the House of Life"), has since been rejected by its author; Černý 1976, p. 169 and compare Westendorf 1965–77, pp. 193 and 539. Conclusive Sahidic examples ⲤⲀϨⲠⲢⲀⲚϢ and ⲤⲀϨⲠⲢⲀⲈⲒϢ are noted by Lucchesi 1975.

1033. For the simple designation "scribe," see the magician *Mry-Rꜥ* in Posener 1985, pp. 16–17; for "good scribe," see Setna II, cols. 3/2, 6/36, 7/6 (*sẖ nfr rmt rḫ*, "good scribes and wise men"), in Griffith 1985, pp. 164–65 and 204–07. For *wp.t n sẖ nfr*, see Setna I, col. 4/23, in Griffith, ibid., pp. 114–15. For *sp n sẖ*, see above, p. 68 and n. 311.

1034. See the remarks of Gardiner 1917, p. 31 and Sauneron 1966, pp. 33–34. See also the comments on the limiting factor of literacy, discussed above, pp. 204–07.

1035. See Gardiner 1917; von Känel 1984, pp. 163–231 and 284–305; and idem 1985, p. 601.

storerooms at the Ramesseum.[1036] Found during the clearance of the bottom of a reused Twelfth Dynasty tomb shaft, the wooden box measured approximately eighteen by twelve by twelve inches and contained twenty-three fragmentary papyri, a bundle of reed pens, four broken ivory "apotropaic knives," and various beads, amulets, and figurines. Included among the last were four female dolls, a Beset[1037] statuette holding snakes, a bronze uraeus "entangled in a mass of hair," and an ivory herdsman carrying a calf. The exterior surface of the box was covered with a white plaster slip, and the figure of a jackal was sketched in black ink atop the lid.

Although the excavator did not recognize the significance of the find, a study of the contents of the papyri revealed the magical nature of the collection, for aside from two literary works, the texts are all ritual, magical, or "medico-magical" in substance.[1038] The associated objects are equally at home within the sphere of magical accouterments:

1036. In the northern corner of the Ramesseum precinct; for discussion, see Quibell 1898, p. 3 and pls. 2–3. Aside from the papyri, the general contents of the box have received no further serious study. Significant inaccuracies flaw the popular treatment in Brier 1980, pp. 46–50, though the brief summary by David (1991, pp. 37–39) notes important similarities between these finds and the discovery of a Beset figurine, clappers, and a Bes mask buried in a "magician's house" at Kahun.

1037. The excavator, unaware of the existence of a female Beset, identified the figure as a dancer wearing a male Bes mask. For Beset, see Bosse-Griffiths 1977. The Ramesseum apotropaic knives and Beset figure are noted on pp. 102–03, though Bosse-Griffiths follows Quibell in describing the image as a nude woman with a mask. The same attribution was given in Wild 1963, pp. 79 and 81. Both Wild and Bosse-Griffiths note the existence of a single Bes mask, but that does not require that the statuette represent a masked figure. Despite a recent attempt to overemphasize ritual masking, the statuette—probably used in healing rituals (Bosse-Griffiths 1977, p. 103)—should be interpreted as the goddess and *not* as a human impersonator; see below, n. 1041. A statue, like a masked priest(ess), is an image used as an intermediary or conduit for divine power. A masked statuette is unnecessarily redundant—an image of an image of a deity. Wolinski 1986 and 1987 provides no cogent proof for her ill-conceived assertion that all deities with "bizarre" or ill-fitting (to Western sensibilities) heads are masked priests. Were such "incongruities" always to be explained by ritual masking, then the Giza sphinx must represent a lion wearing a human mask, criosphinxes would be lions masked as rams, and Horus-Sobek would be a crocodile wearing the mask of a hawk! For these hybrids, see Merz 1978 and te Velde 1980, especially p. 79. This statuette and a comparable example from Kahun are still considered "masked" in David 1991, pp. 37–38.

1038. For the papyri, see Gardiner 1955b, pp. 1–2 (identification as magical) and 7–18 (analysis of contents) and Barns 1956. Selected texts are translated in Borghouts 1978, pp. 43–44 (§§69–70). Brier's statement (1980, p. 46) that the discovery of wax sons of Horus in the tomb shaft was "the first clue that this was a magician's tomb" is not credible. In the first place, these wax figures were explicitly recognized by the excavator as being of the "XXIInd dynasty style" (Quibell 1898, p. 3) and thus intrusive, with *no relation* to the earlier Middle Kingdom box. In the second place, such figures are standard burial equipment, and the use of wax in no way implies that they were intended for a magician (see Raven 1983, pp. 14–16).

amulets (and beads as amulets[1039]) for healing and security, apotropaic knives used to protect infants from demons,[1040] statues of protective deities (the uraeus and Beset), and human figurines. The presence of the goddess Beset conforms to the imagery on the ivory knives where she also appears, with her power over noxious animals indicated by the standard device of the "master of animals" pose, used elsewhere by Heka, Horus, and underworld deities.[1041] As a protective image, the uraeus is common,[1042] and the use of hair as a personal effect or "relic" to strengthen a charm has been noted above for

1039. See Feucht 1975 and compare CT spell 576 (de Buck 1956, p. 191), recited over a bead of carnelian or amethyst to enable a man to copulate in the underworld, in Faulkner 1977, p. 181.

1040. The standard work is Altenmüller 1965. See also idem 1975; idem 1986; and Wildung and Schoske 1984, pp. 26–27.

1041. For Beset on ivory knives, see Altenmüller 1986, pp. 19–20. By seizing beasts (snakes, scorpions, lions, lizards, gazelles, etc.), the central figure displays his or her domination of the animal and the hostile forces which it represents; compare CT spell 885 (de Buck 1961, p. 97): "The snake is in my hand and cannot bite me, and so forth" (Faulkner 1978, p. 49). For a parallel to the Ramesseum figure, see the instructions against snakes in the "Book of the Heavenly Cow," ll. 300–05: "Make a female image standing on your southern side; make a goddess upon her (or "it," i.e., "the side") in her (or "its") middle, (and) a serpent standing on its tail with her hand on its body" (Hornung 1982, pp. 28 and 47). The animals most commonly held are two snakes, which become two staves crossed upon the chest of Heka. For examples, see *inter alia* the images of Heka depicted in te Velde 1970, pls. 27–29 and compare CT spell 993 (de Buck 1961, p. 205): "To Become Him of the Two Wands" (Faulkner 1978, p. 101). Cippi of Horus show the same posture; for references see Kákosy 1980a. For underworld deities, see Piankoff and Rambova 1957, pls. 11 (two snakes held by Heka), 13 (lizard and snake), 18 (lizard), 22 (lizards), and 27 (two snakes) and Fazzini 1975, p. 113, fig. 95 (two Sons of Horus holding lizards and a snake; sculpture from the tomb of Montuemhat). The significance of the gesture is repeated on reliefs where the king grasps his hapless enemies by the hair (often collectively and thus clearly symbolically) before dispatching them as a sacrifice to the god; see above, pp. 115–16. The widespread Egyptian pose is paralleled by, and apparently derives from, the common "master of the animals" image in Mesopotamia; for which see Calmeyer 1972–75; Frankfort 1959, pp. 124–25; and Kantor 1974, pp. 247–48 (no. 210) and 251 (pl. 32).

1042. See the use of four uraei (two *nṯry* and two *wȝḏty*) to guard the cardinal points in temple rituals at Edfu on behalf of the king (Rochemonteix et al. 1984–87, p. 312/13–15) and in the ritual of the House of Life in Pap. Salt 825 on behalf of Osiris (Derchain 1965, pp. 84–86, 141–42, and 13*–14* [col. 12]). The fire-spitting serpents repel enemies and demons at night, and the corresponding vignette, fig. XIX on p. 24* (misidentified as fig. XX on p. 86), has the tag text: "The flame burns for him (*scil.* Osiris) in the dark." On the basis of these rituals, one may restore the text in O. Gardiner 363 (= HO 109,1) as a correspondingly "private" rite (for "NN born of NN," *mn ms n mn.t*) to dispel the assault of dead men and women in the form of nightmares: "Words to be said [over] 4 [ura]ei made of pure clay, with lamps in their mouths. One should be placed in the corner [of every room] in which there is a man or a woman [...] sleeping with a man"; ll. 8–12, in Černý and Gardiner 1957, p. 29 (described only as "A magical spell") and pl. 109,1. The text is now re-edited with commentary in Ritner 1990. With these rites, compare the rite of the four torches in BD spell 137A, in Allen 1974, pp. 113–15.

apotropaic ritual,[1043] and the usage continues in Demotic and Greek papyri (as ουσια).[1044] The appearance of human figures within a magical context now needs little further elaboration. One should note, however, that two of the female images, depicted without legs, correspond to the so-called "concubine" figures used to promote feminine fertility.[1045]

The magical significance of the ivory herdsman has yet to be clarified,[1046] but becomes evident when compared to an identical representation in a fording scene from the Old Kingdom tomb of Ti, in which a herdsman carries a calf into the water to induce the cattle to follow (see figs. 20a and 20b).[1047] Similar fording scenes are not uncommon in tomb relief,[1048] and are regularly accompanied by the recitation of a "water spell":

1043. In the rite of the four balls and the festival of Beḥdet at Edfu; see above, pp. 161 and 210, n. 971. The technique in "sympathetic magic" is called synecdochism, the use of a part of an object or person to represent the whole.

1044. Demotic examples appear in the London and Leiden Magical Pap., vo. 16/7 (woman's hair put in wick for love spell), vo. 17/6 (woman's hair on inscribed lamella placed in mummy's mouth), and vo. 29 (to drive a man mad, tie his hair to that of a dead man); see Griffith and Thompson 1904, pp. 189, 191, and 201. An earlier attestation of the practice is noted in Chabas 1860, p. 184; compare CT spell 892 (de Buck 1961, p. 102), in which hair is tied on the neck, in Faulkner 1978, p. 54. For Greek attestations, see PGM XIXa (found with auburn hair, folded to be placed in a mummy's mouth), in Preisendanz 1931, p. 141 (= Betz 1986, pp. 256–57); PGM LXXXIV (found with a trace of hair), in Kase 1936, pp. 73–74, no. 76 (= Betz 1986, pp. 300–01); and compare PGM IV, ll. 1949–52: "Give me the authority over this spirit of a murdered man, a part of whose body I possess," in Preisendanz 1928, pp. 132–33 (= Betz 1986, p. 72, σκηνους, "corpse" mistranslated "tent"). A general discussion is found in Preisendanz 1913 and for Christian parallels, see Aune 1980, pp. 1536–37.

1045. Quibell 1898, p. 3 and pl. 2, figs. 10–11. For further examples and references, see Wildung and Schoske 1984, p. 139.

1046. Were it not for the undisturbed context of the find, Quibell (1898, p. 3) would have considered the piece intrusive and of Roman date. For the figure, see Quibell, pl. 2.

1047. Wild 1953, pls. 81 and 114. In most such scenes, a spell accompanies this relief. Here, however, the herdsman's statement has generally been interpreted as a caustic remark between laborers: "Hey, shitty (*mḥsḥs pw*), keep the calf away from(?) the nursing cow"; see Erman 1919, pp. 28–29, followed by Kadish 1979, p. 211, n. 30 (as an instance of scatological humor). A reinterpretation of this passage appears in Ogdon 1989, pp. 61 and 69, n. 18, who translates the passage as a magical address to the crocodile, deformed by orthography and derided as excrement: "O crocodile (*mḥs* < *msḥ*), this excrement! (*ḥs pw*)." The remaining text of this line would then continue the address: "May you allow these cattle coming forth from the swamp to go." For the uncertain verb *ỉꜣʿ* in the next line (and sentence?), perhaps compare *ꜣʿʿ*, "to force" or similar in the "Decree of Horemheb," in Helck 1958b, p. 2150/2. This line may constitute a label: "Forcing (?) this nursing calf."

1048. Compare Wild 1953, pls. 79, 113 (goats induced by food and whips), and 124 (calf dragged on rope); Capart 1907, pls. 27–30 (tomb of Ankhmahor, calf dragged on rope); Duell 1938a, pls. 20–21 (calf dragged on rope); and idem 1938b, pls. 168–70 (cattle led by beating, goats by food and beating).

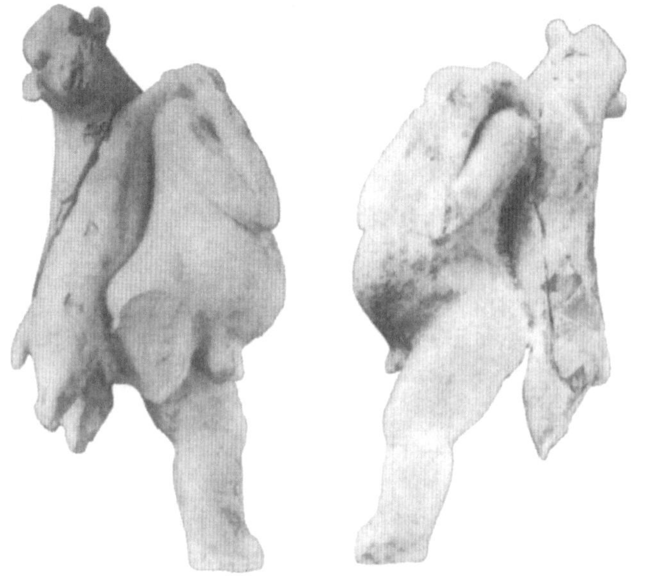

a

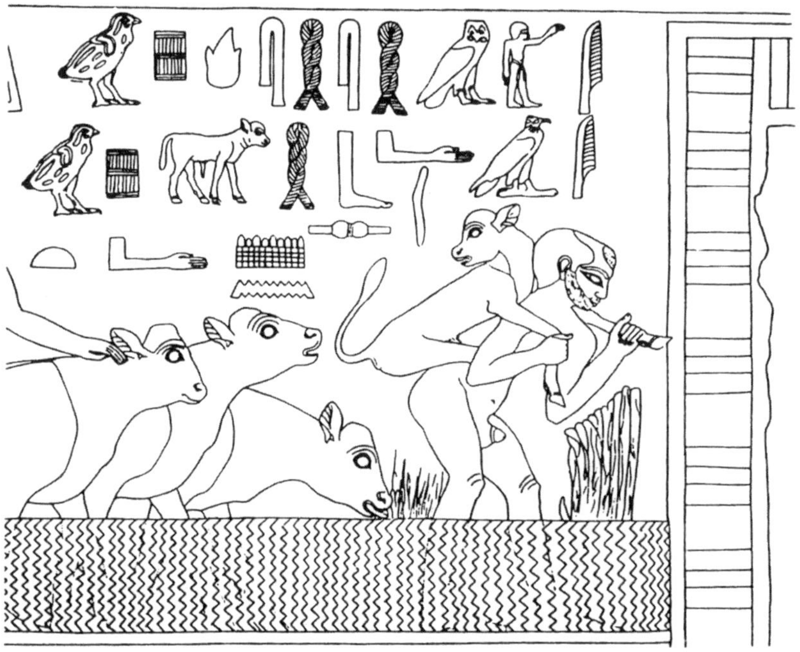

b

Figure 20. (*a*) Broken Ivory Statuette of Herdsman Carrying Calf (after Quibell 1898, pl. 2, fig. 2) and (*b*) Herdsman Carrying Calf (after Wild 1953, pl. 114).

> Crossing the canal by the cattle. Warding off death. Warding off the crocodile by the herdsman: 'Oh herdsman there! Let your face be watchful for this marsh-dweller who is in the water, to prevent these here (*scil.* the cattle) falling a victim to this marsh-dweller. May he come as a sightless one! Let your face be very watchful for him!'[1049]

The Ramesseum ivory herdsman was almost certainly associated with just such a fording rite, probably as a substitute figure over which the charm could be recited during the crossing. It has generally been considered that these spells were recited by the herdsmen themselves,[1050] but closer examination suggests that this was not necessarily the case. Representations of the scene from the tombs of both Ankhmahor and Mereruka do show the herdsmen extending their index finger in a protective gesture,[1051] but the recitation of the spell is left to a single individual at the left of the composition (see fig. 21).[1052] Unlike the boatmen who physically row, gesture, or tow the calf, the speaker sits calmly, a wand in one hand, the other raised to his lips in the traditional attitude of recitation.[1053] This division between recitation and ritual gesture accords with the charm—addressed to the herdsmen in the second person—and is paralleled by a fording spell in the Harris magical papyrus which stipulates that the charms must not be revealed to those outside the House of Life, though a "man of the ship" may execute the ritual act.[1054] In another fording scene from the tomb of Ti, as the herdsmen extend their fingers, they are watched by a lone, standing figure at the left who is dressed in an elaborate kilt and leans upon a staff beside the water (see fig. 22a).[1055] Urged by a herdsman to "(Put) your hand over the water" in the ritual gesture, the man replies instead: "Do not speak so much!"[1056] Distinguished from

1049. From the tomb of Ankhmahor; see Borghouts 1978, pp. 83, (no. 122; translation) and 124 (bibliography). For further examples and variants (Ti, Mereruka, etc.) and discussion, see the preceding note and above, pp. 48, n. 229 and 207, n. 956.

1050. So Erman 1919, pp. 29–31.

1051. For the magical gesture, see Erman, ibid., pp. 30–31; Ogdon 1985; and compare the gesture discussed in Wainwright 1961.

1052. See Capart 1907, pls. 27 and 30 and Duell 1938a, pl. 21. Fording scenes *without boats* apparently never show a special reciter (cf. Wild 1953, pl. 113 and Duell 1938b, pls. 168–70). This may indicate that the herdsmen recited the spell in such cases, or it may represent a compression of the scene. In any case, the presence of the spell above such scenes primarily serves the purpose of *funerary magic*, guaranteeing the safety of the tomb owner's underworld herds and flocks; it may not precisely reflect practices of earthly life.

1053. The figure reproduces the "man-with-hand-to-mouth" determinative for speech: 𓀁 (Gardiner 1973, p. 442 [Sign-list A 2]).

1054. Column 6/10 (§K, 1–4); see above, p. 203, n. 945.

1055. Wild 1953, pl. 124.

1056. See Erman 1919, p. 31.

the herdsmen by dress and demeanor, the lone figure need not be only an amused bystander with a clever retort;[1057] he may be the priest who recites the spell while the herdsmen silently perform the magical gesture. In the upper register of the same wall, an identically dressed figure does serve as "magician," extending the magical gesture at the birth of a calf (see fig. 22b).[1058]

Figure 21. Reciter at Rear of Boat in Fording Scene (after Duell 1938a, pl. 21).

1057. So Erman ibid., p. 31.

1058. Wild 1953, pl. 124. This figure does have a beard, which initially might seem disconcerting on a priest. However, since priestly service was not a full time occupation but performed in rotation (see below, n. 1078), the stringent rules for shaving, purification, dress, et cetera. need only apply during active temple duty. Community magicians were presumably *off-duty* priests, and thus exempt from such restrictions. This supposition is supported by the frequent necessity for specifications regarding ritual purity, clothing, and food taboos within the rubrics of individual spells. The non-exclusive nature of the occupation of lector priest in the Old Kingdom is evident from the inscriptions of Harkhuf (additionally a count, seal bearer, and expedition leader [Sethe 1933, p. 122/13]), and Ankhmahor (also a chief overseer of works [Sethe 1933, p. 202/2]). For the varying social ranks of such priests, see Otto 1975, p. 942. Perhaps comparable to the figure in the tomb of Ti, an "ordinary lector priest" (*ẖry-ḥb ꜥꜣ*) appears within a list of household staff from the Middle Kingdom (Griffith 1898, p. 41 and pl. 14, l. 52 [Pap. Kahun-Gurob 6, l. 52]).

a

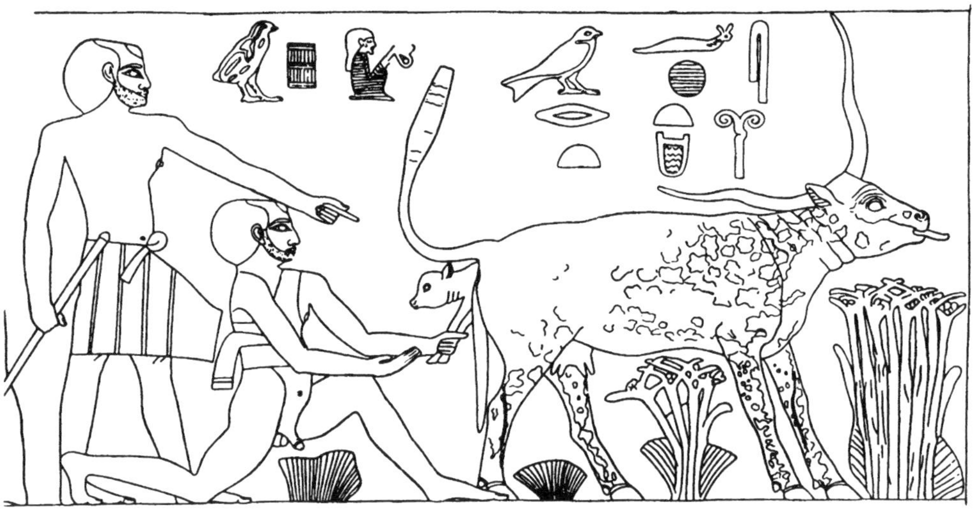

b

Figure 22. (*a*) Magician(?) Beside Fording Scene (after Wild 1953, pl. 124) and (*b*) Magician at Calving Scene (after Wild 1953, pl. 124).

In the Middle Kingdom "Story of the Herdsman," the reciters of these charms are specified as the "knowledgeable ones of the herdsmen."[1059] Though these have been considered merely "informed" ox-herds who had memorized spells of common knowledge,[1060] the phrase used, *rḫ-ḫ.t* (literally, "knower of things"), serves as a technical term for "professional magician" ("one knowing sacred things") from the

1059. Lines 12–13; see above, p. 207, n. 956.

1060. Compare Goedicke 1970, p. 252.

Middle Kingdom through the Greco-Roman periods,[1061] and should be contrasted with the less specific *rḫ*, "wise man" which need have no magical overtones.[1062] This use of *ḫ.t*, "thing" in the sense of "sacred/ritual things" should be compared with the expression *ỉrỉ ḫ.t*, "to perform a ritual offering" (literally, "to do something").[1063] Stressing the central importance of knowledge (of spells, gestures, words of power, etc.) in Egyptian magic, the title *rḫ-ḫ.t* readily betrays its priestly affiliation, since the source of such magical knowledge was the priesthood and the House of Life. Not surprisingly, individuals qualified by *rḫ-ḫ.t* are given priestly titles as well,[1064] and in Ptolemaic decrees the hieroglyphic *rḫ-ḫ.t* is regularly rendered in Demotic as *sḫ pr-ʿnḫ*, "scribe of the House of Life" and in Greek as ἱερογραμματέυς, "sacred scribe."[1065] Thus despite the "every-day" quality of herding magic, the performers of the rite should have been trained magicians and

1061. See *Wb* 2: 443/27–31: *rḫ-ỉḫ.t* and Erichsen 1954a, p. 253: *rḫ-ỉḫy*, "magic" (literally, "knowing things"); contra Goedicke (1970, p. 253), who takes it as a term indicating general knowledge "without entailing any formal education," ostensibly following Brunner (1966). Goedicke, however, misrepresents the analysis of Brunner, who considers that the term basically signifies "den Lebensklugen, der in allen Lagen einen Ausweg weiß; es steht auch für den Zauberer ..." (p. 32). As Brunner further notes, the acquisition of such knowledge requires training ("Der Vater des Merikare rät seinem Sohn zweimal, er solle sich die Tradition einverleiben, um als *rḫ-jḫt* seinen Räten und der schwierigen politischen Lage gewachsen zu sein," p. 32), and the examples gathered by Brunner consist primarily of the famous authors listed in Pap. Chester Beatty 4, who are specified as trained scribes (vo. 2/5) and lector priests (vo. 2/9) with control over magic (vo. 3/9), having "concealed their magic (*ḥkȝw*) from the entire world, (though) it is read in a book of writing." For the passage, see above, p. 38. Similarly, in the literary Pap. D'Orbiney, the term is used of the "scribes and sages" of the palace who are able to interpret a mysterious lock of divinely-created hair (Brunner 1966, p. 32).

1062. *Wb* 2: 445/17–18 and compare the corresponding Demotic *rmt rḫ*, "wise man" or *sḥm.t rmt rḫ.t*, "wise woman" (> ⲢⲘⲢⲀϢ; Crum 1939, p. 308a; Černý 1976, p. 142) in Erichsen 1954a, p. 252 and Thissen 1984, pp. 89–90. Since the term is of general application, it can appear within a magical context; see the description of the magician *Nȝ-nfr-kȝ-ptḥ*, in Setna I, col. 4/3: *sḫ nfr rmt rḫ m-šs pȝy*, "He is a good scribe and a very wise man," in Griffith 1985, pp. 106–07. Note also that a prophetic function has been suggested for the feminine term *rḫ.t*, "wise woman," seemingly used to identify a prophet or seer at Deir el-Medineh; see Letellier 1980; Borghouts 1982, pp. 24–27 (§8); and compare the title *rḫ.t* used of Isis and other goddesses in *Wb* 2: 446/3–5 and Erichsen 1954a, p. 252.

1063. *Wb* 1: 124/9 and compare the fuller form on p. 125/2–3 (*ỉr ỉḫ.t nṯr*).

1064. In Pap. Chester Beatty 4, vo. 2/5–3/11, eight famous authors are described as both *rḫ-ḫ.t* (vo. 2/5 and 3/7) and "lector priests" (vo. 2/9) with control over *ḥkȝ* (vo. 3/9); see above, n. 1061. In the Bentresh stela, the exorcist *Ḏḥwty-m-ḥb* is styled *rḫ-ḫ.t* and is said to be a scribe from the "staff of the House of Life" (*ṯ.t n.t pr-ʿnḫ*); see de Buck 1970, p. 107/8 and 12 (ll. 9 and 11); Edel 1976, pp. 59–63; and Gardiner 1938, pp. 166–67 (no. 32) and 170–79 (for *ṯ.t n.t pr-ʿnḫ*). See also the Demotic Pap. Tebtunis Tait 22, l. 2: *Pȝ-šr-n-gb pȝ ḥm-ntr pȝ rḫ-ỉḫy*, "NN, the prophet and sage," in Tait 1977, pp. 72–73.

1065. See Gardiner 1938, p. 170 and Daumas 1952, pp. 183–85.

not "educated" herdsmen.[1066] This supposition is confirmed not only by the presence of a pertinent figurine in a professional magician's box, but by the heading of the collection of fording spells in the Harris Magical Papyrus, which specifically identifies them as the property of the House of Life and the chief lector priest.[1067]

From the contents of the Ramesseum box, there can be little doubt that its owner could have been qualified by the title *rḫ-ḫ.t*, or by the less praiseworthy *ḥkꜣy*, "magician,"[1068] with professional competence in matters of general medicine, feminine fertility, protection from serpents and demons, childhood ills (perhaps as *ḥkꜣy n kꜣp*, "magician of the nursery"[1069]), and agricultural magic. Scribal training is equally clear from the presence of papyri which would have to be consulted and of pens with which to write amuletic charms. The appearance of state and funerary rituals[1070] among the papyri emphasizes his priestly affiliation, while the literary texts have given rise to the suggestion that he "combined with the sterner purposes of his profession the function of a local story-teller and entertainer."[1071] It is the decoration of the box itself which provides the clearest indication of the professional identity of the Ramesseum magician, for the painted jackal atop the lid reproduces the hieroglyphic title , *ḥry-sštꜣ*, "He who is over the secrets."[1072] Perhaps originally an epithet of Anubis guarding the Canopic chest of Osiris,[1073] the title is applied

1066. The plural genitive (*nw*) in the phrase "knowledgeable ones of the herdsmen" need not imply that the "knowledgeable ones" were actually *members* "of" the herdsmen any more than the phrase "servants of the masters" would imply that the servants were themselves masters.

1067. Column 6/10 (§K, 1–4); see above, p. 203, nn. 944–45.

1068. As the basic term for "magician," *ḥkꜣy* can have both positive and negative connotations. The term, together with its feminine *ḥkꜣy.t*, appears in clearly negative contexts in the "Book of the Heavenly Cow" to describe threatening Egyptian magicians (see above, pp. 22 and 202–03), in a letter of Amenhotep II to his viceroy in Nubia to indicate hostile foreign magicians (see above, n. 623), and in the amuletic decrees to describe both Egyptian and foreign magicians who might bewitch the possessor of the charm (see above, n. 1010).

1069. For the title, see Gardiner 1917, p. 32.

1070. See Sethe 1928a (Pap. Ramesseum B) and Gardiner 1955b, pp. 9–17 (Pap. Ramesseum E).

1071. Gardiner 1955b, p. 1. As Gardiner further notes (p. 1), the combination of magical and literary papyri directly parallels the Chester Beatty library from Ramesside Deir el-Medineh. As at Deir el-Medineh, the literary papyri may have served for scribal teaching or personal pleasure/edification.

1072. *Wb* 4: 298–99. The significance of this feature was lost on Brier (1980, p. 48): "The fact that the box in the magician's tomb had a jackal on it is curious. Anubis, the jackal-headed god, was the god of embalming and had no particular association with magic. A more likely candidate to be painted on a magician's box would be Isis, the goddess of magic."

1073. See Heerma van Voss 1969 and 1971.

to officials with privileged access to cultic mysteries.[1074] By the Middle Kingdom (and thus contemporary with the magician's box), *ḥry-sštꜣ* had become a specific priestly rank.[1075] The involvement of the *ḥry-sštꜣ* in ritual and magic was such that by the Late Period the title was seemingly equated with that of the primary specialist in these areas, the lector priest (*ẖry-ḥb.t*).[1076] Such an involvement is already clear in the Middle Kingdom magician's box.[1077]

That a practicing priest should function as the community magician (thus obviating the necessity—and clientele—for any itinerant practitioner) was undoubtedly neither unusual nor unwieldy. It would certainly have posed no professional difficulty, since except for the very highest ranks, Egyptian priests did not work full time in the temple, but served in groups or "phyles" in rotation.[1078] With four or more such phyles in service, priests would have had fully three quarters of the year off duty, and thus plenty of time for a "private" practice. Combining in himself the roles of composer, compiler, and performer, it is the priest alone who constitutes the "private" magician in ancient Egypt.

As is evident from the title ⲤⲪⲢⲀⲚϢ (< "scribe of the House of Life"), an echo of this relationship between priest and magician survived even in Coptic terminology, when the suppression of pagan cults and clergy had long since recast the magician in the modern stereotype of a secretive, isolated seeker of arcane and forbidden knowledge. Of necessity, the scribal character of the magician remained, and is recognized in the term ⲤⲀϨ Ⲛ̄ ⲢⲈϤⲘⲞⲨⲦⲈ, "magician scribe."[1079] Further Coptic terms for "magician" include the general ϨⲀⲔⲞ[1080] or ⲢⲈϤⲢ̄ϨⲒⲔ, "magician";[1081] the descriptive ⲢⲈϤⲘⲞⲨⲦⲈ (ϨⲚ̄ ⲞⲨ ⲘⲞⲨⲦⲈ), "enchanter"

1074. Including divine, royal, and cosmological secrets; see the range in *Wb* 4: 299.

1075. *Wb* 4: 299/2.

1076. See Derchain 1978. For the magical associations of the rank, compare the title *ḥry-sštꜣ n p.t tꜣ dwꜣ.t*, "overseer of the secrets of heaven, earth, and the underworld" (*Wb* 4: 299/12) with the magical enchantment of earth, heaven, and the underworld effected in Setna I, discussed above, pp. 61–64.

1077. One final question remains with regard to the box: why was it buried in a private tomb with papyri which were presumably temple property? Two answers may be suggested. Since not a single complete manuscript was recovered from the box, the damaged condition of the papyri (and other objects) may have led to their interment, corresponding to the customary burial of damaged sacred utensils, statuary, et cetera. The fragmentary state of the texts was already evident to the excavator; see Quibell 1898, p. 3 and Gardiner 1955b, p. 7, who suggests modern damage to account for the absence of complete texts. Alternatively, the Ramesseum box may represent a simple usurpation of temple property for "private" use, anticipating the practice of the Late Period; for which see above, n. 953.

1078. Discussion and bibliography in Helck 1982.

1079. Orlandi 1980, pp. 44–45, l. 18.

1080. Crum 1939, p. 662b; Černý 1976, p. 277; Westendorf 1965–77, p. 361; Vycichl 1983, p. 293b.

1081. Crum 1939, p. 661a; see above, p. 14.

(literally, "a man who calls [in a call]");[1082] ⲣⲉϥⲛ̄ⲕⲱⲱⲥ ⲉϩⲟⲩⲛ, "necromancer" (literally, "a man who brings in corpses");[1083] ⲣⲉϥⲣ̄ⲡⲁϩⲣⲉ, "sorcerer" (literally, "a man who makes potions");[1084] ⲣⲉϥⲕⲁⲟⲩⲛⲟⲩ, "astrologer" (literally, "a man who places hours");[1085] ⲣⲉϥϫⲉⲙⲧⲁⲩ, "enchanter" (literally, "a man who says words");[1086] ⲣⲉϥϣⲉⲛϩⲓⲛ, "diviner" (literally, "a man who inspects vessels");[1087] ⲣⲉϥϣⲓⲛⲉ, "diviner" (literally, "a man who asks");[1088] and the foreign ⲙⲁⲅⲟⲥ (μάγος) and ⲫⲁⲣⲙⲁⲅⲟⲥ (φαρμακός).[1089] All such terms carry the derogatory stigma still inherent in the modern word "magician."[1090]

1082. Crum 1939, pp. 192a and 196a (s.v. ⲙⲧⲁⲩ) and Westendorf 1965–77, p. 104.

1083. Crum 1939, p. 120b and Westendorf 1965–77, p. 70.

1084. Crum 1939, p. 282b and Westendorf 1965–77, p. 157.

1085. Crum 1939, p. 485a and Westendorf 1965–77, p. 272.

1086. Crum 1939, p. 196a; Černý 1976, p. 94; Westendorf 1965–77, p. 105; and Vycichl 1983, p. 125b.

1087. Crum 1939, p. 685b (which also cites ⲣⲉϥⲙ̄ⲡϩⲓⲛ ⲉϩⲟⲩⲛ, "diviner" literally, "a man who brings in the vessel") and Westendorf 1965–77, p. 377.

1088. Crum 1939, p. 570a.

1089. For these Greek terms, see Crum 1939, p. 196a (s.v. ⲙⲧⲁⲩ).

1090. See the denunciations of various categories of magicians in lists of evildoers in D. W. Johnson 1980, pp. 24–25 (CSCO 415 [text]) and 18 (CSCO 416 [translation]) and Kuhn 1960, pp. 24 (CSCO 206 [text]) and 22–23 (CSCO 207 [translation]).

CHAPTER 6

FROM *ḥkꜣ* TO ϨΙΚ: QUESTIONS OF DEFINITION AND DECLINE

> The Forty-seventh Spirit Uvall, or Vual, or Voval. He is a Duke, Great Mighty and Strong; and appeareth in the Form of a Mighty Dromedary at the first, but after a while at the command of the Exorcist he putteth on Human Shape, and speaketh the Egyptian tongue, but not perfectly.[1]
>
> 1. He can nowadays converse in sound though colloquial Coptic.—Ed.
>
> L. W. de Laurence, ed., 1916, p. 37

RELIGION, MAGIC, AND HEKA

The shift from pharaonic *ḥkꜣ* to Coptic ϩⲓⲕ represented far more than a linguistic development. If the Coptic pairing of ϩⲓⲕ and *magia* opens the way for the legitimate use of the term "magic" in Egyptology, it must not be forgotten that this equation entailed the adaptation of native terminology to accommodate a Roman category further transformed by Christian belief. The resultant changes in religious meaning and social significance could hardly have been greater. Egyptian priests might prove their sanctity through laudatory declarations asserting mastery of *ḥkꜣ* ("Never did any excellent magic [*ḥkꜣ*] remain hidden from me.").[1091] For their Coptic counterparts, however, sanctity was proved by *public denial* of any familiarity with ϩⲓⲕ or *magia*. *Magia* and its Coptic synonym must be understood primarily as terms of disparagement, denoting unaccepted and thus "sub-religious" practices[1092] in which unorthodox gods are made demons and unorthodox worship made crime. Such a connotation is not applicable to *ḥkꜣ*, and one may thus speak of indigenous "Egyptian magic" only with explicit restrictions. Unqualified use of the term necessarily indicates only the Roman, Christian, or modern concept superimposed on ancient practice. But while for both Romans and Christians it was meaningful to speak of "Egyptian magic," the significance and range of such "magic" will have been interpreted differently even by these groups who shared the same terminology but not the same ideology. For either group, even the "orthodox" practices of the other were dismissed as *magia*.[1093] The modern discomfort with the category "magic" is the direct legacy of the inherent subjectivity of this Roman concept.

1091. From the tombs of *Ny-ꜥnḫ-Ppy* and *ꜥnḫ-m-ꜥ-Ḥr*. For the passage, see Sethe 1933, p. 202/2 and Edel 1964, p. 570, §1094.

1092. See the typical assessment in H. I. Bell 1953, p. 74: "But magic is after all no more than the disreputable basement in the house of religion."

1093. Coptic hagiographies are replete with *topoi* of Romans and Christians using the term *magia* at cross-purposes. Saintly "miracles" are consistently described by jailers and governors as ⲙⲁⲅⲓⲁ and the saint as ⲙⲁⲅⲟⲥ; typical examples appear in "The Martyrdom of Macrobius" in Hyvernat 1886, pp. 232, 234–35 and D. N. Bell 1988, pp. 117 and 119: "What shall we do with this magician (ⲙⲁⲅⲟⲥ) ... who is casting multitudes of spells (ⲙⲁⲅⲓⲁ) in the prison"; and in "The Martyrdom of Epima" in Mina 1937, pp. 11 and 53–54: "I swear to you by Jesus, this name through which you do magic (ⲙⲁⲅⲓⲁ) ... Truly, you are a scribal magician (ⲥⲁϩ ⲙ̄ⲙⲁⲅⲟⲥ)." Such accusations invariably lead to a counter-charge by the saint: "The governor ... said to him: 'Teach me, too, to make magic (ⲙⲁⲅⲓⲁ) like you.' ... The saint said to him: 'I myself am no magician (ⲙⲁⲅⲟⲥ), and may it never happen that I practice magic (ⲙⲁⲅⲓⲁ). Nor should this name of magician (ⲙⲁⲅⲟⲥ) be associated with any Christian. It is those who serve idols who have discovered all magic (ⲙⲁⲅⲓⲁ)'" ("The Martyrdom of Macrobius," in Hyvernat 1886, pp. 238–39 and D. N. Bell 1988, p. 122). In the related martyrdoms of Epima and Shenufe, the saint rebuts the charge by transferring it to the pagan clergy, citing the case of the ⲙⲁⲅⲟⲥ Astratole, *high priest* of Ashmunein, who descended into the underworld and escaped only by conversion to

Designed more as a "category of exclusion" (that which is not X) than as a "category of inclusion" (that which is X), the inherited Western concept of "magic" is notoriously difficult to define. Its suggested components are disputed,[1094] and those criteria generally adopted depend primarily upon perceived emotions and attitudes of the practitioner—adding yet another level of subjectivity to a classification already vague. Given the failure of such criteria to delineate an unambiguous sphere of "magic," a new approach was attempted in which "activity" was selected as the diagnostic criterion. Maintaining the traditional interpretation of magic as unorthodox practice, and selecting the "rational causality" of the post-"Enlightenment" to represent orthodoxy, magic in the *modern Western* sense is defined as any activity which seeks to obtain its goals by methods *outside* the simple laws of cause and effect.[1095] Using such a "working definition," the identification of "magical" elements within spells, rituals, literature, and archaeological artifacts is relatively simple, and a brief selection of these are surveyed: circumambulation, spitting, licking, swallowing, the use of images, superposition, trampling, binding, the use of red, breaking, the use of sand, burning, numerological symbolism, piercing, reversal, burial, the use of the dead, and oracular consultations.

This definition of "magic" yields explicit results by accepting certain equally explicit presuppositions. "Magic" is *not* seen as a universal category of equal applicability across time and space (*contra* all early anthropology, certain modern theorists of comparative religion, and most Egyptological treatments). Inherent in the term is the subjectivity of cultural bias, and thus "magic" must be understood with reference to a specific cultural context. This working definition openly recognizes and incorporates the Western bias of the present scholarly category. Rather than intuit the attitude and bias of the ancient (or foreign) practitioner, this approach openly declares those of the researcher. Thus are produced results which are useful for description and organization *within a specific scholarly framework*, but which must not be confused with ancient (or foreign)

Christianity. Astratole's remarkable descent into hell was "magic"; his equally remarkable ascent was not; see Mina 1937, pp. 18–19 and 62–63; Reymond and Barns 1973, pp. 102–03 and 203; and White 1926, pp. 102–03 (where Astratole is ultimately cast as a martyr). The capricious nature of these accusations was already evident to Celsus in his contemporary critique of early Christian propaganda: "Is it not a silly sort of argument to reckon by the same works that one man is a god whilst his rivals are mere 'sorcerers?'" (Hoffmann 1987, p. 66).

1094. See now the overview and critique of Gutekunst 1986 and 1987 and compare Altenmüller 1980.

1095. I.e., the laws of causality as understood by the *modern* researcher. By concentrating exclusively on modern concepts for the modern definition, confusions regarding the perceptions of causality by the *ancient* practitioner become irrelevant, thus obviating the dilemma posed above, pp. 69–70 and the critique of Gutekunst 1986, cols. 1323–24.

interpretation.[1096] Such a treatment is directly analogous to the superimposed use of "verb," "noun," "adjective," et cetera, in analyses of Egyptian grammar, and subject to the same limitations.[1097] Yet while the artificial nature of such grammatical terminology has long been recognized in linguistics, the equally artificial terminology of "magic" and "religion" has generally gone unnoticed. Few would argue that "verb" is an invariable, universal concept, that the Egyptian "verb" must be analyzed exactly as the English "verb," or that the Egyptian "verb" must have been understood similarly by ancient speaker and modern scholar. The previous sentence would no longer be true were "magic" to be substituted for "verb." Scholarly terminology should be recognized for what it is: imposed descriptive approximations and *not* found universal "truisms." In particular, "magic" and "religion" (like "verb") are *Latin* concepts specifically meaningful within *Latin* culture, its derivatives and descendants. They can only represent an artificial framework for study when used of alien cultures.[1098]

The Aristotelian "urge to classify" so central (as to be subliminal) in Western thought often obscures the synthetic nature fundamental to all classification. Almost unavoidable is the resultant tendency to assume that classifications are universally valid "objects" to be discovered rather than artificial (if not arbitrary) tools contrived for descriptive purposes. As a consequence, outmoded classifications are jealously maintained, contrary classifications devised, and new categories are proliferated as ends in themselves.[1099] Such has

1096. This incongruity of modern and ancient categories is equally notable in discussions of Egyptian botany, zoology, anatomy, and color terminology. Thus the color term *wꜣḏ*, conventionally translated "green," included both modern "blue" and "green," while *dšr*, "red" included shades of "orange," "yellow," "pink," et cetera. The danger of confusing Egyptian with modern categorization in these areas is well discussed in Weeks 1979. Mesopotamian color terminology is no less "culturally specific" (see Landsberger 1969).

1097. The artificial nature of traditional grammatical terminology is easily documented: the "adjective" in Coptic is rather a "noun" in an attributive position, "aorist" in Egyptian grammar does not have the same range of meaning as in Greek grammar (from which the term is taken), et cetera. Paralleling the ambiguity of the categories "magic" and "religion," present grammatical categories are also not mutually exclusive, with such terms as "nominalized participles," "nominalized adjectives," and "verbal nouns" (infinitive). Recent attempts to modify terminology produce similarly artificial structures, see the summarizing remarks in J. H. Johnson 1986a, pp. 401–02.

1098. Compare the common designation of American Indian or African "charged substances" as "medicine"—while comparable materials in Europe or the Near East are designated "magic."

1099. See my remarks (1987). A particularly flagrant example of multiplying categories as ends in themselves can be found in the five divisions offered by Gordon for Sumerian "proverbs" (cited in Thissen 1984, p. 8). The suggested technical distinctions between "precept," "maxim," "truism," "adage," and "byword" are obviously arbitrary formulations since the terms are merely synonyms in English. Their descriptive usefulness for modern study is doubtful, and the terms certainly do not derive from, nor do they reflect, Sumerian thought.

clearly been the case with many of the modern discussions of "magic." The anthropological misuse of Evans-Pritchard's Zande category of "witchcraft" is noted above (pp. 10–12), and the attempted "discovery" of this category within Egyptian magic by Borghouts (above, p. 11) displays clearly the inherent weakness of such generalizations, since *in Egypt* "witchcraft" is but a category without content. The cultural strictures on this subsection of "magic" are no less applicable to the concept of "magic" as a whole.

Though generally abandoned in anthropology, the global approach to magic has not been laid to rest. In 1982, sociologist Daniel O'Keefe published *Stolen Lightning: The Social Theory of Magic*, an attempt to present "a general theory of magic: that means a complete explanatory account of the whole thing, past and present, all the provinces, rather than a single hypothesis."[1100] Dismissing contextual studies as "too slack to explain anything,"[1101] O'Keefe propounds a "non-deductive" approach using "theories as data."[1102] The ensuing analysis, synthesis, and generalizations are thus conducted almost entirely within the framework of competing modern Western theoretical interpretations. If the discussions and conclusions thereby engendered say much about these varying theoretical approaches, they say very little about actual practice within individual societies. This is particularly evident where the author strives to incorporate Egyptian evidence. By proclaiming dogmatically that "magic is, in general, a case of expropriating social forces,"[1103] and "symbolism expropriated to protect the self against the social," [1104] O'Keefe enshrines the Western conception of magic as "contrary" activity, antithetical to established religion, state, and society. Egyptian institutionalized "magic" simply *cannot* be seen in these terms, and thus the author is forced to devise a special category ("religious magic") which is only "magical 'in the weak sense'."[1105] By circular argument, O'Keefe finds that established "religious magic" is not (by his definition) true "magic" since it is not

1100. O'Keefe 1983, p. xv.

1101. Ibid., p. xvi.

1102. Ibid., p. xvi.

1103. Ibid., p. 124.

1104. Ibid., p. xviii.

1105. Ibid., pp. 6 and 213–14.

a "peripheral" institution.[1106] Such a generalization certainly obscures more than it clarifies.[1107] Ultimately, O'Keefe's argument is but a tempest within the teapot of Western theory: it shows the ways (and terms) in which the West has construed a problem which the West has devised, and it offers yet another construction. O'Keefe declares that "magic is real" precisely because *his* cultural and theoretical background has utilized the concept, however unsystematically. The title of the work itself betrays this unrecognized cultural bias, for "stolen lightning" refers to the Greco-Roman myth of the theft of fire by Prometheus for mankind—for O'Keefe as for Aeschylus (*Prometheus Bound*) and Shelley (*Prometheus Unbound*) a symbol of the revolt of the individual against authority. In Egypt, "magic" as *ḥkꜣ* was not a theft but a gift from the gods, and thus "stolen lightning" is an inappropriate metaphor, and the implied antithesis of "state religion" and "individual magic" is false. As eloquently phrased by Patrick Grim in a review of *Stolen Lightning*:

> 'Magic,' after all, is a term stemming from *our* cultural traditions, and is laden with the particular associations, ambiguities, and overtones of its place within that cultural tradition. ... [Like 'marriage' and 'political party',] it may be that the notion of 'magic' does not export well. These terms have an established use at home in *our* culture, of course, but that is no guarantee that they will be fruitful or even usable in trying to understand some *other* culture. What a careful reading of the ethnographic data shows, I suggest, is that voodoo and mana and taboo are very different things in their different cultural and historical contexts. ... Perhaps we ignore or distort important differences by calling these all 'magic' or by grouping them all under any one term. Perhaps we will have to learn more about them,

1106. O'Keefe 1983, p. 213. As an example of "true magic" in relation to "religion," O'Keefe (following the religion/magic dichotomy advanced by Budge) calls attention to threats against the gods as religious rites "burlesqued, done backwards or otherwise travestied, because magic has its own aims which are always somewhat illicit and often hostile to religion" (p. 124). While this description fits the "Black Mass" of Christian tradition which was the author's obvious source of inspiration, it is absolutely inapplicable to Egyptian tradition in which such threats are not "burlesques of religious rites" but often an integral, legal part of those religious rites! O'Keefe's notions of what should constitute religion, piety, legality, and magic are rigidly circumscribed by Greco-Roman and Judeo-Christian values; outside this narrow sphere they have limited or no validity.

1107. Compare the extremely oversimplified analysis (merging Marx and Wittfogel) offered by O'Keefe (1983, pp. 366–68), which construes Egyptian religion and magic as government monopolies designed to be tools of domination by promising the "magic goal of immortality." Sumerian religion and magic, though still government monopolies, are somehow less "magical" since "the Sumerian cities, organized on a religious basis, did not preach the magic goal of immortality as did the magician kings of Egypt" (p. 368). This blanket condemnation of "religious magic" (O'Keefe's category) provides no insights into Egyptian (or Sumerian) "religion" or "magic"; it merely presents the author's own opinions on the subject of religion and immortality. O'Keefe's discussion further suffers from the outdated or "popular" sources on which he relies, a common failing of "generalist" historians outside their realm of competency.

> individually and in context, before attempting to deal with them in terms of *any* larger general categories.[1108]

The present study of "magical mechanics" attempts precisely that, an investigation of Egyptian practice "individually and in context." The sharp deviations thus revealed between pharaonic Egyptian and modern Western conceptions of "magic" are unmistakable, and far too significant to be dismissed by uncritically subsuming both categories within a general theory. In scholarly discussion, the two constructs must always be rigorously separated—not subordinated—"otherwise we, in vain, attempt to contain water in a net and catch fish in a shovel."[1109]

The futility of any attempt to subordinate Egyptian to Western notions of "magic" is well represented by Wilfried Gutekunst's discussion of "Zauber" for the final volume of the *Lexikon der Ägyptologie*, a counterpart and foil to Borghouts' presentation of "Magie" in the first volume of the series.[1110] Starting from the pretext that within non-Egyptological literature the German synonyms "Zauber" and "Magie" have on occasion been treated as distinct—though vaguely defined—concepts, Gutekunst undertakes a survey and critique of suggested criteria for determining "magic" on a global scale. While this pretext permits a second discussion of a difficult problem, Gutekunst's article is concerned less with the examination of Egyptian conceptions than with the justification of Western theory. The supposed distinction between "Zauber" and "Magie" rapidly proves to be exclusively a matter of Western speculation, the special nuance of "Zauber" deriving only from its equation with Evans-Pritchard's over-generalized and inapplicable term "witchcraft."[1111]

1108. Grim 1983, pp. 93–95. Grim's conclusions are apt: "... *Stolen Lightning* is *not* a good book. Yet the reasons it is not a good book are important reasons, and themselves have something to tell us about the nature of magic" (p. 93). "All in all, *Stolen Lightning* gives the impression of being a peculiarly *anachronistic* book; it belongs among the great volumes of the nineteenth century anthropological and sociological theory. Those were magnificent pieces of work. But we are well beyond them now" (p. 95).

1109. The sixteenth century neo-pagan philosopher Giordano Bruno commenting on the inability of Aristotelian and contemporary Christian concepts to describe the essence of Egyptian religious *magia*; see Bruno 1964, p. 238 and Yates 1964, p. 213. Though Bruno's interpretation of Egyptian magic was hampered by the limitations and inaccuracies of his sources, his attempt to analyze Egyptian practice *from an Egyptian perspective* remains commendable and revolutionary, predating the scholarly advocates of the "emic" approach by four centuries.

1110. Gutekunst 1986. For Borghouts' article on "Magie," see 1980. Borghouts' methodology is certainly to be preferred, since he derives his theories from an initial presentation of Egyptian evidence. In contrast, Gutekunst presents his "global" theoretical interpretations first, with Egyptian conceptions following as an appendage (§B).

1111. Gutekunst 1986, col. 1336, n. 1.

Of necessity, the Egyptian material covered by Gutekunst is exactly the same as that previously reviewed by Borghouts.

Like the present study, Gutekunst faults traditional definitions of "magic" for their vagueness and imprecision.[1112] In the course of this critique, he also objects to the use of the "natural law of causality" as a universal index of "magical" practice, since many acts deemed "religious" are also outside this "law," and since varying cultures will have their own world view with their own understanding of what constitutes "natural causality."[1113] In an attempt to salvage the general applicability of the Western term "magic," he thus proposes a compromise in which certain "religious" practices would be reclassified as "magic" in a "wider sense," while "magic" in a "narrow sense" would be limited to the sphere of the magician and the magical spell.[1114]

Gutekunst's revival of Roeder's "wide" and "narrow" magic[1115] is hardly more helpful than O'Keefe's "true" and "weak" magic. Nor is the determination of "magic" simplified by making the distinction of "magic versus religion" contingent upon that of "magician versus priest" and "magical spell versus ritual recitation or prayer." As the present study demonstrates and as Gutekunst has tacitly recognized, within the *Egyptian* world view there is no distinction between magician and priest, spell and prayer, nor ultimately between religion and magic since a recognized category of "religion" did not even exist. If reliance upon the "natural law of causality" (or any other criteria, for that matter) produces only a Western interpretation and not a universal definition of magic, it is because "magic" is a distinctly Western concept, and a universal definition simply cannot exist. Each "world view" must be examined individually. In common with Western "magic," Egyptian *ḥkꜣ* represents a force that is secret (*sštꜣ*),[1116] powerful (*ꜣḫ, pḥty*),[1117] and superhuman (*Ḥkꜣ*, *nṯr*).[1118] Beyond these basic characteristics the similarity ends. As *Stolen Lightning* represents a failed attempt to construct a universal definition of magic, Gutekunst's

1112. The examined and rejected criteria for determining "magic" include the attitude of the practitioner (manipulation of versus subjection to higher powers), the dependence of the activity on the law of causality (the definition adopted within this study), the "supernatural" goals of the process, the reliance on "secret and miraculous" powers to effect the goal, and the dichotomy of state/orthodoxy versus individual/private actions.

1113. Gutekunst 1986, cols. 1323–24 (Merkmal 2).

1114. Ibid., col. 1326 (§III).

1115. See above, p. 70.

1116. For the association of *ḥkꜣ* with secrecy (*sštꜣ*), see above, pp. 202–04.

1117. For these terms and their associations with *ḥkꜣ*, see above, pp. 30–35 (*ꜣḫ*) and 25–26 (*pḥty*).

1118. See above, pp. 15–28 (*Ḥkꜣ*) and 26 (*nṯr*).

discussion catalogues the failed attempts to apply such definitions specifically to ancient Egyptian practice.[1119]

No more successful are the recent attempts to substitute alternate global categories for the failed dichotomy of "religion versus magic." Thus the suggested distinction of "calendrical ritual versus crisis rite"[1120] is confounded by such execration texts as the "Apophis Book" which span both categories, being performed at calendrical ceremonies as well as on a daily basis as a "cultic crisis rite" for the protection of the deity and individual suppliants. Since the same text, ritual activity, and performer were involved regardless of whether the ceremony was enacted at regular intervals or when individual need ("crisis") arose, the contrast of calendrical and crisis rites proves to be but a distinction without a difference.

More fundamental objections can be raised against Silvio Curto's suggestion of a tripartite division (derived from anthropological models of civilization stages), in which "magic" describes the world view of the primitive hunter and gatherer (pre-First Industrial Revolution), "religion" that of the post-Revolution farmer, and "neo-magic" the outmoded, irrational survival of archaic "magic" in the "cultural substratum" of the post-Revolution system, ready "to re-emerge whenever advanced culture declines."[1121] Though simple, this system is clearly unworkable as a descriptive paradigm for Egypt, since the world view of the primitive Egyptian hunter (Curto's "magic") is largely unknown and unknowable, and where survival of this world view may be supposed it is not relegated to an inferior cultural substratum, but is fully incorporated in the world view of the "post-Revolution" civilization, leaving no distinction between Curto's "religion" and "neo-magic."[1122] The diachronic "revolutions" in thought which his analysis presupposes simply cannot be traced, though the sources for his theory can. The inspiration for Curto's category of "neo-magic" is certainly Egypt's well-known cultural conservatism with its retention of ancient rites, myths, et cetera throughout its documented ("post-Revolution") history. There is, however, no justification for assuming that these "survivals" were merely outmoded "cultural baggage,"

1119. A similarly negative conclusion regarding the universality of Western theory is now reached in Gutekunst 1987, essentially a re-edition of his study in 1986, cols. 1320–26, but substituting a final rejection of the religious/magic dichotomy (p. 94) for the proposed "compromise" that terminated the earlier study (col. 1326): "*die 'Magie' im alten Ägypten ist eine bestimmte Art von ägyptischer religiöser Praxis, die sich von anderen Arten*—inbesondere dem 'Götterkult' und dem 'Totenkult', der im vorliegenden Rahmen unberücksichtigt geblieben ist—*nicht grundlegend unterscheidet* " (p. 94, emphasis added).

1120. Titiev 1960; cited with approval in Sørensen 1984, p. 6.

1121. Curto 1984, pp. 717–18 further elaborated in 1987.

1122. Compare the direct continuation of the "smiting scene" from pre-dynastic to Roman times (discussed above, pp. 113–16) with no discernible change of meaning or of cultural stratum.

opposed or inferior to contemporary religious concepts. On the contrary, as is witnessed by the continuity of execration practice from the Old Kingdom through the Greco-Roman periods, it seems that traditional religious elements were maintained precisely because they did conform or could be assimilated to contemporary thought.

Underlying Curto's suggestion that a recrudescence of "neo-magic" would accompany the decline of higher civilization is the oft-repeated but fully unsubstantiated belief that "magical" practices increased at the expense of "religion" as Egyptian history "declined" after the New Kingdom,[1123] culminating in the debased and foreign magic of the Greco-Roman eras.[1124] The evidence adduced for this supposed "increase" does not, however,

1123. Curto 1984, p. 731: "Starting from the XIX dynasty the sepulchral furnishings and mummies make an ever more increasing use of amulets and the Stelae of Horus on crocodiles and statues with healing powers become popular." For the supposed rise in magic after the New Kingdom, see Breasted 1968, pp. 223–71; Kákosy 1974, p. 39; and Kadry 1982, p. 204: "In comparison with the pre-ʿAmārna period, magic, in the Ramesside period, came more to the fore than earlier." A similar increase in the Late Period is suggested in Kákosy 1977, col. 1110 and compare Drioton (1928, p. 54), who decried a late tendency to subordinate god to magic, in defiance of the "great tradition" of Egyptian religion, "celle d'une véritable religion de l'Esprit, dont le Code était la loi morale, qu'il importait plus que jamais de défendre contre les empiétements de la magie." Drioton's assessment of an original, pristine Egyptian "great tradition" based on "spirit" and "moral law" free from "impious magic" betrays an obvious Christian bias at odds with all Egyptian evidence for the inherent—and pivotal—role of *ḥkꜣ* in the "great tradition." The supposed late "warning" against magic published in this note by Drioton is in fact a praise of magical healing statues as civic benefactions approved by Re; see above, n. 81. Late Coptic magic has also been seen as evidence of a decline, even while acknowledging its continuity from pre-Christian origins (Drescher 1948, p. 276).

1124. For the dismissal of later Egyptian religion as "dreary formalism" replaced on the popular level by "material" and "trivial" magic, see H. I. Bell 1953, pp. 13 and 71–74. The assumption of "dreary formalism" is no more than an unsubstantiated guess to explain the rise of Christianity at the expense of Egyptian cultic religion. Coptic sources, however, often reveal the devotion of their pagan opponents (in hostile terms, of course) even during the period of the Christian triumph, when pagans were frequently converted by the threat of torture or of property seizure; compare the tale of Macarius of Tkou translated in Lexa 1925, vol. 2, pp. 219–22 and that of Macedonius translated in Budge 1977b, p. 961. Social, political, and economic concerns were certainly factors as important in conversion as religious "formalism"; compare the relative importance of economic versus theological concerns in the writings of the archimandrite Shenute, discussed in Barns 1964, pp. 154–56 and 158. In any case, the popular practice of "material" and "trivial" magic (as understood by H. I. Bell) continued unabated in the Coptic period. Coptic description of contemporary pagan religious texts as "magical" (Barns ibid., p. 153) is meaningless, since in Coptic eyes all pagan religious texts were necessarily "magical." For the supposed "alien character" of late magic, compare the description of Demotic magical texts in Borghouts 1974, p. 17: "Though the mythology is still egyptian for a large part, the spirit is strikingly different from that of earlier magic: productive and destructive magical spells abound (love spells, catching spells, divination procedures, spells for harming people) while the procedures are described in extenso. Evidently, these magical texts cannot be considered the immediate continuation of «older» magic and they should be studied in connection with magical texts from greek and semitic sources." Despite Borghouts' negative characterization, careful scrutiny of these texts reveals that they

reflect a fundamental *qualitative* change in Egyptian thought or practice, merely a *quantitative* increase in the evidence of objects[1125] and actions which had long been central to Egyptian culture: a greater proliferation of amulets, healing statues, magical/ritual papyri, incantations within medical texts, or mention of the god Heka within theological texts. The pivotal role of Heka is fixed in the Old and Middle Kingdoms,[1126] and incantations accompany treatments in the earliest medical texts.[1127] The use of amulets, images, and spells to preserve the living and the dead was an integral element of the Egyptian world view at all periods. The increase in the *availability* of these constant features is a result of the progressive "democratization" of Egyptian religious prerogatives, comparable to the increase in ("magical") funerary texts from the restricted royal Pyramid Texts to the more common upper-class Coffin Texts to the widely distributed, popular Book of the Dead, Book of Breathings, et cetera.[1128] The development of new forms of healing

---

generally share not only the same mythology with older Egyptian spells, but also the same "world view," symbolism, purpose, as well as verbal and ritual methodology. In particular, the present study seeks to demonstrate the direct affiliation of Demotic "love spells, catching spells," and "spells for harming people" with traditional execration procedures (see above, *Chapter 4*). As noted frequently above, the similarity of Demotic spells to the Greek magical papyri most often derives from the common use of older Egyptian sources by bilingual Egyptian scribes; see further the extensive discussion in Ritner 1995.

1125. Compare Ramesside use of the "prisoner motif," discussed above, pp. 122–31, especially n. 585.

1126. See above, *Chapter 1*.

1127. Compare Griffith 1898, p. 10, Prescription XXX (Middle Kingdom). For the misleading distinction between medical and magical cures, see above, pp. 5, 49–57, 78–82, 88–89, and 93–96.

1128. Economic factors in this process cannot be ignored. The development in the New Kingdom of a town-centered bureaucratic and artisan "middle class" with disposable income readily provided the market for such culturally-desirable goods. Had peasants of previous periods been able to afford such objects, an industry would have certainly developed to provide them. Amulets were no less desirable—and no less "magical"—in the Old Kingdom than in the New. The evidence for much of this proliferation (i.e., the "magical" texts on ostraca and papyri) is confined to Deir el-Medineh, whose special religious and economic status is well known; see above, pp. 206–07.

statues in the New Kingdom[1129] does not imply an increase in "magic" any more than the contemporary increase in temple construction implies increased religiosity. Like the temple, amulet, image, and ritualized spell were the primary ingredients of Egyptian ceremonial practice for the duration of its existence. Being the essence of religion, they cannot grow at the expense of religion. Even the presence of foreign elements in the latest Demotic spells does not constitute an "alien magic," divorced from traditional religion. The practice simply continues the syncretistic nature of Egyptian theology, absorbing Nubian, Greek, and Semitic elements[1130] as the New Kingdom had assimilated the gods (Baal, Astarte, Reshep, and Huruna) and spells of its neighbors (Cretan and Semitic).[1131] Far from being stagnant and moribund, late Egyptian religion still assimilated its traditions to contemporary thought. The clearest expression of this dynamic interaction between traditional practice and contemporary thought is found in the Egyptian influence upon the development of Neoplatonist Theurgy ("performing the works of god"), a melding of

1129. E.g., the cippi of "Horus on the Crocodiles," noted above, p. 207, n. 956. These amuletic statuettes are innovations in form only, being part of a continuum of "healing images" attested at all periods that includes not only other small amulets and figures of faience, clay, wax, wood, metal, or stone, but also vignettes on papyrus and large scale images of healing "intermediaries" depicting a deity (the portable image of Khonsu in the Bentresh Stela), the divine king (the "healing statue" of Ramses III), or the blessed dead (Amenhotep son of Hapu's statue at Thebes, the "healing statue" of Djed-ḥor, etc.), and even living and dead sacred animals. The underlying rationale for the effectiveness of such figures was no different than for the cult image in the temple. If that principle is to be called "magic," then "magic" was necessarily a constant element in Egyptian religion that cannot be meaningfully said to have increased or decreased. Even the Amarna period probably does not constitute an exception, since it merely substituted one set of numinous imagery for another. Akhenaton's zealous destruction of figures of Amon is a *traditional* response to the "magical" potency of imagery.

1130. For Nubian spells, see Pap. BM 10588, col. 7, in Bell, Nock, and Thompson 1933, pp. 12–13 (= Betz 1986, p. 289); Ritner 1986a, pp. 98–99; and Griffith and Thompson 1904, p. 193 (vo. 20). Compare also BD spell 164 with the Nubian name of Sakhmet-Bastet (*Ḥrpgkšršb*) in an invocation (Allen 1974, p. 160). For the late fear of Nubian magic, see the romance of Setna II, discussed above, n. 321. For Greek and Semitic elements, see Betz 1986, passim. As often noted, the phenomenon of *vox barbarica* or so-called "magical nonsense words" is probably related to the use of foreign incantations and "names of power"; compare the outlandish names of deities in BD spells 162–65 (Allen 1974, pp. 157–62) and of Apep in the "Apophis Book" (Pap. BM 10188, col. 32/19–40).

1131. Compare Pap. BM 10059, col. 11/4–6, "A conjuration of the Asiatic disease in the speech of Keftiu"; in Wreszinski 1912, pp. 151–52 and 192; Borghouts 1978, p. 37 (no. 57); F. G. Gordon 1932; Wainwright 1931, pp. 27–30; and Goedicke 1984. For Semitic spells, see Lange 1927, pp. 93–94 (col. 11/8–9 = Spell Y, l. 28) and 98 (col. 12/1–5 = Spell Z). Compare also Pap. Ebers 422: "Another remedy for eyes which an Asiatic of Byblos told." The use of foreign magic in the New Kingdom derives from the cosmopolitan character of contemporary society, no longer isolated from cultural contact. For fear of Nubian and Asiatic sorcery, see above, n. 1010.

philosophy, religion, and ceremonial "magic."[1132] In its positive recognition of "magic" as a technique within religion, Theurgy reflects Egyptian notions of *ḥkꜣ* rather than Latin concepts of *magia*, and the term provides perhaps the best designation of Egyptian "magico-religious" theology.

Within its own "world view" Egyptian *ḥkꜣ* was of far more exalted significance than its Coptic descendant or Western approximation. Amoral and quintessentially effective (*ꜣḫ*), a power to which gods, men, and all of nature were subject, it was still the same force whether used by god, king, priest, private individual, rebel, or foreign enemy, whether hostile or beneficent, sanctioned or suppressed. As the pre-eminent force through which the creator engendered and sustained the ordered cosmos, it was necessarily the dynamic "energy" which Egyptian religious ritual sought to channel that it might effect its identical goal, the preservation of the creator's universe. The cultic manipulation of this "energy" by recitation, substance, and ritual thus constituted a sophisticated system of "practical theology,"[1133] a "theurgy" in which the priest quite literally "performed the works of god." Conforming to the classical anthropological terminology of Arnold van Gennep, Egyptian "magical" acts are best understood as the technique of religion, the "magical mechanics" of cultic worship.[1134]

These mechanics are sanctioned not merely by practice, but by patron. "Before duality yet arose," Heka was formed to generate the multiplicity of creation, and the means by which he performed this task illuminates not only the methodology of the force of *ḥkꜣ*, but its larger significance in the Egyptian understanding of the nature of the universe as a whole. Heka did not fabricate the universe *ex nihilo*; rather he *reproduced* as terrestrial "doubles" (*kas*, *kꜣ.w*) the acts and *logos* of the demiurge.[1135] As *Nb-kꜣ.w*, "Lord of Doubles," the "magical" deity Heka thus presides over the dissemination of *consecrated images*, the transformation of a numinous primordial unity into a myriad of *reflected* forms. This "*ka*-theology"[1136] of which Heka is the patron begets the "imagistic principle" which is fundamental to all Egyptian theological speculation on the unity of creation: the

1132. Egyptian sacerdotal influence on Theurgy is clearest in Iamblichus' *De Mysteriis Aegyptiorum*; for the text and translation, see Iamblichus 1966. For Theurgy and its distinction from Greco-Roman *magia* and γοητεία, see now Luck 1985, pp. 20–23. The Egyptian priestly role in contemporary Theurgy is further illustrated in the "Life of Plotinus" (Luck ibid., pp. 218–19).

1133. As coined by te Velde 1970, p. 176.

1134. See van Gennep 1960, p. 13: "... *religion*, whose techniques (ceremonies, rites, services) I call *magic*."

1135. For Heka as the consecrator of the *kas* of the creator, the Lord of *kas* with a "myriad of *ka*-spirits" in his mouth, see CT spells 261 and 648, discussed above, pp. 17 and 23–25.

1136. For the "*ka*-theology" of creation, see Greven 1952, especially pp. 35–41 and Schweitzer 1956.

profusion of deities in the pantheon may be seen as "images" or projections of "one god who made himself into millions,"[1137] animals are the images of both gods and demons,[1138] statues and reliefs are animated images of deity,[1139] the king is both the bodily heir of the creator and his "Living Image" on earth,[1140] priests conduct the cultic liturgy throughout

1137. Evidence from the Old Kingdom reveals that the root meaning of the basic Egyptian word for god is simply "image" (Spiegelberg 1930, pp. 120–21). This unity *and equality* of "the One and the Many" renders the question of "monotheism versus polytheism" irrelevant to Egyptian thought, a dichotomy as alien as that of "magic versus religion." The ultimate unity of the creator and his creation (whether gods, men, animals, etc.) is expressed succinctly in such divine epithets as "the one god who made himself into millions" (*nṯr wꜥ ỉr sw m ḥḥ*), attested from the New Kingdom through the Greco-Roman eras; see the discussion and examples in Zandee 1964, pp. 255–56; Assmann 1983, pp. 186–87 (especially 186/4) and 188–90 (especially 188/7: "who came into being alone, who begot himself as millions"); and idem 1975, pp. 244 and 566 (no. 105/4 and no. 106/7 = idem 1983, pp. 186/4 and 188/7), 290/60 (no. 128), and 293/1 (no. 129); adding *Wb Beleg.* 3, p. 43 to *Wb* 3: 153/12: "who came as one that he might differentiate himself as millions," "who made himself into millions of gods, created from his limbs." Compare also Griffith and Thompson 1904, p. 67 (col. 9/6): "Every god is your name." See also the "pantheistic figures" of divine emissaries discussed in Sauneron 1960 and Ritner 1989b, pp. 111–12.

1138. The function of sacred animals as images of an indwelling god are well known. Thus the "Buchis" bull is literally the "Embodied *ba*" of Re (*bꜣ-ḥr-ḫ.t*); for this ancient etymology of the name, see Fairman 1934, pp. 38–40. For the lion as the image of the king, see above, n. 573. For wild animals in ritual hunting and sacrifice as images of enemies and demons, see above, p. 160 and n. 743. The process is stated succinctly in Pap. Insinger, col. 24/8: "Even the small scarab {is great} through its secret image" ([as the sun god Khepri] Lichtheim 1980, p. 204).

1139. See Hornung 1973. Morenz's sharp distinction between the deity and images of the deity (1973, pp. 318–19, n. 71) reflects modern preoccupation with the category of "idolatry" (the worship of "empty statues"), a concept irrelevant to Egyptian notions of consecrated images.

1140. For the divine birth of the king and the role of Heka within it, see above, n. 110. The king as image of Horus is well known and codified in the royal "Horus name" (Gardiner 1973, p. 72). For the reigning monarch's affiliation with the archetypal "royal *ka*," see L. Bell 1985a; idem 1985b; and Murnane 1985. The king as "living image" is concretely expressed in the royal name "The Living Image of Amon" borne not only by Tutankhamun (*Twt-ꜥnḫ-ꜣImn*), but by virtually all reigning Ptolemies after Ptolemy II (*Sḫm-ꜥnḫ-ꜣImn* for Ptolemies III, IV, V, VIII, IX, and XII; var. *Snn-ꜥnḫ-ꜣImn* for Ptolemy X and Alexander I); see Gauthier 1916, pp. 245, 263, 275, 307, 346, 366 (but correct Gauthier's *ỉry-Mꜣꜥ.t Snn-ꜥnḫ-n-Rꜥ-ꜣImn* to *ỉry-Mꜣꜥ.t-Rꜥ Snn-ꜥnḫ-n-ꜣImn*), and 392. See also the names "Twin of the Living Apis on their Birth-brick" (for Ptolemy VI, ibid., p. 288), "Living Image of Re" (*Tỉ.t-ꜥnḫ-Rꜥ*, for the Meroitic ruler Ergamenes, ibid., p. 424), and "Image of Re" (*Tỉ.t-n-Rꜥ*, for the Meroitic ruler *ꜣIḏḫrỉmn*, ibid., p. 429).

Egypt as the image of the king[1141] and the gods,[1142] royal statues are embodiments of the king,[1143] while private statues and tomb reliefs are animated images of the dead, who are themselves ultimately images of Osiris (as "Osiris so-and-so"), et cetera. Indistinguishable from this pattern of images is the "magical" use of figurines, reliefs, vessels, the dead, animals, plants, et cetera, in funerary cult, execration rite, and medical practice. Ritual acts are no less imagistic, rendering concrete (by encircling, superposition, burning, trampling, etc.) their intangible "doubles" (dominion, superiority, victory, etc.). The effectiveness of "magical" words and names must be understood within the same continuum, the pictorial character of the Egyptian script (with representational determinatives) adding a further bond between the written word and the object which it embodies.[1144]

If the force of *ḥkꜣ* is to be understood primarily as the power of effective duplication or "empowered images," then the techniques discussed within this study constitute "magical mechanics" in both the Western and Egyptian sense—though for very different reasons. The use of *ḥkꜣ* could hardly be construed in Egyptian terms as "activity outside the law of natural causality" since *ḥkꜣ* is itself the ultimate source of causality, the generative force of nature. It is the notion of *ḥkꜣ* which unites the tenets of Egyptian religion to the techniques of Egyptian religion.

ỉw=f pw

1141. Since the king was in theory the chief priest of each temple, he necessarily designated "representatives" to enact his role in daily ritual. In light of the thorough methodology of "designated images" in Egyptian theology, it is possible that these "royal substitutions" should not be considered only polite fictions of convenience. Should some reflected aspect of royal divinity be attributed to the liturgical performer—at least during the performance of the rite? The "royal" attributes of the high priest Herihor are perhaps an elaborate development of such a notion.

1142. Compare the ritual "Songs of Isis and Nephthys" in Pap. Bremner-Rhind, performed by two pure virgins "with the hair of their bodies removed, their heads adorned with wigs, tambourines in their hands, and the names 'Isis' and 'Nephthys' inscribed on their shoulders" (col. 1/2–4 in Faulkner 1933, p. 1 and 1936, pp. 121–22). Comparable to the practice with execration figures, the application of the name (Isis, Nephthys) to the figure (priestess) effects the identity. Masks of Anubis and Bes were used for similar identifications during ritual (Murray 1935–38 and Wild 1963, pp. 78–81). The significance of such masking is distorted beyond reason in Wolinski 1986 and 1987; see above, n. 1037. Priestly impersonators of Anubis regularly appear in funerary ceremonies, and are styled simply *ꜣInpw*, "Anubis" or *rmt-ꜣInpw*, "Anubis-men"; see Faulkner 1951, pp. 48–49: *ỉnk ꜣInpw*, "I am Anubis" (line 6); Reymond 1973, pp. 120–23 (misunderstood, p. 123, n. 12); and de Cenival 1972b, pp. 18, 33, 34, and 57, n. 25. Compare also CT spells 513, 516, and 546.

1143. For this now much-discussed issue, see the seminal study of Habachi (1969). Compare also the remarks of Davies and Davies 1939, p. 155: "the visit of the king and queen ... seems to be by proxy, if indeed statues in Egypt ought to be considered as ranking inferior to the actual person."

1144. For the equation of word and object, cf. the discussion of the seven creative "utterances," above, p. 44 and 46–47.

REFERENCES CITED

The following list comprises only references specifically cited within this volume and should not be considered an exhaustive bibliography of works on Egyptian magic or religion. Alphabetization follows the standard established by the *AEB*.

———————

1934 *ⲠⲒϪⲰⲘ ⲚⲦⲈ ϮⲆⲒⲀⲐⲎⲔⲎ ⲘⲂⲈⲢⲒ* [The Book of the New Testament]. Cairo: Abnaa el Kanisa.

Abdallah, Aly O. A.

1984 "An Unusual Private Stela of the Twenty-First Dynasty from Coptos," *JEA* 70: 65–72.

Aberle, David F.

1966 "Religio-Magical Phenomena and Power, Prediction and Control," *Southwestern Journal of Anthropology* 22: 221–30.

Abu Bakr, Abdel Moneim and Osing, Jürgen

1973 "Ächtungstexte aus dem Alten Reich," *MDAIK* 29: 97–133.

Abusch, Tzvi

1974 "Mesopotamian Anti-Witchcraft Literature: Texts and Studies," *JNES* 33: 251–62.

Alcock, Anthony

1982 "Wicked foxes and bath demons," *GM* 53: 9–10.

1983 *The Life of Samuel of Kalamun by Isaac the Presbyter*. Warminster: Aris & Phillips Ltd.

Allam, Schafik

1973 *Hieratische Ostraka und Papyri aus der Ramessidenzeit*. Volume 1. Urkunden zum Rechtsleben im alten Ägypten, vol. 1/1. Tübingen: Schafik Allam.

Allen, T. George

1949 "Some Egyptian Sun Hymns," *JNES* 8: 349–55.

1974 *The Book of the Dead or Going Forth by Day: Ideas of the Ancient Egyptians Concerning the Hereafter as Expressed in Their Own Terms*. SAOC, vol. 37. Chicago: University of Chicago Press.

Alliot, Maurice

1946 "Les rites de la chasse au filet, aux temples de Karnak, d'Edfou et d'Esneh," *RdE* 5: 57–118.

1949 *Le culte d'Horus à Edfou au temps des Ptolémées*, Vol. 1. BdE, vol. 20/1. Cairo: IFAO.

1954 *Le culte d'Horus à Edfou au temps des Ptolémées*, Vol. 2. BdE, vol. 20/2. Cairo: IFAO.

Altenmüller, Hartwig

1965 *Die Apotropaia und die Götter Mittelägyptens.* Unpublished thesis. Munich: Ludwig Maximillians Universität.

1971 "Eine neue Deutung der Zeremonie des *ꜣIN ꜣIT RD*," *JEA* 57: 146–53.

1972 *Die Texte zum Begräbnisritual in den Pyramiden des Alten Reiches.* ÄgAb, vol. 24. Wiesbaden: Otto Harrassowitz.

1973 "Bemerkungen zum Hirtenlied des Alten Reiches," *CdE* 48, no. 96: 211–31.

1975 "Apotropaikon," *LÄ* 1: cols. 355–58.

1977 "Bemerkungen zum Kannibalspruch," in *Fragen an die altägyptische Literatur*, edited by J. Assmann, E. Feucht, and R. Grieshammer (Eberhard Otto Festschrift). Wiesbaden: Dr. Ludwig Reichert, pp. 19–39.

1979 "Eine Zauberspruch zum 'Schutz des Leibes,'" *GM* 33: 7–12.

1980 "Magische Literatur," *LÄ* 3: cols. 1151–62.

1986 "Ein Zaubermesser des Mittleren Reiches," *SAK* 13: 1–27.

Ammianus Marcellinus

1971 Edited and translated by John C. Rolfe. 3 vols. Cambridge, MA: Harvard University Press.

Andreu, Guillemette

1987 "Le policier *sꜥšꜣ*," *BIFAO* 87: 1–20.

Anthes, Rudolf

1930 "Die Vorführung der gefangenen Feinde vor den König," *ZÄS* 65: 26–35.

1961 "Das Verbum *šni* 'umschliessen, bannen' in den Pyramidentexten," *ZÄS* 86: 86–89.

1974 "Die Berichte des Neferhotep und des Ichernofret über das Osirisfest in Abydos," in *Festschrift zum 150jährigen Bestehen des Berliner Ägyptischen Museums*, edited by Wolfgang Müller. Mitteilung aus der ägyptischen Sammlung, Band 7. Berlin: Akademie-Verlag, pp. 15–49.

Assmann, Jan

1975 *Ägyptische Hymnen und Gebete.* Zurich: Artemis Verlag.

1978 "Eine Traumoffenbarung der Göttin Hathor," *RdE* 30: 22–50.

1983 *Sonnenhymnen in thebanischen Gräbern.* Theben, vol. 1. Mainz am Rhein: Philipp von Zabern.

1984a *Ägypten-Theologie und Frommigkeit einer frühen Hochkultur.* Urban-Taschenbücher, no. 366. Stuttgart: W. Kohlhammer.

1984b "Schöpfung," *LÄ* 5: cols. 677–90.

Audollent, Auguste

1904 *Defixionum Tabellae.* Thèsis, Faculté des Lettres de Paris. Paris: Fontemoing.

Aufrère, Sydney

1982–83 "Caractères principaux et origine divine des minéraux," *RdE* 34: 3–21.

Aune, David E.

1980 "Magic in Early Christianity," in *Aufstieg und Niedergang der römischen Welt*, Part II, Volume 23.2. Berlin: Walter de Gruyter, pp. 1507–57.

Badawi, Ahmad

1956 "Das Grab des Kronprinzen Scheschonk, Sohnes Osorkon's II. und Hohenpriesters von Memphis," *ASAE* 54: 153–77.

Badawy, Alexander

1969 "Illusionism in Egyptian Architecture," in *Studies in Honor of John A. Wilson*, edited by E. B. Hauser. SAOC, vol. 35. Chicago: University of Chicago Press, pp. 15–23.

Baer, Klaus

1960 *Rank and Title in the Old Kingdom*. Chicago: University of Chicago Press.

1964 "The oath *sdfꜣ-try.t* in Papyrus Lee, 1, 1," *JEA* 50: 179–80.

1965 "Ein Grab verfluchen?" *Orientalia* (N. S.) 34: 428–38.

Baines, John

1972 "R. T. Rundle Clark's Papers on the Iconography of Osiris," *JEA* 58: 286–95.

1983 "Literacy and Ancient Egyptian Society," *Man* (N. S.) 18: 572–99.

1985 *Fecundity Figures*. Warminster: Aris & Phillips Ltd.

Baines, John and Eyre, Christopher J.

1983 "Four notes on literacy," *GM* 61: 65–96.

Bakir, Abd el-Moḥsen

1943 "A Donation Stela of the Twenty-Second Dynasty," *ASAE* 43: 75–81.

Balestri, I. and Hyvernat, H.

1924 *Acta Martyrum II*. CSCO, vol. 86. Paris: Imprimerie Nationale.

Barb, A. A.

1963 "The Survival of Magical Arts," in *The Conflict Between Paganism and Christianity in the Fourth Century*, edited by A. Momigliano. Oxford: Clarendon Press, pp. 100–25.

Barguet, Paul

1961 "Un curieux objet votif du Musée du Louvre," *Mélanges Maspero*. I: *Orient ancien*. MIFAO, vol. 66/4. Cairo: IFAO, pp. 7–10.

Barns, John W. B.

1956 *Five Ramesseum Papyri*. Oxford: Oxford University Press.

1964 "Shenute as a Historical Source," in *Actes du Xe Congrès International de Papyrologues Varsovie-Cracovie 3–9 Septembre 1961*, edited by Józef Wolski. Warsaw: Polskiej Akademii Nauk, pp. 151–59.

Barta, Winfried

1968 *Aufbau und Bedeutung der altägyptischen Opferformel*. ÄF, vol. 24. Glückstadt: J. J. Augustin.

1970 *Das Selbstzeugnis eines altägyptischen Künstlers (Stele Louvre C 14)*. MÄS, vol. 22. Berlin: Bruno Hessling.

1980 "Materialmagie und -symbolik," *LÄ* 3: cols. 1233–37.

Basel Museum

1978 *Geschenk des Nils: Aegyptische Kunstwerke aus schweizer Besitz*. Basel: Schweizerischer Bankverein.

Becker, M. J.

1980 "An American Witch Bottle," *Archaeology* 33/2: 18–23.

von Beckerath, Jürgen

1965 "Zur Begründung der 12. Dynastie durch Ammenemes I.," *ZÄS* 92: 4–10.

1975 "Astronomie und Astrologie," *LÄ* 1: cols. 511–14.

Beinlich, Horst

1984 *Die "Osirisreliquien."* ÄgAb, vol. 42. Wiesbaden: Otto Harrassowitz.

Bell, David N.

1988 *Mena of Nikiou. The Life of Isaac of Alexandria & the Martyrdom of Saint Macrobius.* Cistercian Studies Series, vol. 107. Kalamazoo, MI: Cistercian Publications.

Bell, H. Idris

1953 *Cults and Creeds in Graeco-Roman Egypt.* New York: Philosophical Library. (reprinted Chicago: Ares Publishers, Inc., 1975)

Bell, H. Idris; Nock, Arthur D.; and Thompson, Herbert

1933 *Magical Texts from A Bilingual Papyrus in the British Museum.* Proceedings of the British Academy, vol. 17. Oxford: Oxford University.

Bell, Lanny

1985a "Aspects of the Cult of the Deified Tutankhamun," in *Mélanges Gamal Eddin Mokhtar*, Vol. 1, edited by Paule Posener-Kriéger. BdE, vol. 97/1. Cairo: IFAO, pp. 31–59.

1985b "Luxor Temple and the Cult of the Royal *Ka*," *JNES* 44: 251–94.

Bentzen, Aage

1950 "The Ritual Background of Amos I.2–II.16," *Oudtestamentische Studien* 8: 85–99.

von Bergmann, E.

1886 *Hieratische und hieratisch-demotische Texte der Sammlung aegyptischer Alterthümer.* Vienna: Adolf Holzhausen.

Betz, Hans D., ed.

1986 *The Greek Magical Papyri in Translation.* Chicago: University of Chicago Press.

Bietak, Manfred

1981 *Avaris and Piramesse.* Mortimer Wheeler Archaeological Lecture, 1979. Oxford: Oxford University Press.

Bierbrier, Morris

1982 *The Tomb-Builders of the Pharaohs.* London: British Museum.

Biggs, Robert

1980–83 "Kopfkrankheiten," in *Reallexikon der Assyriologie und vorderasiatischen Archäologie*, vol. 6. Berlin: Walter de Gruyter, pp. 210–11.

Bilabel, Friedrich

1934 *Griechische, koptische und arabische Texte zur Religion und religiösen Literatur in Ägyptens Spätzeit.* Heidelberg: Verlag der Universitätsbibliothek.

Bingen, Jean

1969 Review of Georges Michaïlides, "Éléments de synthèse religieuse gréco-égyptienne," *CdE* 44, no. 87: 163.

Birch, Samuel

1863a "Sur un papyrus magique du Musée Britannique," *Revue Archéologique* 7: 119–28.

1863b "Sur un papyrus magique du Musée Britannique," *Revue Archéologique* 8: 427–40.

1876 "Egyptian Magical Text," in *Records of the Past, Being English Translations of the Assyrian and Egyptian Monuments*, Vol. VI: *Egyptian Texts.* London: Samuel Bagster and Sons, pp. 113–26.

von Bissing, Friedrich W.

1907 *Steingefässe.* CGC. Vienna: Adolph Holzhausen.

von Bissing, Friedrich W. and Kees, Hermann

1922 *Untersuchungen zu den Reliefs aus dem Re-Heiligtum des Rathures*, Vol. 1. Abhandlungen der Bayerischen Akademie der Wissenschaften, philosophische-philologische und historische Klasse, vol. 32/1. Munich: Bayerischen Akademie der Wissenschaften.

Björkman, Gun

1974 "A Funerary Statuette of Hekaemsaf, Chief of the Royal Ships in the Saitic Period," *Boreas* 6 [Säve-Söderbergh Festschrift]: 71–80.

Blackman, Aylward M.

1924 *The Rock Tombs of Meir*, Part 4. ASE, vol. 25. London: EES.

1938 "The Use of the Egyptian Word *ḥt* 'House' in the Sense of 'Stanza'," *Orientalia* (N. S.) 7: 64–66.

1945 "The King of Egypt's Grace before Meat," *JEA* 31: 57–73.

Blackman, Aylward M. and Fairman, Herbert W.

1941 "A Group of Texts Inscribed on the Façade of the Sanctuary in the Temple of Horus at Edfu," in *Miscellanea Gregoriana: Raccolta di scritti pubblicati nel I Centenario dalla fondazione del Museo Egizio (1839–1939).* Monumenti Vaticani Archeologia e d'Art, vol. 6. Vatican City: Tipographia Poliglotta Vaticana, pp. 397–428.

1942 "The Myth of Horus at Edfu-II," *JEA* 28: 32–38.

1943 "The Myth of Horus at Edfu-II," *JEA* 29: 2–36.

1944 "The Myth of Horus at Edfu-II," *JEA* 30: 5–22 and 79–80.

Bonner, Campbell

1932 "Demons of the Bath," in *Studies Presented to F. Ll. Griffith*, edited by S. R. K. Glanville. London: EES, pp. 203–08.

1950 *Studies in Magical Amulets Chiefly Graeco-Egyptian.* Ann Arbor: University of Michigan.

Bonnet, Hans

1952 *Reallexikon der ägyptischen Religionsgeschichte.* Berlin: Walter de Gruyter.

Borchardt, Ludwig

1909 "Das Sethtier mit dem Pfeil," *ZÄS* 46: 90–91.

1913 *Das Grabdenkmal des Königs ŚAꜣḤU-REʾ.* Part 2, *Die Wandbilder*. Wissenschaftliche Veröffentlichung der Deutsche Orient-Gesellschaft, vol. 26. Leipzig: J. C. Hinrichs'sche Buchhandlung.

1925 *Statuen und Statuetten von Königen und Privatleuten*, Part 2. CGC. Berlin: Reichsdruckerei.

1929 "Bilder des 'Zerbrechens der Krüge,'" *ZÄS* 64: 12–16.

1930 *Statuen und Statuetten von Königen und Privatleuten*, Part 3. CGC. Berlin: Reichsdruckerei.

1937 *Denkmäler des Alten Reiches*, Part 1. CGC. Berlin: Reichsdruckerei.

Borghouts, Joris F.

1970 *The Magical Texts of Papyrus Leiden I 348. OMRO*, vol. 51. Leiden: E. J. Brill.

1974 "Magical Texts," in *Textes et langages de l'Égypte pharaonique. Cent cinquante années de recherches 1822–1975: Hommage à Jean-François Champollion*, Volume 3, edited by Serge Sauneron. BdE, vol. 64/3. Cairo: IFAO, pp. 7–19.

1978 *Ancient Egyptian Magical Texts.* Nisaba, vol. 9. Leiden: E. J. Brill.

Borghouts, Joris F. (*cont.*)

1980 "Magie," *LÄ* 3: cols. 1137–51.

1982 "Divine Intervention in Ancient Egypt and its Manifestation (*b3w*)," in *Gleanings from Deir el-Medîna*, edited by R. J. Demarée and Jac. J. Janssen. Egyptologische Uitgaven, vol. 1. Leiden: Nederlands Instituut voor het Nabije Oosten, pp. 1–70.

1984 "The Victorious Eyes: A Structural Analysis of Two Egyptian Mythologizing Texts of the Middle Kingdom," in *Studien zu Sprache und Religion Ägyptens. Zu Ehren von Wolfhart Westendorf überreicht von seinen Freunden und Schülern, Band 2: Religion*, edited by F. Junge. Göttingen: F. Junge, pp. 703–16.

1987a "Akhu and Hekau. Two Basic Notions of Ancient Egyptian Magic, and the Concept of the Divine Creative Word," in *La Magia in Egitto ai Tempi dei Faraoni*, edited by A. Roccati and A. Siliotti. Milan: Rassegna Internazionale di Cinematografia Archeologica Arte e Natura Libri, pp. 29–46.

1987b "The Edition of Magical Papyri in Turin: a Progress Report," in *La Magia in Egitto ai Tempi dei Faraoni*, edited by A. Roccati and A. Siliotti. Milan: Rassegna Internazionale di Cinematografia Archeologica Arte e Natura Libri, pp. 257–69.

Bosse-Griffiths, Kate

1973 "The Great Enchantress in the Little Golden Shrine of Tutʿankhamūn," *JEA* 59: 100–08.

1975 "The Use of Disc-Beads in Egyptian Bead-Compositions," *JEA* 61: 114–24.

1976 "Further Remarks on *Wrt Ḥk3w*," *JEA* 62: 181–82.

1977 "A Beset Amulet from the Amarna Period," *JEA* 63: 98–106.

Bothmer, Bernard V.

1982 "On Realism in Egyptian Funerary Sculpture of the Old Kingdom," *Expedition* 24: 27–39.

Botti, Giuseppe and Peet, T. E.

1928 *Il Giornale della Necropoli di Tebe*. Turin: Fratelli Bocca.

du Bourguet, Pierre

1975 "Ensemble magique de la période romaine en Égypte," *Revue du Louvre* 25: 255–57.

1980 "Une ancêtre des figurines d'envoûtement percées d'aiguilles, avec ses compléments magiques, au Musée du Louvre," in *Livre du Centenaire 1880–1980*, edited by Jean Vercoutter. MIFAO, vol. 104. Cairo: IFAO, pp. 225–38.

Boylan, Patrick

1922 *Thoth, the Hermes of Egypt*. London: Humphrey Milford (reprinted Chicago: Ares, 1979).

Brashear, William

1979 "Ein Berliner Zauberpapyrus," *ZPE* 33: 261–78.

Breasted, James H.

1906 *Ancient Records of Egypt*. 5 vols., Chicago: University of Chicago Press.

1930 *The Edwin Smith Surgical Papyrus, Volume 1: Hieroglyphic Transliteration, Translation, and Commentary*. OIP, vol. 3. Chicago: University of Chicago Press.

1968 *The Dawn of Conscience*. New York: Charles Scribner's Sons (reprint of 1933).

Bresciani, Edda

1964 *Der Kampf um den Panzer des Inaros (Papyrus Krall)*. MPER, vol. 8. Vienna: Prachner Verlag.

1975 *L'Archivio Demotico del Tempio di Soknopaiu Nesos*, Vol. 1. Testi e documenti per lo studio dell'antichità, vol. 49. Milan: Cisalpino-Goliardica.

1987 "I grandi testi magici demotici," in *La Magia in Egitto ai Tempi dei Faraoni*, edited by A. Roccati and A. Siliotti. Milan: Rassegna Internazionale di Cinematografia Archeologica Arte e Natura Libri, pp. 313–29.

Bresciani, Edda; Pernigotti, Sergio; and Silvis, M. Paola Giangeri

1977 *La Tomba di Ciennehebu, Capo della Flotta del Re*. Tombe d'età saitica a Saqqara, vol. 1. Pisa: Giardini.

Brichto, Herbert

1975 "The Case of the Sōṭā and a Reconsideration of Biblical Law," *Hebrew Union College Annual* 46: 55–70.

Brier, Bob

1980 *Ancient Egyptian Magic*. New York: William Morrow and Company, Inc.

Brovarski, Edward

1987 *A Table of Offerings. 17 Years of Acquisitions of Egyptian and Ancient Near Eastern Art by William Kelly Simpson for the Museum of Fine Arts, Boston*. Boston: Museum of Fine Arts.

Brown, Peter

1970 "Sorcery, Demons, and the Rise of Christianity from Late Antiquity into the Middle Ages," in *Witchcraft Confessions and Accusations*, edited by Mary Douglas. London: Tavistock Publications, pp. 17–45.

Browne, G. M.; Coles, R. A.; Rea, J. R.; Shelton, J. C.; and Turner, E. G.

1972 *The Oxyrhynchus Papyri*, Volume 41. Graeco-Roman Memoirs, vol. 57. London: EES.

Brugsch, Emil

1889 *La tente funéraire de la princesse Isimkheb provenant de la trouvaille de Déir el-Baharî*. Vienna: Adolphe Holzhausen.

Brugsch, Heinrich

1871 "Bau und Maasse des Tempels von Edfu," *ZÄS* 9: 32–45.

1883–91 *Thesaurus inscriptionum Aegyptiacarum, Altägyptische Inschriften, gesammelt, verglichen, übertragen, erklärt und autographiert*. 6 vols. Leipzig: J. C. Hinrichs'sche Buchhandlung.

1891 *Die Aegyptologie*. Leipzig: Wilhelm Friedrich.

1981 *Recueil de monuments égyptiens*. Hildesheim: Georg Olms (reprint of Leipzig: J. C. Hinrichs'sche Buchhandlung, 1862–85).

Brunner, Hellmut

1966 "Die 'Weisen,' ihre 'Lehren' und 'Prophezeiungen' in altägyptischer Sicht," *ZÄS* 93: 29–35.

1986 *Die Geburt des Gotteskönigs*. 2nd ed. ÄgAb, vol. 10. Wiesbaden: Otto Harrassowitz.

Brunner-Traut, Emma

1988 "Der menschliche Körper-eine Gliederpuppe," *ZÄS* 115: 8–14.

Bruno, Giordano

1964 *The Expulsion of the Triumphant Beast*, translated by Arthur D. Imerti. New Brunswick, NJ: Rutgers University Press.

Bruyère, Bernard

1930 *Mert Seger à Deir el Médineh*. MIFAO, vol. 58. Cairo: IFAO.

de Buck, Adriaan

1935 *The Egyptian Coffin Texts, Vol. 1: Texts of Spells 1–75*. OIP, vol. 34. Chicago: University of Chicago Press.

1937 "The Judicial Papyrus of Turin," *JEA* 23: 152–64.

1938 *The Egyptian Coffin Texts, Vol. 2: Texts of Spells 76–163*. OIP, vol. 49. Chicago: University of Chicago Press.

1947 *The Egyptian Coffin Texts, Vol. 3: Texts of Spells 164–267*. OIP, vol. 64. Chicago: University of Chicago Press.

1951 *The Egyptian Coffin Texts, Vol. 4: Texts of Spells 268–354*. OIP, vol. 67. Chicago: University of Chicago Press.

1954 *The Egyptian Coffin Texts, Vol. 5: Texts of Spells 355–471*. OIP, vol. 73. Chicago: University of Chicago Press.

1956 *The Egyptian Coffin Texts, Vol. 6: Texts of Spells 472–786*. OIP, vol. 81. Chicago: University of Chicago Press.

1961 *The Egyptian Coffin Texts, Vol. 7: Texts of Spells 787–1185*. OIP, vol. 87. Chicago: University of Chicago Press.

1970 *Egyptian Readingbook*. Leiden: Nederlands Instituut voor het Nabije Oosten.

Budge, E. A. Wallis

1899 *The Book of the Dead. Facsimilies of the Papyri of Hunefer, Ånhai, Kerāsher, and Netchemet with Supplementary Text from the Papyrus of Nu*. London: British Museum.

1901 *Egyptian Magic*. London: Kegan Paul, Trench, Trübner and Co., Ltd. (reprinted New York: Dover, 1971).

1904 *The Gods of the Egyptians*. 2 vols. London: Methuen & Co. (reprinted New York: Dover, 1969).

1910 *Facsimilies of Egyptian Hieratic Papyri in the British Museum*. London: British Museum.

1912 *The Greenfield Papyrus in the British Museum*. London: Oxford University Press.

1923 *Facsimiles of Egyptian Hieratic Papyri in the British Museum, Second Series*, HPBM, vol. 2. London: British Museum.

1977a *Coptic Martyrdoms, etc. in the Dialect of Upper Egypt*. Coptic Texts, vol. 4. New York: AMS Press (reprint of London: British Museum, 1914).

1977b *Miscellaneous Coptic Texts in the Dialect of Upper Egypt*. Coptic Texts, vol. 5/2. New York: AMS Press (reprint of London: British Museum, 1915).

Calmeyer, Peter

1972–75 "'Herr der Tiere'; 'Herrin der Tiere'," in *Reallexikon der Assyriologie und vorderasiatischen Archäologie*, Volume 4. Berlin: Walter de Gruyter, pp. 334–35.

Caminos, Ricardo A.

1954 *Late-Egyptian Miscellanies*. London: Oxford University Press.

1958 *The Chronicle of Prince Osorkon*. AnOr, vol. 37. Rome: Pontifical Biblical Institute.

1972 "Another Hieratic Manuscript from the Library of Pwerem son of Ḳiḳi (Pap. B.M. 10288)," *JEA* 58: 205–24.

1987 "Magic for the Dead," in *La Magia in Egitto ai Tempi dei Faraoni*, edited by A. Roccati and A. Siliotti. Milan: Rassegna Internazionale di Cinematografia Archeologica Arte e Natura Libri, pp. 147–59.

Cannon, Walter B.

1942 "'Voodoo' Death," *American Anthropologist* (N. S.) 44: 169–81.

Cannuyer, Christian

1985 "Notules à propos de la stèle du Sphinx," *Varia Aegyptiaca* 1: 83–90.

Capart, Jean

1904 *Les débuts de l'art en Égypte*. Brussels: Vromant & Co.

1907 *Une rue de tombeaux à Saqqarah*, Volume 2. Brussels: Vromant & Co.

1908 "Une liste d'amulettes," *ZÄS* 45: 14–21.

1940 "Avant-propos," in *Princes et pays d'Asie et de Nubie*, by Georges Posener. Brussels: Fondation Égyptologique Reine Élisabeth, pp. 5–9.

1944 "Les anciens Égyptiens pratiquaient-ils déjà la lécanomancie?" *CdE* 19, no. 38: 263.

Capart, Jean; Gardiner, Alan H.; and van de Walle, Baudouin

1936 "New Light on the Ramesside Tomb-Robberies," *JEA* 22: 169–93.

Carter, Howard

1927 *The Tomb of Tut-Ankh-Amen*, Volume 2. London: Cassell & Company.

1933 *The Tomb of Tut-Ankh-Amen*, Volume 3. London: Cassell & Company.

Carter, Howard and Gardiner, Alan H.

1917 "The Tomb of Ramesses IV and the Turin Plan of a Royal Tomb," *JEA* 4: 130–58.

Carter, Howard and Mace, A. C.

1923 *The Tomb of Tut-Ankh-Amen*, Volume 1. London: Cassell & Company.

Cauville, Sylvie

1983 *La théologie d'Osiris à Edfou*. BdE, vol. 91. Cairo: IFAO.

1987 *Essai sur la théologie du temple d'Horus à Edfou*, Volume 1. BdE, vol. 102/1. Cairo: IFAO.

1989 "La chapelle de Thot-Ibis à Dendera édifiée sous Ptolémée Ier par Hor, scribe d'Amon-Rê," *BIFAO* 89: 43–66.

Cauville, Sylvie and Devauchelle, Didier

1985 *Le temple d'Edfou*, Tome 15. MMAF, vol. 32. Cairo: IFAO.

de Cenival, Françoise

1972a *Les associations religieuses en Égypte d'après les documents démotiques*. BdE, vol. 46. Cairo: IFAO.

1972b "Un acte de renonciation consécutif à un partage de revenus liturgiques Memphites (P. Louvre E 3266)," *BIFAO* 71: 11–65.

Černý, Jaroslav

1962 "Egyptian Oracles," in *A Saite Oracle Papyrus from Thebes*, by Richard A. Parker. Providence: Brown University, pp. 35–48.

1964 "An alternative etymology of the Bohairic word for 'interpreter of dreams'," *JEA* 50: 184.

1967 *Le temple d'Amada*, Tome 5. Cairo: Centre de Documentation et d'Études sur l'Ancienne Égypte.

Černý, Jaroslav (*cont.*)

1973 *A Community of Workmen at Thebes in the Ramesside Period.* BdE, vol. 50. Cairo: IFAO.

1976 *Coptic Etymological Dictionary.* Cambridge: Cambridge University Press.

Černý, Jaroslav and Gardiner, Alan H.

1957 *Hieratic Ostraca.* Oxford: Oxford University Press.

Chabas, François J.

1860 *Le papyrus magique Harris.* Chalon-sur-Saône: J. Dejussieu.

1868 "Horus sur les crocodiles," *ZÄS* 6: 99–106.

1909 "Sur un papyrus de formules magiques du Musée de Turin," *Bibliothèque Égyptologique* 13: 45–57.

Chassinat, Émile

1894 "Le livre de protéger la barque divine," *RdT* 16: 105–22.

1928 *Le temple d'Edfou*, Tome 3. MMAF, vol. 20. Cairo: IFAO.

1929a *Le temple d'Edfou*, Tome 4. MMAF, vol. 21. Cairo: IFAO.

1929b *Le temple d'Edfou*, Tome 9. MMAF, vol. 26. Cairo: IFAO.

1930 *Le temple d'Edfou*, Tome 5. MMAF, vol. 22. Cairo: IFAO.

1931 *Le temple d'Edfou*, Tome 6. MMAF, vol. 23. Cairo: IFAO.

1932 *Le temple d'Edfou*, Tome 7. MMAF, vol. 24. Cairo: IFAO.

1933 *Le temple d'Edfou*, Tome 8. MMAF, vol. 25. Cairo: IFAO.

1934a *Le temple d'Edfou*, Tome 13. MMAF, vol. 30. Cairo: IFAO.

1934b *Le temple d'Edfou*, Tome 14. MMAF, vol. 31. Cairo: IFAO.

1952 *Le temple de Dendara*, Tome 5. Cairo: IFAO.

1960 *Le temple d'Edfou*, Tome 10/1–2. MMAF, vol. 27. Cairo: IFAO.

Clark, R. T. Rundle

1959 *Myth and Symbol in Ancient Egypt.* London: Thames and Hudson.

Clère, Jacques J.

1958 "Fragments d'une nouvelle représentation égyptienne du monde," *MDAIK* 16: 30–46.

Cohen, Norman

1970 "The Myth of Satan and his Human Servants," in *Witchcraft Confessions and Accusations*, edited by Mary Douglas. London: Tavistock Publications, pp. 3–16.

Collier, Mark

1986 "A note on the syntax of *ḪPR* and omitted impersonal subjects in late egyptian," *Wepwawet* 2: 15–22.

Conti Rossini, Karolus

1910 *Scriptores Aethiopici, Vitae Sanctorum Indigenarum.* CSCO (O. S.), vol. 24. Leipzig: Otto Harrassowitz.

Corcoran, Lorelei H.

1988 *Portrait Mummies from Roman Egypt.* Unpublished Ph.D. dissertation, Department of Near Eastern Languages and Civilizations, The University of Chicago.

Cowley, A.

1923 *Aramaic Papyri of the Fifth Century B.C.* Oxford: Clarendon Press.

Crompton, Winifred M.

1916 "Two Clay Balls in the Manchester Museum," *JEA* 3: 128.

Crum, Walter E.

1922 "La magie Copte. Nouveaux textes," in *Recueil d'études égyptologiques dédiées à la mémoire de Jean-François Champollion.* Bibliothèque de l'École des Hautes Études. Sciences historiques et philologiques, nr. 234. Paris: Librarie Ancienne Honoré Champion, pp. 537–44.

1934 "Magical Texts in Coptic-II," *JEA* 20: 195–200.

1939 *A Coptic Dictionary.* Oxford: Clarendon Press (reprinted 1972).

1942 "An Egyptian Text in Greek Characters," *JEA* 28: 20–31.

Cumming, Barbara

1982 *Egyptian Historical Records of the Later Eighteenth Dynasty,* Fascicle 1. Warminster: Aris & Phillips Ltd.

Cumont, Franz

1911 *Oriental Religions in Roman Paganism,* translated by Grant Showerman. Chicago: The Open Court (reprinted New York: Dover, 1956).

1937 *L'Égypte des astrologues.* Brussels: Fondation Égyptologique Reine Élisabeth.

Cunen, F.

1960 "Lampe et coupe magiques (PGM, V, 1–52)," *Symbolae Osloenses* 36: 65–71.

Cunliffe, Barry

1983 "The Temple of Sulis Minerva at Bath," *Archaeology* 36/6: 16–23.

Curto, Silvio

1984 "Some Notes Concerning the Religion and Statues of Divinities of Ancient Egypt," in *Studien zu Sprache und Religion Ägyptens. Zu Ehren von Wolfhart Westendorf überreicht von seinen Freunden und Schülern, Band 2: Religion,* edited by F. Junge. Göttingen: F. Junge, pp. 717–34.

1987 "Magia e neomagia," in *La Magia in Egitto ai Tempi dei Faraoni,* edited by A. Roccati and A. Siliotti. Milan: Rassegna Internazionale di Cinematografia Archeologica Arte e Natura Libri, pp. 15–27.

Daniel, Robert W.

1975 "Two Love-Charms," *ZPE* 19: 249–64.

Daressy, Georges

1893 "Notes et remarques," *RdT* 14: 20–38.

1901 *Ostraca.* CGC. Cairo: IFAO.

1903 *Textes et dessins magiques.* CGC. Cairo: IFAO.

1906 *Statues de divinités.* CGC. Cairo: IFAO.

1909 *Cercueils des cachettes royales.* CGC. Cairo: IFAO.

1912 "Pierre-talisman d'Edfou," *ASAE* 12: 143–44.

1916 "La statue d'un astronome," *ASAE* 16: 1–5.

1919a "Statue de Zedher le Sauveur," *ASAE* 18: 113–58.

1919b "Inscriptions tentyrites," *ASAE* 18: 183–89.

Daumas, François

1952 *Les moyens d'expression du grec et de l'égyptien comparés dans les décrets de Canope et de Memphis*. SASAE, vol. 16. Cairo: IFAO.

1958 *Les mammisis des temples égyptiens*. Paris: Société d'Édition «Les Belles Lettres».

Davey, Christopher J.

1985 "Crucibles in the Petrie Collection and Hieroglyphic Ideograms for Metal," *JEA* 71: 142–48.

David, A. Rosalie

1973 *Religious Ritual at Abydos (c. 1300 BC)*. Warminster: Aris & Phillips Ltd.

1991 "Religious Practices in a Pyramid Workmen's Town of the Twelfth Dynasty," *The Bulletin of the Australian Center for Egyptology* 2: 33–40.

Davies, Nina de Garis and Davies, Norman M. de Garis

1939 "Harvest Rites in a Theban Tomb," *JEA* 25: 154–56.

Davies, Nina de Garis and Gardiner, Alan H.

1915 *The Tomb of Amenemhēt*. The Theban Tomb Series, vol. 1. London: EES.

Davies, Norman M. de Garis

1925 *The Tomb of Two Sculptors at Thebes*. Robb de Peyster Tytus Memorial Series, vol. 4. New York: Metropolitan Museum of Art.

1948 *Seven Private Tombs at Ḳurnah*. Mond Excavations at Thebes, vol. 2. London: EES.

1953 *The Temple of Hibis in the Khārgeh Oasis*. Part III: *The Decoration*. PMMA, vol. 17. New York: Metropolitan Museum of Art.

1973 *The Tomb of Rekh-Mi-Rēʿ at Thebes*. 2 vols. PMMA, vol. 11. New York: Arno Press (reprint of New York: Metropolitan Museum of Art, 1943).

Davies, Norman M. de Garis; Gardiner, Alan H.; and Davies, Nina de Garis

1925 *The Tomb of Antefoker, Vizier of Sesostris I, and of his Wife Senet*. The Theban Tomb Series, vol. 2. London: George Allen & Unwin, Ltd.

Davies, W. V.

1976 "'Hands and hearts (Berlin 1157)'—an alternative," *JEA* 62: 176–77.

Davis, Kenneth W. and Gillis, Everett

1989 *Black Cats, Hoot Owls, and Water Witches. Beliefs, Superstitions, and Sayings from Texas*. Denton, TX: University of North Texas.

Davis, S.

1955 "Divining Bowls: Their Uses and Origin. Some African Examples, and Parallels from the Ancient World," *Man* 55: 132–35.

Davis, Wade

1985 *The Serpent and the Rainbow*. New York: Simon and Schuster.

Dawson, Warren R.

1927 "The number 'seven' in Egyptian texts," *Aegyptus* 8: 97–107.

1931 "Notes on Egyptian Magic," *Aegyptus* 11: 23–28.

1932 "Adversaria Aegyptiaca," *Aegyptus* 12: 9–16.

1934 "Studies in the Egyptian Medical Texts—III," *JEA* 20: 41–46.

1938 "The Writing of the Name *Ḥike'*," *JEA* 24: 128.

1945 “The Writing of the Name *Ḥike’*. Second Note,” *JEA* 31: 105.

von Deines, H.; Grapow, H.; and Westendorf, W.

1958 *Übersetzung der medizinischen Texte*. GMAÄ, vol. 4/1. Berlin: Akademie-Verlag.

von Deines, H., and Westendorf, W.

1962 *Wörterbuch der medizinischen Texte*, Volume 2. GMAÄ, vol. 7/2. Berlin: Akademie-Verlag.

Delatte, A. and Derchain, Philippe

1964 *Les intailles magiques gréco-égyptiennes*. Paris: Bibliothèque Nationale.

Demarée, R. J.

1983 *The ꜣḫ ỉkr n Rʿ-Stelae. On Ancestor Worship*. Leiden: Terra BV.

Derchain, Philippe

1961 “Remarques sur la décoration des pylônes ptolémaïques,” *BiOr* 18: cols. 47–49.

1962a “Le rôle du roi d’Égypte dans le maintien de l’ordre cosmique,” in *Le pouvoir et le sacré*, Tome 1, edited by Luc de Heusch. Brussels: Annales du Centre d’Étude des Religions, pp. 61–73.

1962b *Le sacrifice de l’oryx*. Rites égyptiens, vol. 1. Brussels: Fondation Égyptologique Reine Élisabeth.

1965 *Le Papyrus Salt 825 (B.M. 10051)*. Brussels: Palais des Académies.

1974 “Miettes,” *RdE* 26: 7–20.

1978 “Miettes §8. Le chien, le taricheute et l’hiérogrammate,” *RdE* 30: 59–61.

1981 “Anthropologie. Égypte pharaonique,” in *Dictionnaire des mythologies et des religions des sociétés traditionelles et du monde antique*, edited by Yves Bonnefoy. Paris: Flammarion, pp. 46–50.

1989 “Harkhébis, le Psylle-Astrologue,” *CdE* 64, nos. 127–28: 74–89.

Derchain, Philippe and Hubaux, J.

1958 “L’affaire du marché d’Hypata dans la «Métamorphose» d’Apulée,” *L’Antiquité Classique* 27: 100–04.

Desroches-Noblecourt, Christiane

1963 *Tutankhamen. Life and Death of a Pharaoh*. London: George Rainbird Limited.

1985 “The Contribution to Egyptology,” in *La momie de Ramsès II*, edited by L. Balout and C. Roubet. Paris: Éditions Recherche sur les Civilisations, pp. 388–91 (French version pp. 384–87).

Dévaud, Eugène

1912 “Sur le mot saïto-ptolémaïque 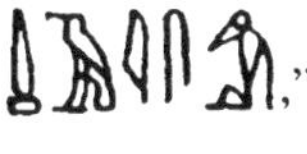,” *ZÄS* 50: 127–29.

Devéria, Théodule

1865 “Le papyrus judiciaire de Turin,” *Journal Asiatique* series 6, vol. 6: 227–61 and 331–77.

1866 “Le papyrus judiciaire de Turin,” *Journal Asiatique* series 6, vol. 8: 154–95.

1867 “Le papyrus judiciaire de Turin,” *Journal Asiatique* series 6, vol. 10: 402–76.

van Dijk, Jac.

1979–80 “The Birth of Horus according to the Ebers Papyrus,” *JEOL* 26: 10–25.

1986 “Zerbrechen der roten Töpfe,” *LÄ* 6: cols. 1389–96.

Diodorus Siculus

1933 Translated and edited by C. H. Oldfather. 12 vols., (Loeb Library). Cambridge, MA: Harvard University Press (reprinted 1968).

Donadoni, Sergio

1973 "II. Le Iscrizioni del Passagio," in "Relazione Preliminare sulla II Campagna di Scavo nella Tomba di Šešonq all'Asasif (1971)," by S. Donadoni, A. Roccati, and S. Bosticco. *Oriens Antiquus* 12: 39–64 (larger article pp. 19–67).

Douglas, Mary

1966 *Purity and Danger: An Analysis of Concepts of Pollution and Taboo.* New York: Praeger.

1970 *Witchcraft Confessions and Accusations.* London: Tavistock Publications.

Drescher, J.

1948 "A Coptic Malediction," *ASAE* 48: 267–76.

Drioton, Étienne

1926 *Les inscriptions. Rapport sur les fouilles de Médamoud 1925.* FIFAO, vol. 3/2. Cairo: IFAO.

1927a *Les inscriptions. Rapport sur les fouilles de Médamoud 1926.* FIFAO, vol. 4/2. Cairo: IFAO.

1927b "Religion et magie.—L'Opinion d'un sorcier égyptien," *Revue de L'Égypte Anciennne* 1: 133–37.

1928 "Religion et magie.—Un avertissement aux chercheurs de formules," *Revue de L'Égypte Anciennne* 2: 52–54.

1939 "Une statue prophylactique de Ramsès III," *ASAE* 39: 57–89.

1942 "Un charme d'amour égyptien d'époque gréco-romaine," *BIFAO* 41: 75–81.

1952 "Une mutilation d'image avec motif," *ArOr* 20: 351–55.

1957 "Une statue de Ramsès III dans le désert d'Almazah," *Pages d'Égyptologie* (*La Revue du Caire*): pp. 53–68.

Duell, Prentice

1938a *The Mastaba of Mereruka Part I.* OIP, vol. 31. Chicago: University of Chicago Press.

1938b *The Mastaba of Mereruka Part II.* OIP, vol. 39. Chicago: University of Chicago Press.

Dümichen, J.

1981 "Geographische Inschriften altägyptischer Denkmäler IV," in *Recueil de monuments égyptiens,* Part VI, by H. Brugsch. Hildesheim: Georg Olms (reprint of J. C. Hinrichs'sche Buchhandlung, Leipzig: 1866).

Dunham, Dows

1967 *Uronarti, Shelfak, Mirgissa.* Second Cataract Forts, vol. 2. Boston: Museum of Fine Arts.

Durkheim, Emile

1965 *The Elementary Forms of the Religious Life.* New York: The Macmillan Co. (reprint of 1915).

Edel, Elmar

1945 "Untersuchungen zur Phraseologie der ägyptischen Inschriften des alten Reiches," *MDAIK* 13: 1–90.

1955 *Altägyptische Grammatik,* Volume 1. AnOr, vol. 34. Rome: Pontifical Biblical Institute.

1964 *Altägyptische Grammatik,* Volume 2. AnOr, vol. 39. Rome: Pontifical Biblical Institute.

1970 *Das Akazienhaus und seine Rolle in den Begräbnisriten des alten Ägyptens.* MÄS, vol. 24. Berlin: Bruno Hessling.

1976 *Ägyptische Ärzte und ägyptische Medizin am hethitischen Königshof.* Opladen: Westdeutscher Verlag.

Edgar, M. C. C.

1905 *Graeco-Egyptian Coffins, Masks and Portraits.* CGC. Cairo: IFAO.

1925 "A Love Charm from the Fayoum," *Bulletin de la Société royale d'archéologie d'Alexandrie* 21: 42–47.

Edgerton, W. F.

1936 "Wooden Tablet from Qâw," *ZÄS* 72: 77–79.

1940 "Egyptian Phonetic Writing, from its Invention to the Close of the Nineteenth Dynasty," *JAOS* 60: 473–506.

Edwards, I. E. S.

1960 *Oracular Amuletic Decrees of the Late New Kingdom.* 2 vols. HPBM, vol. 4. London: British Museum.

1968 "Ḳenḥikhopshef's Prophylactic Charm," *JEA* 54: 155–60.

1976a *Treasures of Tutankhamen.* New York: Metropolitan Museum of Art.

1976b *Tutankhamun: His Tomb and its Treasures.* New York: Metropolitan Museum of Art and Alfred A. Knopf, Inc.

Eliade, Mircea

1959 *The Sacred and the Profane.* New York: Harcourt, Brace & World, Inc.

1971 *The Myth of the Eternal Return.* Princeton: Princeton University.

Ellis, Richard S.

1966 "A Note on Some Ancient Near Eastern Linch Pins," *Berytus* 16: 41–48.

Elsworthy, Frederick

1958 *The Evil Eye.* London: Collier (reprint of London: John Murray, 1895).

Englund, Gertie

1978 *Akh—Une notion religieuse dans l'Égypte pharaonique. Boreas,* vol. 11. Uppsala: University of Uppsala.

Epigraphic Survey, The

1930 *Medinet Habu, Vol. I: Earlier Historical Records of Ramses III.* OIP, vol. 8. Chicago: University of Chicago Press.

1932 *Medinet Habu, Vol. II: Later Historical Records of Ramses III.* OIP, vol. 9. Chicago: University of Chicago Press.

1970 *Medinet Habu, Vol. VIII: The Eastern High Gate with Translations of Texts.* OIP, vol. 94. Chicago: University of Chicago Press.

1980 *The Tomb of Kheruef: Theban Tomb 192.* OIP, vol. 102. Chicago: The Oriental Institute.

1986 *Reliefs and Inscriptions at Karnak, Vol. IV: The Battle Reliefs of King Sety I.* OIP, vol. 107. Chicago: The Oriental Institute.

Erichsen, Wolja

1954a *Demotisches Glossar.* Copenhagen: Einar Munksgaard.

1954b "Aus einem demotischen Papyrus über Frauenkrankheiten," *MIO* 2: 363–77.

Erichsen, Wolja and Schott, Siegfried

1954 *Fragmente memphitischer Theologie in demotischer Schrift (Pap. demot. Berlin 13606)*. Mainz: Akademie der Wissenschaften und der Literatur.

Erman, Adolf

1883 "Die ägyptischen Beschwörungen des grossen Pariser Zauberpapyrus," *ZÄS* 21: 89–109.

1893 "Der Zauberpapyrus des Vatikan," *ZÄS* 31: 119–24.

1901 *Zaubersprüche für Mutter und Kind*. Berlin: Abhandlungen der Königliche Preusissischen Akademie der Wissenschaften.

1907 *A Handbook of Egyptian Religion*, translated by A. S. Griffith. London: A. Constable & Co. (original German edition Berlin: G. Reimer, 1905).

1911 *Hymnen an das Diadem der Pharaonen*. Berlin: Abhandlungen der Königliche Preusissischen Akademie der Wissenschaften.

1919 *Reden, Rufe und Lieder auf Gräberbildern des Alten Reiches*. Berlin: Abhandlungen der Preusissischen Akademie der Wissenschaften.

1933 *Neuaegyptische Grammatik*. 2nd ed. Leipzig: Wilhelm Engelmann.

Evans-Pritchard, E. E.

1937 *Witchcraft, Oracles, and Magic among the Azande*. Oxford: Clarendon Press.

1965 *Theories of Primitive Religion*. Oxford: Clarendon Press.

Eyre, Christopher J.

1984 "A Draughtsman's Letter from Thebes," *SAK* 11: 195–207.

Fairman, Herbert W.

1934 "The Hieroglyphic Inscriptions," in *The Bucheum*, Volume 2: *The Inscriptions*, by Robert Mond and Oliver Meyers. EES Memoir, vol. 41/2. London: EES, pp. 2–52.

1935 "The Myth of Horus at Edfu—I," *JEA* 21: 26–36.

1954 "Worship and Festivals in an Egyptian Temple," *Bulletin of the John Rylands Library* 37: 165–203.

1958 "A Scene of the Offering of Truth in the Temple of Edfu," *MDAIK* 16: 86–92.

1974 *The Triumph of Horus. An Ancient Egyptian Sacred Drama*. Berkeley: University of California Press.

Faraone, Christopher

1985 "Aeschylus' ὕμνος δέσμιος (*Eum.* 306) and Attic judicial curse tablets," *Journal of Hellenic Studies* 105: 150–54.

Faulkner, Raymond O.

1933 *The Papyrus Bremner-Rhind (British Museum No. 10188)*. Bibliotheca Aegyptiaca, vol. 3. Brussels: Édition de la Fondation Égyptologique Reine Élisabeth.

1935 "Some Further Remarks on the Transcription of Late Hieratic," *JEA* 21: 49–51.

1936 "The Bremner-Rhind Papyrus—I," *JEA* 22: 121–40.

1937a "The Bremner-Rhind Papyrus—II," *JEA* 23: 10–16.

1937b "The Bremner-Rhind Papyrus—III," *JEA* 23: 166–85.

1938 "The Bremner-Rhind Papyrus—IV," *JEA* 24: 41–53.

1951 "The Stela of Rudjᶜaḥau," *JEA* 37: 47–52.

1958 *An Ancient Egyptian Book of Hours*. Oxford: Oxford University Press.

1969 *The Ancient Egyptian Pyramid Texts*. Oxford: Clarendon Press.

1973 *The Ancient Egyptian Coffin Texts*, Volume 1. Warminster: Aris & Phillips Ltd.

1977 *The Ancient Egyptian Coffin Texts*, Volume 2. Warminster: Aris & Phillips Ltd.

1978 *The Ancient Egyptian Coffin Texts*, Volume 3. Warminster: Aris & Phillips Ltd.

Fazzini, Richard

1975 *Images for Eternity* (Exhibit catalogue). New York: Brooklyn Museum.

Ferrero, Giovanni

1987 "Simboli e metafore nel mito egizio di Ra e di Iside," in *La Magia in Egitto ai Tempi dei Faraoni*, edited by A. Roccati and A. Siliotti. Milan: Rassegna Internazionale di Cinematografia Archeologica Arte e Natura Libri, pp. 271–84.

Festugière, A. J.

1932 *L'Idéal religieux des grecs et l'évangile*. Paris: J. Gabalda.

1939 "L'Expérience religieuse du médecin Thessalos," *Revue Biblique* 48: 45–77.

Feucht, Erika

1975 "Anhänger," *LÄ* 1: cols. 271–72.

Firth, Cecil M.

1926 "Preliminary Report on the Excavations at Saqqara (1925–1926)," *ASAE* 26: 97–101.

Fischer, Henry G.

1961 "Notes on the Mo'alla Inscriptions and Some Contemporaneous Texts," *WZKM* 57: 59–77.

1973 "Hands and Hearts (Berlin 1157)," *JEA* 59: 224–26.

Fisher, Clarence S.

1917 "The Eckley B. Coxe, Jr. Egyptian Expedition," *The Museum Journal* (The University of Pennsylvania) 8/4: 211–37.

Foucart, G.

1924 "Études thébaines. La belle fête de la vallée," *BIFAO* 24: 1–209.

Frankfort, Henri

1951 *The Birth of Civilization in the Near East*. London: Williams & Norgate (reprinted Garden City, NY: Doubleday, 1959).

Frankfort, Henri; de Buck, Adriaan; and Gunn, Battiscombe

1933 *The Cenotaph of Seti I at Abydos*. 2 vols. EES Memoir, vol. 39. London: EES.

Frazer, Sir James G.

1910 *The Golden Bough. Part 1, The Magic Art and the Evolution of Kings*. New York: The Macmillan Company.

1971 *The Golden Bough*. Abridged ed. New York: The Macmillan Company (reprint of 1922).

Friedman, Florence

1982 Review of Gertie Englund, *Akh—Une notion religieuse dans l'Égypte pharaonique*. *JARCE* 19: 145–47.

1985a "On the Meaning of Some Anthropoid Busts from Deir el-Medîna," *JEA* 71: 82–97.

1985b "The Root Meaning of *ꜣḫ*: Effectiveness or Luminosity," *Serapis* 8: 39–46.

Frymer-Kensky, Tikva

1984 "The strange case of the suspected Sotah (Numbers v 11–31)," *Vetus Testamentum* 34: 11–26.

Gaballa, G. A. and Kitchen, Kenneth A.

1969 "The Festival of Sokar," *Orientalia* (N. S.) 38: 1–76.

Galerie Nefer

1987 *Nefer*. Sale Catalogue, no. 5. Zurich: Galerie Nefer.

1992 *Nefer*. Sale Catalogue, no. 10. Zurich: Galerie Nefer.

Gardiner, Sir Alan H.

1903 "On the Meaning of the Preposition ," *PSBA* 25: 334–36.

1905 "Hymns to Amon from a Leiden Papyrus," *ZÄS* 42: 12–42.

1914 "New Literary Works from Ancient Egypt," *JEA* 1: 20–36.

1915 "Some Personifications. I. *ḤIKE*ʾ The God of Magic," *PSBA* 37: 253–62.

1917 "Professional Magicians in Ancient Egypt," *PSBA* 39: 31–44.

1922 "Magic (Egyptian)," in *Encyclopaedia of Religion and Ethics*, vol. 8, edited by J. Hastings. New York: Charles Scribner's Sons (reprint of London: 1915), pp. 262a–69a.

1925 "The Autobiography of Rekhmerēʿ," *ZÄS* 60: 62–76.

1930 "A New Letter to the Dead," *JEA* 16: 19–22.

1931 *The Library of A. Chester Beatty* (*The Chester Beatty Papyri, No. I*). London: Oxford University.

1932 *Late-Egyptian Stories*. Bibliotheca Aegyptiaca, vol. 1. Brussels: Fondation Égyptologique Reine Élisabeth.

1935 *Chester Beatty Gift*. 2 vols. HPBM, vol. 3. London: British Museum.

1938 "The House of Life," *JEA* 24: 157–79.

1947 *Ancient Egyptian Onomastica*. 2 vols. London: Oxford University Press.

1951 "A Grim Metaphor," *JEA* 37: 29–31.

1952 "Tuthmosis III Returns Thanks to Amūn," *JEA* 38: 6–23.

1955a "A Unique Funerary Liturgy," *JEA* 41: 9–17.

1955b *The Ramesseum Papyri*. Oxford: Oxford University Press.

1961 *Egypt of the Pharaohs*. Oxford: Clarendon Press.

1964 *Egyptian Hieratic Texts: I*. Reinheim: Georg Olms (reprint of Leipzig: J. C. Hinrichs'sche Buchhandlung, 1911).

1969 *The Admonitions of an Egyptian Sage from a Hieratic Papyrus in Leiden (Pap. Leiden 344 recto)*. Hildesheim: Georg Olms (reprint of Leipzig: J. C. Hinrichs'sche Buchhandlung, 1909).

1973 *Egyptian Grammar*. 3rd ed. London: Oxford University Press (reprint of 1957).

Gardiner, Sir Alan H. and Sethe, Kurt H.

1928 *Egyptian Letters to the Dead*. London: EES.

Garitte, Gerardus

1949 *Antonii Vitae Versio Sahidica*. CSCO, vol. 117. Paris: Imprimerie Nationale.

Gauthier, Henri

1916 *Le livre des rois d'Égypte*, Volume 4. MIFAO, vol. 20. Cairo: IFAO.

1925 *Dictionnaire des noms géographiques*, Tome 2. Cairo: Société Royale de Géographie d'Égypte.

van Gennep, Arnold

1960 *The Rites of Passage*. Chicago: University of Chicago Press (reprint of 1909).

Germond, Philippe

1981 *Sekhmet et la protection du monde*. AH, vol. 9. Geneva: Editions de Belles-Lettres.

Ghalioungui, Paul

1983 *The Physicians of Pharaonic Egypt*. DAIK, Sonderschrift 10. Mainz am Rhein: Philipp von Zabern.

Giddy, Lisa L.

1983 "Rapport préliminaire sur la quatrième campagne de fouilles à ʿAyn Aṣīl (Oasis de Dakhleh)," *ASAE* 69: 103–09.

Gilliam, Robyn

1983 "Two Old Kingdom Tombs at Quseir el-Amarna." Unpublished paper given at the American Research Center in Egypt conference, Ann Arbor, Michigan, April 23, 1983.

Gillon, Werner

1984 *A Short History of African Art*. New York: Facts on File.

Gilula, Mordechai

1978 "Hirtengeschichte 17–22 = CT VII 36 m–r," *GM* 29: 21–22.

Glanville, S. R. K.

1939 *A Theban Archive of the Reign of Ptolemy I, Soter*. Catalogue of Demotic Papyri in the British Museum, vol. 1. Oxford: British Museum.

1955 *The Instructions of ʿOnchsheshonqy (British Museum Papyrus 10508)*. Catalogue of Demotic Papyri in the British Museum, vol. 2. London: British Museum.

Goedicke, Hans

1963 "Was Magic Used in the Harem Conspiracy against Ramses III? (P. Rollin and P. Lee)," *JEA* 49: 71–92.

1970 "The Story of the Herdsman," *CdE* 45, no. 90: 244–66.

1972 "The Letter to the Dead, Nag ʿEd-Deir N 3500," *JEA* 58: 95–98.

1984 "The Canaanite Illness," *SAK* 11: 91–105.

1985 "Rudjedet's Delivery," *Varia Aegyptiaca* 1: 19–26.

1988 "The Scribal Palette of Athu (Berlin Inv. Nr. 7798)," *CdE* 63, no. 125: 42–56.

Goetze, Albrecht

1969 "Ritual to Counteract Sorcery," in *Ancient Near Eastern Texts Relating to the Old Testament*, edited by J. B. Pritchard. Princeton: Princeton University Press, p. 347.

Golénischeff, Woldemar

1927 *Papyrus hiératiques*. CGC. Cairo: IFAO.

Gomaà, Farouk

1973 *Chaemwese, Sohn Ramses' II. und Hohenpriester von Memphis*. ÄgAb, vol. 27. Wiesbaden: Otto Harrassowitz.

Goode, William J.

1949 "Magic and Religion: A Continuum," *Ethnos* 14: 172–82.

1951 *Religion among the Primitives*. Glencoe, IL: The Free Press.

Gordon, Cyrus H.

1969 "Ancient Letters to the Dead and Others," *Natural History* 78/2: 94–99.

Gordon, F. G.

1932 "The Keftiu Spell," *JEA* 18: 67–68.

Gorey, Edward

1983 *The Eclectic Abecedarium.* New York: Adama Books.

Goyon, Jean-Claude

1967 "Le cérémonial de glorification d'Osiris du papyrus du Louvre I. 3079 (colonnes 110 à 112)," *BIFAO* 65: 89–156.

1968 "Le cérémonial pour faire sortir Sokaris. Papyrus Louvre I. 3079, col. 112–114," *RdE* 20: 63–96.

1969 "Textes mythologiques I. «Le livre de protéger la barque du dieu»," *Kemi* 19: 23–65.

1970 "Une formule solennelle de purification des offrandes dans les temples ptolémaïques," *CdE* 45, no. 90: 267–81.

1971 "Un parallèle tardif d'une formule des inscriptions de la statue prophylactique de Ramsès III au Musée du Caire (Papyrus Brooklyn 47.218.138, col. x+13, 9 à 15)," *JEA* 57: 154–59.

1972 *Confirmation du pouvoir royal au nouvel an [Brooklyn Museum Papyrus 47.218.50].* BdE, vol. 52. Cairo: IFAO.

1975 "Textes mythologiques II. «Les révélations du mystère des quatres boules»," *BIFAO* 75: 349–99.

1978a "La fête de Sokaris à Edfou à la lumière d'un texte liturgique remontant au Nouvel Empire," *BIFAO* 78: 415–38.

1978b "*Hededyt*: Isis-Scorpion et Isis au Scorpion. En marge du papyrus de Brooklyn 47.218.50—III," *BIFAO* 78: 439–58.

1979 "The Decoration of the Edifice," in *The Edifice of Taharqa*, by R. Parker, Jean Leclant, and Jean-Claude Goyon. Brown Egyptological Studies, vol. 8. Providence: Brown University, pp. 11–79.

Graefe, Erhart

1979 "König und Gott als Garanten der Zukunft (Notwendiger Ritualvollzug neben göttlicher Selbstbildung) nach Inschriften der griechisch-römischen Tempel," in *Aspekte der spätägyptischen Religion*, edited by W. Westendorf. GOF, vol. 9. Wiesbaden: Otto Harrassowitz, pp. 47–78.

Grant, Frederick C.

1953 *Hellenistic Religions.* Indianapolis: Bobbs-Merrill.

Grapow, Hermann

1911 "Bedrohungen der Götter durch den Verstorbenen," *ZÄS* 49: 48–54.

1955 *Von den medizinischen Texten.* GMÄA, vol. 2. Berlin: Akademie-Verlag.

1958 *Die medizinischen Texte in hieroglyphischer Umschreibung Autographiert.* GMÄA, vol. 5. Berlin: Akademie-Verlag.

Grapow, Hermann; von Deines, H.; and Westendorf, W.

1954–73 *Grundriss der Medizin der alten Ägypter.* 9 vols. Berlin: Akademie-Verlag.

Grdseloff, Bernhard

1941 *Das ägyptische Reinigungszelt.* Cairo: IFAO.

1952 "Deux remarques," *ArOr* 20: 482–86.

Grese, William C.

1986a "*PGM* VII.222–49," in *The Greek Magical Papyri in Translation*, edited by Hans D. Betz. Chicago: University of Chicago Press, pp. 122–23.

1986b "*PGM* VIII.64–110," in *The Greek Magical Papyri in Translation*, edited by Hans D. Betz. Chicago: University of Chicago Press, pp. 147–48.

Greven, Liselotte

1952 *Der Ka in Theologie und Königskult der Ägypter des Alten Reiches*. ÄF, vol. 17. Glückstadt: J. J. Augustin.

Grieshammer, Reinhard

1975 "Briefe an Tote," *LÄ* 1: cols. 864–70.

1977 "Flammeninsel," *LÄ* 2: cols. 258–59.

Griffith, Francis Ll.

1898 *Hieratic Papyri from Kahun and Gurob (Principally of the Middle Kingdom)*. London: Bernard Quaritch.

1900 "The Old Coptic magical texts of Paris," *ZÄS* 38: 85–93.

1909a "Papyrus Dodgson," *PSBA* 31: 100–09.

1909b "Additional Notes on the Papyrus Dodgson, Etc.," *PSBA* 31: 289–91.

1972 *Catalogue of the Demotic Papyri in the John Rylands Library Manchester*. 3 vols. Hildesheim: Georg Olms Verlag. (reprint of Manchester: University Press, 1909).

1985 *Stories of the High Priests of Memphis*. Osnabrück: Otto Zeller Verlag. (reprint of Oxford: Clarendon Press, 1900).

Griffith, Francis Ll. and Thompson, H.

1904 *The Demotic Magical Papyrus of London and Leiden*, Vol. 1. Oxford: Clarendon Press.

1909 *The Demotic Magical Papyrus of London and Leiden*, Vol. 3. Oxford: Clarendon Press.

Griffiths, J. Gwyn

1958 "The Horus-Seth Motif in the Daily Temple Liturgy," *Aegyptus* 38: 5–10.

1960 *The Conflict of Horus and Seth from Egyptian and Classical Sources*. Liverpool: Liverpool University Press.

1970 *Plutarch's De Iside et Osiride*. Swansea: University of Wales.

1972 "The Symbolism of Red in Egyptian Religion," in *Ex Orbe Religionum. Studio Geo Widengren XXIV Mense Apr. MCMLXXII Quo Die Lustra Tredecem Feliciter Explevit Oblata Ab Collegis, Discipulis, Amicis, Collegae Magistro Amico Congratulantibus, Pars Prior*, edited by J. Bergman, K. Drynjeff, and H. Ringgren. Leiden: E. J. Brill, pp. 81–90.

1975 *Apuleius of Madauros. The Isis-Book (Metamorphosis, Book XI)*. EPRO, vol. 29. Leiden: E. J. Brill.

1977 "Hermes and the Marrow in a Love-Charm," *ZPE* 26: 287–88.

1985 "An Egyptian Antecedent of ΑΙΩΝΕΡΓΕΤΗΣ," *AJA* 89: 167–68.

Grim, Patrick

1983 "Theories and Magicians (review of Daniel L. O'Keefe, *Stolen Lightning: the Social Theory of Magic*)," *Cross Currents* 33: 93–95.

Grimal, Nicolas-C.

1981a *La stèle triomphale de Pi(ʿankh)y au Musée du Caire JE 48862 et 47086–47089*. MIFAO, vol. 105. Cairo: IFAO.

1981b *Quatre stèles napatéennes au Musée du Caire: JE 48863–48866. Textes et indices*. MIFAO, vol. 106. Cairo: IFAO.

1983 "Rapport préliminaire sur la quatrième campagne de fouilles à ʿAyn Aṣīl (Oasis de Dakhleh). Annexe. Note sur les objects inscrits," ASAE 69: 110–12.

1985 "Les «noyés» de Balat," in *Mélanges offerts à Jean Vercoutter*, edited by Francis Geus and Florence Thill. Paris: Editions Recherche sur les Civilisations, pp. 111–21.

Grimm, Alfred

1987 "Ein Käfig für einem Gefangenen in einem Ritual zur Vernichtung von Feinden," *JEA* 73: 202–06.

1988 "Feind-bilder und Bildverbrennung," *Varia Aegyptiaca* 4: 207–14.

Grinsell, L. V.

1961 "The Breaking of Objects as a Funerary Rite," *Folklore* 72: 475–91.

1973 "The Breaking of Objects as a Funerary Rite: Supplementary Notes," *Folklore* 84: 111–14.

Groll, Sarah I.

1982 "Diachronic Grammar as a Means of Dating Undated Texts," in *Egyptological Studies*, edited by S. Groll. Scripta Hierosolymitana, vol. 28. Jerusalem: Hebrew University, pp. 11–104.

Gunn, Battiscombe

1917 "Interpreters of Dreams in Ancient Egypt," *JEA* 4: 252.

1934 "An Early Egyptian Door-Socket," *The University Museum Bulletin* 5, no. 1: 9, 12–15.

Gutbub, Adolphe

1978 "Éléments ptolémaïques préfigurant le relief cultuel de Kom Ombo," in *Das Ptolemäische Ägypten. Akten des internationalen Symposions 27.–29. September 1976 in Berlin*, edited by Herwig Maehler and Volker Michael Strocka. Mainz am Rhein: Verlag Philipp von Zabern, pp. 165–76.

Gutekunst, Wilfried

1986 "Zauber," *LÄ* 6: cols. 1320–55.

1987 "Wie 'magisch' ist die 'Magie' im alten Ägypten? Einige theoretische Bemerkungen zur Magie-Problematik," in *La Magia in Egitto ai Tempi dei Faraoni*, edited by A. Roccati and A. Siliotti. Milan: Rassegna Internazionale di Cinematografia Archeologica Arte e Natura Libri, pp. 77–98.

Habachi, Labib

1938 "Découvertes de Karnak (1936–1937)," *ASAE* 38: 69–84.

1954 "Khatâʿna-Qantîr: Importance," *ASAE* 52: 443–559.

1969 *Features of the Deification of Ramses II*. ADAIK, vol. 5. Glückstadt: J. J. Augustin.

Habachi, Labib and Ghalioungui, Paul

1971 "The «House of Life» of Bubastis," *CdE* 46, no. 91: 59–71.

Hafeez Abd el ᶜAl, A.

1977 "An Enigmatic Wooden Object Discovered Beside the Southern Side of the Giza Second Pyramid," *ASAE* 62: 103–20.

Haikal, Fayza

1972 *Two Hieratic Funerary Papyri of Nesmin. Part Two, Translation and Commentary*. Bibliotheca Aegyptiaca, vol. 15. Brussels: Fondation Égyptologique Reine Élisabeth.

Hall, Emma Swan

1983 "A Continuation of the Smiting Scene," in *Artibus Aegypti*, edited by H. de Meulenaere and L. Limme. Brussels: Musées Royaux d'Art et d'Histoire, pp. 75–79.

1986 *The Pharaoh Smites His Enemies*. MÄS, vol. 44. Berlin: Deutscher Kunstverlag.

Halliday, W. R.

1967 *Greek Divination*. Chicago: Argonaut (reprint of 1937).

Hamza, Mahmud

1930 "Excavations of the Department of Antiquities at Qantîr (Faqûs District) (Season, May 21st – July 7th, 1928)," *ASAE* 30: 31–68.

Hari, Robert

1976 "La grande-en-magie et la stèle du temple de Ptah à Karnak," *JEA* 62: 100–07.

1984 "La «damnatio memoriae» Amarnienne," in *Mélanges Adolphe Gutbub*. Montpellier: Université Paul Valéry de Montpellier, pp. 95–102.

1985 *La tombe thébaine du père divin Neferhotep (TT 50)*. Geneva: Éditions de Belles-Lettres.

Harris, Marvin

1968 *The Rise of Anthropological Theory*. New York: Crowell.

Hassan, Ali

1976 *Stöcke und Stäbe im Pharaonischen Ägypten bis zum Ende des Neuen Reiches*. MÄS, vol. 33. Munich: Deutscher Kunstverlag.

Hassan, Selim

1941 *Excavations at Giza Vol. 3, 1931–1932*. Cairo: Government Press.

Hayes, William C.

1937 *Glazed Tiles from a Palace of Ramses II at Ḳantīr*. MMA Papers, vol. 3. New York: Metropolitan Museum of Art.

1942 *Ostraka and Name Stones from the Tomb of Sen-Mūt (No. 71) at Thebes*. PMMA, vol. 15. New York: Metropolitan Museum of Art.

1955 *A Papyrus of the Late Middle Kingdom in the Brooklyn Museum [Papyrus Brooklyn 35.1446]*. Brooklyn: Brooklyn Museum.

1990 *The Scepter of Egypt*. 2 vols. Revised Edition. New York: Metropolitan Museum of Art. (1st ed. 1953–59)

Heerma van Voss, Matthew

1969 *Een mysteriekist ontsluierd*. Leiden: E. J. Brill.

1971 "Toetanchamon's schrijn met Anoebis," *ZÄS* 97: 72–74.

1984 "Kontakt met teksten," *Phoenix* (Leiden) 30: 25–34.

Heimer, Marc

1981 "Une statuette d'envoûtement en albâtre du Moyen Empire," *RdE* 33: 134–37.

Helck, Wolfgang

1954 *Untersuchungen zu den Beamtentiteln des ägyptischen Alten Reiches*. ÄF, vol. 18. Glückstadt: J. J. Augustin.

1955a "Eine Stele des Vizekönigs *Wśr-Śt.t*," *JNES* 14: 22–31.

1955b *Urkunden der 18. Dynastie*, Part 17. Urk. 4, part 17. Berlin: Akademie-Verlag.

1957 *Urkunden der 18. Dynastie*, Part 19. Urk. 4, part 19. Berlin: Akademie-Verlag.

1958a *Urkunden der 18. Dynastie*, Part 21. Urk. 4, part 21. Berlin: Akademie-Verlag.

1958b *Urkunden der 18. Dynastie*, Part 21. Urk. 4, part 22. Berlin: Akademie-Verlag.

1961 *Urkunden der 18. Dynastie. Übersetzung zu den Heften 17–22*. Berlin: Akademie-Verlag.

1969 *Der Text der "Lehre Amenemhets I. für seinen Sohn."* Kleine ägyptische Texte. Wiesbaden: Otto Harrassowitz.

1970 *Die Lehre des Dwꜣ-Ḫtjj. Teil I*. Kleine ägyptische Texte. Wiesbaden: Otto Harrassowitz.

1971 *Die Beziehungen Ägyptens zu Vorderasien im 3. und 2. Jahrtausend v. Chr*. 2nd rev. ed. ÄgAb, vol. 5. Wiesbaden: Otto Harrassowitz.

1982 "Phyle," *LÄ* 4: col. 1044.

1984 "Schamane und Zauberer," in *Mélanges Adolphe Gutbub*. Montpellier: Université Paul Valéry de Montpellier, pp. 103–08.

Herbin, François-René

1988 "Les premières pages du Papyrus Salt 825," *BIFAO* 88: 95–112.

Hermann, Alfred

1966 "Magische Glocken aus Meroe," *ZÄS* 93: 79–89.

de Heusch, Luc

1968 "Les sociétés initiatiques traditionnelles d'afrique centrale: analyse structurale des rites et des mythes," *Annuaire, École Pratique des Hautes Études*. V^{e} section, vol. 76 (1968–1969), Paris: Sorbonne, pp. 77–85.

Hodjash, Svetlana and Berlev, Oleg

1982 *The Egyptian Reliefs and Stelae in the Pushkin Museum of Fine Arts, Moscow*. Leningrad: Aurora Art Publishers.

Hölscher, Uvo

1932 *Excavations at Ancient Thebes 1930/31*. OIC, vol. 15. Chicago: University of Chicago Press.

1941 *The Excavation of Medinet Habu, Vol. III: The Mortuary Temple of Ramses III, Part I*, translated by Mrs. Keith C. Seele. OIP, vol. 54. Chicago: University of Chicago Press.

Hoenes, Sigrid-Eike

1976 *Untersuchungen zu Wesen und Kult der Göttin Sachmet*. Bonn: Rudolf Habelt Verlag.

Hoffmann, R. Joseph

1987 *Celsus. On the True Doctrine*. New York: Oxford University Press.

Hofmann, Inge and Tomandl, Herbert

1986a "Bemerkungen zu einem meroitischen Gefangenentypus," *Varia Aegyptiaca* 2: 101–11.

1986b *Unbekanntes Meroe.* Beiträge zur Sudanforschung, Beiheft 1. Vienna and Mödling: Institut für Afrikanistik der Universität Wien.

Hopfner, Theodor

1974 *Griechisch-ägyptischer Offenbarungszauber*, Volume 1. Amsterdam: Adolf M. Hakkert (revised edition of Leipzig: 1921).

Horner, G. W.

1922 *The Coptic Version of the New Testament in the Southern Dialect.* Vol. 6, *The Acts of the Apostles.* Oxford: Clarendon Press.

Hornung, Erik

1963 *Das Amduat. Die Schrift des verborgenen Raumes.* 2 vols. ÄgAb, vol. 7. Wiesbaden: Otto Harrassowitz.

1966 *Geschichte als Fest. Zwei Vorträge zum Geschichtsbild der frühen Menschheit.* Darmstadt: Wissenschaftliche Buchgesellschaft.

1967 *Das Amduat. Die Schrift des verborgenen Raumes.* Vol. 3, *Die Kurzfassung. Nachtrag.* ÄgAb, vol. 13. Wiesbaden: Otto Harrassowitz.

1968 *Altägyptische Höllenvorstellungen.* ASAW, vol. 59/3. Berlin: Akademie-Verlag.

1973 "Bedeutung und Wirklichkeit des Bildes im alten Ägypten," in *Kunst und Realität*, edited by Elisabeth Schmid, Erich Hornung, Hermann Fillitz, Hanspeter Landoldt, Karl Pestalozzi, and Fritz Gnirss. Akademische Vorträge, gehalten an der Universität Basel, vol. 8. Basel: Verlag von Helbing und Lichtenhahn, pp. 35–46.

1975 *Das Buch der Anbetung des Re im Westen (Sonnenlitanei) nach den Versionen des Neuen Reiches*, Volume 1. AH, vol. 2. Geneva: Editions de Belles-Lettres.

1976 *Das Buch der Anbetung des Re im Westen (Sonnenlitanei) nach den Versionen des Neuen Reiches*, Volume 2. AH, vol. 3. Geneva: Editions de Belles-Lettres.

1979 *Das Buch von dem Pforten des Jenseits nach den Versionen des Neuen Reiches*, Volume 1. AH, vol. 7. Geneva: Editions de Belles-Lettres.

1980 *Das Buch von dem Pforten des Jenseits nach den Versionen des Neuen Reiches*, Volume 2. AH, vol. 8. Geneva: Editions de Belles-Lettres.

1982 *Der ägyptische Mythos von der Himmelskuh. Eine Ätilogie des Unvollkommenen.* OBO, vol. 46. Freiburg: Universitätsverlag.

Horsley, G. H. R.

1981 *New Documents Illustrating Early Christianity*, Volume 1. North Ryde, Australia: Macquarie University.

van der Horst, Peter Willem

1984 *Chaeremon. Egyptian Priest and Stoic Philosopher. The Fragments Collected and Translated with Explanatory Notes.* EPRO, vol. 101. Leiden: E. J. Brill.

Hughes, George R.

1958 "A Demotic Letter to Thoth," *JNES* 17: 1–12.

1968 "A Demotic Plea to Thoth in the Library of G. Michaelides," *JEA* 54: 176–82.

1969 "The Cruel Father. A Demotic Papyrus in the Library of G. Michaelides," in *Studies in Honor of John A. Wilson*, edited by E. B. Hauser. SAOC, vol. 35. Chicago: University of Chicago Press, pp. 43–54.

Hughes, George R. (*cont.*)

1986 "An Astrologer's Handbook in Demotic Egyptian," in *Egyptological Studies in Honor of Richard A. Parker*, edited by Leonard H. Lesko. Hanover and London: Brown University Press, pp. 53–69.

Husson, Constance

1977 *L'Offrande du miroir dans les temples égyptiens d'époque gréco-romaine*. Lyon: Université de Lyon.

Hyvernat, Henri

1886 *Les actes des martyrs de l'Égypte tirées des manuscrits coptes de la Bibliothèque Vaticane et du Musée Borgia*. Paris: Ernest Leroux.

Iamblichus

1966 *Jamblique, Les mystères d'Égypte*, edited and translated by Édouard des Places. Paris: Société d'Édition «Les Belles Lettres».

Ibrahim, Mohiy E. A.

1975 *The Chapel of the Throne of Re of Edfu*. Bibliotheca Aegyptiaca, vol. 16. Brussels: Fondation Égyptologique Reine Élisabeth.

Jacquet-Gordon, Helen K.

1962 *Les noms des domaines funéraires sous l'Ancien Empire égyptien*. BdE, vol. 34. Cairo: IFAO.

James, E. O.

1963 Review of A. Momigliano, *The Conflict between Paganism and Christianity in the Fourth Century*. *Folklore* 74: 572–73.

James, T. G. H.

1962 *The Ḥekanakhte Papers and Other Early Middle Kingdom Documents*. PMMA, vol. 19. New York: Metropolitan Museum of Art.

Jankuhn, Dieter

1972 *Das Buch "Schutz des Hauses" (s3-pr)*. Bonn: Rudolf Habelt Verlag.

Janssen, Jac. J.

1975 *Commodity Prices From the Ramessid Period*. Leiden: E. J. Brill.

Jelínková-Reymond, Eve

1956 *Les inscriptions de la statue guérisseuse de Djed-ḥer-le-Sauveur*. BdE, vol. 23. Cairo: IFAO.

Jéquier, Gustave

1940 *Le monument funéraire de Pepi II*. Vol. 3: *Les approches du temple*. Cairo: IFAO.

Johnson, D. W.

1980 *A Panegyric on Marcarius Bishop of Tkôw Attributed to Dioscorus of Alexandria*. 2 vols. CSCO, vols. 415–416. Louvain: Catholic University of Louvain.

Johnson, Janet H.

1975 "The Demotic Magical Spells of Leiden I 384," *OMRO* 56: 29–64.

1977 "Louvre E 3229: A Demotic Magical Text," *Enchoria* 7: 55–102.

1986a "'Focussing' on Various 'Themes,'" in *Crossroad. Chaos or the Beginning of a New Paradigm*, edited by Gertie Englund and Paul J. Frandsen. CNI Publications, vol. 1. Helsingør, Denmark: Carsten Niebuhr Institute, pp. 401–10.

1986b "The Role of the Egyptian Priesthood in Ptolemaic Egypt," in *Egyptological Studies in Honor of Richard A. Parker*, edited by Leonard H. Lesko. Hanover: Brown University, pp. 70–84.

1986c "*PDM* xiv.1–149," in *The Greek Magical Papyri in Translation*, edited by Hans D. Betz. Chicago: University of Chicago Press, pp. 195–203.

1986d "*PDM* xiv.594–620," in *The Greek Magical Papyri in Translation*, edited by Hans D. Betz. Chicago: University of Chicago Press, p. 228.

1986e "*PDM* Suppl. 168–84," in *The Greek Magical Papyri in Translation*, edited by Hans D. Betz. Chicago: University of Chicago Press, p. 329.

Jonckheere, Frans

1955 "Le 'Préparateur des Remèdes' dans l'organisation de la pharmacie égyptienne," in *Ägyptologische Studien*, edited by O. Firchow (Festschrift Grapow). Berlin: Akademie-Verlag, pp. 149–61.

Jordan, David R.

1975 "A Curse Tablet from a Well in the Athenian Agora," *ZPE* 19: 245–48.

1985 "The Inscribed Gold Tablet from the Vigna Codini," *AJA* 89: 162–67.

Junker, Hermann

1903 *Über das Schriftsystem im Tempel des Hathor in Dendera*. Berlin: August Schaefer.

1910a "Die Schlacht- und Brandopfer und ihre Symbolik im Tempelkult der Spätzeit," *ZÄS* 48: 69–77.

1910b *Die Stundenwachen in den Osirismysterien, nach den Inschriften von Dendera, Edfu und Philä dargestellt*. Vienna: Alfred Hölder.

1947 *Giza VIII*. Vienna: Akademie der Wissenschaften.

1955 "Die Feinde auf dem Sockel der Chasechem-Statuen und die Darstellung von geopferten Tieren," in *Ägyptologische Studien*, edited by O. Firchow (Festschrift Grapow). Berlin: Akademie-Verlag, pp. 162–75.

1958 *Der grosse Pylon des Temples der Isis in Philä*. Vienna: Akademie der Wissenschaften.

1959 "Vorschriften für den Tempelkult in Philä," *Studia Biblica et Orientalia* 3: Oriens Antiquus (= *Analecta Biblica* 12): 151–60.

Junker, Hermann and Winter, Erich

1965 *Das Geburtshaus des Tempels der Isis in Philä*. Vienna: Hermann Böhlaus.

Kadish, Gerald E.

1979 "The Scatophagus Egyptian," *SSEA Journal* 9: 203–17.

Kadry, Ahmed

1982 *Officers and Officials in the New Kingdom*. Studia Aegyptiaca, vol. 8. Budapest: Université Loránd Eötvös.

von Känel, Frédérique

1984 *Les prêtres-ouâb de Sekhmet et les conjurateurs de Serket*. Bibliothèque de l'École des Hautes Études, Section des Sciences Religieuses, nr. 87. Paris: Presses Universitaires de France.

1985 Review of P. Ghalioungui, *The Physicians of Pharaonic Egypt*. *BiOr* 42: col. 601.

Kaiser, Werner

1958 "Zur vorgeschichtlichen Bedeutung von Hierakonpolis," *MDAIK* 16: 183–92.

1967 *Ägyptisches Museum Berlin*. Berlin: Staatliche Museen Berlin.

Kákosy, László
1974 "Die weltanschauliche Krise des Neuen Reiches," *ZÄS* 100/1: 35–41.
1977 "Heka," *LÄ* 2: cols. 1108–10.
1980a "Horusstele," *LÄ* 3: cols. 60–62.
1980b "Magische Stelen," *LÄ* 3: cols. 1162–64.
1987 "Some Problems of the Magical Healing Statues," in *La Magia in Egitto ai Tempi dei Faraoni*, edited by A. Roccati and A. Siliotti. Milan: Rassegna Internazionale di Cinematografia Archeologica Arte e Natura Libri, pp. 171–86.

Kambitsis, Sophie
1976 "Une nouvelle tablette magique d'Égypte. Musée du Louvre, Inv. E. 27145- IIIe/IVe siècle," *BIFAO* 76: 213–23.

Kantor, Helene J.
1974 "Ägypten," in *Frühe Stufen der Kunst*, edited by Machteld J. Mellink and Jan Filip. Propyläen Kunstgeschichte, vol. 13. Berlin: Propyläen Verlag, pp. 227–56.

Kaplony, Peter
1969 "Das Hirtenlied und seine fünfte Variante," *CdE* 44, no. 87: 27–59.
1970 "Hirtenlied, Harfnerlieder und Sargtext-Spruch 671 als verwandte Gattungen der ägyptischen Literatur," *CdE* 45, no. 90: 240–43.

Kase, Edmund H.
1936 *Papyri in the Princeton University Collections*, Vol. 2. Princeton: Princeton University Press.

Kees, Hermann
1912 *Der Opfertanz des ägyptischen Königs*. Leipzig: J. C. Hinrichs'sche Buchhandlung.
1915 "Nachlese zum Opfertanz des ägyptischen Königs," *ZÄS* 52: 61–72.
1924 "*Nbḏ* als Dämon der Finsternis," *ZÄS* 59: 69–70.
1930 "Kulttopographische und mythologische Beiträge. 5. 'Ḥike, der Älteste des heiligen Platzes des Urbeginns'," *ZÄS* 65: 83–84.
1942 "Bemerkungen zum Tieropfer der Ägypter und seiner Symbolik," *Nachrichten von der Gesellschaft der Wissenschaften zu Göttingen, Philologisch-Historische Klasse*, pp. 71–88.
1980 *Der Götterglaube im alten Ägypten*. Berlin: Akademie-Verlag (reprint of Leipzig: J. C. Hinrichs'sche Buchhandlung, 1956).

Keimer, Ludwig
1933 "Materialien zum altägyptischen Zwiebelkult," *Egyptian Religion* 1: 52–60.

Kemp, Barry J.
1973 "Photographs of the Decorated Tomb at Hierakonpolis," *JEA* 59: 36–43.

Kendall, Timothy
1982 *Kush: Lost Kingdom of the Nile*. Brockton, MA: Brockton Art Museum.

Kertesz, Trude
1976 "The Breaking of Offerings in the Cult of Hathor," *Tel Aviv* 3: 134–36.

Kitchen, Kenneth
1983a *Ramesside Inscriptions*, Volume 5. Oxford: B. H. Blackwell.
1983b *Ramesside Inscriptions*, Volume 6. Oxford: B. H. Blackwell.

Klakowicz, Beatrix E.

1980 "The Funerary Papyrus of *ʾIhḏ* (P. Palau Rib. inv. 68)," *Studia Papyrologica* 19: 9–38.

Klasens, Adolf

1952 *A Magical Statue Base (Socle Behague) in the Museum of the Antiquities of Leiden*. OMRO, vol. 33. Leiden: E. J. Brill.

Koenen, Ludwig

1968 "Die Prophezeiungen des 'Töpfers'," *ZPE* 2: 178–209.

1970 "The Prophecies of a Potter: A Prophecy of World Renewal Becomes an Apocalypse," in *Proceedings of the Twelfth International Congress of Papyrology*, edited by Deborah H. Samuel. American Studies in Papyrology, vol. 7. Toronto: A. M. Hakkert Ltd., pp. 249–54.

1984 "A Supplementary Note on the Date of the Oracle of the Potter," *ZPE* 54: 9–13.

Koenig, Yvan

1981 "Les effrois de Keniherkhepeshef (Papyrus Deir el-Médineh 40)," *RdE* 33: 29–37.

1982 "Deux amulettes de Deir el-Médineh," *BIFAO* 82: 283–93.

1987a "A propos des textes d'envoûtement de Mirgissa (Nubie)," in *La Magia in Egitto ai Tempi dei Faraoni*, edited by A. Roccati and A. Siliotti. Milan: Rassegna Internazionale di Cinematografia Archeologica Arte e Natura Libri, pp. 301–12.

1987b "La Nubie dans les textes magiques «l'inquiétante étrangeté»," *RdE* 38: 105–10.

1989 "Nouveaux textes Rifaud II (document E)," *CRIPEL* 11: 53–58.

1990 "Les textes d'envoûtement de Mirgissa," *RdE* 41: 101–25.

Königlichen Museen zu Berlin

1905 *Hieratische Papyrus aus den Königlichen Museen zu Berlin*, Volume 2. Leipzig: J. C. Hinrichs'sche Buchhandlung.

Korostovtsev, Mikhaïl

1947 "Stèle de Ramsès IV," *BIFAO* 45: 155–73.

1973 *Grammaire du neo-égyptien*. Moscow: L'Académie des Sciences de l'U. R. S. S.

Kramer, Samuel N.

1969a "Lamentation over the Destruction of Ur," in *Ancient Near Eastern Texts Relating to the Old Testament*, edited by J. B. Pritchard. Princeton: Princeton University Press, pp. 455–63.

1969b "Lamentation over the Destruction of Sumer and Ur," in *Ancient Near Eastern Texts Relating to the Old Testament*, edited by J. B. Pritchard. Princeton: Princeton University Press, pp. 611–19.

Kropp, Angelicus M.

1930–31 *Ausgewählte koptische Zaubertexte*. 3 vols. Brussels: Fondation Égyptologique Reine Élisabeth.

Kruchten, Jean-Marie

1985 "Un instrument politique original: la «belle fête de *pḥ-nṯr*» des rois-prêtres de la XXIe dynastie," *BSFE* 103: 6–26.

1986 *Le grand texte oraculaire de Djéhoutymose*. Monographies Reine Élisabeth, vol. 5. Brussels: Fondation Égyptologique Reine Élisabeth.

Kuchman, Liza

1977–78 "Egyptian Clay Anthropoid Coffins," *Serapis* 4: 11–22.

Kuentz, Charles

1925 *Deux stèles d'Aménophis II*. BdE, vol. 10. Cairo: IFAO.

1928 *La bataille de Qadech*. MIFAO, vol. 55. Cairo: IFAO.

Kuhn, K. H.

1960 *Pseudo-Shenoute on Christian Behaviour*. 2 vols. CSCO, vol. 206–07. Louvain: Catholic University of Louvain.

1978 *A Panegyric on Apollo Archimandrite of the Monastery of Isaac by Stephen Bishop of Heracleopolis Magna*. 2 vols. CSCO, vol. 394–95. Louvain: Catholic University of Louvain.

Kurth, Dieter; Thissen, Heinz-Josef; and Weber, Manfred

1980 *Kölner ägyptische Papyri (P. Köln ägypt.)*, Volume 1. Papyrologica Coloniensia, vol. IX. Opladen: Westdeutscher Verlag.

La Barre, Weston

1985 *Muelos: A Stone Age Superstition about Sexuality*. New York: Columbia University Press.

Lacau, Pierre

1904 "Textes Religieux," *RdT* 26: 59–81.

1909 *Stèles du Nouvel Empire*. CGC. Cairo: IFAO.

1914 "Suppressions et modifications de signes dans les textes funéraires," *ZÄS* 51: 1–64.

1921–22 "Les statues «guérisseuses» dans l'ancienne Égypte," *Monuments Piot* 25: 189–209.

Lambert, Wilfred G.

1957–58 "An Incantation of the Maqlû Type," *AfO* 18: 288–99.

Landsberger, Benno

1969 "Über Farben im Sumerisch-akkadischen," *JCS* 21: 139–73.

Lange, Hans O.

1927 *Der magische Papyrus Harris*. Copenhagen: Andr. Fred. Høst & Søn.

Lansing, Ambrose

1933 "The Egyptian Expedition. The Excavations at Lisht," *BMMA* 28 (November [section II]): 4–26.

1947 "An Old Kingdom Captive," *BMMA* (N. S.) 5 (February): 149–52.

Lanzone, Ridolfo V.

1974 *Dizionario di Mitologia Egizia*, Volume 1. Amsterdam: John Benjamins B. V. (reprint of Turin: 1881–84).

Lauer, Jean-Philippe

1931 "Remarques sur les monuments du Roi Zoser à Saqqarah," *BIFAO* 30: 333–60.

1969–70 "Les statues de prisonniers du complexe funéraire de Pépi Ier," *BIE* 51: 37–45.

Lauer, Jean-Philippe and Leclant, Jean

1969 "Découverte de statues de prisonniers au temple de la pyramide de Pépi I," *RdE* 21: 55–62.

de Laurence, L. W., ed.

1916 *Goetia. The Lesser Key of Solomon*. Chicago: De Laurence, Scott & Co.

Leclant, Jean

1968 "Éléments pour une étude de la divination dans l'Égypte pharaonique," in *La Divination*, Volume 1, edited by André Caquot and Marcel Leibovici. Paris: Presses Universitaires de France, pp. 1–23.

1977 "Gotteshand," *LÄ* 2: cols. 813–15.

1979 *Recherches dans la pyramide et au temple haut du Pharaon Pépi Ier à Saqqarah.* Scholae Adriani De Buck Memoriae Dicatae, vol. 6. Leiden: Nederlands Instituut voor het Nabije Oosten.

Lefébure, Eugène

1902 "Le vase divinatoire," *Sphinx* 6: 61–85.

Lefebvre, Gustave

1931 "La statue «guérisseuse» du Musée du Louvre," *BIFAO* 30: 89–96.

1949 "Rouge et nuances voisines," *JEA* 35: 72–76.

Legrain, Georges

1906 *Statues et statuettes des rois et de particuliers.* CGC. Cairo: IFAO.

1917 "Le logement et transport des barques sacrées et des statues des dieux dans quelques temples égyptiens," *BIFAO* 13: 1–76.

Lehner, Mark and Lacovara, Peter

1985 "An enigmatic object explained," *JEA* 71: 169–74.

Lepsius, C. Richard

1972–73 *Denkmäler aus Ägypten und Äthiopien.* 12 vols. (always cited by subsuming 6 Abteilungen). Geneva: Édition de Belles-Lettres (reprint of Berlin: Nicolaische Buchhandlung, 1849–59).

Lesko, Leonard

1972 *The Ancient Egyptian Book of Two Ways.* Berkeley: University of California Press.

Letellier, Bernadette

1980 "La destinée de deux enfants, un ostracon ramesside inédit," in *Livre du Centenaire 1880–1980,* edited by Jean Vercoutter. MIFAO, vol. 104. Cairo: IFAO, pp. 127–33.

Levi, Peter

1975 "The prose style of the magical papyri," in *Proceedings of the XIV International Congress of Papyrologists,* edited by P. J. Parsons, J. R. Rea, E. G. Turner, and R. A. Coles. Graeco-Roman Memoirs, vol. 61. London: EES, pp. 211–16.

Lévi-Strauss, Claude

1950 "Introduction à l'oeuvre de Marcel Mauss," in *Sociologie et anthropologie,* by Marcel Mauss. Paris: Presses Universitaires de France.

Lewis, Naphtali

1977 "A Ban on False Prophets: P. Coll. Youtie 30," *CdE* 52, no. 103: 143–46.

Lexa, François

1925 *La magie dans l'Égypte antique.* 3 vols. Paris: Paul Geuthner.

1926 *Papyrus Insinger.* Paris: Paul Geuthner.

Lichtheim, Miriam

1973 *Ancient Egyptian Literature,* Volume 1. Berkeley: University of California Press.

1976 *Ancient Egyptian Literature,* Volume 2. Berkeley: University of California Press.

1980 *Ancient Egyptian Literature,* Volume 3. Berkeley: University of California Press.

1983 *Late Egyptian Wisdom Literature.* OBO, vol. 52. Freiburg: Universitätsverlag.

Liddell, H. G.; Scott, R.; and Jones, H. S.

1940 *A Greek-English Lexicon.* Oxford: Clarendon Press.

Lindsay, Jack

1971 *Origins of Astrology*. New York: Barnes and Noble.

Littauer, M. A. and Crouwel, J. H.

1985 *Chariots and Related Equipment from the Tomb of Tutʿankhamūn*. Tutʿankhamūn's Tomb Series, vol. 8. Oxford: Griffith Institute.

1987 "'Unrecognized Linch Pins from the Tombs of Tutʿankhamon and Amenophis II': A Reply," *GM* 100: 57–61.

Lloyd, Alan B.

1975 "Once More Hammamat Inscription 191," *JEA* 61: 54–66.

Lobel, E. and Roberts, C. H.

1954 *The Oxyrhynchus Papyri, Part XXII*. Graeco-Roman Memoirs, vol. 31. London: EES.

Logan, Thomas

1976 "Papyrus Harkness," in *Studies in Honor of George R. Hughes*, edited by Edward F. Wente and Janet H. Johnson. SAOC, vol. 39. Chicago: The Oriental Institute, pp. 147–61.

López, Jesús

1982 *Ostraca Ieratici N. 57320–57449*. Catalogo del Museo Egizio di Torino, vol. 3/3. Milan: Istituto Editoriale Cisalpino-La Goliardica.

Lorton, David

1977 "The Title 'Book of Knowing the Creations of Re and of Felling Apophis': A Grammatical Note on the Titles and Headings of Egyptian Religious Compositions," *GM* 23: 55–63.

Lucchesi, Enzo

1975 "A propos du mot copte 'Sphransh,'" *JEA* 61: 254–56.

Luck, Georg

1985 *Arcana Mundi*. Baltimore: Johns Hopkins University Press.

Lüddeckens, Erich

1943 "Untersuchungen über religiösen Gehalt, Sprache und Form der ägyptischen Totenklagen," *MDAIK* 11: 1–188.

MacDonald, George

1981 *Lilith*. Grand Rapids, MI: Wm. B. Eerdman (reprint of 1895 edition).

MacMullen, Ramsay

1966 *Enemies of the Roman Order: Treason, Unrest and Alienation in the Empire*. Cambridge, MA: Harvard University Press.

1984 *Christianizing the Roman Empire (A.D. 100–400)*. New Haven: Yale University Press.

Malinine, Michel

1934 "Un fragment de l'enseignement d'Amenemhat Ier," *BIFAO* 34: 63–74.

Malinowski, Bronislaw

1948 *Magic, Science and Religion and Other Essays*. Glencoe, IL: The Free Press.

el Mallakh, Kamal and Brackman, Arnold C.

1978 *The Gold of Tutankhamen*. New York: Newsweek Books.

Mallet, Dominique

1909 *Le Kasr el-Agoûz*. MIFAO, vol. 11. Cairo: IFAO.

Mallon, Alexis

1926 *Grammaire Copte avec bibliographie, chrestomathie et vocabulaire*. 3rd ed. Beirut: Imprimerie Catholique.

Maltomini, Franco

1979 "I Papiri greci," in "Nuovi Papiri Magici in Copto, Greco e Aramaico," by Edda Bresciani, S. Pernigotti, F. Maltomini, and P. Marrassini. *SCO* 29: 94–112 (larger article pp. 15–130).

Marcillet-Jaubert, Jean

1979 "Tabella Defixionis Augustodunensis," *ZPE* 33: 185–86.

Mariette, Auguste

1873 *Dendérah. Description générale du grand temple de cette ville*, Volume 4. Paris: A. Franck.

1976 *Les mastabas de l'Ancien Empire*. Hildesheim: Georg Olms (reprint of Paris: F. Vieweg, 1889).

Martin, Geoffrey T.

1979 "A Block from the Memphite Tomb of Ḥoremḥeb in Chicago," *JNES* 38: 33–35.

1985 *The Tomb-Chapels of Paser and R'ia at Saqqâra*. EES Memoir, no. 52, London: EES.

1989 *The Memphite Tomb of Ḥoremḥeb Commander-in-Chief of Tut'ankhamūn*. I. *The Remains, Inscriptions, and Commentary*. EES Memoir, no. 55. London: EES.

Martin, Hubert, Jr.

1986 "*PGM* VII.505–28," in *The Greek Magical Papyri in Translation*, edited by Hans D. Betz. Chicago: University of Chicago Press, pp. 131–32.

Martin, Karl

1984 "Sand," *LÄ* 5: cols. 378–79.

Marwick, Max

1970 *Witchcraft and Sorcery*. Middlesex, England: Penguin Books.

Maspero, Gaston

1902 "Un cercueil de chien et un hypocéphale en terre cuite," *ASAE* 3: 283–85.

Maspero, Gaston; Gauthier, Henri; and Bayoumi, Abbas

1939 *Sarcophages des époques persane et ptolémaïque*. CGC. Cairo: IFAO.

Massart, Adhémar

1957 "The Egyptian Geneva Papyrus MAH 15274," *MDAIK* 15: 172–85.

1959 "A propos des «listes» dans les textes funéraires et magiques," *Analecta Biblica* 12: 227–46.

Mattha, Girgis and Hughes, George R.

1975 *The Demotic Legal Code of Hermopolis West*. BdE, vol. 45. Cairo: IFAO.

Mauss, Marcel

1972 *A General Theory of Magic*, translated by Robert Brain. London: Routledge and Kegan Paul (reprint of Paris: *L'Année sociologique* 1902–03).

McCullough, W. S.

1967 *Jewish and Mandaean Incantation Bowls in the Royal Ontario Museum*. Toronto: University of Toronto Press.

Meeks, Dimitri

1976 "Notes de lexicographie," *RdE* 28: 87–96.

1980 *Année lexicographique*, Volume 1 (1977). Paris: D. Meeks.

Meeks, Dimitri (*cont.*)

1981 *Année lexicographique*, Volume 2 (1978). Paris: D. Meeks.

1982 *Année lexicographique*, Volume 3 (1979). Paris: D. Meeks.

Meier, Gerhard

1937 *Die assyrische Beschwörungssammlung Maqlû. AfO* Beiheft, nr. 2. Berlin: Im Selbstverlage des Herausgebers.

1941–44 "Der zweite Tafel der Serie bīt mēseri," *AfO* 14: 139–52.

1966 "Studien zur Beschwörungssammlung Maqlû," *AfO* 21: 70–81.

Merrifield, Ralph

1987 *The Archaeology of Ritual and Magic*. New York: New Amsterdam Books.

Merton, Robert K. and Nisbet, R. S.

1971 *Contemporary Social Problems*. New York: Harcourt Brace Jovanovich.

Merz, Richard

1978 *Die numinose Mischgestalt*. Religionsgeschichtliche Versuche und Vorarbeiten, vol. 36. Berlin: Walter de Gruyter.

Metzger, Martin

1985 *Königsthron und Gottesthron*. 2 vols. AOAT, vol. 15. Kevelaer: Verlag Butzon & Bercker.

Metzler, D. and Hoffmann, H.

1977 "Zur Theorie und Methode der Erforschung von Rassismus in der Antike," *Kritische Berichte* 5: 5–20.

de Meulenaere, Herman

1964 "Cultes et sacerdoces à Imaou (Kôm el-Hisn) au temps des dynasties Saïte et Perse," *BIFAO* 62: 151–71.

1967 "Horus de Hebenou et son prophète," in *Religions en Égypte hellénistique et romaine, Colloque de Strasbourg 16–18 mai 1967*, edited by Philippe Derchain. Travaux des Centres d'Études supérieures spécialisé d'Histoire des Religiones des Strasbourg. Paris: Presses Universitaires de France, pp. 21–29.

1981 "Le signe hiéroglyphique ," *BIFAO* 81 Supplément (Bulletin du Centenaire): 87–89.

Meyer, Gudrun

1990 "Das Hirtenlied in den Privatgräbern des Alten Reiches," *SAK* 17: 235–84.

Meyer, Marvin W.

1986 "*PGM* IV.475–829," in *The Greek Magical Papyri in Translation*, edited by Hans D. Betz. Chicago: University of Chicago Press, pp. 48–54.

Michaïlides, Georges

1966 "Le dieu Bès sur une stèle magique," *BIE* 42–43: 65–85.

1968 "Éléments de synthèse religieuse gréco-égyptienne," *BIFAO* 66: 49–88.

Mina, Togo

1937 *Le martyre d'Apa Epima*. Cairo: Service des Antiquités de l'Égypte.

Möller, Georg

1909a *Hieratische Paläographie*. Vol. 1. Leipzig: J. C. Hinrichs'sche Buchhandlung.

1909b *Hieratische Paläographie*. Vol. 2. Leipzig: J. C. Hinrichs'sche Buchhandlung.

1912 *Hieratische Paläographie.* Vol. 3. Leipzig: J. C. Hinrichs'sche Buchhandlung.

1913 *Die beiden Totenpapyrus Rhind des Museums zu Edinburg.* Demotische Studien, vol. 6. Leipzig: J. C. Hinrichs'sche Buchhandlung.

1920 "Das Amtsabzeichen des Oberrichters in der Spätzeit," *ZÄS* 56: 67–68.

Momigliano, Arnaldo

1963 *The Conflict Between Paganism and Christianity in the Fourth Century.* Oxford: Clarendon Press.

Mond, Robert and Meyers, Oliver

1934 *The Bucheum.* 3 vols. EES Memoir, no. 41. London: EES.

Montet, Pierre

1928 "Notes et documents pour servir à l'histoire des relations entre l'ancienne Égypte et la Syrie," *Kêmi* 1: 19–28.

1947 *Les constructions et le tombeau d'Osorkon II à Tanis.* La nécropole royale de Tanis, vol. I. Paris: Jourde et Allard.

1961 *Géographie de l'Égypte ancienne.* Part 2: *La Haute Égypte.* Paris: Librairie C. Klincksieck.

Morenz, Siegfried

1958 "Eine Wöchnerin mit Siegelring," *ZÄS* 83: 138–41.

1973 *Egyptian Religion*, translated by Ann Keep. Ithaca: Cornell University Press (original German edition Stuttgart: 1960).

1975 *Religion und Geschichte des alten Ägypten.* Cologne: Verlag Böhlau.

1984 *Gott und Mensch im alten Ägypten.* 2nd ed. Zurich: Artemis Verlag.

Moret, Alexandre

1902 *Le rituel du culte divin journalier en Égypte.* Paris: Ernest Leroux.

1906 "La magie dans l'Égypte ancienne," in *Conférences faites au Musée Guimet, Annales du Musée Guimet, Bibliothèque de vulgarisation*, Volume 20. Paris: Ernest Leroux, pp. 241–81.

1931 "La légende d'Osiris à l'époque thébaine d'après l'hymne à Osiris du Louvre," *BIFAO* 30: 725–50.

1938 "Le rite de briser les vases rouges au temple de Louxor," *RdE* 3: 167.

de Morgan, Jacques

1895 *Kom Ombos*, Volume 1. Catalogue des monuments et inscriptions de l'Égypte antique, Series I, vol. II. Vienna: Adolphe Holzhausen.

1909 *Kom Ombos*, Volume 2. Catalogue des monuments et inscriptions de l'Égypte antique, Series I, vol. III. Vienna: Adolphe Holzhausen.

Müller, Hans W.

1964 *Ägyptische Kunstwerke, Kleinfunde, und Glas in der Sammlung E. und M. Kofler-Truniger, Luzern.* MÄS, vol. 5. Berlin: Verlag Bruno Hessling.

Müller, W. Max

1902 Review of Adolf Erman, *Zaubersprüche für Mutter und Kind. OLZ* 5, no. 8/9: 345–49.

Munro, Peter

1972 "Zu einigen ägyptischen Terrakotta-figuren," *GM* 2: 27–32.

Murnane, William J.
1985 "False-doors and Cult Practices inside Luxor Temple," in *Mélanges Gamal Eddin Mokhtar*, Volume 2, edited by Paule Posener-Kriéger. BdE, vol. 97/2. Cairo: IFAO, pp. 135–48.

Murray, Margaret A.
1935–38 "Ritual Masking," in *Mélanges Maspero*. I: *Orient ancien*, edited by Pierre Jouguet. MIFAO, vol. 66/1. Cairo: IFAO, pp. 251–55.

Myśliwiec, Karol
1972 "À propos des signes hiéroglyphiques 'ḥr' et 'tp'," *ZÄS* 98: 85–99.

Naveh, Joseph and Shaked, Shaul
1985 *Amulets and Magic Bowls. Aramaic Incantations of Late Antiquity*. Jerusalem: Magnes Press.

Naville, Édouard
1883 *Inscription historique de Pinodjem III grand prêtre d'Ammon à Thèbes*. Paris: Maisonneuve et Cie.

1886 *Das aegyptische Todtenbuch der XVIII. bis XX. Dynastie aus verschiedenen Urkunden zusammengestellt und herausgegeben*. 2 vols. Berlin: A. Asher & Co.

1892 *The Festival-Hall of Osorkon II in the Great Temple of Bubastis (1887–1889)*. EEF Memoir, no. 10. London: Kegan Paul, Trench, Trübner & Co.

1896 *The Temple of Deir el Bahari*. Part 2. EEF Memoir, no. 14. London: EEF.

Nebe, Ingrid
1986 "Werethekau," *LÄ* 6: cols. 1221–24.

Nelson, Harold H.
1931 *Medinet Habu Reports*. OIC, vol. 10. Chicago: University of Chicago Press.

1949 "The Rite of 'Bringing the Foot' as Portrayed in Temple Reliefs," *JEA* 35: 82–86.

Neugebauer, Otto and Parker, Richard
1969 *Egyptian Astronomical Texts. III. Decans, Planets, Constellations and Zodiacs*. Brown Egyptological Studies, vol. 6. Providence: Brown University Press.

Newberry, Percy
1899 *The Amherst Papyri*. London: Bernard Quaritch.

Nicholson, Frank W.
1897 "The Saliva Superstition in Classical Literature," *Harvard Studies in Classical Philology* 8: 23–40.

Nims, Charles F.
1948 "The Term *HP* 'Law, Right' in Demotic," *JNES* 7: 243–60.

Nock, Arthur D.
1961 *Conversion*. Oxford: Oxford University Press (reprint of 1933).

Nur el Din, M. A. A.
1974 *The Demotic Ostraca in the National Museum of Antiquities at Leiden*. Collections of the National Museum of Antiquities at Leiden, vol. 1. Leiden: E. J. Brill.

O'Connor, David and Silverman, David
1979 "The University Museum in Egypt. The Past," *Expedition* 21/2: 4–45.

von Oefele, Felix

1904 "Astrologisches in der altägyptischen Medizin," *ZÄS* 41: 117–25.

Ogden, J. M.

1973 "Cylindrical amulet cases," *JEA* 59: 231–33.

1974 "An additional note on 'Cylindrical amulet cases'," *JEA* 60: 258–59.

Ogdon, Jorge R.

1979 *Las manipulaciones mágicas en el antiguo Egipto.* Estudios Egiptológicos, vol. 1. Asunción-Buenos Aires.

1982 "CT VII, 36 *i–r* = Spell 836," *GM* 58: 59–64.

1985 "Studies in Ancient Egyptian Thought, I. The Hand and the Seal," *Discussions in Egyptology* 1: 27–34.

1986 "*Ḏnỉ.t*: Jar of Embalming?" *Discussions in Egyptology* 6: 21–32.

1989 "Discussions in Ancient Egyptian Thought, IV. An Analysis of the 'Technical' Language in the Anti-snake Magical Spells of the Pyramid Texts (PT)," *Discussions in Egyptology* 13: 59–71.

O'Keefe, Daniel

1983 *Stolen Lightning: The Social Theory of Magic.* New York: Vintage Books. (reprint of Continuum Publishing Company, 1982).

O'Leary, De Lacy

1930 "The Arabic Life of S. Pisentius," in *Patrologia Orientalis*, vol. 22, edited by R. Graffin and F. Nau. Paris: Firmin-Didot et Cie, pp. 313–488.

O'Neil, Edward N.

1986 "*PGM* IV.1928–2005," in *The Greek Magical Papyri in Translation*, edited by Hans D. Betz. Chicago: University of Chicago Press, pp. 72–73.

Orlandi, Tito

1980 *Eudoxia and the Holy Sepulchre. A Constantinian Legend in Coptic.* Testi e Documenti per lo Studio dell'antichità, vol. 67. Milan: Cisalpino-Goliardica.

Osing, Jürgen

1976a "Ächtungstexte aus dem Alten Reich (II)," *MDAIK* 32: 133–85.

1976b *Die Nominalbildung des Ägyptischen.* 2 vols. Mainz am Rhein: Philipp von Zabern.

Otto, Eberhard

1960 *Das ägyptische Mundöffnungsritual.* 2 vols. ÄgAb, vol. 3. Wiesbaden: Otto Harrassowitz.

1971 "Gott als Retter in Ägypten," in *Tradition und Glaube. Das frühe Christentum in seiner Umwelt*, edited by Gert Jeremias, H.-J. Kuhn, and H. Stegemann. Göttingen: Verlag Vandenhoeck & Ruprecht, pp. 9–22.

1975 "Cheriheb," *LÄ* 1: cols. 940–43.

Parássoglou, George M.

1976 "Circular from a Prefect: Sileat Omnibus Perpetuo Divinandi Curiositas," in *Collectanea Papyrologica* (Texts Published in Honor of A. C. Youtie), edited by Ann Ellis Hanson. Bonn: Rudolf Habelt Verlag, pp. 261–74.

Parker, Richard A.

1959 *A Vienna Demotic Papyrus on Eclipse- and Lunar-Omina*. Brown Egyptological Studies, vol. 2. Providence: Brown University Press.

Parker, Richard; Leclant, Jean; and Goyon, Jean-Claude

1979 *The Edifice of Taharqa*. Brown Egyptological Studies, vol. 8. Providence: Brown University Press.

Pax, W.

1957 "Circumambulatio," in *Reallexikon für Antike und Christentum*, Volume 3, edited by T. Klauser. Stuttgart: Anton Hiersemann, pp. 143–52.

Peet, Thomas Eric

1930 *The Great Tomb-Robberies of the Twentieth Egyptian Dynasty*. Oxford: Clarendon Press.

Pellegrini, Astorre

1907 "Piccoli testi copto-sâîdici del Museo archeologico di Firenze," *Sphinx* 10: 141–59.

Pestman, P. W.

1982 "Who were the Owners, in the 'Community of Workmen', of the Chester Beatty Papyri," in *Gleanings from Deir el-Medîna*, edited by R. J. Demarée and Jac. J. Janssen. Egyptologische Uitgaven, vol. 1. Leiden: Nederlands Instituut voor het Nabije Oosten, pp. 155–72.

Petrie, Sir W. M. Flinders

1898 *Deshasheh*. EEF Memoir, no. 15. London: EEF.

1902 *Abydos. Part I, 1902*. EEF Memoir, no. 22. London: EEF.

1906 *Researches in Sinai*. New York: E. P. Dutton and Co.

1972 *Amulets*. Warminster: Aris & Phillips Ltd. (reprint of London: Constable & Company Ltd., 1914).

1974 *Objects of Daily Use*. Warminster: Aris & Philips Ltd. (reprint of London: British School of Archaeology in Egypt, 1927).

Petrie, Sir W. M. Flinders; Griffith, F. Ll.; and Murray, A. S.

1888 *Tanis. Part II. Nebesheh (AM) and Defenneh (Tahpanhes)*. EEF Memoir, no. 4. London: Trübner.

Petrie, Sir W. M. Flinders; Sayce, A. H.; Griffith, F. Ll.; and Spurrell, F. C. J.

1974 *Tell el Amarna*. Warminster: Aris & Phillips Ltd. (reprint of London: Methuen & Co., 1894).

Philips, Alan K.

1986 "Observation on the Alleged New Kingdom Sanatorium at Deir el-Bahari," *GM* 89: 77–83.

Piankoff, Alexandre

1935–38 "Une statuette du dieu Ḥeka," in *Mélanges Maspero*. I: *Orient ancien*, edited by Pierre Jouguet. MIFAO, vol. 66/1. Cairo: IFAO, pp. 349–52.

1942a "Le livre des Quererts. 1er tableau," *BIFAO* 41: 1–11.

1942b *Le livre du jour et de la nuit*. BdE, vol. 13. Cairo: IFAO.

1944 "Le livre des Quererts. Seconde division," *BIFAO* 42: 1–14.

1958–60 "The Osireion of Seti I at Abydos during the Greco-Roman Period and the Christian Occupation," *BSAC* 15: 125–49.

1964 *The Litany of Re*. New York: Bollingen Press.

1969 *The Pyramid of Unas*. New York: Bollingen Press (reprint of 1968).

Piankoff, Alexandre and Rambova, N.

1954 *The Tomb of Ramses VI*. New York: Bollingen Press.

1955 *The Shrines of Tut-Ankh-Amon*. New York: Bollingen Press.

1957 *Mythological Papyri*. New York: Bollingen Press.

Piantelli, Mario

1987 "Note sulla storia di Iside e Ra," in *La Magia in Egitto ai Tempi dei Faraoni*, edited by A. Roccati and A. Siliotti. Milan: Rassegna Internazionale di Cinematografia Archeologica Arte e Natura Libri, pp. 285–99.

Pleyte, Willem

1868 *Le Papyrus Rollin*. Leiden: E. J. Brill.

Pleyte, Willem and Rossi, Francesco

1869–76 *Papyrus de Turin*. 2 vols. Leiden: E. J. Brill.

Pliny

1975 *Natural History*, Volume 8, edited and translated by W. H. S. Jones (Loeb Library). Cambridge, MA: Harvard University Press (reprint of 1963).

Pocock, David

1972 "Foreword," in *A General Theory of Magic*, by Marcel Mauss, translated by Robert Brain. London: Routledge and Kegan Paul (reprint of Paris: *L'Année sociologique* 1902–03), pp. 1–6

Polotsky, Hans J.

1971 "An Egyptian Epithet for a Learned Scribe," in *Collected Papers* by Hans J. Polotsky. Jerusalem: Hebrew University, p. 319 [Hebrew; English summary in *AEB* 1948, no. 605].

Porten, Bezalel

1986 *Select Aramaic Papyri from Ancient Egypt*. Institute for the Study of Aramaic Papyri. n.p.: Bezalel Porten.

Porter, Bertha and Moss, Rosalind

1939 *Topographical Bibliography of Ancient Egyptian Hieroglyphic Texts, Reliefs, and Paintings*. Vol. 6: *Upper Egypt: Chief Temples*. Oxford: Clarendon Press.

1972 *Topographical Bibliography of Ancient Egyptian Hieroglyphic Texts, Reliefs, and Paintings*. Vol. 2: *Theban Temples*. 2nd rev. ed. Oxford: Clarendon Press.

Posener, Georges

1939a "Nouveaux textes hiératiques de proscription," in *Mélanges syriens offerts à Monsieur René Dussaud, Tome 1*. Bibliothèque Archéologique et Historique, tome 30. Paris: Libraire Orientaliste Paul Geuthner, pp. 313–17.

1939b "Nouvelles listes de proscription (Ächtungstexte) datant du Moyen Empire," *CdE* 14, no. 27: 39–46.

1940 *Princes et pays d'Asie et de Nubie*. Brussels: Fondation Égyptologique Reine Élisabeth.

1946 "Les criminels débaptisés et les morts sans noms," *RdE* 5: 51–56.

1949 "Les signes noirs dans les rubriques," *JEA* 35: 77–81.

1956 *Littérature et politique dans l'Égypte de la XIIe dynastie*. Paris: Librairie Ancienne Honoré Champion.

1958 "Les empreintes magiques de Gizeh et les morts dangereux," *MDAIK* 16: 252–70.

Posener, Georges (*cont.*)

1963a "Aménémopé 21, 13 et *bjꜣj.t* au sens d'«oracle»," *ZÄS* 90: 98–102.

1963b "Sur la valeur phonétique *ꜣṯ* > *ꜣt* du signe 𓄫," *RdE* 15: 127–28.

1966 "Les textes d'envoûtement de Mirgissa," *Syria* 43: 277–87.

1969 "Sur l'emploi euphémique de *ḫftj(w)* «ennemi(s)»," *ZÄS* 96: 30–35.

1971 "À la recherche de nouveaux textes d'envoûtement," in *Papers in Jewish Demography 1969: Proceedings of the Fifth World Congress of Jewish Studies*, edited by U. O. Schmelz, P. Glikson, and S. Della Pergola. Jerusalem: The World Union of Jewish Studies, pp. 144–49.

1974 "Philologie et archéologie égyptiennes," *Annuaire du Collège de France* 74: 397–404.

1975a "Ächtungstexte," *LÄ* 1: cols. 67–69.

1975b "Philologie et archéologie égyptiennes," *Annuaire du Collège de France* 75: 405–11.

1976a "Philologie et archéologie égyptiennes," *Annuaire du Collège de France* 76: 435–42.

1976b "Notes de transcription," *RdE* 28: 146–48.

1977 "Philologie et archéologie égyptiennes," *Annuaire du Collège de France* 77: 503–11.

1980 *Catalogue des ostraka hiératiques littéraires de Deir el Médineh*. DFIFAO, vol. 20/3. Cairo: IFAO.

1984 "Une nouvelle statuette d'envoûtement," in *Studien zu Sprache und Religion Ägyptens. Zu Ehren von Wolfhart Westendorf überreicht von seinen Freunden und Schülern, Band 1: Sprache*, edited by F. Junge. Göttingen: F. Junge, pp. 613–19.

1985 *Le Papyrus Vandier*. Bibliothèque Genérale, vol. 7. Cairo: IFAO.

1987 *Cinq figurines d'envoûtement*. BdE, vol. 101. Cairo: IFAO.

Posener-Kriéger, Paule

1968 "Remarques sur l'ensemble funéraire de Neferirkareʾ Kakai à Abu Sir," in *Festschrift für Siegfried Schott zu seinem 70. Geburtstag*, edited by W. Helck. Wiesbaden: Otto Harrassowitz, pp. 112–20.

1982 "Les travaux de l'Institut Français d'Archéologie Orientale en 1981–1982," *BIFAO* 82: 379–96.

Poupon, Gérard

1981 "L'accusation de magie dans les Actes apocryphes," in *Les Actes apocryphes des apôtres: Christianisme et monde païen*, edited by François Bovon, Michel van Esbroeck, Richard Goulet, Eric Junod, Jean-Daniel Kaestli, Françoise Morard, Gérard Poupon, Jean-Marc Prieur, and Yves Tissot. Publications de la Faculté de théologie de l'Université de Genève, nr. 4. Geneva: Labor et Fides, pp. 71–93.

Praetorius, Franz

1911 "Bemerkungen zu Takla Ḥawāryāt," *ZDMG* 65: 781–93.

Preisendanz, Karl

1913 "Sexuelles auf griechischen Zauberpapyri," *Sexual-Probleme* 9: 614–19.

1928 *Papyri Graecae Magicae*, Volume 1. Leipzig: B. G. Teubner. (reprinted Stuttgart: B. G. Teubner, 1973).

1931 *Papyri Graecae Magicae*, Volume 2. Leipzig: B. G. Teubner. (reprinted Stuttgart: B. G. Teubner, 1974).

Pritchard, James B.

1954 *The Ancient Near East in Pictures*. Princeton: Princeton University Press.

1969 *Ancient Near Eastern Texts Relating to the Old Testament*. 3rd ed. Princeton: Princeton University Press.

Quack, Joachim F.

1989 "Sur l'emploi euphémique de *ḫft* «ennemi» en démotique," *RdE* 40: 197–98.

Quaegebeur, Jan

1984 "Divinités égyptiennes sur des animaux dangereux," in *L'animal, l'homme, le dieu dans le Proche-Orient ancien* (Actes du Colloque de Cartigny 1981), edited by Philippe Borgeaud, Yves Christe, and Ivanka Urio. Les Cahiers du Centre d'Étude du Proche-Orient Ancien, vol. 2. Louvain: Éditions Peeters, pp. 131–43.

1985 "On the Egyptian Equivalent of Biblical *Ḥarṭummîm*," in *Pharaonic Egypt, the Bible and Christianity*, edited by Sarah Israelit-Groll. Jerusalem: Hebrew University, pp. 162–72.

1987 "'Horo sui coccodrilli'. Elementi per una interpretazione nuova," in *La Magia in Egitto ai Tempi dei Faraoni*, edited by A. Roccati and A. Siliotti. Milan: Rassegna Internazionale di Cinematografia Archeologica Arte e Natura Libri, p. 187.

Quibell, J. E.

1898 *The Ramesseum*. Egyptian Research Account, vol. 2. London: Bernard Quaritch.

1900 *Hierakonpolis. Part I*. Egyptian Research Account, vol. 4. London: Bernard Quaritch.

1902 "Rapport," *ASAE* 3: 254–58.

1908 *Excavations at Saqqara (1906–1907)*. Cairo: IFAO.

Radwan, Ali

1969 *Die Darstellungen des regierenden Königs und seiner Familienangehörigen in den Privatgräbern der 18. Dynastie*. MÄS, vol. 21. Berlin: Verlag Bruno Hessling.

Randall-MacIver, D.; Mace, A. C.; and Griffith, F. Ll.

1902 *El Amrah and Abydos*. EEF Memoir, no. 23. London: EES.

Ranke, Hermann

1935 *Die ägyptischen Personennamen*, Volume 1. Glückstadt: J. J. Augustin.

Raven, Maarten J.

1978–79 "Papyrus-Sheaths and Ptah-Sokar-Osiris Statues," *OMRO* 59–60: 251–96.

1982 "Corn-Mummies," *OMRO* 63: 7–38.

1983 "Wax in Egyptian Magic and Symbolism," *OMRO* 64: 7–47.

Ray, John

1972 "Two Inscribed Objects in the Fitzwilliam Museum, Cambridge," *JEA* 58: 247–53.

1976 *The Archive of Ḥor*. London: EES.

Reich, Nathaniel J.

1910 "Ein demotischer Kaufpfandvertrag," *Sphinx* 13: 238–62.

1914 *Papyri juristischen Inhalts in hieratischer und demotischer Schrift aus dem British Museum*. Vienna: Alfred Hölder.

Rea, John

1977 "A New Version of P. Yale Inv. 299," *ZPE* 27: 151–56.

Redford, Donald B.

1975 "Studies on Akhenaten at Thebes, II: A Report on the Work of the Akhenaten Temple Project of the University Museum, The University of Pennsylvania, for the Year 1973–4," *JARCE* 12: 9–14.

Reinisch, Leo

1873 *Aegyptische Chrestomathie*. Vienna: Wilhelm Braumüller.

Reisner, George

1905 *The Hearst Medical Papyrus*. University of California Publications, Egyptian Archaeology, vol. I. Leipzig: J. C. Hinrichs'sche Buchhandlung.

1913 "New Acquisitions of the Egyptian Department," *MFA Bulletin* 11, no. 66: 53–66.

Rémondon, Roger

1953 "Un papyrus magique Copte," *BIFAO* 52: 157–61.

Revillout, Eugène

1888 *Corpus Papyrorum Aegypti*, Volume 2. Papyrus démotiques du British Museum. Paris: Ernest Leroux.

Reymond, Eve A. E.

1969 *The Mythical Origin of the Egyptian Temple*. Manchester: Manchester University Press.

1973 *Catalogue of Demotic Papyri in the Ashmolean Museum I. Embalmers' Archive from Hawara*. Oxford: University Press.

1977 *From the Contents of the Libraries of the Suchos Temples in the Fayyum II. From Ancient Egyptian Hermetic Writings*. MPER, vol. 11. Vienna: Brüder Hollinek.

1983 "From the contents of a temple library," in *Das Römisch-byzantinische Ägypten. Akten des internationalen Symposiums 26.–30. September 1978 in Trier*, edited by Günter Grimm, Heinz Heinen, and Erich Winter. Aegyptiaca Treverensia, vol. 2. Mainz am Rhein: Philipp Von Zabern, pp. 81–83.

Reymond, Eve A. E. and Barns, J. W. B.

1973 *Four Martyrdoms from the Pierpont Morgan Coptic Codices*. London: Oxford University Press.

Ridley, R. T.

1973 *The Unification of Egypt*. Deception Bay, Australia: Shield Press.

Riefstahl, Elizabeth

1968 *Ancient Egyptian Glass and Glazes in the Brooklyn Museum*. Brooklyn: Brooklyn Museum.

Ritner, Robert K.

1984a "A Property Transfer from the Erbstreit Archives," in *Grammata Demotika. Festschrift für Erich Lüddeckens zum 15. Juni 1983*, edited by Heinz-Josef Thissen and Karl-Theodor Zauzich. Würzburg: Gisela Zauzich Verlag, pp. 171–87.

1984b "A Uterine Amulet in the Oriental Institute Collection," *JNES* 43: 209–21.

1986a "Gleanings from Magical Texts," *Enchoria* 14: 95–106.

1986b "Unrecognized Decorated Linch Pins from the Tombs of Tutankhamon and Amenhotep II," *GM* 94: 53–56.

1987 Review of Heinz Thissen, *Die Lehre des Anchscheschonqi (P. BM 10508)*. *BiOr* 44: cols. 641–46.

1989a "So-called 'Pre-dynastic Hamster-headed' Figurines in London and Hanover," *GM* 111: 85–95.

1989b "Horus on the Crocodiles: A Juncture of Religion and Magic in Late Dynastic Egypt," in *Religion and Philosophy in Ancient Egypt*, edited by W. K. Simpson. Yale Egyptological Studies, vol. 3. New Haven: Yale University Press, pp. 103–16.

1989c Review of Emma Brunner-Traut, "Der menschliche Körper-eine Gliederpuppe," (*ZÄS* 115 [1988]: 8–14). *SAMPh* 17: 42.

1990 "O. Gardiner 363: A Spell Against Night Terrors," *JARCE* 27: 25–41.

1991 Review of M. Heerma van Voss et al., eds., *Studies in Egyptian Religion: Dedicated to Professor Jan Zandee*. *JNES* 50, no. 3: 209–13.

1995 "Egyptian Magical Practice under the Roman Empire: the Demotic Spells and their Religious Context," in *Aufstieg und Niedergang der römischen Welt*, Part II, Volume 18.5. Berlin: Walter De Gruyter, pp. 3333–79.

Ritter, Edith K.

1965 "Magical-Expert (*Āšipu*) and Physician (= *Asû*): Notes on Two Complementary Professions in Babylonian Medicine," in *Studies in Honor of Benno Landsberger on His Seventy-Fifth Birthday, April 21, 1965*, edited by H. Güterbock and Th. Jacobsen. AS, vol. 16. Chicago: University of Chicago Press, pp. 299–321.

Roccati, Alessandro

1970 *Papiro Ieratico n. 54003. Estratti magici e rituali del Primo Medio Regno*. Turin: Edizioni d'Arte Fratelli Pozzo.

1973 "I. Le Iscrizioni della Scala," in "Relazione Preliminare sulla II Campagna di Scavo nella Tomba di Šešonq all'Asasif (1971)," by S. Donadoni, A. Roccati, and S. Bosticco. *Oriens Antiquus* 12: 23–37 (larger article pp. 19–67).

Rochemonteix, Le Marquis de; Chassinat, E.; Cauville, Sylvie; and Devauchelle, Didier

1984–87 *Le temple d'Edfou*, Volume I. MMAF, vol. 10. Cairo: IFAO (revised edition of Paris: Ernest Leroux, 1892).

Roeder, Günther

1928 Review of François Lexa, *La magie dans L'Égypte antique*. *Gnomon* 4, no. 4: 196–201.

Roquet, Gérard

1980 "Niveaux de représentation du code graphique égyptien: phonétique et phonologique," in *Livre du Centenaire 1880–1980*, edited by Jean Vercoutter. MIFAO, vol. 104. Cairo: IFAO, pp. 73–90.

1984 "La réécriture: facteur critique de l'étymologie," in *Studien zu Sprache und Religion Ägyptens. Zu Ehren von Wolfhart Westendorf überreicht von seinen Freunden und Schülern, Band 1: Sprache*, edited by F. Junge. Göttingen: F. Junge, pp. 355–85.

Rossi, Francesco

1887 *I papyri copti del Museo egizio di Torino*, Volume 1. Turin: E. Loescher (reprint of Reale accademia delle scienze di Torino. Memorie. Series 2, vol. 35, 1884).

1893 "Un nuovo codice copto del Museo Egizio di Torino contenente la vita di S. Epifanio ed i martiri di S. Pantoleone, di Ascla, di Apollonio, di Filemone, di Ariano e di Dios con versetti di vari capitoli del «Libro di Giobbe»," in *Atti della Reale Accademia dei Lincei*. Reale Accademia dei Lincei, Anno CCXC, 1893, Serie Quinta, Classe di Scienze Morali, Storiche e Filologiche, Volume I, Partie 1ª: Memorie. Rome: Reale Accademia dei Lincei, pp. 3–136.

Roth, Ann Macy

1991 *Egyptian Phyles in the Old Kingdom: The Evolution of a System of Social Organization*. SAOC, vol. 48. Chicago: The Oriental Institute.

Rowe, Alan

1938 "New Light on Objects Belonging to the Generals Potasimto and Amasis in the Egyptian Museum," *ASAE* 38: 157–95.

1939 "Three New Stelae from the South-Eastern Desert," *ASAE* 39: 187–94.

Rühlmann, Gerhard

1964 "Der Löwe im altägytpsichen Triumphalbild," *Wissenschaftliche Zeitschrift der Martin-Luther Universität Halle-Wittenberg* 13: 651–58.

1971 "Deine Feinde fallen unter deine Sohlen," *Wissenschaftliche Zeitschrift der Martin-Luther Universität Halle-Wittenberg* 20: 61–84.

Rüterswörden, Udo

1976 "Vernichtungssymbolik in Ugarit," *GM* 19: 51–55.

Saʿad, Ramadan

1970 "Les travaux d'Aménophis IV au IIIe pylône du temple d'Amon Reʿ à Karnak," *Kemi* 20: 187–93.

Sadek, M.

1971 Review of Serge Sauneron, *Le papyrus magique illustré de Brooklyn*. *Bulletin of the American Society of Papyrologists* 8, no. 4: 113–14.

Säve-Söderbergh, Torgny

1941 *Ägypten und Nubien. Ein Beitrag zur Geschichte altägyptischer Aussenpolitik*. Lund: Håkan Ohlssons Boktryckeri.

Samson, Julia

1978 *Amarna. City of Akhenaten and Nefertiti*. Warminster: Aris & Phillips Ltd. (reprint of 1972).

Sander-Hansen, C. E.

1937 *Die religiösen Texte auf dem Sarg der Anchnesneferibre*. Copenhagen: Einar Munksgaard.

1956 *Die Texte der Metternichstele*. AnAe, vol. 7. Copenhagen: Einar Munksgaard.

Satzinger, Helmut

1987 "Acqua guaritrice: le statue e stele magiche ed il loro uso magico-medico nell'Egitto faraonico," in *La Magia in Egitto ai Tempi dei Faraoni*, edited by A. Roccati and A. Siliotti. Milan: Rassegna Internazionale di Cinematografia Archeologica Arte e Natura Libri, pp. 189–204.

Sauneron, Serge

1951 "Aspects et sort d'un thème magique égyptien: les menaces incluant les dieux," *BSFE* 8: 11–21.

1959 *Quatre campagnes à Esna*. Esna, vol. 1. Cairo: IFAO.

1960 "Le nouveau sphinx composite du Brooklyn Museum et le rôle du dieu Toutou-Tithoès," *JNES* 19: 269–87.

1961 "La légende des sept propos de Méthyer au temple d'Esna," *BSFE* 32: 43–48.

1962a "Les conditions d'accès à la fonction sacerdotale à l'époque gréco-romaine," *BIFAO* 61: 55–57.

1962b *Les fêtes religieuses d'Esna aux derniers siècles du paganisme*. Esna, vol. 5. Cairo: IFAO.

1966 "Le monde du magicien égyptien," in *Le monde du sorcier: Égypte, Babylone, Hittites, Israël, Islam, Asie Centrale, Inde, Nepal, Cambodge, Viet-Nam, Japon*, edited by Denise Bernot, Anne-Marie Esnoul, Paul Garelli, Yves Hervouet, Marcel Leibovici, Jean-Paul Roux, Serge Sauneron, and Jean Yoyotte. Sources Orientales, vol. 7. Paris: Éditions du Seuil, pp. 27–65.

1968 *Le temple d'Esna III*. Esna, vol. 3. Cairo: IFAO.

1970a *Le papyrus magique illustré de Brooklyn*. Brooklyn: Brooklyn Museum.

1970b "Le rhume d'Anynakhté (Pap. Deir el-Médinéh 36)," *Kemi* 20: 7–18.

1975 *Le temple d'Esna VI*. Esna, vol. 6. Cairo: IFAO.

1982 *L'Écriture figurative dans les textes d'Esna*. Esna, vol. 8. Cairo: IFAO.

1989 *Un traité égyptien d'ophiologie*. Bibliothèque Générale, vol. 11. Cairo: IFAO.

Sauneron, Serge and Yoyotte, Jean

1952 "Le texte hiératique Rifaud," *BIFAO* 50: 107–17.

Schäfer, Heinrich

1905 *Urkunden der älteren Äthiopenkönige*. Urk. 3. Leipzig: J. C. Hinrichs'sche Buchhandlung.

Scheurleer, R. A. Lunsingh

1984 *Egypte Eender en Anders*. Amsterdam: Allard Pierson Museum.

Schoske, Sylvia

1986 "Vernichtungsrituale," *LÄ* 6: cols. 1009–12.

Schoske, Sylvia and Wildung, Dietrich

1985 *Entdeckungen, Ägyptische Kunst in Süddeutschland*. Mainz am Rhein: Philipp von Zabern.

Schott, Siegfried

1928 "Die Zeremonie des 'Zerbrechens der roten Töpfe,'" *ZÄS* 63: 101.

1929 *Urkunden mythologischen Inhalts. Bücher und Sprüche gegen den Gott Seth*. Urk. 6. Leipzig: J. C. Hinrichs'sche Buchhandlung.

1930a Note 2, p. 107, in R. Eilmann, A. Langsdorff, and H. E. Stier, "Bericht über die Voruntersuchungen auf den Kurûm el-Ṭuwâl bei Amrîje," *MDAIK* 1: 106–29.

1930b "Die Bitte um ein Kind auf einer Grabfigur des frühen Mittleren Reiches," *JEA* 16: 23.

1930c "Drei Sprüche gegen Feinde," *ZÄS* 65: 35–42.

1955 "Ein ungewöhnliches Symbol des Triumphes über Feinde Ägyptens," *JNES* 14: 96–99.

1956 "Totenbuchspruch 175 in einem Ritual zur Vernichtung von Feinden," *MDAIK* 14: 181–89.

Schulman, Alan R.

1988 *Ceremonial Execution and Public Rewards*. OBO, vol. 75. Göttingen: Vandenhoeck & Ruprecht.

Schweitzer, Ursula

1956 *Das Wesen des Ka*. ÄF, vol. 19. Glückstadt: J. J. Augustin.

Segal, Alan F.

1981 "Hellenistic Magic: Some Questions of Definition," in *Studies in Gnosticism and Hellenistic Religions Presented to Gilles Quispel on the Occasion of his 65th Birthday*, edited by R. van den Broek and M. J. Vermaseren. EPRO, vol. 91. Leiden: E. J. Brill, pp. 349–75.

van Seters, John

1964 "A Date for the 'Admonitions' in the Second Intermediate Period," *JEA* 50: 13–23.

van Seters, John (*cont.*)

1966 *The Hyksos. A New Investigation.* New Haven: Yale University.

Sethe, Kurt

1904 *Hieroglyphische Urkunden der Griechisch-Römischen Zeit.* Urk. 2. Leipzig: J. C. Hinrichs'sche Buchhandlung.

1907 *Urkunden der 18. Dynastie*, Part 1. Urk. 4, part 11. Leipzig: J. C. Hinrichs'sche Buchhandlung.

1908 *Die altaegyptischen Pyramidentexte*, Volume 1. Leipzig: J. C. Hinrichs'sche Buchhandlung.

1910 *Die altaegyptischen Pyramidentexte*, Volume 2. Leipzig: J. C. Hinrichs'sche Buchhandlung.

1916 *Von Zahlen und Zahlworten bei den alten Ägyptern.* Strassburg: Karl J. Trübner.

1926 *Die Ächtung feindlicher Fürsten, Völker und Dinge auf altägyptischen Tongefässscherben des Mittleren Reiches.* Berlin: Akademie der Wissenschaften.

1927 *Urkunden der 18. Dynastie*, Part 1. Rev. ed. Urk. 4, part 1 [1906]. Leipzig: J. C. Hinrichs'sche Buchhandlung.

1928a *Dramatische Texte zu altaegyptischen Mysterienspielen.* UGAÄ, vol. 10. Leipzig: J. C. Hinrichs'sche Buchhandlung.

1928b "Zu der Zeremonie des Zerbrechens der roten Töpfe," *ZÄS* 63: 101–02.

1930a *Urkunden der 18. Dynastie*, Part 2. Rev. ed. Urk. 4, part 2 [1906]. Leipzig: J. C. Hinrichs'sche Buchhandlung.

1930b *Urkunden der l8. Dynastie*, Part 3. Rev. ed. Urk. 4, part 3 [1906]. Leipzig: J. C. Hinrichs'sche Buchhandlung.

1930c *Urkunden der l8. Dynastie*, Part 4. Rev. ed. Urk. 4, part 4 [1906]. Leipzig: J. C. Hinrichs'sche Buchhandlung.

1933 *Urkunden des Alten Reiches.* 2nd ed. Urk. 1. Leipzig: J. C. Hinrichs'sche Buchhandlung.

1934 "Miszelle," *ZÄS* 70: 134.

1935a *Übersetzung und Kommentar zu den altägyptischen Pyramidentexten*, Volume 1. Hamburg: J. J. Augustin.

1935b *Übersetzung und Kommentar zu den altägyptischen Pyramidentexten*, Volume 2. Hamburg: J. J. Augustin.

1935c *Übersetzung und Kommentar zu den altägyptischen Pyramidentexten*, Volume 3. Hamburg: J. J. Augustin.

1935d *Übersetzung und Kommentar zu den altägyptischen Pyramidentexten*, Volume 4. Hamburg: J. J. Augustin.

1962a *Übersetzung und Kommentar zu den altägyptischen Pyramidentexten*, Volume 5. Hamburg: J. J. Augustin.

1962b *Übersetzung und Kommentar zu den altägyptischen Pyramidentexten*, Volume 6. Hamburg: J. J. Augustin.

1983 *Ägyptische Lesestücke.* Hildesheim: Georg Olms. (reprint of Leipzig: 1928).

Sethe, Kurt and Partsch, Josef

1920 *Demotische Urkunden zum ägyptischen Bürgschaftsrechte vorzüglich der Ptolemäerzeit.* Leipzig: B. G. Teubner.

Sheridan, Richard Brinsley
1981 *The Rivals*, edited by C. J. L. Price. Oxford: Oxford University Press.

Shinnie, Peter L. and Bradley, R. J.
1981 "The Murals from the Augustus Temple, Meroe," in *Studies in Ancient Egypt, the Aegean, and the Sudan*, (Essays in honor of Dows Dunham), edited by William K. Simpson and W. M. Davis. Boston: Museum of Fine Arts, pp. 167–72.

Shorter, Alan W.
1935 "Notes on Some Funerary Amulets," *JEA* 21: 171–76.
1936 "A Magical Ostracon," *JEA* 22: 165–68.
1937 "The Papyrus of Khnememḥab in University College, London," *JEA* 23: 34–38.
1938 *Catalogue of Egyptian Religious Papyri in the British Museum*. London: British Museum.

Simpson, William Kelly
1963 *Papyrus Reisner I*. Boston: Museum of Fine Arts.
1969 *Papyrus Reisner III*. Boston: Museum of Fine Arts.
1970 "A Late Old Kingdom Letter to the Dead from Nag' Ed-Deir N 3500," *JEA* 56: 58–64.
1972a "Acquisitions in Egyptian and Ancient Near Eastern Art in the Boston Museum of Fine Arts. 1970–1971," *The Connoisseur* 179 no. 720: 113–22.
1972b "A Relief of the Royal Cup-Bearer Tja-wy," *Boston Museum Bulletin* 70, no. 360: 68–82.
1973 "Ptolemaic-Roman Cartonnage Footcases with Prisoners Bound and Tied," *ZÄS* 100/1: 50–54.
1974 *The Terrace of the Great God at Abydos: The Offering Chapels of Dynasties 12 and 13*. Pennsylvania-Yale Expedition, vol. 5. New Haven: Peabody Museum and Philadelphia: University Museum.

Simpson, William K.; Faulkner, Raymond O.; and Wente, Edward F.
1973 *The Literature of Ancient Egypt. An Anthology of Stories, Instructions, and Poetry*. New ed. New Haven: Yale University Press.

Śliwa, Joachim
1973 "The God Nkiw-mnt," *ZDMG* 123: 6–8.

Smith, Jonathan Z.
1978 *Map is Not Territory*. Leiden: E. J. Brill.
"Birth Upside Down or Right Side Up?," pp. 147–71.
"The Temple and the Magician," pp. 172–89.
"Good News is No News: Aretalogy and Gospel," pp. 190–207.

Smith, Mark
1977 "A New Version of a well-known Egyptian Hymn," *Enchoria* 7: 115–49.
1979 *The Demotic Mortuary Papyrus Louvre E. 3452*. Unpublished Ph.D. dissertation, Department of Near Eastern Languages and Civilizations, The University of Chicago.
1987 *The Mortuary Texts of Papyrus BM 10507*. Catalogue of Demotic Papyri in the British Museum, vol. 3. London: British Museum.

Smith, Morton
1973 *Clement of Alexandria and a Secret Gospel of Mark*. Cambridge, MA: Harvard University Press.
1978 *Jesus the Magician*. San Francisco: Harper and Row.

Smith, Morton (*cont.*)

1983 "On the Lack of a History of Greco-Roman Magic," in *Althistorische Studien*, (Hermann Bengston Festschrift), edited by Heinz Heinen. Historia Einzelschriften, vol. 40. Wiesbaden: Franz Steiner Verlag, pp. 251–57.

1984 "*The Eighth Book of Moses* and How it Grew (P LEID. J 395)," in *Atti del XVII Congresso Internazionale di Papirologia (Napoli, 19–26 maggio 1983)*, Volume 2. Naples: Centro Internazionale per lo Studio dei Papiri Ercolanesi, pp. 683–93.

1986 "*PGM* XIII.1–734," in *The Greek Magical Papyri in Translation*, edited by Hans D. Betz. Chicago: University of Chicago Press, pp. 172–89.

Smith, William Stevenson

1967 "Two Archaic Egyptian Sculptures," *Boston Museum Bulletin* 65, no. 340: 70–84.

Smither, Paul C.

1939 "A Coptic Love-Charm," *JEA* 25: 173–74.

1941 "A Ramesside Love Charm," *JEA* 27: 131–32.

1942 "An Old Kingdom Letter Concerning the Crimes of Count Sabni," *JEA* 28: 16–19.

Sørensen, Jørgen

1984 "The Argument in Ancient Egyptian Magical Formulae," *AcOr* 45: 5–19.

Sourdive, Claude

1984 *La main dans l'Égypte pharaonique*. Berne: Peter Lange.

Spalinger, Anthony J.

1988 "A Hymn of Praise to Akhenaten," in *The Akhenaten Temple Project*. Vol. 2: *Rwd-mnw, Foreigners and Inscriptions*, edited by Donald Redford. Aegypti Texta Propositaque, vol. I. Toronto: Akhenaton Temple Project, pp. 29–33.

Speleers, Louis

1935 *Traduction, index, et vocabulaire des textes des pyramides égyptiennes*. Brussels: Imprimerie Sainte Catherine.

1947 *Textes des cercueils du Moyen Empire égyptien*. Brussels: 159 Avenue Marie-José.

Spencer, A. Jeffrey

1979 "The Brick Foundations of Late-Period Peripteral Temples and their Mythical Origin," in *Glimpses of Ancient Egypt: Studies in Honour of H. W. Fairman*, edited by John Ruffle, G. A. Gaballa, and Kenneth A. Kitchen. Warminster: Aris & Philipps Ltd., pp. 132–37.

Spiegelberg, Wilhelm

1901 "Der Name des Tentyritischen Gaues," *RdT* 23: 101–02.

1902 *Demotische Papyrus aus den königlichen Museen zu Berlin*. Leipzig: Giesecke & Devrient.

1906 *Die Demotischen Denkmäler II. Die Demotischen Papyrus. Tafeln*. CGC. Strassburg: Elsässische Druckeri.

1910 *Der Sagenkreis des Königs Petubastis*. Demotische Studien, vol. 3. Leipzig: J. C. Hinrichs'sche Buchhandlung.

1912 *Demotische Texte auf Krügen*. Demotische Studien, vol. 5. Leipzig: J. C. Hinrichs'sche Buchhandlung.

1914 *Die sogenannte Demotische Chronik des Pap. 215 der Bibliothèque Nationale zu Paris.* Demotische Studien, vol. 7. Leipzig: J. C. Hinrichs'sche Buchhandlung.

1917a *Der ägyptische Mythus vom Sonnenauge (der Papyrus der Tierfabeln—"Kufi") nach dem Leidener demotischen Papyrus I 384.* Strassburg: Strassburger Drukerei.

1917b "Der demotische Papyrus Heidelberg 736," *ZÄS* 53: 30–34.

1920a "Ein Bruchstück des Bestattungsrituals der Apisstiere (Demot. Pap. Wien Nr. 27.)," *ZÄS* 56: 1–33.

1920b "Neue Schenkungsstelen über Landstiftungen an Tempel," *ZÄS* 56: 55–60.

1922 "Horus als Arzt," *ZÄS* 57: 70–71.

1924 "Miszellen—  *ḏd mdw* im Koptischen," *ZÄS* 59: 160.

1925 "Demotica I," *Sitzungsberichte der Bayerischen Akademie der Wissenschaften, Philosophisch-philologische und historische Klasse* (Munich) 6: 1–49.

1930 "*nṯr.w* 'Götter' = 'Bilder,'" *ZÄS* 65: 119–21.

1932a "Aus der Geschichte vom Zauberer Ne-nefer-ke-Sokar," in *Studies Presented to F. Ll. Griffith,* edited by S. R. K. Glanville. London: EES, pp. 171–80.

1932b *Die demotischen Denkmäler, III: Demotische Inschriften und Papyri.* CGC. Berlin: Reichsdruckerei.

Staehelin, Elisabeth

1970 "Bindung und Entbindung," *ZÄS* 96: 125–39.

Stefanski, Elizabeth

1939 "A Coptic Magical Text," *AJSL* 56: 305–07.

Sternberg-el-Hotabi, Heika

1987 "Die Götterdarstellungen der Metternichstele," *GM* 97: 25–70.

1989 "Horusstele des Anchpachered, Sohn des Djedheriuefanch," *SAK* 16: 275–87.

Steuer, Robert O.

1948  *(wḫdw) Aetiological Principle of Pyaemia in Ancient Egyptian Medicine.* Supplements to the Bulletin of the History of Medicine no. 10. Baltimore: Johns Hopkins University Press.

Steuer, Robert O. and Saunders, J. B. de C. M.

1959 *Ancient Egyptian and Cnidian Medicine.* Berkeley: University of California Press.

Stricker, B. H.

1954 "De strijd om het pantser van Koning Inahrow," *OMRO* 35: 47–64.

Suys, Émile

1935 *La sagesse d'Ani.* AnOr, vol. 11. Rome: Pontifical Biblical Institute.

Tait, W. John

1976 "The Fable of Sight and Hearing in the Demotic *Kufi* Text," *AcOr* 37: 27–44.

1977 *Papyri from Tebtunis in Egyptian and in Greek.* Texts from Excavations, vol. 3. London: EES.

Tambiah, S. J.

1968 "The Magic Power of Words," *Man* (N. S.) 3: 175–208.

Tambiah, S. J. (*cont.*)

1973 "Form and Meaning of Magical Acts: A Point of View," in *Modes of Thought*, edited by R. Horton and R. Finnegan. London: Faber and Faber, pp. 199–229.

Tavenner, Eugene

1916 *Studies in Magic from Latin Literature*. New York: Columbia University Press.

Tedlock, Dennis

1985 *Popol Vuh*. New York: Simon & Schuster.

Tefnin, Roland

1991 "Les têtes magiques de Gizeh," *BSFE* 120: 25–37.

Théodoridès, Aristide

1967 "De la prétendue expression juridique *pnʿ r mdt*," *RdE* 19: 111–21.

Thissen, Heinz J.

1984 *Die Lehre des Anchscheschonqi (P. BM. 10508)*. Bonn: Rudolf Habelt Verlag.

1987 "Ambres und Amenthes," *GM* 95: 79–84.

1991 "Ägyptologische Beiträge zu den griechischen magischen Papyri," in *Religion und Philosophie im alten Ägypten: Festgabe für Philippe Derchain zu seinem 65. Geburtstag am 24. Juli 1991*, edited by Ursula Verhoeven and Erhart Graefe. Orientalia Lovaniensia Analecta, vol. 39. Louvain: Uitgeverij Peeters and Departement Oriëntalistiek, pp. 293–302.

Thomas, Keith V.

1971 *Religion and the Decline of Magic*. London: Weidenfeld and Nicholson.

Thompson, Herbert

1932 *The Coptic Version of the Acts of the Apostles and the Pauline Epistles in the Sahidic Dialect*. Cambridge: Cambridge University Press.

1940 "Two Demotic Self-Dedications," *JEA* 26: 68–78.

Thompson, R. Campbell

1971 *Semitic Magic*. New York: Ktav Publishing House (reprint of 1908).

Titiev, Mischa

1960 "A Fresh Approach to the Problem of Magic and Religion," *Southwestern Journal of Anthropology* 16: 292–98.

Tomandl, Herbert

1986 "Die Thronuntersätze vom Amuntempel in Meroe und Jebel Barkal. Ein ikonographischer Vergleich," *Varia Aegyptiaca* 2: 63–72.

Traunecker, Claude

1983 "Une chapelle de magie guérisseuse sur le parvis du temple de Mout à Karnak," *JARCE* 20: 65–92.

1987 "Une pratique de magie populaire dans les temples de Karnak," in *La Magia in Egitto ai Tempi dei Faraoni* , edited by A. Roccati and A. Siliotti. Milan: Rassegna Internazionale di Cinematografia Archeologica Arte e Natura Libri, pp. 221–42.

Tsukimoto, Akio

1985 *Untersuchungen zur Totenpflege (kispum) im alten Mesopotamien*. AOAT, vol. 216. Kevelaer: Verlag Butzon & Bercker.

Uphill, Eric

1963 "The Sed-Festivals of Akhenaton," *JNES* 22: 123–27.

1965 "The Egyptian Sed-Festival Rites," *JNES* 24: 365–83.

1967 "The Nine Bows," *JEOL* 6: 393–420.

Vachala, Bretislav

1976 "The Residence of the Cat goddess Bastet," *Nový Orient* 31: 299–301 (Czech; German synopsis by the author in *AEB* 1976, p. 243).

Valbelle, Dominique

1985 *«Les ouvriers de la tombe» Deir el-Médineh à l'époque ramesside*. BdE, vol. 96. Cairo: IFAO.

1990 *Les neuf arcs*. Paris: Librairie Armand Colin.

Vandier, Jacques

1961 *Le Papyrus Jumilhac*. Paris: Centre National de la Recherche Scientifique.

Varille, Alexandre

1968 *Inscriptions concernant l'architecte Amenhotep fils de Hapou*. BdE, vol. 44. Cairo: IFAO.

te Velde, Herman

1970 "The God Heka in Egyptian Theology," *JEOL* 21: 175–86.

1977 *Seth, God of Confusion*. Probleme der Ägyptologie, vol. 6. Leiden: E. J. Brill.

1980 "A Few Remarks upon the Religious Significance of Animals in Ancient Egypt," *Numen* 27: 76–82.

1986 "Scribes and Literacy in Ancient Egypt," in *Scripta Signa Vocis. Studies about Scripts, Scriptures, Scribes, and Languages in the Near East presented to J. H. Hospers by his pupils, colleagues and friends*, edited by H. L. J. Vanstiphout, K. Jongeling, F. Leemhuis, and G. J. Reinink. Groningen: Egbert Forsten, pp. 253–64.

Vergote, Joseph

1959 *Joseph en Égypte*. Louvain: Université de Louvain Institut Orientaliste.

Verner, Miroslav

1985 "Les statuettes de prisonniers en bois d'Abousir," *RdE* 36: 145–52.

Vernus, Pascal

1974 "Sur une formule des documents judiciaires de l'époque ramesside," *RdE* 26: 121–23.

1978 "Un témoignage cultuel du conflit avec les éthiopiens," *GM* 29: 145–48.

1985 "La rétribution des actions: à propos d'une maxime," *GM* 84: 71–79.

Vikentiev, Vladimir

1943 "Quelques mots énigmatiques dans un texte astronomique," *ASAE* 43: 115–31.

Vila, André

1963 "Un dépôt de textes d'envoûtement au Moyen Empire," *Journal des Savants*, pp. 135–60.

1973 "Un rituel d'envoûtement au Moyen Empire Égyptien," in *L'Homme, hier et aujourd'hui. Recueil d'études en hommage à André Leroi-Gourhan*, edited by Marc Sauter. Paris: Éditions Cujas, pp. 625–39.

Vittmann, Günther

1982 Review of Dieter Kurth, Heinz J. Thissen, and Manfred Weber, *Kölner ägyptische Papyri*, Volume 1 (P. Köln ägypt.; *Papyrologica Coloniensia*, vol. IX). *Enchoria* 11: 119–28.

Vittmann, Günther (*cont.*)

1984a "Ein Amulett aus der Spätzeit zum Schutz gegen Feinde," *ZÄS* 111: 164–70.

1984b "Ein Zauberspruch gegen Skorpione im Wadi Hammamat," in *Grammata Demotika. Festschrift für Erich Lüddeckens zum 15. Juni 1983*, edited by Heinz-Josef Thissen and Karl-Theodor Zauzich. Würzburg: Gisela Zauzich Verlag, pp. 245–56.

1989 "Zur Verständnis des demotischen Zauberspruchs im Wadi Hammamat," *Discussions in Egyptology* 13: 73–78.

Volten, Aksel

1937 *Studien zum Weisheitsbuch des Anii.* Det Kongelige Danske Videnskabernes Selskab, Historisk-filologiske Meddelelser 23/3. Copenhagen: Levin & Munksgaard.

1942 *Demotische Traumdeutung (Pap. Carlsberg XIII und XIV Verso).* AnAe, vol. 3. Copenhagen: Einar Munksgaard.

1945 *Zwei altägyptische politische Schriften. Die Lehre für König Merikarê (Pap. Carlsberg VI) und die Lehre des Königs Amenemhet.* AnAe, vol. 4. Copenhagen: Einar Munksgaard.

Vycichl, Werner

1983 *Dictionnaire étymologique de la langue Copte.* Louvain: Peeters.

1984 "Un royaume dans un pot de lentilles. Une histoire de magie copte recueillie en 1936 à Farchout (Haute Égypte). L'Origine du mot *hik* «magie»," in *Mélanges Adolphe Gutbub.* Montpellier: Université Paul Valéry de Montpellier, pp. 233–37.

Wainwright, G. A.

1931 "Keftiu," *JEA* 17: 26–43.

1932 "Letopolis," *JEA* 18: 159–72.

1961 "The Earliest Use of the Mano Cornuta," *Folklore* 72: 492–95.

Walker, Jim

1990 "The Place of Magic in the Practice of Medicine in Ancient Egypt," *The Bulletin of the Australian Centre for Egyptology* 1: 85–95.

van de Walle, Baudouin

1940 "Remarques paléographiques sur les textes similaires de Berlin," in *Princes et pays d'Asie et de Nubie*, by Georges Posener. Brussels: Fondation Égyptologique Reine Élisabeth, pp. 99–109.

1967 "L'Ostracon E 3209 des Musées Royaux d'Art et d'Histoire mentionnant la déesse scorpion Ta-Bithet," *CdE* 42, no. 83: 13–29.

Walters, Stanley D.

1970–71 "The Sorceress and her Apprentice," *JCS* 23: 27–38.

Wångstedt, Sten V.

1965–66 "Demotische Ostraka aus der Sammlung des Ashmolean Museums in Oxford," *OrSu* 14–15: 16–44.

1981 "Demotische Ostraka. Varia II," *OrSu* 30: 5–36.

Ward, William

1982 *Index of Egyptian Administrative and Religious Titles of the Middle Kingdom.* Beirut: American University of Beirut.

Weber, Manfred

1977 "Harimsverschwörung," *LÄ* 2: cols. 987–91.

1980 "Lebenshaus I," *LÄ* 3: cols. 954–57.

Weeks, Kent

1979 "Art, Word, and the Egyptian World View," in *Egyptology and the Social Sciences*, edited by Kent Weeks. Cairo: American University in Cairo Press, pp. 59–81.

Weigall, Arthur

1907 "A Report on Some Objects Recently Found in Sebakh and Other Diggings," *ASAE* 8: 39–50.

Weill, Reymond

1914 "Monuments égyptiens divers," *RdT* 36: 83–101.

Weinstein, James

1973 *Foundation Deposits in Ancient Egypt.* Unpublished Ph.D. dissertation, The University of Pennsylvania.

Weiss, M.

1969 "The Pattern of the 'Execration Texts' in the Prophetic Literature," *IEJ* 19: 150–57.

Wenig, Steffen

1978 *Africa in Antiquity*, Volume 2. Brooklyn: Brooklyn Museum.

Wente, Edward F.

1975–76 "A Misplaced Letter to the Dead," *OLP* 6/7 (Miscellanea Vergote): 595–600.

1982 "Mysticism in Pharaonic Egypt?" *JNES* 41: 161–79.

Wessetzky, Vilmos

1984a "Anmerkungen über das Gottesbuch des Königs," in *Studien zu Sprache und Religion Ägyptens. Zu Ehren von Wolfhart Westendorf überreicht von seinen Freunden und Schülern, Band 2: Religion*, edited by F. Junge. Göttingen: F. Junge, pp. 963–66.

1984b "Die Bücherliste des Tempels von Edfou und Imhotep," *GM* 83: 85–89.

West, James K.

1971 *Introduction to the Old Testament.* New York: The Macmillan Company.

Westendorf, Wolfhart

1965–77 *Koptisches Handwörterbuch.* Heidelberg: Carl Winter.

1966a "Beiträge aus und zu den medizinischen Texten," *ZÄS* 92: 128–54.

1966b *Papyrus Edwin Smith. Ein medizinisches Lehrbuch aus dem alten Ägypten.* Hubers Klassiker der Medizin und Naturwissenschaften, vol. 9. Bern: Hans Huber.

1970 "Beiträge aus und zu den medizinischen Texten," *ZÄS* 96: 145–51.

Westenholz, Joan and Aage

1977 "Help for Rejected Suitors: The Old Akkadian Love Incantation MAD V 8," *Orientalia* (N. S.) 46: 198–219.

White, Hugh G. Evelyn

1926 *New Texts from the Monastery of Saint Macarius.* The Monasteries of the Wadi ʾN Natrûn Part I. PMMA, vol. 2. New York: Metropolitan Museum of Art.

Whitehouse, Helen

1990–91 "To Seal the Mouth of all Snakes," *The Ashmolean* 19: 4–6.

Wiedemann, Alfred

1905 *Magie und Zauberei im alten Ägypten*. Der Alte Orient, vol. 6. Leipzig: J. C. Hinrichs'sche Buchhandlung.

Wilcken, Ulrich

1927 *Urkunden der Ptolemäerzeit*, Volume 1. Berlin: Walter de Gruyter.

1935 *Urkunden der Ptolemäerzeit*, Volume 2. Berlin: Walter de Gruyter.

Wild, Henri

1953 *Le tombeau de Ti. Fascicule II: La chapelle*. MIFAO, vol. 65/2. Cairo: IFAO.

1963 "Les danses sacrées de l'Égypte ancienne," in *Les danses sacrées: Égypte Ancienne, Israël, Islam, Asie Centrale, Inde, Cambodge, Bali, Java, Chine, Japon*, edited by Denise Bernot, Anne-Marie Esnoul, Paul Garelli, Yves Hervouet, Marcel Leibovici, Jean-Paul Roux, Serge Sauneron, and Jean Yoyotte. Sources Orientales, vol. 6. Paris: Éditions du Seuil, pp. 33–117.

Wildung, Dieter

1973 "Der König Ägyptens als Herr der Welt? Ein seltener ikonographischer Typus der königsplastik des Neuen Reiches," *AfO* 24: 108–16.

1977a *Imhotep und Amenhotep*. *MÄS*, vol. 36. Munich: Deutscher Kunstverlag.

1977b "Erschlagen der Feinde," *LÄ* 2: cols. 14–17.

1977c "Feindsymbolik," *LÄ* 2: cols. 146–48.

Wildung, Dieter and Schoske, Sylvia

1984 *Nofret—Die Schöne*. Exhibition catalog. Mainz am Rhein: Philipp von Zabern.

Wilkinson, John Gardiner

1878 *Manners and Customs of the Ancient Egyptians*. 3 vols. (revised edition by Samuel Birch) London: John Murray.

Wilkinson, Richard H.

1985 "The Coronational Circuit of the Walls, the Circuit of the *ḤNW* Barque and the Heb-Sed 'Race' in Egyptian Kingship Ideology," *SSEA Journal* 15/1: 46–51.

Williams, Bruce

1985 "Nubian Publications Project. Serra East," *Oriental Institute 1984–1985 Annual Report*. Chicago: The Oriental Institute, pp. 44–46.

Williams, Ronald J.

1976 "Some Fragmentary Demotic Wisdom Texts," in *Studies in Honor of George R. Hughes, January 12, 1977*, edited by Edward F. Wente and Janet H. Johnson. SAOC, vol. 39. Chicago: The Oriental Institute, pp. 263–71.

Wilson, John A.

1946 "Egypt: The Nature of the Universe," in *The Intellectual Adventure of Ancient Man*, by Henri Frankfort, H. A. Frankfort, John A. Wilson, Thorkild Jacobsen, and William A. Irwin. Chicago: University of Chicago Press, pp. 31–61.

1951 *The Burden of Egypt*. Chicago: University of Chicago Press.

1952 "A Note on the Edwin Smith Surgical Papyrus," *JNES* 11: 76–80.

1969a "The God Amon as Healer and Magician," in *Ancient Near Eastern Texts Relating to the Old Testament*, edited by J. B. Pritchard. Princeton: Princeton University Press, p. 369.

1969b "The God and His Unknown Name of Power," in *Ancient Near Eastern Texts Relating to the Old Testament*, edited by J. B. Pritchard. Princeton: Princeton University Press, pp. 12–14.

1969c "The Execration of Asiatic Princes," in *Ancient Near Eastern Texts Relating to the Old Testament*, edited by J. B. Pritchard. Princeton: Princeton University Press, pp. 328–29.

1969d "The Instruction of King Amen-em-het," in *Ancient Near Eastern Texts Relating to the Old Testament*, edited by J. B. Pritchard. Princeton: Princeton University Press, pp. 418–19.

Winter, Erich

1967 *Der Entwurf für eine Türinschrift auf einem ägyptischen Papyrus*. Nachrichten der Akademie der Wissenschaften in Göttingen I. Philologisch-historische Klasse. Göttingen: Vandenhoeck & Ruprecht.

Wissa Wassef, Cérès

1971 *Pratiques rituelles et alimentaires des Coptes*. BdEC, vol. 9. Cairo: IFAO.

de Wit, Constant

n.d. *Le rôle et le sens du lion en l'Égypte ancienne*. Luxor: Gezirat el Bairat.

1956 "Some Values of Ptolemaic Signs," *BIFAO* 55: 111–21.

1961 "Inscriptions dédicatoires du temple d'Edfou," *CdE* 36, no. 71: 56–97; *CdE* 36, no. 72: 277–320.

Wolf, Walther

1929 "Der Berliner Ptah-Hymnus," *ZÄS* 64: 17–44.

Wolinski, Arlene

1986 "Ancient Egyptian Ceremonial Masks," *Discussions in Egyptology* 6: 47–53.

1987 "Egyptian Masks: The Priest and His Role," *Archaeology* 40/1: 22–29.

Wolohojian, Albert

1969 *The Romance of Alexander the Great by Pseudo-Callisthenes*. New York: Columbia University.

Worrell, William H.

1929–30 "A Coptic Wizard's Hoard," *AJSL* 46: 239–62.

Wortmann, Dierk

1968a "Neue magische Texte," *Bonner Jahrbücher* 168: 56–111.

1968b "Das Blut des Seth (P. Colon. inv. 3323)," *ZPE* 2: 227–30.

Wreszinski, Walter

1912 *Der Londoner medizinische Papyrus (Brit. Museum Nr. 10059) und der Papyrus Hearst*. Leipzig: J. C. Hinrichs'sche Buchhandlung.

1913 *Der Papyrus Ebers*. Leipzig: J. C. Hinrichs'sche Buchhandlung.

1926 "Bäckerei," *ZÄS* 61: 1–15.

Wright, G. R. H.

1979 "The Egyptian Sparagmos," *MDAIK* 35: 345–58.

Wünsch, Richard

1898 *Sethianische Verfluchungstafeln aus Rom*. Leipzig: B. G. Teubner.

Yates, Frances A.

1964 *Giordano Bruno and the Hermetic Tradition*. Chicago: University of Chicago Press.

Yoyotte, Jean

1961 "Les principautés du delta au temps de l'anarchie libyenne (Études d'histoire politique)," *Mélanges Maspero*. I: *Orient ancien*, edited by Pierre Jouguet. MIFAO, vol. 66/4. Cairo: IFAO, pp. 121–81.

1973 "Fouilles à Tanis. Rapport sur la XXIVe campagne (1968–1969)," *ASAE* 61: 79–86.

1980–81 "Héra d'Héliopolis et le sacrifice humain," in *Annuaire, Ecole Pratique des Hautes Études*. Ve section, vol. 89: 31–102.

Žába, Z.

1956 *Les maximes de Ptaḥḥotep*. Prague: Éditions de l'Académie Tchécoslovaque de Sciences.

Žabkar, Louis

1968 *A Study of the Ba Concept in Ancient Egyptian Texts*. SAOC, vol. 34. Chicago: University of Chicago Press.

Zandee, Jan

1948 "De Hymnen aan Amon von Papyrus Leiden I 350," *OMRO* 28: 1–158.

Zandee, Jan

1960 *Death as an Enemy according to Ancient Egyptian Conceptions*. Leiden: E. J. Brill.

1964 "Hymnical Sayings, addressed to the Sun-god by the High-priest of Amūn Nebwenenef, from his Tomb in Thebes," *JEOL* 18: 253–65.

1972 "Sargtexte, Spruch 75. Fortsetzung (Coffin Texts I 348 b–372 c)," *ZÄS* 98: 149–55.

1973 "Sargtexte, Spruch 77 (Coffin Texts II 18)," *ZÄS* 100/1: 71–72.

1975–76 "Sargtexte um über Wasser zu verfügen (Coffin Texts V 8–22; Sprüche 356–362)," *JEOL* 24: 1–47.

Zauzich, Karl-Theodor

1976 "Die schlimme Geschichte von dem Mann der Gottesmutter, der ein Gespenst war," *Enchoria* 6: 79–82.

1978 "Neue literarische Texte in demotischer Schrift," *Enchoria* 8/2: 33–38.

1983 "Das Lamm des Bokchoris," in *Festschrift zum 100-jährigen Bestehen der Papyrussammlung der Österreichischen Nationalbibliothek: Papyrus Erzherzog Rainer (P. Rainer Cent.)*, edited by Josef Zessner-Spitzenberg. 2 vols. Vienna: Verlag Brüder Hollinek, pp. 165–74.

1985 "Abrakadabra oder Ägyptisch? Versuch über einen Zauberspruch," *Enchoria* 13: 119–32.

Zibelius, Karola

1984a "Speichel," *LÄ* 5: cols. 1125–26.

1984b "Zu 'Speien' und 'Speichel' in Ägypten," in *Studien zu Sprache und Religion Ägyptens. Zu Ehren von Wolfhart Westendorf überreicht von seinen Freunden und Schülern, Band 1: Sprache*, edited by F. Junge. Göttingen: F. Junge, pp. 399–407.

Ziegler, Christiane

1979 "À propos du rite des quatre boules," *BIFAO* 79: 437–39.

Zivie, Christiane

1976 *Giza au deuxième millénaire*. BdE, vol. 70. Cairo: IFAO.

GENERAL INDEX

EGYPTIAN WORDS

COPTIC WORDS

GREEK WORDS

INDEX OF TEXTS AND OBJECTS CITED

KEY

BT	=	Biblical Text	PL	=	Palette
BX	=	Box	PM	=	Parchment
CA	=	Cartonnage	PT	=	Pot
CL	=	Clay	SB	=	Statue Base
CO	=	Coffin	SD	=	Sandal
DS	=	Door Socket	SN	=	Stone
FG	=	Figurine	ST	=	Stela
FT	=	Footcase	TB	=	Tablet
MS	=	Manuscript	VA	=	Vase
O	=	Ostracon	WO	=	Wood
PAP	=	Papyrus			